D1413960

CAMBRIDGE LATIN AMERICAN STUDIES

EDITORS

MALCOLM DEAS   CLIFFORD T. SMITH
JOHN STREET

26

LAND AND LABOUR
IN
LATIN AMERICA

THE SERIES

LAND AND LABOUR IN LATIN AMERICA

ESSAYS ON
THE DEVELOPMENT OF AGRARIAN CAPITALISM
IN THE NINETEENTH AND TWENTIETH CENTURIES

EDITED BY
KENNETH DUNCAN and IAN RUTLEDGE
with the collaboration of
COLIN HARDING

CAMBRIDGE UNIVERSITY PRESS

CAMBRIDGE

LONDON · NEW YORK · MELBOURNE

Published by the Syndics of the Cambridge University Press
The Pitt Building, Trumpington Street, Cambridge CB2 1RP
Bentley House, 200 Euston Road, London NW1 2DB
32 East 57th Street, New York, NY 10022, USA
296 Beaconsfield Parade, Middle Park, Melbourne 3206, Australia

© Cambridge University Press 1977

First published 1977

Photoset and printed in Malta by
Interprint (Malta) Ltd.

Library of Congress Cataloguing in Publication Data
Main entry under title:
Land and labour in Latin America.
(Cambridge Latin American studies; 26)
Includes index.
1. Haciendas – Latin America – Addresses, essays, lectures.
2. Agricultural laborers – Latin America – Addresses, essays, lectures.
3. Latin America – Rural conditions – Addresses, essays, lectures.
I. Duncan, Kenneth, 1944–   II. Rutledge, Ian.   III. Harding, Colin.   IV. Series.
HD1471.L3L36   338.1'098   76–11076
ISBN 0 521 21206 5

CONTENTS

Contents

TABLES

Tables
ix

FIGURES

MAPS

ACKNOWLEDGEMENTS

Most of the papers collected in this volume were originally presented at a Symposium, 'Landlord and Peasant in Latin America and the Caribbean', held in December 1972 at King's College, Cambridge, under the joint auspices of the Centre of Latin American Studies, University of Cambridge, and the Institute of Latin American Studies, University of London, and with financial assistance of the Joint Council for Latin American Studies of the American Social Science Research Council.

More than for most books, it is true to say that innumerable people have helped in one way or another with the preparation of this volume. Our special thanks are due to the following: Professor Christopher Platt and his successor as Director of the Centre of Latin American Studies at Cambridge, Dr Brian van Arkadie; Dr Harold Blakemore of the Institute of Latin American Studies, London; and Dr Bryce Wood of the Ford Foundation in New York. Hilary Prior provided most valuable assistance not only in organizing the symposium but also in the early preparation of the manuscript, a task which was later completed by Marion Piper. The maps, graphs, and plates were designed and prepared by Ric Bryant, Chris Cromarty, and Alick Newman, whose invaluable skill, advice and patience has been much appreciated. Malcolm Deas of St Antony's College, Oxford, and the staff of the Cambridge University Press have been extremely helpful and understanding at all stages of the preparation of this book. Finally we would like to thank all those who participated in the original meeting and those who have subsequently contributed to the volume; their willingness to exchange ideas and to proffer and accept advice has not only lightened our editorial load but also made it a rewarding and worthwhile experience.

K. D. D.

I. R.

C. H. H.

CHAPTER I

Introduction: patterns of agrarian capitalism in Latin America

The development of capitalist agriculture has had a wide variety of effects upon pre-existing agrarian societies in Latin America. The forms it has assumed have in part been determined by variations in such factors as climate, ecology, demographic structure and history, ethnic patterns, and land tenure. The central theme of this volume is that such variations, whilst important in explaining localized phenomena, should essentially be seen as aspects of a basic process of change from one mode of production to another in the rural sector.

This is not of course a new idea, and indeed a number of writers, especially in the fields of economic history and social anthropology, have already dealt with many of the questions of particular relevance to the theme of this volume. Broadly speaking, their various approaches can be divided into three different levels of generalization. First, there are those works principally concerned with identifying the general mode of production in contemporary Latin American agriculture, in which the argument has centred around the question of whether the social organization of agriculture is essentially feudal or capitalist. Secondly, there is a more limited amount of theoretical discussion relating to the different types of agricultural enterprise to be found in Latin America, in which the principal distinction is drawn between the *hacienda* and the plantation. Finally, there is a very considerable body of literature dealing with types of peasantry and rural labour, where discussion concentrates upon the role-structure of rural economic life.

The mode of production in Latin American agriculture

It has been argued by many development theorists that the countries of Latin America, and indeed most other developing nations, are in a stage of transition between a 'traditional' and 'modern' society. As this transition takes place, a kind of hybrid society is created which displays the characteristics of 'structural dualism'.[1] A society in transition is therefore a 'dual society' containing two (or more)[2] sectors or sub-societies. For example, the French geographer Jacques

Map I

Lambert refers to an important group of countries in which there exists 'a numerical balance ... between two parts of the population, of which one presents the characteristics of developed societies, and the other those of archaic societies',[3] and the American political scientist C. W. Anderson describes the typical Latin American country as containing 'specific enclaves of modernity and the prenational and premodern remainder'.[4] Referring specifically to Brazil, Lambert states that a part of the population 'belongs fully to a developed national society and state', but the remainder 'still displays the characteristics, almost intact in certain rural areas, of an archaic culture which had disappeared in Western Europe several centuries ago'.[5]

The traditional sector of the dual society is often assumed to be geographically isolated from the modern (and usually urban) zone, lacking adequate transport facilities and communications.[6] Production is thought to be organized largely on a household basis, and firms and formal credit mechanisms hardly exist.[7] The economy is predominantly agricultural, lacking integration into the national market and frequently oriented towards subsistence activities.[8] The stratification system is portrayed as being extremely rigid and based mainly on ascribed roles and statuses.[9] Above all, the social and economic structure of the traditional society in Latin America is held to be dominated by the existence of the archaic *latifundio*, the vast, underutilized manorial estate which is barely integrated into the national market but which provides its owner with immense social and political power.[10]

Such is the view of Latin America's agrarian society held by those writers who either explicitly or implicitly adopt the dualist perspective; the only significant exception admitted is in references to the 'modern' plantation agriculture of the coastal zones. It can be seen that particular emphasis is laid upon the alleged lack of integration into the national market, and it is often claimed that bringing about this integration would result in the modernization of the *latifundia* system. This state of affairs has been taken by some writers of the dualist school as evidence that Latin America's rural society is essentially fuedal.[11] The view that agriculture in Latin America is feudal or semi-feudal is also to be found in the works of certain marxist writers, although it should be pointed out that their argument has been based mainly on the apparent persistence of serfdom within the *latifundio* system rather than on any belief that this system is an economically isolated or closed one.[12]

The idea that rural society in Latin America is feudal has been strongly criticized by A. G. Frank and others. Frank rejects the view that Latin American agriculture was in any way outside the capitalist system. He stresses that the agrarian economy of the region has been deeply involved in the international market economy since the European Conquest, and he concludes that Latin America had become thoroughly capitalist as early as the sixteenth century.[13] In his essay on Brazilian agriculture he shows that the allegedly isolated and feudal northeastern region was fully incorporated into a market economy, and he underlines the importance of commercial agriculture in all parts of Brazil.

Clearly, for Frank, production for the market is taken to be the

defining characteristic of capitalism. This is stated most explicitly in a
footnote to his essay on Brazilian agriculture:

It once seemed to me to be useful to distinguish 'inside the farm' from 'outside
the farm' . . . I thought . . . that this distinction might help avoid the confusion
of calling agriculture 'feudal' when the 'outside' relations are evidently capitalist
but the 'inside' ones are not. But I now think that all relations are fundamentally
affected by the capitalist structure of the economy, and I can no longer
recommend this distinction.[14]

In other words, according to Frank, the incorporation of an agricultural
estate into the national or international market 'affects' its internal social
relations of production and makes them capitalist ones. But what can
Frank mean by this?

Normally production relations are described as being capitalist when
they are based upon a system of free wage labour as opposed to serfdom,
slavery, or some other form of extra-economic coercion. There is a
considerable amount of historical evidence that, under certain conditions, agrarian systems have become integrated into the world capitalist
market without any accompanying development of free wage labour;
and indeed, in many cases, their integration resulted in an actual intensification of pre-capitalist forms of surplus extraction. Marx, Weber, and
a number of modern writers have discussed some important examples of
this phenomenon.[15] However, Marx, for one, makes it quite clear that
only where free wage labour is the rule can we speak of a capitalist mode
of production.

Consequently, whilst many students of Latin American agrarian
society would accept Frank's criticism of the dualist theory with
its implication that the *latifundia* are primarily a type of closed
economy, at the same time they would reject his view that a market-
oriented society is necessarily a thoroughly capitalist one. In particular,
historians such as Rodolfo Puiggrós and Ernesto Laclau have strongly
criticized the suggestion that the mode of production in colonial Latin
America was capitalist simply because it was involved in a market
economy.[16] In doing so they have drawn attention to the widespread
existence of unfree labour and extra-economic coercion in colonial Latin
America – forms of production relations which have in some cases
persisted well into the twentieth century.

In a sense, Frank's argument that Latin American agrarian society
has been thoroughly capitalist since the Conquest in the sixteenth
century shuts the door on a number of important and interesting questions. It certainly may be misleading to speak of feudalism in relation

to Latin American agriculture, but nevertheless the major social and economic changes which have occurred in the rural societies of this region from the second half of the nineteenth century onwards can best be interpreted as the transition from a type of pre-capitalist mode of production to a capitalist one. Clearly, Frank's position pre-empts any discussion of this transition process – a process, moreover, which is as yet incomplete in many parts of Latin America.

The part played by market forces in the transition process towards free wage labour has been both complex and varied. Under certain conditions the expansion of the capitalist market has brought about the fairly rapid development of free wage labour as the principal form of labour organization; but in other circumstances the impact of the market has seen an initial and sometimes lengthy period of intensified labour coercion which has only later resulted in the development of free wage labour. Yet again, in a different situation, increased output of some commercial crops has been obtained by remunerating free wage labourers partly in money and partly in the usufruct of land, so that for a time a kind of hybrid peasant/wage labourer has predominated. In other words, a number of distinct patterns of agrarian capitalist development can be identified in the different regions of Latin America.

Types of agricultural enterprise

One of the most important attempts to distinguish between the different types of large estate in Latin America and the Caribbean was presented by Eric Wolf and Sidney Mintz in 1957, when they drew a basic distinction between the plantation and the *hacienda*; and it is worth quoting in full their definitions of these two types of large landed estate.[17] The *hacienda* is 'an agricultural estate, operated by a dominant landowner and a dependent labour force, organized to supply a small-scale market by means of scarce capital, in which the factors of production are employed not only for capital accumulation but also to support the status aspirations of the owner'.[18] In comparison, the plantation is 'an agricultural estate, operated by dominant owners (usually organized into a corporation) and a dependent labour force, organized to supply a large-scale market by means of abundant capital, in which the factors of production are employed primarily to further capital accumulation without reference to the status needs of the owners'.[19]

Wolf and Mintz pointed out that it would be erroneous to think of some necessary sequential stage of development leading from the *hacienda* to the plantation. They also dismissed the idea of the *hacienda* as being a closed, subsistence economy and they stressed that '*Haciendas* and plantations are characteristically the products of the expansion of the world economy, particularly since the fifteenth century. Both are geared to the sale of surpluses produced into an outside market.'[20] Wolf and Mintz went on to discuss differences in labour recruitment and organization, land use, market behaviour, and so on.

Although some of the alleged differences between the two types of agricultural enterprise can be questioned, in general this scheme has provided a useful starting point for the analysis of Latin American agrarian society, and other writers in discussing regions other than those considered by Wolf and Mintz have utilized this basic model and modified it to add to the original classification.[21] Nevertheless, in so far as it is based on essentially static criteria, this particular form of typological elaboration falls short of present requirements. Here we are concerned not so much with static models of agrarian organization as with dynamic historical patterns of agrarian change. We would argue, for example, that the *hacienda* is normally in a state of tension or flux, in which the conflicting interests of landowner and peasant eventually lead to a transformation of the enterprise. Similarly, the modern plantation as defined by Wolf and Mintz is itself the outcome of a historical process of development, very frequently from a slave plantation system. In this respect, the earlier paper by Mintz which studied the historical pattern of change from slave plantation to modern plantation in Puerto Rico is of greater relevance to the theme of this volume.[22] A further example of this type of approach, which deals with some of these processes of socio-economic change, is Solomon Miller's study of the proletarianization of tenant farmers in a highland *hacienda* in Peru.[23] Miller showed how a traditional type of *hacienda* was taken over by a capitalist enterprise and rationalized with the intention of improving profitability. He also described the accompanying economic and social disruption, which uprooted the Indian tenant farmer and sped him along the road to proletarianization – in many cases literally, by compelling him to seek work as a cane-cutter in the lowland sugar plantations. One of the most interesting points to emerge from Miller's paper concerns the changing functions of labour tenancy in the *hacienda*. He showed that, under certain conditions, labour tenancy could be retained by the 'modernizing' *hacienda*; a rationalized version of this essentially pre-capitalist form of labour organization could be made to function in the economic interests of the *hacienda*'s new corporate management.

This casts considerable doubt upon those theories (e.g. Wolf and Mintz) which interpret labour tenancy as evidence of prestige- or status-orientation or of a non-profit-maximizing mentality on the part of the *hacienda*'s owner or owners. Indeed, the alleged distinction between forms of agricultural enterprise which are prestige-oriented and those which are profit-oriented is a false dichotomy. The owners of *haciendas* may be just as greedy for profits as the owners of plantations, who in turn may be just as status-conscious as the *hacendados*.

Types of peasantry and rural labour

It is not our intention here to go over the whole debate about what constitutes a peasant or even to give a definitive classification of the various categories of peasant and rural labour to be found in Latin America. Rather, we wish to focus attention on some of the problems and difficulties encountered in attempts to identify and isolate distinct types of peasantry and rural labour and, in so doing, to suggest the importance of integrating this kind of analysis into a general historical model of agrarian change.

We may begin by looking at the basic difficulty of distinguishing between those country people in Latin America who could be called peasants and those who could be termed rural labourers or rural wage workers. A number of social anthropologists and sociologists have attempted definitions of the peasantry in Latin America. Robert Redfield's studies of the peasants of central Mexico and the Yucatán peninsula provided some of the first theoretical analysis, but in much of his earlier writing Redfield made little distinction between peasants and primitives and tended to regard geographical and economic isolation as being a defining property of peasant communities. Peasants were included in his category of 'folk society' − a society whose economy is based almost entirely on subsistence production and among whose members only a minimal degree of social and economic differentiation has developed.[24] Later, however, Redfield recognized that the peasantry must be defined in relation to a broader social structure, and their defining characteristics must be elicited, in part, from their economic and political subordination to other social groups − landowners, state functionaries, and so on. Moreover, Eric Wolf and others have pointed out that in fact many peasant groups were fully incorporated into the international capitalist market.[25] A further dimension was added to the Latin American peasantry when it was realized that large numbers of small cultivators not only were involved in production for the market but also spent a considerable part of their labour time working for others, either for wages or for remuneration in kind. Thus in 1964 Richard Adams came to the conclusion that 'the simple, concrete distinction between the independent operator and the wage labourer has become meaningless. An extreme case is the peasant. Although the term once referred only to an independent operator, now it is much more commonly applied to an individual who must spend part of his time working either for his peers or for large landholdings'.[26] However, if the distinction between peasant (i.e. small, family farmer) and rural labourer has become difficult to draw, it does not follow that one can say that such a distinction is meaningless. Essentially, this analytical confusion has stemmed from the desire of certain anthropologists and sociologists to discover some kind of 'essence' of the peasantry, some immutable and transcendant characteristics which could provide a basis for the idea of an archetypal 'peasant society'. Anthony Leeds has presented a formidable criticism of this kind of approach; he argues for a methodological separation of 'persons' and 'roles' in studying agrarian societies.[27] Leeds points out that empirical evidence refutes the idea of fixed and universal peasant communities: on the contrary, detailed studies have shown that in the rural society of Latin America and many other parts of the world there is considerable fluctuating movement both into and out of peasant roles. On the other hand, this does not mean that peasants can no longer be distinguished from rural labourers, as Adams seemed to suggest. Indeed the analytical distinction, insofar as it refers to social and economic roles, remains of crucial importance – especially since the methodology embodied in this approach requires that attention also be paid to the general societal processes which determine the overall role-structure and the processes of change within it. Implicit in Leeds's argument is the view that the Latin American peasantry should be studied through a historical model of the development of agrarian capitalism and the spread of wage labour in the countryside.

But if the study of Latin American peasants and rural labourers must be grounded in a more general analysis of the mode of production, then certainly a theoretical discussion of the latter cannot proceed without detailed reference to the former, which is precisely the omission in A. G. Frank's writings. It will be recalled that Frank saw Latin American agriculture as being thoroughly capitalist and therefore 'ripe' for the transition to socialist production. This conclusion was based merely on the evidence of capitalist marketing arrangements, without any systematic analysis of the forms of labour organization and production relations within Latin American agriculture. By ignoring these internal mechanisms, which constitute the real basis of change from one mode of production to another, Frank failed to recognize the extent to which certain types of agrarian system have remained pre-capitalist and as such presented serious obstacles to the development of socialist agriculture. By the same measure Frank also failed to identify the conditions under which a relatively smooth and rapid transition to socialist agriculture may occur. This brings us back to a discussion of the general characteristics of rural wage labour in Latin America.

Mintz has argued that the rural wage labourer, especially the plantation proletarian, develops a way of life and cultural values which differ markedly from those of the small peasant farmer.[28] According to Mintz, the plantation wage labourer lacks the peasant's sense of attachment to the land; he obtains his food and clothing by store purchases rather than by domestic production; he wants higher wages and more stable employment rather than a plot of land of his own; and he is likely to have experience of trade union activity and some degree of political awareness. This suggests that the presence of a labour force of this type must facilitate a transition to socialist agriculture based on large-scale state farming units, and in fact this is largely confirmed by Juan Martínez Alier's study of the agrarian basis of the Cuban Revolution.[29] Martínez Alier has demonstrated that in Cuba the socialization of agriculture came about largely as a result of pressures and demands from the rural labourers in the sugar plantations. Although the Cuban plantation workers are shown to be in some respects less proletarian in their outlook and behaviour than the Puerto Rican rural labourers described by Mintz, they nevertheless recognized that their basic needs for regular stable employment and higher incomes could be satisfied by the conversion of the plantations into collectives or state farms. Consequently the Cuban sugar plantation workers fully supported and collaborated with the Revolutionary Government's plans to socialize Cuban agriculture.

Plantation labourers are not, however, a homogeneous social group. Mintz's paper on the plantation proletariat probably over-generalizes on the basis of the Puerto Rican example, where a fairly advanced degree of proletarianization had been reached. Moreover Mintz seems primarily to have been discussing the permanent plantation labourers, giving less attention to the seasonal cane-cutters who, in some plantation regions, are temporary migrants from fairly distant areas of peasant agriculture. Indeed, in many plantation economies the labour force is highly differentiated. In the sugar cane industry, for example, four main categories of labour can usually be identified: permanent factory workers, seasonal factory workers, permanent field workers, and seasonal field workers. To take but one concrete example, the Argentine sociologists Miguel Murmis and Carlos Waisman have shown that there are very significant differences between the categories of labour in the sugar cane industry of Tucumán, in northwest Argentina, with respect to social origins, political awareness, and class consciousness.[30]

In certain cases occupational differentiation may be combined with, and intensified by, ethnic divisions within the labour force. During the 1930s, for example, the sugar cane industry in the provinces of Salta and Jujuy, in northern Argentina, recruited labour from a great variety of sources. *Criollo* peasants from different provinces of northwest Argentina mingled with highland Indians from both Argentina and Bolivia, and Indians from the lowland Chaco region of these two countries, to form a labour force of extreme occupational and ethnic differentiation. The occupational and ethnic structure of the labour force in one plantation complex at this period – that of the *Ingenio* San Martín del Tabacal in the province of Salta, in about 1935 – can be illustrated as follows:

	Factory workers	Field workers
Permanent workers	Criollos (Salta)	Chiriguanos (Bolivian Chaco)
Seasonal workers	mainly Criollos	Criollos (Catamarca) Highland Indians (Argentina) Highland Indians (Bolivia) Matacos (Argentine Chaco)

(Salta and Catamarca are provinces of northwest Argentina. 'Criollos' is a term used to describe the bulk of the population in northwest Argentina who are of mixed blood. Chiriguanos and Matacos are two tribes of the vast Chaco region which covers parts of both Argentina and Bolivia. The Chiriguanos had migrated permanently to Salta.)

A very similar situation of ethnic and occupational diversity within the plantation labour force can be observed in the coffee industry of Guatemala, where the complex occupational hierarchy and the division between permanent (*colono*) and seasonal (*jornalero*) workers is reinforced by the widely varying linguistic and cultural backgrounds of the different Indian groups who make up the bulk of the plantation labour force, compared to the ladino overseers and administrative or technical staff.

In our view, the characteristics of the labour force pertaining to any given agrarian system depend to a large extent upon the precise way in which the agrarian system has developed out of the previous mode of production. Throughout this introductory survey, emphasis has been placed on the need to get away from simple, static typologies and instead to try to understand what might be called the dynamics of each agrarian system – the processes of socio-economic change arising from the interaction of the various components of a given mode of production. An important example of what we mean is provided by the Chilean labour regime known as *inquilinaje*.

Frequently the *inquilino* of central Chile has been presented as the classic case of the labour-service tenant – the archetypal peasant of a traditional agrarian society. However, the studies of Góngora, Bauer, Kay, and others[31] have indicated how important it is to study the changes in the conditions of *inquilinaje* which have accompanied the varying conditions of labour supply, market circumstances, and technical innovations in cereal agriculture. Until about 1860 it seems that the *inquilino*, whilst undoubtedly poor, nevertheless enjoyed a certain degree of freedom in his economic activities. Basically, his situation was that of a tenant who paid rent, including some labour rent, to the landlord, but in most other respects he remained largely independent. Moreover, the labour obligations which the *inquilino* owed to the landlord were fairly light. Indeed, it is possible that some *inquilinos* became quite substantial farmers in their own right.

After 1860 the situation began to change. The expansion of the export grain trade encouraged landowners to increase direct cultivation, a process which required rural labour on a much greater scale than hitherto. The landowners' solution to this problem was to increase the labour-service obligations of their existing *inquilinos*, as well as to settle new *inquilinos* with higher labour obligations on their estates. The *inquilinos* still retained their own plots of land, although they were generally smaller than was the case before 1860. But from about 1930 onwards technical improvements combined with rational capitalist logic resulted in a process of gradual encroachment on the *inquilinos'* plots, which were increasingly incorporated into the area of direct cultivation in return for the payment of increased money wages and other benefits. Thus by the 1960s the typical *inquilino* approximated more closely to a permanent rural wage labourer than to a labour-service tenant. On the other hand, the degree and extent of proletarianization was less than in, say, the case of the Cuban plantation worker, and Cristóbal Kay's paper in this volume refers to a limited re-emergence of a peasant economy on expropriated estates in Allende's Chile – a phenomenon which invites comparison with the relatively smooth transition to socialist agriculture in Cuba.

These brief remarks on the Chilean *inquilino* show how important it is to advance beyond the stage of mere typologies which categorize static examples of peasantry and rural labour, and to begin to study the different social groups within a historical perspective which is grounded in a relevant sociological model of agrarian change.

Such a model must incorporate, as one of its basic features, the long-run trend towards proletarianization in the rural sector since the mid nineteenth century. This process has intensified since the Second World War, and one of the most notable features of rural Latin America in the mid-1960s was the continuing growth in the numbers of landless and semi-landless rural labourers as a result both of population increase in smallholding communities and of the proletarianization of labour-service tenants brought about by technical improvements in agriculture and other forms of capitalist rationalization. The CIDA reports on the land tenure system in seven countries in Latin America provided much evidence on this subject; for example, the report on Ecuador (which is generally assumed to have one of the most traditional agrarian structures) stated that 'The technological transformation of agriculture always brings with it changes in the basic social status of the direct producers which principally affect their form of labour organization and the manner of remuneration. One of the most common occurrences has been the change from being remunerated with a plot of land to being a free wage worker.'[32]

Marx's discussion of the crucial relationship between the emergence of free wage labour on a large scale and the development of capitalism is perhaps too well known to need repetition here.[33] In our view it provides a key to the understanding of the major social and economic forces at work in rural Latin America since the mid nineteenth century. But the trend towards rural proletarianization has been neither uniform (i.e. proceeding at the same pace in all regions) nor uninterrupted. It follows that we should try to specify the particular conditions under which different patterns of agrarian capitalist development take place. Eventually one would hope to be able to specify, with a fair degree of rigour and exactitude, the relationships between all the relevant variables – labour organization, labour supply, land tenure patterns, market conditions, etc. Inevitably such a task is beyond the scope of this book, but it is hoped that at least a preliminary stage of systematization can be reached by linking the study of agrarian capitalist development to a discussion of some of the basic ecological, demographic, and ethnic variations to be found in the different regions of Latin America.

Broadly speaking, two main types of analysis have predominated in the study of regional patterns in Latin America. The traditional geographical approach, which has also been followed by some rural sociologists, has been to focus on particular crops such as coffee, sugar cane, cotton, etc. and then to generalize, on the basis of certain well-known cases, about the particular 'farming type' associated with each crop.[34] This farming type is usually assumed to impart its main characteristics to the general social structure of the agricultural region in question. An alternative approach, favoured by many social anthropologists, has been to identify particular 'culture areas' in Latin America. The social and economic structure of these culture areas is assumed to be strongly influenced by their predominant ethnic features and the pattern of relationships between the different ethnic groups of the region.[35]

Taken separately, neither approach is entirely satisfactory. With respect to the 'farming type' argument, it has already been pointed out that a given crop, e.g. sugar cane, can be cultivated under widely varying social and economic conditions. Sugar cane economies have differed markedly with respect to their ethnic and socio-cultural environment (compare northeast Brazil with northwest Argentina or coastal Peru), their class structure (compare the three-class structure of factory owners, plantation owners, and rural labourers in coastal Peru or northeast Brazil), and their position in the national and international capitalist market (production for export in Cuba and Peru; production for the internal market in northwest Argentina). Similar marked variations can be found in the case of coffee cultivation. The 'culture areas' approach similarly over-generalizes by failing to recognize the major differences which are introduced into a given culture area by different productive modes. A good example of this can be seen in the famous study by Fernando Ortiz which compared sugar cane cultivation with tobacco-growing in Cuba.[36] The plantation structure of the former contrasted markedly with the small peasant farmer society of the latter, although both existed within a common culture area, namely the Caribbean. Similar important differences in social and economic organization can be observed in northeast Brazil between the sugar cane areas and cacao-growing areas, although both parts of the region share a common (predominantly Negro) culture.

Clearly, one solution to the problem would be to combine the two approaches and use them to develop a more complex system of classification. To a large extent this is what we have done in organizing the papers for this volume, although, as we have already stressed, our approach involves an emphasis upon dynamic, historical patterns of change within particular agrarian regions rather than the simple elaboration of the regional differences *per se*. Moreover, our point of departure is not to use only agricultural and ethnic criteria but also the ecological and demographic factors from which the former should not be separated.

In Latin America the European Conquest and subsequent colonial rule brought a spatial patterning of the population which was crucially related to the attempts of the Europeans to harness labour for their profit-making enterprises. The brutal physical coercion which was inherent in the mode of production associated with a pre-capitalist, but nevertheless mercantile and commercially oriented, economic system brought with it the displacement of human beings on a vast scale. From the silver mines of Potosí, high on the Andean *altiplano*, to the sugar cane plantations of the Caribbean and the northeast coast of Brazil, the mercantile–colonial economy forcibly created huge new concentrations of population, while in other parts of the New World, vast stretches of territory for which the Europeans had no immediate use were left under the sway of marauding tribes of hostile Indians.

With the development of industrial capitalism in Europe from the late eighteenth century onwards, the agrarian systems of Latin America experienced important new market conditions and new possibilities for making money. However, the development of agrarian capitalism took place within the context of a demographic and social structure which was the legacy of an earlier mode of production. Inevitably this produced very different patterns of capitalist development within the varying conditions established by the previous economic system. The total number of identifiable patterns is undoubtedly very great indeed; however, in our opinion, the papers included in this volume fall into four main groupings, each of which can be broadly identified with a common set of ecological and demographic conditions governing the demand for and supply of rural labour. The following are the four main situations:

(i) Where an expanding commercial agriculture seeks to mobilize *local* labour resources without recourse to labour from other areas.

(ii) Where an expanding commercial agriculture not only seeks to mobilize local labour but also looks for labour in other, more distant regions of the country (we could call this *peri-local* labour to distinguish it from the third category of labour).

(iii) Where local and peri-local labour is insufficient or difficult to mobilize, and *foreign* (European) immigrant labour is recruited for agricultural production.

To these three can be added a fourth which is somewhat different from the others in that we are dealing with an area of pre-capitalist commercial agriculture which experiences a radical change in the status and freedom of movement of local labour:

  (iv) Where slavery is in decline, or has been abolished, and new
       methods of holding the existing labour force and recruiting new
       labour have to be devised.

These four cases constitute ecological configurations which coincide with large but clearly identifiable geographical areas. Let us now examine these in more detail. In so doing we shall also refer more explicitly to the actual historical forms in which agrarian change has occurred in these regions.

(i) The transition from traditional hacienda *to capitalist estate* (Principal locations: cereal/livestock zones of Mexico, central Chile, and the Andean highlands)

In this situation the expansion of commercial agriculture occurred in areas where there already existed a local labour force in more or less sufficient numbers for the type of farming undertaken. This labour force, frequently of Indian or *mestizo* peasants, was typically distributed between existing *haciendas* (where some form of labour tenancy prevailed) and neighbouring smallholdings or communal lands. In order to rationalize production and increase output for the market, the *hacienda* tried in a variety of ways to extend its direct control over its own land. This process involved the conversion of tenants into wage labourers, though a distinction should be drawn here between stock-raising and grain-producing estates, the labour requirements of the latter being considerably greater than of the former. On stock-raising estates in the Peruvian Andes, the proletarianization process meant the attempted eviction of many of the tenant shepherds and their sheep from the lands of the *hacienda*, and the conversion of the remainder into wage-earning shepherds. On the cereal-growing estates where labour requirements were higher, the *hacienda* attempted to extend its control over both the local internal and external peasantry, with a view to incorporating them more closely into the *hacienda*'s own production system. However, circumstances were not always favourable for this to occur, and the *hacienda* sometimes found it was fighting a losing battle against a recalcitrant peasantry.

(ii) *The development of a plantation economy with labour recruitment from highland peasant communities* (Principal locations: tropical lowlands and piedmont areas of the Andean countries)

Here the expansion of commercial agriculture occurred in areas where local labour was insufficient to meet the needs of the enterprise, especially with regard to seasonal harvest labour. To solve this problem labour was recruited from other regions of the country, these frequently being highland areas which supported a numerous peasant population, often Indians practising subsistence agriculture. In such cases quite distant and distinct ecological and cultural areas were incorporated into a structural whole with the original plantation area. In some areas the highland peasants were completely unprepared for the transition to wage labour, and in such cases various forms of extra-economic coercion were used, for a time, in their recruitment, although in other cases this was not necessary and financial inducements sufficed.

(iii) *The development of commercial agriculture using European immigrant labour* (Principal locations: south central Brazil and the Argentine *pampas*)

In this case the expansion of commercial agriculture took place in areas where local labour was insufficient and where there were no regional reserves of labour as in case (ii). Moreover, in this situation we are dealing with an ecological zone in which there existed vast amounts of un-cultivated land waiting to be opened up for agricultural exploitation. Consequently there was a heavy demand for permanent as well as seasonal labour, this permanent labour being required for the tasks of preparing the virgin soil and establishing new farms or plantations. Since this type of agricultural development occurred principally in the more temperate southern parts of Latin America, it was possible to attract large numbers of European immigrant labourers to work these lands. Typically, immigration schemes offered the immigrant labourer the possibility of eventually establishing himself as an independent farmer, but the extent to which this occurred varied very greatly.

(iv) *The transition from slave plantation to capitalist plantation* (Principal locations: sugar cane zones of northeast Brazil, Colombia, and the Caribbean)

Here we are dealing with an old zone of commercial agriculture (usually sugar cane) established during the early colonial period when labour supply problems were solved by the mass importation of Negro slaves. In the nineteenth century, the decline and eventual abolition of slavery, together with technological advances, compelled the plantation owners to find new methods of labour organization and recruitment. The plantation owners' success in converting the ex-slaves and descendants of slaves into wage labourers depended upon a number of factors, of which the prevailing land tenure pattern and population density were the most important. However, in a number of cases the plantation owners undoubtedly failed in their attempts to secure a smooth transition from the old slave economy to that of a modern capitalist plantation. Not unnaturally, many ex-slaves associated the plantation itself with slavery and, finding themselves free of the latter, also wished to be free of the former.

In some respects this *schema* has certain similarities with that utilized by the social anthropologist Marvin Harris in his study *Patterns of race in the Americas*.[37] Harris proposed a threefold division for studying the people and cultures of Latin America and the Caribbean. The major areas he distinguished were: (i) the Highlands (from Mexico south through Central America along the highlands to northern Chile), where the main culture types are American Indians, Europeans, and their admixtures; (ii) the tropical and semi-tropical lowlands (including the Caribbean islands), where Africans, Europeans, and their mixtures prevail; and (iii) the temperate south, peopled in the main by Europeans. This schema is undoubtedly useful as a general regional breakdown on the basis of ethnic and cultural criteria, and to this extent it is somewhat similar to the 'culture areas' approach discussed above. However, ethnic or cultural criteria are simply not sufficient for a regional analysis which is intended to serve as a basis for studying the different patterns of agrarian capitalism in Latin America. For example, the agrarian systems of the tropical or sub-tropical lowlands are by no means all of the 'African culture' type. The plantation economy of northwest Argentina, to give one instance, developed in an area where Negro slavery had barely existed and where labour was largely recruited from highland Indian communities. Moreover, the *hacienda* type of enterprise, which Harris seems to identify with the 'Highland/Indian' culture group, existed well outside the limits he specifies: central Chile is a case in point. In other words, whilst Harris's system of classification is adequate for his purposes, it is not entirely suitable for ours, and for this reason we believe it is valuable to maintain the fourfold division already described.

It is not our intention to assert that these four patterns of agrarian development are the sole identifiable types or the only ones of interest. We are aware that the studies included in this volume ignore certain cases which some may regard as being as interesting and important as those which have been listed. We should have liked to include, for example, material on the banana plantation system of Central America, Colombia, and Ecuador and on the cattle ranches of Argentina, Uruguay, Paraguay, and southern Brazil. Equally, we should emphasize that by grouping the case studies along the lines already specified we are not suggesting that within each group the individual case studies show precisely the same pattern of development. What we do suggest, however, is that all the individual case studies pertaining to each group illustrate a basic problem or set of problems which had to be dealt with by the respective rural social classes. For example, in the case of the changing *hacienda* system, both landlords and peasants, from conflicting standpoints, faced the problem of determining the precise role of independent peasant production within the overall *hacienda* system; or to take another example, in the case of the plantation system, which used highland peasant labour on a seasonal basis, both plantation owners and peasants, in different ways, faced the problem of how to make seasonal wage labour consistent with the continuing existence of the peasant community. Clearly, the ways in which these problems were dealt with and solved were determined by more detailed sets of circumstances, which naturally vary among the individual case studies, but in our view this merely reinforces the need to establish some general parameters within which the detailed historical analysis may be undertaken.

NOTES

1. The idea of structural dualism and the 'dual society' was first introduced by J. H. Boeke in relation to the Dutch East Indies, although Boeke suggested that the idea was applicable to all underdeveloped countries; see J. H. Boeke, *Economics and economic policy of dual societies* (N. V. Haarlem, 1953). The concept of the dual society has been applied to Latin America by the following writers, amongst many others: Jacques Lambert, *Amérique Latine: structures sociales et institutions politiques* (Paris, 1963); Manning Nash, 'Social prerequisites of economic growth in Latin America and South East Asia', *Economic Development and Cultural Change* XII, 3 (1964); Gino Germani, *Política y sociedad en una época de transición* (Buenos Aires, 1966). A dualistic perspective is also used implicitly by C. W. Anderson, *Politics and economic change in Latin America* (Princeton, 1967).
2. Nash, 'Social prerequisites', uses the expression 'multiple society' instead of 'dual society'.
3. Lambert, *Amérique Latine*, p. 51.
4. Anderson, *Politics and economic change*, p. 34.
5. Lambert, *Amérique Latine*, p. 56.
6. Ibid., pp. 105–6.
7. Nash, 'Social prerequisites', p. 231.

8. Germani, *Política y sociedad*, p. 118; Anderson, *Politics and economic change*, pp. 49–50, 61–2.
9. Nash, 'Social prerequisites', p. 229; see also B. F. Hoselitz, 'Social stratification and economic development', *International Social Science Journal* XVI, 2 (1964).
10. Lambert, *Amérique Latine*, pp. 85–93; Nash, 'Social prerequisites', p. 229.
11. This is clearly implied in Lambert's statement regarding the existence in Brazil of 'an archaic culture which had disappeared in Western Europe several centuries ago' (*Amérique Latine*, p. 44).
12. See for example, José Carlos Mariátegui, *Siete ensayos de interpretación de la realidad peruana* (Lima, 1928), especially the essay 'El problema de la tierra'.
13. A. G. Frank, *Capitalism and underdevelopment in Latin America* (New York, 1967), p. viii.
14. Ibid., p. 266.
15. See Karl Marx, *Capital*, vol. 1 (London, 1970), pp. 236–7. See also Marx, *Capital*, vol. 3 (Moscow, 1966), p. 332; Max Weber, *The theory of social and economic organization*, ed. Talcott Parsons (New York, 1947), p. 142; Weber, 'Capitalism and rural society in Germany', in *From Max Weber*, ed. H. Gerth and C. Wright Mills (London, 1948); Maurice Dobb, *Studies in the development of capitalism* (London, 1963), chapter 2; Barrington Moore, *The social origins of dictatorship and democracy* (London, 1969), pp. 433–6.
16. See Rodolfo Puiggrós, 'Los modos de producción en Iberoamérica', *Izquierda Nacional* III (1966); Ernesto Laclau, 'Modos de producción, sistemas económicos y población excedente; aproximación histórica a los casos argentino y chileno', *Revista Latinoamericana de Sociología* II (1969), pp. 276–316; Laclau, 'Feudalism and capitalism in Latin America', *New Left Review* LXVII (1971), pp. 19–38.
17. Eric R. Wolf and Sidney Mintz, 'Haciendas and plantations in Middle America and the Antilles', *Social and Economic Studies* VI, 3 (1957), pp. 380–412.
18. Ibid., p. 380.
19. Ibid., p. 380.
20. Ibid., p. 385.
21. See, for example, Manuel Diégues Júnior, *Establecimentos rurais na América latina* (Geneva, 1963); Marshall Wolfe, 'Rural settlement patterns and social change in Latin America: notes for a strategy of rural development', *Economic Bulletin for Latin America* X, 1 (1965), pp. 1–21.
22. Sidney Mintz, 'The culture history of a Puerto Rican sugar cane plantation, 1876–1949', *Hispanic American Historical Review* XXXIII (1953), pp. 224–47.
23. Solomon Miller, 'Hacienda to plantation in northern Peru: the process of proletarianization of a tenant farmer society', in Julian H. Steward (ed.), *Contemporary change in traditional societies*, 3 vols. (Chicago and London, 1967), vol. 3.
24. Robert Redfield, *The folk culture of Yucatan* (Chicago, 1941).
25. Eric R. Wolf, 'Types of Latin American peasantry', *American Anthropologist* LVII, 3 (1955), pp. 452–71.
26. Richard Adams, 'Rural labor', in *Continuity and change in Latin America*, ed. J. J. Johnson (Stanford, Calif., 1964), pp. 49–78.
27. Anthony Leeds, 'Mythos and Pathos: some unpleasantries on peasantries' (abstract in chapter 19 below).
28. Sidney Mintz, 'The folk–urban continuum and the rural proletarian community', *American Journal of Sociology* LIX, 2 (1953), pp. 136–43; see also the same author's

20   *Introduction*

'The rural proletariat and the problem of rural proletarian consciousness' (mimeographed), 1972.

29. Juan Martínez Alier, 'The peasantry and the Cuban Revolution', *St. Antony's Papers* 22 (Oxford, 1970), pp. 137–58.
30. Miguel Murmis and Carlos Waisman, 'Monoproducción agro-industrial, crisis y clase obrera: la industria azucarera tucumana', *Revista Latinoamericana de Sociología* II (1969), pp. 344–82.
31. See Mario Góngora, *Origen de los 'inquilinos' de Chile central* (Santiago de Chile, 1960); Arnold Bauer, 'Chilean rural labor in the nineteenth century', *The American Historical Review* LXXVI, 4 (1971); Cristóbal Kay, 'The development of the Chilean hacienda system, 1850–1973' (chapter 5 in this volume).
32. Comité Interamericano de Desarrollo Agrícola (CIDA), *Tenencia de la tierra y desarrollo socio-económico del sector agrícola – Ecuador* (Washington, 1965), p. 136.
33. See Marx, *Capital*, vol. 1, pp. 167–76. See also V. I. Lenin, *The development of capitalism in Russia* (Moscow, 1967).
34. See the regional cases described in J. H. Steward (ed.), *The people of Puerto Rico* (Urbana, Ill., 1956); also R. S. Platt, *Latin America: countrysides and regions* (New York, 1943); and an early study by C. E. Jones, 'Agricultural regions of South America', *Economic Geography* IV (1928), pp. 1–30, 159–86, 267–94; V (1929), pp. 109–40, 277–307; VI (1930), pp. 1–36.
35. A good example of this approach is to be found in A. L. Kroeber, *Cultural and natural areas of native North America*, 2nd edn (Berkeley, Calif., 1958); the same approach is also implicit in J. H. Steward (ed.), *Handbook of South American Indians*, 7 vols. (Washington, 1946–59).
36. Fernando Ortiz, *Contrapunteo cubano del tabaco y el azucar* (Havana, 1940).
37. Marvin R. Harris, *Patterns of race in the Americas* (New York, 1964).

PART I

The transition from traditional *hacienda* to capitalist estate

David Brading's paper constitutes the essential introduction to Part I, since it provides a useful point of departure for examining the development of the *hacienda* system. The *haciendas* of the Bajío of Mexico exemplify the economic and social difficulties encountered by pre-capitalist cereal agriculture – low profitability, unstable market conditions, and above all an underlying tension between the demands of demesne cultivation and the encroachments of tenant farming. Indeed, in the particular case studied by Brading it seems that the land-owning class had practically lost this struggle even before the great Mexican agrarian revolution of 1910–17. Jan Bazant's paper takes a similar starting point, showing the conflict between large landowners and the various categories of tenant labour settled on the periphery of their estates. However, in the *haciendas* of San Luis Potosí, unlike the Bajío, during the latter part of the nineteenth century the landowners were relatively successful in gradually restricting the rights of their tenants and successfully converting their *peones* into an increasingly impoverished class of day-wage labourers, stripped of the meagre privileges and security of the pre-capitalist agrarian society.

Arnold Bauer and Ann Hagerman Johnson deal in considerable detail with the changes in land tenure and land use during the period of expanding cereal agriculture in Chile. They show that the extension of cultivation took place mainly within the boundaries of existing estates through the conversion of previously unused land, and that there was in fact little or no change in the actual pattern of land ownership. (A similar point is made by Juan Martínez Alier in his paper on the Peruvian highlands.) However, whilst Bauer and Johnson show that the rural labour force was mobilized mainly on the basis of intensifying the tenant-labour system rather than by going over to wage labour, Cristóbal Kay's paper, which covers a longer time-period, demonstrates how changes in the *hacienda* system eventually resulted in the emergence of a landless rural proletariat. At the same time, in the last part of his paper Kay suggests that the process of land reform under the Allende Government (1970–3) tended, albeit unintentionally, to re-establish the independent peasant enterprise, often at the expense of the collective and social requirements of the newly expropriated estates.

The paper by Juan Martínez Alier, which deals with different types of *haciendas* in the central Sierra of Peru, continues the main theme of Part I – the protracted struggle between the landowner, who wishes to discipline, to control, and ultimately to proletarianize his peasant labour force, and the peasant himself, who seeks more and more independence for his own farming or stock-raising activities and greater security of tenure over the land he holds, within or bordering on the *hacienda*. Martínez Alier describes in detail how attempts by the *hacienda* to proletarianize its work force have been resisted by the Indian shepherds of the central Sierra, and he casts doubt on the traditional view of the Peruvian tenant-labour system, which, he argues, was by no means as disadvantageous to the Indian peasant as is usually assumed – hence the desire of the *hacienda* owners to abolish the system and introduce more rational and capitalistic forms of labour organization.

Whilst the first papers in Part I examine the patterns of agrarian change resulting from the mobilization of local labour resources in the specific socio-economic and ecological context of the traditional cereal or livestock *hacienda* worked by *mestizo* or Indian tenant labour, it is important to emphasize that this is not the only situation under which local labour resources have been recruited for capitalist agriculture in Latin America. In addition to the transition from slave plantation to capitalist plantation (which is dealt with as an analytically separate pattern in Part IV), at least one other case may be considered here. The paper by Ciro Cardoso discusses the development of capitalist estates using local free wage labour, against a background very different from that already described. The coffee estates of Costa Rica studied in this paper emerged out of a relatively well-established smallholder society in which medium-sized *haciendas* existed alongside the smaller farms. However, although the coffee estates were in general unable to expropriate the lands of the smallholder class, the coffee *hacendados* achieved a considerable degree of economic and social control over the smallholders in other ways. Not only did the larger estate-owners dominate the smallholders through the former's control of the processing and marketing stages of the coffee industry, but they also directly employed many smallholders and their families as seasonal labourers in the harvesting of the crop.

CHAPTER 2

Hacienda profits and tenant farming in the Mexican Bajío, 1700–1860

DAVID BRADING[1]

Introduction: the diversity of the Mexican hacienda

In the common usage of Mexico the term '*hacienda*' simply meant a large estate. It designated an extensive tract of contiguous land held under single ownership, be it of an individual, a family, or an institution. Usually, it implied the presence of a *casco*, which included a set of buildings to house the *mayordomo* (administrator) or the owner, and corrals for livestock or barns for grain. It suggested some degree of formal exploitation of the territory in question, either for pasture or for cultivation. The term offered little guide to physical extension.[2] In the Bajío it was customary to restrict its application to properties which at least encompassed a *sitio de estancia de ganado menor*, that is to say, 18 *caballerías* or about 780 hectares. Many estates, especially in the arid north, were much larger; the Tetillas in Zacatecas covered no less than 200,000 hectares. By contrast, in Tlaxcala mere farms were at times called *haciendas*.[3] Similarly, the term embraced all types of agricultural activity. A *hacienda* could be a sugar plantation, a ranch for cattle and sheep, or a farm which grew cereals, regardless of the fact that each class of enterprise differed markedly in its deployment of labour, capital, and land.[4] To compound the problem of definition, a *hacienda* did not necessarily constitute a single unit of production; in many districts landowners rented a considerable portion of their land to tenant farmers. In this diversity the Mexican large estate resembled its medieval counterpart, of which Georges Duby wrote that 'The destiny of every manor was individual and its structure unique.'[5]

The physical environment and local history of each region profoundly modified the internal organization of the Mexican *latifundio*. A *hacienda* which grew maize in the tropical coastlands of Veracruz obviously differed from an equivalent estate in the temperate Valley of Toluca; equally important, the latter differed from a *hacienda* in the Bajío because although they shared a similar climate the sequence of human settlement was quite distinct. The regions of Mexico are characterized by diverse patterns of land tenure and labour supply in addition to the more obvious

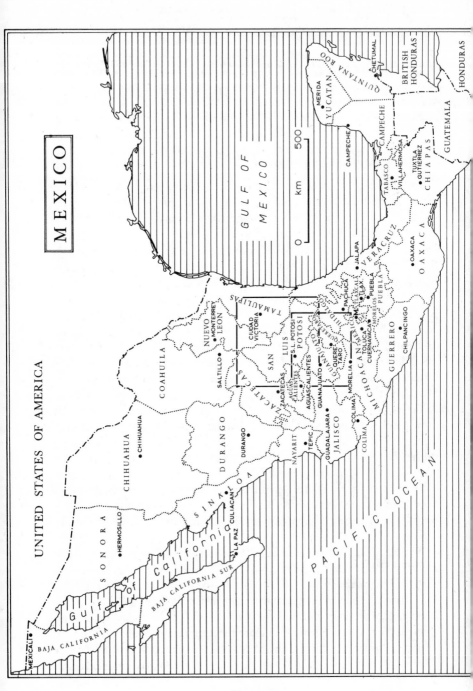

Map 2

determinants of altitude and rainfall. A key consideration here is the presence or absence of a long-established Indian peasantry with communal traditions of land tenure. Within its borders Mexico possessed agrarian analogues of both Peru and Chile. Hitherto, both contemporary travellers and later historians have concentrated their attention upon the historic estates with their fortified *cascos* and many square miles of territory. The sugar plantations of Morelos and the great stock-raising *estancias* of the north have frequently figured as veritable archetypes of the Mexican *hacienda*. By contrast, the estates of moderate dimensions which cultivated wheat and maize have been neglected despite their numerical predominance.

The purpose of this paper is to examine the evolution of the *hacienda* in the Mexican Bajío, a clearly defined region lying four days' horse-ride north of the capital. In part, my aim is to test certain hypotheses advanced by Andrés Molina Enríquez and Enrique Florescano. The main drift of their argument is that although the *hacienda* existed to provide its owner with an income, the actual profits taken from cereal production were low and intermittent.[6] The chief innovation of this paper is the emphasis placed upon tenant farming. The stratification of agrarian society in this part of Mexico is highly reminiscent of the Chile described by Mario Góngora.[7]

The Bajío

Although the Bajío lies at the core of the modern Mexican republic, historically and geographically the region stands at the frontier which separates the inhospitable wastelands of the great Mesa del Norte from the fertile valleys of the central plateau. The series of connected basins which cover most of the state of Guanajuato and a part of Querétaro once formed vast lakes lined by volcanoes so that their rich soil derives from thick lacustrine sediment mixed with alluvial mud and volcanic ash of the Tertiary Age.[8] To the north, in the districts of Dolores and San Luis de la Paz, the western flanks of the Sierra Madre join with the Sierra Gorda to form a band of hills with thinner, less productive soils. All local rivers drain southwards into the great Río Lerma. Almost the entire region falls within the limits of the *tierra templada*, with average heights of 1,500 to 2,000 metres. Lowland temperatures range from 14 °C in January to 22 °C in May. The estimated average annual precipitation in the state of Guanajuato is 580 mm, with about 80 per cent of all rain falling in the four summer months, June to September. This pattern of heavy summer rains preceded by a dry hot spring in large measure deter-

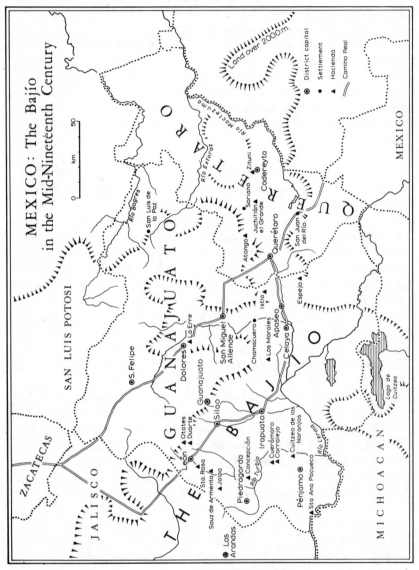

Map 3

mines both the range of natural vegetation and the limits of traditional agriculture. Apart from the tree-covered Sierra, the open plains of the Bajío supported, albeit in more luxuriant form, much the same variety of cactus scrub, low wooded thickets of *mezquite*, and dense seasonal grass that are still to be found in the steppelands of the north. Maize flourished in this climate, but wheat, if it were to survive the dry winter months, required the assistance of irrigation or close proximity to running water. Pasture was perforce extensive and dependent on permanent springs or rivers. The considerable variations in both the intensity and incidence of the summer rains made harvest yields unpredictable. In thirty-one observed years at Celaya no less than seventeen were described as dry or poor years.[9]

Historically the Bajío, save at the southern fringe, lay outside the confines of the Tarascan and Aztec empires and at the time of the Spanish Conquest was inhabited by semi-savage hunting and food-gathering Indians known collectively as Chichimecas. The initial colonization was a joint venture of both Spaniards and Indians, with groups of Otomíes and Tarascans pushing northwards into the area. As was to be expected, the more fertile south – Apaseo, Yuriria, and Acámbaro – attracted the first settlers; here the Crown granted *encomiendas* and in 1571 chartered the town of Celaya to encourage Spanish agriculturalists. Due east, Querétaro was founded by an Otomí chieftain but was soon transformed into a Spanish city. Further north, the spread of settlement was tardy and sparse. The discovery of silver at Zacatecas and the subsequent Chichimeca wars prompted the establishment of San Miguel el Grande (1555), San Felipe (1562), and León (1576) as garrison towns and way stations on the great road north.[10] The steady expansion of the silver mines at Guanajuato, situated in the local Sierra, completed the first phase of colonization.

In the eighteenth century the Bajío emerged as the pacemaker of the Mexican economy. Guanajuato replaced Zacatecas as the leading silver producer in New Spain, and Querétaro became the chief centre for the manufacture of woollen textiles. Other towns such as Celaya, San Miguel, and León also housed extensive artisan industries. The country-side shared in this new prosperity, benefiting from the expansion in urban consumption. Equally important, population increased more rapidly than elsewhere in Mexico, so that whereas in 1742 the area which later formed the state of Guanajuato was inhabited by 156,140 persons, by 1793 that total had risen to 397,924. At the close of the century, the province supported about 10 per cent of the Mexican population. The capital, with its dependent circle of mining villages, contained 55,000

persons, and just across the border the city of Querétaro possessed
nearly 30,000 inhabitants. By this time only 44 per cent of the intend-
ancy's population were classified as Indians, the remainder passing as
castas or Spaniards.[11] On the eve of Independence the Bajío thus formed
a prosperous intermediary zone quite distinct from either the central
valleys with their blend of *latifundia* and Indian villages or the scattered
mining camps and vacant ranges of the north. It was distinguished by a
high degree of urbanization based upon thriving textile and mining
industries, matched by a relatively dense population of predominantly
casta extraction and a prosperous agriculture.

In the countryside three main types of land tenure can be discerned.
Each had a separate legal origin. In the first place, the Crown rewarded
those Indians who settled in the Bajío with the usual communal titles of
landownership for their villages.[12] Their leaders also obtained allotments
of considerable extension. Unfortunately, little is known about the
history of either type of holding. At the close of the eighteenth century
the Intendant of Guanajuato reported that the majority of the sixty-two
Indian villages located in his province had lost or sold their land. Indeed,
most Indians were listed for the purposes of tributary collection as
vagos (vagrants), living scattered individually in *haciendas, ranchos,* and
towns.[13] Apparently they had not maintained their communal traditions
and were well advanced on the road to acculturation.

The second class of landholding was the *rancho,* a term which was
originally employed to describe physical settlement but which slowly
came to denote a large farm or a small property. Occasionally a dismembered portion of a *hacienda,* the *rancho* more commonly took its
start from a *cabildo merced.* Each town council had the power to grant its
citizens small tracts of land of about 2 to $3\frac{1}{2}$ *caballerías* – that is, 85 to 150
hectares.[14] At first these grants required viceregal confirmation, but after
1640 recipients usually obtained royal warrant for a few *pesos* during the
periodic inspections of the *juez de composiciones.* In León the *cabildo*
continued to issue grants of this nature throughout the seventeenth
century to a wide range of citizens including a few Indians as well as
castas and Spaniards.

The history of the Mexican *rancho* has yet to be written. Much depended upon the location of the property and the resources of its owner.
In some instances two or three *cabildo* grants were combined to form a
small estate, a miniature *hacienda* usually called a *labor.* In other cases
the laws of inheritance effectively dissolved the original tract into a
series of plots. Within these clusters of *minifundia* there frequently
operated a continuous process of aggregation and fragmentation of farm

lands. At times of course neighbouring *haciendas* purchased adjacent strips. By 1793 the Intendant of Guanajuato counted 360 independently owned *ranchos* in his province, along with another 1,046 units of the same denomination which formed parts of larger estates.[15]

The rise of the predominant type of land tenure, the *hacienda*, has been eloquently described by François Chevalier. With few exceptions the 448 *haciendas* listed by the Intendant in 1793 traced their origin to the late sixteenth and early seventeenth centuries, when the viceroys distributed most territory in the Bajío in *mercedes* of *sitios de estancia*, either for *ganado mayor* or *ganado menor*. Many *haciendas* situated on the fertile open plains stretching from Celaya to León never extended much beyond two or three of these square land grants which respectively comprised 1,755 and 780 hectares.[16] Some estates, however, especially those bordering the uplands of the west and north, finally encompassed as many as twenty or forty *sitios* through acquisition of multiple grants, further purchase, and outright annexation of unoccupied sections. All land held without due title received legal title from the *juez de composiciones*. Despite their early possession, as late as 1700 many *sitios* served for little more than rough pasture and sold for about 500 *pesos*. Boundaries between estates remained unmapped so that litigation between landowners was common. To avoid further encroachment from neighbours, many *hacendados* encouraged Indians or *castas* to settle on their land as tenants. It is clear that at the beginning of the eighteenth century much of the Bajío had yet to be cleared of its dense cover of natural vegetation. A hundred years later, however, its landscape reminded a European traveller of the plains of Lombardy.[17] Behind this physical transformation lay the creation of a complex and changing structure of agricultural production.

Tenants and capital investment

As a newly colonized territory with a network of towns set down in a wilderness, the Bajío offers the historical geographer ideal conditions for the application of location theory. Following Von Thünen, it should be possible to devise a sequence of maps illustrating the stages by which the increase in urban population and its demand for foodstuffs provoked the expansion of the penumbra of cultivated land which surrounded each town, until the entire countryside – soil quality permitting – was cleared, drained, and brought under the plough.[18] The great herds of cattle and sheep which in the seventeenth century still dominated the plains were steadily eliminated or driven northward where pasture was abundant and cheap. The textile industries of Querétaro and San Miguel turned to Nuevo León and Coahuila for their supply of wool.[19] In the Bajío itself the first emphasis upon stock-raising changed to a system of mixed farming, which in its turn was replaced by a concentration on the cultivation of cereals. Needless to say, the slow unfolding of this process varied from place to place and was modified by the nature of local terrain; hill districts were obviously best left to livestock. Similarly, the high costs of transport by mule team imposed effective limits on the extension of agriculture into districts situated at some distance from urban markets. In such marginal areas a combination of stock-raising with maize-growing offered the best chance for profit.

The movement towards a more intensive exploitation of land required considerable mobilization of labour and capital. Yet since the Bajío lacked the long-established Indian communities which in the central valleys of Mexico and Puebla acted as virtual reservoirs of agricultural manpower, labour was scarce and relatively expensive. All *sirvients acomodados*, as resident workers were called, expected a weekly ration of maize and a monthly wage of three or four *pesos*. At these rates the annual wage bill of twenty *peones* employed on a permanent basis ranged from 750 to 1,000 *pesos*, the equivalent in capital value of a small farm of 3 *caballerías* (128 hectares) or of an entire *sitio* of pasture land. In consequence of this high expense, it was not uncommon at the start of the eighteenth century for landlords to owe their workers considerable sums of unpaid wages. In 1707, for example, the owners of Cuitzeo de los Naranjos, an estate situated in Pénjamo, owed their *peones* 818 *pesos* for past services and a further 1,319 *pesos* on current account.[20] The same year ninety-three workers in the neighbouring Corralejo *hacienda* had claims to no less than 11,558 *pesos* from their bankrupt employer.[21] At this point in time, labour was in shorter supply than land and hence, comparatively speaking, was more valuable.

To resolve the problem, landowners kept only a small number of regular workers and instead hired men by the day for the sowing and harvesting of their crops. To ensure a sufficient supply of seasonal labour (as well as to gain additional income) they threw open a considerable portion of their land to tenant farmers. Here, arrangements varied greatly from estate to estate, and the absence of written contracts prevents any clear or certain description of the system. Later evidence suggests that in some cases, but not all, tenants were expected to assist the landlord in the harvest, their services being rewarded at the standard daily rate. In effect, therefore, although rents were defined or measured in monetary terms, as so many *pesos* for such an extent of land, at least part if not all of the cost was satisfied by the provision of labour. In this fashion the landowner utilized his most abundant resource – land – to attract what he most needed – seasonal labour.

In the long run, however, the decision to establish a numerous body of tenant farmers threatened the economic viability of the average *hacienda*. For the steady expansion of urban demand made it advantageous for the tenants to sell their produce on the open market and to use the receipts to pay rents in cash, hiring *peones* to satisfy such labour obligations as were still expected. The *haciendas* of the Bajío thus encountered competition from smallholders, both independent *rancheros* and tenants, or *arrendatarios* as they were termed. In consequence maize prices – drought years apart – remained obstinately low throughout the century, since the demographic increase was still more than matched by the supply of land. As late as 1806 the owner of the great Istla *hacienda* in Apaseo complained that with corn prices at 5 *reales* a *fanega* sales would not cover the costs of production and maintenance.[22]

In general, it can be argued that once tenancy arrangements became common, landlords eventually would have to abandon direct cultivation of maize on unirrigated land. The Russian economist A. V. Chayanov has demonstrated that in traditional agriculture, where wages form the chief cost of production, peasant farmers will tend to oust capitalist landowners from the market.[23] Backed by his family, accustomed to low levels of subsistence, the peasant can increase his labour input to survive crop prices which are simply uneconomic for an agriculturalist dependent on hired workers. Indeed, when prices fall the peasant is inclined to expand production at the point where the landlord is obliged to suspend operations. In the Bajío, this tendency first became manifest at the margin, in districts most distant from urban markets, where only the *rancheros*, either as tenants or proprietors, could absorb the extra transport costs of their locality by further increments of labour for returns just sufficient to maintain their families.

In some measure, our hypothesis is contradicted by the essential periodicity of Mexican agriculture. Florescano has argued that most *haciendas* made their profit in times of poor harvests when they obtained high prices for grain held over from previous years. Similarly, each summer before harvest began corn prices rose.[24] Thus, provided he possessed ample dry storage space, the *hacendado* could ride out smallholder competition by awaiting the most propitious season to release his grain. Such a policy of course required considerable cash reserves, since workers had to be paid even if the crop was not sold. To cover these costs of operation, most *haciendas* sought supplementary income from stock-

raising or from other crops. But the most reliable source of additional
revenue was precisely the cash rents of their tenants. In many instances
the rents or labour of the tenants thus kept the *hacienda* in production
until the inevitable drought years brought their profit.

The surest way of escaping smallholder competition was to invest
capital in the construction of barns, dams, and water tanks, since irrigation permitted the cultivation of wheat, a more profitable crop than
maize. Moreover the assurance of a relatively permanent supply of water
averted the danger of livestock dying from drought. In the middle years
of the eighteenth century the owner of the Jalpa *hacienda*, situated in San
Pedro Piedragorda, borrowed at least 30,000 *pesos* to build four dams of
such dimensions that even today a casual sightseer might mistake them
for natural lakes.[25] In Celaya the Espejo estate possessed a massive dam
which carried an inventory value of 18,000 *pesos*.[26] In effect, the marked
increase in the appraised value of most *haciendas* in the Bajío derived as
much from such improvements as from the rise in the price of land. In
1707 the Cuitzeo de los Naranjos, an estate which comprised just over
100 *caballerías* (4,250 hectares), was worth only 7,653 *pesos*, excluding
livestock from the calculation. By 1791 its inventory value was appraised
at 22,485 *pesos*, a threefold increase, in good part based upon the construction of a dam, a flour mill, a fruit garden and stone walls, and the
irrigation of 2 *caballerías* for wheat.[27]

A second course of action open to the landowner was to abandon direct
cultivation and become a mere rentier. At the close of the eighteenth
century many *haciendas* were leased for periods of three to seven years.
In more extreme cases, some estates were rented in sections to a numerous
group of tenants. For absentee landlords the advantage of this practice
was that although income was probably lower than the possible yield
from direct exploitation, it avoided any further capital investment and
eliminated the risks and worry inevitably connected with enterprises
dependent on unpredictable weather. For a later period Molina Enríquez
has commented on the tendency of Mexican landlords to seek low-risk,
sure-yielding forms of income.[28] The larger the estate, the more likely
was its owner to be ready to rest content with a certain but relatively low
return upon the capital value of his land.

An illustration of this latter trend was provided by the Mariscales de
Castilla, the greatest landowners in the Bajío. During the decade 1700–9
the current Mariscal, resident in Mexico City, received an annual net
income of 16,608 *pesos* from an entire chain of *haciendas* which stretched
from La Erre in San Miguel to La Concepción in Piedragorda and
Pénjamo.[29] This vast aggregation of territory served as a sheep farm, with

wool and beasts for slaughter, along with lesser derivative items such as tallow and skins, forming the main source of revenue. Apparently there was no attempt at cultivation except by means of tenants, whose rents amounted to 4,669 *pesos*, or 11.6 per cent of total gross receipts. Costs of operation were high, running at over 17,000 *pesos* a year to be paid in either cash or cloth. But then, at some as yet unknown point in the next sixty years, the Mariscales de Castilla abandoned sheep-farming and became rentiers. In 1772, their general manager disclaimed any knowledge of the number of Indians resident on three *haciendas* situated in Irapuato, San Miguel, and Piedragorda.[30] These estates were let to no fewer than 594 listed tenants, who paid a combined rent of 21,820 *pesos*. Many of these farmers, so the manager explained, hired seasonal labour for harvest and in some cases sublet part of their land. In 1792 the census enumerated 205 Spanish and *casta* tenants resident on La Erre, Indians being excluded from the count.[31]

Needless to say, most *haciendas* avoided such extreme reactions, since their owners lacked the resources for extensive capital investment and needed the profits that could still be obtained from demesne farming. Moreover, the variegated nature of their terrain encouraged the persistence of stock-raising alongside cereal production. To comprehend their situation at mid-century, let us examine with some care the record of the Juchitlán el Grande, an estate situated to the northeast of Querétaro between the small towns of Soriano and Cadereyta and thus standing at the very edge of our region. With its subordinate *ranchos* of Santa Rosa, Los Panales, San José Curacupes, and Zituni, it comprised at least 39 large *sitios* (over 68,800 hectares), but since most of this land was stony or mountainous, in 1752 the entire estate with livestock was only worth 89,894 *pesos*.[32] Its Church mortgages had climbed to 36,540 *pesos*, and in addition the owners had raised another 17,332 *pesos* from private individuals. In 1752, with unpaid interest at 6,213 *pesos*, the creditors embargoed the *hacienda* and installed an administrator. The sketchy accounts he later submitted form the basis of our discussion (see Table 1).

Basically, the Juchitlán offered its owners three main sources of income: maize-growing, goat-herding, and ground rents. The product of the small herds of 190 cattle, 300 sheep, and 100 brood-mares, combined with occasional sales of barley and beans, complete the picture. Most of the land was used for pasture. The 30 *sitios* of the Panales *rancho* supported a herd of about 11,000 goats, which in the decade 1753–62 yielded an average income of 1,810 *pesos* from the annual slaughter of 1,830 animals. Some thirty flocks of sheep and goats from Huichiapán and El Mezquital were pastured on these fields each year at a cost of 900 *pesos* a year. An

TABLE I *Hacienda Juchitlán and Los Panales: production and income, 1752–72*

Year	Harvest (*fanegas*)	Sales[a] (*fanegas*)	Product (*pesos*)	Average price (*reales* per *fanega*)	Number of goats slaughtered 1753–62[b]	
					chivatos[c]	*cabras viejas*[d]
1752	5,211	n.a.	n.a.			
1753	3,353	n.a.	n.a.		746	263
1754	2,566	2,437	1,276	4.1	1,689	340
1755	1,211	1,601	1,601	8	1,216	456
1756	4,107	3,328	4,074	9.8	1,346	551
1757	1,802	138	137	8	1,400	451
1758	1,643	1,687	1,639	8	1,334	539
1759	854	1,145	1,245	8.7	1,444	624
1760	3,141	1,488	2,178	11.7	1,200	610
1761	1,932	2,747	4,157	12.1	1,398	669
1762	2,194	281	475	13.5	1,532	516
1763	1,759	567	702	10		
1764	274[e]	1,780	920	4.1		
1765	3,423	—[f]	—	—		
1766	6,836	—[f]	—	—		
1767	3,630	1,169	380	2.6		
1768	3,385	3,132	1,315	3.3		
1769	1,339	1,818	1,136	5		
1770	910	890	1,144	10.2		
1771	859	519	797	12.3		
1772	77	210	341	13		
Total	50,506	24,937	23,517	7.5	13,305	5,019

[a] Maize sold derives from harvest of previous calendar year.
[b] Goat sales: figures available only for 1753–62.
[c] Kids: sold at 9 *reales* each.   [d] Old goats: sold at 5 *reales* each.
[e] Little sown.   [f] No sales.
Source: AGN, Tierras 827.

unspecified income was derived from maguey plants. There is reference to four or five *tlachiqueros de mezcal* (distillers of *mezcal*, an alcoholic beverage) who periodically set up small distilleries within the *hacienda*. One individual moved about with eighteen workers cutting firewood and milking the *magueys*; he paid 30 *pesos* a month rent.

In the two farms located at Juchitlán itself and at Santa Rosa, about 2,412 *fanegas* were produced each year if we take the average for the period 1754–70. Actual sales amounted to just under 60 per cent of harvests, the remainder presumably being consumed by the *peones* or left to rot. At an overall price of 7.4 *reales* a *fanega*, the average yield for these years came to 1,316 *pesos*. Marked variations occurred both in actual crop production and the prices obtained. The superabundant harvests of the mid-1760s, a phenomenon common throughout New Spain, proved specially disastrous with little grain finding a market.

The permanent work force was not large. The *mayordomo* of the Juchitlán was assisted by two *caporales* to mind the horses, four cowboys for the cattle, a general help, and eighteen *gañanes* for the maize farms. In Los Panales the *mayordomo* had eighteen shepherds, and at Curacupes the slaughterhouse required a guard. In all, the wage bill came to 1,940 *pesos* a year, with the two *mayordomos* taking 120 and 160 *pesos* each. The *caporales*, cowboys, guard, and assistant were paid 4 *pesos* each month, and the shepherds and *peones* 3 *pesos*. In addition they received a maize ration. The Juchitlán *mayordomo* took 8 *pesos* a month in cash and 2 *pesos* in maize; but he also had free pasture for his livestock and enjoyed the customary right of milking the *hacienda* goats during the rainy season to make cheese which he then sold for his personal profit. There is no mention in these documents of debt peonage.

Rental of cultivated land constituted the third main source of income. The entire *rancho* of Zituni was leased for 500 *pesos* a year, whether to one or many individuals is not stated. Ground rents in Juchitlán and Panales on average yielded 1,586 *pesos* a year. A detailed enquiry made in 1763 listed twenty-two persons in Los Panales who together paid 272 *pesos* in rent, the sums ranging from 1 to 40 *pesos*. Of these entries some sixteen had held their land since at least 1752 and another three since 1754. The Indians of San Antonio Bernal, a small neighbouring village, rented a small *rancho* for 25 *pesos*. In Juchitlán the variations were greater, the situation more fluid. That year sixty-six persons paid a combined rent of 1,245 *pesos*. One man paid 125 *pesos* for an entire *sitio*, and another paid 100 *pesos*. Here, far fewer tenants – twenty-six – remained in their farms for the entire decade. Some fourteen had only entered in the last two years. Moreover, within the *hacienda* itself there was a considerable degree of movement. One Indian, Pedro Felipe, started the decade with a rent of 3 *pesos* and finished by paying 30 *pesos*. Juan Manuel Cabrera leased one *rancho* for 40 *pesos*, and then changed to another which cost him 100 *pesos*. These increases all sprang from the greater area taken by the tenants. In another case, however, reference is made to an individual who for two years paid only 9 *pesos* since he had 'opened new land'. In the third year the rent for his same tract rose to 33 *pesos*. The 1752 inventory revealed that the tenants cultivated more land than the owners – 172 *fanegas de sembradura* compared to 44 in both Panales and Juchitlán. The average rent was 8 *pesos* a *fanega de sembradura*.

If our calculations are correct, then in the period 1753–62 the Juchitlán yielded an average yearly gross income of 6,544 *pesos*, taken from the following sources:

Maize sales:	1,748 *pesos*
Goat sales:	1,810 *pesos*
Ground rents:	2,086 *pesos*
Pasture rents:	900 *pesos*

If this annual figure be divided into the appraised estate value of 90,000 *pesos*, it results in a return on capital of 7.1 per cent. However, it seems likely that the wage bill of 1,940 *pesos* has to be subtracted from the gross receipts, so that the net return was closer to 5.1 per cent, a more plausible rate for such a *hacienda*. But since the 5 per cent interest on the ecclesiastical mortgages and other charges amounted to 3,189 *pesos* a year, the owners in fact received a mere 1,415 *pesos* a year. Small wonder they fell into debt; in part they must have lived off the loans they raised as much as on income.

The Hacienda San José de Duarte

As the population of the Bajío increased, so, compared with the first half of the eighteenth century, the value of land rose and the value of labour declined. Landowners now sought to exploit all the resources of their estates. In particular, they seized the opportunity to raise rents and, in some cases, to demand additional labour services from their *peones* and tenants. In 1804 the tenants of the Santa Rosa, a large *hacienda* situated close to León, complained that Baltazar Muciño, who had leased the entire property for 3,200 *pesos* a year, was steadily raising their rents, in one case from 25 *pesos* to 60, and in another from 333 *pesos* to 400. Furthermore, he expected them to assist him at harvest or send *peones* in their place, an obligation, so they claimed, hitherto unknown in the Santa Rosa.[33] He also forbade them to set up lime furnaces on their farms, a traditional supplement to their income.

Similar cases at the other end of the Bajío indicate that this was no isolated incident but rather part of a general trend. In Querétaro, on a *hacienda* called Atongo, a group of Indian tenants were accustomed to pay 6 *pesos* for every *fanega de sembradura* they rented, along with free rights to pasture and firewood. In return, they worked for the landlord, when required, for 1 *real* a day. But in the 1790s, so they complained, a new administrator raised their rents to 10 *pesos* a *fanega*, charged them for pasture, forbade them to touch the *magueys* or to cut firewood, and summoned them to work most days of the week, still at the old rate of 1 *real*. In response, the owner asserted that in fact their services were only required for the harvest. The charges for pasture were low, and firewood for personal use remained free. To quell the disturbance, however, he expelled the four leaders of the protest from the estate.[34] In the absence of written contracts all tenancy agreements expired each year, renewal depending upon custom and verbal assent.

In 1807 José Mora, the father of the Liberal theorist, leased the *hacienda* of Los Morales in Chamacuero, a subordinate district of Celaya.[35] He found that the standard rent of 10 *pesos* a *fanega de sembradura* was satisfied by the tenants providing a yoke of oxen and a *peón* two days a week when needed, a service which was credited to their account at the rate of 2 *reales* a day. Pasture for their oxen, and by customary extension for all their livestock, was free, but for firewood and *tuna* (the fruit of the *maguey* plant) they supplied another six days' work each year. Similarly, the *arrimados*, or squatters, who dwelt on the tenant farms were expected to work for the landlord twelve days a year. In addition, the *hacienda* also housed several gangs of *gañanes*, *peones* paid 8 *reales* for a six-day week, who had their own gardens and free pasture for their animals. Dissatisfied with this complicated system, Mora proposed to pay all workers, tenants and *peones* alike, $1\frac{1}{2}$ *reales* a day. Tenants were no longer obliged to provide plough teams, but they could still pay their rent in labour services. In addition, Mora now charged them for pasture and commuted the work requirement for firewood and *tuna* into a cash payment of 12 *reales*. So also the *arrimados* were obliged to pay 2 *pesos* a year in lieu of seasonal assistance. Presumably he also exacted more rigorous service from the *gañanes*, since he complained that some acted as if they owned the estate, rarely working more than one or two days a week. His reforms provoked such unrest that he called upon the local magistrates to help him expel several protesters from the *hacienda*.

These examples all point in the same direction. Under conditions of labour scarcity, with land in abundant supply, landowners settled tenants on their estates, offering them a free run of its resources in return for low rents and seasonal assistance. By the close of the eighteenth century mounting prosperity combined with the demographic expansion to bring more land under cultivation. Labour was relatively plentiful. In consequence, as the value of land rose, landowners moved both to raise rents and to restrict former customary rights to free pasture, firewood, and *tuna*. Exploitation of marginal resources often became an important item of total receipts. Much the same trend can be observed in the local silver mining industry. There, the traditional bait to lure workers into a dangerous occupation had been a share of the ore. But in the 1790s the chief mine-owners of Guanajuato terminated this arrangement and instead paid their men a daily wage, albeit of 8 to 10 *reales* as compared to the 1½ *reales* plus maize rations of the agricultural labourer.[36] This drive to put the relation of worker and employer upon a strict wage basis sprang as much from a quest for survival as from a demand for further gains. As competition in the corn market became more intense, the margin between profit and loss grew ever tighter. It is quite possible that by the beginning of the nineteenth century the *hacienda* which concentrated upon the cultivation of maize on unirrigated land was already an economic anachronism. Proof for this hypothesis, however, can only come from a close examination of surviving account books. Here we must rest content with one case study.

The *Hacienda* San José de Duarte was situated about ten miles east of the town of León. It encompassed 103 *caballerías* or about 4,370 hectares, of which up to one-third was deemed suitable for cultivation, the remainder abutting on to the mountainous ridges which here line the plains of the Bajío. To obtain an impression of the estate it is necessary to return to 1758, when a formal inventory was taken (see Table 2).

In accordance with its broken and partly mountainous terrain, which was similar to that of the neighbouring *hacienda*, Otates y Tlachiquera (see Map 4, page 40), the Duarte concentrated upon maize-growing and stock-raising; major irrigation for wheat was apparently not feasible. Despite common assertions to the contrary, this type of *hacienda* obviously required a considerable outlay of capital if it was to yield a profit. Its financial success depended upon a numerous herd of oxen for ploughing, ample dry storage in stone-built barns so as to await the best season or year for sale, and an expensive mule team to carry grain to market when and where prices were the most inviting. The volume of production was high, and the yield upon the quantity sown was remarkable. In response to an official inquiry, the owner declared that he generally sowed 40 *fanegas* of maize, from which in good years he expected to reap 4,000 *fanegas*, and in poor years 1,000.[37] The inventory shows that the barns still held 2,432 *fanegas* from 1756, alongside 3,862 unthreshed *fanegas* from the December harvest of 1757. Tithe records report that the *hacienda* produced an average of 2,141 *fanegas* for the years 1761 to 1767. Its tenants (of whom the inventory makes no mention) produced 393 *fanegas*, just under a fifth of the landlord's output.[38] At this time the *hacienda* employed thirty-nine workers whose debts amounted to 496 *pesos*, an average of 13 *pesos* each, or the equivalent of three to four months' wages.[39]

For the years 1811 to 1818, relatively detailed accounts of the Duarte's operations were deposited in the municipal archive by the trustee for the current owner, an elderly, infirm spinster.[40] Their value is enhanced by

TABLE 2   *Hacienda San José de Duarte: inventory, January 1758*

	Value (*pesos*)	Total value (*pesos*)
Land		10,775
pasture: 82 *caballerías*	5,000	
arable: 21 *caballerías* at 275 *pesos*	5,775	
Buildings		8,199
house and chapel	2,010	
2 barns	3,000	
walls: 9,000 metres	2,109	
other buildings	1,080	
Equipment	249	249
Workstock		3,151
173 oxen at 7 *pesos*	1,211	
37 heifers at 5 *pesos*	185	
16 mule teams at 25 *pesos*, and		
3 mule teams at 12 *pesos*	436	
59 saddle mules at 16 *pesos*	944	
75 horses at 5 *pesos*	375	
Livestock		5,331
52 cattle at 5 *pesos*	260	
12 calves at 1 *peso*	12	
340 brood-mares at 2–3½ *pesos*	764	
53 ponies at 1 *peso*	53	
166 mules, 1–5 years, at 11 *pesos*	1,826	
23 mules, 1–2 years, at 6 *pesos*	138	
23 mules, new-branded, at 4 *pesos*	92	
36 donkeys at 1–12 *pesos*	213	
2,412 sheep and lambs at 2–12 *reales*	1,746	
145 goats at 2–8 *reales*	73	
223 pigs at 1–6 *reales*	154	
Maguey: 20,000 plants	4,000	4,000
Produce		4,067
maize: 2,432 *fanegas* (previous harvest)		
and 3,862 *fanegas* (just harvested), both		
at ½ *peso* a *fanega*	3,147	
soap	567	
other produce	353	
Total		35,772

Source: AHML, 1758–9, 31, inventory taken 26 January 1758.

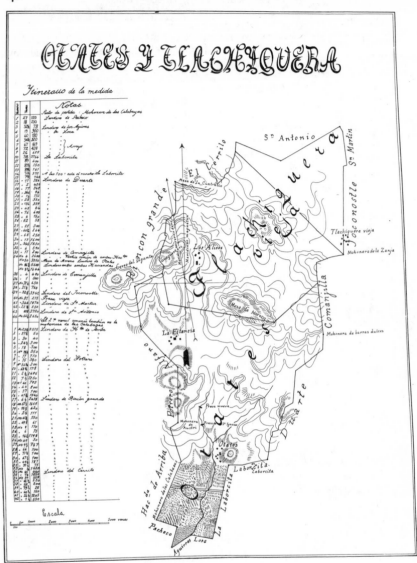

Map 4

TABLE 3 *Hacienda San José de Duarte: accounts rendered, 1811–18 (pesos).*

	1811	1812	1813	1814	1815	1816	1817	1818	Total
Income									
Maize	5,767	1,376	1,998	1,141	4,443	2,028	6,884	2,167	25,804
Cane	1,003	572	145	216	200	96	48	92	2,372
Minor crops	407	249	11	298	13	36	73	54	1,141
Livestock	535	516	255	—	23	33	—	126	1,488
Pulque	203	43	—	195	113	147	231	61	993
Rents	1,474	1,440	1,461	1,260	1,086	911	1,145	904	9,681
Misc.	162	17	19	—	18	—	—	—	216
Total	9,551	4,213	3,889	3,110	5,896	3,251	8,381	3,404	41,695
Debts paid	285	66	47	57	—	—	113	168	736
Peones' debts	541	789	627	474	(500)	(500)	693	526	4,650
León interest	175	177	28	36	29	29	186	188	848
Cash in hand	1,880	1,199	1,270	—	—	(470)	—	—	4,819
Grand total	12,432	6,444	5,861	3,677	(6,425)	(4,250)	9,373	4,286	52,748
Expenses									
Annual wages	4,408	3,114	2,874	2,657	(2,400)	(2,400)	2,219	2,550	22,622
Seasonal wages	306	70	162	257	87	72	112	196	1,262
Costs	657	851	829	464	884	1,367	1,728	2,586[a]	9,366
Chapel	94	85	83	271	(100)	(102)	—	—	262
Debts	296	94	151	386	1,472	—	332	34	1,380
Balance to mayordomo	—	—	—	—	—	—	1,223	22	3,103
Total	5,761	4,214	4,099	4,035	4,943	3,941	5,614	5,388	37,995
To owner	5,472	960	2,148	1,114	1,012	1,532	3,781	499	16,518
Grand total	11,233	5,174	6,247	5,149	5,955	5,473	9,385	5,887	54,513
Balance	+1,199	+1,270	−386	−1,472	(+470)	(−1,223)	−12	−1,601	—
Annual profit	4,791	1,031	492	28	2,954	−161	4,982	−1,080	13,037

Note: Figures in brackets are extrapolations.
[a] includes purchase of bulls, 1,150 *pesos* (see p. 44).
Sources: AHML, 1811(4)–28; 1814–32; 1815(1)–5; 1818(1)–1.

TABLE 4   *Hacienda San José de Duarte; maize production and sales, 1811–18*

	Stock (*fanegas*)	Harvest (*fanegas*)	Sales[a] (*fanegas*)	Income (*pesos*)	León price: average (*reales* per *fanega*)
1811	240	3,706	2,179	5,767	20.3
1812	404	3,720	609	1,376	17
1813	2,380	3,213	1,582	1,998	14.2
1814	2,250	2,100	1,206	1,141	8
1815	2,271	1,970	2,333	4,443	16
1816	770	1,977	951	2,028	18
1817	937	1,759	2,125	6,884	27.7
1818	—	2,173	1,010	2,167	18
Total		20,618	11,995	25,804	

[a] Sales include all grain issued on account to *peones*.
Sources: as for Table 3.

TABLE 5   *Hacienda San José de Duarte: maize consumption, 1811–18 (fanegas)*

Sown	184
To owner	675
Peón rations	4,049
Sold on account to *peones*	2,990
Sold in *hacienda*	2,113
Sold in León	6,892
Church tithes	1,739
Miscellaneous	255
Stolen	1,961
Total	20,858

Sources: as for Table 3.

their coincidence with the period of Insurgency and the invasion of Javier Mina. The estate suffered considerable depletion of its livestock but managed to maintain maize production at a time when many *haciendas* were obliged to suspend operations. In consequence the high price obtained from the sale of maize offset the losses incurred in capital value. Tables 3, 4, and 5 present a reconstruction of these accounts. Unfortunately damp destroyed the summaries for 1815 and 1816 so that, although most entries can be calculated from itemized records, certain key strands of information are missing. Figures in brackets are extrapolated estimates.

In these years the chief business of the Duarte, from which it drew over 60 per cent of its gross receipts, was the cultivation of maize, with an average production of 2,514 *fanegas*, a figure influenced by the renewal of the Insurgency after 1813. Just under 60 per cent of the harvest was actually sold, of which 2,990 *fanegas*, i.e. 14 per cent of the total, was purchased by the *hacienda peones* at prices somewhat lower than the market rate. These workers, the *sirvientes acomodados*, took as their free rations another 20 per cent of the crop. The remainder went to pay the tithe, went to feed the owner, was sown, was used for livestock feed, or was stolen. The owner took about 84 *fanegas* a year for household consumption. The amount set aside for sowing was remarkably small and implies yields ranging from eighty-two to one in 1812 to sixty-eight to one in 1817. The volume and value of sales varied markedly from year to year. Half of all revenue came from the high returns of the two years 1811 and 1817. It is noticeable that between 1813 and 1815 large stocks of grain – over 2,000 *fanegas* – had to be stored. With the confiscation of its mule team, the *hacienda* either sold its produce on the estate or sent it to León. The one-day journey to town cost no less than 1 *real* a *fanega*, a sum easily absorbed by the overall average price of 16 *reales* a *fanega*. Possession of a town barn in León permitted the owner to await the most favourable moment to sell his grain. In 1815, for example, all maize from Duarte was sold in León during the summer weeks between 17 June and 31 August.

The *hacienda* also regularly planted small quantities of barley and beans, but the object here was internal consumption, for both workers and stock, with only occasional sales. Despite the large plantation of *magueys*, the return on *pulque* was low, ranging from 100 to 200 *pesos* a year. An unexpectedly high income derived from the sale of *caña* or Indian cane, although here the disparity between 1811 and subsequent years reduces the overall value of this entry. In addition, the *huerta* or garden produced green chile which was sent to both León and Guanajuato, although after 1812 production seems to have dwindled. In sum, these minor crops supplied one-tenth of the gross receipts. In the two years 1811 and 1812, however, this proportion rose to 18 per cent, so that here we perhaps encounter some measure of the effects of the Insurgency.

The livestock accounts require careful examination. In 1811 the Duarte possessed 185 oxen, 201 mules, 80 saddle horses, and herds of 378 cattle and 264 brood-mares. Apart from the elimination of sheep and goats, these numbers were remarkably similar to those recorded in the 1758 inventory. The documents reveal an intimate relation between the working stock and the breeding herds. In 1811, 21 young bulls were converted into plough oxen, permitting the discard of an equal number of presumably ageing beasts. In the two succeeding years another 13 and 16 animals respectively were transferred. Thus the herd of cattle served a twofold purpose: apart from the sales which provided an additional, albeit minor, source of income, the herd replenished and maintained the plough oxen at small cost to the owner. The broodmares likewise fulfilled a dual function. In 1811 they provided 7 additions to the mules and 32 to the saddle horses; no doubt in other years a proportion would also have been sold. In 1812 this balance between work stock and breeders was broken. The insurgents stole 249 head of cattle; another 40 were sold; and with only 55 left, the yield of calves was barely sufficient to replace minor thefts. By 1818 the number of oxen had dropped through natural wastage to 102, so that the owner was then obliged to invest no less than 1,150 *pesos* in the purchase of 100 fresh oxen. By then the cattle herd amounted to 48 head. During the same year the *hacienda* lost most of its saddle horses and mules. In 1812 and 1813, 87 mules were stolen by the insurgents, and another 65 were appropriated by the royal army. By 1818 further thefts left the *hacienda* with no more than 16 mules. At the same time the insurgents took 71 horses and the royalists 25; after 1814 no saddle horses were listed. By contrast, however, the herd of brood-mares survived. Over the years 1814 to 1817, 149 were stolen, but these losses were offset by natural increase, so that in 1818 they still numbered 274 head. These severe losses prevent any reliable estimate of the relative importance of income derived from the sale of livestock. In both 1811 and 1812 it amounted to over 500 *pesos*, or 7.6 per cent of the combined income of these two years. The prime importance of the herds lay in the replenishment of the working stock.

The success of the Duarte in maintaining production throughout these years can be attributed to the large number of workers who were employed on a permanent basis. In 1812 maize rations were issued to thirty-four men. The cost of this labour force was high, since over a period of eight years the wage bill averaged 2,830 *pesos* a year in addition to an annual supply of 506 *fanegas* of maize. The role of debt in binding men to the estate is difficult to estimate. In 1812, the thirty-four *sirvientes acomodados* owed their employer 765 *pesos*, an average of 22 *pesos* each, about equal to half a year's wage. Part of this debt, however, probably came from the additional maize purchased by the *peones*. For the harvest and other seasonal tasks labourers were hired at a daily rate of 2 *reales*. In 1812 about thirty men were employed for short periods of time, most of them recruited from the tenants or their families.

About a quarter of gross revenue over the eight years came from rents, at an annual average of 1,212 *pesos*. Three distinct types of land were held in tenancy. In 1811, nineteen persons paid 246 *pesos* for an unspecified area of irrigated land suitable for the cultivation of green chile and other vegetables. Another forty-eight men rented just over 75 *fanegas de sembradura*, which at the current rate of 10 *pesos* a *fanega* yielded the owner 756 *pesos*. Finally, another fifty-four persons described as *moradores* paid 472 *pesos* for their *asientos* or dwelling-places and for *ranchos* or pasturage. One individual in this last group paid 200 *pesos* for what was obviously an entire *rancho*. It should be noted that persons in the first two categories paid on average 13 and 15 *pesos* a head; the plots of land they rented were thus rarely larger than 2 *fanegas*.

Some indication as to the extension of land held in tenancy can be obtained from a later inventory drawn up in 1843. At that time the total area of arable land in the Duarte was estimated at 195 *fanegas*, of which 12 *fanegas* were irrigated and hence were described as the *huerta*. According to this measure 6 *fanegas de sembradura* were reckoned as the equivalent of a *caballería* – that is to say, each comprised about 7 hectares. In 1843 the rent for ordinary land was still assessed at 10 *pesos* a *fanega*. The area under irrigation, however, was let in plots fifty paces square, at the rate of 60 *pesos* a *fanega*.[41] If these measures be applied to the *hacienda* of 1811, we find that with 76 *fanegas* let out of 183 *fanegas* suitable for maize, and 4 out of 12 irrigated *fanegas*, the Duarte leased just over a third of its arable land.

Little can be said about this class of tenant farmers, or *arrendatarios*, as they were invariably called. As far as can be ascertained, all tenure was customary, based upon verbal or informal agreement; contracts were not notarized and apparently did not carry any guarantee of renewal beyond the year in question. No doubt, however, some farmers remained on one *hacienda* for a lifetime; others came and went quite rapidly. In these years the area in the Duarte under tenancy varied remarkably – as a consequence, we may presume, of the turmoil of the invasion of Javier Mina. The extension let for maize-growing reached a peak of 89 *fanegas* in 1813, fell to 13 in 1816, and rose again to 56 by 1818. We may note that in 1817 the *mayordomo* himself rented 4 *fanegas* for maize and another 1½ *fanegas* of the *huerta*. Whether other permanent employees of the *hacienda* also rented land cannot be discovered. Finally, there is no indication that these tenant farmers acted as sharecroppers, save for one reference in 1816 to the *medieros* of the *huerta*; but these men are apparently distinct from the tenants of that year.

To calculate the actual profit of the Duarte in these eight years, we first have to subtract the cash in hand carried over from 1810 (1,880 *pesos*) and the final debit balance of 1818 (1,601 *pesos*). Thus the true profit was 13,037 *pesos* or an average of 1,629 *pesos* a year, the equivalent of a 4 or 5 per cent return upon the capital value of the estate. The true source of this profit makes a nice question. It is startling to note that for three years 1812 to 1814 the fixed wage bill (8,645 *pesos*) exceeded the value of all sales of produce (7,053 *pesos*). Only the high yields of 1811, 1815, and 1817 justified the continuance of maize cultivation. The record of the Duarte thus corroborates the theory of Florescano. Judging from this perspective, we can say that the function of rents was to provide a steady flow of cash sufficient to cover the wage bill and to offset the fluctuations of the corn market. The practice also permitted the landlord to share in the benefits of good harvests. One last query remains: would it not have been more profitable to have rented the entire *hacienda*? At a uniform rate of 10 *pesos* a *fanega de sembradura*, annual receipts upon arable land would have amounted to 1,950 *pesos*, a greater sum than the net return of 1,629 *pesos*. But these years of turmoil were sufficiently exceptional to invalidate the value of our evidence when pushed to such extreme conclusions. At the very least, however, our calculations demonstrate that for *haciendas* like the Duarte the margin between profit and loss was both narrow and uncertain.

The Hacienda Sauz de Armenta

The effect of the Insurgency and the economic depression which followed the attainment of Independence was to hasten the abandonment of direct cultivation by landlords in favour of a system of tenant farming or sharecropping. Many owners first let their entire estates and then, to meet their debts, sold outlying farms or proceeded at once to the final division of their *haciendas*. In many cases, only the survival of massive Church mortgages in the form of *capellanías* and *censos* presented an obstacle to such measures. During the 1850s the enactment of the Laws of the *Reforma* finally cancelled these inherited debts and hence removed the last legal barriers to the partition of many an estate.[42] It was in this decade, for example, that the Santa Ana Pacueco, a vast *latifundio* stretching from Pénjamo to Las Arandas in Jalisco was offered for sale to a numerous group of *rancheros*.[43] So also, in direct consequence of the *Reforma*, its neighbour in Pénjamo, the Cuerámaro, the property of a relogous order, was expropriated and eventually divided into at least fifteen *ranchos*.[44] Further west in the district of San José de Gracia, the *hacienda* called Guaracha was partitioned among more than fifty individual purchasers in the years 1861 and 1862.[45]

It should be emphasized that this trend was already in operation in the decades before the enactment of *Desamortización*. Between 1827 and

1851 the owners of the Jalpa sold up to 379 *caballerías* of land situated in Las Arandas and adjacent districts.[46] Similarly, it was in the 1840s that the *casco* village of Cuitzeo de los Naranjos was divided into over seventy-seven plots for sale to their occupants.[47] In effect, at this time there was a pronounced tendency for *haciendas* to dissolve into their component parts, that is into the farms previously held by tenants. How many estates were so partitioned and in which districts they were mainly to be found remains a subject for future research. Cases occurred in parts of Guanajuato, Jalisco, Michoacán, and Zacatecas. In general the process was most perceptible in the hill districts which bordered the Bajío rather than on the open plains where fertile land and close urban markets still offered high profits to the landlord either as rentier or cultivator. Even here, however, several *haciendas* were divided among heirs, and sections were sold to enterprising farmers. Needless to say, *haciendas* with irrigated lands largely escaped this trend. The owners of the Jalpa retained their most fertile land and used the receipts obtained from the sale of outlying sections both to repair the dams and other irrigation works damaged by the insurgents and to install a modern flour mill.

Further insight into the complex economic evolution of the *hacienda* in the Bajío can be secured from the accounts of the Sauz de Armenta, an estate which lay about twenty miles to the south of León. In 1708 the entire *hacienda*, then comprising 105 *caballerías* or about 4,460 hectares, was sold for 6,000 *pesos*, its 24 plough oxen, 64 cattle, and 165 remaining beasts being included in the price. In fact, since the estate carried two Church mortgages worth 3,900 *pesos*, the purchaser had to find only 2,100 *pesos*.[48] Half a century later the tithe records indicate a thriving enterprise which in the three years 1756–8 produced an average 2,913 *fanegas* of maize, 137 ponies, 80 mules, 103 calves, and 940 lambs.[49] In the years which followed, the stock-raising side of its activities declined to be replaced by a greater concentration on maize-growing. By 1793 the *hacienda* maintained no less than 172 plough oxen.[50] But then a disputed inheritance resulted in the division of the estate, so that when an inventory was taken in 1823 the remaining nucleus consisted of 59 *caballerías* or about 2,500 hectares. (See Table 6.)

Following the declaration of this inventory, much of the livestock was sold to satisfy the claims of several heirs.[51] Since the actual owner was a young child, the *mayordomo* appointed by the guardian was ordered to submit regular accounts which were then deposited in the municipal archive to avoid future litigation. When in 1827 the new manager entered his duties he found only 25 plough oxen, 24 other cattle, 102 brood-mares, and 11 mules. Testamentary division had thus entailed

Map 5

TABLE 6   *Hacienda Sauz de Armenta: inventory, June 1823*

	Value (*pesos*)	Total value (*pesos*)
Land		15,400
pasture: 32 *caballerías*		
(20 at 100 *pesos*; 12 at 50 *pesos*)	2,600	
arable: 10 *caballerías* at 600 *pesos*	6,000	
rented: 17 *caballerías* at 400 *pesos*	6,800	
Buildings		6,322
house	1,492	
chapel	902	
barns	348	
dam	2,751	
other buildings	829	
Workstock		2,060
72 oxen at 16 *pesos*	1,152	
19 mules at (mostly) 30 *pesos*	520	
37 horses at 10 *pesos*, and 3 horses at 6 *pesos*	388	
Equipment	208	208
Livestock		2,643
46 cattle at 12–4 *pesos*	582	
25 calves at 4 *pesos*	100	
131 brood-mares at 6 *pesos*	786	
92 ponies at 2–8 *pesos*	349	
10 donkeys at 6–7 *pesos*	62	
549 goats at 5–14 *reales*	582	
86 sheep at 4–12 *reales*	120	
46 pigs at 1–2 *reales*	62	
Produce		660
maize: 300 *fanegas* at 2 *pesos* a *fanega*	600	
beans: 12 *fanegas* at 5 *pesos* a *fanega*	60	
		27,293

Source: AHML 1827(3)–26, inventory taken 2 June 1823.

a severe undercapitalization of the estate. The small herd of cattle could not maintain, still less expand, the existing stock of oxen. Similarly, the handful of mules could not meet the seasonal transport requirements. Moreover, the low number of plough oxen suggests that the area of land under cultivation was probably far less than the 10 *caballerías* listed in 1823.

It is evident that by 1827 the Sauz de Armenta differed markedly from the usual stereotype of the Mexican *hacienda*. Whereas according to our calculations about a third of arable land in the Duarte was let to tenant farmers, in the Sauz that proportion in all likelihood approached three-quarters. During the twelve years 1827 to 1838, no less than 69 per cent of its gross income derived from rents. Moreover, if we are to trust the accounts presented by the *mayordomo*, the home farm – the demesne, so to speak – failed to cover its costs of operation, so that in effect its continued operation was subsidized from rents. Clearly, with the estate under wardship, the Sauz suffered from weak management, so that we should be cautious in using this case for any general interpretation. At the very least, however, it indicates that when absentee ownership was combined with insufficient capital investment, direct cultivation of maize was exposed to considerable risks, not to say losses.

The majority of the *arrendatarios* were probably substantial farmers rather than mere squatters. In 1831 some forty men paid a total rent of 1,136 *pesos*.[52] Of these, the six who paid under 8 *pesos* (charged at the rate of 10 *pesos* a *fanega de sembradura*) were called *terrazgueros*. At the other end of the scale, the brother-in-law of the owner was assessed at 116 *pesos*. Excluding these extremes, there remain thirty-three men with an average rent of 30 *pesos* each, the *mayordomo* himself paying 32 *pesos*. The more prosperous farmers obviously enjoyed the assistance of hired hands. In 1822 a local census enumerated 525 persons or 115 families as resident in the Sauz de Armenta. Now since the owner at most maintained nine permanent workers as *sirvientes acomodados*, it is clear that about half the heads of families were labourers employed by the *ranchos*. Thus the *hacienda* housed two distinct classes of men – tenant farmers and mere labourers – even if at the lower end of the scale considerable overlap occurred. The so-called debt *peones* were probably better off than either the poorer tenants or the hired hands.

Upon turning to the accounts rendered by the *mayordomo*, we encounter a dismal story of failure, the result either of managerial ineptitude or adverse market conditions. Part of the trouble, however, can be attributed to the insufficient quantity of livestock left from the testamentary apportionment. In 1827 the estate owned 25 oxen and a herd of 24 cattle; twelve years later numbers had risen to 44 oxen and 38 cattle. During this period the *mayordomo* sold 18 ageing oxen for 192 *pesos*, recruited 22 young bulls from the increase of the herd, but was furthermore obliged to purchase another 49 oxen, at a cost of 583 *pesos*, to replenish the plough teams. Much the same pattern applied to the mules, with the number increasing from 11 beasts in 1827 to 29 in 1839. Over the years 46 young males were obtained from the broodmares; 21 were sold for 366 *pesos*, but in 1836 an entire team of 17 head was acquired for 405 *pesos*. About the only positive entry in the livestock account was the herd of brood-mares, where in addition to the young mules already mentioned, sporadic sales of ponies brought in another 277 *pesos*. In all, over a twelve-year period, purchase of stock cost 1,311 *pesos* as against 903 *pesos* realized from sales. These figures explain the maintenance of relatively large herds of cattle and mares on *haciendas* such as Duarte. Granted an abundance of pasture, it was surely cheaper to breed working stock and to sell the surplus rather than to purchase replacements.

The major cause of the *hacienda's* problems, however, came from the failure to find a market for its maize, the only product of importance. Each year the estate harvested maize – on average about 410 *fanegas* – but in only eight out of twelve years did it sell appreciable quantities. Situated twenty miles or more from León, the nearest urban market, with transport costs at 1½ *reales* a *fanega*, the Sauz de Armenta was apparently unable to compete with *haciendas* like the Duarte which in addition to their greater proximity possessed greater storage capacity. Tables 7, 8, and 9 summarize the results.

In all the *hacienda* sold 58 per cent of maize produced between 1827 and 1838, with the overall price averaging 13 *reales* a *fanega*. The rations for kept *peones* consumed just over one-fifth of output, a proportion similar to that of the Duarte. Broken down by year, the performance appears yet more damning. After a reasonable year in 1827, the *hacienda* did not sell any noticeable quantity of maize until 1831, and then it obtained an average of only 8.7 *reales* per *fanega*. Indeed it was not until 1835 that the estate did well, selling almost 550 *fanegas* at an average price of 19 *reales*. In both 1831 and 1834 the Sauz had to carry stocks of over 1,000 *fanegas*. It was presumably this failure which drove the *mayordomo* to reduce the wage bill by sowing all maize *a medias* – that is to say, on some unspecified sharecropping basis. After 1830 only six to nine men were retained as permanent workers, entitled to maize rations and paid a monthly wage of four *pesos*. Their principal task was the care of livestock. The harvest and other seasonal jobs were undertaken with labour hired by the day. Even so the home farm of the Sauz showed a consistent loss. Spread over the twelve-year period, the sale of all produce yielded an annual average of 541 *pesos*, whereas wages and annual costs equalled 526 *pesos*. When, however, we add the costs of transport, taxes, the repair of equipment, and the replacement of livestock, the total operating cost rises to an annual 785 *pesos*, a sum well in excess of income. In effect, therefore, the operation of the farm was subsidized

TABLE 7 *Hacienda Sauz de Armenia: accounts, 1827–39 (pesos)*

	1827	1828	1829	1830	1831	1832	1833	1834	1835	1836	1837	1838–9[a]	Total
Income													
Maize	912	14	17	—	811	407	—	557	1,294	753	176	165	5,126
Minor produce	45	51	12	10	60	—	29	20	18	10	—	—	255
Livestock	100	21	76	281	9	57	18	122	27	89	32	71	903
Rents	991	1,073	1,153	1,149	1,101	1,201	1,153	1,224	1,290	1,464	1,347	1,429	14,584
Misc.	—	6	27	16	57	50	4	16	23	3	10	—	212
Peones' debts	81	89	188	—	—	—	—	—	—	—	—	—	358
Total	2,129	1,254	1,473	1,456	2,038	1,724	1,204	1,959	2,652	2,319	1,565	1,665	21,438
Carried forward	1,039	1,318	1,200	475	459	719	1,033	703	981	708	920	518	—
Annual totals	3,168	2,572	2,673	1,931	2,497	2,443	2,237	2,262	3,633	3,027	2,485	2,183	22,477
Costs													
Annual wages	364	521	688	509	340	382	346	343	324	362	326	334	4,839
Seasonal wages	177	90	135	167	275	112	93	64	45	115	7	202	1,482
Costs	136	87	183	78	304	205	88	287	104	268	180	127	2,047
Livestock purchase	80	138	51	4	—	—	163	96	113	542	104	20	1,131
Management	595	—	589	146	204	172	120	196	265	233	157	167	2,844
Total	1,352	836	1,646	904	1,123	871	810	986	851	1,520	774	850	12,523
Expenditure													
To owner	228	266	218	208	208	268	454	358	258	311	977	655	4,409
Interest payments	270	270	270	270	270	270	270	270	270	170	170	120	2,890
Litigation, guardian	—	—	—	91	177	—	—	68	46	106	46	60	594
Capital redemption	—	—	—	—	—	—	—	—	1,500	—	—	500	2000
Total	498	536	488	569	655	538	724	696	2,074	587	1,193	1,335	9,893
Grand total	1,850	1,372	2,134	1,473	1,788	1,409	1,534	1,682	2,925	2,107	1,967	2,185	22,416
Balance carried	1,318	1,200	539[b]	458	719	1,033	703	981	708	902	518	—	—

[a] The 1838 account was carried through into April 1839.
[b] 64 *pesos* not carried, unaccounted.
Sources: AHML, 1830(1)–2, 1831(1)–7; 1832(2)–4; 1835(1)–2; 1836(1)–2; 1837(2)–26; 1838(2)–23; 1839(1)–13

TABLE 8   *Hacienda Sauz de Armenta: maize production and sales, 1827–38.*

	Stock (*fanegas*)	Harvest[a] (*fanegas*)	Sales (*fanegas*)	Income[b] (*pesos*)	Prices in León: average (*reales*)
1827	408	154	430	912	17.2
1828	11	249	5	14	—
1829	135	227	11	17	—
1830	211	931	—	—	—
1831	1,000	733	774	811	8.7
1832	796	501	336	407	10
1833	831	446	—	—	—
1834	1,083	452	393	577	11
1835	994	144	546	1,294	19.2
1836	134	464	409	753	14.8
1837	42	162	71	176	20
1838	21	454	113	165	10
Total	—	4,917	3,088	5,126	—

[a] Tithes already deducted from harvest.
[b] Taxes already deducted from income.
Sources: as for Table 7.

TABLE 9   *Hacienda Sauz de Armenta: maize consumption, 1827–38 (fanegas)*

To owner	42
Sown	157
For livestock	170
Peones' rations	1,109
Sold to *peones*	116
Sales in León	2,972
Lost or unaccounted	759
Total	5,325

Source: as for Table 7.

from rents. As Table 7 demonstrates, rents provided 69 per cent of the gross income, whereas maintenance of the *hacienda* as a productive unit absorbed nearly 45 per cent of all income.

In general, the Sauz de Armenta yielded a remarkably low return upon invested capital. The young owner received a derisory 367 *pesos* a year from an estate still worth about 25,000 *pesos*. However, to this sum must be added the annual 270 *pesos* paid in interest upon the 5,400 *pesos* of Church mortgages charged on the estate. If in addition we add the fees of the guardian, litigation costs, capital redemption, and, more important, the salary of the *mayordomo*, then the potential yield of the estate rises to 14,318 *pesos* or an annual 1,193 *pesos*, the equivalent of 4.4 per cent return upon capital value. Even so, this sum is still lower than the 1,219 *pesos* obtained from rents. Clearly, the attempt at direct cultivation had proved a miserable failure; the owner would have been better served if his guardian had leased the entire *hacienda*.

The aftermath

As yet we know little about the agricultural history of the Bajío during the Porfiriato (1876–1910) so that our remarks here must be treated with all due caution. One fact appears to be certain: in contrast to the trend in Morelos and in the far north, there were few attempts made in the Bajío to expand the physical area of the great estate. Indeed, since between 1882 and 1910 the recorded numbers of *ranchos* and of *haciendas* both increased, presumably the average size of these units diminished. Some *haciendas* were divided and outlying portions of farmland were sold to *rancheros*. At the same time, the laws of inheritance worked to break down the *ranchos* into *minifundia*.[53] Table 10 indicates the dimension of the changes.

Since the *desamortización* decrees of the *Reforma* had lifted the burden of ecclesiastical debt from their estates, landowners were free to offer their property as security for a fresh round of loans and mortgages. By 1909 many *hacendados* were as much in debt to the banks as they had once been to the Church.[54] No doubt, however, if this capital was em-

TABLE 10 *Number of haciendas and ranchos in the State of Guanajuato, 1810–1910*

	1810	1882	1910
Haciendas	474[a]	442	534
Ranchos	416	2,716	3,999
State population	576,600	968,113	1,081,561

[a] Includes 29 *estancias*.

Sources: F. Navarro y Noriega, *Memoria sobre la población de México* (Mexico, 1943), foldpaper; *Memoria del Estado de Guanajuato* (1882), no. 46; G. M. McBride, *Land systems of Mexico* (New York, 1923), pp. 78, 98; El Colegio de México, *Estadísticas sociales del Porfiriato 1877–1910* (Mexico, 1956), p. 7.

ployed to improve agricultural production, and in particular to introduce modern methods of irrigation, such estates became more profitable concerns. During the same period the construction of railways opened access to more distant markets, although transport costs still remained high for cheap, bulky commodities like maize. Equally important, profit margins surely benefited from the failure of agricultural wages to rise at a rate commensurate with the overall increase in prices.[55] These considerations indicate that the revival and expansion of the Mexican economy in the late nineteenth-century probably brought a temporary arrest to the underlying movement to divide the great estate of the Bajío into its component parts. But at the same time the reported prevalence of sharecropping arrangements, if it be a true statement of the case, suggests that many landowners, far from investing in improvements, simply abandoned all further pretence at direct cultivation.[56] In consequence they no longer needed cash rents to pay the wages of their *peones*; and with grain prices rising, they may well have found it more profitable to let their land on a sharecropping basis. All these complex and varying responses to the new opportunities of this period still await their historian.

As the Revolution of this century drove landowners to the edge of bankruptcy, the final destruction of the great estate appeared unavoidable. Evidence is fragmentary. As early as 1919 the owner of the Otates in León sold his *hacienda* to a company formed to organize its *fraccionamiento*.[57] Similarly, in 1930 the owner of the great Jalpa *latifundio* carved out no fewer than 89 plots for sale to individual purchasers. In León a detailed land survey was made to facilitate the partition of estates in that district. Thus, prior to the great cycle of land distribution inaugurated by Lázaro Cárdenas, a stage in which the communal holdings of the *ejidos* became the favoured type of agrarian landownership, in much of the Bajío many *haciendas* had already been surveyed, partitioned into small properties, and sold to a numerous group of *rancheros*. Far from being a sharp break with the past, these transactions were an almost natural consequence of the complex structure of agricultural production which had developed over the course of three centuries. It is significant that in 1960, whereas in the State of Morelos 82 per cent of all land was held by *ejidos*, and in Puebla 51 per cent, in the State of Guanajuato 62 per cent of the land was owned privately by smallholders.[58] It was the rise of the *ranchero* class which first threatened the economic survival of the *hacienda* and then demanded its partition. It is the same class which has profited the most from the changes in landownership brought about by the Revolution.

NOTES

1. Research for this paper was undertaken with the assistance of a Foreign Area Fellowship and a further grant from the American Social Science Research Council. I wish to thank Eric Van Young for his aid in transcribing a part of the data.
2. See, for example, William B. Taylor, *Landlord and peasant in colonial Oaxaca* (Stanford, Calif., 1972), pp. 121–35.
3. Isabel González Sánchez (ed.), *Haciendas y ranchos de Tlaxcala en 1712* (Mexico, 1969).
4. See Eric R. Wolf and Sidney W. Mintz, 'Haciendas and plantations in Middle America and the Antilles', *Social and Economic Studies* VII, 3 (1957), pp. 380–412.
5. Georges Duby, *Rural economy and country life in the medieval west* (London, 1968), p. 171.
6. Andrés Molina Enríquez, *Los grandes problemas nacionales* (Mexico, 1909), pp. 80–106; Enrique Florescano, *Estructuras y problemas agrarios de México 1500–1821* (Mexico, 1971), pp. 125–46.
7. See Mario Góngora, *Origen de los 'inquilinos' de Chile central* (Santiago de Chile, 1960); Jean Borde and Mario Góngora, *Evolución de la propiedad rural en el Valle de Puangue*, 2 vols. (Santiago de Chile, 1956).
8. Robert C. West, 'Surface configuration and associated geology of Middle America', in Robert Wauchope (ed.), *Handbook of Middle American Indians*, vol. 1: *Natural environment and early cultures* (Austin, Texas, 1964), pp. 44–9.
9. Jorge L. Tamayo, *El problema fundamental de la agricultura mexicana* (Mexico, 1964), p. 30; Carlos Manuel Castillo, 'La economía agrícola en la región de el Bajío', in *Problemas agrícolas é industriales de México* VIII (1956), pp. 8–13; Philip L. Wagner, 'Natural vegetation of Middle America', in Wauchope (ed.), *Handbook of Middle American Indians*, vol. 1, pp. 222, 255–7.
10. Wigberto Jiménez Moreno, *Estudios de historia colonial* (Mexico, 1958), pp. 57, 81–9.
11. D. A. Brading, *Miners and merchants in Bourbon Mexico 1763–1810* (Cambridge, 1971), pp. 223–33; Eric R. Wolf, 'The Mexican Bajío in the eighteenth century: an analysis of cultural integration', in Munro S. Edmundson (ed.), *Synoptic studies of Mexican culture* (New Orleans, 1957).
12. Pedro Rojas, *Acámbaro colonial* (Mexico, 1967), pp. 143–50.
13. Wolf, 'The Mexican Bajío', p. 191; Brading, *Miners and merchants*, pp. 227–9.
14. François Chevalier, *La formación de los grandes latifundios en México* (Mexico, 1956), pp. 48, 226.
15. Archivo General de la Nación, Mexico City (hereafter cited as AGN), Historia, 523, f. 76.
16. For these measures see Charles Gibson, *The Aztecs under Spanish rule* (Stanford, 1964), p. 276. A *sitio de ganado mayor* comprised just over 41 *caballerías*, and a *sitio de ganado menor* had 18 *caballerías*; a *caballería* was the equivalent of 42.5 hectares.
17. Alexander von Humboldt, *Ensayo político sobre el reino de la Nueva España* (Mexico, 1966 (first Spanish edition in 1822)), p. 69.
18. See Peter Hall (ed.), *Von Thünen's isolated state* (London, 1966); Michael Chisholm, *Rural settlement and land use* (London, 1968), pp. 25–32.
19. Miguel Ramos Arispe, *Memoria sobre el estado de las provincias internas de oriente* (Mexico, 1932), pp. 85–92.
20. Archivo Histórico Municipal de León (hereafter cited as AHML), 1708–10, 20, Inventory declared, 19 November 1707.

21. AGN, Vínculos 236–3, Inventory taken, 25 January 1707.
22. AGN, Bienes nacionales 1865–64, 1 September 1806.
23. A. V. Chayanov, *On the theory of peasant economy*, ed. Daniel Thorner *et al*. (Homewood, Ill., 1966), pp. 6–9, 39–42, 88–90.
24. Enrique Florescano, *Precios del maíz y crisis agrícolas en México 1708–1810* (Mexico, 1969), pp. 88–91, 122–39; Florescano, *Estructuras y problemas agrarios*, pp. 128–48.
25. AGN, Bienes nacionales, 85–37, 26 April 1749; AGN, Vínculos 221–3.
26. AGN, Civil 120–2, Inventory, 2 June 1755. The dam was 1,400 metres wide and provided irrigation for 18 *caballerías* with 500 *fanegas de sembradura* for wheat.
27. AHML, 1708–10, 20, Inventory, 19 November 1707; Archivo Notarial de León (hereafter cited as ANL), 14 July 1791.
28. Molina Enríquez, *Los grandes problemas nacionales*, pp. 92–103.
29. See AGN, Vínculos 117 (the entire volume).
30. Archivo General de Indias (hereafter cited as AGI), Mexico 1370, Manager's report, 4 February 1772.
31. See AGN, Padrones 24.
32. The clearest inventory of estate is in AGN, Tierras 2646, 7 September 1753. Our discussion of the internal organization of Juchitlán is taken from the three volumes AGN, Tierras 826–8.
33. AHML, 1798–9, 1; AHML, 1807, 27, tenants' complaint, 8 March 1804.
34. AGN, Vínculos 5–3, Indian protest, 9 March 1802.
35. For this case see AGN, Tierras 1383–3, Expulsion of leaders, March 1808. See also José María Luis Mora, *Obras sueltas* (Mexico, 1963), p. 169.
36. Brading, *Miners and merchants*, pp. 146–9, 288–91.
37. AHML, 1757–8, 8, statement, 21 February 1757.
38. Archivo Casa Morelos, Morelia (hereafter cited as ACM), 846.
39. AHML, 1758–9, 31, Inventory, 26 January 1758.
40. The sources of the subsequent discussion are inserted in Table 3.
41. Archivo Histórico de Guanajuato, Bienes difuntos, 1843–5, Inventory, 1 February 1844. Compare this measure with Charles Gibson, *The Aztecs under Spanish rule*, where a *fanega de sembradura* is reckoned as 3.5 hectares or about 12 to a *caballería*. Leovigildo Islas Escárcega, *Diccionario rural de México* (Mexico, 1961), p. 121, asserts that the area ranged from 3 to 10 hectares.
42. For an excellent discussion see Jan Bazant, *Alienation of Church wealth in Mexico* (Cambridge, 1971), pp. 181–2, 197–8.
43. Paul S. Taylor, *A Spanish–Mexican peasant community: Arandas in Jalisco, Mexico* (Berkeley, Calif., 1933), pp. 13, 26–8.
44. Jan Bazant, *Los bienes de la Iglesia en México 1856–75* (Mexico, 1971), Appendix 21, pp. 340–8, 'Fraccionamiento de las haciendas en el Bajío'. This valuable study is not included in the English version of the book, *Alienation of Church wealth in Mexico* (Cambridge, 1971).
45. Luis González, *Pueblo en vilo* (Mexico, 1968), pp. 94–8.
46. Multiple entries in notarial register: see ANL, 19 and 28 November 1827; 29 April and 24 May 1828; 25 May 1842; 3 July, 12–13 September, and 28 October 1843; 22 March 1844; 13–25 November 1848; 24 April 1851.
47. Multiple entries in notarial register: see ANL, 28–9 February, 12 and 29–30 March, 1 April, 30 August, 27 September, and 24 October 1844; 26 February, 27 July, and 31 December 1846; 17–18 January 1847; 11 February 1848.
48. ANL, 7 April 1708.
49. ACM, 851.

50. AHML, 1793–4, 4, 30 October 1793.
51. The sources of the subsequent discussion are shown in Table 7.
52. Included in the total of 1,136 *pesos* is 35 *pesos* charged to one peasant but unpaid (see Table 7).
53. For a similar trend see González, *Pueblo en vilo*, pp. 139–43.
54. Daniel Cosío Villegas, *La historia moderna de México: el porfiriato, la vida económica*, 2 vols. (Mexico, 1965), vol. 2, pp. 837–8, 848–50, 858–63.
55. Cosío Villegas, *El porfiriato*, vol. 1, pp. 5–26; Francisco Bulnes, *El verdadero Díaz y la revolución*, 2nd edn (Mexico, 1960), p. 218.
56. Moisés González Navarro, 'El porfiriato, vida social', in Daniel Cosío Villegas (ed.), *Historia moderna de México* (Mexico, 1957), pp. 133–4, 222.
57. AHML, Titles of Otates.
58. Leopoldo Solís, *La realidad económica mexicana: retrovisión y perspectivas* (Mexico, 1970), p. 201.

CHAPTER 3

Landlord, labourer, and tenant in San Luis Potosí, northern Mexico, 1822–1910

JAN BAZANT

In northern Mexico, where population was sparse and land plentiful, large estates predominated; their size, roughly speaking, increased with aridity and distance from Mexico City. In the state of San Luis Potosí, situated in what might be called the middle north, *haciendas* covered an average area of about fifteen square leagues; that is, between 25,000 and 30,000 hectares each. The few Indian villages that existed – there had been no sedentary population in northern Mexico before the Conquest – were also well endowed with land, some of them originally having been granted some thirty-six square leagues each by the colonial government. Estates naturally made frequent inroads into these communal holdings, thereby expanding at the expense of the Indian villages. The opposite process also took place occasionally, at least after Mexico became independent in 1821.

The population of the old-established Indian villages was not very large, and it would seem that in the early nineteenth century they did not supply the *haciendas* with much of the required seasonal labour; instead the estates had to rely almost entirely on their own permanent labourers. Another source of seasonal labour arose in time, eventually replacing the old villages. The estates were enormous, and in the beginning only the land around the *casco* – the farm buildings – was cultivated, and the rest was given over to extensive cattle-grazing. The *peones* or farm labourers lived in the *casco*, leaving the rest of the estate virtually uninhabited, except for a few small, scattered ranches where the cattle herds were kept and where the herders lived. But as a result of the gradual increase in population in the eighteenth and nineteenth centuries, small settlements or hamlets (*rancherías*) began to appear in the outlying areas of the *haciendas*. The origins of these settlements are not clear; perhaps they were founded by surplus *peones* from the *haciendas* themselves, or by peasants from the freeholding villages. Others again may have come from the nearby mining towns. From the *hacendados'* point of view, this amounted to illegal occupation of their land; they were mindful of the colonial legislation which permitted these new settlers to claim as their own the land on which they lived and which they worked.

But the process once begun was irreversible, and the *hacienda* thus preferred to legalize the status of its resident population. The settlers were assigned a rent, a fixed amount being charged for the house site together with a variable annual rent, depending on the area they had under cultivation and the number of cattle they kept on the *hacienda* lands. Squatters thereby became tenants. At least one village, the settlement of Ahualulco, was later alleged to have been founded by the *hacendado* who had presumably settled a group of families on his property under specific, favourable conditions. It is an open question how many such settlements of tenants originated in a contract – not necessarily a written one – between settlers and a landowner eager to increase his revenues, and how many were begun through the illegal occupation of certain areas of the *hacienda* by the landless poor. The situation was clearly different from that prevailing in central Mexico, where old-established villages with written privileges were common. Whatever their origin, by the nineteenth century many settlements of tenant farmers dotted the landed estates of San Luis Potosí.

In this essay we shall describe the relationship between *haciendas* on the one hand and labourers, tenants, and sharecroppers on the other. Our information has been derived from the private archives of two *haciendas*: San Diego, situated to the east of the city of San Luis Potosí, on a fertile, well-watered plain near the town of Río Verde, where the altitude of 1,000 metres made the climate sufficiently attractive for the cultivation of sugar cane in spite of frequent and sometimes severe winter frosts; and the *Hacienda* Bocas, some forty kilometres north of the state capital, at an altitude of 1,700 metres, which was mainly devoted to cattle-raising and maize- and wheat-growing.[1]

The Hacienda San Diego

The archives of the *Hacienda* San Diego are fragmentary and throw most light on the social aspects of *hacienda* life and organization. The main activity of this large *hacienda*, which in the early years of Independence covered over 27,800 hectares, was the cultivation of sugar cane by irrigation, and the manufacture of brown, unclayed sugar known as *piloncillo* for sale in the city of San Luis Potosí. Secondary activities included maize cultivation and the exploitation of the *hacienda*'s forest resources. From the probably incomplete lists for the year 1822 it appears that there were at least 250 *arrendatarios*, or tenants, on the estate, which would indicate a minimum population of about 1,000 people. Sometimes it is difficult to distinguish between *arrendatarios* properly so called, who were

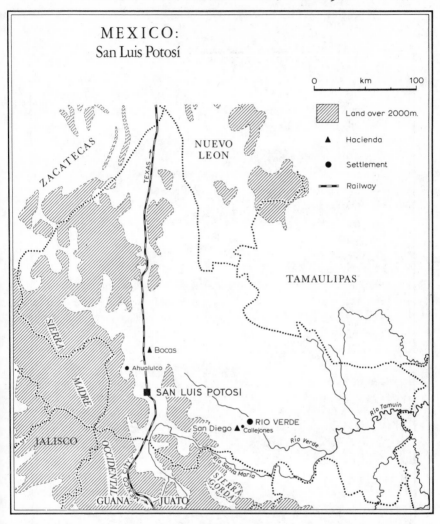

Map 6

men living with their families on *hacienda* land, and landless peasants
who lived in settlements outside the *hacienda* and simply rented land
belonging to the *hacienda* for cultivation. Such was the case of the
inhabitants of Callejones, a hamlet situated, as its name indicates, along
a road bordering the *hacienda*. Across the way from their huts the irrigated *hacienda* lands were devoted at least in part to sugar cane, and

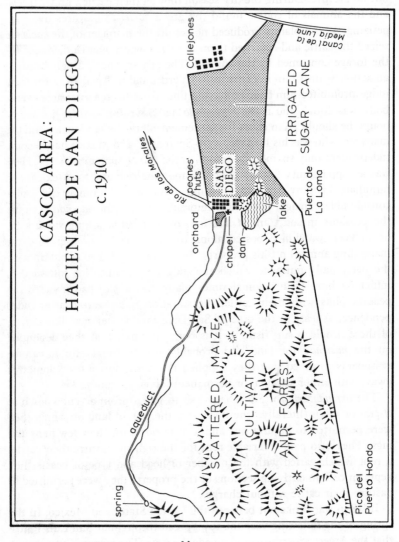

Map 7

so they were allotted lands for growing maize on a distant *rancho*, or remote section of the estate. The people of Callejones had some cattle, but no pasture. During the dry season they let their cattle wander freely, and the animals of course found the green *hacienda* pastures more appetizing. As complaints produced no result, the manager of the *hacienda* seized the cattle and returned them to their owners against payment for the forage consumed by the animals. The peasants accordingly brought an action against him in court in Río Verde, and in April 1822 the local judge prohibited him from collecting fines from his tenants; now everybody was equal, and if the *hacendado* had anything against his neighbours, he should go to court for settlement. Both the landowner and the manager, who was his brother, were Spaniards, and Mexico had become independent only six months before, at the end of September 1821. Here was an opportunity for the poor to annoy the rich and for Mexicans to humiliate haughty Spaniards. Hungry and thirsty animals can cause considerable damage; but it was impracticable for the *hacendado* to sue the peasants in court and it was too costly to build a long stone wall, or to keep watchmen posted along the *hacienda* boundaries to drive marauding animals off his property. So the *hacendado* had to put up with the petty daily nuisance which the judge, no doubt, had intended to inflict on him. If in colonial times many *hacendados* had invaded the peasant plots with their cattle, the situation was reversed after Independence, at least in the case of San Diego and Callejones. The daring of these people is surprising if it is borne in mind that they depended on the *hacienda* for land and probably also for work, for it can be reasonably assumed that they supplied the *casco*, only a few kilometres away, with either seasonal or permanent labour, or both.

The *arrendatarios* of San Diego had to pay a ground rent known as *el piso* or *pisaje* (literally, 'the floor') for the plot of land on which they were permitted to build a hut and a little *corral* for their few hens and pigs. They also paid a variable rent for the right to pasture their cattle, a rent which varied with the number of head and type of beasts they kept; on certain outlying sections of the property they were permitted to pasture their cattle without charge.

In 1846 war broke out between the United States and Mexico. In the spring of the following year the fear spread throughout San Luis Potosí that the American army would invade the state. The owner of San Diego, the son of a Spanish father and a Mexican mother, invited his *arrendatarios* to form, at his expense and under his command, a *guerrilla* against the invader. He offered to waive the rent on both *el piso* and their animals for the duration of the campaign, and promised to feed their families in their absence. It is significant that he did not address himself to the *peones permanentes*, who were resident in the *casco*, but only to the *arrendatarios* who were used to an independent life, to horseback riding and shooting wild beasts in the forest. The American army did not proceed south, however; its strategy was different, and the *guerrilla* of Río Verde never materialized. It is not even known how the *arrendatarios* reacted to their master's proclamation. However, the fact that such an invitation was possible shows that the relations between the *hacendado* and at least the more prosperous of his tenants could not have been totally bad.

The poorer *arrendatarios*, who did not earn enough to pay their rent, who were in debt and were sometimes forced to pay it in other ways or run the risk of being evicted, may have had different feelings. With Mexico's defeat, despair spread among the ruling classes and starvation among the poor. It was therefore no surprise that the peasantry rose up against the established order in the Sierra Gorda mountains, south of San Diego. They succeeded in capturing the district of Río Verde, the prefect of which was a cousin of the *hacendado* of San Diego. He himself had once been the manager of San Diego, and he now decided to avenge some real, or imagined, wrongs inflicted on him by the wealthy branch of the family. He therefore drew up for the rebels a programme designed to satisfy the demands of both tenants and labourers on the local *haciendas*. Among other things *arrendatarios* 'shall have land at a moderate rent, never paying a share of the harvest'. *Hacendados* often found it more convenient to have sharecroppers instead of straightforward tenants, especially if their share amounted to more than half the crop.[2] 'The *arrendatarios* shall not pay *pisaje* or rent for work-animals . . . They shall not do any *faena*; every service will be justly paid.' (*Faena* was occasional unpaid compulsory work performed by labourers and tenants on Sundays.) The *peones* or labourers 'shall be paid in cash or in goods of good quality and at the prevailing local prices'. Finally, the *haciendas* with more than 1,500 inhabitants – equivalent to at least 300 *peón* families – in their *casco* should become villages; as villages were traditionally granted a certain minimum area of land for both house-building and agricultural use, it meant in practice the confiscation of the core area of the *hacienda*. It is not certain if the population of the *hacienda* of San Diego was large enough to fall into this category; at any rate, the *hacendado* resolved to offer armed resistance to the rebellion, his property was sacked and burned, and the dam was blown up. The federal army suppressed the uprising in October 1849.

The Hacienda Bocas

In the Bocas territory there were no mountains where the guerrillas could hide; but the basic situation was not very different. Juan Pérez Gálvez, who had bought the property of almost 75,000 hectares in 1844, began to encroach on the fields and orchards (*huertas*) of Ahualulco, a village located on *hacienda* lands. During the unsettled conditions accompanying the war with the United States, the peasants revolted, and the governors of San Luis Potosí and Zacatecas – Ahualulco was then just across the state boundary – advised the landowner to give up his 'improvements'. The landowner was willing to cede to the village the so-called *fundo legal*, an area of 1 square kilometre, but Ahualulco claimed to have been granted one square league of land, equal to 17.5 square kilometres, by the owner of Bocas towards the end of the eighteenth century. On the neighbouring *Hacienda* Cruces, belonging to the same person, a village with 800 inhabitants was granted one square league of land by the State Congress in 1850.

For the examination of labour relationships and land tenure in Bocas, the year 1852 has been selected. At that time the main products of this cattle *hacienda* were wool, hides, skins, and tallow, which were sold in Querétaro, Mexico City, and other major Mexican cities. The *hacienda* also produced large quantities of *mezcal*, an alcoholic 'firewater' distilled from *agave* juice, which comes from the *maguey*, a plant which was found in a semi-wild state on *hacienda* territory. In addition several commercial varieties of chile (red) peppers, maize, wheat, barley, and leguminous plants such as beans, chickpeas, and lentils were grown. Wheat and chile peppers were cultivated with irrigation.

The *hacienda* had both permanent and seasonal labourers at its disposal. The former, called *sirvientes permanentes* (permanent servants), had access to a patch of land for a house and *corral*, and a plot for growing food, free of charge. Most *sirvientes permanentes* lived 'in the *casco*', grouped around the *hacienda* buildings, the owner's or manager's residence, and the chapel. Some of those responsible for herding the cattle lived on the *ranchos*; because of the distances involved, a few *ranchos* were run as completely separate agricultural enterprises. All *sirvientes permanentes* were subject to a rigorous discipline: this was the price that had to be paid for their traditional, unwritten rights and privileges.

There were about 400 *sirvientes permanentes* in Bocas; inevitably their number fluctuated in the course of the year, the lowest – 325 – being

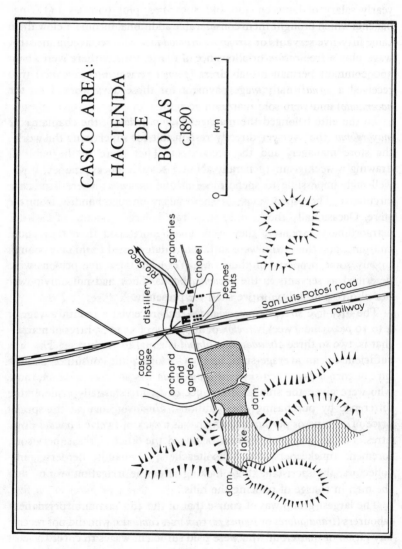

CASCO AREA:
HACIENDA
DE
BOCAS
c.1890

0   1
km

granaries

chapel

Rio seco

distillery

peones' huts

San Luis Potosí road

railway

casco house

orchard and garden

lake

dam

dam

dam

Map 8

registered in December, when it would seem that some of them returned to their original homes to harvest their own maize crops. They can be divided into three groups. At the top were five people each earning a yearly salary of between 300 and 800 *pesos*, plus bonuses and fringe benefits which brought them considerable additional income. Below them came fifty-five servants or *sirvientes acomodados* who received a monthly wage plus a free *ración* or allowance of maize. Finally there were about 360 common permanent labourers (*peones permanentes comunes*) who received a *jornal* (daily wage payment for those days worked for the *hacendado*) and were sold maize on account.

To the elite belonged the manager (*administrador*), the chaplain, the *mayordomo* (the overseer directly responsible for supervising the work), the store manager, and the accountant. They were in the habit of drawing a weekly sum (generally about 3 *pesos*) as pocket money. It was well-nigh impossible to spend more on the *hacienda*, where little cash circulated. They spent most of their salary on merchandise from the store. Occasionally they would withdraw a larger amount of cash for extraordinary expenses; they were given more food than they could consume, and those who were sufficiently determined could save enough to buy some property of their own. Yet even these five persons were described as servants in the *hacienda* books. They had not only power but also responsibility, as we shall see presently.

The fifty-five *sirvientes acomodados* each received a monthly wage of 4 to 10 *pesos* and a weekly *ración* or allowance of 15 to 23 litres of maize – that is, two to three *almudes* (one *almud* is equal to 7.6 litres).[3] This was sufficient for an average-sized family, for one adult consumed about a litre of corn a day. Each *sirviente acomodado* was assigned a *ración*; those who were given the smaller allowance of 15 litres usually made up the difference by purchasing one additional *almud* of corn at the special price of 1.50 pesos per *fanega*, which was a sack of twelve *almudes* or 91 litres. To this group of workers belonged the office clerks, supervisors, foremen, timekeepers, two schoolteachers, cowhands, herders, rent-collectors, the sacristan, those looking after the irrigation works, and the men in charge of policing the hills.

The largest group was of course that of the 360 'common' permanent labourers (*trabajadores* or *peones permanentes comunes*) who did not receive any *ración* of maize but who were paid sufficient wages to cover the cost of the maize they had to purchase for themselves and their families. Two hundred and sixty-five of them received the daily wage or *jornal* of 1½ *reales*, equal to 1.30 *pesos* a week or 5.60 pesos a month. The remaining ninety-five, called *muchachos* or 'boys', were paid a *jornal* of 1 *real* –

that is, 1 *peso* a week or 3.75 pesos a month; their ages were not indicated, but judging from their surnames, they were the sons of older *peones permanentes*, who were starting out on an independent life of their own. Sundays were regarded as ordinary workdays; there were roads to be repaired or a chapel to be built. Sunday work was of course paid at the normal daily rate. Hence, at Bocas, at least for the *peones*, the hated *faenas* did not exist. On the other hand *peones* were not paid for the days on which they did not work, and these were many, including of course occasional Sundays. Such a large number of wage labourers clearly required constant supervision; the function of many of the fifty-five *sirvientes acomodados* consisted of seeing to it that the *peones* who had turned up for work early in the morning were kept at their tasks all day. The older *peones* usually took home 23 litres of maize every week, or about a hundred litres a month. These amounts were charged to their accounts at the rate of 1.50 *pesos* per *fanega*, the same price at which maize was granted to the *sirvientes acomodados*. The *muchachos* usually took about half this amount, from which it can be deduced that at least some of them had wives but as yet no children – perhaps only a few infants. Thus *peones permanentes* spent between a quarter and a third of their income on maize.

Peones permanentes, including the *sirvientes acomodados*, normally cultivated a small patch of maize on land which the *hacienda* allowed them free of charge. This was a concession to the age-old tradition of the Mexican Indians. In mid-1852 at least half the *peones permanentes* purchased one *almud* of seed grain each from the *hacienda*. The high price of 3.75 pesos per *fanega* resulted from the fact that this was selected grain, and this perhaps explains why not everyone bought it. One *almud* of seed was sufficient for about 3,000 square metres of land; the harvest from this of course varied, but in general each plot yielded sufficient maize to feed one or perhaps even two adults for a year.

The *peones permanentes* certainly received enough of this basic food-stuff. The *sirvientes acomodados* had free maize: the mass of *peones per-manentes comunes* bought it at a fixed concessionary price and moreover obtained some from their own plot of land. On exceptional occasions they bought small quantities of maize from the *hacienda*'s *troje* (granary) at the commercial price, which fluctuated between 2 and 3 *pesos* a *fanega*, or in other words up to twice as much as the special price. Why did they not buy all their maize at the special reduced price? The main reason was that the *hacienda* merely wished to guarantee the *peones*' basic subsistence needs, and therefore each one was assigned a certain amount of maize which he could obtain at the reduced price; if he wished for any extra then he had to pay the full commercial price.

Peones permanentes obtained everything else at the *tienda de raya*, the *hacienda* store. The most frequent weekly item was the *recaudo*, which included all kinds of food (except maize), beverages, and tobacco. They occasionally purchased the meat of animals specially slaughtered by the *hacienda*, a pair of sandals, and some coarse cotton cloth (*manta*). *Manta* was sold to the *peones* at the current local price. From the extant archives it has been possible to estimate the gross profit of the store at a not unreasonable 33 per cent. No sales of alcoholic beverages are recorded in the *hacienda* archives – the risk of disturbances was probably too high.

Each *peón permanente* had a current account to which his earnings and payment of debts were credited and his expenses and amounts borrowed were debited. On 31 December 1852, 220 *peones permanentes* owed the *hacienda* almost 1,500 *pesos*; the *hacienda* owed eighty-two others a total of 450 *pesos*; and finally 133 *peones* owed the *hacienda*, or were themselves owed by the *hacienda*, sums of less than 1 *peso*, and in some cases nothing at all. Hence almost 30 per cent of the *peones permanentes* did not owe the enterprise anything, which is quite contrary to the general impression that all or practically all the *hacienda* work force were indebted and deliberately kept in this situation by the *hacienda*, which wanted to hold a reluctant labour force. On 1 January 1852 the total indebtedness had amounted to 2,800 *pesos*; it had thus been reduced by nearly a half in the course of the year. In most cases those who had begun the year with a debt ended the year still in debt. Most families or individuals owed some money; further research might show the origin of this indebtedness. Some families and individuals clearly preferred to be creditors; those with ambition could eventually withdraw their small savings from the *hacienda* and become independent operators on a small scale, for Bocas put no obstacles in their way. It is not known how many *peones* left the *hacienda* with their account paid off. The records listed only those who had left either with a credit or a debit. In 1852, 120 former *peones permanentes* who had left the *hacienda* still owed more than 1,000 *pesos*, a sum which obviously could not be collected. In turn the *hacienda* owed about 200 *pesos* to thirty other men who had left without claiming the money owed them.

The situation of seasonal labourers (*peones eventuales, peones temporales,* or *alquilados*) was less satisfactory. They did not have the benefits enjoyed by the *peones permanentes* such as a house site, a parcel of land for cultivation, credit at the *hacienda* store, and maize at the concessionary price. Given the distance of the *hacienda* from the nearest villages, it can be assumed that during the harvest season they dwelled on the *hacienda* in temporary huts (*chozas provisionales*). Five hundred of them worked on the *pizca*, the maize harvest, at the beginning of 1852. Their numbers then declined sharply and dwindled to half a dozen at the end of July, when many of the workers were busily engaged in sowing their maize crop in their home villages or *rancherías*. In September and October, when the maize was being cultivated, their numbers rose to between 200 and 300. A few *peones temporales* could earn up to 3 *reales* a day, or 10 *pesos* a month, assuming they worked for the whole month, which of course they rarely did. The vast majority earned between 1 and 1½ *reales* daily. This pattern of wage distribution was very similar to that of the *peones permanentes*. Of the 500 *peones temporales* engaged in harvesting maize, approximately twenty-five earned 3 *reales*, 325 earned 1½ *reales*, and 150 were each paid 1 *real* per day. Their nominal wages were thus about the same as those of *peones permanentes*, but in fact their real wages were much lower. They received half their wages 'in silver', the other half being paid in maize at the current commercial price. For example, at the beginning of November they worked an average of three days a week; towards the end of the month they worked more. Between 160 and 210 *peones temporales* bought 100 *fanegas* of grain at 2 *pesos* a *fanega* in November; each *peón* thus obtained maize for two people. It is not known how they disposed of the cash element in their wages. They could of course have bought additional amounts of maize on the *hacienda*, or anywhere else for that matter. Nor is it known what they did with the rest of their time, or if they were in fact employed or not. If they were not, was it for lack of opportunity or other reasons? One thing only is certain: the majority of the *peones temporales* on Bocas were *arrendatarios* on the same *hacienda*.

In the middle of the nineteenth century the *arrendatarios* on Bocas were supposed to pay rent or *pisaje* for their house site, at the flat rate of 5 *pesos* a year; they also paid half a *peso* a year for one *almud* of maize land (that is the area required to plant one *almud* of seed grain, which worked out at about 3,000 square metres). This was the minimum amount of agricultural land that could be rented; in practice much larger areas were frequently involved. A figure of twelve *almudes* or 1 *fanega* of land, equal to about 3.6 hectares, rented for 6 *pesos*, was not uncommon. Pasture rents were paid at so much per head of cattle, the animals being allowed to roam freely on certain sections of the *hacienda* which were reserved for tenants. The annual charge was one-twentieth of a *peso* for a sheep or a goat, and one-fourth of a *peso* for each cow, ox, or bullock.

In 1852 there were 794 tenants living on Bocas – a population of 4,000 people at most. They lived scattered in about a dozen *rancherías* and another dozen smaller settlements. If we add to this the *peones per-*

manentes and their families, who probably numbered not more than 1,500 people, given the large number of *muchachos* without children, the total permanent population of the *hacienda* amounted to between 5,000 and 5,500 people. Seasonal migrant workers are not included in this figure.

The *arrendatarios* can be roughly divided into three groups. Firstly there were those who rented both crop and pasture land, including a few who rented only crop land. Secondly there were a few *arrendatarios* who rented only pasture land, and did not grow any crops. Lastly, the most numerous and poorest group paid only ground rent or *pisaje*. Their exact number cannot be ascertained, because their individual accounts in many cases indicate only their accumulated debt, without specifying its origin. As debts mainly amounted to between 10 and 15 *pesos*, it can reasonably be assumed that this was ground rent for two or three years, and that they did not grow any maize or keep any animals, for in this case the debt would have been different. However this may be, those who had only a house site together with those who kept only a few sheep or goats were in the majority. In order to earn the money to pay their 5 *pesos* a year rent, they had to work as *peones eventuales* for the *hacienda*, for the larger tenants, or for the sharecroppers on Bocas, or possibly also on the neighbouring *haciendas*. Alternatively, they might be independent craftsmen or small traders.

The *arrendatarios* who rented both farm land and pasture were in a minority; moreover, it is again necessary to distinguish between small tenants, who rented only one *almud* of land, and large tenants, who might rent 1 *fanega* of land, or even more. The former, who were much more numerous, had to find some way of supplementing the yield from 3,000 square metres of crop land, which was insufficient to feed a family. There was a very marked contrast indeed between this group of tenants and the *peones permanentes*, who also cultivated one *almud* of maize land each, but who had to pay for neither their land nor their house sites, and who moreover had steady jobs and were supplied with maize at a reduced price. It may well be imagined that many tenants hoped to become *peones permanentes* and to exchange their freedom for the harsh discipline of life on the *hacienda*, for freedom often meant hunger whilst servitude seemed to be more than compensated for by a full stomach. On the other hand, the large tenants who rented at least 1 *fanega* of land and owned several dozen head of cattle did not have to hire themselves out to others; on the contrary, they often employed poor tenants themselves. Information on this point is unfortunately lacking, for the *hacienda* recorded only the rent of its tenants, but not their earnings, costs, or expenses. The 794 tenants owed the *hacienda* 14,594 *pesos*, ten times as much as the *peones permanentes* (seasonal labourers as such had no debts). Almost all tenants were indebted to the *hacienda*, and very few made payments on account. The debt tended to increase with time and for all practical purposes was regarded as irredeemable. The *hacienda* might just as well have cancelled it, but this would have demoralized the few tenants who had paid their debts and would have given encouragement to those who refused to pay. For either rents were excessive, or tenants had no intention of paying them; the latter possibility cannot be discounted in view of the 1849 uprising. We shall presently see how the *hacienda* found a way out of this impasse.

The 200 or so sharecroppers or *aparceros* were included in the list of the 794 tenants; they received agricultural land from the *hacienda* in exchange for a share of the harvest, but this did not exempt them from the obligation to pay *pisaje* or the rent for pasturing their animals. The *hacienda* paid half the harvesting costs; this probably helped to mitigate the sharecroppers' resentment of being supervised. At harvest time some of the *aparceros* employed as many as a dozen or more labourers, paying them $1\frac{1}{2}$ *reales* a day. It would appear from the names in the account books that others hired their own sons, paying them the standard wage. Further research might reveal if *aparceros* rose from poor tenants, from *peones permanentes*, or from both types of worker. Some such mobility surely existed; at present it can only be surmised from family names that reappear at different times among the different social groups.

To sum up, the population of Bocas consisted basically of *peones permanentes* and *arrendatarios*; in the middle were both *peones temporales* and *aparceros*, the latter being a combination of tenants, wage-earners and sub-contractors. Future research might also indicate downward mobility, however. The prospects of moving up the social ladder probably seemed slight to most tenants, who were frequently poorer than the *peones permanentes*. To them, the upper groups must have seemed inaccessible.

It is well known that tenants constituted a vast pool of reserve labour on Mexican *haciendas*. But in Bocas, at least, they were not always willing to work for the enterprise. The *hacienda* would then resort to the use of force – *haciendas*, after all, had their own armed guards. Since practically all the tenants owed the *hacendado* money, he could always argue that he was only trying to collect what was his due, although of course this was against the law. The *hacienda* could also put pressure on its indebted workers by threatening to take away their animals – again an illegal procedure. Perhaps this was the only way, since the courts were too slow. Bocas also instituted a *faena* (unpaid work), which had to be performed by the *aparceros* and which consisted of gathering maize straw. Those who could afford to do so sent a son or a *peón* in their stead, but everyone complained. It so happened that labour was scarce when the *hacienda* most needed it, at harvest time, when the tenants were busy harvesting their own crops, to which they naturally gave preference. In some cases, however, the impression is that they simply did not feel like working for the *hacienda* or that they preferred other easier work.

This then was the main area of conflict. Tension frequently mounted each December, and in 1853 it exploded. When tenants on an outlying *rancho* refused to carry out some urgent work on the *agave* plants, protesting their ignorance of the cultivation techniques, the manager ordered their huts to be torn down, thereby adding fuel to the fire. On 15 March 1853 the *hacienda* workers 'mutinied'. From the scanty information available it is possible to deduce that a group of men attempted to disarm the *hacienda* guards – nothing more. It also seems, so far as it has been possible to identify the participants, that they were *arrendatarios* rather than *peones*. They were taken to jail in San Luis Potosí. The *mayordomo* also lost his job and was imprisoned; perhaps he showed suspicious lenience towards the culprits. The accounts reveal that most *peones* abstained from work in the first few weeks following the mutiny. The situation soon returned to normal, however, and only an insignificant number of workers lost their jobs. The *hacienda* preferred to keep its organization intact.

Discipline on the *hacienda* was easily restored, but nevertheless the *arrendatarios* kept on causing problems. We can now appreciate that their non-payment of rent was mainly due to their extreme poverty, but after the 1849 rebellion there was an element of doubt. The *hacendado* suspected their motives and in some cases attributed it to disobedience. In 1853 the manager of Bocas compiled for the first time a separate 'list of evicted, insolvent, and deceased tenants', which amounted to almost 250 persons who owed a total of 4,264 *pesos*. Naturally enough this amount was written off as a total loss by the *hacienda*. The 'insolvent' tenants were those who were unable to clear their debts either by working them off or by pledging their animals as security. The indebted tenants still on the *hacienda* were expected to pay cash; if they were unable to pay, they were expected to work off the debt themselves or to send a son or a *peón* in their place. If the worse came to the worst, they were liable to have their animals confiscated. Insolvent tenants of course faced the danger of being evicted. Pressure was combined with incentives; tenants were offered the opportunity to reduce their debt by working for Bocas as *peones temporales*. The tenant then received a daily wage of 2 *reales* instead of the usual 1½, with the extra half-*real* being credited to his account. Consequently, although his net wage remained the same, at least his debt would slowly be reduced. For the *hacendado* the extra half-*real* could be seen as a loss, but the method could at least be expected to improve relations with the *arrendatarios*. The debt could also be reduced by forcing tenants to become sharecroppers, with a part of the harvest being credited to their account. Thus, in 1864 the *hacendado* tried to force the villagers of Ahualulco to become *aparceros*, but they complained to the authorities, alleging that, as they were fairly prosperous already, they would suffer badly if they were obliged to become sharecroppers. By such means the total indebtedness of the tenants of Bocas was reduced from 15,000 *pesos* in 1852 to 8,000 *pesos* in 1865.

Changes in labour organization on Hacienda Bocas, 1870–94
The risks of having such a large number of tenants and labourers on Bocas were, no doubt, constantly on the *hacendado*'s mind. It might possibly have led him to carry out a deliberate policy of gradually restricting their numbers. There were probably other motives for this, such as the desire to economize during a period of economic stagnation, the causes of which are not clear. Further research might throw some light on the decline of the maize harvest at Bocas. It is probable that the change in ownership was a contributing cause; by 1870 the *hacienda* was the property of the Farías brothers, and it was under their management that the new policy took shape. Up to then, *peones* residing on the *hacienda* were always described as '*permanentes*'. Although they had no written contract, the *hacendado* felt bound to give them reasonably steady employment, and we have seen, perhaps in contrast to some other *haciendas*, that *peones* were not kept at Bocas against their will. Perhaps by as early as 1852 there were too many of them on the *hacienda*, and this might explain the willingness of the landowner to let them go; and yet they were regarded – and regarded themselves – as a part of the *hacienda*. All this changed with the publication of the Civil Code at the end of 1871. The Code recognized only three types of wage contracts: domestic service, service remunerated by a daily wage or *jornal*, and piece-work. There was no mention of the traditional and permanent ties between a labourer and his job. Certainly the Code specified that those labourers hired for a certain length of time could not be dismissed without just cause, but the idea of a permanent contract was foreign to the liberal authors of the Code, who wished to introduce maximum freedom

for both labourer and employer. Thus at a stroke *peones permanentes* became *jornaleros* who could be dismissed at any time.

In the first months of 1872, apart from an administrative staff of ten, Bocas had sixty *acomodados* who enjoyed the free *ración* of maize, and 275 *peones* earning the traditional wage. A few of them appear to have been the same individuals who had been recorded twenty years before; judging from their surnames, most of them were probably the sons of the 1852 *peones*. The total work force of 345 at the service of the *hacienda* was much smaller than twenty years earlier. The number of clerks and supervisory staff had increased, whilst the number of those actually engaged in agricultural work had diminished. More important was the fact that the term '*sirvientes permanentes*' had been dropped, and the ordinary *peones* (not the *acomodados*) were now called *alquilados*, or hired hands, the term previously used in Bocas for seasonal labourers. At the beginning this change of terminology was not consistent, and to a casual observer it might have seemed accidental. It is doubtful if the *peón* noticed this subtle change in his legal situation, which was completed in 1876. By December of that year, Bocas had a staff of six *dependientes* (clerks), sixty *acomodados*, and only forty-three *peones* who would formerly have been described as '*permanentes*', though of course no such adjective was now used. All the other former *peones permanentes* were now included in the list of seasonal or day-labourers, as *alquilados* or *jornaleros*. The numbers of workers in these categories thus increased from about 300 to 454.

All these groups of *hacienda* workers continued to earn the same wages as before, but as a result of a bad harvest in 1875 the concessionary price of maize was raised in January 1876 from 1.50 *pesos* to 2.25 *pesos* per *fanega*. Previously, it should be recalled, all *peones permanentes* had had the right to purchase maize at the concessionary price; but now most of them had been transformed into *jornaleros* or day-labourers who had to buy their maize supplies at the prevailing commercial rates, which by now had risen to 3 *pesos* a *fanega*. Consequently, for the overwhelming majority of *peones* the price of maize had doubled without any corresponding increase in wages. These developments had a curious outcome: by the end of 1875 employees and workers had a net credit of 1,091 *pesos* outstanding against the *hacienda*. A minority of them owed the estate 683 *pesos*, whilst the *hacienda* owed the majority a total of 1,774 *pesos*. In the space of twenty-three years debtors had become creditors; the situation had been turned upside down. However, by increasing the price of maize, the *hacienda* debt to the *peones* was practically wiped out in a very short time, being reduced to 255 *pesos* by February 1876.

The management clearly acted as if the *hacienda* had no need of its workers. The fact that most *peones* clung to their jobs in spite of their deteriorating social and economic situation shows that few better opportunities existed elsewhere.

The owners of Bocas also took advantage of the Civil Code to change their relationship with their tenants. Until then, the *arrendatarios* had understood their tenancy to mean the right to occupy a piece of land for an indefinite period of time in exchange for the payment of a low fixed rent. By tradition, Mexican Indians (and peasants in general) were deeply attached to the soil; even if the land were not their own, in the course of time they came to regard it as such – an attitude which was not to the landowner's liking or advantage. The Civil Code now specified that leases previously extended for an indefinite period of time would automatically expire after three years. Hence the leases then in force would all expire at the end of 1874, and thereafter the landlord was free to raise rents as he wished. In accordance with the prevailing liberal spirit, rents as well as wages were to be agreed upon by the contracting parties. Lessees of course were free not to accept new rents, but in this case they had to go elsewhere. However, the gradual increase in population tended to push up rents everywhere, so tenants were faced with a difficult situation. The Civil Code gave *aparceros* a better deal, as it regarded them as the partners of the landowner. Should they harvest the crops without letting him know, however, the penalty would be double payment. In other words, if the agreed share was 50 per cent, they stood to lose the entire harvest to the landowner.

In 1874, the *hacendado* of Bocas had two booklets printed: *Conditions to which shall be subject those persons wishing to become or remain tenants of the Hacienda Bocas for 1875*, and *Conditions of sharecropping on the lands of the Hacienda Bocas for 1875, subject to amendments for subsequent years by the landowner*. Ground rent or *pisaje* was raised from 5 *pesos* to 10 *pesos* a year; for 1 *fanega de sembradura* of land (3.6 hectares) rents went up to between 9 and 12 *pesos* according to the quality of the land, again an increase of 100 per cent; for one head of cattle, to 0.75 *pesos* per annum, an increase of 200 per cent; for one goat or one sheep, to 0.18 *pesos*, a rise of 260 per cent. The manager was to determine which lands were to be used for pasture and which would be rented for crops. If he so wished, he could give a tenant a parcel of land other than the one that had previously been cultivated by him for years. The written leases were to be for three years, after which the *hacendado* could modify or renew them as he wished. As the tenants did not respond to the *hacienda*'s invitation to sign the contracts, Bocas raised the rents for 1876 even higher: *pisaje* went up to 12 *pesos*, cattle rents to 1 *peso* per head, and goats and sheep to one-fourth of a *peso* per head.

The first booklet defined a house-site as a plot sufficient for a three-room dwelling, including the kitchen, together with an adjacent *corral*. The rent was to be double if there were more rooms. Obviously some tenants had been accustomed to sharing their huts with another family in order to share the rent. This was now explicitly prohibited. Married sons often lived with their parents; according to the new regulations, while there could be no limitation on the size of the lessee's family, other families sharing the same house could not exceed six persons in all. If they did, the rent would again be doubled. If the manager could not prevent the natural increase in population, he could at least prevent strangers settling in the tenant's houses. A traditional rule of hospitality was that a family would offer its house to landless and homeless friends, *compadres*, and relatives, who would eventually form families of their own and so swell the numbers of the needy. Henceforth, these so-called *arrimados* were to be excluded from the lands of the *hacienda*. Should a tenant admit an *arrimado* into his house, he was liable to immediate expulsion from the *hacienda*.

Anticipating all manner of difficulties with the tenants, the rules forbade them to build houses of brick (all houses were of course built at the tenants' expense); the *hacendado* also reserved to himself the right to move tenants about from one part of the *hacienda* to another at will. Tenants could only live in the twenty-seven specified *ranchos*, each one of which was restricted to a maximum of forty families; hence the total number of lessees on Bocas was limited to about 1,000. The management had the right to move families from those *ranchos* considered over-populated to other, less crowded ones. Tenants were to pledge their animals as security; they were expected to help the *hacienda* recapture fugitive criminals without receiving any payment; and they were re-quired to perform extra *faenas* in return for a wage equal to that paid to the seasonal labourers. Widows and orphans were to be exempted from paying rent for three years. The relationship between landlord and tenant was more than a simple lease according to the Civil Code; the tenant was still a potential *peón*, with many obligations but also some rights. The regulations no doubt incorporated some old usages and customs, but they made life more difficult than before for the tenants unless they agreed to become sharecroppers.

According to the second set of rules, sharecroppers were to continue to pay the traditional *pisaje* of 5 *pesos*, or half of what the ordinary tenants were to pay. Furthermore, they were entitled to free pasture for four

animals and to a small free plot, over and above the land allocated to
them for sharecropping, on which they could grow anything they wished.
The *hacienda* was to provide the land – a minimum of half a *fanega* and
a maximum of 3 *fanegas* (more than 10 hectares) – and seed, oxen, and
farm implements. In this case sharecroppers were to receive two-fifths
of the harvest, for according to an old custom one-fifth of the crop was
'for the oxen', that is, for their owner. In sharecropping by halves,
tenants were to supply their own oxen and implements. They were forbidden to sublet their contract without written permission from the
manager, for this was apparently a common means of exploiting poorer
tenants. Finally, in order to encourage the growing of wheat and barley,
the *hacienda* offered *aparceros* who would grow these crops a half share
in the harvest together with a yoke of oxen. The *hacienda* reserved the
best lands for its own crops, and also preferential use of irrigation
water. Tenants thus found it to their advantage to become sharecroppers,
the poor ones sharecropping 'by the fifth' and the more prosperous ones
sharecropping by halves. Most of them cultivated 1 *fanega de tierra de
sembradura* each.

As a result of these various pressures, the total number of tenants
decreased. By 31 December 1876 there were only 491 left, about 300
less than a quarter of a century earlier; their total debt amounted to
7,624 *pesos*. Of 304 'former' tenants, 95 were dead, 138 were 'absent',
having left of their own accord, 32 had been evicted, mostly for 'defects
of character' or for failing to pay their rent, and finally there were 39
insolvent tenants, who were perhaps due for eviction. Of the 491 tenants
then on the *hacienda*, 253 were *aparceros* who were no longer required
to pay *pisaje*, as the *hacienda* had evidently waived its right to charge
them 5 *pesos* a year; and 159 were plain tenants, most of whom were
very poor and had no cattle. These tenants were charged 12 *pesos* per
annum for *pisaje*; their occupations are unknown, but they did not rent
any land for cultivation. The remaining seventy-nine were *hacienda
peones* who rented some land for their own use, but paid no ground rent
for their hut. By 1894 almost all the tenants on Bocas had been transformed into sharecroppers; their total indebtedness amounted to 3,124
pesos. The management of Bocas had obviously succeeded in bringing
hacienda tenants under control, and perhaps even in wringing some
profit from them.

Hacienda Bocas before the 1910 Revolution
With some exceptions, *peones* and *arrendatarios* were traditionally
minded and shrank from the idea of being independent; they yearned

for security both for themselves and for their generally numerous families. Thus, even though the *peones* of Bocas were deprived of their security of tenure and their standard of living was reduced by about a half, they tended to stay on as *jornaleros*. However, there is evidence to suggest that this began to change before the end of the nineteenth century. After the completion of the Mexico City–San Luis Potosí–Monterrey–Texas railway in 1888, the more ambitious of the young, unmarried *peones* were free to go north, to the booming cotton plantations of La Laguna, to the new industrial factories of Monterrey, and even further north, across the border into the United States. After all, there was a railway station just opposite the *casco* of Bocas.

At the end of 1899, Bocas was sold to the García brothers, the third change of ownership in less than sixty years, and the situation of the *peones* was further simplified. In January 1904 the *hacienda* had eighteen *dependientes* who were paid a monthly salary, and 407 labourers, all of whom belonged to a single group of workers since the distinction between *alquilados* and *acomodados* had been abolished; no evidence of maize allowances is to be found. Most of the 407 *peones* were different from those listed ten years earlier. As the wages were exactly the same as they had been half a century before – though of course *reales* were now converted to *centavos* – and since the general price level was now much higher, many *peones* must have decided to leave the *hacienda* of their own free will. Since no lists of former *peones* were compiled at that time, or have not survived, it is impossible to determine their numbers. Their place was taken by other labourers. It is also probable that many tenants emigrated from Bocas in search of better opportunities elsewhere. In 1904, a rumour spread that other *haciendas* in the state were luring away the *peones* from Bocas with offers of higher wages. Five years before the outbreak of the Revolution, the *hacendado* finally resolved to raise the basic daily wage from 20 *centavos* – slightly more than $1\frac{1}{2}$ *reales* – to 25 *centavos*.

Conclusions

The records of the *Hacienda* Bocas show that its *peones* became impoverished during the second half of the nineteenth century and that its tenants gradually improved their standard of living by becoming sharecroppers. In contrast to the *peones*, the *aparceros* did not suffer as a result of the steadily increasing price of maize; on the contrary, it would seem that they profited by it.

No comparable set of data exists for the *Hacienda* San Diego, nor to my knowledge for any other *hacienda* in the State of San Luis Potosí. Hence it is impossible to know if the same patterns of change took place on other *haciendas* in the region, much less on those of the Bajío, the eastern part of which is near the southwestern boundary of San Luis Potosí. In the first place, the *haciendas* of the Bajío were generally much smaller than those of San Luis. In fact, in Guanajuato the term '*hacienda*' also meant an area of five square leagues – that is, 8,778 hectares. This would seem to indicate that the average size of a *hacienda* in the heart of the Bajío was about one-third of that prevalent in San Luis. Secondly, *haciendas* in the Bajío were devoted mainly to cereals, both wheat and maize, whereas in San Luis, with the exception of those located in the warmer and more humid eastern part of the state, they were given over mainly to cattle-raising and the production of *mezcal*. Finally, because of the greater climatic variations in the north, the *haciendas* of San Luis Potosí relied more heavily than their counterparts in the Bajío on costly irrigation works and *trojes* or storage barns.

There can be no doubt that the *haciendas* of San Luis Potosí were commercial, profit-seeking enterprises, at least after 1840. Whenever possible, they produced for the market, as exemplified by maize cultivation. *Haciendas* sold maize to their *peones* by charging it to their current account together with purchases from the store and cash loans. They also had the alternative of buying maize grown by other independent peasant producers and re-selling it to their *peones*. The fact that they chose to grow it themselves, both directly and through sharecroppers, indicates the profitability of maize cultivation – not to mention that of other crops and products – at least as far as the large *haciendas* of San Luis Potosí in the second half of the nineteenth century are concerned.

NOTES

1. The archives of *Hacienda* San Diego are the property of Sr Octaviano Cabrera and are kept in his home in the city of San Luis Potosí. The archives of *Hacienda* Bocas are located on the *hacienda* itself. For further details concerning the contents of this archive, and other aspects of life on the *hacienda*, see J. Bazant, 'Peones, arrendatarios y aparceros en Mexico, 1851–1853', in *Historia Mexicana* XXIII, 2 (El Colegio de México, 1973), pp. 330–57. The archives deal mainly with social aspects of life on the *hacienda* and are less concerned with its economic organization.
2. In many cases *haciendas* could extract more money from tenants by converting them into sharecroppers. However, those tenants who owned a yoke of oxen and a plough tended to oppose this, as they would normally fare better by working for themselves. But most tenants were very poor, and it can be assumed that they welcomed the opportunity to become either sharecroppers or, if possible, *peones*. The second reason was that most *haciendas* were responsible for security in their own

territory. They obviously disliked having starving tenants and thus offered them the means of earning their daily *tortillas*.

3. The following figures are used in this essay:

1 *peso* = 8 *reales*
1 *fanega* = ½ *carga* = 12 *almudes* = 91 litres
1 *almud* = 7.6 litres
1 *almud de tierra de sembradura* = 3,000 square metres
1 *fanega de tierra de sembradura* = 3.6 hectares.

BIBLIOGRAPHY

So far there is little written material available on the Mexican *hacienda* in the nineteenth and twentieth centuries. The following works deal with the *hacienda* system in general: George McCutcheon McBride, *The land systems of Mexico* (New York, 1923); Frank Tannenbaum, *The Mexican agrarian revolution* (New York, 1929); Nathan L. Whetten, *Rural Mexico* (Chicago, 1948); Moisés González Navarro, *Raza y tierra: la guerra de castas y el henequén* (Mexico, 1970); N. Reed, *The caste war of Yucatán* (Stanford, Calif., 1964); Eyler N. Simpson, *The ejido: Mexico's way out* (Chapel Hill, N. C., 1937); M. Mörner, 'The Spanish American hacienda: a survey of recent research and debate', *Hispanic American Historical Review* LIII, 2(1973), pp. 183–216; J. Coatsworth, 'Railroads, land-holding, and agrarian protest in the early Porfiriato', *Hispanic American Historical Review* LIV, 1 (1974), pp. 48–71; Moisés González Navarro, 'Tenencia de la tierra y población agrícola, 1877–1960', *Historia Mexicana* XIX, 1 (1969), pp. 62 – 86; F. Katz, 'Labor conditions on haciendas in Porfirian Mexico: some trends and tendencies', *Hispanic American Historical Review* LIV,1 (1974), pp. 1 – 47.

Detailed studies of specific *haciendas* can be found in Manuel Gamio (ed.), *La población del Valle de Teotihuacán*, 3 vols. (Mexico, 1922); R. S. Platt, *Latin America: countrysides and regions* (New York, 1943), particularly pp. 20 – 67, which describes a number of *haciendas* in different parts of Mexico; Ezio Cusi, *Memorias de un colono* (Mexico, 1969) contains the recollections of a former *hacendado*; Charles H. Harris, *The Sánchez Navarros: a socio-economic study of a Coahuilan latifundio, 1846 – 1853* (Chicago, 1964); François Chevalier, 'The north Mexican hacienda, eighteenth and nineteenth centuries', in A. R. Lewis and R. McGann (eds.), *The New World looks at its history* (Austin, Texas, 1963), pp. 95–107; Edith Boorstein Couturier, 'Modernización y tradición en una hacienda: San Juan Hueyapán, 1902–1911', *Historia Mexicana* XVIII, 1 (1968), pp. 35–55. Good accounts of life on the *hacienda* are contained in the novels of M. Azuela, *Los de abajo* (Mexico, 1915), published in English as *The underdogs* (New York, 1962), and J. López Portillo y Rojas, *La parcela*, 2nd edn (Mexico, 1945). Contemporary descriptions of *hacienda* life by foreign visitors are also useful: J. L. Stephens, *Incidents of travel in Yucatán*, 2nd edn, 2 vols. (Norman, Okla., 1962; first published London, 1841); C. M. Flandrau, *Viva Mexico*, 2nd edn (Urbana, Ill., 1964) which describes life on a coffee plantation; P. F. Martin, *Mexico of the twentieth century* (London, 1907); and

J. K. Turber, *Barbarous Mexico* (Chicago, 1911). Finally, the following books deal with *haciendas* from the village point of view: J. Sotelo Inclán, *Raíz y razón de Zapata* (Mexico, 1943); J. Womack, Jr, *Zapata and the Mexican Revolution* (London, 1969); P. Friedrich, *Agrarian revolt in a Mexican village* (Englewood Cliffs, N. J., 1970); and O. Lewis, *Life in a Mexican village* (Urbana, Ill., 1951).

CHAPTER 4

Land and labour in rural Chile, 1850–1935

ARNOLD BAUER and ANN HAGERMAN JOHNSON

The agrarian sector continues to present a baffling problem in Chile. Over the past decade, new tenure patterns and labour systems have been formed, reformed, and shattered through movements led by urban cadres – frequently armed with little more than passionately held assumptions. Despite the interest and energy recently focused on the countryside, remarkably little is known about the formation and nature of rural society. Usually illiterate, rural people wrote few memoirs or confessions; not owning land, rarely hired by contract, and usually disposed to toil without complaint (or having little hope of legal redress), they left little trace in the written records and are only dimly perceived through the eyes of travellers. Even in fairly recent times one is forced to infer the workers' existence from the volume of their output or the nature of the demands placed on them. One way to get at the elusive subject of rural society is by examining the more statistically visible agrarian units – *haciendas*, medium and small farms – around which labour was organized. That is the aim of the present paper. We present first a statistical picture of changes in land distribution under the impact of expanding markets during the century up to 1935,[1] and then we discuss the way the lower rural society adapted to the new conditions.

Although writers, with tiresome predictability, describe Chile as a 'long thin land of contrasts', many are inclined to generalize about the central nucleus.[2] But even here the broken terrain and micro-climates produce a variety of geographic patterns that should be kept in mind. One such region is the department of La Ligua, a valley lined with a narrow fringe of irrigated land in the midst of rolling dry hills, some one hundred miles north of Santiago and just below the arid *norte chico* (see Map 9). Here, in 1854, eight sprawling *haciendas* – five of which grew out of a single colonial entail – contained 143,000 of the department's 149,000 hectares of arable and grazing land. The remaining 6,000 hectares were divided among some 150 proprietors. A general picture of land distribution can be seen in Table 11.

La Ligua was not unique; other regions had a similar mix of irrigated

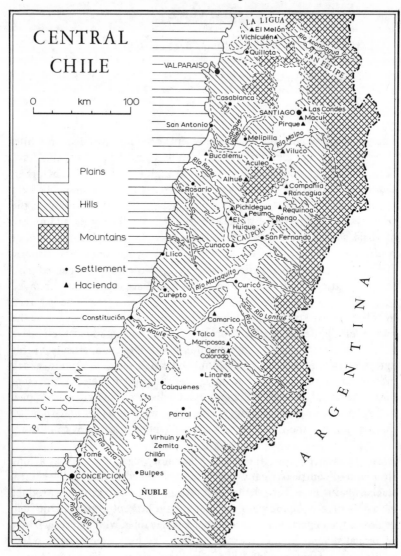

Map 9

and thin, dry pasture land. Rafael Baraona's careful and at times poetic
study of Putaendo treats a similar valley; both areas were exceptional for
extremely skewed distribution as well as low productivity. Landowners
in La Ligua as a whole produced an income of only 67 *centavos* per
hectare in 1854.[3]

TABLE 11   *Land distribution in La Ligua, 1854*

Category in hectares	0–5	6–20	21–50	51–200	201–1,000	1,001–5,000	over 5,000	Total
No. of owners	95	40	9	4	5	1	8	162
Percentage of owners	58.6%	24.6%	5.6%	2.6%	3.1%	0.6%	4.9%	100%
Total hectares	243	394	252	385	3,006	1,570	142,850	148,700
Percentage of total hectares	0.2%	0.3%	0.2%	0.3%	2.0%	1.0%	96.0%	100%

Soruce: Archivo Nacional (Santiago), *Colección de Hacienda*, vol. CCCIV (1854–6), p. 36.

TABLE 12   *Land distribution in San Felipe, 1854*

Category in hectares	0–5	6–20	21–50	51–200	201–1,000	1,001–5,000	over 5,000	Total
No. of owners	353	134	40	22	5	2	—	556
Percentage of owners	63.4%	24.2%	7.1%	4.0%	0.9%	0.4%	—	100%
Total hectares	739	1,421	1,423	1,839	1,607	3,227	—	10,256
Percentage of total hectares	7.2%	13.8%	13.8%	17.9%	15.7%	31.6%	—	100%

Source: Archivo Nacional (Santiago), *Colección de Hacienda*, vol. CCCIV (1854–6), no page.

The department of San Felipe, only a few miles to the south, was a quite different sort of place. Landowners in this small but well-watered and fertile valley tended to the vine, planted fruit trees, and enjoyed a lively commerce with Santiago and Valparaíso. The land was nearly all irrigated and was more evenly divided (see Table 12). In fact, the largest *hacienda* was M. J. Hurtado's San Regis, which held just under 5,000 hectares; and the highest-yielding estate, according to the tax records, produced 17,500 *pesos* for Francisco Videla on only 2,800 hectares.[4]

Finally, a third example of local variety within central Chile: the department of Caupolicán. Situated in the heartland of agricultural Chile, Caupolicán represents perhaps better than any other department the classic *criollo* rural society. Already important in the eighteenth century for their production of grain and beef, the larger *fundos* prospered under the impact of nineteenth-century markets. Around these estates, whose owners were frequently elected to the national congress, turned

TABLE 13   *Land distribution in Caupolicán, 1854*

Category in hectares	0–5	6–20	21–50	51–200	201–1,000	1,001–5,000	over 5,000	Totals
No. of owners	358	440	164	90	36	21	5	1,114
Percentage of owners	32.1%	39.5%	14.7%	8.1%	3.2%	1.9%	0.5%	100%
Total hectares	1,067	4,783	5,263	8,945	17,268	43,448	103,608	184,382
Percentage of hectares	0.6%	2.6%	2.9%	4.9%	9.4%	23.6%	56.0%	100%

Source: Archivo Nacional (Santiago), *Colección de Hacienda*, vol. CCCIV (1854–6), no page.

the economic and social life of the countryside. The *pulpería* or *fundo* store sold or advanced on credit local produce (flour, spirits) and imports such as sugar and cottons. The estate's chapel, *fiestas*, rodeos, and races served as focal points for rural society. By the mid nineteenth century there were twenty-six *fundos* that averaged some 5,600 hectares each, and together these contained about 80 per cent of the total agricultural land. Below these large farms, over 1,100 medium farmers and smallholders shared the remaining land. Table 13 indicates the land distribution in Caupolicán in the middle of the nineteenth century. It is a pattern about midway between the examples of La Ligua and San Felipe and is reasonably typical of central Chile.[5]

Because there are no published acreage data for the rest of the nineteenth century, and in fact none until 1919, we must infer changes in land distribution from the data on annual estate income taken from the tax rolls. The first of these – for 1854 – is presented in Table 14.[6] Now, if the tax rolls do provide a rough picture of income distribution and a general idea of earnings in the agricultural sector, they cannot be used as a substitute for acreage distribution, since the size of a holding was but one rather unimportant determinant of its value.[7] The explanation lies in the nature of Chilean agriculture at mid-century – a system that had changed very little from the colonial years. The California and Australian gold strikes, by providing a modest and ephemeral market for Chilean produce (wheat and flour) in the early 1850s, gently stimulated the countryside. But except for those farms within reach of Santiago or the ports, rural Chile lay neglected, with droves of scrawny cattle, stretches of weeds, the occasional cultivated plot. *Haciendas* of potential value such as Cerro Colorado (13,000 hectares) or Mariposas (16,000), in south central Talca, yielded only 5,100 and 2,500 *pesos* respectively.[8]

TABLE 14 *Annual income of rural properties in central Chile, 1854*

Category in pesos	$25–99	$100–199	$200–499	$500–999	$1,000–5,999	$6,000 and over	Total
No. of properties	12,403	3,130	1,957	748	717	145	19,100
Percentages of properties	64.9%	16.4%	10.2%	3.9%	3.8%	0.8%	100%
Total income (pesos)	$143,712	$469,500	$733,875	$561,000	$2,324,000	$1,552,643	$5,784,730
Percentage of total income	2.5%	8.1%	12.7%	9.7%	40.2%	26.8%	100%

Source: Sociedad Nacional de Agricultura, *Boletin* I (Santiago, 1854), Table I.

TABLE 15 *Annual income of rural properties in central Chile, 1874*

Category in pesos	$25–99	$100–199	$200–499	$500–999	$1,000–5,999	$6,000 and over	Total
No. of properties	17,000	6,015	3,103	1,012	1,475	323	28,928
Percentage of properties	58.8%	20.8%	10.7%	3.5%	5.1%	1.1%	100%
Total income (pesos)	$200,000	$902,250	$973,350	$759,000	$3,229,220	$3,846,929	$9,910,749
Percentage of total income	2.0%	9.1%	9.8%	7.7%	32.6%	38.8%	100%

Source: Impuesto agrícola, rol de contribuyentes (Valparaíso, 1875).

As one moved in toward Santiago from the outlying departments, estates were worth much more. In Caupolicán, *haciendas* of about the same combination of irrigated, level, and hilly land as Cerro Colorado or Mariposas normally yielded two or three times as much income. In the relatively small department of Santiago itself, thirty-two estates of over 5,000 *pesos'* income were reported. These were rarely over 3,000 hectares and often much smaller.[9]

What one had, then, in mid-nineteenth-century Chile was not huge *haciendas* toward the centre and smaller properties on the periphery, but rather a country where unused land was already held in large private estates and where markets were so weak that if a 20,000-hectare *hacienda* meant many tenants and servants, hundreds of horses and hounds, it actually provided little in the way of cash income. All this began to change rapidly with the advent of steam and rail. By 1874, central Chile was moving to a quicker economic rhythm as nitrates in the north and still-high grain prices enabled Chileans to sell wheat to England (1874 was the peak year in grain exports), and as more prosperous local cities required food. What this meant for agriculture can be partially seen in the new survey of annual income carried out in 1874 (see Table 15).[10]

Two points here are unmistakable: first, rural Chile underwent rapid changes during those years as both the number of holdings and their productivity showed a marked increase. Secondly, the large holders, not the smaller farmers, benefited most from the expansion. The change – undoubtedly much greater than shown here, since large incomes tended to be undervalued and the small ones more easily seen – is revealed in the Lorenz curves of Figure 1, which shows the increased concentration of rural income.

Again, the figures do not clearly indicate the change in land distribution. But from the data that appear later – for 1917 and 1935 – the direction of change can be inferred. It is not that new large estates were put together in the later nineteenth century – they were already there – but rather that they became much more productive and began to show up on the rolls. Besides that, several of the huge colonial *haciendas* were sub-divided. Whereas in 1854 there were 717 estates earning over 1,000 *pesos*, by 1874 the number more than doubled to 1,474. This was also true of the really high-income estates: their number grew from 145 in mid-century to 323 twenty years later. In short, all sizes of property gained, but the number of the wealthy properties increased much faster. We can say in general that economic expansion beginning in the 1860s confirmed and consolidated the large estate in its dominant role and made others profitable. If we add that rural wages remained low through-

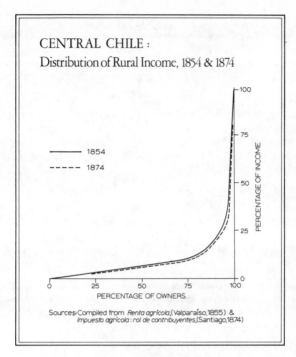

Fig. 1

out the nineteenth century, we can better understand why it was in these years and not in those of the colonial aristocracy that the landed estate and its owners loom so large in the social and political life of the nation.

From 1917 to the present, the data on land distribution improve. Beginning in 1919, the first published acreage figures appeared (for 1917), and they have continued to do so regularly since.[11] Again, it is appropriate to look at a number of distinct zones within central Chile. In the small department of La Ligua little actually changed. The extremely skewed distribution of 1854 remained remarkably constant down to 1923. Twelve large livestock *haciendas* grew out of the eight that were present in 1854, but as the owners extended the agricultural area within each estate the average size actually increased, from 18,000 hectares in 1854 to around 19,000 in 1923. The number of smaller properties increased slightly but their share of La Ligua's surface declined. Table 16 shows the development of land distribution in La Ligua between 1854 and 1923.

TABLE 16   *Land distribution in La Ligua, 1854 and 1923*

Category in hectares	0–5	6–20	21–50	51–200	201–1,000	1,001–5,000	over 5,000	Total
1854								
No. of owners	95	40	9	4	5	1	8	162
Percentage of owners	58.6%	24.6%	5.6%	2.6%	3.1%	0.6%	4.9%	100%
Total hectares	243	394	252	385	3,006	1,570	142,850	148,700
Percentage of hectares	0.2%	0.3%	0.2%	0.3%	2.0%	1.0%	96.0%	100%
1923								
No. of owners	190	57	12	4	7	5	12	287
Percentage of owners	66.2%	19.9%	4.2%	1.4%	2.4%	1.7%	4.2%	100%
Total hectares	325	507	391	528	3,443	13,483	226,523	245,200
Percentage of hectares	0.1%	0.2%	0.2%	0.2%	1.4%	5.5%	92.4%	100%

Sources: Archivo Nacional (Santiago), *Colección de Hacienda*, vol. CCCIV (1854–6), p. 36. Dirección General de Estadística, *Anuario estadístico*, vol. VII (Santiago, 1924), pp. 4–5.

In San Felipe, where land in 1854 was more equally distributed, there was a trend toward greater inequality. Although there were no really large *haciendas* (none over 5,000 hectares), those in the 1,001–5,000 category tripled their share of the land between 1854 and 1917, and the amount doubled by 1965.[12] Here as elsewhere, landowners increased the amount of agricultural land within the estate through irrigation or clearing. The medium and smaller properties (6–200 hectares) increased in number through both sub-division and internal expansion and kept the same average size and roughly the same share of land. At the very bottom there was a sharp increase among *minifundistas* – to 1,706 by 1965. Table 17 demonstrates the change in land distribution in this fertile department over the past century. By 1965, the prosperous 'yeoman farmers' for which this department is noted were still there, but they were being eclipsed by the larger estates.

Once again, let us turn to Caupolicán, our paradigm for central Chile. Here we can clearly see the changes among large estates and the development of *minifundia* (see Table 18). The dwarf holdings multiplied between 1854 and 1917. The medium to small properties (6–50 hectares) stayed about the same down to 1917, but there were 115 more medium to large *fundos* (51–1,000 hectares) than in 1854, and 13 more very large

TABLE 17 *Land distribution in San Felipe, 1854, 1917, and 1965*

Category in hectares	0–5	6–20	21–50	51–200	201–1,000	1001–5,000	over 5,000	Total
1854								
No. of owners	353	134	40	22	5	2	—	556
Percentage of owners	63.4%	24.2%	7.1%	4.0%	0.9%	0.4%	—	100%
Total hectares	739	1,421	1,423	1,839	1,607	3,227	—	10,256
Percentage of hectares	7.2%	13.8%	13.8%	17.9%	15.7%	31.6%	—	100%
1917								
No. of owners	978	134	35	28	8	6	—	1,189
Percentage of owners	82.3%	11.3%	2.9%	2.4%	0.7%	0.5%	—	100%
Total hectares	1,023	1,283	1,027	2,906	4,006	11,038	—	21,283
Percentage of hectares	4.8%	6.0%	4.8%	13.6%	18.6%	51.9%	—	99.2%
1965								
No. of owners	1,706	272	61	49	6	9	—	2,103
Percentage of owners	81.1%	12.9%	2.9%	2.3%	0.3%	0.4%	—	100%
Total hectares	2,352	2,812	2,135	5,325	2,500	19,500	—	34,624
Percentage of hectares	6.8%	8.1%	6.2%	15.4%	7.2%	56.3%	—	100%

Sources: Archivo Nacional (Santiago), *Colección de Hacienda*, vol. CCCIV (1854–6), no page. *Anuario estadístico* (Santiago, 1917), pp. 6–7. *Censo nacional agropecuario* (Santiago, 1964–5), vol. VI.

haciendas. These increased numbers reflect sub-division and the increased use by the owners of the estates' land.

What can be said about central Chile as a whole in the twentieth century? The pattern that emerged out of the vigorous growth of the later nineteenth century is partly revealed in the 1917 survey (see Table 19). Here we have a statistical picture of a rural scene made familiar through countless novels and memoirs and the increasingly vociferous attacks of its critics. Yet the figures alone give a distorted view. It may be that some 47 per cent (nearly three million hectares) of central Chile was held by only 216 estates, but much of these larger *haciendas*, although designated as agricultural land in the statistics, was often 'natural pasture' or hills and scrub land. The more profitable estates were usually smaller *fundos* with 200 to 1,000 hectares of irrigated land. The increase

TABLE 18   *Land distribution in Caupolicán, 1854 and 1917*

Category in hectares	0–5	6–20	21–50	51–200	201–1,000	1001–5,000	over 5,000	Total
1854								
No. of owners	358	440	164	90	36	21	5	1;114
Percentage of owners	32.1%	39.5%	14.7%	8.1%	3.2%	1.9%	0.5%	100%
Total hectares	1,067	4,783	5,263	8,945	17,268	43,448	103,608	184,382
Percentage hectares	0.6%	2.6%	2.9%	4.9%	9.4%	23.6%	56.0%	100%
1917								
No. of owners	3,041	555	162	163	78	31	8	4,038
Percentage of owners	75.3%	13.7%	4.0%	4.0%	1.9%	0.8%	0.2%	100%
Total hectares	4,212	5,353	4,780	17,483	43,214	59,565	108,535	243,142
Percentage hectares	1.7%	2.2%	2.0%	7.2%	17.8%	24.5%	44.6%	100%

Sources: Archivo Nacional (Santiago), *Colección de Hacienda*, vol. CCCIV (1854–6), no page. *Anuario estadístico* (Santiago, 1917), pp. 10–11.

in the number of these more manageable units, along with their more intensive cultivation, was a significant development and should substantially alter the view of a rural Chile as dominated by 'sprawling feudal domains'. The quality of land, especially its access to water, is of paramount importance.[13]

And the trend toward sub-division and increased use continued over the next two decades. Now two million more hectares were brought into use, and nearly 7,000 new farms of between 21 and 1,000 hectares appear in the 1935 statistics. It is not the size of the estate that critics should have condemned but rather the method of exploitation. Although there are several notable exceptions, Chilean landowners increased agricultural output up to 1930 simply by increasing the inputs of land and men: little technical improvement took place. McBride's classic description of Chile in the 1930s leaves the unmistakable impression of a backward agriculture.[14] But far more detrimental than a presumed maldistribution of land – one can easily argue that most irrigated *fundos* in 1935 were viable economic units – was the condition and use of rural labour. Let us now turn to that other factor of production and follow the social impact of the expanding market and changing land distribution.

TABLE 19 *Land distribution in central Chile, 1917 and 1935*

Category in hectares	0–5	6–20	21–50	51–200	201–1,000	1001–5,000	over 5,000	Totals
1917								
No. of owners	26,033	13,627	6,268	4,867	2,131	731	216	53,873
Percentage of owners	48.2%	25.3%	11.7%	9.0%	4.0%	1.4%	0.4%	100%
Total hectares	41,987	127,851	196,878	469,843	943,913	1,539,538	2,898,212	6,218,222
Percentage of hectares	0.7%	2.1%	3.2%	7.6%	15.2%	24.8%	46.6%	100%
1935								
No. of owners	59,922	22,482	9,799	6,995	3,143	939	246	103,526
Percentage of owners	57.9%	21.7%	9.5%	6.8%	3.0%	0.9%	0.2%	100%
Total hectares	95,385	239,602	315,732	690,452	1,360,718	1,909,702	3,504,698	8,116,289
Percentage of hectares	1.2%	2.9%	3.9%	8.5%	16.8%	23.5%	43.2%	100%

Sources: Oficina central de Estadística, *Anuario estadístico de la República de Chile*, vol *VII: agricultura* (Santiago, 1917–18), pp. 6–14. Direción General de Estadística. *Censo de agricultura: 1935–6* (Santiago, 1938), pp. 125, 248, 268.

The changes in land distribution and use just described were accompanied by changes in the rural labour system.[15] There were two important groups of working men – service tenants and day labourers – and both responded to economic, geographic, and psychological imperatives. A larger market and the sub-division of large properties into more efficient farming units obviously created a need for more workers. There is no doubt that landowners extended cultivation of the estates. The amount of land used for agriculture grew tremendously from the 1860s down to 1935 – the increase was from six to eight million hectares between 1917 and 1935 – and this expansion required large inputs of labour because the farming system itself was little changed. And unlike, say, Argentina or Australia, workers were already present in rural Chile; they needed only to be induced to work or encouraged to work more.

It is important to see just how estates were organized and to understand the alternatives. As the market grew, why did landowners not, for example, rent sections of their estates to tenant farmers, who in turn (one has in mind here the English model) might have hired wage labour? Or why were estates not modernized by introducing more machinery or by moving to a more impersonal and effective system? Why did Chilean landowners apparently insist on a demesne system where the owner (or administrator, usually a close relative) manages the entire estate and directly employs large numbers of service tenants and *peones*, a system similar to the classic manor of Eastern Europe?

The answer is partly geographic. In the *de rulo* or unirrigated *haciendas*, found especially on the gentle slopes of the Coastal Range or in the vast tracts reaching into the Cordillera, sub-leasing and sharecropping arrangements were not uncommon.[16] Sometimes these *haciendas* contained tens of thousands of hectares, and the problems of management, especially the prevention of cattle theft, were quite beyond the capacity of a single owner. Where cereals were sown, yields were low and crop failure likely while the acreage required was huge. Under these circumstances, many owners were reluctant to venture out of Santiago into these rather bleak regions and preferred to take a lower income in the form of rents rather than beat their heads against the hard facts of nature. Others could be found in the sparse middle stratum of society or from among the most reliable in the smallholder communities who would take the risks. Besides that, owners of dryland *haciendas* really had little choice, partly because they did not have irrigated land to attract sufficient numbers of service tenants. Only a few *inquilinos* could be accommodated on these estates that sloped away toward the Cordillera or the Coastal Range. Although often holding huge tracts of land, these *haciendas*, where skinny cattle picked their way through sparse grass or nibbled tree leaves off lower branches (or *ramonear*, in the local verb that describes this unnourishing practice), were often rented or share-cropped, and additional men were hired from the dusty hamlets and nearby squatter settlements. One must be careful not to mistake the solution worked out on these *haciendas* for part of a general trend. Geography remains a basic determinant in the formation of rural labour systems.

Irrigation canals drew a cultural trench along the edges of the level central valley. Within these boundaries one finds, by 1935, smaller farms of 400, 500, or 600 hectares, entirely managed by one man and worked with direct labour. These smaller estates in the verdant central valley had little difficulty in attracting men who would work in exchange for an acre or two of good land. Far from needing coercive devices such as debt or force to hold a labour force, *fundos* could select from a line of applicants the best workers in the rural society. The Chilean farmer wanted – indeed still wants – his own land, even if only a tiny plot. But since this was rarely possible, the next best thing was access to irrigated land on the *fundo*.

Still, these economic and geographic conditions are only the most apparent reasons for the peculiar development of Chile's rural society. The less tangible but perhaps more important explanations lie in the perceptions and values of the people themselves. Although not all landowners believed the *bajo pueblo* to be irredeemably hopeless, most certainly felt that it would take a great deal of time and education to make a responsible farmer out of the ordinary *huaso* (the general term for a rural worker, which in itself suggests a dull, and often laughable, rustic). Many landowners felt that irresponsibility and sloth were deep racial characteristics of the lower orders (a product of the Andalusian/Araucanian mixture) and that increased pay would only lead to greater vice.[17] To entrust a member of this class with the independent management of a section of the *fundo* would have been seen as simple madness.[18] For his part, the *inquilino*, faced with a countryside dominated by estate agriculture, became reconciled to his fate. He undoubtedly felt himself fortunate to occupy his *posesión* and to enjoy, often enough, the benevolent paternalism of the owner. The picture we are sometimes given of *inquilinos* groaning under the oppression of a vicious master is rarely confirmed by the evidence. *Inquilinos* were not driven particularly hard – much more was expected of day labourers – and there were distinct limits to an owner's capacity to apply pressure. Loyalty to estate and owner were often repaid by security of tenure. Until the 1930s there were few cases of *inquilino* protest, and even today they remain the most conservative of rural inhabitants.[19]

At the same time, estate ownership still conferred prestige, and, quite apart from the fact that from the 1860s on farming was increasingly profitable, it also permitted a style of life greatly valued in the *criollo* tradition and one that was not without a measure of charm and pleasure. Summers on the *fundo*, with its shady corridors of poplar trees; the barbeques and new wine; the celebrations and traditional *fundo* festivities; the deferential treatment by dozens of servants; the satisfaction of commanding and being unquestioningly obeyed; all this was gratifying in a way not revealed by the account books, and it helped determine the nature of the *fundo* labour force. The desire of the landowner to have stable, obedient, and even subservient workers always at his beck and call can be seen in those *fundos* near the large cities. Even here, where one imagines a nearby source of reserve labour, owners settled *inquilinos* on valuable land to ensure the presence of the kind of labourer they wanted.[20]

Let us turn now to the more specific changes that took place on these irrigated valley *fundos* over the years between the 1860s and 1935. In the mid nineteenth century most of these estates already had a number of service tenants.[21] The precise number is difficult to isolate in the statistics on occupation, since owners, renters, staff, and all other permanent residents were lumped together under the rubric '*agricultores*'.[22] Descriptions of individual estates and an understanding of tenure changes and agricultural output, however, enable one to infer the direction of change. From the 1860s on, landowners settled more and more service tenants on their estates. The meagre and even squalid conditions that these new settlers considered an improvement is, of course, a measure of their choice. But there is no denying that *inquilinos* considered themselves – and indeed were – fortunate to live on a *fundo*, a position that placed them a full cut above the *peón* or wage labourer. Through the late nineteenth century and into the twentieth, the institution of *inquilinaje* matured and gradually took on the characteristics familiar in recent times. Smaller and more intensively worked estates and heavier demands for labour put increased demands on the *inquilinos*, and under this pressure their perquisites – land, pasturage, rations – were reduced, and more labour was required of each *inquilino* household. By 1935 we have a fairly reliable statistical picture of the service tenantry (see Table 20). Although *inquilinos* (here the term refers to heads of households) themselves made up about 30 per cent of the total rural labour force, they

TABLE 20   *Composition of the rural labour force in central Chile, 1935*

Categories	*Inquilinos* (head of households)	*Peones* or *gañanes* (workers who are members of *inquilino* households)	*Afuerinos* (workers who are not members of *inquilino* or *empleado* households)	*Empleados* (blacksmith, carpenter, warehouse keeper, etc.)	Total workers
No. of workers	58,701	64,889	54,785	18,492	196,867
Percentage of total	29.8%	33.0%	27.8%	9.4%	100.0%

Source: Dirección General de Estadística, *Censo de agricultura: 1935–6* (Santiago, 1938), pp. 34, 265, 284, 498.

provided the *fundo* with nearly 65,000 more workers out of their own households. These *'peones o gañanes, miembros de la familia de inquilinos'*, were just that: sons or brothers or even more distant relatives who lived as *allegados* in the *inquilino* house. These were the *'obligados'* or extra hands required by the landowners of the service tenants, and their large number here reflects the mounting pressure applied to the service tenantry, the culmination of a process begun some seventy years earlier. There has been some confusion over this matter, because Correa Vergara's widely quoted *Agricultura chilena* gives only the figures for the number of *inquilinos* and their percentage of the total work force.[23] Thus it has often been assumed that the importance of service tenantry was shrinking and that landowners were turning to a wage-labour system. But as the figures in Table 20 show, down to 1935 at least, one finds in the central valley not a proletarianization of the rural work force, but, on the contrary, an intensification of an older paternalistic system.

Besides its need for service tenants, Chilean agriculture required additional workers for roundups and grape and grain harvests. The development of this second main segment of the rural labour force is tied directly to the proliferation of dwarf holdings or *minifundia*. Towards the middle of the nineteenth century, one has the impression from eyewitness accounts, partly corroborated in the statistics, of an extraordinary mass of 'floating' population.[24] By 1935 many of these people had come to form loose clusters of households that transformed the settlement pattern of rural Chile. The estates were able to draw on this more or less stable reservoir for seasonal labourers, while the countryside acquired the characteristic estate/*minifundia* polarization that has lasted up to the present. The growth of *minifundia* began much earlier than is commonly supposed, but its development is somewhat clouded by statistical difficulty.

Let us begin with the nineteenth-century sources. The 1854 tax roll attempted to list all properties of an annual income of 25 *pesos* or more, but unfortunately there is no way of knowing how many properties existed below this minimum figure. In the manuscript worksheets of this tax roll we found that several of the *funditos* evaluated at 25 *pesos* had no more than a half hectare. It would seem that only the tiniest of plots – the sort found at the back of rude huts of the pigsty/chicken coop/garden patch syndrome, still found in rural hamlets – were the only properties left out.[25]

If we do not know the number under 25 *pesos* in 1854, the problem is more perplexing for 1874, for then the minimum was raised to 100 *pesos*. It was obvious that such a policy left out many farms, and the Sociedad Nacional de Agricultura (SNA) managed to persuade the government to carry out a special survey in 1881 to count the smallholders ignored by the previous tax rolls: Here a definitional problem enters as well: were the smallholders rural or urban? Ambiguity on this point continues down to the present, as we shall see; but let us first attempt to make sense out of the data at hand. The 1881 survey is a good place to start our examination of the smallholder problem. The survey found, in central Chile, 57,578 rural properties (*fundos rústicos*) that had been left off the 1874 roll. A handful of these were large properties inadvertently overlooked in 1874, but the rest were in the 'less than 100 *pesos*' category. The 10,000 worksheet pages of this remarkably detailed survey – information was gathered on acreage, quality of land, animals, and production – have not been uncovered, but the SNA published a 'pre-report' in the 1881 *Treasury yearbook* that gives the gross numbers of properties by *subdelegación* (the political division within a department), and local newspapers published complete lists of proprietors, giving their annual income – often only 4 or 5 *pesos*.[26] This astonishing growth of tiny plots reflects the changing settlement pattern of central Chile and the impact of agricultural expansion. Although several of the new *minifundistas* were undoubtedly ex-*inquilinos* or relatives, a great many were floating seasonal workers and squatters who came to settle in quasi-urban clusters and hamlets – the *caseríos*, *aldeas*, and *villorios* – that sprang up everywhere during these years, who grew a few vegetables and kept a pig or chickens, and who supplemented this meagre income with wages earned on the large estates. It was never entirely clear to census-takers whether these properties should be called urban or rural, and of course both the reality and the definition were constantly changing. The 1881 survey considered as 'rural' all householders who did not pay the night watchman or lighting tax (*derecho de sereno y alumbramiento*) and thus must have included almost everyone outside the large provincial towns. This too, must have reflected reality, since at this time few proper towns existed; the bulk of provincial villages were functionally rural.[27]

In 1935–6, the statistical service tried to resolve the problem by categorizing proprietors by their produce: the 'principal' ones produced livestock, cereals and garden crops; the 'secondary' ones anything but those items. It is undoubtedly these 'secondary' producers that best correspond to the type of *minifundistas* that emerged in the 1860s and 1870s and that constituted the majority of dwarf holdings in 1935.[28]

Finally, we offer Table 21 to illustrate in a rough way the development of the Chilean smallholder between 1854 and 1945. The smallholders came into existence to satisfy the need for a more stable *hacienda* work force and have lingered on as a marginal class, by and large ignored by landlord and reforming governments alike.

TABLE 21   *Estimates of dwarf holdings in central Chile, 1881, 1935, and 1965*

	1881	1935	1965
No. of holdings of 0–5 hectares	40,000	59,922	78,095

Sources: Estimates adapted from *Memoria de Hacienda* (Santiago, 1881), 'Anexo Sociedad Nacional de Agricultura', pp. 28–41; Dirección General de Estadística, *Censo de agricultura: 1935–6* (Santiago, 1938); *Censo nacional agropecuario 1964–65* (Santiago).

By 1935 the floating mass of men who had provoked so much comment in the mid nineteenth century had disappeared. Most of this class was absorbed by the transformed agrarian structure which required higher labour quotas and could, up to a point, absorb some of the population increases through fragmentation of the *minifundia*. But rural population grew faster than labour requirements, and beyond a point fragmentation was devastating. The resulting population pressure was at first somewhat relieved through migration to the northern mines and to newly opened Araucanía in the south. There was also some minimal emigration to Peru and Argentina. Within central Chile itself, the population was likewise on the move. Men went to Valparaíso to work on the dock and railway projects, and both men and women – but especially women – moved to the cities, attracted by the wealth of the prospering upper class.

The flow to the cities accelerated in the twentieth century, the tide increasing with each successive decade. The sexual composition of this migration confirms what we have been saying about Chilean society. Wealth generated by the export of nitrate and copper spread through an ever-growing bureaucracy and multiplied the ranks of the Santiago wealthy. The offices and large houses of this commercial–bureaucratic city required flocks of maids and washerwomen, and as the word spread, thousands of young women sought employment in the capital. There was less opportunity for men in the pre-industrial city while at the same time an unmechanized agriculture could employ a great many male workers. Inexorably, however, as population grew while the need for field hands decreased, men too followed the rails and the new roads into the cities, but their numbers lagged behind the female migration. Sexual imbalance can be clearly seen in the 1930 census. In rural communities such as Requínoa or Palmilla (province of Colchagua), the number of single men aged 20 to 29 was almost double the number of unmarried women, while Santiago was 54 per cent female in 1930. The social and psychological implications of these sex ratios – in both Santiago and the countryside – are now just beginning to be understood; but for those who stayed behind, economic expansion clearly meant the persistence of a traditional rural social system.

NOTES

1. For this paper we were fortunate to be able to use for the first time fragments of the manuscript worksheets of the 1854 *catastro*. These give detailed information on the amount and quality of land, livestock, and vineyards. We are grateful to Mr. R. McCaa for pointing out the usefulness of this source.

2. All of the data we present in this paper, unless otherwise noted, are for the region called the *núcleo central*, which stretches from the province of Aconcagua in the north to Ñuble in the south. In 1854 these were roughly the limits of agricultural activity, since world markets had not yet discovered the desert nitrate or copper or doomed the Araucanian Indians below Concepción, and the area today remains the heartland of rural Chile. Another definition is in order. Although *fundo*, *hacienda*, and *latifundio* are often used interchangeably in Chile, by '*hacienda*' we mean a large estate (usually over 5,000 hectares), normally dedicated to livestock and cereals, and by '*fundo*' we mean a smaller, usually irrigated estate, devoted to mixed farming including dairy and vineyards. The English word 'estate' describes both *hacienda* and *fundo*; the somewhat charged '*latifundio*' is not used.

3. Archivo Nacional (Santiago), *Colección de Hacienda*, vol. IV (1854). The total landed income in 1854 in La Ligua was reckoned at approximately 95,000 *pesos* (Rafael Baraona *et al.*, *Valle de Putaendo* (Santiago, 1960)).

4. Archivo Nacional (Santiago), *Colección de Hacienda*, vol. CCCIV (1854–6).

5. San Vicente de Tagua-Tagua, a *comuna* in Caupolicán, was selected as a test case for the 1955 agricultural census: '*La Comuna de San Vicente puede considerarse como representativa de la región del Valle Central* . . .', Dirección de Estadística y Censos, *III censo nacional agrícola ganadero (1955)* (Santiago, 1960), vol. 6, p. XV.

6. We have used, up to now, the incomplete manuscript worksheets on which the published 1854 *catastro* was based. The published *catastro* gives only the owner's name of farm, annual income, and amount of tax; it says nothing about the acreage of land. The only two published tax rolls are the *Estado que manifiesta la renta agrícola* . . . *establecida en substitución del diezma por la ley de 25 de oct. de 1853* (Valparaíso, 1955); *Impuesto agrícola: rol de contribuyentes* (Santiago, 1874); *Indice de proprietarios rurales* . . . (Santiago, 1908). The 1834 *catastro* lacks the province of Colchagua and is found in manuscript in Biblioteca Nacional, Archivo Nacional, *Colección de la contaduría mayor, Vol. Catastro* (1834).

7. That the tax figures provide an imperfect tool is obvious. Landowners themselves often complained about unfair evaluation: see 'El avalúo de los fundos rústicos', Sociedad Nacional de Agricultura, *Boletín* VI (1874), pp. 81–92; 'Impuesto agrícola', ibid. IX (1878), pp. 301–6. Jean Borde felt that any investigation based on the tax rolls would be marked by a 'dangerous fantasy' (Jean Borde and Mario Góngora, *Evolución de la propiedad rural en el Valle del Puangue*, 2 vols. (Santiago, 1956), vol. I, p. 141.

8. Archivo Nacional (Santiago), *Colección de Hacienda*, vol. CCCV (1855). (The difference in this case is that Cerro Colorado contained more irrigated land.)

9. For example, Antonio Larrain's estate had only 750 hectares and was listed at 6,000 *pesos*' annual income; J. A. Gandarillas had 785 hectares for 6,500 *pesos* (Archivo Nacional (Santiago), *Colección de Hacienda*, vol. IV (1854)).

10. 'Impuesto agrícola', and the summary published in Sociedad Nacional de Agricultura, *Boletín* VI (1874), pp. 409 ff.

11. Apart from the *Anuarios estadísticos* that begin in the 1860s and supply detailed acreage figures in 1919, the Dirección de Estadística y Censos had carried out four agricultural censuses, in 1935–6, 1943, 1954–5, and 1964–5.

12. Since it is difficult to isolate San Felipe in the 1935–6 data, we have included the 1965 figures to provide an idea of recent trends.

13. An excellent source that reveals, much more clearly than the gross statistics do, the reality of Chilean rural structure is Juvenal Valenzuela O., *Album de informaciones agrícolas: zona central de Chile* (Santiago, 1923). This work, the product of several years of conscientious research, gives detailed information on nearly two thousand of the most important rural properties.

14. George McBride, *Chile: land and society* (New York, 1936).

15. For earlier developments, see Arnold J. Bauer, 'Chilean rural labor in the nineteenth century', *The American Historical Review*, LXXVI, 4 (October 1971), pp. 1059–82.

16. This is the impression gained from numerous archival references (see Bauer, 'Chilean rural labor', p. 1064); the accounts of individual *haciendas* such as El Peumo (Sociedad Nacional de Agricultura, *Boletín* VI (1874–5), pp. 306–8); and Pichedegua.

17. The Sociedad Nacional de Agricultura, *Boletín*, has several articles on the theme of rural hopelessness and vice; for an interesting article on racial interpretation, see Francisco Encina *et al.*, 'La subdivisión de la propiedad rural en Chile en 1919', reprinted in *Mapocho* V (Santiago, 1966), pp. 20–9.

18. McBride, *Chile*, p. 178.

19. Brian E. Loveman, 'Property, politics, and rural labor: agrarian reform in Chile, 1919–72' (unpublished dissertation, Indiana University, 1973), based on the records of the Oficina del Trabajo, deals with labour unrest.

20. Juvenal Valenzuela O., *Album*, points out the presence of *inquilinos* even on *fundos* on the very city limits of Santiago.

21. For the earlier period, Mario Góngora, *El origen de los 'inquilinos' de Chile Central* (Santiago, 1960) is useful.

22. Before the 1935–6 census the only population census that specifies *inquilinos* is that of 1813.

23. Luis Correa Vergara, *Agricultura chilena*, 2 vols. (Santiago, 1938), vol. 1, p. 162.

24. Bauer, 'Chilean rural labor', pp. 1070–2.

25. Archivo Nacional, *Colección de Hacienda*, vol. CCCIV (Santiago, 1854–6). (The measure of land in pre-metric Chile was the *cuadra*, or 1.57 hectares.)

26. The 'pre-report' is in *Memoria de Hacienda* (Santiago, 1881), 'Anexo Sociedad Nacional de Agricultura', pp. 28–41. Most of the local newspapers that published lists of these newly found smallholders have been lost. We examined those from Talca, Rancagua, and San Felipe.

27. Carlos Hurtado, *Concentración de población y desarrollo económico: el caso chileno* (Santiago, 1966), pp. 167–71.

28. Dirección General de Estadística, *Censo de agricultura: 1935–6* (Santiago, 1938), pp. 4–8, 125, 248, 268.

CHAPTER 5

The development of the Chilean *hacienda* system, 1850–1973

CRISTOBAL KAY[1]

The nature of the hacienda system: the conflict between landlord and peasant enterprises

In this paper I shall attempt to explain the changes in the Chilean *hacienda* system which has dominated rural society since colonial times. Although the *hacienda* system has until recently retained many of its traditional features, largely by maintaining its economic, social, and political predominance in the countryside, nonetheless it has experienced cumulative changes which have gradually undermined the unity of the *hacienda* as a system, transforming it from a large multi-farm estate, characterized by a complex of traditional landlord–peasant relationships, to a single-farm estate, characterized by farm manager–wage labour relationships. The pressures for change have come from sources largely external to the *hacienda* system. Among the important causes of the transformation of the Chilean *hacienda* system must be mentioned the changes in the market (both internal and external), the growth of the urban population, and the increasing radicalization and political organization of the urban working class and later of the peasantry. This analysis will focus on the changes which these factors provoked in the *hacienda* system, particularly in its labour structure.

Perhaps I should spare a few lines explaining my conceptual approach to the problem, especially in the hope that other analysts might find it useful when studying landlord–peasant relationships in regions dominated by the large landed estate. I shall adopt the 'multi-enterprise approach' first presented by Rafael Baraona in his study on the nature of the *hacienda* in the Ecuadorean Sierra.[2] The multi-enterprise approach views the *hacienda* system as a conflicting unity between two types of agricultural enterprise: the landlord and the peasant. It is the changing relationships between these two types of enterprise which explain the historical dynamic of the *hacienda* system. Herein lies the contribution of the multi-enterprise approach, which views the *hacienda* system as a complex of conflicting economic and social relationships between peasants and landlords, centred around the landlord's estate where are concentrated most of the natural resources and from which

the landlord extracts an agricultural surplus using the unpaid or partially remunerated labour of the peasantry.[3]

Most of the labourers employed by the *hacienda* or demesne enterprise
live within the territorial boundaries of the *hacienda*,[4] and an important
proportion obtain a subsistence production from their tenancies, largely
if not completely using their own means of production. Those peasants
who live outside the territorial boundaries of the *hacienda* may also use
some of its resources such as pastures, woods, or arable land, or they
may work as seasonal wage labourers on the landlord or demesne enterprise (*empresa patronal*), or even on the peasant enterprise of the *hacienda*.
Tenants pay labour, kind or money rent in return for the use of the
estate's resources.[5] Thus we have three types of economy within the
hacienda system: the landlord economy, the peasant economy of tenant
farmers within the property of the *hacendado* (internal peasant enterprise), and the peasant economy situated nearby and related to the
hacienda (external peasant enterprise).

Besides being a productive system, the *hacienda* system is also a social
system. The *hacienda* might have its own school, church, *pulpería* (store),
and other similar services. The administration of these services and of
justice is controlled by the landlord who uses this control to assert his
paternalistic authority over the peasantry. Links with the urban culture,
society, and polity are largely the monopoly of the landlord class.

Within a *hacienda* system various conflicts arise between the landlord
economy and the peasant economy, and sometimes minor conflicts arise
between the internal and external peasant enterprises. The essential long-
term conflict – the basic contradiction of the system – is over the appropriation or control of agricultural resources (land, water, woods, pastures)
and of the labour force. The conflict between the peasant and landlord
economies implies the development of one and, sooner or later, the
disappearance of the other.

The development of the landlord enterprise leads in the end to the
appropriation of the peasant tenures. Thus, at the very least, the peasant tenant is transformed into a proletarian, and his family's livelihood
comes to depend on selling their labour power in the market for a wage.
This we can call the internal proletarianization process. The landlord
enterprise becomes a medium- or large-scale unit which employs mainly
permanent wage labour. If this expansion of the landlord enterprise also
produces the expropriation or sale of the external peasant enterprise,
we can speak of an external proletarianization process. (Of course this
tendency may also occur through population growth or a process of

socio-economic differentiation within the peasantry, or for a number of other reasons.)

On the other hand, should the peasant economy develop,[6] either by a gradual process of acquisition (buying the land), or rapidly by expropriation (reform or revolution),[7] the peasants gain ownership over their own plots of land and over the landlord enterprise. Before the final dissolution of the *hacienda* system in favour of the peasantry occurs, a process of increasing control (but not proprietorship) over the natural resources of the *hacienda* generally takes place. This happens either when landlords give peasants access to arable land, pastures, woods, or water in return for rent payments, or when they are forced to accept *de facto* land invasions. If this extension of control stems from the internal peasant enterprise, we can speak of an internal siege (*asedio interno*); if the origin lies in the external peasant enterprise, of an external siege (*asedio externo*). Although in this case the peasants dismember the *hacienda* system to their own benefit, a peasant economy is not necessarily maintained. In certain cases a socio-economic differentiation process takes place, with some peasants expanding their landed property to become farmers and others losing most or all of their land to become wage labourers employed by the farmer. Whichever way this conflict over resources is resolved, it will conclude in the dissolution of the *hacienda* system, as the close interaction between the peasant economy and the landlord economy ceases to exist.

Another source of conflict between the landlord and peasant enterprises refers to market opportunities. The question arises of which enterprise takes advantage of the expanding market – either internal or external – for agricultural products.[8] Partially connected with this is the conflict over the use of the labour of the peasant economy. This occurs most notably in the case of an expanding market which requires more labour in both the peasant and landlord enterprises and competition for labour results.[9] The political and urban resources conflict arises over the allocation and distribution of economic resources which the state and private economic institutions assign to the rural sector.

Thus the intensity of the conflicts between the landlord enterprise and the peasant enterprise over agricultural resources, capital, and labour is influenced by variations in population density, changes in demand for agricultural products, developments in agrarian technology, and changes in the allocation of political resources.

I propose in this paper to give an interpretation of the transformation undergone by the *hacienda* system in Chile and to make some contrib-

ution towards creating a model for the development of the the Latin
American *hacienda* system in order to facilitate comparative studies.[10]

The consolidation of the hacienda system from the 1850s to the 1880s

The traditional *hacienda* of the first half of the nineteenth century
procured a self-sufficiency in agricultural consumer goods and produced only a small marketable surplus. There were few incentives
for increasing production, as the urban market was small, and the
rural population obtained its own means of subsistence. The demand
for wheat from Peru had been dwindling since the Wars of Independence and was relatively insignificant during the first half of the
century.[11] This lack of commercial opportunities for the *haciendas*
explains the absence of intensive farming and the dedication of land
to extensive livestock rearing. The breeding of cattle required only
a few labourers, whose labour services were remunerated with
production and consumption fringe benefits. This was convenient, as
land was abundant, and it kept monetary outlays to a minimum.
Except for the few weeks of the harvesting season, external labour
was rarely employed. These seasonal *peones* were paid a small wage
and in many cases simply received their food and lodging. The low
level of agricultural activity, and the land tenure system, meant that
the rural sector was heavily overpopulated, and we find frequent
references to vagrancy and *ocio* (idleness) in the literature of the
time.[12]

In Chile various types of *inquilinos* or labour-service tenants existed,
distinguished mainly by the size of the land leased to them and the number of animals they were allowed to pasture on the *hacienda* (*talajes*).
Their labour obligations varied accordingly. For example, *inquilinos* who
provided a second labourer – commonly referred to as a *sobre-peón* – received a double-sized land lease. Others only received a half-sized land
lease and therefore only had a 'half obligation' – *inquilinos de media
obligación*.[13]

The *inquilino* received two plots of land as production fringe benefits.
One was the *cerco* or garden plot, which was a piece of land around the
house in which the *inquilino* family lived. Food crops, fruit trees, and
small animals such as pigs and hens were kept on the *cerco*. The other plot
of land was larger and was not in any set location, as it had to conform to
the rotational pattern of the *hacienda*'s system of cultivation. The *inquilino* also had rights to pasture a specified number of animals on the estate.
As consumption fringe benefits, he received the house and sometimes the

right to collect wood from the forest. For the days the *inquilino* worked on the landlord's enterprise, he would receive his lunch, and bread for breakfast and dinner. The *inquilino* was under an obligation to supply the *hacienda* enterprise with one or more *peones obligados* (obligatory workers) nearly all the year around. When the *peón obligado* performed the labour services, he would receive the *inquilino*'s food ration. This explains why the *peón obligado* was also referred to as *reemplazante*, since he replaced the labour duty of the *inquilino*. If the *peón reemplazante* was contracted from outside the *inquilino*'s household, the *inquilino* would in addition pay him a supplementary wage of half pay (*media paga*). It was obviously only the richer *inquilinos* who could afford to do this. In those cases where livestock farming was important, the *inquilino* had to provide his wife's or daughters' labour to milk the cows. The size of the land lease (*regalía tierra*) given to *inquilinos* varied according to the fertility of the soil, the type of crop grown, his position within the labour force (largely determined by the number of years of service and degree of 'loyalty' expressed to the landlord), and above all the number of labourers he provided for the demesne – that is, the amount of labour rent paid to the landlord.

Thus the *inquilino* performed a dual function. On the one hand, he was a producer exploiting a piece of land for which he paid a rent; on the other hand, he was an agricultural labourer working on the landlord's estate (except in those cases where he was able to contract a *reemplazante*). As the *hacienda* system was transformed, one of these functions inevitably tended to predominate.

The period of agricultural inactivity came to an end towards 1849, when new markets for Chilean wheat opened up in the Pacific territories of California and, later, Australia. These markets, however, were short-lived, since after 1859 these countries started producing their own wheat; and California became in time a successful competitor in the international wheat market. As the Pacific market declined, a new customer for Chilean wheat was found in the Atlantic – England. (See Table 22.) Although after 1880 Chile continued exporting large quantities of wheat and flour, their value diminished as the international price fell steadily from a maximum of 64.5 shillings for 480 lb of wheat in 1867 to 26.1 shillings in 1900.[14] This fall in price had profound effects on Chilean agriculture, provoking a displacement from those regions which had traditionally produced wheat (the central region) to the newly colonized regions of the south (see Table 23).

Judging from secondary evidence, particularly the rate of growth of wheat production, there is no doubt that the agricultural sector per-

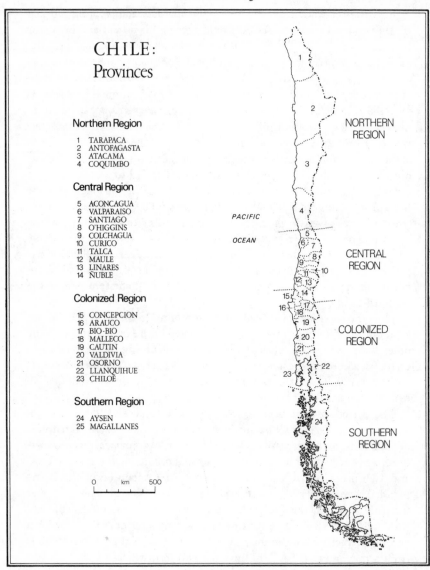

Map 10

formed well – especially in comparison with this century. For example, the annual rate of growth of wheat production was 3.8 per cent between 1860 and 1908 (see Table 23), whilst the annual rate of population growth was 1.35 per cent between 1865 and 1907 (see Table 24).

TABLE 22   *Total average annual exports of Chilean wheat and flour, 1844–5 to 1901–5 (hundreds of tons)*

1844–5	102.4
1846–50	257.6
1851–5	378.1
1856–60	292.2
1861–5	685.2
1866–70	1,282.2
1871–5	1,524.1
1876–80	1,102.6
1881–5	1,350.9
1886–90	882.4
1891–5	1,455.6
1896–1900	739.2
1901–5	385.2

Source: Sergio Sepúlveda, *El trigo chileno en el mercado mundial* (Santiago, 1959), pp. 127–8.

TABLE 23   *Chile: rates of annual growth of wheat production by region, 1860–1908 (per cent)*

	Central region	Colonized region[a]	Chile Total
1860–1908	1.9%	5.9%	3.8%
1860–80	5.3%	1.9%	5.3%
1880–1908	–1.0%	7.9%	0.9%

[a] Colonized region: La Frontera (provinces of Concepción, Arauco, Bío-Bío, Malleco, and Cautín) and Los Lagos (provinces of Valdivia, Osorno, Llanquihue, and Chiloé).
Source: C. Hurtado, *Concentración de la población y desarrollo económico: el caso chileno* (Santiago, 1966), Table 16, p. 161. Calculations based on data from *Anuarios estadísticos* (Santiago, various years).

TABLE 24   *Chile: annual population growth rate by region, 1865–1907 (per cent)*

Total population	1.35%
Rural population	0.8%
Rural population: central region	0.2%
Rural population: colonized region[a]	2.3%

[a] See note [a] to Table 23.
Source: Hurtado, *Concentración de la población*, Table 2, p. 144.

From 1860 to 1880 wheat production grew by 5.3 per cent annually. This growth was possibly due to the existence of reserves of land capable of being incorporated into wheat production, to the transfer from livestock-rearing to wheat cultivation, and to the abundance of labour. After 1880 the central region changed back to livestock-rearing, and the southern provinces started expanding wheat cultivation, achieving the high rate of 7.9 per cent annually through the colonization of new land and the abundance of cheap rural labour which migrated from the central region. (See Tables 23 and 24.)

Undoubtedly the growth of foreign markets[15] generated important transformations in the Chilean countryside, particularly in production, in incomes, and in the labour structure of the *hacienda* system, which I shall now proceed to examine. This analysis will focus on the central region, as the *hacienda* system was less important in the recently colonized regions.

As an example of the impact created by the external market, land dedicated to cereals increased from approximately 130,000 to 400,000 hectares between 1850 and 1875. This enormously increased the demand for labour, a demand which was easily satisfied owing to the existence of a large number of unemployed rural labourers. Bauer estimates that central Chile required between 35,000 and 50,000 additional workers for harvesting the grain during this period.[16] The question is, which economy expanded most to satisfy the increased wheat demand – the landlords' or the peasants'? The answer to this question largely depended on how the landlords responded, since they controlled most of the agricultural resources.

The landlord could respond to the increased wheat demand in a number of ways. Firstly, he could rent out parcels of land to peasants in return for a kind or money rent, thus effectively becoming a rentier. Conditions were unfavourable for the adoption of this alternative on a large scale, however, as peasants were poorly equipped with the instruments of production (they lacked the necessary working capital to be able to respond to the new wheat demand) and thus were unable to pay high rents. On the other hand political conditions were not so favourable as to fully guarantee the property rights of the estate,[17] and there was no assurance that the economic development of the peasant enterprise implied in this alternative could be kept in check. Nevertheless, the renting-out of land for cash or indirect labour systems (such as share-cropping) took place and was more common among those estates which lacked capital to expand wheat production,[18] those where yields were low due to the poor quality of the soil, and those which faced labour shortages. A sharecropping arrangement was entered into with the better-equipped peasant enterprises (*empleados, mayordomos,* and the richer *inquilinos*) and often with external peasant enterprises. For the landlord the advantage of this contract was that the sharecropper supplied all the labour and sometimes half of the working capital. The landlord provided the land and the other half of the working capital (or occasionally more through credit). Sometimes *hacendados* paid part of the harvest labour costs and the *mediero* (sharecropper) paid half the threshing costs. Produce was divided in half after subtracting any credit given to the *mediero*. Sharecropping in vegetables also became more common in this period, as landlords tried to minimize money payments by paying labourers partially with food produced on their own estates.[19] Sharecropping in vegetables was convenient, as the landlord did not have to divert his own labour and capital equipment from wheat production. Moreover, vegetable cultivation required constant care and attention. As a landlord himself wrote:

Vegetable production, more than any other crop, entails a wide variety of tasks which have to be carried out at set times throughout the year, such as weeding, irrigating, earthing-up, and many others, which means that a proprietor may neglect his other agricultural activities. The shortage of labour also makes it difficult for the owner to undertake the cultivation of this crop.

The sharecropper, who has a direct interest in producing as much as possible, takes more care of his small plot of vegetables, employing his wife, children, and relatives, thus introducing to the estate workers whom the landlords otherwise would not be able to attract.

The vegetable harvest generally takes place at the same time as the wheat harvest and so is often delayed and damaged due to the lack of labour. When this happens, the crops suffer and go to waste. Beans fall out of their pods and a large proportion is lost. However, under the sharecropping system the produce is harvested satisfactorily, as it is in the *inquilino*'s interest to obtain the greatest quantity possible from the land he has worked.

On other occasions, harvesting equipment, such as carts for transport, bullocks, and horses for threshing, is being used for the grain harvest and is therefore not available for vegetables. Meanwhile the *inquilino* seldom lacks such materials, as it is easy for him to find a cart and animals to undertake his small harvest.[20]

The second and more common response of *hacendados* to the increased wheat demand was to expand demesne cultivation by increasing the labour-rent payments of the existing *inquilinos*, by settling more labour-service tenants on the estate, and by employing seasonal wage labourers. As labour was abundant and cheap, this second alternative ensured greater profitability than money- and kind-rent leases. The newly settled *inquilinos* received smaller land allotments than the traditional *inquilinos* for the same labour obligations, but this was partially compensated by a reduced or supplementary wage – that is, one below the normal wage rate of *peones*. In certain cases these new tenants, called in some areas *inquilinos-peones*, (cottage-garden labourers), received only a *cerco*. They were often selected from the resident labour force living in the *inquilino*'s household either as relatives or as contracted *peones obligados*.[21] However it is difficult to judge the relative importance of this new type of tenant labourer.[22]

This settling of *peones obligados* as *inquilinos-peones* and the higher wages of *peón* labour which resulted from the increased demand for labour meant that *inquilinos* became less able to contract *peones reemplazantes* and so began to fulfil the labour obligations themselves. Those *inquilinos* who continued to employ *peones reemplazantes* outside of the family not only paid them with food, lodging, and minor payments as before but now had to '*arreglarle un salario*' – that is, they had to supplement the low wage of the landlord to make it equal to the normal wage for *peón* labour.[23]

Many of the *regalías* (perquisites) given to the *inquilinos* were allocated specifically as '*regalía p'a trigo*' (land allotment for wheat) so as to increase the estate's output of wheat. This clearly indicates that the *inquilino* was at least partially integrated into the commercial market.

The other type of *regalía* was '*regalía p'a chacra*' or land leased for vegetables. The latter became more common, especially after the demand for wheat exports fell.

In view of the seasonal character of wheat production, it was not profitable to settle all the extra labour required. Seasonal labour worked on the landlord's estate for food, drink, lodgings, and a small wage. Although the seasonal labourers received a significantly higher wage than the *inquilinos*, they were not employed all the year round and could be easily dismissed when no longer required. Neither did they put any pressure on the land resources of the estate. However, the employment of seasonal labour (*peones ambulantes* or *forasteros*) had its dangers. The *trabajador libre*, according to writings of the time, '*es trabajador sin Díos ni Ley de espíritu fuerte y aventurero*' ('is a godless and lawless worker with a strong and adventurous spirit') and the '*principal propagador de reivindicaciones*' (principal propagator of the worker's claims). In short, he was a trouble-maker on the estate. He was often accused of petty theft and drunkenness, and many landlords argued that although his wages were miserable there was little point in raising them as they would only be squandered on women and drink.[24] Seasonal labour was provided by the rural migrants and vagabonds, and, more important, by the surplus labour of the nearby *minifundia* peasant enterprises.

During the major wheat-exporting period more labour was paid on a piece-work basis (the *tarea* or *trato*)[25] to encourage a faster rhythm and longer hours of work. Work by *tarea* was mainly used during the harvesting period, when it was important to bring in the harvest before the weather could damage the crop and lower the return. This system also required less supervision from the estate administration. The wage per *tarea* was often three to four times higher than the daily rate.[26]

In conclusion the wheat export boom strengthened the landlord's enterprise, which adjusted to the new market opportunities by extending grain cultivation. Thus, apart from some coastal external *minifundia* areas situated near ports, which produced wheat for the export market but eventually suffered from serious soil erosion, it was largely the landlords who reaped the benefits of the growth in wheat exports. The large surplus fund of rural labour facilitated this alternative and meant that production could be increased without the need of large financial resources, merely by extending the labour-service tenant system. More *inquilinos* were settled with higher labour rents. However this was partially compensated by a supplementary wage for labour services. For the first time also the landlord enterprise employed seasonal wage labour on a large scale. Thus the second half of the nineteenth century witnessed the extension and consolidation of the *hacienda* system based on the labour-service tenancy arrangements, but it also showed the first signs of a proletarianization process which took place on a large scale only after the 1930s. The signs of this process included the growing overpopulation experienced by the external peasant enterprise areas, which expressed itself in the growing movement of population from the rural to the urban regions from the second half of the nineteenth century onwards,[27] and in the increasing number who sought a tenancy or seasonal wage employment on the *hacienda*. The beginnings of a proletarianization process was also evidenced by the fact that landlords came increasingly to view the internal peasant enterprise as a source of cheap permanent wage labour rather than as a source of rent.[28]

The disintegration of the Chilean hacienda system: the proletarianization of the labour-service tenant

Between the 1880s and the 1920s new agricultural areas were incorporated into wheat and later livestock production. Thus, the *hacienda* system was extended to other regions of the country and generally stabilized its labour structure. However, changes occurred, mainly in farming efficiency.[29] The period 1900 to 1930 witnessed the highest per capita rate of growth of agricultural production so far this century.[30] During this time the internal market for agricultural products also expanded, owing to the high rate of rural-to-urban migration.

The main factor responsible for the proletarianization of the labour tenant was the rapid mechanization of the estates from the 1930s onwards. From the beginning of this century to the 1930s, the *haciendas* greatly increased the irrigated crop area (which doubled for the whole country)[31] and so increased the demand for labour. This was the last period when *inquilinos* were settled on the *haciendas*. After the late 1920s the cultivated area ceased to increase, the main sources of output growth being the introduction of machinery and the more extensive use of modern inputs such as fertilizers and pesticides. Industrial crops also became increasingly important. These factors contributed to the increase both in land and, especially, in labour productivity.[32]

The increase in the productivity of the *hacienda* enterprise meant that the payment of production fringe benefits became more costly for the landlord, and a substitution process set in, replacing land leases by kind and (above all) money payments. *Inquilinos* were expelled and additional wage labourers employed. In this section I shall analyse the particular ways in which the labour-service tenant was proletarianized.

The tenant peasant enterprise occupied approximately one-fifth of the cultivated land and produced about a quarter of the total output of the *hacienda* system of central Chile in 1955.[33] By 1965, however, tenants occupied one-seventh of cultivated *hacienda* land, and their contribution to the total production of the *hacienda* fell to a fifth.[34] Taking the whole of Chile, the land leased on a sharecropping basis remained more or less the same between 1955 and 1965, whereas the land leased in *regalía* to labour-service tenants diminished by about one-sixth.[35] As for the stock of livestock, in 1955 approximately one-fifth of the cattle and half of the horses of the *hacienda* belonged to the tenant peasant enterprise.[36] These data partially reflect the growing unprofitability of the *regalía* system for the landlords, compared to other more favourable ways of employing labour.

The proletarianization of the labour-rent tenant occurred in the following ways:

(a) Their absolute number and relative proportion in the labour force employed by the *hacienda* enterprise diminished.[37] *Inquilinos* became less important within the total economically active agricultural

population. Their proportion of the rural population diminished from a
maximum of 21 per cent in 1935 to 12 per cent in 1955 and 6 per cent in
1965 (the latest official data available).[38]

(b) The amount of land leased to *inquilinos* decreased, and so their
production became less significant within the *hacienda* system.

(c) Grazing rights were reduced, thus restricting the *inquilino*'s
capacity to produce and accumulate.

(d) The landlord economy, through its possession of machinery,
expanded its productive participation in the *inquilino*'s enterprise
by undertaking the ploughing and/or harvesting of the *inquilino*'s
land.[39]

(e) The *inquilino*'s function as labour supplier, via the *reemplazante*,
disappeared. Increasingly, *inquilinos* performed these labour services
themselves, working as *peones obligados*, as they no longer had the
economic capacity to hire and maintain *peones reemplazantes*. (The
inquilinos would supplement the low cash wage which the *reemplazante*
received from the landlord.)[40] In 1955 approximately a quarter of the
total labour days worked on the *inquilino*'s enterprise came from hired
wage labour.[41] However, in 1965 the *inquilino* had to rely almost entirely on his unpaid family labour, as he no longer had the financial
means available to contract outside labour.[42] Increasingly, also, the
members of the *inquilino* family worked as *voluntarios* (resident seasonal
wage labourers) on the *hacienda* enterprise so as to procure additional
income for the deteriorating *inquilino* household, especially when the
level of the *voluntario* wage approached the higher wage paid to *afuerinos*
(outside seasonal wage labourers). When wages increased, the *peones
reemplazantes* were no longer dependent on the supplementary wage of
the *inquilino* and dealt directly with the landlord. As landlords no
longer required the *inquilino*'s function as a source of external hired
labour, they had even more reason to decrease production fringe benefits.

(f) The *hacienda* enterprise was compelled by legislation to pay an
increasing proportion of the *inquilino*'s minimum wage in cash; the cash
proportion rose from 25 per cent in 1953, when minimum-wage legislation was introduced, to 75 per cent in 1965. The proportion of the
inquilino's income derived from his role as a wage labourer thus increased. It is estimated that in the early 1940s[43] approximately a third of
his total income was in cash, and by 1965 this had risen to a half.[44]

(g) The number of implements and draught animals owned by
the *inquilinos* steadily declined. By 1965, almost half did not possess an
iron plough, and two-thirds lacked draught animals.[45] This reduction

in the instruments of production is perhaps the clearest expression of the proletarianization of *inquilinos*.

For the increasingly proletarianized *inquilino*, the *media* (tenancy subject to a sharecropping system) was almost the only way open to economic betterment[46] and to the maintenance of his peasant enterprise. The land given in *media* to the *inquilino-mediero* was usually twice as large as the land given in *regalía*. *Medias* were generally confined to those *inquilinos* who were better capitalized and who possessed a larger household labour force.[47] In 1965, out of the total land leased to *inquilinos*, two-thirds was in *regalías* and one-third in *medias*. The increasing proletarianization of the internal peasant enterprises meant that by 1965 only 13 per cent of the total cultivated land was cultivated by them. Of the total land, 2 per cent was given in sharecropping to outside *medieros*, who did not work as labourers on the *hacienda* enterprise. (See Table 25.)

Rural wage labourers[48] were increasingly important in the total labour supply of the estate. Landlords employed two types of wage labour. One was the *voluntario*, whose origin lay partially with the *peón reemplazante* and who lived in the *inquilino* household. As he lived on the estate he was permanently available, but the landlord only employed him when necessary, paying a wage and food ration for days worked. The *voluntario* was called 'volunteer' because, unlike the *peón obligado*, he was not forced to work on the *hacienda* enterprise but only did so if he wished to and when required by the landlord.

The other type of wage labourer employed by the estates was the *afuerino*. He was termed 'outsider' because he did not live permanently

TABLE 25 *Distribution of total cultivated land in the hacienda system of central Chile, according to type of tenements, in 1965 (per cent).*

Held as *regalías* by *empleados*	2	
Held as *regalías* by *inquilinos*	6	
Total held as *regalías*		8
Held as *medias* by *inquilinos*	3	
Held as *medias* by non-residents	2	
Total held as *medias*		5
Total cultivated by peasant enterprises		13
Total cultivated by *hacienda* enterprise		87

Source: Landlord's survey, ICIRA, *Fundo project, 1965 – 66.*

on the estate, nor was he attached to it. *Afuerinos* were either small landed proprietors, village labourers, or migrant labourers (*torrantes*). About 10 per cent of *afuerinos* were also *minifundistas*; 10 to 15 per cent fulfilled obligations as *reemplazantes* of *inquilinos*; approximately 10 per cent also undertook urban-rural employment (small trading in villages and countryside, working on road construction, and the like); and the remaining 65 to 70 per cent were unemployed during various months of the year – that is, they were 'full-time' *afuerinos*.[49] About 90 per cent of *afuerinos* worked regularly as such, and 85 per cent were employed as *afuerinos* for more than six months of the year.[50] Although the *afuerinos*' position was still precarious, there was a tendency towards stabilization as they were employed for longer periods by the same estate.[51]

It is worth noting the absence of 'pure' wage labour in the labour structure of the *hacienda*. One scarcely finds mention of agricultural workers who were employed on a yearly contract and given a fixed weekly or monthly cash wage payment.

Within the labour structure of the *hacienda* we must also mention the *empleados* (administrative strata) concerned with the running of the estate. Employed on a yearly contract and remunerated with a monthly salary and at times a tenancy as an incentive (*regalía* and / or *media*), they often received a share in the profits to encourage higher productivity on the estate.

Table 26 presents the average labour structure of the *hacienda* enterprise in 1965. Approximately 80 per cent of the total labour days worked

T A B L E 26   *Labour structure of the hacienda enterprise in central Chile, 1965*

Labour Category	Percentage of *haciendas* which do not employ this labour category	Average number of days worked per labourer per annum[a]	Average number of labourers employed per *hacienda*[a]	Percentage distribution of total working days per annum[b]
Empleados	2%	300	5	13%
Inquilinos	1%	254	23	46%
Voluntarios	8%	188	16	23%
Afuerinos	15%	67	38	18%

[a] Statistical average: refers only to those *haciendas* which effectively employ that labour category.

[b] Calculated on the total number of working days on all *hacienda* enterprises; therefore includes those *haciendas* which do not employ a specific labour category.

Source: Landlords' survey, ICIRA, *Fundo project 1965–66*.

were supplied internally, the remainder being provided by the *afuerinos*. However, the number of *afuerinos* was equivalent to the number of *inquilinos* and *voluntarios* taken together, which shows that during the periods of high labour demand outside labour was as important as the resident labour force. From this table it will be noted that the internal resident labour force (*empleados* and *inquilinos*) accounted for the greatest number of working days per year, followed by the semi-permanent resident labour (*voluntarios*), and finally the seasonal non-resident labour (*afuerinos*).

As we have already mentioned, the conflict between the *hacienda* enterprise and the peasant enterprise over natural resources was resolved in favour of the former. In view of this, it is more correct to consider land leases as a means of remunerating labour at a lower cash wage cost than as a means of obtaining rent payments. In fact it was only during the second half of the last century that a supplementary or marginal monetary wage (often paid in kind) was paid to *inquilinos*, and when this was first introduced it was only paid for those labour days which exceeded the customary labour rent. The land lease was still largely considered as a rent income in labour for the *hacienda* enterprise. As late as 1927 we find evidence that some landlords viewed the *inquilinaje* as a renting system (although rather conveniently so, as landlords wanted to avoid establishing a labour contact with *inquilinos* which would commit them to respecting the existing labour legislation). In a letter to the Director of the Labour Office a landlord wrote the following:

I really can't see how landlords can sign labour contracts like the ones you send me, as the *inquilino* system is not a 'labour contract' but an agreement by the owner to rent a small piece of land to the *inquilino*, the rent being determined by the quality, quantity, and location of the land.

The *inquilino* pays the rent, according to what has been agreed, in (a) cereals, (b) harvesting tasks, (c) various agricultural duties like rounding up cattle, rodeo, ploughing, reaping, fallowing, and finally the obligation to provide a *peón* to work on the *fundo* the whole year round or for periods of four, six or eight months, depending on what has been agreed.[52]

Labour-service tenancy and sharecropping were only convenient for the landlord as long as labour rent and kind or money rent remained higher than the profit he could obtain by exploiting the rented land himself. As soon as cash wages of *inquilino* labour increased at a faster rate than wages of pure wage labour on the one hand, and land productivity of the *hacienda* enterprise increased – pushing up profits per hectare of the demesne – on the other hand, a substitution process in favour of pure wage labour took place.

Labour legislation and mechanization from the 1950s onwards pushed up the cost of *inquilino* labour and the economic advantage of *inquilinaje* disappeared, thus explaining its being superseded by *voluntario* and *afuerino* labour.[53] According to my calculations based on the ICIRA *Fundo project* data (see Table 27, column 1), the cash cost for the landlord of employing *inquilino* labour in 1965 was already slightly higher than that of employing *voluntario* and *afuerino* labour. Traditionally the opposite used to be the case, especially as the *afuerinos* received no production fringe benefits and were employed only seasonally. If we take into account the implicit or opportunity cost for the landlord of the land leased to *inquilinos*, then the cost of *inquilino* labour increases to about 60 per cent higher than that of *voluntarios* and *afuerinos* (see Table 27, column 2).[54] Thus landlords intensified their efforts to reduce the *raciones de tierra* of the *inquilinos*, or even to evict them. They did not, however, diminish the land leased on a sharecropping basis to the *inquilinos*, as this was a very profitable way of indirectly employing labour.

Although the petty mode of production of the peasant economy might

TABLE 27 *Average labour cost per day worked by different labour categories employed by the hacienda enterprise in central Chile, 1965 (E^O of 1965)[a]*

Labour category	Average cash cost per day worked[b] (1)	Average cash and non-cash cost per day worked (inc. *regalia*[c] and *media*[d]) (2)	
Empleados	14.0	16.0	
Inquilinos	} 6.1	} 7.5	8.3
Inquilino-Medieros			4.6
Voluntarios	} 4.7	} 4.7	
Afuerinos			

[a] 1965 exchange rate: $U.S. 1.00 = E^O 3.6.
[b] Cash cost includes direct cash wage plus social security payments plus consumption fringe benefits and *participaciones* (share in profits), in cases where these exist.
[c] Land leased in *regalías* to the labourers has been valued at the average profit per arable hectare obtained by the *hacienda* enterprise – that is, E^O 400.
[d] The wage cost of *inquilino-mediero* labour is lower than the *inquilino*'s, as the former pay money or kind rent for the land leased on a sharecropping basis. The landlord's yearly profit is estimated at E^O 300 per hectare for the land leased in *media* to *inquilino-medieros*.
Source: Landlords' survey, ICIRA, *Fundo project 1965–66*.

be less efficient than large-scale capitalist production, peasants were often able to earn more working on their own piece of land than as wage labourers – even if they had to pay rent – by working longer hours per day, by employing family labour, and so on. Thus, for example, although real rural wages had greatly increased during 1965 the earnings of *inquilinos* per man-day worked on the tenancy were more than double the wage per day worked on the *hacienda* enterprise (see Table 28).

Tenants preferred to become wage labourers only if the loss in earnings resulting from giving up the tenancy was smaller than the additional yearly earnings they obtained as wage labourers. As Table 28 indicates, this was obviously not the case in Chile in 1965, and this is one of the reasons why *inquilinos* resisted becoming pure rural proletarians. However, there are other considerations to be borne in mind. As a wage labourer the *inquilino* was subjected to market forces to a greater degree. For instance, he might be unemployed during certain periods, and in an inflationary economy such as the Chilean his real wage would tend to fall. Since he was a tenant, his income would increase with rising prices; his standard of living would be less prone to fluctuations, as a percentage of his production would be destined for family consumption; and he and his family were likely to be less liable to unemployment.[55] *Medieros*, however, according to Table 28, were likely to gain by transferring some labour to the *inquilinaje* system, becoming partial wage labourers, and thereby qualifying for family allowances and social security benefits which were enforced and greatly increased after 1964.

In summary, the main forces behind the proletarianization process after the 1930s, until the initiation of the land reform period in the second half of the 1960s, were the following. Firstly, mechanization extended the land cultivated by the *hacienda* enterprise, thus restricting the pasture and forest rights of tenants and reducing the land given as *raciones*. Land became scarcer and more productive, thus raising its opportunity cost. Mechanization also had the effect of reducing the ratio of labour per hectare. Secondly, the *hacienda* enterprise began to improve crop yields through the use of modern inputs and the reallocation of land to those crops which increased the profit rate per hectare (largely the new industrial crops such as sugar beet, linseed, sunflower seed, and rape seed). Thirdly, as the cash costs of *inquilino* labour increased proportionally more than those of *voluntarios* and *afuerinos*, and even surpassed them by 1965, the pressure for proletarianizing tenants became even greater. The proletarianization process of the external peasant enterprises occurred simultaneously. The fragmentation of the external *minifundia* drove more peasants into the seasonal labour market, thus depressing wages.

I shall now consider briefly the impact of urbanization and the political system on the break-up of the *hacienda* system. The develop-

T A B L E 28   *Earnings per man-day and per year of tenants and wage labourers in central Chile, 1965 (E^O of 1965)[a]*

	Voluntarios and afuerinos[b]	Inquilinos	Inquilino-medieros	Medieros
Earnings per man-day worked on *hacienda* enterprise[c]	4.7	6.1	6.1	—
Earnings per man-day worked on tenancy[d]	?	13.0	9.3	5.4
Total earnings per man-day worked[e]	4.7(?)	8.9	8.2	5.4
Total earnings per man-day[f]	4.7(?)	5.6	5.4	5.1
Total earnings of household per year[g]	1,000 – 2,000(?)	3,500	4,400	4,400
Total value of production of tenancy per year	?	2,000	6,600	14,500

[a] 1965 exchange rate: $U.S. 1.00 = E^O 3.6.

[b] *Voluntarios* and *afuerinos* might have had additional earnings, the *voluntarios* from a garden plot (around 30 per cent of them had *cercos*) and the *afuerinos* from their own small peasant property or tenancy (about 20 per cent). No reliable figures on the unemployment rate exist for these labourers. Thus, except for earnings per man-day worked on the *hacienda* enterprise, most of the data could not be calculated with exactness for this labour category.

[c] These earnings include daily wage plus consumption fringe benefits and family allowances expressed on a per-day-worked basis.

[d] These earnings are per man-day worked and include the days worked by the family members on the tenancy expressed on a man-day basis. Costs of production (including money or kind rents) have been subtracted from the total value of production to obtain total earnings.

[e] These total earnings per day worked are a weighted average of the sum of [c] and [d].

[f] Similar to [e] but earnings have been expressed on the basis of total available man-days and therefore include the days of unemployment.

[g] Similar to [f] but includes also other non-agricultural earnings by family members. The figure of E^O 1,000–2,000 is an estimate and refers only to *voluntarios*.

Source: ICIRA, *Fundo project 1965–66*.

ment of capitalism in Chile has led to the increasing economic importance of the urban sector. This in turn has stimulated a greater commercialization of agriculture and the development of an urban
resources conflict between the peasant and landlord economies. By
urban resources we mean those economic resources largely controlled
by urban-based groups, a control which is generally greater when most
of the surplus comes from the industrial or mining sector, as is the case
in Chile. Peasants and landlords compete for credit, inputs, and markets
for agricultural products. If the peasant economy is able to capture these
urban resources, its entrepreneurial capacity will be strengthened and
the peasant enterprise will develop. In Chile the 'urban resources' are
subordinated to 'political resources'. The state administrative network
of social and economic services has spread into the countryside only
in recent decades. Whether these services are assigned to the landlord
economy or to the peasant economy depends on which social class
controls the political system, especially the state machine. Thus the
allocation of state urban resources is determined by the political system –
that is, by the class which controls the 'political resources'. The allocation of private urban resources is determined by the market system, or
in other words by those economic groups who control the market.

The advances in agricultural technology and the development of
new inputs[56] have enabled the peasantry to achieve higher outputs
from their own pieces of land. This has increased the relative importance
of capital in relation to land and has made the availability of capital
crucial. Until recently, landlords monopolized state and commercial
credits and in turn were the main suppliers of credit to the tenants,
charging a higher rate of interest than the state credit.[57] On the output
side, the peasants' surplus production was increasingly sold to urban
middlemen and sometimes to agencies of the state, instead of to the
landlord economy.

In the 1950s, the extension of the franchise to the peasantry increased their political participation, and political parties started to
compete for the peasant vote. In return for political allegiance, the
parties promised legislation to improve the peasants' economic and
social position. The political parties in government used the state bureaucracy to channel economic resources to the peasants and to supervise
the implementation of social legislation. Thus the state became a
'political entrepreneur'. Those political parties not in power used active
party members as their 'political entrepreneurs', offering private economic resources and political power to the peasantry. The state introduced
minimum-wage and social-security legislation, but this was only half-

heartedly controlled, and evasions were frequent before the land reform period. The state also controlled, and in some cases fixed, agricultural prices. These fixed prices became known as 'political prices', and they reflected the growing political power of the organized working class and dominance of industrial interests over the agrarian sector.

Thus the landlord enterprise managed to dominate the *hacienda* system by modernizing and expanding its economy and effectively proletarianizing the internal peasant enterprise. But, as the landlord no longer allocated tenancies or offered stable employment, he gradually lost his source of legitimacy and paternalistic control over peasants. Thus the very technological innovations which the landlords introduced themselves turned the internal peasant enterprise into a stumbling block for the *hacienda*'s full capitalist development; therefore the *hacienda* as a socio-economic system was undermined from within.

Furthermore the spread of urban and political resources into the agrarian sector accelerated the dissolution of the *hacienda* system. The penetration of urban commercial and political interests exposed the peasantry to new economic and social groups. It 'opened up' the the *hacienda* system and uprooted the entrepreneurial and socio-political control of the landlords.

The final contradiction arose when the landlord economy, after successfully proletarianizing the peasantry and preventing any possible economic expansion of the peasant economy, was itself expropriated. The situation is even more startling when we take into account the fact that land reform was not primarily initiated as a result of a peasant movement[58] but was introduced by urban-based interest groups who exploited the landlord–peasant conflict for electoral ends. The landlords lost the battle in the arena of urban politics, thus transforming their former economic victory into a political defeat.

The expropriation of the hacienda system: the land reform process, 1965–73

The agrarian reform can be divided into two phases. The first phase of limited expropriation and capitalist modernization coincided with the Christian Democrat government of Eduardo Frei (1965–70). The second phase of total expropriation and liquidation of the landlord *hacienda* system, and its replacement by the collective *hacienda* system, coincided with the Allende government (1971–3).

The policy of the Christian Democrat government towards the agricultural sector was twofold. On the one hand, during their six-year mandate, about 10 per cent of the *hacienda* system was expropriated, and a transitional organization – the *asentamiento* – was introduced, in which the land and other resources became state property and were managed jointly by the peasants and bureaucrats of CORA (Corporación de la Reforma Agraria), the state land reform agency. The *asentamientos* included *asentados* (the ex-*inquilinos*) and *socios* (the ex-*voluntarios*). The former retained their rights to production fringe benefits and had a voice and vote in the administrative council and assembly. The latter had neither production fringe benefits nor voting rights. After a trial period of three to five years the property and management of the *asentamiento* were to be transferred to the peasants, who could either choose a co-operative form of exploiting the land or split the *asentamiento* into parcels farmed individually but maintaining a loose co-operative organization. On the other hand, the government policies were aimed at increasing the efficiency of the non-expropriated estates, thus strengthening the large-scale agricultural capitalist enterprise.

These modernizing economic policies increased certain agricultural prices and established a stable price policy, so as to give incentives and security to the agricultural producer. Public investment in agriculture increased, mainly in the form of new irrigation projects, housing, and credits. Large amounts of public credits were directed to the rural sector, especially towards those large, efficient producers who undertook modernization plans, such as importing farm machinery and equipment. The government also increased taxation and the minimum agricultural wage, thus forcing an increase in the productivity of land and labour on the estates. Through these positive incentives of price and credit policies and the negative incentives of increased wages, tax legislation, and the threat of expropriation, the Christian Democrat government effectively achieved the modernization of the *haciendas*,[59] cutting out the inefficient producer without always having to expropriate. These stick-and-carrot policies of modernization were enforced by an extension of the agrarian bureaucracy and by the massive syndicalization of the peasantry.

Thus the agrarian policy of the Frei government represented a reform strategy based on three pillars – the expropriation of large and inefficiently exploited estates, the organization of rural labour under government sponsorship, and an increase in rural incomes through the enforcement of minimum wages and job security – the underlying strategy being the creation of a peasant base of political support for the Christian Democrat party.

The Christian Democrat agrarian policy was ambiguous, reflecting the conflicting interests of the different social groups represented by that party. During the implementation of the land reform programme, increased labour costs resulted in large-scale expulsion of labour from the *haciendas*. The government, in response to mounting political pressure from the peasants, introduced legislation which restricted the right to dismiss agricultural labourers. Landlords also began to sub-divide their *haciendas* amongst family members and relatives to escape the land reform law which stipulated that any estate over eighty 'basic' hectares[60] was liable to expropriation. In response to this evasion, the government introduced legislation which controlled and limited the sub-division of large *haciendas*. Thus landlords were faced with contradictory policies in their modernization effort, for they were not able to expel their redundant labour force, nor were they able to sub-divide their estates so as to work them more intensively. The legal restrictions conflicted with underlying economic and technological pressures. Sooner or later the *hacienda* enterprise had to reduce its labour force and eliminate the resource-use payments, thus signing the final death certificate of the *inquilinaje* system. However they were not able to do so without a struggle, as the increasing unionization of the peasantry (mainly the resident labour force) created new social pressures against the final proletarianization of the *inquilinos*, and union demands often specified an extension of the resource-use payment as a way of increasing rural incomes and security for labourers. Therefore the government-sponsored unionization of rural labourers also constituted an obstacle to the full modernization of the estates.

The Christian Democrat land reform was not without its socially negative aspects. It created both economic and political divisions amongst the peasantry. Economically, only a minority of unionized peasants acquired access, and later property rights, to the expropriated *haciendas*. This privileged group of rural labourers were the so-called *asentados* (literally the 'settled'). Politically, the trade union legislation encouraged the adherence of agricultural labourers to various trade unions, each controlled by a different political party. This had the effect of dividing peasants politically, sometimes even at the farm level. The unionized peasants (*inquilinos* and *voluntarios*) could exert pressure to expropriate estates, defend their employment, and demand higher wages. Peasants who were not unionized, largely the *afuerinos*, due to their seasonal and migrant nature,[61] were the first ones to suffer from the rising rural unemployment and were excluded from the benefits of expropriation.

The differentiation of the peasantry created by the land reform even went so far that the new beneficiaries, the *asentados*, continued to employ *afuerinos* as the landlord had done before.[62] *Afuerinos* were often employed to work on the collective land, freeing the *asentado* to dedicate his labour time to his own parcel of land. The *asentados* benefited from the costly investments which the state made on the *asentamientos*. CORA paid an *anticipo* (an advance on yearly profits) to the *asentados* for days worked, but as the *asentamientos* did not make large profits, and sometimes even suffered losses, the government was actually subsidizing the production unit. Moreover state credits given to the *asentamientos* were frequently not repaid.[63] One of the limitations on the extension of the land reform was its enormous financial cost.[64]

Another peasant group neglected by the land reform process was the external peasant enterprise, which did not receive access to land; thus the problems of overpopulation in the *minifundia* areas remained unsolved. Nor did the external peasant enterprises receive significant financial aid from the state to purchase modern inputs or introduce investments which would raise the productivity of the land and create new employment opportunities.

As the benefits of the land reform were confined to a very small group[65] and expropriation advanced at a very slow pace, peasant demands and actions became more radical. The *pliegos de peticiones* (labour petitions) not only demanded higher wages but called for the expropriation of the estates. When this was rejected, peasants increasingly took to direct action, initiating for the first time in rural social history the large-scale seizure of estates (*tomas*).[66] The government responded with force, and the declared policy became '*el predio tomado no será expropiado*'[67] ('the occupied farm will not be expropriated'). Rural discontent grew, and although two-thirds of unionized peasants belonged to peasant confederations affiliated to the Christian Democrat party, this party ceased to have a clear control over them. The Christian Democrats had even less control over the non-unionized peasants who comprised over half the total peasant population in 1970. Under these circumstances, Allende received a majority vote among the rural male population and was elected president in 1970 under the banner of the Unidad Popular (UP) — a coalition of left-wing parties.

The legacy of the first phase of the land reform process was the emergence of a new land tenure system. The expropriated estates were divided into the *asentamiento* and the *reserva* (reserve). The law recognized that expropriated landlords had the right to a *reserva* which could not exceed eighty 'basic' hectares.[68] (This did not apply to those estates expropriated because of absenteeism or manifest mal-exploitation.) As mentioned before, many estates had tried to avoid the land reform by sub-dividing their land into *parcelas*, carrying out a spontaneous and private land reform of their own. Often, however, this was no more than a fictitious partition, as estates were sub-divided among family members and administered as a unit. Although legislation was passed in 1967 limiting this practice, it was not always strictly enforced. Yet other estates remained intact, probably on account of their higher degree of modernization. Preliminary figures from a study which re-interviewed the estates included in the ICIRA *Fundo project* of 1965–6 indicate that, of the *haciendas* existing in 1965–6, the following changes had taken place by 1970–1: 39 per cent remained intact as a *hacienda* unit; 26 per cent had been sub-divided, giving rise on average to 3.6 *parcelas* on each ex-estate; and 35 per cent had been expropriated,[69] being transformed into *asentamientos*.[70] The expropriations were only partial, as in slightly fewer than half the expropriated *haciendas* the landlords were able to retain a *reserva* (that is, a smaller estate).

The Frei land reform process resulted in the creation of the peasant estates (the *asentamientos*), the maintenance of the old, large but modernized landed estate, and the formation of many new medium-sized to smaller single-farm estates (the *reservas* and *parcelas*), whose number practically doubled. Thus the *hacienda* system – understood as an inter-related unity between landlord and peasant enterprise – practically vanished.[71] As expropriated landlords retained their machinery, this resulted in the capitalization of the *reservas*, the location of which the landlord was free to choose. He thus kept for himself not only the best land but also most of the infrastructure (barns, cow sheds, irrigation works, chicken farm, fruit plantations, and so on).[72]

The Allende government continued the land reform using the same legislation but radicalized its application by expropriating all *haciendas* regardless of their efficiency.[73] Fewer reserves were granted, and their size was reduced from 80 to 40 'basic' hectares. Whilst 60 per cent of the expropriated landlords retained a *reserva* under Frei, this figure fell to 10 per cent under Allende.[74] Politically motivated to eliminate the landlord class and to transfer power to the peasantry,[75] Unidad Popular completed the expropriation phase of the land reform in 1972, expropriating twice as many estates in two years as the Christian Democrats had done in six. In mid-1972 the reformed sector accounted for a little under half of the total irrigated land and just over a third of the land in 'basic' hectares. The peasants in the reformed sector still constituted a privileged minority, as they comprised less than 15 per cent of the total rural labour force.[76] However, private capitalist farming maintained a hold

TABLE 29   *Chile: distribution of farms according to size, 1965 and 1972*

Size	Percentage of farms		Percentage of land	
('basic' hectares)	1965	1972	1965	1972
Less than 5	81.4%	79.3%	9.7%	9.7%
5.1 to 40	14.5%	14.6%	22.2%	24.6%
40.1 to 80	2.1%	4.1%	12.8%	27.3%
Over 80	2.0%	0.1%	55.3%	2.9%
Reformed sector	—	1.9%	—	35.5%
Total	100.0%	100.0%	100.0%	100.0%

Source: S. Barraclough (co-ordinator of project), *Diagnóstico de la reforma agraria chilena (noviembre 1970 – junio 1972)*, ICIRA (Santiago, 1972), p. III-3.

in the countryside, as the Frei land reform had created a new sector of modern medium-sized farms falling in the range of 40 to 80 'basic' hectares, which the Allende government did not expropriate. In 1965 these farms accounted for only 12.8 per cent of the land, but by 1972 this figure had increased to 27.3 per cent (see Table 29). Their importance in terms of agricultural production was even greater on account of their high productivity.

In view of the social and economic disadvantages of the *asentamiento*, the main difficulty of the Allende government was to find an alternative organization which would prejudice neither peasant political support nor the long-run socialistic aims of the government. Meanwhile, it continued to form *asentamientos*.

In August 1971 the parties of the Unidad Popular finally agreed on the CERA (*Centro de Reforma Agraria*) and the *Centro de Producción*. The latter was less important, being confined to those estates which were highly capitalized and often had an industrial character, such as wood industries and livestock-breeding centres. It was a large state enterprise *(hacienda estatal)*, operated with pure wage labourers[77] and managed jointly with government representatives as in the nationalized industries of the social property sector.

The CERA was intended as a transitional structure. It was a large co-operative which united a number of adjacent estates into one unit of optimum size, incorporating the maximum number of permanent members to help solve unemployment. Unlike the *asentamiento*, the CERA was to be characterized by the social and economic equality of the peasants, all of whom were to be equal partners in the co-operative; like those of the *asentamiento*, the workers of the CERA were guaranteed an equal minimum wage through the *anticipo*. Each peasant worker was entitled to the use of a house and *goce* (piece of land) plus specified rights for pasturing animals. However, the total land of the peasant households could not exceed one-fifth of the CERA's arable land. As was not the case with the *asentamiento*, part of the profits were to be invested internally in social services and buildings; another part was to go to a community development fund for the entire region. The state was to assure technical assistance, machinery, and credits, but the CERA was to be an accountable private enterprise, with its production plan financed by a loan from the state bank.[78]

The CERAs came under heavy attack from the opposition parties and aroused the suspicions of the peasantry, largely because of the 'disappearance' of part of the profits into a community fund and because of the incorporation of the seasonal labourers (*afuerinos*) as permanent members.[79] In response to this the government was forced to devise an alternative organization, the peasant committee (*comité campesino*), which represented an uncertain compromise between the CERA and the *asentamiento*. In summary, in 1972 about 45 per cent of the expropriated *haciendas* were *asentamientos*, 45 per cent *comités* and the remainder were CERAs and production centres (*Centros de Producción*).[80]

The more socialized forms of organization failed in their original intentions. Peasants showed a clear preference for limiting the numbers of members and maximizing their private plots and pasture rights. This resulted in a considerable expansion of the peasant economy within the estates to the detriment of the collective land. For example, in 1971–2 about 15 per cent of total cultivated land on the *unidades reformadas* ('reformed units') were farmed as *goces*. From 1965, the extent of *goces* seems to have doubled at least.[81] Collective cultivation was neglected, and peasants even surreptitiously appropriated produce from the collective part and used communal machinery and implements for private purposes.[82] The deterioration of collective production can be explained by various factors. Firstly, the payment of the *anticipo* did not provide any economic incentives, since it had become a fixed monthly payment, which did not vary according to number of days worked, effort displayed, skills required, and tasks performed on the collective land by each member. Secondly, the lack of machinery and equipment, together with insufficient supplies of seeds and fertilizers, resulted in much collective land being left uncultivated or under-exploited. Thirdly, the agrarian bureaucracy gave insufficient technical advice, training, and supervision to the reformed units. Finally, and perhaps most important, the growth of the black market in foodstuffs from mid-1972 provided an additional economic incentive for peasants to develop their peasant enterprise at the expense of the collective, as private produce could be sold for high prices on the black market whilst collective produce was largely sold at official prices through the state marketing agencies.

In spite of all the above-mentioned factors which encouraged the expansion of the peasant economy, peasants in the reformed sector did not normally want to split the collective up into private plots, since by so doing they would have faced accumulated debts, would have had to pay for the land, and would no longer receive the *anticipo* and state-subsidized credits, machinery, seeds, and fertilizers. Thus the question arises if we are in the presence of a new type of *hacienda* system in which the owner of the land is the state and the peasants are wage labourers, who receive a wage in the form of the *anticipo* from the state as well as usufruct of land and pasture in return for working on the collective land, the produce of which is appropriated by the state. I do not intend to attempt to answer this question here but merely raise the point.[83]

Conclusions

It is possible to depict four phases in the development of the Chilean *hacienda* system since the middle of the last century. The first phase was characterized by the consolidation of the *hacienda* system due to the significant expansion of the external market for wheat and flour. Landlords responded by extending the labour tenant system, settling more *inquilinos* with higher labour-rent payments and smaller tenancies. This was compensated for by the introduction of a supplementary wage. However, as the increased production of wheat was achieved without the aid of mechanization, the demand for labour (especially seasonal labour) increased enormously. Thus, together with the expansion of the internal peasant enterprise, seasonal rural wage labour was employed to a significant degree for the first time.

The second phase of the *hacienda* system was identified by its progressive disintegration. The crisis occurred owing to a rise in the value of land, brought about by a growth of the internal market through large-scale rural-to-urban migration, and to the increasing mechanization of the estates. This crisis of the multi-farm estate was characterized by the growing proletarianization of both tenant farmers and *minifundistas*. The internal peasant enterprise was reduced in size and number, and the *inquilino* was obliged to work more labour days on the landlord enterprise. He ceased to be a producer paying a rent and became a permanent wage labourer receiving a monetary wage plus production and consumption fringe benefits. The proletarianization of the external peasant enterprise was exemplified by the peasants' growing need to work as temporary wage labourers on the *hacienda* enterprise. *Voluntarios* and *afuerinos* replaced *inquilinos* as the dominant labour force of the estates.

The third phase of the *hacienda* system was short but intense, coinciding with the changes introduced by the Christian Democrat land reform policy. This land reform was the outcome of the increased power of the organized working class as well as the greater presence of the peasantry in national politics. The Christian Democrat land reform was however only the logical conclusion of the disintegration process of the *hacienda* system, which had been under way for some decades. It speeded up this process, modernizing the *haciendas* through mechanization and through their sub-division into single-farm estates, thus making the labour-tenant system obsolete. Mechanization created growing unemployment, especially among those of the external peasant enterprises who had worked as *afuerinos*. Only a fifth of the *hacienda* system was expropriated in this period. Peasant co-operatives (*asentamientos*) were formed, but solely for the internal resident labour force, and *afuerinos* were effectively excluded from the land distribution. The land reform of the Christian Democrats generated its own contradictions by bringing to the fore a massive peasant unionization and by creating obstacles to the elimination of production fringe benefits, the large scale expulsion of surplus labour from the estates, and the sub-division of the over-large *haciendas*. Thus the modernization of the *hacienda* system and its full transformation into single-farm estates clashed with the demands of the newly formed peasant unions, which demanded not only higher wages and more production fringe benefits but also a more rapid and extensive expropriation policy.

The fourth phase opened in 1970 with the government of the Unidad Popular coalition. In response to the growing radicalization of the peasantry (expressed in increasing *tomas* or land seizures), the Allende government speeded up the land reform process and in just two years expropriated all *haciendas*. The government attempted to incorporate *afuerinos* into the benefits of land distribution, but without much success except in the Mapuche Indian *minifundia* region. Unidad Popular also failed to restrict the amount of land controlled privately on the expropriated farms. On the contrary, the peasant economy expanded considerably by multiplying or enlarging *goces* (individual plots of land) and by privately appropriating the collective resources. Thus a new type of *hacienda* system would seem to be emerging in the Chilean country-

side, based on a conflicting relationship between the peasant economy
and the collective economy which is formally under the control of the
agrarian state bureaucracy. Paradoxically the revolutionary land reform
of Unidad Popular resurrected the multi-farm estate, although with the
intention of initiating a process of transition to socialism.

Postscript

The above account was written before the violent overthrow of the
Unidad Popular government. The major achievement of Allende's agrarian reform was the final expropriation of all estates larger than 80
'basic' hectares – which amounted to over 60 per cent of Chile's irrigated
land – and the transformation of the landlord *hacienda* system into a
collective *hacienda* system, thereby resulting in a significant increase
in the peasant's standard of living. The historical conflict between landlords and peasants was resolved in favour of the latter, with the peasantry
gaining over most of the agricultural resources of the *hacienda* system.

The collective *hacienda* system, however, has had a short life, as the
military junta plans to sub-divide the expropriated estates by granting
reservas of 40 'basic' hectares or over to all landlords expropriated who
did not receive *reservas* under Unidad Popular, and by splitting the
remainder up into small peasant holdings to be sold to selected members
of the reformed units. Co-operative ownership will only be retained
on those few estates which have major investments in forestry and livestock. The military government intends to hand over expropriated
land as private property to landlords and peasants within a period of
three to five years. The *reservas* will be the first to be returned and will
greatly strengthen the 40-to-80-'basic'-hectare farm sector, which will
increase numerically by about a third. This will become the dominant
sector in the countryside in terms of land, capital, and production. At
the other end of the spectrum, most of the resultant peasant holdings
will be less than 5 'basic' hectares, thus joining the *minifundia* or small
farm sector, which is already the most numerous and contains the largest
proportion of the rural population.

Thus although the military government cannot reverse the expropriation process by fully reconstituting the traditional landlord *hacienda*
system, it is eliminating both the co-operative and collective *hacienda*
systems. Under these circumstances, the disappearance of the *hacienda*
system will not benefit the majority of the peasantry, as only a small
percentage will gain access to rural proprietorship. It may be that even
amongst those who receive small holdings, it will not be long before

they are forced to join the ranks of the rural proletariat as a result of the continued processes of socio-economic differentiation resulting from the unequal patterns of capitalist development.

NOTES

1. In the shaping of my ideas on Chilean rural economy and society I have greatly benefited from discussions in the past with Rafael Baraono and Alexander Schejtman. I wish to express my appreciation to them but do not hold them responsible for all the views expressed in this paper. My thanks also are due to Andre G. Frank for drawing my attention to the extensive report by Karl Kaerger on Chilean agriculture at the turn of the century, and to Brian Loveman for making available his vast collection of documents from the Chilean Labour Archives.

2. R. Baraona, 'Una tipología de las haciendas en la sierra ecuatoriana', in O. Delgado (ed.), *Reformas agrarias en América Latina* (Fondo de Cultura Económica, Mexico, 1965), pp. 688–96. See also chapter 1 of C. Kay, 'Comparative development of the European manorial system and the Latin American *hacienda* system: towards a theory of agrarian change in Chile' (unpublished Ph.D. thesis, University of Sussex, 1971).

3. In common English usage the concept of 'peasant' implies entrepreneurship and proprietorship. Unless specified otherwise, I employ the concept of 'peasant' in its widest meaning – that is, any rural cultivator who derives his main livelihood from agricultural pursuits ('*campesino*' in Spanish). Thus the peasantry in the Latin American sense would include small landed proprietors (who, together with their families, cultivate the land, perhaps employing additional wage labourers), tenants, and agricultural wage labourers.

4. Note that I distinguish between the *hacienda* system and the *hacienda*. The *hacienda* is the landlord's exclusive property whereas the *hacienda* system includes land belonging to those peasants who are linked by a wage or rent relationship to the *hacienda*.

5. Kind- or money-paying tenants are known by a wide variety of terms throughout Latin America. They are referred to as *medieros* and *aparceros* in Chile; *camayos*, *concertados*, and *yanaconas* (coastal region) in Peru; *partidarios* in Ecuador; *aparceros* in Colombia; *habilitados* in Argentina; and *arrendatarios* in most of Latin America. Labour-rent tenants are called *inquilinos* in Chile; *huasipungueros*, *cuadreros*, *arrimados*, *colonos*, and *yanaperos* in Ecuador; *allegados*, *colonos*, and *yanaconas* (Sierra region) or *arrendires* (Cuzco and Selva region) in Peru; *peones acasillados* in Mexico; *terrazgueros*, *colonos*, and *concertados* in Colombia.

6. For an analysis of the concept of peasant economy, see A. V. Chayanov, *The theory of the peasant economy*, transl. and ed. D. Thorner *et al.* (Homewood, Ill., 1966); and J. Tepicht, 'The complexities of the peasant economy' (mimeographed) (Universidad de Chile, Santiago, 1970).

7. The expropriation alternative does not necessarily come about as a result of a previous development of the peasant economy; on the contrary, it might be due to the increasing proletarianization of the peasantry.

8. The development of the market, especially of the foreign market, generally causes an uneven regional development. Those *hacienda* systems near to the market or to

export ports benefit more than those which because of their peripheral location face higher transport costs. This was particularly significant in previous centuries, when transport costs were a relatively high percentage of the value of total produce. The market stimulus also provokes an unequal development between the landlord and peasant economies.

9. This conflict over what has been called '*usura de tiempo*' (literally 'usury of time') is reflected in the following complaint by a sharecropper: 'We have to cut the landlord's wheat first and only afterwards the sharecropper's, thus endangering the sharecropper's harvest.' Archivo Dirección del Trabajo, Ministerio del Trabajo (Santiago, 1941).

10. For an attempt to apply this multi-enterprise approach to other Latin American countries, see the valuable team study directed by R. Baraona on Ecuador: Comité Interamericano de Desarrollo Agrícola (CIDA), *Tenencia de la tierra y desarrollo socio-económico del sector agrícola – Ecuador* (Washington, 1965). See also Kay, 'Comparative development of the European manorial system and the Latin American *hacienda* system', chapter 4, which deals with Peru and Bolivia. Unfortunately our limited knowledge of other Latin American cases and the scarcity of historical material and research make this task difficult. However, research currently being undertaken on Peruvian and Mexican agrarian history – particularly on the *hacienda* – looks very promising. See, among others, Juan Martínez Alier's paper in this book (chapter 6).

11. It is estimated that on average only 135,000 metric *quintals* (1,350 tons) of wheat were exported yearly to Peru before 1850. This would not have required more than 15,000 hectares of land. See A. J. Bauer, 'Expansión económica en una sociedad tradicional: Chile central en el siglo XIX', *Historia*, no. 9 (Instituto de Historia, Universidad Católica de Chile, Santiago, 1970), p. 145.

12. See M. Góngora, *Vagabundaje y sociedad fronteriza en Chile (Siglos XVII a XIX)*, Cuadernos del Centro de Estudios Socio-Económicos, no. 2 (Santiago, 1966), pp. 29–37.

13. M. J. Balmaceda, *Manual de hacendado chileno* (Santiago, 1875): Part IV was republished by the Instituto de Capacitación e Investigación en Reforma Agraria, Convenio FAO–Chile (ICIRA) in *Recopilación de lecturas sobre el hombre y la tierra* (Santiago, 1970), pp. 42–5. G. Izquierdo, *Un estudio de las ideologías chilenas: la sociedad de agricultura en el siglo XIX*, Publicación del Centro de Estudios Socio-Económicos (Santiago, 1968), pp. 185–7.

14. Hurtado, *Concentración de la población*, pp. 159–60.

15. Although the external market for wheat was significant in stimulating agricultural production, it should not be overestimated in relation to the whole economy. For example, agricultural exports maximized their contribution to foreign-exchange earnings in 1860, when they accounted for 17.3 per cent of the value of total exports. In 1900 this figure had fallen to only 3.7 per cent. (Hurtado, *Concentración de la población*, p. 71.)

16. A. J. Bauer, 'Chilean rural labor in the nineteenth century', *The American Historical Review* LXXVI, 4 (1971), p. 1078.

17. Karl Kaerger, *Landwirtschaft und Kolonisation im Spanischen Amerika* (Leipzig, 1901), p. 193.

18. Bauer, 'Chilean rural labor', p. 1064.

19. According to the owner of the well-known *hacienda* El Principal, Sr Salvador Izquierdo, who wrote a thesis for his degree in agronomy, published by the SNA

(Sociedad Nacional de Agricultura) in 1833, the advantage of *chacarería* (vegetable cultivation) undertaken by the sharecroppers was that 'it supplied the workers and the owner of the estate, which is especially convenient because of the high price of vegetables, particularly beans' (cited in Izquierdo, *Un estudio de las ideologías chilenas*, p. 303).

20. Ibid., pp. 304–5.

21. The landlord preferred to promote and contract labour resident on the estate, as this ensured greater control and generally greater reliability due to their long-time family dependence on the owners of the estate.

22. Bauer, 'Chilean rural labor', p. 1076, mentions the case of the large and well-known estate of Viluco (south of Santiago) which settled 200 *peones sedentarios* or *inquilinos-peones*, each of whom received a house and a garden plot of half a *cuadra* (0.75 hectare).

23. For data on wages of *peón* labour from 1830 to 1880, see Bauer, 'Chilean rural labor', p. 1080. Unfortunately there are still no representative national or regional statistical data on items such as types and size of land leases, types and amounts of rent payments, and so on. Available case study data provide insights, but they have limitations and can often be misleading when used to discover national long-term historical trends. This lack of statistically representative data in Chilean agrarian history is being gradually overcome, however, by the valuable research of historians like M. Góngora, A. J. Bauer, M. Carmagnani, and others.

24. See Kaerger, *Landwirtschaft und Kolonisation*, p. 134.

25. '*Tarea*' literally means 'task' and refers to the amount of work necessary to earn the wage. A *tarea* tended to reflect the work a good labourer normally managed to complete in one day. For example, a *tarea* for cutting wheat used to be one-sixth of a *cuadra* (0.25 hectare) (Kaerger, *Landwirtschaft und Kolonisation*, pp. 129–30).

26. Bauer, 'Chilean rural labor', p. 1078. Kaerger, *Landwirtschaft und Kolonisation*, pp. 126 and 130, estimates that in 1898 wages by *tarea* were only twice the level of normal wages.

27. Hurtado, *Concentración de la población*, Tables 2 and 3, pp. 144–5.

28. For the best historical analysis of the *arrendatarios-inquilinos* when *inquilinos* were mainly viewed as labour-rent tenants, see M. Góngora, *Origen de los 'inquilinos' de Chile central* (Santiago, 1960), pp. 83–104. To determine more objectively the way in which the *inquilinaje* system should be viewed (that is, as a source of labour rent or of wage labour) we would have to compare the amount of labour rent paid by the *inquilino* with the amount of wage payment received from the land-lord. In strictly economic terms, if the former amount is larger than the latter the *inquilino* can be viewed as a lessor partially paid with a supplementary wage; if the reverse is the case, as a wage labourer partially paid with supplementary production fringe benefits.

29. M. Ballesteros and T. E. Davis, 'El crecimiento de la producción y el empleo en sectores básicos de la economía chilena', *Cuadernos de Economía* II, 7 (Universidad Católica de Chile, Santiago, 1965), p. 22.

30. Ballesteros and Davis, 'El crecimiento de la producción', pp. 13, 15.

31. Hurtado, *Concentración de la población*, p. 176.

32. Ibid., p. 115.

33. These estimates can only be regarded as indicating orders of magnitude, as it is very difficult to single out exact data for the *hacienda* and its components, the tenant peasant enterprise and the landlord enterprise, from the census data. Estimates based

136 *Cristóbal Kay*

on CIDA, *Chile: tenencia de la tierra y desarrollo socio-económico del sector agrícola* (Santiago, 1966) pp. 63, 159, 162; on Chile, *III censo nacional agrícola ganadero 1955, resumen general del país*, vol. 4 (Dirección de Estadísticas y Censos, República de Chile, Santiago, 1960); and on ICIRA, *Fundo project 1965–66*, typescript (Santiago, n.d.).

34. ICIRA, *Fundo project 1965–66*.
35. Chile, *III censo nacional agrícola ganadero 1955*, vol. 4; and Chile, *IV censo nacional agrícola ganadero 1965, resumen general del país* (Dirección de Estadísticas y Censos, Santiago, 1969).
36. Chile, *III censo nacional agrícola ganadero 1955*, vol. 4. The properties of over 200 hectares are taken as being representative of *haciendas*. Unfortunately no comparative data exist for 1965.
37. Chile, *III censo nacional agrícola ganadero 1955, IV censo nacional agrícola ganadero 1965*.
38. Kay, 'Comparative development of the European manorial system and the Latin American *hacienda* system', Table 5–12, p. 113 (page-reference to mimeographed version of thesis). The figures for central Chile are higher than those indicated here for the whole of Chile, as *inquilinos* were more common in the central zone, where they made up 35 per cent of the total rural labour force in 1935.
39. According to data from ICIRA, *Fundo project 1965–66*, in about 10 per cent of estates the lease was actually taken over by the *hacienda* enterprise, and the *inquilino* received the equivalent in produce of what he had previously reaped from the soil. This was called '*ración cosechada*' or 'harvested allowance'; it revealed the *inquilino*'s deteriorating entrepreneurial and productive capacity.
40. According to a study of the Putaendo valley during the mid-1950s, the supplementary wage paid by the *inquilino* fluctuated between two-thirds and three-quarters of the *reemplazante*'s total wage income (R. Baraona *et al.*, *Valle de Putaendo: estudio de estructura agraria* (Santiago, 1961), p. 236).
41. Data from Chile, *Aspectos económicos y sociales del inquilinaje en San Vicente de Tagua-Tagua* (Departamento de Economía Agraria, Ministerio de Agricultura, Santiago, 1960), p. 46.
42. ICIRA, *Fundo project 1965–66*.
43. Chile, *Veinte años de legislación social*, Dirección de Estadísticas (Santiago, 1945), p. 93.
44. ICIRA, *Fundo project 1965–66*.
45. Ibid.
46. Clearly landlords considered it to be so too, as the following quotation shows: 'on the estate there exists a sharecropping system with the *inquilinos* which notably improves the work opportunities for themselves and their families and consequently the possibility of increasing their incomes' (Archivo Dirección del Trabajo (Santiago, 1957)).
47. For a penetrating analysis of the *inquilinaje* system in central Chile which also uses data from the ICIRA *Fundo project 1965–66*, see Alexander Schejtman, 'Peasant economies within the large *haciendas* of central Chile' (unpublished B.Litt. thesis, Oxford University, 1970).
48. Rural wage labourers generally received only a monetary wage payment in return for their labour power.
49. H. Zemelman, *El afuerino*, ICIRA (mimeographed) (Santiago, 1966), p. 13, based on data from ICIRA, *Fundo project 1965–66*.

50. Zemelman, *El afuerino*, p. 12.
51. About a third of *afuerinos* had been employed more than once by the same estate (Ibid., p. 26).
52. Archivo Dirección del Trabajo (Santiago, 1927). Other examples of landlords referring to the *inquilinaje* as a renting system are given as late as 1938 in letters to the Dirección del Trabajo.
53. The number of *voluntarios* and *afuerinos* increased by 46 per cent between 1955 and 1965, whilst the number of *inquilinos* decreased by 44 per cent (Chile, *III censo nacional agrícola ganadero 1955*, and *IV censo nacional agrícola ganadero 1965*).
54. *Afuerinos* and *voluntarios* tended to work longer than the eight-hour day of the *inquilino* on the *hacienda* enterprise. This was so because *afuerinos* and *voluntarios* undertook much more work on a piece-work basis (*a trato*) which encouraged them to work longer than the legal eight-hour working day, but *inquilinos* preferred to spend the extra daylight hours working on their own tenancy and thus undertook little if any piece-work. Data from ICIRA, *Fundo project 1965–66*, reveal that 70 per cent of the days worked by *afuerinos* and 45 per cent worked by *voluntarios* on the *hacienda* enterprise were on a piece-work basis.
55. For a detailed analysis of the economic rationale of the labour and tenancy structure of the *hacienda* system in central Chile, based on the ICIRA *Fundo project* data, see P. Ramírez, *Cambios en las formas de pago de la mano de obra agrícola*, ICIRA (Santiago, 1968); A. Schejtman, 'Peasant economies'; and Kay, 'Comparative development of the European manorial system and the Latin American *hacienda* system', chapter 6, pp. 136–79.
56. We refer to inputs such as improved seeds, pesticides, fertilizers, and so on. Unlike machinery, they have the advantage of greater divisibility; also, they do not replace labour, which is the abundant factor of production on the peasant enterprise.
57. C. Nisbet, 'Interest rates and imperfect competition in the informal credit market in rural Chile', *Economic Development and Cultural Change* XVI, 1 (October 1967), pp. 73–90; E. Feder, 'Feudalism in agricultural development: the role of controlled credit in Chile's agriculture', *Land Economics* XXXVI, 1 (1960), pp. 92–108.
58. A vast and organized peasant movement only got under way in Chile after the land reform process had started. However, this is not to deny the long history of acute conflict in the countryside and the persistent struggle of the peasantry against the landlords, as documented in the comprehensive study by B. Loveman, 'Property, politics, and rural labor: agrarian reform in Chile, 1919–72' (unpublished Ph.D. dissertation, Indiana University, 1973).
59. W. R. Ringlien, 'Economic effects of Chilean national expropriation policy on the private commercial farm sector, 1964–69' (unpublished Ph.D. dissertation, University of Maryland, 1971).
60. The 'basic' hectare is a hectare of best-quality irrigated land, or the equivalent. In the central and southern region the equivalent of eighty 'basic' hectares could reach over 900 hectares of arable land, thus maintaining relatively large holdings.
61. A. Affonso *et al.*, *Movimiento campesino chileno*, 2 vols. ICIRA (Santiago, 1970).
62. Wage labourers employed by *asentamientos* constituted about 30 per cent of the total labour force, according to a study using 1968 data. See J. Echeñique, 'Las expropiaciones y la organización de *asentamientos* en el período 1965–70', in *Reforma agraria chilena: seis ensayos de interpretación*, ICIRA (Santiago, 1970), p. 106.
63. I. Ribeiro, *Política financiera de la reforma agraria (1965–69)*, ICIRA (mimeographed) (Santiago, 1970).

64. Chile, *Reforma agraria chilena, 1965–70*, CORA (Santiago, 1970), pp. 69–79.
65. Out of the 100,000 peasant families promised to benefit from the land reform process, at the end of the Frei government only 21,000 had actually received land. The total rural labour force is over 700,000.
66. E. Klein, 'Conflict between rural workers and landowners in central Chile' (unpublished Ph.D. thesis, University of Sussex, 1973).
67. In practice many of the estates taken over by peasants were later expropriated.
68. ICIRA, *Exposición metódica y coordinada de la ley de reforma agraria de Chile* (Santiago, 1968).
69. The percentage of expropriated *haciendas* is much higher than the national average, as the estates included in the sample were taken from the larger *haciendas*, above 150 'basic' hectares, which were the first to be expropriated by the Frei government.
70. D. Stanfield and M. Brown, *Changes in land tenure in the large farm sector in Chile's central valley between 1966 and 1971* (draft, mimeographed), Land Tenure Center, University of Wisconsin (Santiago, 1973), Table II, p. 10.
71. However, in some cases new links were established between the *asentamiento* and the *reserva*, such as the renting of farm machinery and even the supply of credit by the landlords to the peasant co-operative. *Reservas* were in some cases over-capitalized as landlords 'dismantled' the expropriated estate by transferring all their farm equipment to the *reserva*. The landlords also often kept or sold live-stock. Both machinery and livestock were left to the expropriated owners to dispose of as they wished.
72. Non-expropriated *haciendas* and *parcelas* also benefited from the large imports of farm machinery and from sales of farm machinery from those *haciendas* which did not retain a *reserva*. Thus the large-scale private farm sector increased in efficiency.
73. For an analysis of the agrarian policy of the Unidad Popular government, see D. Lehmann, 'Agricultura chilena y el período de transición', *Sociedad y Desarrollo* III (Centro de Estudios Socio-Económicos, Santiago, 1972), pp. 101–44; P. Winn and C. Kay, 'Agrarian reform and rural revolution in Allende's Chile', *Journal of Latin American Studies* VI, 1 (May 1974), pp. 135–59; I. Roxborough, 'Agrarian policy in the Popular Unity government', Institute of Latin American Studies, Glasgow University, *Occasional Papers* no. 14 (1974); and C. Kay, 'Chile: an appraisal of Popular Unity's agrarian reform', Institute of Latin American Studies, Glasgow University, *Occasional Papers* no. 13 (1974).
74. Data from a study on the land reform process by a research team from ICIRA (typescript) (Santiago, 1972), chapter 2, p. 3.
75. On the various ways in which peasants have increased their power, see C. Kay, 'La participación campesina', in *La economía chilena en 1971* (Instituto de Economía, Universidad de Chile, Santiago, 1972), pp. 537–56.
76. S. Barraclough (co-ordinator of project), *Diagnóstico de la reforma agraria chilena (Noviembre 1970 – Junio 1972)*, FAO–PNUD–ICIRA (Santiago, 1972) pp. III-3 and III-8. A summarized version of this voluminous report is available in S. Barraclough and A. Affonso, 'Diagnóstico de la reforma agraria chilena', *Cuadernos de la Realidad Nacional* no. 16 (Santiago, April 1973) pp. 71–123.
77. Theoretically this was so, but in actual fact agricultural labourers received some production fringe benefits although on a much smaller scale than the *asentamientos* or the CERAs.
78. On the CERA see Chile, CORA, *Organización transitoria de la nueva area de reforma agraria: los centros de reforma agraria* (mimeographed) (Santiago, 1971).

79. The political opposition to the Allende government partly succeeded in mobilizing its peasant base (mainly members of the Christian-Democrat-controlled Confederación de Asentamientos) against the CERAs, by falsely arguing that peasants would lose their property rights to the house and *goce* and would receive few, if any, production fringe benefits.

80. Barraclough, *Diagnóstico de la reforma agraria chilena*, p. III-19; data refer to early 1972.

81. Ibid., pp. III-8, III-12; Appendix, Table II. See also Table 25, p. 116 above, which shows that the land held in *regalía* by *inquilinos* (of which almost half is *goce*) was 6 per cent of total cultivated land of the *hacienda* in 1965–6.

82. O. Brevis (co-ordinator of project), *Proyecto análisis de las unidades reformadas en la IV zona de reforma agraria*, ICIRA (mimeographed) (Santiago, 1972); and M. Langand and A. Peña, *Relaciones de producción en un sector de comuna*, ICIRA (mimeographed) (Santiago, 1973).

83. Eric R. Wolf would refer to the multi-farm-estate reformed units as an 'administrative domain': see his *Peasants* (Englewood Cliffs, N.J., 1966), pp. 50–9. As A. V. Chayanov (*The theory of the peasant economy*) theorized that the peasant economy existed under the feudal, capitalist, and socialist modes of production, it is perhaps not too far-fetched to argue that the *hacienda* system might also exist under various modes of production. For a comparison of *hacienda* and manorial systems in different historical periods see C. Kay, 'Comparative development of the European manorial system and the Latin American *hacienda* system', *Journal of Peasant Studies* II, 1 (1974), pp. 69–98.

CHAPTER 6

Relations of production in Andean *haciendas*: Peru

JUAN MARTINEZ ALIER[1]

This paper presents some tentative conclusions based on the archives of a few expropriated *haciendas*. The material so far collected in Lima filled five or six lorries, and they will allow several books to be written by several people. A large part of the new archive consists of account books. A much smaller and sometimes very juicy part (perhaps one quarter of a lorry-load in all) consists of correspondence between *hacienda* managers and landowners, or *hacienda* managers and *comunidad* authorities, and so on. All this either has been catalogued or is in the process of being catalogued. It belongs almost totally to the twentieth century. A great digestive capacity will be needed to work through this material. One also needs a stomach as strong as that of a *llama* (the Andean cameloid), since the diet includes massacred, beaten-up, and blacklisted Indians. However, one of my tentative conclusions is that the Indians' resistance to the expansion of the *haciendas* made landowners behave carefully, if not kindly.

A relevant consideration, in order to properly assess the value of the records collected in Lima, is that those *haciendas* which kept many records are surely not typical, modal *haciendas*, but they are nevertheless crucial to an understanding of the efforts made at rationalization and the resistance they provoked. One might argue that some landowners were able to expand their *haciendas* and rationalize their labour systems only because other, more traditional, and wiser *hacendados* did not follow suit in this dangerous disruption of the rules of the game.

External and internal encroachment

By 'expansion of the *haciendas*' I mean the effective exercise of the rights of property inside *hacienda* boundaries. I do not mean either the shifting of *hacienda* limits beyond those established in the original land grants by the Crown, or the creation of new *haciendas* on *comunidad* land ('capturing' communities, as this has been called). My impression is that few *haciendas* were founded after the eighteenth century; there is now an easy method to establish this, and also the frequency of changes in

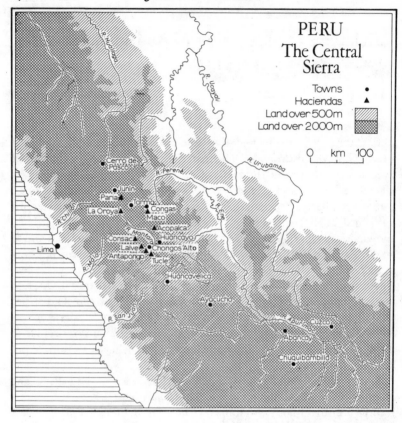

Map 11

ownership, by studying the summaries of property titles included in the *expediente de afectación* for each expropriated *hacienda*. Many of the *haciendas*, however, existed only on paper. Landowners were not able to make peasants pay anything at all for the use of *hacienda* land. The history of *haciendas* is therefore the history of how landowners attempted to get something out of the Indians who were occupying *hacienda* lands. In some cases (notably sheep *haciendas*) twentieth-century landowners went to the extreme of trying to dislodge the Indians.[2]

Though I have studied the central Sierra more than the southern Sierra, I suspect that the fantastic increase (shown in Chevalier's article) in the number of *haciendas* in Puno, as wool prices went up in the early decades of this century, reveals only the fact that *haciendas* which had long existed on paper became proper *haciendas* – that is, *haciendas* able to get something out of the Indians or even to dislodge some of them. The increase does not necessarily indicate that new property titles were granted or forged. In the central Sierra, my impression is that all *haciendas* had some sort of titles going back to colonial times.

However, such titles have been disputed, and what from the landowner's point of view might look like the effective occupation of his own *hacienda* lands, from the Indians' point of view might look like encroachment. The titles have been in doubt not only, and not mainly, because of their lack of precision. There has been time enough since the colonial period to conduct proper land surveys.

It would be difficult to improve upon the following account of such disputes, which I think deserves full transcription:

A problem of importance and of much worry which originated back in the days when the Cerro de Pasco purchased the *haciendas*, is the matter of boundary and land disputes. Seldom does a week go by without a boundary controversy. It might be livestock passing onto our grounds or a *'comunidad'* claiming parts of our land as their property. When the Corporation purchased all the *haciendas* back in 1924 to 1926, they received the property from the original owners with the boundaries *status quo*. Some of the boundaries were natural terrain features such as rivers or mountain ridges, but none were marked with any concrete pyramids as permanent and defined boundary markers.

Several years after the purchase of the *haciendas*, boundary disputes arose and many were settled through the intervention of a Government arbitrator. When they were settled, the Government issued a decree legalizing the boundary and the Ganadera constructed concrete markers along the agreed boundary. Many sections of our outside boundaries are still without concrete markers, and most of the adjacent *'comunidades'* and private owners of these unmarked sections, continue to claim that their land overlaps beyond the boundary we are defending.

These land claims are made through the Dirección de Asuntos Indígenas, Ministerio de Justicia. Both parties concerned are called to Lima to present our titles before an arbitrator and try to reach a solution. It is a regular occurrence that the communities involved do not recognize our titles to the land, and claim that we have taken the land away from them. And then the arbitrator tries to get us to give a little strip of our land to the *'comunidad'* in order to solve the situation peacefully. Naturally we object and state we are the rightful owners and will not cede one square metre. The meeting adjourns and the problem is prolonged until a later date. In the meantime the *'comunidad'* keeps pushing its livestock onto this disputed land, and often gets the *Senadores* and *Diputados* of their *Departamentos* and *Provincias* to put pressure on the Government to decide in favour of the *'comunidad'*.

These disagreements last for one to ten years, and during this time our boundary riders are constantly fighting to protect our land. On several occasions

our boundary riders have been cursed, clubbed and hit with rocks by our neighbours. That is when we have to back our men, and go out personally to show
our support. It is not very comforting to face and argue with fifty to two
hundred half-drunken members of an opposing 'comunidad' while standing on
the land they claim as theirs. I ceded a small strip under these circumstances
once, and I regret it to this day, but I learned to withhold my strongest objections until they are much fewer in numbers and usually in my office or some
other safe place.

We must continue to protect our land and get every foot of our boundary
clearly marked with concrete pillars, in order to build wire fences for better
protection.

There are two weaknesses that make our battles long and hard. One is the
Government's lack of firm support to the rightful private land owners who
occupy the land disputed. Anytime the 'comunidad' claims a piece of our land,
we have to prove that we own it, yet in many cases they do not have even a
piece of paper that resembles a legal title. Other times they have forged titles
which they use to force the issue. The Government agency gives the 'comunidades' moral support, encouragement and confidence in these affairs, instead of
reprimanding them for their unauthorized, unorthodox and illegal procedures.

The other weakness is the poor description or method of designating the
boundaries of our titles, which leaves much in doubt. In some instances, a title
will describe our north boundary as such and such a 'comunidad' but does not
name any reference points between us. In other cases the titles will name
mountains or areas, but over the years and generations, the mountains or areas
have assumed other names and the original names have long passed from the
minds of the old-timers. In these cases we have to depend upon the 'squatter's
right' or physical possession to keep us put. In two early cases, the 'comunidades'
took possession of our land and pushed us off. We have had lawsuits pending for
years on these two cases, yet no verdict has been given.

At present we have fifteen land disputes pending. The one with the Community
of Tusi has been going on since 1914, and it is still a perennial headache. They
occupy about 5,000 acres of *Hacienda* Paria, our good land, and are still trying to
take more. We cannot afford to relax along our boundaries or else we will be
taken.

We will soon start fencing our outside boundaries which have been settled
by Government decree and marked with concrete pyramids. We trust that we will
be able to settle all boundary disputes in the near future and fence them in as soon
as they are settled. We can anticipate further trouble after the boundaries are
fenced, such as wire cutting and fence stealing, but we will be ready to meet it
when the time comes.[3]

This was written in the peaceful Odría period (1948–56). Actually,
when the time of troubles came around 1960, the lands of the Corporation, like those of many other landowners, were invaded. So far we
have only a highly coloured account of such events, provided by the

novelist Manuel Scorza in *Redoble por Rancas* and *Historia de Garabombo el invisible*. A true history might prove even more sensational than Scorza's contrived epic, in which the peasants, though able to talk with their horses, appear as very primitive, politically inarticulate rebels.

Along with the external encroachment of *comunidades* upon *hacienda* lands, there is also the more interesting encroachment from within, for which Baraona has coined the phrases *asedio externo* and *asedio interno*.[4] In 1955, in the *haciendas* of the Cerro de Pasco Corporation (in all, some 300,000 hectares) there were 52,000 sheep (or, rather, sheep plus some horses and cattle reduced to sheep units) which belonged to workers and shepherds (*huacchilleros*). This was 17.33 per cent of the total number of sheep units. In less efficiently run *haciendas*, the ratio could go up to 50 per cent or more. In even less efficient *haciendas*, it would be difficult to know the ratio, since they surely did not bother to keep a control on numbers.[5]

In 1955, the Cerro de Pasco Corporation started a further campaign to reduce the number of *huaccha* sheep, as they are called, by setting an upper limit of 250 sheep units per worker or *huacchillero*, and also by increasing wages in inverse proportion to the number of *huaccha* sheep. This system had already been proposed by Peruvian landowners, though not implemented with any great success. From the landowners' point of view, having so many alien sheep in their own *haciendas* looked like a form of internal encroachment. From the *comunidades*' point of view, the prospect of having these sheep thrown onto their already over-crowded pasture lands was disturbing. Landowners were well aware of this, and they seem to have refrained from pushing *huaccha* livestock off the *haciendas*, knowing that this would give *comunidades* additional reasons for invading. Displaced Indians, whether they were formally members of outside *comunidades* or not (shepherds were, as a rule, in the central Sierra), were likely to have to fall back on *comunidad* resources. Thus, one reason why a wage-labour system had not been introduced in the Fernandini *haciendas* (also some 300,000 hectares) was 'so as to avoid the turmoil that would arise from the displacement of men and animals which would put pressure on the *comunidades*'.[6] Internal encroachment could be reduced only at the risk of increasing external encroachment.

Restrictions on the geographical mobility of labour

Before I go on to consider the efforts that were made to change the labour system, and the methods which the Indians resorted to in order to resist such attempts, one point must be clarified. This is the fundamental question of restrictions on the geographical mobility of labour. If *huacchilleros* and *colonos* had been unable to leave the estates, then landowners could have used their monopoly power, very much as slave-owners were able to do in plantation America, to make them pay dearly in labour services for their own subsistence. If they could freely leave the estates, then it is wrong to talk of 'monopsony' or 'oligopsony' in the labour market. Even if the *haciendas* were very large, land was not 'mono-polized' – there were at least several hundred large landowners in Peru. As it was, the landowners got the worst of three possible worlds. *Huacchilleros* and *colonos* were not serfs or wage labourers (or sharecroppers or cash tenants). They had cheap access to *hacienda* resources and at the same time could not be prevented from leaving the estates.

I think that Baraona's remark on *huasipungueros* in Ecuador applies generally: 'free *peones*' income is inferior to that of *huasipungueros*';[7] and therefore it would have been pointless for the *huasipunguero* to leave the estate and join the ranks of the day labourers. Similarly, Jan Bazant has found that in the *Hacienda* Bocas, in San Luis Potosí, Mexico, around 1850, the economic condition of the resident population was superior to that of casual labourers.[8] Bauer asserts with great vigour that *inquilinos* in Chile were free to leave, had they so wished.[9] A detailed study of one *hacienda* in the Yanamarca Valley, in the central Sierra in Peru, concludes that 'the most extreme of these sanctions [against *colonos*] was expulsion from the *hacienda* lands'.[10] There are of course references in the literature to the geographical immobility of *colonos* in recent times, though not many in scholarly literature. For instance, Tullis has claimed that in the central Sierra of Peru *colonos* were not free to move. But his authority for this view is Ciro Alegría – winner, as Tullis tells us, of the First Latin American Prize Novel Contest, held in the United States.[11]

More worthy of consideration is the view put forward, for instance, by Macera,[12] and also by Chevalier on Mexico,[13] that in colonial times debt peonage was used – that is, the intended burdening of *hacienda* labourers with debts beyond their capacity to repay them, as a means to tie them to the estate. Though I am not qualified to comment on the colonial period, and while there is little information on the Peruvian Andes in the nineteenth century, some points are worth mentioning. One consideration is that debt peonage, in the sense suggested, was at most a second-best solution as compared to serfdom proper. Charles Gibson makes the point that 'an Indian worker bent on leaving his *hacienda* could find occasion to do so despite his indebtedness', and, further, that it was the Indians themselves who wished to get in-debted:

As monetary values came to occupy a large role in Indian society . . . the *hacienda* offered a regular or irregular income. To Indians who had lost their land (largely, of course, to *haciendas*) the *hacienda* provided a dwelling and a means of livelihood . . . the *hacienda* was an institution of credit, allowing Indians freely to fall behind in their financial obligations without losing their jobs or incurring punishment.[14]

In one sheep *hacienda* I have studied, a system somewhat akin to debt peonage was used into the 1950s. The *huacchilleros* guaranteed repayment of the money advanced to them on becoming *huacchilleros* with their own *huaccha* sheep. This system was not used in the bigger firms, such as Cerro de Pasco Corporation, Sociedad Ganadera del Centro, or Fernandini. But in *Hacienda* Antapongo, once the initial expense of an advance had been made, and a contract for one year signed with the prospective *huacchillero* who was to take care of *hacienda* sheep, the landowner, perhaps making a virtue out of necessity, would attempt to get services for his money and to reduce labour turnover by retaining *huacchilleros* who were indebted, not allowing them to leave. If they left, some of their own *huaccha* sheep would be embargoed, either with or without the surrounding *comunidad* authorities' co-operation. If, against the rules of the *hacienda*, they left with their own *huaccha* sheep, the co-operation of the Guardia Civil for the detention of the *prófugo* would be sought, sometimes with success and sometimes not. Care was taken in Antapongo for debts not to grow larger than a few weeks' wages, and always to remain much below the value of the debtor's own livestock. I know of no case where the job was inherited because of debt, though there are cases of debts being not only tacitly but also explicitly waived for widows.

The word *prófugo* also appears sometimes in the records of other *haciendas*, used for *huacchilleros* who left before their period of contract was over, but no steps were taken to make them come back. The situation might have been different in other *haciendas*, and in earlier times. Indeed, assuming that *haciendas* were in difficulties over recruiting labour to work on the *hacienda*'s own (demesne) lands, because neither the Indians within nor those without wanted to work, and assuming that large advances had therefore to be made (large in relation to wages), then of course debts might have been widespread. One may find statements by landowners to the effect that it was a good idea for the *huacchilleros* to be a little in debt so that they would not leave for the mines. This sort of statement was made, for instance, at the beginning of this century by the manager of *Hacienda* Consac, of Sociedad Ganadera Junín, one of the *haciendas* later bought by the Cerro de Pasco Corporation. In my view, it was equivalent to saying that in order to keep people on the job you have to pay them the going rate, either as a lump sum in the form of an advance, or little by little as wages. Of course, once an Indian got into debt, the landowner, like any other creditor, did not like the debt to be defaulted, although naturally this did happen from time to time.

What the coastal *haciendas* or the mines did through *enganche*, thus ensuring that Sierra *minifundistas* remained in the new proletarian jobs, the Sierra *haciendas* did mostly by allowing *huacchilleros* and *colonos* free use of *hacienda* resources to the extent necessary for their standard of living to be higher than that of labourers in the labour market; though it is actually most misleading to talk of *haciendas* 'allowing' the use of *hacienda* resources, since typically the landowners had not been asked for permission. One always has to keep in mind the basic conflict on the legitimacy of *haciendas*, which manifested itself in the dubious legality of proper titles, in the periodic invasions, and in the reluctance of *colonos* and *huacchilleros* to reciprocate for their use of *hacienda* resources.

Here it is important to consider why some landowners came to think that it would be in their economic interest to change the labour system. The situation is rather complex because we have at least two main types of highland *haciendas*: sheep *haciendas* and agricultural *haciendas*, as I shall call them (with some simplification, since sometimes it is a question of two different main patterns of land use inside each *hacienda*). Their economics differ markedly, since there are considerable economies of scale in sheep-farming.

Resulting from this, we find different patterns of land tenure and use of labour: free use of *hacienda* resources in a more or less distant past; use of resources paid for with money (for instance, the *arrendatarios de pastos*) or in kind (*arrendatarios* who paid *hierbaje*: one sheep per year out of every ten, for example); use of resources paid for with labour services, called *faenas*; use of resources plus a small cash wage paid for with labour services (this was the most common system – shepherds working under this system were called *huacchilleros*, cultivators were generally called *colonos*). The alternatives would have been to turn *huacchilleros* into wage-paid shepherds and to turn *colonos* either into wage labourers or (more profitably to landowners) into sharecroppers or cash tenants. There would be two reasons for choosing the alternative system in the case of sheep-farming: first, the lack of incentive to work, given the lack of links between remuneration and performance; secondly, the economic superiority (in the sense of lower land and capital unit costs) of large-scale sheep-farming, absent in arable agriculture. There would be only one economic reason for choosing one of the alternatives in the case of agricultural *haciendas*: the lack of incentive to work, for the same stated reason. In the case of sheep *haciendas*, the displacement of *huaccha* sheep and the turning of *huacchilleros* into wage-paid shepherds would also allow internal fencing and would perhaps make it profitable (depending on fencing and wage costs) to dismiss shepherds.

As a background to the study of such alternative systems of labour use, one would need to have figures on the income accruing to *huacchilleros* and *colonos* from the use of *hacienda* resources, and to compare it to their wages in order to show that we are dealing more with peasants than with labourers. Figures on their total income (both from the use of *hacienda* resources and from such little wages as they got) must then be compared with the wages earned by pure labourers, to show that we are dealing with peasants who were doing better than labourers, no extra-economic coercion therefore being needed to keep them on the estates. Finally, and looking at it from the landowners' point of view, the cost of the prevailing labour system must be estimated as compared to the stated alternatives. The cost arose from the loss in income from the lands occupied by *huacchilleros* and *colonos*, but the system also provided benefits in that lower money wages were paid than in the purely wage-labour market, though it is also the case that these lower wages were accompanied by lower effort, for instance shorter working hours by the *colonos*.

'Peasant income' and 'wage income'

Let us first look at some figures on the ratio of 'peasant income' to 'wage income' for *huacchilleros* and *colonos*. These and the following figures are offered more to illustrate the reasoning I am following than to prove points which will remain in doubt until further work is done.

It is difficult to know how many *huaccha* sheep any *huacchillero* had. *Hacienda* records list shepherds and the *huaccha* sheep nominally belonging to each of them, but it is not certain that they were in fact owned by them. Sometimes (but how often and to what extent we do not know) *huacchilleros* managed to make *mishipa* livestock appear as *huaccha* livestock, by introducing livestock belonging to people outside as if it were their own, either charging a rent or not, in the case of relatives. Sometimes they are alleged to have operated a joint system of *huaccha* sheep ownership (perhaps inside families) while taking turns at becoming *huacchilleros*. Leaving this aside, one can estimate the number of *huaccha* sheep units per *hacienda huacchillero* (or worker) at never less than 100. In the 1920s, there had been a free allowance of up to 300 sheep in the Fernandini *haciendas*. As we have seen, in the Cerro de Pasco Corporation *haciendas* nearly 20 per cent of all sheep units belonged to *huacchil-*

leros and other workers in the mid-1950s, while the number of man-years per thousand sheep units was only a little above two, an average, broadly speaking, of one hundred *huaccha* sheep units per *huacchillero* (or other workers). This was the most efficient sheep-farming enterprise in Peru.

Accepting, then, this minimum figure of one hundred *huaccha* sheep per *huacchillero*, let us briefly examine the distribution of a shepherd's income between 'peasant income' and 'wage income'. I shall use the figures provided by the general manager of the Fernandini *haciendas* in 1947 (consumption of meat not included):[15]

> 100 sheep with 2 pounds of wool each,
>   at S/.1.50 per pound   S/. 300
> 50 sheep sold, at S/.20 each,
>   replaced by births   S/.1000
>   S/.1300

This would mean a daily wage of S/.3.60 per hundred sheep units, and while it might have been an exaggeration to call them 'small capitalists', as the manager did, they were undoubtedly peasants rather than wage labourers, since the wages they got from the *hacienda* were around one *sol* per day.

Looked at from the landowners' viewpoint, not all the returns the *huacchilleros* got from their *huaccha* sheep could be counted as a loss to the *hacienda*, since the return came not only from the use of *hacienda* pastures but also from the capital invested in *huaccha* sheep. The scales of wage increases, in inverse proportion to the number of *huaccha* sheep which were proposed and sometimes implemented by some landowners, give an estimate of the landowners' own view of the costs attributable to *huaccha* sheep. Thus, the manager of the Fernandini *haciendas* was ready in 1947 to pay S/.3.50 per day to those who gave up all their *huaccha* sheep, and S/.2.00 to those with up to one hundred. I plan to do more systematic work on this, but I think the figures tally in a general way with those from other *haciendas*. The implicit cost to the *hacienda* (it was not only land rent, as we shall see later) was thus estimated at S/.1.50 per hundred *huaccha* sheep a day, while the *huacchilleros* were estimated to be making S/.3.60 per hundred *huaccha* sheep a day. This figure of S/.3.60 included both returns on the capital they had invested in sheep (S/.2.10), and the unpaid rent (S/.1.50).

It should be noted again that S/.3.60 is probably a low estimate in the sense that the average *huacchillero* was able to keep considerably more than one hundred *huaccha* sheep, although, on the other hand, both the average of two pounds of wool production per sheep and the birth rate might be considered on the high side for *huaccha* sheep.

Let us now consider briefly one agricultural *hacienda*, the *Hacienda* Maco, near Tarma, of 2,750 hectares, of which 70 were devoted yearly to potato-growing (on both *colonos'* lands and demesne lands) with a seven-year rotation. Potato production then was carried out on a total acreage of 490 hectares, of which six-sevenths were in fallow, the rest of the *hacienda* being permanent pasture land. In 1946 the Indians had 65 per cent of the agricultural land and 30 per cent of the pasture land – agricultural land was said to be fifty times as valuable.[16] At some time in the past, *colonos* had been doing even better: 'Formerly the *colonos* sowed approximately six times as much as the *hacienda*, which had an acreage of 10 hectares.'[17] This source goes on: 'As the *hacienda* has increased its potato acreage to 30 hectares, the *colonos'* acreage has decreased from 60 to 40 hectares.' Thus we have a progressive reduction from 60 hectares in an unspecified past, to 45.5 in 1946, to 40 in 1959. This was a *hacienda* where one of the first unions was formed, and one of the first real strikes took place in the agitated period 1945 to 1947. The punishment inflicted on the *colonos* who led the strike was dismissal from the *hacienda*.

In *Hacienda* Maco, as in agricultural *haciendas* in general, once land-owners were able to impose their hold and claim their rights, the system used appears to have been a straight system of labour services (with no money wages paid) in exchange for the use of *hacienda* land. With time, small cash wages began to be paid, and the trend was towards increased use of wages. There were two reasons for this. First, there was pressure from the *colonos* themselves, who wanted to keep their plots but also to get higher wages. Secondly, the landowners attempted to wean the peasants away from the lands they occupied by offering them cash wages for the days worked on *hacienda* demesne lands; however, since from the landowners' point of view the peasants were paid well enough by the use of *hacienda* resources (they were probably doing better than the labourers without land, the obvious point of comparison), landowners were naturally reluctant to pay cash wages comparable to those of the outside labour market. The alternative was to increase *faenas* as much as possible. The figures for Maco are interesting because they come from a rationalizing *hacienda*. Nevertheless, they show the greater importance of 'peasant income' as compared to 'wage income'. It was considered in 1946 that the *colonos* had to work twelve work-days (*tareas*) a month to pay the rent for their plots (*chacras*); for example, the wages for the twelve work-days were considered to equal 20 per cent of the value of the production from their plots, this 20 per cent being considered a fair rent. That is, 'peasant income' was taken to be five times as large as 'wage income'.

Our first conclusion then is that 'peasant income' was higher than 'wage income' in the total income of both *huacchilleros* and *colonos*. A second important consideration is that their total income was probably higher than the wages drawn by landless labourers. Thus, in 1947, when *huacchilleros* in the Fernandini *haciendas* (assuming only 100 sheep each) were estimated to be making S/.4.60 per day, every day of the year (S/.1.00 as daily wage, and S/.3.60 from their sheep), casual labourers were earning at most S/.3.00 per day, which would buy some 15 kilogrammes of potatoes at farm prices. The Prefect's report on *Hacienda* Maco (1946) states that daily cash wages for *colonos* were about 50 per cent of those earned by *maquipureros* (day labourers); but cash wages were only 20 per cent of total income, as has been stated. Though further research is needed, there are grounds for assuming that *huacchilleros* and *colonos* did better than landless labourers. Perhaps the strongest evidence in favour of this conclusion are the threats of dismissal against those who seriously misbehaved. In 1949, *chacras* were taken away from the most 'subversive' *colonos* of *Hacienda* Maco, at the same time that the demands from several people from the neighbouring *comunidad* of Congas asking to become *colonos* were refused, as Maco already had too many people on its agricultural land and too many *huaccha* sheep on its pasture land.[18]

The particularly bellicose *colonos* of *Hacienda* Chinche also formed a union and went on strike in 1945. One of the union's initial demands was that the landlord be prevented from carrying out his policy of 'systematic evictions'. The *acta de conciliación* which was finally signed allowed the landlord to expel only the *colonos* who did not perform the stipulated labour services in payment for their potato-growing plots.[19] I might be wrong, but I think that proper serfs would not have been threatened with eviction but rather corporally punished, since expulsion would have been tantamount to setting them free to go to the cities and, anyway, would have been outside the feudal landlord's set of possible choices.

This same point was made by the owner of Maco himself. Writing to his lawer, Carlos Rizo Patrón, he quoted from a petition which the *maqueños* had addressed to the President of the Republic: 'When we ask for some benefits or complain about the abuses against us, we are thrown into the dungeon and we are threatened with expulsion.' There was indeed a dungeon in Maco, under the chapel. But then, Ing. Mario

Cabello had this contribution to make to the comparative study of serfdom: 'This typically medieval picture, of feudal castles and haughty seigneurs, so impressively described, has been damaged by including, let us say, a democratic automobile in a medieval scene. For the threat of expulsion is to the Inquisition-like, medieval procedures very much as a 1942 automobile is to the litters of those times.' He added that one single *colono* had left voluntarily in the last ten years, while the *hacienda* often received applications for entry which could not be granted because all the land was already occupied. The correspondence received by *Hacienda* Maco provides further evidence of this.[20]

There is no denying that there was physical violence, even in *haciendas* which produced records. The institutionalization of violence appears in the remark in 1949 by the manager of *Hacienda* Acopalca – later a top-ranking official in the current land reform – that an Indian who answered him back had duly got *su pateadura*.[21] Though I think that the really effective violence was meted out by the police and the army, and not so much by the *haciendas*' staff, one will have to explain in due course why violence had not yet become the monopoly of the state. One might even eventually discover that there was a pattern of violence to force *colonos* and *huacchilleros* to work on demesne lands instead of letting them enjoy and peacefully expand their own plots of land and pasture rights. Even then, the analogy with serfdom would be inappropriate, in that eviction would have been no punishment for a serf. Mario Vásquez overlooks this simple point when he plainly states: 'Apart from the fully entitled *peones* and *colonos*, there exist also the *"yanapacuc"*, *"yanapakoj"*, *"satjatas"*, *"puchurunas"*, *"chacrate"*, or *"pisante"*, who are individuals who are not members, like *peones*, of the *hacienda*, many living under the economic tutelage of their parents or brothers, and who in theory are not obliged to labour services but who nevertheless perform labour services from time to time, *out of fear of being evicted from the hacienda*.'[22]

Such threats of expulsion (drawn from Alberti, Kapsoli, and Vásquez, and from the papers of *Hacienda* Maco) all refer to agricultural *haciendas* or, as in Chinche, to mixed *haciendas*. In purely pastoral *haciendas* there can remain even less doubt as to the lack of restrictions from above to geographical mobility; and indeed some landowners, keener to push peasants off than to keep them on, soon learned to turn the attack on 'feudalism' into a defence of capitalism:

by the introduction of a modern sheep-farming practice it will not only become more difficult to steal sheep, but all the ills attendant upon [the present] penning and shepherding system can be removed. At present, it may be said that the farmer is at the mercy of the Indian shepherd ... Usually each flock of 500 is grazed by an Indian who also pastures on the farm 200–300 sheep of his own and needless to say his own sheep receive more attention than do those of the *patrón* ... The farmer ... may dip his own sheep, but the Indian will not submit to having his interfered with, so that where there are Indian sheep on a farm the complete eradication of scab will be impossible ... This difficulty may be overcome by the introduction of a paddock system ... This system will also put an end to the unsatisfactory relations between *patrón* and Indians, and facilitate the complete emancipation (or dispossession) of the latter ... Under the new system, the Indian will be compelled to keep his sheep on his own ground, leaving the *patrón* free to improve and develop his farm to the lasting benefit of the country and himself. He will then be able to pay his Indians a much higher rate of wages, thus lifting him from the state of semi-slavery in which he now finds himself ... By the establishment of a paddock system Peru will be converted into a stockbreeder's Utopia.[23]

One finds some evidence that living, and even working, on a *hacienda* has long been a desirable alternative for some people. The beginning of a *colono*–landlord relationship is described as follows in a book published in the 1920s: 'A family which is too poor, which has no land and even less a home to live in, demands entry into a *hacienda*.'[24] This is also the implication of the figures cited by Cornblit,[25] from a census at the end of the eighteenth century in the provinces where the *mita* was enforced. Nearly half the Indians were *indios forasteros*, and one-fourth 'lived sheltered' in the *haciendas*. The *indios forasteros* either were escaping from the *mita* or had already served in the mines and were free labourers. Perhaps there was a wide free labour market – cities preceded *haciendas*, in America – and one may assume that those who sheltered in the *haciendas* did so because they did not see any better economic alternative either in their communities, if they belonged to one, or in the wage-labour market.

There is, however, the question of why, if there was no restriction to mobility, there was the need to import slaves and coolies to work on the coastal *haciendas*, and why methods such as the *enganche* were needed to bring Indians down to the coast. One answer would be that Indians did economically better in the *haciendas* (and also, of course, as *minifundistas* in *comunidades*) than they could on the coast at the wages the coastal *haciendas* were prepared to pay. The high risks of malaria and other coastal diseases at the time should also be taken into account. The economic explanation, however, does not account for the apparent reluctance of the unattached Indians to move. Another factor might be that the framework of social relations in the Sierra was such that, even without restrictions on mobility imposed from above, the Indians (including *hacienda* Indians) would not leave because they had links of kinship and beliefs which gave meaning to their lives. Here one would have to consider the Sierra economy, from the Indians' point of view, not only as a source of employment and livelihood, but also as providing a godfather for one's children, a patron saint for one's community, and so on. The potential economic advantage to be gained by leaving could not be traded for the loss in non-economic relations. I myself remain unconvinced by this argument. One further argument is that Indians were such poor workers that it actually was cheaper to import coolies.

A recent book by Antonio Díaz Martínez provides a compilation of interviews with *colonos* in the mid-1960s. Here is a conversation with the wife of a *colono*:

He is at work, but his wife receives us kindly. Three children, with no shoes, play on the ground. The house is a single room, of twenty-five square metres, with mud walls and a roof of cane leaves. A small verandah at the front of the room is used as a kitchen and dining room. Food is being cooked in a stewpot resting on stones. In a corner of the small patio, there is a small pen with three pigs and five hens. She says they also have five goats, one cow, and one donkey, which are grazing. Both she and her husband speak only Quechua and have never been to school. Before, they had a *chacrita*, and they grew some wheat, and maize, but now they have been thrown out, onto the hillside, and she thinks that their fields will probably produce nothing, because of lack of water. She adds that many young peasants have left for the coast, in search of work, and that they themselves do not leave because they are not sure of finding a job.[26]

Indeed, with such an assortment of domestic animals and children and with no knowledge of Spanish, they were wise not to leave. The point is that this woman thought in terms of alternative employment possibilities. She was dissociating the economic aspects of her life from other social and political aspects, in the way that people living in a capitalist system are accustomed to do, though the labour system can hardly be described as capitalist. We do not know whether Peruvian peasants learnt to think in terms of alternative employment possibilities only in the 1960s. I would imagine they learnt much earlier than that.

Resistance to change in the labour system

The *Hacienda* Maco is the only agricultural Sierra *hacienda* for which we have, so far, good catalogued records in the new archive. No determined attempt was made there to change to a system of wage labour or (better still, from the landowner's point of view) to sharecropping or cash tenancy. But I think there was a clear perception of the disadvantages of the existing labour system. Thus, to quote from a letter from the owner to the manager:

Formerly they worked alternate weeks, one for the *hacienda* and one for themselves. According to the collective agreement of 8 October 1947, they now have the obligation to work fifteen days a month as a minimum, that is, four days a week from Monday to Thursday (and six hours a day). If we made them work on Fridays and Saturdays, apart from the fact that we should then pay them the Sunday wage which would add 17 per cent to labour costs (Sunday wage to be paid if six days have been worked), the following week they will not come to work because they will need time to attend to their own activities. Organization is thus broken and disorder begins. The workers start work when they wish or are able, and tasks are not finished on the expected date, as much because of the lack of people [to work on the *hacienda* demesne land] as because of the low productivity of those who work, since those who come lack willingness to work because they are working against their own particular interests while the rest are attending their own crops.[27]

One would normally expect small-scale cultivation rather than wage labour in unmechanized agriculture, since the labour of the peasant family has a lower valuation if put to work for the family than as wage labour for the *hacienda*. This is a relevant consideration when comparing wage labour to tenancy. When comparing labour-service tenancy to either wage labour or sharecropping (or cash tenancy), the relevant consideration is that, while in sharecropping or cash tenancy or wage labour performance is or can be linked to remuneration, labour-service tenancy does just the opposite. The suspicion may be entertained that a system whereby the higher one's remuneration (that is, the more *hacienda* resources at one's disposal), the less time available and the less need to work on *hacienda* demesne lands, is not a system conducive to profit maximization, and it will only be used, as in a system of serfdom, when there are institutional restrictions on mobility and therefore where the production forgone from the land occupied by the serfs does not represent a cost to the estate.

A system was proposed in Maco whereby money wages were increased considerably (up to three times) for the work-days worked over and above the compulsory work-days. In 1946, the Prefect's report had considered the alternative of substituting a sharecropping system, rejecting it on the spurious grounds that lack of motivation to work, because of a reduced level of needs, would actually result in decreased production. The allegation is not convincing since the *colonos* went on strike asking for a big increase in money wages, which presumably were not to be hoarded.

Thus, in the case of agricultural *haciendas* there is some slight evidence of a move towards a wage-labour system, and no evidence (as yet) has been uncovered of a move towards sharecropping or cash tenancy. We know that such changes did not generally occur in agricultural *haciendas*, except perhaps in a few isolated cases. However, the point is not to state whether the changes did actually occur, but rather to understand the motives landowners had for wanting such changes to take place, and to understand the reasons why these changes did not occur. Descending from these hypothetical levels to actual instances, some cases can be documented of moves towards a wage-labour system in sheep *haciendas*.

I have mentioned before the attempts made in this direction in both the Fernandini and the Cerro de Pasco Corporation *haciendas*. I shall mention here the earliest of such attempts which we so far have on record, though I would not be surprised if earlier ones are subsequently found. In 1945, the manager of *Hacienda* Laive of the Sociedad Ganadera del Centro, Ing. Rigoberto Calle, explained that the reason why wool production per *hacienda* sheep had decreased in one year from 4.48 to 4.18 pounds had to do with the excessive number of animals in the *hacienda* :

When I arrived in Laive, the first question I attempted to cope with was the *huaccha* problem; but when I tried to explain to the *huacchilleros* the new system of increased wages with a discount for *huaccha* sheep, there was a reaction on their part which ended with a sort of attempted strike. Seeing this, I had no other alternative but to relent, telling them that they were to work under the same conditions as before.[28]

Another difficulty he saw in reducing the *huaccha* allowance was that dissatisfied *huacchilleros* would go to the neighbouring *haciendas*, Antapongo and Tucle. To prevent this, he suggested that an agreement should operate among the three *haciendas* (and was operated, though not always with success) to blacklist *huacchilleros* who left one *hacienda* to go and work in one of the other two. In this way, 'when the neighbouring *comunidades* overflow with sheep, we shall be able to get good *huacchilleros* without difficulty and with a lower number of *huaccha* sheep than they now have'. One is inclined to think that the procedure was lacking in wisdom; to substitute *asedio externo* for *asedio interno* was really no solution at all. The three *haciendas* were partly invaded in 1946 despite the fact that no actual reduction of *huaccha* sheep had yet taken place. I am not implying that they were invaded because the Indians got wind of such plans. They were invaded because of the changed political situation in Lima, where a reformist government had taken power the previous year. But it was unwise to propose such methods while lacking the necessary force.

The economic reason why landowners were prepared to pay higher wages to *huacchilleros* who gave up their *huaccha* sheep – even perhaps to the point of increasing *huacchilleros'* total income – was that landowners could make more money out of the pasture land with their own improved sheep than the *huacchilleros* could with their native stock. If not, they might have considered a system of money rents or of rents in kind, adapting perhaps the institution of *hierbaje*. But wool production per *hacienda* sheep was more than twice as high, the birth-rate was also higher, and so was meat production. *Haciendas* had imported new breeds, and they were large enough to separate the different sheep by age and kind, allocating pastures to them according to technical needs, ensuring that all lambs were born in the appropriate season, and so on. *Huaccha* sheep, moreover, not only occupied valuable pasture land but might also interbreed with *hacienda* sheep and transmit diseases. Steps were taken to prevent such losses, like separating *huaccha* sheep from those of the owners, compulsory dipping, and compulsory castration of *huaccha* rams. Furthermore, stealing was made easier by the fact that *huacchilleros* had their own sheep which they could sell. It might be possible in due course to quantify the cost to the *haciendas* of such measures.

Of course, had it been absolutely impossible to turn *huacchilleros* and *colonos* into wage labourers (or sharecroppers or cash tenants) or to dislodge them, then the land they occupied would have had no real cost to the *hacienda*. In practice, they were rarely turned into wage labourers or sharecroppers or cash tenants, or dislodged, but there was no legal obstacle to doing so – rather the opposite, since wage labour (or even sharecropping or cash tenancy) was far more respectable than 'serf' labour. Naturally, the legal provisions are not the heart of the matter. What we need to know is whether landowners considered they suffered a loss in income because of the land occupied by *huacchilleros* and *colonos*.

Some, perhaps many, landowners certainly did believe this. After all, the system implied that the land occupied by *colonos* and *huacchilleros* was recognized by all parties as belonging in some sense to the landlord. This is why *colonos* and *huacchilleros* were paid either no money wages or money wages inferior to those of outside labourers, since they also received a remuneration from the *hacienda* in the form of use of *hacienda* land. It would be absurd to argue that landowners were not aware of this fact. If they saved in money wages it was because of the loss in income from land occupied by *colonos* and *huacchilleros* – they could make comparisons with the production from their own demesne lands and with the wages paid in the labour market. If relatively few landowners made attempts to turn *colonos* and *huacchilleros* into wage labourers or sharecroppers or cash tenants, or to dislodge them altogether, I would strongly argue that this was not because landowners had not noticed that they were prevented from gaining income from the occupied lands, but rather because they felt unable to make such profitable changes or were even afraid of the Indians' reaction. They had to behave in a paternalistic fashion because they were short of power. Eulogio Fernandini's manager wrote in 1929: 'there is no Indian around these parts who does not say that they can take any advantage they like of *taita* Eulogio, because *taita* Eulogio is afraid of them'.[29]

Although, as has been said, *colonos* and *huacchilleros* were getting higher 'peasant incomes' than 'wage incomes', their main grievance appears to have been over their low money wages. The strike in Maco in 1946 was to demand an increase in the *colonos*' daily wage from one *sol* to four *soles*. But, although there undoubtedly was a long-term trend towards cutting down on their use of *hacienda* resources, *colonos* and *huacchilleros* also resisted such attempts with some success. I believe that their way of putting up resistance was based in part on the use of cultural differences to further their economic interests. Thus, one finds the manager of the Hacienda Laive complaining: 'They argue that the traditional custom has been to admit *huaccha* sheep without charge and that this system should continue, even with the increased wages. And, as you know, the Indian, being a good Indian, is like a piece of granite when he is not willing to understand.'[30]

Such a breakdown in vertical communications proves rather damaging to the theories of W. F. Whyte, F. Lamond Tullis, and other writers of the same school on Peruvian *haciendas*, though it is only fair to remark that such evidence was not available to them.[31]

I have focused in this paper on the labour system internal to the *hacienda*, and on some factors which impinged upon the landowners' decisions on land tenure and use of labour. Their field of decision was rather limited. Throughout I have abstained from bringing in such external factors as the demographic situation and market opportunities, and I have scarcely referred to the general political situation (that is, the political complexion of Lima governments, which is not totally exogenous since it tends to respond to some extent to the threats from the Sierra). Such factors are clearly relevant in that they might have increased or decreased the attractiveness of a change in the labour system. But I think that, with this qualification, it is advisable to leave such external factors aside so that due emphasis may be given to internal factors.

The trend towards wage labour (or, in agricultural *haciendas*, towards sharecropping or cash tenancy) did not make much progress because of the unwillingness of the Indians to give up the *hacienda* resources they freely used, and because of the landowners' inability to overcome their resistance. In Peru, a head-on collision was narrowly averted in 1945–7 and again in the early 1960s. In 1945–7 it was probably due to the APRA leaders' refusal to support the unions that had started to flourish in Sierra *haciendas* and which Aprista agents helped to set up; in the 1960s, to the state's taking over when the landowners gave up; and in both periods, to straight violence from the police and the Army.

The novelty of my tentative conclusions, which turn prevailing interpretations upside down, or perhaps inside out, results from the fact that the *hacienda* records now available allow us to look at things from the point of view of the landowning class. Landowners were not even strong enough to have the communities' land brought into the market. More energy is usually devoted to denouncing the sporadic lack of compliance with the legislation which made communities's land inalienable than to analysing its significance as an exceptional measure in a capitalist society. One would expect, going through the debates on this topic, to find references to the fear of Indian rebellions.

Although the new archive of *hacienda* papers contains many letters from *comunidades*, petitions from *colonos* and *huacchilleros*, and so on, in order to understand better the situation from the Indians' point of view one would of course need to learn Quechua and do field work. One might speculate, for instance, on the reasons why *huacchilleros* refused to cut down the number of their own sheep even though landlords were perhaps ready to increase their remuneration to a level which would more than offset this loss. Perhaps Indian *huacchilleros* were affectually attached to their sheep. The word *huaccha* also means 'orphan' and 'poor'. Perhaps they realistically thought, and still think, that despite any short-term mutual benefits, in the long run a dispossessed *huacchillero*, and the sons and daughters of a dispossessed *huacchillero*, would not fare very well in the depressed Peruvian labour market. Landlords (and nowadays land reform authorities and SAIS managers)[32] would also point out with some justification that the pasture land allowance did not benefit the poor *huacchillero* as much as it did the relatively rich sheep-owners of the internally differentiated surrounding communities. There is also the question of complementarity with other activities at a lower ecological level. For instance, the oxen needed to plough the land of the *comunidad* of Chongos Alto had access to the pastures of, or could be bought cheaply from, *Hacienda* Antapongo, provided that the *comunero* who used the pasture land or bought the oxen agreed to work for the *hacienda* for a period of time. The records of *Hacienda* Antapongo contains many references to this practice. Lack of access to *hacienda* pasture would thus produce negative secondary effects on the communities' economy, apart from the loss of the direct returns (meat, wood, dung for fuel, and so on).

Finally, and from the Indians' viewpoint, one would also like to see whether it can be argued – as I think it can – that the remarkable resilience of Indian cultural life comes partly from the fact that their culture has been an instrument against landowners who wanted to rationalize labour systems, to settle boundary questions, to buy *comunidad* land, and so on. This would be in contrast to the view that 'explains' the lack of Indian 'integration' by lack of schools, as if it had been in the Indians' interest to 'integrate', to become 'castilianized'.[33]

There remains the question of accounting for other interpretations, interesting because of what they say about their authors. There is, for instance, what I like to call the village shopkeeper's view. Indians are assumed to have been 'feudally' abused and exploited since they were not paid good cash wages to spend in the shops, and on top of it they are assumed to have been burdened with debts in the *haciendas' cantinas* (or *tiendas de raya*, in Mexico). *Hacienda* unions in Peru in 1945–7 sometimes asked that *cantinas* be installed in the *haciendas* so that the peasants would have no need to travel to the villages and towns.

By looking at things from the landowners' viewpoint, attention has been drawn in this paper to the actual roles of the Indians as historical agents. A common urban ideology in Peru sees the Indians as absolutely crushed under the weight of landowners' domination, at the same time proclaiming the Indian as the bearer of national redemption along the lines popularized in Mexico. The inheritor of Inca greatness was expected to eventually step forth onto the stage of history, hopefully draped in a Peruvian flag. Such millenarian hopes on the part of the ideologues conveniently postponed the precise hour at which the Indian was expected to step forth, and simultaneously raised the Indian above the sordid materialistic considerations of the class struggle.[34] By blaming landowners for deliberately preventing Indian 'integration', this ideology also had the virtue of eschewing the painful question of whether Peru is or is not, and should or should not be, a nation. The identification of deplorable backwardness with Quechua-speaking comes out clearly in the censuses, where Indians who speak Quechua have been additionally classified as illiterate, which is rather like calling Puerto Ricans illiterate because they cannot read English.

The meaning of the current land reform is still ambiguous. In the pastoral *haciendas*, the government's intention is to continue the rationalization process which private landowners had no power to carry through. However, in the agricultural *haciendas* in the Sierra the situation is less clear-cut, since many of them are too small and too poor to pay for the bureaucrats needed for rationalization. Although attempts are being made to form larger units (as in Pampa de Anta and elsewhere), the government may eventually decide that this is too difficult and too dangerous. One cannot help reflecting that a land reform representing different class interests, carried out by personnel enjoying the Indian peasants' confidence, would not find it so difficult to push through measures such as substituting improved sheep for *huaccha* sheep, which ideally should be to everybody's advantage.

NOTES

1. The recovery and cataloguing of papers from expropriated *haciendas* is one of the undoubted benefits of the land reform in Peru. This work is being carried out by Centro de Documentación Agraria, Lima, with institutional support from the Tribunal Agrario, Seminario de Historia Rural Andina of San Marcos University, and other Peruvian institutions. Financial support comes mostly from the Joint Committee on Latin American Studies of the American Social Science Research Council and the American Council of Learned Societies. I am very indebted to all these institutions, and in particular to Dr Guillermo Figallo, President of the Tribunal Agrario. The idea of collecting ex-*hacienda* records was born at the Instituto de Estudios Peruanos. Members of the Centro de Documentación Agraria gave assistance in locating the *haciendas* on Map 11.
2. As pointed out by François Chevalier, 'Témoignages littéraires, et disparités de croissance: l'expansion de la grande propriété dans le Haut-Pérou au XXᵉ siècle', *Annales Économies, Sociétés, Civilisations* XXI, 4 (1966), pp. 315–31.
3. Centro de Documentación Agraria (hereafter CDA), Cerro de Pasco Corp., Ganadera Division, Interdepartmental correspondence, R. H. Wright to J. W. Henley, 5 July 1952.
4. Comité Interamericano de Desarrollo Agrícola (CIDA), *Tenencia de la tierra y desarrollo socio-económico del sector agrícola – Ecuador* (Washington, 1965).
5. Rigoberto Calle, *Producción de ovinos* (Universidad Agraria La Molina, Lima, 1968), pp. 34–5.
6. CDA, 'Informe sobre salarios de la Sociedad Agrícola y Ganadera Algolán S.A. presentado por el Ing. C. F. Peña a la Asociación de Criadores de Lanares del Perú', 6 April 1962.
7. CIDA, *Tenencia de la tierra*, p. 151.
8. Jan Bazant 'Peones, arrendatorios y medieros en México: la hacienda de Bocas

hasta 1867', in Enrique Florescano (ed.), *Haciendas, latifundios y plantaciones en América Latina* (Mexico, 1975 – see note 1 to chapter 18 below).

9. A. Bauer, 'Chilean rural labor in the nineteenth century', *The American Historical Review* LXXVI, 4 (1971), pp. 1059–82.

10. G. Alberti, 'The breakdown of provincial urban power structure and the rise of peasant movements', *Sociologia Ruralis* XII (1972), pp. 315–33.

11. F. Lamond Tullis, *Lord and peasant in Peru* (Cambridge, Mass., 1970), p. 123.

12. P. Macera, 'Feudalismo colonial americano', *Acta Historica* (Szeged, Hungary, 1971), pp. 3–43.

13. François Chevalier, *La formation des grands domaines au Méxique: terre et société aux XVIᵉ–XVIIᵉ siècles* (Paris, 1952).

14. C. Gibson, *The Aztecs under Spanish rule* (Stanford, Calif., 1964), pp. 252–5.

15. CDA, Algolán, 'Correspondencia Administrador General – Eulogio Fernandini', 20 March 1947.

16. CDA, Sociedad Ganadera del Centro, 'Correspondencia e informes: Administración General, 1938–49'. Informe del Prefecto de Junin al Ministerio de Justicia y Trabajo, 20 February 1946.

17. CDA, Hacienda Maco, 'Correspondencia Director-Gerente a la Administración 1946–67', 27 September 1959.

18. CDA, Hacienda Maco, 'Correspondencia Administrador al Director-Gerente 1944–49', 26 August 1949.

19. W. Kapsoli, 'Los movimientos campesinos en Cerro de Pasco, 1880–1963' (unpublished dissertation, Universidad Nacional Mayor de San Marcos, Lima, 1971), pp. 38, 41.

20. CDA, Hacienda Maco, Documentos varios, décadas 1940–50–60, letter of 8 January 1946, accompanying 'El memorial de los maqueños'. Ing. Mario Cabello had written a thesis in 1927 on *Hacienda* Udima, in Lambayeque (there is a copy in Universidad Nacional Agraria, Lima), where he proposed expanding demesne lands at the expense of *colonos*, or *pachaqueros* as they are called in Udima. Its part-owner, the manager Ricardo de la Piedra, complained after the land reform of 1969: 'Who would possibly have bought this *hacienda* from us, so full of people and with so little *hacienda* livestock?' (I am grateful to Douglas Horton for this quotation and for information on Udima and on Ing. Cabello's thesis.)

21. CDA Sociedad Ganadera del Centro, Hacienda Acopalca, 'Correspondencia Administrador-Gerente, 1947–64'. 'Patear' means 'to kick'. There was a court case, and the incident was reported in the press, prompting an enquiry from the general manager in Lima.

22. Mario Vásquez, *Hacienda, peonaje y servidumbre en los Andes peruanos*, Monografías Andinas no. 1 (Lima, 1961). Vásquez was much involved in the famous Vicos project, which no student of Peruvian *haciendas* can ignore. The absence of any reference to the unions of 1945–7 in Vásquez's work is due, to put it kindly, to easily remedied ignorance, since the best records of such events have been kept in the Ministerio de Trabajo y Comunidades (as it is now called). It was unscientific to select for study, on grounds of political expediency and not of historical relevance, only one of the possible types of change in the *hacienda* system. At least two alternative situations should have been considered: no change (or accurate study of the situation previous to the Cornell takeover), and change through unions.

23. 'Huacauta sheep ranch', *West Coast Leader*, 16 March 1922, pp. 6–7 (I am grateful to Geoff Bertram for this reference). A version of this article appeared in Spanish

164 *Juan Martínez Alier*

in *La vida agrícola*, 3–4, (Lima, April 1926). *Hacienda* Huacauta, near Chuqui-
bambilla, in Puno, belonged to a Bedoya & Revie company. (I am grateful to Colin
Harding for this information.)

24. A. Serruto, *Monografía del distrito de Pichacani*, cited in G. Espinoza and C. Mal-
pica, *El problema de la tierra* (Lima, 1970), p. 311.
25. O. Cornblit, 'Society and mass rebellion in eighteenth-century Peru and Bolivia',
St Antony's Papers 22 (Oxford, 1970), p. 25.
26. A. Díaz Martínez, *Ayacucho, hambre y esperanza* (Ayacucho, 1969), pp. 228–9.
27. CDA, Hacienda Maco, 'Correspondencia Director-Gerente a la Administración
1946–67', 27 September 1959.
28. CDA, Sociedad Ganadera del Centro, Hacienda Laive, 'Correspondencia Administrador-Gerente', 8 March 1945
29. CDA, Algolán, 'Correspondencia Administrador General – Eulogio Fernandini,
1928–30', 12 November 1929.
30. CDA, Sociedad Ganadera del Centro, Hacienda Laive, 'Correspondencia Administrador-Gerente,' 3 February 1945.
31. The views of this school are contained in J. Matos Mar, J. Cotler, G. Alberti, J.
Oscar Alers, F. Fuenzalida, and L. K. Williams, *Dominación y cambios en el Perú
rural* (Lima, 1969).
32. Sociedad Agrícola de Interés Social, a large cooperative-style enterprise created
by the land reform in many areas of the Peruvian Andes.
33. It should be pointed out, however, that the demand for schools often appears in the
lists of *colonos'* grievances. It is also true that while the recent change in official
terminology (from *indio* to *campesino*) does not necessarily mean any improvement for
the people in question, and while being called and behaving as an Indian was an
advantage in land invasions and in defending a peasant mode of life, on the other
hand landlords themselves sometimes found it useful to call them Indians since some
forms of struggle were then, in a way, implicitly denied to them. Thus, the manager
of *Hacienda* Laive commented on the unions in 1947, 'this is an entirely grotesque
thing, because the Indians do not even know how to pronounce the well-known
terms such as *comandos, sectores, departamento de capacitación, enlaces*' (CDA,
Sociedad Ganadera del Centro, Hacienda Laive, 'Correspondencia Administrador-
Gerente, 1940–51', 1 July 1947).
34. I have used in this paragraph notes made by Geoff Bertram on an early draft of
this paper.

CHAPTER 7

The formation of the coffee estate in nineteenth-century Costa Rica

CIRO F. S. CARDOSO

The background

In any discussion of the development of the coffee economy in nine-teenth-century Latin America, it is quite common to contrast the case of Brazil – with its moving frontier and the transition from slave labour to massive European immigration – with the situation in Spanish America, where land for coffee expansion was generally less abundant, and where a numerically significant immigration process did not occur. Nevertheless, even restricting ourselves to the Spanish American case, it is possible to identify significant variations in land tenure, labour patterns, and so on. Limiting our field still further to Central America alone, striking differences can be easily perceived between the history of coffee cultivation in Costa Rica – with its early origins, and with the absence of any large-scale process of land concentration, and its effects on the organization of the labour market – and the Guatemalan and Salvadorean experiences – in which coffee expansion only really got under way after a fierce struggle that set the new coffee bourgeoisie against the dominant social and economic groups inherited from colonial times, and which exhibited features of land and labour control al-together different from those found in Costa Rica. This essay deals mainly with the peculiarities of the Costa Rican case.

Geographical and ecological factors

The expansion of coffee production in nineteenth-century Costa Rica was restricted almost entirely to one small area, the intermontane valley known as the Meseta Central or Valle Central.[1] Extending for 70 kilo-metres from west to east, and with an average width of 20 kilometres, the Meseta Central covers a total area of 2,700 square kilometres, at an average altitude of about 1,000 metres. Situated between the volcanic Cordillera Central to the north and the precordillera of the Talamanca range to the south, the Meseta Central is divided into two sections by the foothills of the Talamanca; the western part, the San José valley, which covers three-quarters of the total area, is drained by the Río

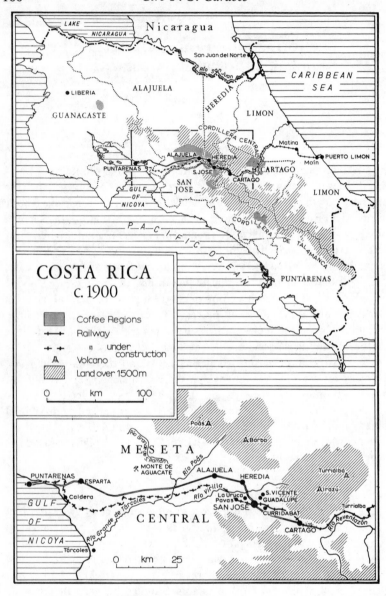

COSTA RICA
c.1900

Coffee Regions
Railway
under construction
Volcano
Land over 1500m

0   km   100

Map 12

Grande de San Ramón and the Río Virilla, which unite to flow into the Gulf of Nicoya; to the east is the Agua Caliente basin, which empties into the Caribbean. Coffee cultivation originated in the San José valley – where ideal conditions of soil, temperature, rainfall, and altitude for the production of high-quality mountain coffee are found together – and by the end of the last century had expanded as far as the Turrialba and Reventazón valleys, transition zones between the Meseta Central and the Atlantic lowlands where the more humid conditions impose serious problems for harvesting, processing, and transporting the coffee crop, which almost invariably must be done in the rain.

Three main soil types are found in this zone: in the northern part, volcanic soils derived from the outpourings of the Poás, Barba, Irazú, and Turrialba volcanoes; alluvial soils along the river valleys; and the heavily eroded laterite soils of the steeply northward-sloping foothills of sandstones and conglomerates to the south of the Meseta Central. Coffee was first cultivated on the rich volcanic soils of the north, and later along the equally fertile riverine alluvial strips; and, from time to time, even the laterites, which are generally unsuitable for coffee, being poor and rather infertile, have been utilized for coffee planting.

Climatically the Meseta Central shows marked variations. In the eastern part, around Cartago, where the Atlantic influence predominates, there is only one dry month, April; more towards the centre, around San José, the dry season extends from December to April; and in the western portions, around Alajuela, where the Pacific influence is predominant, the wet and dry seasons are more clearly defined. The natural vegetation of the Meseta Central consists of sub-tropical rain forests, whilst in the Turrialba and Reventazón valleys, where there is practically no dry season, tropical rain forest tends to predominate.

The historical background

The relative strength of the colonial institutions is one of the most important elements in explaining both the subsequent patterns of social and economic change and the pace of structural transformations experienced by each Latin American country in the decades following political independence. In this respect it is possible in the Central American case to contrast the coffee societies of Guatemala and El Salvador with that of Costa Rica. By the time of Independence from Spain, strongly entrenched interest groups had developed in both Guatemala and El Salvador. The liberal reforms demanded by the expansion of commercial coffee cultivation were only put into effect following the decline of the world market for dyestuffs during the

1860s and 1870s, and after a bitter struggle between rival groups in
Guatemala in the 1870s and in El Salvador between 1881 and 1886.
In the meantime Costa Rica, which had been the poorest and least
populous colony on the isthmus, because of the relatively weaker
influence of its colonial background moved straight into the coffee era
a little more than a decade after Independence in 1821, without any
significant internal upheavals. Nevertheless, three factors suggest that
it would be wrong to underestimate the importance of the country's
colonial past. First, as Samuel Z. Stone has shown, the majority of the
large coffee planters and *beneficiadores* or processors[2] were descended
from the important families of the Conquest and the colonial era.
Secondly, the capital which financed the first – and most difficult –
stages of coffee production seems to have been accumulated, admittedly
in modest amounts, by these families, at least in part from other economic
activities carried on during the colonial period: cacao and tobacco
production, the extraction of *palo brasil* (a dyewood), and so on. Finally,
the isolation and economic backwardness of colonial Costa Rica, though
it ensured that coffee would not have any serious competitors, also meant
that a series of major obstacles had to be overcome before large-scale
production could be undertaken. These problems, arising from an inadequate demographic and economic infrastructure, included labour
shortages, the absence of technical knowledge and experience, lack of
international commercial contacts, insufficient capital, lack of a transport network, and so on.[3]

   During the last decades of the colonial regime and the first years after
Independence – say, from 1780 to 1832 – it was obvious that an export
crop was needed on which to base a viable economy. Coffee, introduced
sometime between 1791 and 1808,[4] was at first regarded as only one
possibility among many, and it only became firmly established in the
1830s.

   At the time of its Independence in 1821 Costa Rica was still a primitive
country, virtually cut off from the commercial and technical life of the
times, and extremely backward even in comparison with the other parts
of Central America. Such a situation emerges from the account by John
Hale, who visited the country in 1825:

The low level of commercial exchange which this province has had with other
parts of the world can be seen from the following: the arms and pans of the
scales are of roughly carved wood; the weights consist of stones picked up in
the streets and tested in some shop or other. People look on foreign products as
miraculous articles; not even the useful wheelbarrow, without which our canals
and other great enterprises could not have been undertaken, has been im-

ported; they have no notion of the utensils made by the cooper; they do not use the spindle, and the machinery for planting cotton and cleaning coffee would be a novelty to them. Nobody in the entire province has yet seen a boiler. In short, there are hundreds of modern inventions and articles of daily use which are completely unknown there ... The few artisans to be found in Costa Rica have to struggle with the crudest tools, and it is surprising that they can carry out their work at all with such unsuitable instruments ... They have neither spades nor hoes of iron and in no part of the province have they ever seen a garden rake. Agriculture and horticulture are more than a century behind Europe and the United States. Almost all tools are made of wood, as iron is very scarce and consequently extremely dear.[5]

Less than ten years later, with the beginnings of coffee expansion, the situation started to change rapidly, and in due course Costa Rica came to be

the first nation (in Central America) to possess a railway linking the capital with the two oceans, the first to light its cities by electricity, the first in educational matters after having been at the same low level as its neighbours, the first to have a decent road network, and although it was not the first to have a newspaper (in fact it was one of the last on the Continent), it came in time to have the largest number of newspapers per inhabitant in Central America.[6]

There can be little doubt that the coffee-growing elite exercised a decisive influence over the political life of the country, a power which has been the subject of a number of detailed and copiously documented studies by Stone.[7] Apart from foreign loans, the coffee export tax was the one great source of possible financing for important projects. The road to the port of Puntarenas, the National Theatre, and on several occasions payment of the foreign public debt or the interest outstanding on it were all financed from the duties raised on coffee exports. In short, the growth of the coffee industry in the nineteenth century ushered in a new era of dependent capitalism in Costa Rica.[8]

Coffee production in Costa Rica experienced three main periods of growth in three major areas of the country. Until the late 1840s it was confined almost exclusively to the Meseta Central; then from the mid nineteenth century onwards it spread out towards the heavily forested western edges of the Meseta Central, in the province of Alajuela. Finally, in the 1890s, and closely related to the railway developments of the time, the coffee zone expanded into the Reventazón and Turrialba valleys, to the east of the Meseta Central.[9]

In this paper I shall confine my discussion to the growth of coffee production in the nineteenth century in the Meseta Central, the oldest and by far the most important coffee zone in Costa Rica; according to the available statistics, in 1890 it contained approximately 20,000 of the 26,000 *manzanas* (a *manzana* is equal to 0.69 hectares) then planted to *cafetales* (coffee groves) in Costa Rica.[10]

Factors influencing coffee production in the nineteenth century

The land

Three main types of land system formed the basis for coffee expansion: (1) the appropriation of waste or public lands; (2) the dissolution of communal forms of property; and (3) private land transactions.

Appropriation of waste or public lands. At the time of Independence, Costa Rica had a population of less than 60,000. The Indian population, which had never been very numerous, was by now reduced to a very small group. The Meseta Central was the only area of the country which could boast a relatively high density of population. But, with the exception of a few old-established areas of settlement such as El Mojón, San Vicente, and Guadalupe, *terrenos baldíos* (waste or public lands), which were the property of the state, were plentiful even here on the Meseta.

From its early years, the expansion of coffee production tended to reinforce and extend the fragmented smallholding structure inherited from the colonial period.[11] To encourage coffee cultivation (and, to begin with, other crops as well) first at the local and then at the national level, the government simplified the procedures for acquiring *terrenos baldíos* free of charge and for buying public lands (*tierras públicas*) at low prices; it did away with the tithe (*el diezmo*) on coffee and certain other crops, and later abolished it altogether; and in 1832 there was even a provision for government subsidies for coffee growers 'with proper guarantees and securities'.[12]

During the first four decades of independent life, several laws were published covering the methods of appropriation of waste lands. A decree issued in 1824 tried to encourage their purchase. A law passed in 1854 decreed that no more than 10 *caballerías* of land (a *caballería* equals 45 hectares or 65 *manzanas*) could be sold to any one individual. Regarding prices, we must differentiate between those charged for *tierras de legua* and those charged for *tierras de caballería*. *Tierras de legua* were all those lands located within a radius of three leagues around all population centres of more than 3,000 inhabitants. This radius was increased in 1846 to five leagues around San José, and four leagues around the other main urban areas of Cartago, Heredia, and Alajuela. Because of their proximity to the major towns, prices for these lands were much higher than for the *tierras de caballería*, which lay beyond this circle. Before 1839, areas of *terreno baldío* wanted by buyers were required to be measured by land surveyors and then sold in public auction. In that year the price of public lands was fixed at 3 *pesos* per *manzana* for *tierras de legua*, and 50 *pesos* per *caballería* for *tierras de caballería*. The price demanded for the *tierras de legua* was raised to 4 *pesos* per *manzana* in 1851; that for the *tierras de caballería* was lowered to 25 *pesos* per *caballería* in 1842, raised again to 50 *pesos* in 1850, and then to 100 *pesos* in 1858; in any case these lands were still cheap. Regulations covering the level of interest rates, forms and terms of payment, and the method of sale – by public auction or otherwise – changed frequently. As a matter of fact, late payments were frequently tolerated, and eventually even the failure to pay was not punished.[13]

The conditions of sale of the *terrenos baldíos* have been described by Ephraim George Squier, who visited the country in the mid-1850s and commented:

In regard to the 'valdios', the immigrant will find it next to impossible to obtain information concerning their position from the government; he must inquire of the inhabitants of the country, more especially in the districts bordering on the wilds where he wishes to purchase. When he has obtained the requisite information, he must have the lands measured and land-marks established. His application to the government must enclose a full description of the section he has chosen. This application is called 'denouncing the land', the price of which is then fixed. The applicant takes possession, paying a certain amount thereon and a yearly interest of four per cent on the remainder. There have been cases – some remaining to the present day in *statu quo* – where the purchaser (a native of influence) has been allowed to take possession, retain, and cultivate, without paying anything more than the yearly interest of four per cent.'[14]

Squier's observations suggest how the role of political influence tended to some extent to counteract the trend towards 'rural egalitarianism' and indeed to favour the concentration of property through the disposal and occupation of the *terrenos baldíos*. His statement is confirmed by a famous scandal which erupted between two well-known Costa Rican figures of the last century, Braulio Carrillo and Juan Rafael Mora.[15]

The great ease with which waste lands could be obtained often led to their acquisition for purely speculative purposes, without due regard to the legal requirement to bring these lands into cultivation. However, as the cultivation of lands remote from the towns involved too great an expense, only the *tierras de legua* were in great demand before about 1858.[16]

TABLE 30   *Disposal of* terrenos baldíos *in Costa Rica, 1584–1890*

Period	Land sold (hectares)	Land granted (hectares)
1584–1821	77,487	12,127
1822–39	56,439	13,896
1840–50	28,450	3,853
1851–60	53,769	34,413
1861–70	35,783	6,389
1871–80	52,329	34,727
1881–90	54,535	86,225
Total	358,792	191,630

Source: *Gaceta Oficial*, 'Memoria de Hacienda y Comercio, del Secretario de Estado Ricardo Montealegre' (San José, 16 July 1896). The slight difference between Tables 30 and 31 in the total figures for lands sold is contained in Montealegre's figures.

TABLE 31   *Disposal of* terrenos baldíos *in Costa Rica, by province, 1584–1890*

Province	Land sold (hectares)	Land granted (hectares)
San José	80,771	39,163
Cartago	46,378	52,500
Heredia	18,402	7,767
Alajuela	121,893	49,767
Guanacaste	48,264	4,476
Puntarenas	20,148	11,416
Limón	22,934	26,541
Total	358,790	191,630

Source: As for Table 30.

Tables 30 and 31, which are based on a report prepared by Ricardo Montealegre, a Costa Rican Treasury Minister of the 1890s, present figures for the sales and grants of *terrenos baldíos* from 1584 to 1890. The colonial period is taken as a whole in Table 30. Unfortunately, the provincial figures given by Montealegre (see Table 31) do not give the breakdown between the colonial and the national periods, but Table 30 would seem to suggest that the structure of landed property really only took on its present form in the period after Independence.[17]

Dissolution of communal forms of landed property

In the early years of the nineteenth century, several laws and decrees were passed which were intended to break up one of the main forms of communal landholding, the *propios de los pueblos* (municipal common lands), but they only seem to have been enforced between 1841 and 1851, when they were used for the extension of coffee-growing.[18] In sharp contrast to other parts of Latin America where the process has been exhaustively studied, the expropriation of other forms of common land, such as the communal lands of the various Indian groups, was not a very important or characteristic feature of Costa Rica during the last century.[19]

Land transactions

In the decade following Independence, land prices were low and land was of little value. In 1825, according to John Hale, 'land, lodgings and life' were 'dirt cheap' in Cartago and San José.[20] With the development of coffee exports from 1832 onwards, land prices began to rise rapidly, particularly for those lands suitable for coffee, and more especially for coffee lands in the vicinity of San José. Black volcanic soils were at first preferred for the establishment of coffee plantations, with the dark red soils of the alluvial valleys as second choice. These lands in fact occupy a relatively small total area in the Meseta Central, and this helps in part to explain the wide disparities between the price of coffee land and the price of all other types of land in Costa Rica; contiguous blocks of land were frequently valued at quite different prices per unit of area. Moreover the actual price of any piece of land was influenced by a number of other factors, such as the presence or absence of markets and roads, the provision of buildings, *beneficio*, or processing machinery, existence of established coffee groves, and so on; the coffee bushes themselves were sometimes reckoned separately. Carl Scherzer pointed out that the sale price was generally determined by the net yield; a property whose income was 1,000 *pesos* a year was worth 4,000 *pesos*, which meant that, in a country where it was possible to obtain annual interest rates of up to 25 per cent, capital was expected to double in value inside four years. The increase in the price of coffee lands from the 1830s onwards, as well as the rise in the number of transactions and the growth of land speculation in general, have been well documented. It is equally certain that apart from occasional downward fluctuations which were linked to temporary falls in coffee prices, as happened in 1849, the remaining years of the nineteenth century were characterized by relentlessly rising land prices and a steady increase in both the number and the value of land transactions. Wagner and Scherzer were probably not exaggerating when they claimed that the value of land on the Meseta Central had increased twenty or even thirty times between the 1820s and the 1850s.[21] Figure 2 shows land transactions for the period from 1782 to 1850 as recorded by

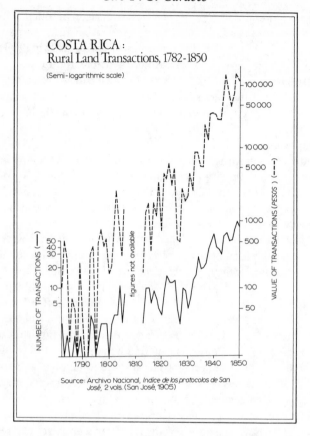

Fig. 2

the *Protocolos* (Registers) for San José: the effects of coffee expansion on land prices can be clearly seen.

However, it is in fact very difficult to measure accurately the changes in the price of land per unit of area in the coffee zone. Both Stone and the present author have attempted to do this, using data from the *Protocolos* for San José and the other cities of the Meseta Central. Whilst these records contain details of land transactions, it is frequently impossible to calculate the unit price of land, since the area being sold is seldom specified. Moreover, as we have seen, land prices varied a great deal even within the same region and the same locality, according to a number of factors which are not always stated in the registers of transactions. In these circumstances any average prices would be very misleading, as they would have to be based on a very small proportion of the cases registered. Nevertheless the broad outlines are clear enough: the volume of land transactions increased markedly, at the same time as the price of coffee land rose sharply. In 1840 the price of a *manzana* of land in the vicinity of San José seldom exceeded 100 *pesos*, or on the odd occasion 150 *pesos*; by 1849–50 land was changing hands at 200 or 300 *pesos* a *manzana*, and on odd occasions even reaching 500 *pesos*. In 1840 8 *manzanas* of good land in La Uruca, in the coffee zone, were exchanged for 130 *manzanas* in Limón, on the Atlantic coast; and, in 1850 land planted with sugar cane in Alajuela, quite close to San José, was sold for 20 *pesos* a *manzana*. Numerous advertisements in the local press announcing the sale of estates in the San José area serve to confirm the very high price of coffee lands during the 1850s, 1860s, and 1870s. The rapid development of coffee and the relatively small supply of land suitable for coffee cultivation, in the area around San José, account for the contrast between the price of coffee land in Costa Rica and that in Guatemala around the middle of the last century. In 1858 a *manzana* of coffee land could cost an average of 150 to 200 *pesos* on the outskirts of the Costa Rican capital, whilst around Escuintla, in the heart of the Guatemalan Pacific piedmont coffee zone, a *manzana* of land equally suitable for coffee growing could be had for 40 or 50 *pesos*, and a little further from that city for 8 or 10 *pesos*.[22]

The degree of land concentration is a matter of some dispute. At least from 1840 onwards there is evidence that some coffee-growers were trying to buy up the small lots or parcels bordering on their own lands. People who wished to increase their holdings were favoured by the legal disposition by which the seller had to give notice of the proposed sale to each of his neighbours in turn, beginning with the one who had the most land bordering on the seller's own, as neighbours had first refusal on buying the land. On the basis of an analysis of the land transactions registered in the *Protocolos*, F. Moretzsohn de Andrade reached the conclusion that a very small group of coffee-growers were buying up peasants' lands on a large scale. Nevertheless, as both Stone and Hall have shown, although a good proportion of these transactions took place within the small group of the richest coffee-growers, each of whom sought to build up a single estate in a relatively large block of land by buying or exchanging small plots, few of them met with much success, and the biggest coffee plantations often remained discontinuous, fragmented into a number of small or medium-sized lots sometimes several kilometres apart. Using abund-ant documentation from a wide variety of sources, including the *Protocolos*, the Register of Property (begun in 1867), and the coffee census of

1935, Hall has shown beyond any reasonable doubt that the number of relatively large *haciendas* or estates was always very small, while the small farms were numbered in thousands. It is known that the financing of the small producers by the large growers, which might involve loss of land in the event of failure to repay the loan, was an important factor leading to land concentration, particularly when small farmers were ruined in periods of crisis or bad harvests. However, very few quantitative data exist on this subject. Carlos Meléndez Chaverri has suggested that, owing to the extremely high land prices in the Meseta Central coffee zone in the 1850s, many peasants in that region preferred to sell their plots and, with the small amount of capital thus raised, apply for *terrenos baldíos* in the new areas of agricultural colonization then being opened up, such as in the province of Alajuela. Again no quantitative data are available to confirm this assertion, though it would seem quite plausible. However, if such causes of land concentration were as important as some authors claim, they would undoubtedly be recorded in the cadastral surveys: but this is not the case. What the available data do show for the Meseta Central – and this goes for the whole period between 1840 and 1935 – is briefly the following: Firstly, there was an absolute predominance of small farms, in terms both of numbers and of the total area of land occupied, and there was a marked tendency for even these to be divided up, through inheritance, into tiny plots of land. Secondly, some fairly large and important properties were consolidated, though these were very few in number and were often composed of several separate pieces of land; their existence is confirmed by an examination of the existing statistics on rural property and on coffee production and exports. Thus, for example, of the 3,000 tons of coffee harvested in 1846, 500 tons or a sixth of the total were produced on the *fincas* (farms) belonging to the Montealegre family and to Juan Rafael Mora. Thirdly, the Costa Rican 'great estate' of the Meseta Central – that is, farms or blocks of farms amounting to more than 50 *manzanas* (34.50 hectares) – would scarcely be regarded as even a medium-sized property in the other coffee-producing countries of Latin America. The most important coffee-producing *hacienda* known to have existed on the Meseta Central, belonging to the Rohrmoser family and formed between 1892 and 1938 to the west of San José, only covered about 875 *manzanas* (about 604 hectares), which is in no way comparable, for example, to the great coffee *fazendas* of Brazil. Finally, the most important properties were situated predominantly in those areas of the Meseta Central which had been least developed before the expansion of coffee production, to the west and southeast of San José, around Pavas, La Uruca, Curridabat, and other localities.[23]

The causes of these local peculiarities of land tenure in the major coffee zone in Costa Rica – *sui generis* in overall Latin American terms – were mainly the chronic and extremely serious shortage of labour, which will be analysed later; the excessively high price of land; and the limited financial resources of the principal coffee-growers. On the problem of capital shortage, Stone has demonstrated how even the wealthiest families had occasionally to pool their resources to make important land purchases. Land transactions were normally made on the basis of ten- or even twenty-year mortgages; and payment was sometimes made in coffee. In 1866, for example, a coffee estate of 40 *manzanas*, valued at 17,000 *pesos*, was to be sold according to the following conditions: 2,500 *pesos* to be paid immediately, and the remaining 14,500 *pesos* in annual instalments, at 6 per cent interest 'during the total number of years required, in order that the buyer can pay off the principal with the crop alone'. The members of the great families preferred to marry within their own circle, and group cohesion was further strengthened by the fact that their members were perpetually in one another's debt.[24]

In 1839, when John Lloyd Stephens arrived in Costa Rica, the Meseta Central was covered with 'rich coffee plantations', and in his book he noted that 'seven years before the whole plain was an open waste'. Undoubtedly this remark exaggerated the situation prior to coffee expansion, but it is nonetheless true that that period of Costa Rican history, between 1832 and the great depression following the crisis of 1929, was strongly marked by a 'moving frontier' of internal colonization associated with the vigorous expansion of coffee cultivation. With respect to the Meseta Central, the physical expansion of the coffee estates had more or less come to an end by the late 1880s, with the occupation of all the waste lands (the *terrenos baldíos*). Subsequent expansion took place, on farms already established, by the steady substitution of coffee production for alternative types of agricultural activity, with increasingly serious consequences, as we shall see presently. It is difficult to estimate the cultivated area of the coffee zone with any degree of accuracy before the agricultural censuses of the 1880s: perhaps 500 *manzanas* (345 hectares) planted with coffee in 1838, according to Hall's calculations, which probably underestimate the true figure; more than 4,200 hectares of *cafetales* in 1857, according to Solano; 20,000 *manzanas* (13,800 hectares) around 1890; and about 40,000 *manzanas* (27,600 hectares) in 1935.[25]

Labour

There is general agreement that labour was very scarce in Costa Rica throughout the last century. Robert Glasgow Dunlop, who visited the country in 1844, observed that 'the labourers are now hardly sufficient for working all the estates which are planted', so that wages – which were 2 *reales* (about a shilling) per day – should, according to him, tend to increase.

The available data on wages paid on the Meseta Central to *peones* (landless rural workers employed throughout the year on the estates) or *jornaleros* (day labourers, who generally also possessed their own plots of land for subsistence food-crop cultivation) seem to confirm this upward trend (see Table 32).

Around 1853 Scherzer put the number of *peones* working in coffee cultivation at only 'about 2,000 labourers'; according to him, one *peón* was able to care for about 5,000 coffee bushes, or to clear two acres of forest land in eight days. In 1857 French commercial sources remarked that the shortage of labour was the most important obstacle to an even greater expansion of coffee cultivation; but the problem was much more serious than usual at that particular time, as a cholera epidemic which had raged since 1856 had wiped out 7 per cent of the Costa Rican population. Anthony Trollope, who visited Costa Rica in 1859, noted that 'labour is extremely scarce and very dear ... in the neighbourhood of San José a man's labour is worth a dollar a day and even at that price it is not always to be had'. Writing in 1886, Joaquín Bernardo Calvo again confirmed the shortage of labour; using data from the 1883 census, he showed that there were then only 18,278 *jornaleros* and 7,479 estate-owners out of a total population of 182,073.[26]

TABLE 32   *Monthly wage rates for* peones *and* jornaleros *in the Meseta Central, Costa Rica, 1844 to 1869–70*

	Wage per month
1844	7 *pesos* 4 *reales*
1849	11 *pesos* 2 *reales*
1853	8 to 9 *pesos*
1856	15 *pesos* to 18 *pesos* 6 *reales*
1869–70	25 to 30 *pesos*

Sources: R. G. Dunlop, *Travels in Central America* (London, 1847), p. 50; L. F. Molina, *A brief sketch of the Republic of Costa Rica* (London, 1849: Public Record Office, London, Foreign Office 21, no. 2); Archivo Nacional, San José, *Hacienda*, no. 7297 (1853); 'Comunicaciones de Gobernadores', documento no clasificado, 13 August 1856, 'Planilla de los gastos habidos en las Pavas'; *Hacienda*, no. 7312, 1869–70: 'Libro de abonos'.

Demographic factors

During the middle and later years of the nineteenth century, Costa Rica experienced what was, for that country, an unprecedented demographic increase, with an average annual growth rate, according to the most reliable censuses we have for the period – those of 1844, 1864, and 1883 – of 2.5 per cent. According to Stone this seems to have been stimulated by the expansion of the coffee industry. Nevertheless, starting as it did from the very low baseline of the 1820s, in absolute terms Costa Rica still had a relatively small population at the beginning of this century, even given the comparatively small size of the country. The great majority however were concentrated in the westernmost parts of the Meseta Central – that is, in the main coffee zone. In 1884 the three central provinces of San José, Heredia, and Alajuela supported 54,022 inhabitants out of a national total of 79,982; in 1864, 82,168 out of 120,499; and in 1883, 127,185 out of 182,073 (see Table 33).

There was no large-scale immigration. Although ever since the early years of the Republican period the government had devoted considerable efforts to fostering the agricultural colonization of the country, they did not do so with a view to solving the problem of labour shortages in the coffee zone. Instead, they were concerned with the colonization of the lowland tropical rain-forest areas with peasant proprietors from Europe, whilst at the same time carefully avoiding Negro and Chinese immigration. Numerous colonization schemes followed one after another during the nineteenth century, but all were failures, for a number of reasons.

TABLE 33   *Costa Rica: population growth, 1801–1904*

	Population
1801	52,591
1809	c. 50,000–60,000
1823	57,146
1844	79,982
1864	120,499
1883	182,073
1892	243,200
1900	307,499
1904	331,840

Sources: Alberto Sáenz Maroto, *Historia agrícola de Costa Rica* (San José, 1970), pp. 771–3. Philippe Périer, 'Algunas observaciones sobre una civilización del café', *Revista de Filosofía de la Universidad de Costa Rica* (San José, 1961), pp. 29–42. Joaquín Bernardo Calvo, *Apuntamientos geográficos*, p. 31.

In the second half of the century the numbers of informal European immigrants – Germans, English, French, Spanish, and later Belgians and Italians – slowly but steadily increased, attracted in particular from the 1840s onwards by the prospects of making a fortune in the expanding coffee industry. These immigrants, however, were not peasant proprietors or agricultural wage labourers; most of them already possessed some capital, and nearly all went in for coffee-processing and marketing. Several of them entered the small circle of the coffee elite, either by alliance or by association, and became its most wealthy and influential members; good examples of this sort of men were J. Millett and L. de Vars Tournon (French), B. Espinach (Spanish), J. Dent (English), von Schrötter (German), and so on. A few of them even took out Costa Rican citizenship, but there were also cases of course of foreign merchants – particularly amongst the Germans, the English, the Americans, and the French – who around the middle of the century made a fortune in San José and immediately emigrated to other countries. Despite the earlier prohibitions, West Indian and Chinese immigrants arrived towards the end of the century with the express purpose of working on the Atlantic Railway and later in the banana plantations; but for many years they were forbidden to move from the Atlantic zone to the Meseta Central.[27]

The property structure

The pattern of land tenure was undoubtedly the most important factor affecting the structure and organization of coffee production in nineteenth-century Costa Rica. The large number of small proprietors and the peasant smallholding structure, which were inherited from the colonial period and which expanded in the first years of Independence, have already been noted. Dunlop stated that 'every family has a small coffee or sugar plantation', and in the same vein T. F. Meagher observed:

For me the most satisfactory of the country's agricultural statistics is the capital fact that two-thirds of its population is composed of landowners. Almost every man has his farm, his mules, his chickens, his pigs and his patch of coffee or sugar-cane. The same individuals we had seen with bare feet and torn clothing coming down the Aguacate winding through jungle beyond the Barranca, carrying coffee to the port, were owners as well as carters.[28]

The fact that he had a small plot of land did not deter the peasant from working on the side as a carter or as a *peón*: 'After their work on their own plots is finished, the owners of the small farms themselves go and take jobs on the big estates or work with their carts and mules in hauling fruit and other articles.'[29]

But it is nevertheless a fact that the widespread distribution of the small property structure limited the supply of labour. The availability of *terrenos baldíos* in the zones around the Meseta Central, coupled with the increasing pressure on land resources through demographic growth on the Meseta Central itself, acted as a powerful stimulus to the constant expansion of agricultural colonization in frontier zones increasingly removed from the main coffee zone. The labour structure and organization of the few large coffee *haciendas* had to be adapted to this fact, and these estates had to make do with only a relatively small number of permanently resident landless labourers (*peones*), taking on as temporary harvest hands (*jornaleros*) large numbers of men, women, and children, not only from the small surrounding peasant plots but also from the local urban centres: during the harvest and processing period San José became almost a ghost town, abandoned by its inhabitants. The coffee-owners tried to ensure the greatest speed in the gathering of the beans by paying piece-rates; but, even so, in some years the harvest – which was normally gathered in November and December – had still not been completed by April because of labour shortages.[30]

Capital

Because of the shortage of coin in circulation during the colonial period – and even to some extent during the first half of the last century – cacao took its place as a medium of currency. In 1825, John Hale noted the insignificance of commercial life in Costa Rica and the acute shortage of minted money; the predominant media of exchange were gold ingots and silver bars, although the first steps towards the minting of coins had already been taken.[31] The atmosphere was very different when Stephens arrived in 1839: 'San José is, I believe, the only city that has grown up or even improved since the independence of Central America ... the city ... exhibited a development of resources and an appearance of business unusual in this lethargic country.'[32] But the truth is that with the beginnings of coffee expansion Costa Rica was already ceasing to be a 'lethargic country' by the 1830s. The problem of financing Costa Rican coffee production during the last century has not yet been studied in depth using the available primary sources. Besides, since most of the historians who have studied the country's economic and financial history (such as Cleto González Víquez, Tomás Soley Güell, and Eduardo Alvarado) rarely cite their sources, it is difficult to make categorical or well-founded statements on this subject. It would seem, however, that the first stages of coffee expansion, perhaps up to the commencement of regular exports to England in 1843, were financed with relatively small amounts of capital, accumulated within the country itself during the colonial period and the first years of Independence from cacao and tobacco cultivation, the export of *palo brasil*, and the extraction of precious metals from the mines of Monte del Aguacate, which had been discovered in 1815 and exploited particularly after 1820 with the help of a small group of European immigrants. There has recently been considerable debate over the role of these mines in the Costa Rican development process. Carlos Araya Pochet has argued that the capital generated from the mining operations was important for the initial financing of the coffee industry, but José Luis Vega Carballo has shown from more reliable documents that the levels of gold and silver production were always low and that there is good reason to believe that the profits derived from mining operations went mainly to England. Any influence that the mining sector might have had on the growth of coffee cultivation was at best indirect; for example the Spaniard Buenaventura Espinach, who had made a fortune in mining, was responsible for the introduction of the wet-processing technique into Costa Rica in 1838, an innovation which was decisive in ensuring the success of Costa Rican coffee in European markets.[33]

During the first phase of coffee expansion, processing techniques were generally very primitive and required little in the way of capital investment. But with the staggering increase in the price of land, technical progress, the growing cost of labour, and the sustained increase in the demand for the product, increasingly large injections of capital became necessary, and these could only come from external financing. Since high-quality coffee was well known and highly esteemed by British consumers, commercial houses in London and Liverpool began to advance credits against future harvests, channelling them through the Costa Rican commercial houses and companies engaged in the coffee trade which were established in increasing numbers by the large coffee-growers from the 1840s onwards. These commercial houses in turn granted credits to the small producers who, because of the mechanism of the rural credit system, were quickly drawn into economic dependence on the large coffee-producers and on the merchants. In some cases this may even have resulted in the ultimate loss of their lands, since for various reasons they were unable to meet their debts.[34] Naturally the export trade was itself a source of foreign exchange, and as well as encouraging increased consumption – particularly the consumption of luxury goods by the great coffee families – the profits from this trade were partially reinvested in the productive sector, for the purchase of machinery, agricultural implements, and so on. Both the system of coffee credit and the imports of consumer goods and capital equipment constituted links in the chain of dependence binding Costa Rica's capitalist development to Great Britain.

The profits from coffee exports could be very considerable. The total cost of production of a *quintal* (46 kilogrammes) of coffee in 1846, including the upkeep of the farm, the cleaning and pruning of bushes, and the harvesting and processing of the crop, amounted to 2.5 *pesos*. The price of coffee in San José in February–April 1846 was 5 *pesos* a *quintal*; transport to Puntarenas cost more or less 1 *peso* a quintal. Dunlop estimated that the profit made by the merchant who bought the coffee in San José and sent it to the port would then be 20 per cent. Scherzer quoted a concrete case of the actual yield of a coffee *finca* in 1852: 25 per cent of the capital invested, with all expenses subtracted. He calculated that it was possible to count on 'completely safe investments of 12 to 15 per cent'. According to French sources a *quintal* of coffee, including transport to Puntarenas, cost the planter from 6 *pesos* to 6 *pesos* 2 *reales* in 1858, while in Europe it was worth 18 to 20 *pesos*.[35]

On 2 July 1857, the government of Juan Rafael Mora made a contract with the merchant Crisanto Medina to create the Banco Nacional Costarricense, which was to receive deposits, give credit, and issue notes. Loans were to be made by contract, and interest could not be greater than 1 per cent per month. The creation of this bank, which was formally inaugurated on 1 January 1858, seemed to present a dangerous threat to the coffee-growers and merchants who practised usury at the expense of the small proprietors and used it as a form of social control. They also feared that Mora, who was himself the biggest coffee exporter in the country, would, with his friends, come to dominate the entire economic and financial life of Costa Rica. They thus brought about a *coup d'état* which toppled the President, who was eventually shot. A French document of that year explained that the bank had ceased operations not only because of opposition from the usurers but also because of 'losses caused by the collapse of a Liverpool firm connected with Central America'.[36] During the following decade credit-giving establishments multiplied in number; the most important was the Banco Anglo-Costarricense, established in 1863. Limited companies also grew up in the fields of interest-bearing loans, coffee financing, and the purchase of landed property. However, it is important to point out that in nineteenth-century Costa Rica these banks never functioned as dispensers of short- and medium-term rural credit, which continued to be advanced through the established mechanisms of advance payment for the crop by British importers to the large growers, processors, and merchants, who in turn extended credit at high rates of interest to the smallholders.[37]

Cultivation and processing techniques
In the nineteenth century, whilst coffee cultivation methods remained rather primitive, *beneficio* (processing) techniques became increasingly mechanized and technically specialized. Nevertheless, if Hale's description of cultivation methods in 1825 (quoted above) is taken as the starting point, even field cultivation techniques were improved to a considerable extent, since the introduction of coffee brought ploughs, sowers, weeders, hand-carts, spades, rakes, hoes, scythes, hatchets, machetes, and so on, all of which were made of metal, whereas previously wooden implements had predominated.[38] But the best proof of the extensive nature of the agricultural techniques applied to coffee cultivation was the progressive decline in the average yield per hectare, already evident in the oldest and most important coffee zone, the Meseta Central, in 1881, and later confirmed by the quantitative data available for the twentieth century. On the best lands of the Meseta, the yield was 20 *fanegas* of coffee beans a *manzana* in 1909 (a *fanega* equals 399.84 litres), and only 9.5 *fanegas* a *manzana* in 1956. Total production for the whole country has tended to increase steadily in absolute terms, even though it has sometimes suffered violent cyclical fluctuations and depressions, and it is interesting to note that the volume of the 1898 crop, which was admittedly exceptional, was not equalled for another thirty years. Production increases did not, however, keep pace with the constant increase in the cultivated area, nor were they related to the length of time that coffee groves or *cafetales* had been established. Falling yields were due to the steady impoverishment of the soil, through the persistent failure of the *finqueros* to replace the exhausted mineral and organic substances.[39]

The preparation of forest land for coffee cultivation followed the traditional slash-and-burn methods found throughout many parts of Latin America and other tropical regions. Trees were haphazardly felled by axe, and the branches and undergrowth hacked to pieces with machetes. After being left to dry in the sun for several weeks, the desiccated debris was cleared off by burning: the resulting ashes frequently constituted the only fertilizer available for the young coffee trees which were subsequently planted in the clearings. But it should not be forgotten that several centuries of human occupation and settlement on the Meseta Central had already resulted in the clearing of much of the natural forest vegetation cover. Coffee plantations were here developed not only on the forested *terrenos baldíos* but also on already-established *fincas* (farms), supplanting sugar-cane, the production of subsistence foodstuffs, and cattle-raising. Since in Costa Rica – unlike Brazil, where coffee was regarded as essentially a migratory, frontier crop – the coffee groves were established as permanent plantation enterprises, this limited use of fertilizers was a very serious matter. Only the wealthiest growers had sufficient financial resources and technical expertise to import *guano* from Peru or to manufacture fertilizer from bones. Another serious problem, particularly on the steeply sloping foothills of the southern Meseta Central, was soil erosion; in the second half of the nineteenth century the custom was introduced of planting shade trees to protect the coffee bushes from winds and excessive rainfall and to protect the soil against erosion.[40]

Dunlop has provided us with the best contemporary account of coffee cultivation and processing:

A coffee plantation in Costa Rica produces a crop the third year after it is planted, and is in perfection the fifth year. The coffee trees are planted in rows, with a space of about three yards between each and one between each plant, resembling in appearance hedges of the laurel bay. The weeds are cut down and the earth slightly turned with a hoe three or four times in the year; and the plant is not allowed to increase above the height of six feet for the facility of gathering the fruit. The coffee tree here begins to flower in the months of March and April, and the berry ripens in the plain of San José in the months of November and December, strongly resembling a wild cherry in form and appearance, being covered with a similar sweet pulp.

As soon as the crimson colour assumed by the ripe fruit indicates the time for cropping, numbers of men, women and children are sent to gather the berry, which is piled in large heaps to soften the pulp for forty-eight hours, and then placed in tanks through which a stream of water passes, where it is continually stirred to free it from the outer pulp; after which it is spread out upon a platform, with which every coffee estate is furnished, to dry in the sun; but there still exists an inner husk which, when perfectly dry, is, in the smaller estates, removed by treading the berry under the feet of oxen; and, in the larger, by water mills, which bruise the berry slightly to break the husk, and afterwards separate it by fanners.[41]

At the time of Dunlop's visit to Costa Rica in 1844 only a few of the most important *fincas* had mills, or any other machinery, driven by water power from the Río Virilla. In 1851 an article published in the *Gaceta Oficial* observed that Costa Rican coffee 'is processed unevenly and without much care'. By 1857, when Solano spent some months in the country, the use of *beneficio* machinery was beginning to spread.[42] A year later

Meagher witnessed the co-existence of the old and new methods of processing the crop, as well as providing us with a valuable insight into the peasant mentality:

Pedro was outside his hut, crushing a handful of coffee in a mortar the size of a roadmender's mallet, perhaps bigger ... In the wealthiest plantations, this primitive implement has gone the same way as the venerable local plough, and has been replaced by safer and more reliable machinery. It is imported from England, and the name of Barnes and Co. engraved on bronze plates is well known in the valleys of Cartago and San José, as it is associated with the making of Costa Rica's principal product; but Pedro feels unshakeable reverence towards old things, and his poverty leads him to reject such innovations and gives him a feel for the dignity of work and limits him to the capability of his muscles.[43]

An indication of the progressive mechanization of the *beneficio* process can be found in the applications for privileges, patents, and exclusive rights to manufacture and sell coffee-processing machinery, made either by the inventors, both local and foreign, or by their representatives, and also in the advertisements for machinery which appeared in the local press (see Table 34).

Obviously the increasing technical complexity and costliness of the various processing techniques contributed to the concentration of this stage of production in a few large estates, which increasingly came to buy the unprocessed coffee beans from the small producers. Around 1888 there were only about 256 *beneficios* in Costa Rica, whilst four years earlier Calvo had calculated that there were 7,490 coffee *fincas* in the country. Some of the large producers such as Dent, Montealegre, Tournon, and von Schrötter each owned several *beneficios*, which meant of course an even greater concentration of the processing sector in a limited number of hands.[44]

Coffee marketing and trade

Transport

Despite the small size of the country, its rugged broken topography and the fact that the major coffee zone is located inland in the intermontane valley have for a long time created serious problems for the transport of the coffee crop from the production areas to the ports of export. By opening up hitherto inaccessible lands and by reducing freight costs, the road to the Pacific port of Puntarenas and, later, the Atlantic Railway were very important in stimulating the initial expansion of the coffee plantations westwards towards the province of Alajuela, from the mid nineteenth century onwards, and later eastwards via the railway into the valleys of the Reventazón and Turrialba, between 1890 and 1935.

TABLE 34   *Costa Rica; introduction of new coffee-processing machinery in the nineteenth century*

	Designer/Patentee	Machine
1841/2	Benito Dengo	Machine for grinding and cleaning the outer shells of coffee beans
1847	Meacock of Jamaica	Machine for processing coffee (manufactured in Birmingham)
1850	Luís Tonkin	Machine for cracking the coffee beans
1851	Thomas and James Russel	Steam dryer (introduced by James Young)
1862	John Hedges Ledgerwood & Canfield	Machine for processing coffee
1863	E. H. Bennett (New York)	Machine for threshing coffee beans
1866	Luciano Tartière	Machine for steam-drying coffee
1867	E. Bradway	Stove for drying coffee
1867	Bruno Carranza	Machine for processing coffee
1868	Daniel Lombard	Machine for cracking and shelling coffee beans.
1871	Arturo Morrell (agent for Alberto Angell)	Machine for shelling, cleaning, and polishing coffee beans
1871	Manuel Dengo	Machine for grinding and drying coffee beans
1872	Cruz Blanco	Machine for processing coffee
1878	Marcus Mason	Improved version of Ledgerwood's machine
1879	M. A. Velázquez, B. Burgi, & M. V. Dengo	Machine for threshing and polishing coffee beans

Sources: Archivo Nacional, *Congreso*, nos. 7770 (24 December 1841–11 January 1842); 5268 (18–21 January 1850); 5811 (14–28 July 1862); 5817 (26 May – 30 July 1862); 5753 (14 July – 4 August 1862); 9825 and 9827 (4 June 1866); 6890 (16 April – 6 June 1866); 6625 (June 1867); 7033 (2 January – 15 June 1868); 9259 (20 May 1868); 7127 (20 December 1871); 6861 (13 February – 4 April 1872); 8435 (22 September 1879). *Gaceta Oficial*, 1 March 1851; 12 December 1863; 24 December 1867; 22 November 1872; 25 April 1874; 12 September 1874; 30 March 1878. Hall, 'Some aspects of the spread of coffee cultivation', pp. 42–3.

A road capable of taking ox-drawn carts was needed to carry the coffee from the Meseta Central to Puntarenas. The Sociedad Económica Itineraria, created in 1843 and composed almost entirely of the large coffee producers, took on the responsibility of having it built, between 1844 and

1846. In 1845, and again in 1867, a tax was levied on coffee exports to finance the construction and maintenance of the road from San José to Puntarenas (or, as was then the intention, the road joining the Atlantic and the Pacific). From January to April, thousands of carts laden with coffee would travel between the coffee zone and Puntarenas. Travellers were particularly fond of this picturesque sight, which they frequently described. The carters (*carreteros*) were accompanied by their wives and daughters, whose job it was to prepare their meals. Each cart could carry 6 or 7 *quintales* (600 to 700 pounds) of coffee, and costs ranged from 15 to 20 *pesos* a ton around 1857.[45]

The ships carrying the coffee to Europe and the Atlantic coast of the United States generally took the Cape Horn route, which lengthened the voyage considerably. The building of the Panama Railway linking the Atlantic and Pacific Oceans opened up another possibility; Juan Rafael Mora, during his period in office, signed a contract with the Pacific Mail Steamship Company, to ensure that their ships called at Puntarenas from 1856 onwards. The coffee transported in this way to Panama was taken by rail to the Atlantic coast and then shipped to Europe and the United States; but because of the high customs tariffs at Panama the Cape Horn route tended to be preferred.[46]

Nevertheless, in order to secure a cheaper and quicker link with the markets of Europe and the eastern seaboard of the United States, it was felt necessary to open a route to the Atlantic and to build a new port on the Caribbean coast. From the 1880s onwards this newly established outlet, Puerto Limón, began to attract an increasingly large proportion of the country's coffee export trade, a trend which was reinforced by the opening in 1890 of the Atlantic Railway, an enterprise whose tortuous origins were intimately linked with the beginnings of the banana industry in Costa Rica. Even the largest ships could tie up at the quay, and coffee could be loaded direct from the trains. As a result of the competition between the two ports, freight charges fell considerably. Thus, for example, in 1870 the English Royal Mail Company charged £5 15s a ton from Puntarenas to Southampton, but by 1886 the tonnage rates had fallen to £4 between Puntarenas and the European ports, and to £2 between Puerto Limón and the same ports. The Pacific Railway was also under construction at this time but was not completed until 1910.[47]

Organization of the coffee trade

Coffee dominated Costa Rica's export trade from the 1840s onwards, as can be seen in Table 35, even though the last two figures clearly reflect the serious coffee depression of 1897 to 1907.

TABLE 35 *Costa Rica: coffee exports as a percentage of total exports, 1885–1900*[a]

1885	75.43
1887	83.88
1890	94.38
1892	88.04
1895	83.27
1898	74.38
1900	60.11

[a] Calculated on contemporary exchange rates.
Source: Rodrigo Facio Brenes, *Estudio sobre economía costarricense* (San José, 1942), p. 32.

The main buyers of Costa Rican coffee in the nineteenth century were Great Britain, France, the Hanseatic cities of Germany, the United States, Chile, and Peru. But no other country had anywhere near the same importance as Great Britain in Costa Rica's import and export trade; commercial and financial links were established at an early date and lasted much longer than those with most other Latin American countries, beginning to weaken significantly only with the First World War. The coffee trade with Chile was important from 1832 until the start of regular direct exports to England in 1843, whereupon it steadily decreased until it disappeared altogether; however, the coffee was only processed in Chile and re-exported to Europe.[48]

Coffee purchases were paid for when the contract was signed, even though the product was only delivered some months later. Payment was often made half in imported merchandise and half in money. Costa Rican export houses such as Fernández y Montealegre, Mora y Aguilar, Fernández y Salazar, and Cañas y Montealegre, linked to British consignment houses (or German houses operating from England), were formed from 1844 onwards; many of them were only short-lived. Imports of English cotton cloth, competing with the small textile factories of Cartago, brought about the collapse of the domestic industry around the middle of the century.[49]

Cyclical fluctuations
Five major coffee crises can be identified during the last century:

(1) The general economic situation provoked by the events of 1847 and 1848 in Europe, which brought on Costa Rica's first serious coffee crisis, though it did not have long-lasting effects. When the price of coffee fell on the world market, many coffee plantations went bank-

rupt, the price of land dropped for a brief period, and credit restrictions were imposed in 1849.[50]

(2) The crisis of 1857–8, caused by the cholera epidemic of 1856 brought back by the troops who had been fighting Walker in Nicaragua: thousands of people died, and the coffee harvest was seriously affected, both through lack of harvest hands and through a shortage of carters to haul the coffee to the ports.

(3) The crisis of 1874–5, which reflected the great European financial crisis of 1873 and caused some credit restrictions.

(4) The crisis of 1884–5, which was the consequence of a bad harvest and a drop in the price of coffee.

(5) The 1897 crisis, which was by far the most serious of the century, and was connected with world-wide over-production followed by a period of low prices and depression. This lasted until roughly 1907. At the same time the crisis in the *peso*, the Costa Rican unit of currency – not only because of the problems in the coffee market but also because of the silver crisis (since it was a currency based on the silver standard) – gave rise to the creation of a new national currency, the

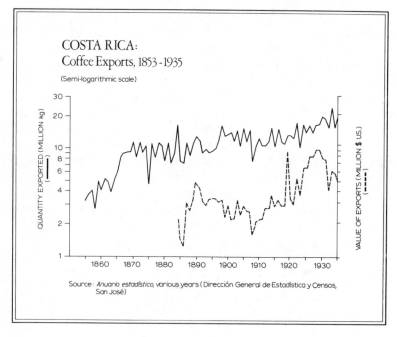

COSTA RICA:
Coffee Exports, 1853-1935

(Semi-logarithmic scale)

Source: *Anuario estadístico*, various years (Dirección General de Estadística y Censos, San José)

Fig. 3

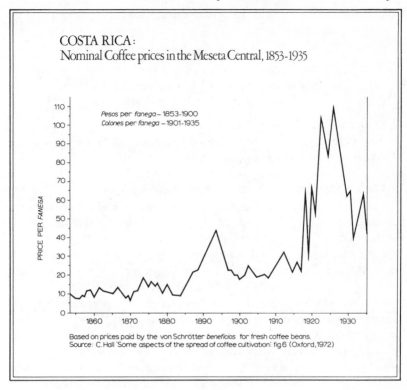

COSTA RICA:
Nominal Coffee prices in the Meseta Central, 1853-1935

Pesos per *fanega* – 1853-1900
Colones per *fanega* – 1901-1935

PRICE PER *FANEGA*

Based on prices paid by the von Schrötter *beneficios* for fresh coffee beans.
Source: C. Hall 'Some aspects of the spread of coffee cultivation' fig.6 (Oxford, 1972)

Fig. 4

colón, and the adoption of the gold standard.[51] Figures 3 and 4 show some of these crises, and the general cyclical fluctuations and trends of coffee exports and prices during the period under review.

From the time when stable links were first established with the European markets in the 1840s until the end of the century, coffee maintained its complete domination over the entire Costa Rican export trade. Dependence on a single product meant that the national economy suffered heavily from the effects of these recurrent coffee crises. But with the sole exception of the 1897 crisis these were not followed by long periods of depression, and coffee prices maintained a long-run upward curve until the 1890s, when world-wide over-production (largely attributable to Brazil) caused a drastic fall in prices. This long-term upward curve encouraged the growth of coffee production in Costa Rica, achieved, as we have seen, by the constant expansion of the area planted to coffee. The high quality of Costa Rican coffee meant that its prices did not fall as much as those of other producer countries, even when there was a crisis on the world coffee market.

Basic characteristics of the Costa Rican coffee estate during the nineteenth century

I shall now sum up by presenting a synthesis of the various different factors outlined above, in an attempt to delineate more clearly the specific features of the Costa Rican coffee *hacienda*.

Factors of production and relations of production

We have seen that several factors, the most decisive of which was the chronic scarcity of labour during the whole of the period under study, meant that the degree of control over the land exercised by the Costa Rican coffee bourgeoisie remained very slight; the small farm continued to be the dominant feature of the rural landscape, and even today the size of the largest coffee *haciendas* scarcely exceeds 500 hectares. Nevertheless this small number of larger properties (even when divided into several separate blocks) and the surrounding small farms, which also produced coffee, functioned and interacted in much the same patterns of domination and dependence as those which characterized the *latifundia–minifundia* complex. As the expression 'large property' refers to a highly relative and extremely variable phenomenon depending on countries and even regions, I would argue that it is permissible to use the term in the case of Costa Rica: the largest coffee *haciendas* in the period under study represented the greatest concentration of land compatible with the specific circumstances of this and the other factors of production in the country.

There is no doubt, however, that it was not control over the land which enabled the coffee bourgeoisie to achieve a high degree of economic, social, and political dominance. Rather it lay in their ability to manipulate and combine the three basic monopolies which were fundamental to the coffee trade: the control of rural credit and the processing and marketing of the crop. These monopolies were secured and maintained by an early and close association with British capital. In many cases, in fact, the *beneficiadores* or processors took little interest in extending their coffee plantations, and indeed some of them even came to concentrate entirely on the preparation and marketing of the beans they purchased, without cultivating coffee plantations themselves. Large coffee processors such as von Schrötter, the Knohr brothers, Tournon,

and Dent acquired *beneficios* long before they had any coffee plantations; in any case a large *beneficio* or processing mill bought from its
fifty or sixty clients much more coffee than was produced on the estate
where it was itself located.

These monopolies acted interdependently. The money received from
the import houses in London and Liverpool by the coffee growers, who
were also merchants, was the advance payment for the future harvest.
This meant that the Costa Rican entrepreneurs won out if the price of
coffee fell between the sale of the crop and its delivery several months
later, but lost if the price went up. The coffee bourgeoisie, which controlled exports and consequently the inflow of foreign exchange, also
paid in advance part of the value of the coffee crop that the small farmers
who used their *beneficios* promised to sell them after the harvest. This –
and the frequent requirement of written contracts – enabled them to
lay down certain quality levels for the coffee beans from the small *fincas*
and allowed them to exercise a high degree of pressure and social control
over the small farmers, which was necessary to guarantee them the
additional labour needed on a large scale for the harvesting and processing of their own coffee. It also permitted the large growers to transfer
part of the losses they might suffer to the peasants: since they advanced
to the owners of small parcels only a part of the payment for the beans
that they would deliver at harvest time, leaving the final reckoning until
after the harvest and export of the product, it was always possible for
them to claim that they had made a loss and to pay less than they had
promised. As they were unable to compete with the highly mechanized
operations of the large *beneficios*, since coffee produced using primitive
manual techniques was unacceptable internationally, and because they
needed the credit represented particularly by the advances on the
sale of their crop to the *beneficios*, the smallholders were dependent
on the small elite group of large growers. If they had a bad harvest they
could find themselves in the situation of being unable to deliver a
sufficient quantity of coffee to the *beneficio* to cover the money already
received and meet the very high interest charges. They then ran the risk
of losing their holdings, or at the very least of becoming even more
dependent on the credit and purchasing mechanisms manipulated by
the *beneficio*.

To summarize, the particular demographic, historical, and ecological
conditions of the country permitted the survival and even the expansion
of the smallholding property structure, at the same time as the control
of rural credit and the processing and marketing of coffee underwrote the
economic, social, and political supremacy of the small ruling group.

The absence of a significant colonial past, the limited labour supply, the land tenure system, and the existence throughout the period under consideration of plentifully available *terrenos baldíos* kept wages high, and also explain why, although personal dependence was not altogether absent, the Costa Rican *peón*, both permanent and casual, was basically an employee, a wage labourer and not a 'serf '.[52]

The attitude of the state towards the labour market was for the most part one of non-intervention. The police regulations issued in 1850 decreed that rural wage labourers had to conclude a contract with their employers establishing the wage, the duration, and the condition of work. If the employee fell sick, his employer was required to help him, but the labourer would have to repay this help later on, under conditions that were to be agreed upon. Of course, successive Costa Rican governments were well aware of the constant labour shortage, but they were at a loss as to how to solve this problem; in fact, their attempts to find a solution, such as the re-enactment of the very old laws against vagrancy and begging in 1883, were always completely ineffective.[53]

To advance our knowledge and understanding of the relations of production in the Costa Rican coffee sector, the logical steps to be taken in the future are, firstly, to examine systematically the few available private archives of coffee-growers and processors, in order to analyse in detail the evolution both of wages and of the economic situation of coffee, as well as of the mechanisms of dependence and exploitation; and, secondly, to undertake a series of case studies of historical demography in the coffee zones, which will permit – as there are no overall national statistics before 1935 (probably because the smallholders organized themselves and came into open conflict with the *beneficios* only after 1922) – detailed knowledge of the cyclical and local variations of the labour supply, beyond the few isolated and unreliable figures which some sources give for the country as a whole.

The qualitative specialization of Costa Rican coffee production

The natural conditions of the Meseta Central were ideal for the production of high-quality coffee. The type of coffee grown during the nineteenth century was of the *coffea arabica* variety, the so-called blue coffee of Santo Domingo. Although production was very important in relation to the small population, needless to say it could never compete in absolute terms with a country like Brazil. In the best years, coffee exports from Costa Rica never represented more than 1 or 2 per cent of world exports. Given the country's situation, everything favoured specialization and the production of a high-quality highland coffee, taking much greater care over the picking, preparation, and selection of the beans than was the case in Brazil.[54] A characteristic of the coffee zone of the Meseta Central, underlined by all the travellers in the last century, was the neatness of the rural landscape and the careful attention given to the fields, as opposed to the general picture in the rest of Central and Latin America generally.[55]

The repercussions of coffee expansion on the agriculture of the Meseta Central

The historical conditions in which coffee expansion occurred, in a country overwhelmingly devoted to subsistence agriculture by small-holding peasants, meant that the best lands and the greater part of the available labour force were tied to coffee monoculture. The absence of competitive or alternative economic activities; the high price of land in the Meseta Central, making only one product of high commercial value able to compensate for the initial investment; British credits, directed specifically into coffee production; the close commercial dependence on England, which ruled out the development of manu-facturing industries financed from coffee income (these were anyway hindered by internal structural conditions) – all these tended to strength-en the pattern of monoculture which was already solidly entrenched when coffee prices took a downturn in the 1890s.

When the supply of *terrenos baldíos* on the Meseta Central was exhausted, around the end of the nineteenth century, the process which had already begun several decades earlier was accelerated, and sub-sistence agricultural activities such as maize, beans, sugar-cane, meat, and dairy cattle were steadily displaced by coffee, though some pastures and cane-fields were retained for feeding the draught animals. One of the most serious consequences of the growing monoculture was the crisis in the subsistence production of basic domestic foodstuffs. Whilst Hale in 1825 was able to describe a country where life was 'dirt cheap', over the years coffee expansion drove the cultivation of food-crops on the marginal lands, and the small proprietors themselves increasingly concentrated their efforts on coffee. It is true that, long before the growth of coffee production, Costa Rica had suffered serious problems in food supply, but the food shortages worsened notably during the nineteenth century, while prices rose considerably. Already in 1841, faced with a food shortage, the government tried to force the coffee growers to plant bananas 'on the boundaries of their estates'. In the 1850s, Wagner and Scherzer observed that life was very expensive in San José, and that many of the foodstuffs were imported. To a certain extent, of course, this fact also reflects the diversification of consumption patterns linked to the growth of trade; but it cannot wholly account for the fact that by that time cereal prices were between twenty and thirty times higher than they had been in the 1820s. Many similar cases could be quoted. Wheat-growing, which had previously been fairly important, collapsed after 1860 in the face of competition from flour from California and Chile. Food production in the neighbourhood of the coffee zone was guaranteed to a certain extent by the colonization of *terrenos baldíos* by pioneer settlers going out to *abrir montaña* (the clearing of virgin forest lands for cultivation), but, mainly because of serious transport problems, this expansion of the agricultural area was unable to compensate for the land lost by subsistence farming to coffee cultivation in the central part of the country. The Costa Rican government passed a number of laws forbidding the export of grains and cattle and encouraging their importation, setting maximum prices for basic foodstuffs at times of acute shortage, and so on, but these measures never added up to an effective solution to the problem.[56]

Conclusion

Some features of coffee expansion in Costa Rica recall the 'classic' aspects of dependent capitalist export agriculture found in so many Latin American countries during the nineteenth and twentieth centuries. Nevertheless, its peculiarities contain an interesting lesson. In other analyses of the *latifundia* in Ibero-America, a great deal of emphasis is commonly placed on the monopolization of the best and most extensive lands by the great landowners in order to explain the high degree of social and economic control they exercise in the countryside. The Costa Rican case demonstrates that it is possible to achieve sufficient economic, social, and political control without this, in so far as the dominant class succeeds in monopolizing other key sectors of the productive process, such as capital and marketing.

NOTES

1. See Dirección General de Estadística y Censos, *Atlas estadístico de Costa Rica* (San José, 1953); Tulia Quirós Amador, *Geografía de Costa Rica* (Instituto Geográfico Nacional, San José, 1954); Miguel Obregón Lizano, *Geografía patria*, 4th edn, 4 vols. (San José, 1932), vol. 1; Carolyn Olive Hall, 'Some effects of the spread of coffee cultivation upon the landscape of Costa Rica in the nineteenth and twentieth centuries' (unpublished D. Phil. thesis, Oxford University, 1972), pp. 78–83.
2. In this paper we shall take the term '*hacienda*' to be equivalent to an estate, and '*finca*' to a farm; but the two are used interchangeably in Costa Rica, and in

practice little distinction is made between the two. The term 'plantation' is here used to simply signify 'planted ground' and should not be confused with the special and more limited meaning usually associated with the word; 'coffee planters' means merely those who plant coffee.

3. Edelberto Torres Rivas, *Interpretación del desarrollo social centroamericano*, 2nd edn (Editorial Universitaria Centroamericana (EDUCA), San José, 1971), pp. 63–73. The 'long wait' referred to by Tulio Halperín Donghi in *Historia contemporánea de América Latina*, 2nd edn (Madrid, 1970), pp. 134–206, was in fact a very brief period in the Costa Rican case. See also Samuel Z. Stone, 'Los cafetaleros: une étude des planteurs de café au Costa Rica' (unpublished doctoral thesis, University of Paris, 1968); Hall, 'Some effects of the spread of coffee cultivation', pp. 20 – 8.

4. Cleto González Víquez, '¿ Quién trajo el café a Costa Rica?', *Revista del Instituto de Defensa del Café de Costa Rica* XVIII (San José, April 1936), pp. 363–6, says that coffee was introduced from Jamaica in 1808; on the other hand, Guillermo Echeverría Morales, *Breve historia del café: cómo llegó a Costa Rica* (San José, 1972), pp. 27–31, suggests that it was introduced from Martinique in 1791. Several alternative dates between 1791 and 1808 have been mentioned by other authors.

5. John Hale, *Six months' residence and travels in Central America* (New York, 1826), quoted in Ricardo Fernández Guardia (ed.), *Costa Rica en el siglo XIX, Antología de viajeros*, 2nd edn (EDUCA, San José, 1970), pp. 32–3.

6. Samuel. Z. Stone, 'Los cafetaleros', *Revista de Ciencias Jurídicas* XIII (Universidad de Costa Rica, San José, 1969), pp. 167–217.

7. Ibid.; see also, by the same author, 'Algunas aspectos de la distribución del poder político en Costa Rica', *Revista de Ciencias Jurídicas* XVII (San José, 1971), pp. 105–30.

8. Rodrigo Soley Carrasco, 'Influencia de la industria del café en la economía nacional: historia del impuesto sobre el café ', *Revista del Instituto de Defensa del Café de Costa Rica* LIII (San José, 1939), pp. 57–62. The basic documents for the history of the coffee tax during the nineteenth century are to be found in the *Congreso* series of the Archivo Nacional de Costa Rica, San José.

9. Hall, 'Some effects of the spread of coffee cultivation', pp. 104 –27.

10. Data taken from the *Anuario estadístico* for 1890, and quoted in Hall, 'Some effects of the spread of coffee cultivation', pp. 28, 87–91.

11. The fragmented smallholding farm structure of colonial Costa Rica was caused, in part, by the scarcity of Indian population and partly by the lack of sufficient capital to buy enough African slaves. No gold or silver mines were discovered, and the various attempts to create important tropical plantations all failed, so that the majority of the admittedly few Spanish settlers were obliged to occupy themselves in cultivating subsistence foodstuffs on small farms. See Murdo J. Macleod, *Spanish Central America: a socioeconomic history, 1520–1720* (Berkeley and Los Angeles, Calif., 1973).

12. Rodrigo Facio Brenes, *Estudio sobre economía costarricense* (San José, 1942), p. 23; on the suppression of the tithe, see Archivo Nacional, *Congreso*, no. 149 (7 July 1825), no. 1953 (31 March 1835), and no. 1882 (1 September 1835); Tomás Soley Güell, *Historia económica y hacendaria de Costa Rica*, 2 vols. (San José, 1947–9), vol. I, pp. 130, 167, 216–19, 271–2; Archivo Nacional, *Congreso*, no. 3351 (8 April 1832). In the *Congreso* and *Historia Municipal* sections of the Archivo Nacional there are numerous documents of *terrenos censitarios* (tithe lands) in Pavas, and documents on the disposal of municipal lands. See also the decree of President Mora,

28 July 1851, published in the *Gaceta Oficial*, 16 August 1851, p. 1; labourers who were able to cultivate waste lands of from one to ten *manzanas* for a period of ten years could obtain title to these lands.

13. *Gaceta Oficial*, 'Memoria de Hacienda y Comercio del Secretario de Estado Ricardo Montealegre', 16 July 1896, pp. 732–5. See also Hall, 'Some aspects of the spread of coffee cultivation', pp. 54, 89.

14. E. G. Squier, *The States of Central America* (New York, 1858), p. 479; Francisco Solano Astaburuaga, *Republicas de Centro América* (Santiago, 1857), quoted in Fernández Guardia, *Costa Rica en el siglo XIX*, p. 311.

15. Braulio Carrillo, the then dictator, gave Mora's lands to another person. See the document published by the *Revista del Archivo Nacional* (San José, 1966), pp. 139–74.

16. *Gaceta Oficial*, 'No oficial', 16 June 1858, pp. 1–2; 'Memoria del Ministro de Hacienda, Guerra y Marina al Congreso de 1858', 1 September 1858, pp. 1–2; 'Memoria de Hacienda', 16 July 1896.

17. Compare with the similar argument proposed for the Honduran case by Héctor Pérez Brignoli, 'Economía y sociedad en Honduras durante el siglo XIX. Las estructuras demográficas', *Estudios Sociales Centroamericanos* VI (San José, September–December 1973), pp. 51–82.

18. *Gaceta Oficial*, 'Memoria de Hacienda', 16 July 1896. Archivo Nacional, *Congreso*, no. 1755, 'Exposición del Poder Ejecutivo' (13 November 1834), and no. 3371, 'Decreto de la Asamblea Constitucional' (14 November 1834); *Hacienda*, no. 6896, 'Informe del Gobernador de Cartago al Ministro' (7 May 1851).

19. Archivo Nacional, *Congreso*, no. 673, 'Exposición de Poder Ejecutivo al Congreso Representativo' (23 October 1827); *Hacienda*, no. 7006, 'Solicitud de varios vecinos de Cartago' (25 November 1869). These documents, which describe the dispossession of Indian communities in Los Tejeros (a district of Cartago) and in the valley of Orosi, show that the problem of the expropriation of lands held by Indian communities was not entirely unknown.

20. Hale, quoted in Fernández Guardia, *Costa Rica en el siglo XIX*, p. 24.

21. Robert Glasgow Dunlop, *Travels in Central America* (London, 1847), p. 4; and Squier, *The States of Central America*, pp. 455–6, 480 (Squier noted that each old coffee plant was worth $\frac{1}{2}$ *real*, and every new bush $1\frac{1}{2}$ *reales*.) Moritz Wagner and Carl Scherzer, *La república de Costa Rica en Centro América*, transl. Jorge A. Lines (San José, 1944), pp. 194–5: the authors travelled extensively in Costa Rica during 1853 and 1854. (The book was originally published in German as *Die republik Costa Rica in Central Amerika* (Leipzig, 1856).) According to the figures given by Joaquín Bernardo Calvo in his *Apuntamientos geográficos, estadísticos e históricos* (San José, 1887), p. 153, during the period from the creation of the Register of Property and Mortgages on 1 September 1867 until 31 March 1886, 57,639 estates had been registered, with a value of 38,807,531 *pesos*; and 46,329 estates, to the value of 38,964,909 *pesos*, had been disposed of. Moreover, in the later years of this period both the number and the value of landed transactions increased significantly.

22. Samuel Z. Stone has very kindly lent me his working notes on this subject. The documents which enable some study to be made of the variations in land prices during the first half of the last century are the sale contracts contained in the *Protocolos de San José* (Archivo Nacional), nos. 491–572. Squier, *The States of Central America*, p. 480, gives an average of 100 to 150 *pesos* per *manzana* for lands in

the neighbourhood of San José around 1857. His observations are confirmed by other sources: the figures he quotes are in fact a little lower than the actual price for coffee lands at that time. See also for example, the advertisements in the *Gaceta Oficial*, 21 June 1856, p. 470; 13 January 1858, p. 4; 1 September 1858, p. 4; 6 December 1859, p. 3; 24 March 1866, p. 4; 25 November 1871, p. 4. The comparison between San José and Escuintla is taken from *Annales du commerce extérieur: Amérique Centrale et Amérique du Sud* (Paris, 1867), Vol. 1 (1843–66), section *Faits commerciaux*, VI (1858), p. 3. See also Hall, 'Some effects of the spread of coffee cultivation', pp. 101–4.

23. The *Protocolos de San José* sometimes quote cases of the purchase of small parcels of land adjacent to established coffee groves or *cafetales*. On 18 May 1840, for example, a coffee planter bought a house and land situated 'next to the purchaser's coffee plantation' for 75 *pesos*, a figure which suggests that it must have been a small farm (Archivo Nacional, *Protocolos de San José*, no. 522, fol. 16; other transactions conducted along the same lines can be found in *Protocolos de San José*, no. 522, fol. 71, and no. 523, fol. 135). Juan Rafael Mora and the Montealegre family were connected with the most important land transactions registered in the *Protocolos de San José* between 1840 and 1850. For other figures given in the text see Squier, *The States of Central America*, p. 480; Solano, in Fernández Guardia, *Costa Rica en el siglo XIX*, p. 324; Anthony Trollope, *The West Indies and the Spanish Main* (London, 1859), pp. 278–9; Calvo, *Apuntamientos geográficos*, p. 150. See also Hall, 'Some aspects of the spread of coffee cultivation', pp. 99–104; Stone, 'Los cafetaleros' (1968), pp. 87–96; F. Moretzsohn de Andrade, 'Decadência do compesinato costarriquenho', *Revista Geográfica* LXVI (Rio de Janeiro, 1967), pp. 135–52; Carlos Meléndez, *Dr José María Montealegre* (Academia de Geografía e Historia de Costa Rica, San José 1968), p. 150.

24. Stone, 'Los cafetaleros' (1968), pp. 87–96; Wagner and Scherzer, *La república de Costa Rica*, p. 195n; *Gaceta Oficial*, 24 March 1866, p. 4.

25. J. Ll. Stephens, *Incidents of travel in Central America, Chiapas and Yucatan*, 2 vols. (London, 1841), Vol. 1, pp. 352–3; Solano, in Fernández Guardia, *Costa Rica en el siglo XIX*, p. 307; Hall, 'Some aspects of the spread of coffee cultivation', pp. 87–91; *Gaceta Oficial*, 'La crisis económica', 2 April 1881, pp. 2–3.

26. Dunlop, *Travels in Central America*, p. 50; Wilhelm Marr, *Reise nach Central-Amerika*, 2 vols. (Hamburg, 1863), quoted in Fernández Guardia, *Costa Rica en el siglo XIX*, p. 136; Trollope, *The West Indies and the Spanish Main*, p. 278; Wagner and Scherzer, *La república de Costa Rica*, pp. 197, 202; Calvo, *Apuntamientos geográficos*, pp. 35, 47; *Faits commerciaux* V (1857), p. 10.

27. Torres Rivas, *Interpretación del desarrollo social centroamericano*, p. 85; Hall, 'Some aspects of the spread of coffee cultivation', pp. 51–7; Wagner and Scherzer, *La república de Costa Rica*, p. 103; Trollope, *The West Indies and the Spanish Main*, pp. 278–9.

28. Dunlop, *Travels in Central America*, p. 45. See also Trollope's comments: 'the people are not idle ... and they love to earn and put by money; but they are very few in number; they have land of their own, and are materially well off' (*The West Indies and the Spanish Main*, p. 278). Thomas Francis Meagher, 'Holidays in Costa Rica', *New Monthly Magazine* (New York), December 1859 – February 1860, quoted in Fernández Guardia, *Costa Rica en el siglo XIX*, p. 369.

29. Solano, in Fernández Guardia, *Costa Rica en el siglo XIX*, p. 324.

30. Dunlop, *Travels in Central America*, pp. 49–50; Hall, 'Some aspects of the spread

of coffee cultivation', pp. 51–7. *Gaceta Oficial*, 'No oficial', 16 June 1856, pp. 1–2; 'Comentario: tranquilidad, café', 14 February 1852, pp. 1–2; 'Cosecha', 14 April 1852, p. 2.

31. Hale, in Fernández Guardia, *Costa Rica en el siglo XIX*, pp. 32–3.

32. Stephens, *Incidents of travel*, Vol. I, pp. 358–9.

33. Carlos Araya Pochet, 'La minería y sus relaciones con la acumulación de capital y la clase dirigente de Costa Rica 1821–1841', and José Luis Vega Carballo, 'La coyuntura económica general y del comercio exterior en Costa Rica durante el siglo XIX', both papers presented to the First Central American Congress on Demographic, Economic and Social History, held in Costa Rica in February 1973, and reprinted in *Estudios Sociales Centroamericanos* V (San José, May–August 1974), pp. 31–64 and 157–85 respectively. See also Alberto Quijano, *Costa Rica ayer y hoy (1800–1939)* (San José, 1949), p. 14; Calvo, *Apuntamientos geográficos*, pp. 99–100; Hall, 'Some aspects of the spread of coffee cultivation', pp. 25–6, 30, 41, 45.

34. José Luis Vega Carballo, 'Actividades inglesas en Costa Rica: el siglo XIX', mimeographed paper presented to the Second Symposium on Economic History of Latin America, Rome, 1972. See also Facio, *Estudio sobre economía*, pp. 27–31; *Gaceta Oficial*, 25 January 1851, 14 February 1863, 5 December 1863, and 15 October 1864: all contain advertisements dealing with the financing of coffee exports.

35. Dunlop, *Travels in Central America*, p. 50; Wagner and Scherzer, *La república de Costa Rica*, p. 196n; *Faits commerciaux* VI (March 1858), p. 3.

36. Squier, *The States of Central America*, p. 473; *Faits commerciaux* VII (December 1858), p. 12, and IX (November 1858), p. 11. Archivo Nacional, *Hacienda*, no. 1184, 'Reformas al contrato entre Crisanto Medina y el Gobierno' (29 December 1857); *Gaceta Oficial*, 'Documento – Banco', 2 January 1858; *Gaceta Oficial*, 'Contrato entre don Crisanto Medina y el Ministerio de Hacienda', 12 June 1858.

37. Calvo, *Apuntamientos geográficos*, pp. 115–16; Hall, 'Some aspects of the spread of coffee cultivation,' pp. 37–41. *Gaceta Oficial*, 22 November 1873; *Gaceta Oficial*, 'Exposición de varias personas con el objeto de fundar un banco de crédito', 9 September 1876. Archivo Nacional, *Congreso*, nos. 7770 (24 December 1841– 11 January 1842), 5268 (18–21 January 1850), 5811 (14–28 July 1862), 5817 (26 May–30 July 1862), 5753 (14 July – 4 August 1862), 9825 and 9827 (4 June 1866), 6890 (16 April – 6 June 1866), 6625 (June 1867), 7033 (2 January – 15 June 1868), 9259 (20 May 1868), 7127 (20 December 1871), 6861 (13 February – 4 April 1872), 8435 (22 September 1879). *Gaceta Oficial*, 1 March 1851, 12 December 1863, 24 December 1867, 22 November 1872, 25 April 1874, 12 September 1874, 30 March 1878.

38. Compare note 5 above; see also Jorge Carranza Solís, *Monografía del café*, 2 vols. (San José, 1933), vol. I, p. 24.

39. Figures for 1909 and 1956 are quoted in Carmen S. de Malavassi y Belén André S., 'El café en la historia de Costa Rica' (unpublished thesis, Universidad de Costa Rica, San José, 1958), pp. 35–6; see also Hall, 'Some aspects of the spread of coffee cultivation,' pp. 85–6.

40. Wagner and Scherzer, *La república de Costa Rica*, p. 202; Hall, 'Some aspects of the spread of coffee cultivation', pp. 83–6. Regarding the limited use of fertilizers, see *Gaceta Oficial*, 2 April 1881; 20 January 1858, p. 2; 'No oficial', 16 June 1858, pp. 1–2; 30 April 1877, p. 2.

41. Dunlop, *Travels in Central America*, p. 49; Squier, *The States of Central America*, pp. 455–6; Wagner and Scherzer, *La república de Costa Rica*, p. 196.

42. Dunlop, *Travels in Central America*, p. 44; Solano, quoted in Fernández Guardia, *Costa Rica en el siglo XIX*, pp. 307–8; *Gaceta Oficial*, 1 March 1851.

43. Meagher, quoted in Fernández Guardia, *Costa Rica en el siglo XIX*, p. 437.

44. Paul Biolley, quoted in Stone, 'Los cafetaleros' (1968), pp. 112–13; Calvo, *Apuntamientos geográficos*, p. 47. See also Hall, 'Some aspects of the spread of coffee cultivation', pp. 41–51.

45. Stone, 'Los cafetaleros' (1968), p. 90; Archivo Nacional, *Congreso*, nos. 4974 (18–19 November 1845) and 6613 (13 May – 6 June 1867); Stephens, *Incidents of travel*, Vol 1, pp. 349–50; Squier, *The States of Central America*, pp. 456, 460; Solano, quoted in Fernández Guardia, *Costa Rica en el siglo XIX*, pp. 308, 313; Meagher, quoted ibid., pp. 349–50.

46. Carranza Solís, *Monografía*, p. 24; *Faits commerciaux* V (September 1857), p. 11, and VIII (June 1859), p. 8; Calvo, *Apuntamientos geográficos*, p. 108.

47. Calvo, *Apuntamientos geográficos*, pp. 108–9, 115, 126, 130. The voyage from Puntarenas to Europe via Cape Horn lasted at least five months, whilst from Limón to Europe it took only six weeks.

48. *Annales du commerce exterieur*, passim; Calvo, *Apuntamientos geográficos*, p. 114; Stone 'Los cafetaleros' (1968), p. 60. Costa Rica already had commercial relations with Chile before 1832. J. Haefkens, *Centraal Amerika, uit een geschiedkundig, aardrijkskundig en statistiek oogpunt beschouwd* (Dordrecht, 1827), published in Spanish as *Viaje a Guatemala y Centro América* (Guatemala City, 1969), p. 288, mentions exports of maize from Costa Rica to Chile and Peru, through Puntarenas, in the first years of independence. On the other hand a document in the Archivo Nacional (*Hacienda*, no. 6999 (1833)) demonstrates that coffee was being exported direct to Great Britain from as early as 1833; see Vega Carballo, 'El nacimiento de un régimen de burguesía dependiente: el caso de Costa Rica', *Estudios Sociales Centroamericanos* VI (San José, September–December, 1973) pp. 83–118.

49. *Faits commerciaux* XIV (June 1866), p. 10; Dunlop, *Travels in Central America*, p. 50; Calvo, *Apuntamientos geográficos*, p. 42; Stone, 'Los cafetaleros' (1968), p. 60; Carranza Solís, *Monografía*, p. 25.

50. Wagner and Scherzer, *La república de Costa Rica*, p. 196; Facio, *Estudio sobre economía*, p. 33.

51. *Gaceta Oficial*, 'No oficial', 22 November 1873, pp. 2–3; ibid., 9 September 1876; Hall, 'Some aspects of the spread of coffee cultivation', pp. 29–33.

52. On the aspects dealt with here, see Stone, 'Los cafetaleros' (1968), pp. 100–35; and Hall, 'Some aspects of the spread of coffee cultivation', pp. 41–51, which uses data from the private archives of Tournon and von Schrötter.

53. *Gaceta Oficial*, 'Reglamento de policía', 2 March 1850; 'No oficial', 16 June 1856, pp. 1–2; 'Carta de A. Pinto a T. Guardia', 20 February 1871, p. 1; 'No oficial', 22 November 1873, pp. 2–3. Archivo Nacional, *Congreso*, no. 9014 (16 June – 18 July 1883).

54. Stone, 'Los cafetaleros' (1968), pp. 100–35; Wagner and Scherzer, *La república de Costa Rica*, p. 195. On the experiments with a new variety, *coffea liberica*, see *Gaceta Oficial*, 4 January 1878, pp. 1–2; 23 June 1876, pp. 3–4; 19 May 1880, p. 3.

55. Stephens, *Incidents of travel*, Vol. 1, pp. 352–3; Dunlop, *Travels in Central America*, pp. 45, 51; Marr, quoted in Fernández Guardia, *Costa Rica en el siglo XIX*, p. 161; Meagher, quoted ibid., pp. 371–2.

56. Soley Güell, *Historia económica*, Vol. 1, p. 169; Wagner and Scherzer, *La república de Costa Rica*, pp. 102–4; Calvo, *Apuntamientos geográficos*, pp. 31, 44; Gerhard Sander, *La colonización agrícola de Costa Rica*, 2 vols. (San José, 1962–4); Hall, 'Some aspects of the spread of coffee cultivation', pp. 91–8.

PART II

The development of a plantation economy with labour recruitment from highland peasant communities

The establishment of new labour-intensive plantation systems in tropical low-land or piedmont areas, where the supply of local labour was insufficient to meet the increased demand, led to a search for new sources of labour, especially seasonal labour, and in many cases this resulted in the recruitment of Indian or *mestizo* peasants from the adjacent highland areas. In the case studied by Ian Rutledge, varying degrees of direct coercion were involved in the process of labour mobilization.

Ultimately, the increased susceptibility of the Indian agricultural labourer to a system of material incentives, combined with demographic growth in the highlands, made the early modes of labour organization irrelevant to the needs and conditions of the time. The process of agrarian change (as exemplified by the replacement of debt peonage by a national system of *mandamiento*) and the reluctance of the planter oligarchy to allow the emergence of free wage labour and a pure plantation proletariat are eloquent indices of the economic and political distortions induced by the dominance of a system of plantation monoculture, developed under conditions of dependent capitalism.

Rutledge's paper also deals with the general theoretical question of the relationship between the expansion of capitalist forms of agricultural production and pre-capitalist modes of labour recruitment, but the particular form of labour coercion described in this paper owed more to a deliberate policy of land monopolization in the highlands than to direct coercion by the state. However, given the immense power of the provincial oligarchy in the region studied by Rutledge, the line between direct and indirect coercion of labour (i.e. the distinction between the use of political and economic measures) is a difficult one to draw. On the other hand, Rutledge argues that the element of coercion involved in the recruitment of highland Indians in northern Argentina should be seen within a broader process that was leading, in time, to the proletarianization of the highland peasantry and their conversion into free (albeit seasonal) wage labourers.

The remaining three papers in Part II deal with cases in which the degree of extra-economic coercion used in the recruitment of highland labourers was either minimal or completely non-existent. The papers by Peter Klarén and Henri Favre deal with migration of Indians from the Peruvian Sierra to the coastal sugar and cotton plantations. Klarén's paper on the sugar industry presents a general account of the development of the plantation system, leading to a discussion of the contracting of highland Indians for the cane harvest. As in the Argentinian case, the sugar planters were at first obliged to resort to various forms of coercion to 'persuade' Indians from the traditional peasant communities of the Sierra to come down and work on the coastal plantations, where, in spite of harsh working and living conditions, they received incomes which could never have been obtained by agricultural labour in the highlands. But over the years, as these seasonal migrant workers became more deeply enmeshed in the wage economy, the labour regime became freer and more typically capitalist in organization. In time the migrations from the highlands created in the coastal region a new type of labour force which was to play an important role in the social and political developments of the country. Favre's paper considers in great detail the ecological and demographic changes (and the related changes in land ownership) which compelled members of Indian Sierra *comunidades* to seek temporary work on the coastal cotton plantations. Favre argues that the Indians succeeded in integrating wage labour into their social and cultural system in a manner which actually fortified their traditional way of life. This accommodation between peasant culture and wage labour contrasts equally with the case of outright rejection of wage labour, discussed in Part I by Martínez Alier, and with the case of reluctant and antagonistic acceptance described by Michael Taussig in Part IV.

The final paper, by Malcolm Deas, presents the history of a single coffee estate in Cundinamarca, Colombia. Using a wealth of graphic archival material, Deas examines the production relations of the estate with its permanent workers and also with the more numerous seasonal labourers; both of these groups were mainly recruited from the highland *Sabana* region. Deas describes the extremely free and independent position of the labour force, which not only came to work on the estate voluntarily but also appears to have been able to pick and choose its own forms of remuneration.

Deas's paper concludes by describing the problems faced by the estate during the frequent periods of political revolution and civil war in Colombia. It might be suggested that herein lies one of the extreme contrasts with the cases of Guatemala and El Salvador. (Whereas in Colombia the landowning class was bitterly divided and the state weak and fragmented, the opposite seems to have been the case in Guatemala, and the state openly collaborated with the landowning oligarchy to mobilize seasonal labour at times of greatest demand.)

CHAPTER 8

The integration of the highland peasantry into the sugar cane economy of northern Argentina, 1930–43

IAN RUTLEDGE[1]

Introduction

Most studies of plantation systems, and especially those dealing with sugar cane economies, have concentrated on cases where the product is sold for export on the international market, and it has become more or less a commonplace to think of 'plantation economy' as being synony-mous with 'export economy'. However, in the case of Argentina there developed in the latter part of the nineteenth century a large and economically important plantation system whose product was destined almost entirely for a protected internal market. This sugar cane economy was based largely in the northwestern province of Tucumán, but later expanded further to the north into the provinces of Salta and Jujuy. Protected by high tariff barriers and liberally financed by banking credits, the Argentine sugar industry of the late nineteenth and early twentieth centuries provides one of the first examples of 'import sub-stitution' in Latin America. However, despite these apparently modern and economically progressive features, the internal logic of the planta-tion system inevitably asserted itself in the field of production relations and patterns of labour recruitment, with the result that, for a certain period, a modern and technologically advanced agro-industry operated labour policies which were manifestly backward and coercive. In Tucu-mán these features were somewhat mitigated by factors which cannot be dealt with in this paper, but in the provinces of Salta and Jujuy arch-aic forms of production relations predominated until as late as the early 1940s. This paper describes the historical process whereby the high-land peasantry of northwestern Argentina was mobilized for seasonal labour in the sugar cane plantations of Salta and Jujuy, and it tries to explain the rationale of a plantation system involving an ecological configuration of sub-tropical lowland commercial agriculture integrated to some extent with zones of highland subsistence agriculture.

BOLIVIA

BRAZIL

PARAGUAY

JUJUY
SAN SALVADOR
DE JUJUY

SALTA
SALTA

FORMOSA

CATA-
MARCA
SAN MIGUEL
DE TUC.
TUCUMAN STE.

CHACO

FORMOSA

MISIONES

RESISTENCIA

CATAMARCA

SANTIAGO
DEL
ESTERO

CORRIENTES
POSADAS

LA RIOJA

CORRIENTES

SANTA FE

SAN
JUAN

LA
RIOJA

SAN JUAN

CORDOBA

SANTA
FE

ENTRE
RIOS
PARANA

URUGUAY

MENDOZA

SAN
LUIS

CORDOBA

MENDOZA

SAN
LUIS

BUENOS AIRES
LA PLATA

SANTA ROSA

LA PAMPA

BUENOS
AIRES

NEUQUEN

NEUQUEN

RIO NEGRO

VIEDMA

CHUBUT

RAWSON

**PROVINCES
OF
ARGENTINA**

SANTA CRUZ

RIO GALLEGOS

TIERRA DEL FUEGO

USHUAIA

SOUTH PACIFIC OCEAN

SOUTH ATLANTIC OCEAN

CHILE

0   km   1000

Map 13

The Indian communities of the Puna Jujeña prior to
their integration in the sugar cane economy

In the highland areas of the provinces of Jujuy and Salta, the land tenure system acquired its basic form under Spanish colonial rule. Vast tracts of land were handed out, particularly during the eighteenth century, as *mercedes* (royal property grants), which contained within their territory settled Indian communities of cultivators and herdsmen. Until around 1810 the recipients of these land grants used the Indians as quasi-serfs to work the estates they had acquired, and after this date, when

Map 14

forced labour was abolished by the national government, the Indians continued to be subject to the landowners' power by having to pay them an annual money rent (*arriendo*) for the land they cultivated, or a payment per head of livestock which they pastured on the lands of the *haciendas* (*pastaje*). In 1874–5 the Indians of the Puna *Jujeña* (*altiplano* or high plateau of Jujuy) rebelled against their landlords, but they were bloodily suppressed. According to one observer, the Swedish anthropologist Eric Boman, who visited the Puna in 1903, the situattion of the highland peasantry differed little at this time from what it must have been like before the rebellion.

The land is divided up among a small number of landlords, almost all of whom live in the town of Jujuy. Each property has an enormous extent and is occupied by a hundred or more Indians, who must give up to the landlord the greater part of the production of their small flocks of sheep and, in addition, give personal service when it is required. The greater part of the owners never visit their lands in the Puna but are content from time to time to send an agent to settle Indian problems and return with supplies.[2]

However, Boman's account may have somewhat exaggerated the extent to which the *hacienda* system had survived the traumas of the period of agrarian revolt and its aftermath. Not only did the Indians continue to agitate for the return of the lands to their own communities, but they also appear to have kept the level of rents they paid down to a level which eventually brought into question the economic viability of the *hacienda* system. According to Benjamín Villafañe, the Governor of Jujuy, in 1927 the Indians of the Puna paid *pastaje* at the following rates: between 6 and 10 *pesos* per year per hundred sheep; 1 or 2 *pesos* per head of cattle; from 40 to 60 *centavos* per donkey or horse; and 40 to 50 *centavos* per *llama*.[3] Villafañe argued that these payments were extremely low (although he did not present figures for the *arriendo*), and while this may be propaganda, it does seem to be the case that at this time the landowners of the Puna were finding their traditional occupations as rentiers less and less remunerative, as I shall show later.

Whereas in the departments of Yaví, Cochinoca, and Rinconada, together with the highland parts of the department of Humahuaca, the *latifundio* still prevailed in the 1920s, in the department of Santa Catalina a different pattern of land tenure had emerged in the first part of the twentieth century.[4] Between 1914 and 1920 a considerable number of Indians bought the lands they rented from their landlords. This occurred especially in the district of Puesto Grande, which contained some of the best pasture land in the department.[5] Each Indian received a parcel of land, which was measured and marked out by an engineer who then supervised the fencing-off of the parcels.[6] Precisely why this occurred we do not know, although it might be conjectured that the Indians in this department had achieved a certain balance of social and economic power with their landlords which persuaded the landlords to cut their losses and sell up.[7] However, whatever the factors lying behind this event, its result was the creation of a class of small peasant proprietors who enjoyed a much greater degree of freedom and independence than the Indians who continued to live in the *haciendas*. Indeed, Villafañe argued that the main reason for dissatisfaction and agitation among the peasants living in the *haciendas* of the Puna was that they wanted to become owners of the land, as had occurred in Santa Catalina and some other parts of the province.[8]

The Indians' social and economic life probably differed little in the late 1920s from the observations made by Boman in 1903. The mainstay of the Indian economy continued to be the raising of sheep, whose wool was either woven into domestic textiles called *baracán* or sold directly to the *mestizo* merchants and storekeepers who dominated the commercial life of the Puna; *baracán* was also probably sold to the merchants, although it is quite likely that the Indians took it directly to market themselves in the Bolivian markets of Talina, Tupiza, and Tarija, which they frequently visited. Within the Puna there was considerable specialization in economic activity. Thus in Yaví there was a certain amount of agriculture – mainly alfalfa, potatoes, and *quinoa* – in Rinconada gold-washing was an important economic activity, and in Santa Catalina gold-washing and textile production were probably about equally important. A certain number of Indians also went to work as labourers in the larger gold and lead mines worked by foreign companies such as La Eureka and El Torno in Santa Catalina, and Pan de Azúcar in Yaví.

For the most part the Indians lived in nucleated villages consisting of simple *adobe* houses surrounding the beautiful white churches constructed by the Spanish, although some Indians lived in scattered settlements on the vast pasture lands, where they tended their herds of sheep and *llamas*. Religion played an important part in their lives, as indeed it still does today. This religion was, however, a complex mixture of Catholic and pre-Columbian beliefs:[9] the *Pachamama* ('mother-earth') continued to be worshipped alongside the Virgin Mary; propitiatory offerings were made not only to the Indians' patron saints such as San Juan (the patron saint of shepherds and sheep) and San Antonio (patron saint of *llamas*) but also to the pre-Columbian *apachetas*, monuments of white stones dedicated to the *Pachamama*. These religious practices remained almost all that was left of the Indians' pre-hispanic culture. In 1863 Martin de Moussy had reported that the Indians still spoke Quechua (which had replaced Ckunza, the original language of the Atacamas), but in the 1870s schools were established in the Puna, and the Indians began to learn Spanish. The acculturation of the highland Indians also affected customs of clothing and dress; already in 1903, Boman had observed that the majority of the Indians wore European dress,[10] and we may assume that by the late 1920s the Indians were largely acculturated in both language and dress.

The most important agents of this process were the *mestizo* store-owners who dominated the local economy. These men introduced new goods into the local market, although not always necessarily to the advantage of the local Indian population. Thus, in Cochinoca, Boman refers to two *mestizo* merchants who sold alcohol made from sugar cane which they bought from the *ingenios* (sugar factories) in the San Francisco Valley.[11] The store-owners and itinerant merchants of the Puna also made a comfortable living out of trading gold. The Indians sold the gold they prospected to the merchants, who then made a profit of 100 per cent in reselling it in the lowland regions.[12]

Little information is available on the Indians' family organization, although it appears that lengthy trial marriages were common and that common-law relationships were as important as legitimate unions. Boman refers to a custom, in a *hacienda* called El Moreno in the department of Cochinoca, in which the *hacendado* conducted a yearly mass marriage of all the young couples suspected of enjoying sexual relations; the Indians were compelled to line up in the open air, and a priest, specially brought in for the task, then conducted the ceremony.[13] In other cases, however, the Indians probably continued many years in common-law unions before receiving church marriage.

Boman noted that the Indians of the Puna had little inclination towards regular wage labour. Sometimes they worked in the mines to earn a little money but soon returned to their traditional pastoral life, which they clearly preferred. This refusal to submit to disciplined wage labour made Boman conclude that there was little chance of the Indians becoming 'civilized'.[14] Europeans have not infrequently raised this complaint against the indigenous peoples of colonial territories who have shown themselves to be unwilling to submit meekly to the rigours of capitalist exploitation; the solution normally adopted has been to hasten the natives' 'civilization' by some form of direct compulsion which, although not intended to permanently enslave or enserf the indigenous population, nevertheless forces them to work for the capitalist. As I shall show later in this chapter, this type of solution was adopted in the 1930s towards the Indians of the Puna by the *ingenios*, in their search for further supplies of seasonal plantation labour.

Sugar and politics in the provinces of Jujuy and Salta during the 1930s

During the nineteenth century it was in the small but heavily populated province of Tucumán that the sugar industry enjoyed its major development. In 1894, whereas Salta had only one *ingenio* (San Isidro) and Jujuy three, there were thirty-six in Tucumán.

However, in the 1920s the sugar industry in the northernmost provinces of Jujuy and Salta had begun to expand more rapidly than in Tucumán. An important boost to the industry in the province of Salta was given by the foundation in 1919 of a new *ingenio* near the town of Orán, at the top of the San Francisco Valley. This was *Ingenio* San Martín del Tabacal which eventually came to be, after Ledesma, the second biggest *ingenio* in Argentina. In 1920 Jujuy and Salta together contributed only 15.7 per cent of the total national sugar production compared with Tucumán's 82.3 per cent, but by 1930 the share of Jujuy and Salta had increased to 25.3 per cent, while Tucumán's share had fallen to 72.1 per cent.

In 1930, the worldwide economic crisis posed problems for the Argentine sugar industry as it did for other sectors of the economy. The sugar producers feared that a fall in prices in the world market, together with the threat of dumping by certain exporting countries, would eliminate the tariff advantage which Argentine sugar enjoyed. Fortunately for the sugar producers, on 6 September 1930 a military coup overthrew the Radical government of President Hipólito Yrigoyen, and the new Provisional Government was sympathetic to the interests of the sugar industry.

On 5 February 1931, the National Sugar Commission, representing all the sugar-producing provinces, petitioned the Provisional Government to increase the tariff on imported sugar. On the following day an additional duty of 4 gold *centavos* per kilo was imposed raising the total duty per kilo to 25 *centavos*.[15] The provincial oligarchies of the northwest were delighted with this action. Benjamín Villafañe, now National Senator for Jujuy, went as far as to remark in one of his publications that, whereas the Radicals had persecuted the industry, the Provisional Government had 'arrived to restore it to life'.[16]

The additional tariff protection does not appear to have prevented

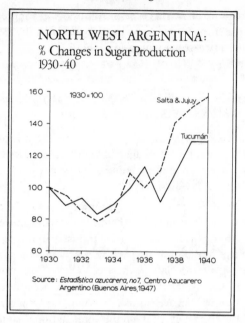

Fig. 5

an initial drop in sugar production, but over the whole ten-year period from 1930 to 1940 its effects were certainly beneficial. During a period which for most of the capitalist world was one of crisis and stagnation, the production of sugar in Argentina expanded from 382,994 metric tons in 1930 to 540,631 metric tons in 1940.[17] It should be noted, however, that the overall rate of increase was faster in Jujuy and Salta than in Tucumán (see Figure 5).

TABLE 36 *Salta and Jujuy: area cultivated with sugar cane, by ingenio, 1930 and 1940 (hectares)*

Province	Ingenio	1930	1940
Jujuy	La Esperanza	4,110	5,371
Jujuy	Ledesma	6,699	7,207
Jujuy	Río Grande	2,810	2,346
Salta	San Martín del Tabacal	4,805	7,616
Salta	San Isidro	1,032	1,262
	Total	19,456	23,802

Source: Estadística azucarera no. 7, Centro Azucarero Argentino (Buenos Aires, 1947).

Production data for the individual *ingenios* were not published for the years 1930 to 1940; however, figures are available for the area cultivated with cane (see Table 36). It will be noted that the biggest expansion of the area cultivated with cane in this period took place in the plantations of *Ingenio* San Martín del Tabacal in Salta.

This period of expansion of the sugar industry coincided with the re-establishment of the political power of the sugar oligarchy of the northwest. The Provisional Government which seized power in 1930 was strongly representative of the conservative forces of the northwest and was headed by General José Félix Uriburu, a prominent member of the oligarchy of Salta, whose family had been among the pioneers of the sugar industry. In addition, the power of the sugar oligarchy was amply displayed by the political positions and offices held by the owners of the two largest *ingenios* in Salta and Jujuy. Herminio Arrieta, owner of *Ingenio* Ledesma in Jujuy, was the National Deputy of Jujuy in the Congress from 1934 to 1938, and from 1938 to 1943 he represented Jujuy in the Senate.[18] Robustiano Patrón Costas, owner of *Ingenio* San Martín del Tabacal, enjoyed even higher political status. From 1932 until 1943 he was Senator for Salta in the Congress; he was also President of the Senate in the same period, interim President of the nation in 1942, and President of the Partido Demócrata Nacional (Conservative Party) between the years 1931 and 1935. In 1943 he was the Conservative candidate for the Presidency and would probably have been elected President but for the military coup of 1943.[19]

At the local level, the political power of the *ingenios* showed itself in two ways: first in the relationship between the *ingenio*-owners and the provincial governments, and secondly in the relationship between the *ingenios* and the provincial legislatures.

In both cases the *ingenios'* most important political instrument was the political party. In Salta the Partido Demócrata Nacional, a strongly conservative organization, was dominant throughout the 1930s. From 1932 until 1943 all the Governors of Salta were members of the Partido Demócrata Nacional. As was pointed out earlier, the party's President from 1931 to 1935 was Robustiano Patrón Costas, owner of *Ingenio* San Martín del Tabacal.

Jujuy was very similar. After the military coup of September 1930, the Conservatives, and the few Radicals who resented the reforming tendencies of Hipólito Yrigoyen, banded together to form the so-called Partido Popular.[20] This followed a common practice in the province where the anti-Yrigoyen Radicals tended to ally with the Conservatives.[21]

This alliance lasted until 1940, when the Radicals of the province re-united, and a Radical Governor was elected. The leader of the local Conservative party during the 1930s was Herminio Arrieta, owner of *Ingenio* Ledesma.

In Salta, *Ingenio* San Martín's relationship with the provincial government reached its apogee in 1936 with the election of Luis Patrón Costas, the brother of Robustiano, to the Governorship of the province, a post he held until 1940. In Jujuy the relationship between the *ingenios* and the provincial government, although equally close, appeared to be complicated somewhat by the existence of the powerful mining interest. In fact, however, the mining and sugar interests were closely intertwined. An important group of businessmen had interests in both industries and at the same time enjoyed the close co-operation of the provincial government.[22] The extent of this co-operation was amply demonstrated in the mid-1930s when the Governor of the province, Pérez Alisedo, was accused of instructing the provincial police to assassinate a Spanish miner who was obstructing the speculations of these businessmen in the tin industry. In a subsequent debate on the affair in the Senate, Herminio Arrieta came strongly to the defence of the Governor of Jujuy.[23] Precisely what Arrieta's role was in the affair is not clear, but he was generally regarded as being closely related to the Pichetti company. The national newspaper *Crítica* echoed the sentiments of many when it stated that 'Jujuy is in danger of falling not into the hands of a specific political group but into the trammels of a rapacious combination of dubious interests linked to the speculative mining industry and to the position of power which one of the *ingenios* of the province wants to create for itself: *Ingenio* Ledesma.'[24]

The influence of the *ingenios* on the provincial governments was undoubtedly an important way in which they protected and promoted their interests in these provinces, but of equal importance was their relationship with the provincial legislatures. The *ingenios'* control over vast tracts of land throughout the provinces of Salta and Jujuy, together with the control they thereby exercised over the local Indian peasantry, made it easy for them to gain the election of their own nominees in the elections for the provincial legislatures. This political control was exercised largely through the *ingenios'* agents, the *contratistas* (labour contractors). In the rural areas of the provinces, the *contratistas*, who were frequently also store-owners, enjoyed a position of local power and authority. They recruited seasonal labourers for the *zafra* (cane harvest), often by securing a dependent clientele of peasants who were indebted to them for goods bought at their stores.[25] However, according to Deputy Juan Solari's Congressional report of 1937, 'in addition to workers', the *contratistas* 'also recruit votes'.[26] Indeed, the *contratistas* were themselves frequently nominated as candidates and duly elected. For example, one of the most important *contratistas* of *Ingenio* Ledesma, Lázaro Taglioli, was deputy for the department of El Carmen in Jujuy in the 1930s, and Mamerto Salazar, the *contratista* and administrator of Patrón Costas' estates in the department of Yaví, was also deputy for that department between 1932 and 1942.[27]

The recruitment of seasonal labour in the highlands of Jujuy and Salta

The relationship between economic power and political power is frequently a complex and subtle one which resists one-sided determinist arguments, whichever viewpoint they are taken from. It could no doubt be argued that the great wealth accumulated and enjoyed by the sugar oligarchy of the northwest had facilitated their acquisition of an important degree of power and influence in the national political structure; but it could also be pointed out that this political power itself enabled them to promote their own economic interests and increase their accumulation of wealth.[28] Similarly, at the local level, the *ingenios*' economic power as the largest employers of labour in the area gave them the political power to engineer the election of their own nominees. However, the *ingenios*' political power did, in turn, facilitate their acquisition of labour for the cane harvest, especially in areas where a landless rural proletariat had not yet emerged, and where the *ingenios*' increasing demand for seasonal labour had to be met through the use of a certain amount of compulsion. The way in which this occurred will now be explained.

Towards the end of the 1920s many of the landowners of the Puna began to look for ways of disposing of their *haciendas* which would be more economical than continuing their traditional rental contracts with their Indian *arrenderos*. As stated earlier, in the department of Santa Catalina, the landowners had sold their lands to the *arrenderos* themselves; however, in the other departments of the Puna the *hacendados* looked for more remunerative arrangements. In the early 1920s Benjamin Villafañe, first as National Deputy for Jujuy, and later as the province's Governor, had sought to persuade the national government to provide money for the purchase of these estates. Villafañe presented this plan with a good deal of pseudo-radical talk about expropriation and the plight of the Indians; however, it is not unlikely that he was acting with the full agreement of many of the landlords themselves. As he himself stated, the owners of the great *haciendas* of the Puna such as the *latifundia* of Yaví and Rinconada, and Rodero and Negra Muerta in the department of Humahuaca, 'offer all kinds of possibilities for their acquisition'.[29] The fact that the Radical government in Buenos Aires neglected to take up this offer probably reflects their doubts about just who was to be the main beneficiary of the 'expropriation'.

However, around 1929 or 1930 the *hacendados* of the Puna found a new customer. The *Haciendas* Rodero and Negra Muerta in the highlands of the department of Humahuaca were bought by Robustiano Patrón Costas and his business associates for the sum of 41,000 *pesos*.[30] Shortly after, many of the *haciendas* in the highlands of Jujuy and Salta were either rented or bought outright by the sugar *ingenios*, of which the most avaricious land-grabber was *Ingenio* San Martín del Tabacal in Salta, owned by Patrón Costas and his associates. Table 37 gives a list of the *haciendas* which were controlled (either owned or rented) by Patrón Costas during the period from 1930 to 1949. This list has been drawn up from a plan for the expropriation of these estates which was presented in the Congress by the Peronist Senator for Jujuy in 1949.[31] It can be seen that the total area of land in the provinces of Jujuy and Salta which was controlled by Patrón Costas in this manner amounted to 930,236 hectares. Map 14 (p. 207) shows the departments in the provinces of Jujuy and Salta which were brought under the economic and political control of Patrón Costas and his associates as a result of this policy of land accumulation.

Whether or not all the *ingenios* of Jujuy and Salta adopted this policy of land accumulation is uncertain. Much of our evidence for the dramatic changes in land tenure which occurred at this time in Jujuy and Salta is drawn from debates in the National Congress during 1949, when bills were presented by the Peronist Senators for Jujuy and Salta for the expropriation of the *latifundia* in the highlands of these two provinces.[32] The speakers in the Senate debates referred to this policy of land accumulation as being carried out by 'the *ingenios*' (plural), and the list of *haciendas* which were to be expropriated was far in excess of those estates controlled by *Ingenio* San Martín del Tabacal. It seems, therefore, that although no *ingenio* is mentioned other than San Martín del Tabacal, more than one *ingenio*, and perhaps all of them, adopted the policy of land accumulation in some degree. However the method used to control land in the highlands was probably that of renting land rather than purchasing it outright, since the list of estates which appears in the *Diario de Sesiones* of the Senate shows the vast majority to still be in the ownership of the traditional landowning families of the highland regions.

Why did the *ingenios* accumulate such vast amounts of low-value land

TABLE 37   *Haciendas in the provinces of Salta and Jujuy controlled by the Patrón Costas family and associates, c. 1930–49*

Hacienda	Size (hectares)	Department and province	Owned or rented	Owner
Rodero y Negra Muerta	164,500	Humahuaca, Jujuy	owned	*Ingenio y Refinería* San Martín del Tabacal, S.A.
Yaví	100,000	Yaví, Jujuy	rented	Hortensia Campero de Figueroa
Hornillos	16,000	Santa Victoria, Salta	owned	*Ingenio* San Martín
Santa Victoria	223,496	Santa Victoria, Salta	rented	Hortensia Campero de Figueroa
San Andrés	129,247	Orán, Salta	owned	*Ingenio* San Martín
Santiago	171,943	Iruya, Salta	owned	Compañía Territorial del Norte, S.A.[a]
Lurucatao y Entre Rios	125,000	Molinos, Salta	owned	Abel Ortiz and Robustiano Patrón Costas
Total amount of land controlled	930,236			

[a] This was a 'front' company for *Ingenio* San Martín del Tabacal.
Sources: Diario de Sesiones, Cámara de Senadores, 10 August 1949, pp. 1177–8, and 21 September 1949, p. 1891.

in the highlands of Jujuy and Salta? This same question was raised in the Senate in 1949, in connection with the plan to expropriate these estates in the Puna of Jujuy and in the Calchaquí Valley of Salta and turn them over to the Indians. In long and detailed debates in August and September of 1949, the Peronist Senators for Jujuy and Salta explained the rationale behind the *ingenios'* massive acquisitions of land.[33]

They showed that it was not so much the land itself which the *ingenios* required, but the potential labour force which lived in the territory they had acquired, which could now be forced into performing seasonal labour in the cane harvest.

Why – I say – have these great industrialists of the *ingenios* of the north made
these investments? Because in these same lands they have the human material
which can be transported to the *ingenios*, and in abnormal and inhuman conditions.[34]

They [the Indians] constituted the cannon-fodder of the *ingenios*; this was the
principal motive for the monopolization of these vast tracts of land.[35]

The system worked as follows. In the *haciendas* which had been
rented by the *ingenios*, the Indian *arrenderos* became the sub-tenants of
the *ingenio* owners. In the *haciendas* which had been bought outright the
Indians simply received a new landlord. In both cases the Indians' rental
payments were transformed from payments in money and goods into
payments in labour. The Indians had to pay their rent in labour services
in the plantations of the *ingenios*, working for six months of the year as
cane-cutters during the *zafra*.

An example of this system is provided by the *Hacienda* Yaví.[36] This
hacienda formed part of the estates of the Campero family. Having been
temporarily expropriated from 1877 to 1893 by the provincial government, the *hacienda* was regained by the Campero family in the latter year;
around 1930 it was let by the owner, Hortensia Campero de Figueroa, to
Robustiano Patrón Costas, owner of Ingenio San Martín del Tabacal.
Patrón Costas installed his own administrator in the *hacienda*, a man
named Mamerto Salazar, who was also given the job of *contratista* for the
area. Mamerto Salazar soon became an important and powerful person
in the highlands of Jujuy and was, in due course, elected Deputy to the
Provincial Legislature, a position he held from 1932 to 1942.[37] At the
beginning of the *zafra*, Salazar's task was to round up all the Indians who
owed labour services to Patrón Costas, load them into cattle trucks, and
ship them off to the plantations. The most brutal methods were used to
ensure that the maximum number of Indians fulfilled their 'obligations'
during the *zafra*. The manner in which they were transported to the
ingenios was well documented by contemporary writers, officials, and
politicians. In 1942, for example, the Federal Inspector in the province
of Jujuy described how the *contratista* and his agents forced the Indians
into trucks for the long journey to the *ingenio* using 'the whip and other
fearsome means of flagellation'. Salazar himself was personally denounced by the Federal Inspector for putting his political powers as
Deputy at the service of *Ingenio* San Martín del Tabacal and for oppres-
sing the Indians.[38] Once delivered to the plantations, the Indians were
set to work cutting and loading cane under a rigid and harsh discipline
which was meted out by armed overseers.[39] One can well imagine the

suffering of the highland Indians, accustomed to living in a cool and dry climate, compelled to do heavy manual labour in the sub-tropical heat and humidity of the San Francisco Valley. With regard to wages, the various accounts of the system are unclear as to whether the Indians received any payment for their work. It seems, however, that if they did receive any payment it was no more than was sufficient to pay for the food and other rations which they bought from the notoriously extortionate *proveedurías* or company stores.[40] Indeed, the whole intention of the land accumulation policy operated by the *ingenios* seems to have been to acquire seasonal labour at a 'price' which was well below the market rate.

The exorbitant prices charged by the *ingenios'* *proveedurías* were the cause of violent conflict in at least one *ingenio* at this time. In *Ingenio* La Esperanza the cane-peelers (seasonal workers) went out on strike in June 1943, protesting about their low wages and the prices charged by the *proveedurías*. They marched on the sugar factory calling on the factory workers to come out and support them, but on approaching the buildings they were fired upon by the plantation police; four workers were killed and a large number were wounded.[41] The strike was denounced as being organized by 'outside agitators'; however, the Federal Inspector in the province apparently recognized the justice of the workers' demands and ordered *Ingenio* La Esperanza to increase wages and lower the prices in its *proveeduría*.[42]

Although it is probable that all the *ingenios* adopted this policy of land accumulation, in one degree or other, in order to obtain seasonal labourers, there can be no doubt that it was *Ingenio* San Martín del Tabacal in Salta which used it on the greatest scale. A number of economic factors help to explain this *ingenio*'s widespread use of the policy of land accumulation. Firstly, it should be remembered that sugar production was at this time, and still is, a highly labour-intensive industry, requiring very large numbers of seasonal workers during the *zafra*. Figure 6 shows the numbers of permanent (all-year-round) and seasonal or temporary field workers in the four main sugar-producing departments of Jujuy and Salta in 1937.[43] It will be noted that the number of seasonal workers is roughly double that of permanent workers. It will also be noted that it is in the department of Orán in Salta that the greatest number of seasonal workers are employed: it was in this department that *Ingenio* San Martín del Tabacal was situated.

The amount of seasonal labour employed in the sugar cane *zafra* is roughly proportional to the area harvested. The large number of seasonal workers employed by *Ingenio* San Martín del Tabacal simply reflects the

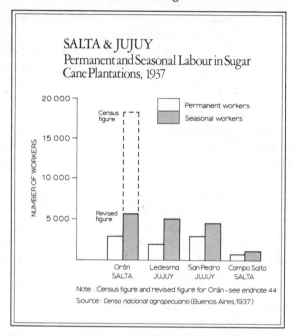

Fig. 6

fact that this *ingenio* had the largest area of land in sugar cane.[44] More-over, it will be recalled from Table 36 (p. 212) that it was in this *ingenio* that the cultivated area expanded most rapidly in the 1930s. It is prob-able, therefore, that it was the particularly heavy requirements for seasonal plantation labour in this *ingenio* which led it to adopt the policy of land accumulation and coerced labour recruitment on such a large scale.

The political power enjoyed by the *ingenios* of Jujuy and Salta was intimately connected with the methods of labour recruitment they employed. In order to maintain this system of recruitment, a whole apparatus of legalized oppression was required. The abuse of political power by the *ingenio*-owners was denounced in the Senate during the debates of 1949 on the agrarian question in Jujuy and Salta.

The authorities of these provinces, in the terrible era of the oligarchies, above all when the dark ages reappeared between 1930 and 1943, the justices of the peace and the municipalities, were all in the service of the big capitalists and landlords. And by choice or by force they [the Indians] had to go to the sugar *ingenios* to work.[45]

Up to the advent of the Peronist period ... the overseers of the greater part of these *latifundia* ... were employed as police; so that the orders of the landlord also had political force, the force of law.[46]

The recruitment of seasonal labour in the province of Catamarca

Apart from the peasantry of Jujuy itself, the *ingenios* of the province (and those of Salta) also recruited seasonal labour from the province of Catamarca and from Bolivia. In 1933 the labour department of the province of Jujuy reported that in that year the nineteen *contratistas* registered in the province recruited 5,544 workers, of which 1,761 came from the province of Catamarca and a large but unspecified proportion consisted of Bolivians resident in the province.[47] The employment of Bolivian labour was at that time quite important to the sugar industry in Jujuy and Salta; large numbers of Indians from the departments of Potosí, Chuquisaca, and Tarija had begun to migrate to the sugar plantations after the termination of the War of the Chaco (1932–5).[48] However, this source of labour was as yet fairly limited in comparison with what it was to become in the 1940s and 1950s. The Mataco and Toba Indians of the Argentine Chaco also provided a source of seasonal labour in the plantations at this time, but their importance appears to have been gradually diminishing, partly because their numbers were decreasing, and also because they were considered unsatisfactory workers.[49] Probably the most important single group of seasonal workers in the plantations of Jujuy at this time were the impoverished peasants of Catamarca.

Since the civil wars of the mid nineteenth century, the previously insurgent provinces of Catamarca and La Rioja had fallen gradually into extreme poverty and backwardness. In La Rioja this appears to have been largely the result of the decline of the traditional cattle trade with Chile. In Catamarca it was the gradual sub-division of the land in the areas of irrigated *minifundia* which was primarily responsible for the increasing poverty of the peasants. In various departments of Catamarca the growth of population in areas where the amount of cultivable land was strictly limited by the lack of irrigation water led to extreme sub-division of the peasant plots by inheritance (*herencias*), bringing about the gradual impoverishment of the peasant population. This occurred especially in the departments of Santa María, Andalgalá, and Belén.

In the midst of this poverty there arrived the *contratistas* seeking seasonal labour for the plantations of Jujuy, Salta, and Tucumán.[50] The system of recruitment was described in detail by Deputy Juan

Antonio Solari in his Congressional report on working conditions, delivered in the Congress in 1934:

The traders or *conchabadores*[51] operate like this: in the small villages far from the railway stations, they set up grocery stores in which they sell almost exclusively maize and salt, the staple necessities of the poor, which are extremely cheap but which nevertheless give a profit of 50 per cent. The sale of these commodities continues all year and is conducted on credit [*a libreta*], the bill at the end of the year amounting to, say, 80 to 100 *pesos*. The purchaser promises, almost always in writing, to pay the bill with what he earns in the *zafra*, and he also promises to accept the store-owner as an intermediary [*contratista*] between himself and the *ingenio*. When the period of the harvest arrives, each *contratista* sends his workers to the *ingenio* in goods trains, and the exploitation enters into another phase. The *contratista* sells the labour he commands at piece-rate, and he also pays his workers in the same way. But he retains as profit the difference between the price he is paid by the *ingenio* for the labour and what he pays the workers, in addition to the profit arising from his grocery trade throughout the whole year.[52]

According to another report, the amount deducted by the *contratista* from the workers' true wages (the official wage bill paid by the *ingenios*) varied between 15 per cent and 30 per cent;[53] bearing in mind that in addition were deducted the sums owing to the *contratista* in his capacity as store-owner, it is not surprising that about 60 per cent of the workers coming from Catamarca, who had been the subject of an official study, returned from the *zafra* absolutely penniless.[54] However, the situation of these workers was even more desperate than that. The *contratistas* maintained a hold on their workers by arranging that they remained permanently indebted to them from year to year, so that they became more or less permanently attached to the *ingenios* in a type of debt bondage. Juan Solari described this practice as follows:

I have ... the pass-book [*libreta*] of a man who works all one year and who, by chance, as in almost all other cases has to return to the plantation the next year, even though he doesn't want to, since it so happens that he has a debt balance of 12.2 *pesos*, which allows the *contratista* to hold him subject, bound to work in the next harvest, for the next *zafra*.[55]

Integration and proletarianization

The integration of the highland peasantry of Jujuy and the peasantry of Catamarca into the national capitalist economy was accomplished by the creation of forms of labour recruitment which were extremely repressive and in some respects reminiscent of earlier colonial forms of labour recruitment. On the other hand they also differed in important respects, both with regard to their form and their intention, from the type of production relations which predominated during the colonial period and which were based entirely upon extra-economic coercion.

The repressive forms of production relations described in this paper were distinct from those characteristic of a feudal or any other kind of pre-capitalist economy. The *ingenios* were highly capitalized and technologically advanced enterprises, and their brutal methods of obtaining labour can hardly be blamed on a 'traditional mentality' or 'feudal outlook'. Indeed their behaviour appears to have been based on rational capitalistic criteria, as I shall now try to show.

It has already been pointed out that the sugar cane industry demanded very heavy inputs of seasonal labour during the six-month *zafra*. However, the expansion of the industry in Jujuy and Salta from 1880 onwards brought with it a rising demand for this type of seasonal labour. The highlands of Jujuy and Salta contained considerable numbers of potential labourers, but their attachment to the land as peasant producers presented a serious obstacle to their conversion into wage labourers. The principal desire of the Indian inhabitants of these areas was not to become salaried workers but to obtain the ownership of the lands they rented from the *latifundistas*[56] – a preference which was intensified by the Indians' traditional belief that the lands of the Puna and the Calchaquí Valley justly belonged to their own communities. In this situation the *ingenios* were faced with the necessity of *creating* a work force by coercion, and they accomplished this by monopolizing the lands on which the Indians lived and worked and using their political power to dragoon the population into working for them. To this extent the system was quite similar to the historical pattern of capitalist development in other parts of the world.[57] However one important difference from the classical pattern of proletarianization should be noted. The Indians were not totally 'divorced from the means of production' in the manner described by Marx.[58] They were permitted to remain on their lands on the condition that they worked in the plantations during the *zafra*. It is this pattern of labour services alternating with subsistence activity on their own lands which makes it tempting to interpret this sytem as a type of serfdom; however, it has already been indicated that such a conclusion would be misleading. The question we must ask is: Would it have served the *ingenios*' interests to completely expel the Indians from their lands and create a totally landless proletariat, as occurred, for example, in parts of Great Britain in the eighteenth and nineteenth centuries? The answer is probably 'no'. The type of labour force re-

quired by the *ingenios* had the following two very specific characteristics:
(1) it was to be employed for, at the most, only half the year;[59] and
(2) it needed to be on hand and ready to start production *en masse* at the
   precise time decided by the *ingenios*, since delays in harvesting could
   result in enormous losses once the sugar factories had commenced
   operation.

Under these conditions a completely landless proletariat would not
necessarily be the best kind of labour force. In particular there would
always be the risk that after the harvest season it would drift away to the
cities and fail to return the following year. In the last extremity, of
course, the *ingenios* could have paid the seasonal workers high enough
wages to maintain them for the rest of the year and thereby ensure their
loyalty to the sugar industry. However, a much more economical solution lay open to them at this time. By permitting the Indians to remain
on their own lands, the *ingenios* not only ensured that they would remain
in the area, ready for work when required, but also placed upon the
Indians the burden of supporting themselves throughout the 'dead
season' by their own subsistence activities.

Finally, the most important differences should be noted between the
production relations of the sugar industry in the 1930s and those of the
colonial *encomienda* in northern Argentina. The first difference is with
regard to the form and degree of the coercion practised by the *ingenios*
against the Indians. Whereas in the colonial *encomienda* and the *mita*
the coercion was designed to maintain a permanently unfree or servile
labour force, the compulsory labour services which were established after
1930 in the highlands of Jujuy were only binding upon those Indians
who, of their own volition, wished to remain living on the lands of the
Puna: they could, by moving away, legitimately free themselves at once
from the duty to work in the *zafra*. This opportunity did not exist for the
Indian who was subject to *servicios personales*, who could, if necessary, be
forcibly retained in the *encomienda*. In Jujuy in the 1930s the brutal
methods of labour recruitment constituted, on the other hand, the primary phase in the proletarianization of the Indian peasantry, a phase
which in other parts of the world has also frequently been accompanied
by a considerable degree of direct coercion. Secondly, it has been shown
that this proletarianization was only partial, in the sense that the Indians
were not completely divorced from the means of production; however, I
believe that this incomplete process of proletarianization is to be explained not by any 'feudal outlook' on the part of the *ingenio*-owners, but
by reference to the specific technological requirements of the sugar
industry, which created a pattern of demand for labour with extremely
heavy seasonal variations.

The same technological requirements determined the system of labour recruitment in Catamarca (and later in Bolivia), although in a somewhat different manner. As we have seen, in Catamarca there was no need for the *ingenios* to adopt measures to divorce the peasants from their means of production, since this had already occurred to a large extent with the impoverishment of the local economy. However, the problem still remained of maintaining a secure and reliable work force, which could be counted on to arrive *en masse* for the beginning of the *zafra*. In this case the solution adopted by the *ingenios* was the widespread use of the *contratista* system, which tied the peasants to the plantation system indirectly, via the labour contractors and the system of debt bondage which they employed.

Nevertheless, both in the case of the peasants of Catamarca and in that of the highland Indians of Jujuy, the events related constituted only the primary phase in their proletarianization. For the process to be fully completed it would be necessary for the coercive aspects of labour recruitment to disappear, being replaced by a more voluntary system of wage labour: this could only occur when wage levels and working conditions in the plantations were significantly improved. The completion of the process of proletarianization also required, however, that wage labour be provided to the peasants on a year-round basis, eventually eliminating their agricultural subsistence activities. The first of these conditions was to be largely fulfilled as a result of government intervention in the period from 1943 to 1955, but although the agricultural subsistence activities of the highland peasantry were to decline steadily in importance, the provision of all-year-round wage work to the Indians has so far remained unattainable.[60]

NOTES

1. This paper is an extended version of an essay previously published in David Rock (ed.), *Argentina in the twentieth century* (London, 1975). The research on which it is based was conducted under the guidance of Professor Miguel Murmis of the Centro de Investigaciones en Ciencias Sociales, Buenos Aires.
2. Eric Boman, *Antiquités de la région andine de la république Argentine et du désert d'Atacama*, 2 vols. (Paris, 1908), Vol. 2, p. 472.
3. Benjamín Villafañe, *El Irigoyenismo* (Jujuy, 1927), p. 30.
4. For political and administrative purposes Argentina is divided into provinces, which are in turn sub-divided into departments; these departments are further sub-divided into districts.
5. I was informed of these transactions in Santa Catalina by Srta Lucía Rueda, a retired schoolteacher and local historian, and by the School Inspector and Chief Census Officer of Santa Catalina, Sr Peñaloza.
6. Personal communication from Srta Rueda.

7. In some parts of the department, it should be mentioned, the *hacienda* continued to exist – for example, in the districts of La Ciénaga and El Angosto, where the Saravia family owned land.
8. Villafañe, *El Irigoyenismo*, p. 31.
9. See A. J. Buntig, 'El catolicismo popular en la Argentina', *Criterio* (Buenos Aires), November 1968 and January 1969.
10. Boman, *Antiquités de la région andine*, Vol. 1, p. 65.
11. Ibid., vol. 2, p. 577.
12. Ibid., vol. 2, p. 696.
13. Ibid., vol. 2, p. 472.
14. Ibid., vol. 2, p. 476.
15. Deputy Américo Ghioldi, *Diario de Sesiones*, Cámara de Diputados, 26 April 1932, p. 787.
16. Benjamín Villafañe, *La región de las parias* (Buenos Aires, 1934) p. 145.
17. *Estadística azucarera* no. 7 (Centro Azucarero Argentino, Buenos Aires, 1947).
18. Strictly speaking, Arrieta was not the 'owner' of the *ingenio* but the major shareholder in the company which owned it. However, the term 'owner' is used as a shorthand device in referring to the individuals mentioned in this section (Arrieta and Patrón Costas).
19. During this period the sugar oligarchy of Tucumán was also strongly represented in the national political power structure; Juan Simón Padros, owner of Ingenio Aguilares, was Deputy for the province from 1932 to 1936.
20. Benjamín Villafañe, *El asesinato de Rafael Tauler, perpetrado por las autoridades* (Buenos Aires, 1938) pp. 35–6.
21. See Villafañe, *El Irigoyenismo*, p. 31.
22. This was the company Pichetti, Pirquitas y Compañía Limitada, to which the following individuals belonged: Alberto Pichetti, Andrés Galinski, Pérez Alisedo (the Governor of Jujuy), and the brothers Walter and Stephen Leach (Villafañe, *El asesinato de Rafael Tauler*, p. 105). Walter and Stephen Leach were co-founders (with their four other brothers) of the firm Leach Hermanos which owned *Ingenio* La Esperanza, and they continued as major shareholders in the limited company Leach Argentine Estates. They were, as partners in the Pichetti, Pirquitas company, part-owners of the tin mines of Pirquitas in the Puna of Jujuy, and they also possessed asphalt mines in the department of San Pedro. Alberto Pichetti and Andrés Galinski, who also owned part of the Pirquitas tin mines, expanded into the sugar business in 1940 when they installed a new *ingenio*, Ingenio San Andrés, in the department of Santa Bárbara, Jujuy; however this does not appear to have been a successful venture, as the *ingenio* ceased operation after a few years.
23. See Senator Herminio Arrieta, *Diario de Sesiones*, Cámara de Senadores, 19 May 1938, pp. 125–39.
24. *Crítica* (Buenos Aires), 7 May 1942.
25. See the Congressional report of Deputy Juan Solari, *Trabajadores del norte argentino* (Buenos Aires, 1937), especially pp. 78–9.
26. Ibid., p. 77.
27. Nicolás González Iramaín, *Tres meses en Jujuy* (Buenos Aires, 1942), p. 142.
28. Since the late nineteenth century, the political influence of the sugar producers had enabled them to expand the industry far beyond the limits which were desirable for the national economy as a whole by massive tariff protection, export premiums to finance the disposal of surpluses, credits from the banking sector, and the pro-

vision of railway transport. In the 1930s, there was added to this list the provision of state-financed irrigation works in the provinces of Salta and Jujuy.

29. Benjamín Villafañe, *El atraso del interior* (Jujuy, 1926), p. 52.
30. Leopoldo Abán, 'Cruenta y larga lucha por la reinvindicación de la Puna', *Pregón* (Jujuy), 6 March 1970.
31. See I. D. Rutledge, 'Perón's little-known land reform', *Bulletin of the Society for Latin American Studies* no. 15 (October 1972), pp. 20–6.
32. See the *Diarios de Sesiones* of the Cámara de Senadores, debates of 10 August, 8 September, and 21 September 1949.
33. The statements of Peronist Senators might possibly be queried as being politically biased. However, there is no reason to believe this is the case with respect to the question at issue. Indeed, there is much complementary evidence to support their argument, including the report of González Iramaín (a Conservative) and the recent anthropological study of Yaví by Roberto Ringuelet and his associates (see note 36 below).
34. Senator Ernesto Bavio, *Diario de Sesiones*, Cámara de Senadores, 8 September 1949, p. 1660.
35. Senator Alberto Durand, ibid., 8 September 1949, p. 1661.
36. Much of the following description is drawn from Roberto Ringuelet, Guillermo Rubén, Carlos West Ocampo, and Mario Murias, 'Migración y organización social en Yaví' (unpublished thesis, Escuela de Antropología, Universidad Nacional de La Plata, 1970).
37. González Iramaín, *Tres meses en Jujuy*, p. 142.
38. Ibid., p. 134.
39. The use of armed overseers has been documented by Carmen Paula Muñoz, 'La desintegración de la comunidad chiriguana en el Ingenio San Martín del Tabacal' (mimeographed), Facultad de Filosofía y Letras, Universidad Nacional de Buenos Aires (Buenos Aires, 1964), p. 27.
40. See the remarks of Senator Ernesto Bavio, *Diario de Sesiones*, Cámara de Senadores, 8 September 1949, p. 1660.
41. 'Entre obreros cañeros y la policía hubo un tiroteo en Jujuy', *La Razón* (Buenos Aires), 22 June 1943.
42. 'Obtienen considerables mejoras los obreros de Ingenio La Esperanza', *La Razón* (Buenos Aires), 13 July 1943.
43. The *Censo nacional agropecuario* of 1937 gives the number of seasonal plantation workers in the department of Orán, Salta as 18,232, compared with a permanent labour force of 2,978. In my view the number of seasonal workers given here must be extremely inflated. As far as we know there were at this time no major differences in agricultural technology between this department (this is the department in which was situated *Ingenio San Martín*) and the others which might account for this extremely high proportion of seasonal workers. It is therefore concluded that the figure given in the census is in error. To obtain a more realistic estimate of the number of seasonal workers, an average ratio of seasonal workers to cultivated cane land has been calculated from the remaining three departments, and the number of hectares cultivated in cane in the department of Orán has then been multiplied by this factor, giving a seasonal plantation labour force of 5,483, which seems much more reasonable.
44. In 1937, *Ingenio* San Martín del Tabacal, had 7,616 hectares in cane; Ledesma, 6,129; La Esperanza, 4,740; Río Grande, 1,919; and San Isidro, 1,744 (*Estadística*

azucarera no. 7, 1945). These are the figures for the area cultivated with cane. Strictly speaking, my argument requires data for the area *harvested*, which are not available. However, I believe there would be little difference between the two sets of figures, since climatic conditions in northwest Argentina do not as a rule allow cane to be left over the winter period without being cut, or the harvest to be staggered as occurs in Peru and in parts of Colombia (see the article by Michael Taussig, p. 404 below).

45. Senator Ernesto Bavio, *Diario de Sesiones*, Cámara de Senadores, 8 September 1940, p. 1660.
46. Senator Alberto Durand, ibid., 8 September 1940, p. 1661.
47. Solari, *Trabajadores del norte argentino*, p. 80.
48. Avila Echazú, 'Las migraciones de braceros bolivianos a la Argentina', *Mundo Nuevo* no. 30 (Paris, 1968), p. 28.
49. The ex-manager of the *lote* La Ciénaga of *Ingenio* La Esperanza, Sr P.H., informed the writer that the Matacos and Tobas were poor workers. They were 'lazy' and 'dirty'. Other sources refer to their habit of eating large amounts of the cane they cut.
50. The *ingenios* of Tucumán employed workers mainly from Tucumán, Santiago del Estero, and Catamarca.
51. '*Conchabador*' is another name for '*contratista*'.
52. Solari, *Trabajadores del norte argentino*, pp. 78–9.
53. Alfredo Palacios, *Pueblos desamparados* (Buenos Aires, 1944), p. 122.
54. Palacios, *Pueblos desamparados*, p. 122.
55. Solari, *Trabajadores del norte argentino*, p. 119.
56. Villafañe, *El Irigoyenismo*, p. 31.
57. See, for example, Giovanni Arrighi, 'Labour supplies in historical perspective: a study of the proletarianization of the African peasantry in Rhodesia', *Journal of Development Studies* VI, 3 (1970).
58. Karl Marx, *Capital* (London, 1970), vol. 1, chap. 26, pp. 713–16.
59. I am speaking here of the majority of the labour force; there were, of course, some permanent workers.
60. This subject is dealt with at length in I. D. Rutledge, 'Agrarian change and integration in an interior province of Argentina: a sociological and historical study of Jujuy, c.1550–1960' (unpublished Ph.D. thesis, Faculty of Economics and Politics, University of Cambridge, 1973). A brief discussion of the events of 1943–55 in northern Argentina can be found in Rutledge, 'Perón's little-known land reform', pp. 20–6.

CHAPTER 9

The social and economic consequences of modernization in the Peruvian sugar industry, 1870–1930

PETER F. KLARÉN[1]

In the late nineteenth and early twentieth centuries, Peru – not unlike other Latin American countries – saw a large segment of its economic structure converted into a modern, export-oriented agro-industrial complex, designed to fill the basic raw-material needs of the rapidly industrializing nations of the northern hemisphere. Although Peru did not have a Porfirio Díaz to speed this process along, it nevertheless counted on a *'científico'*-like Civilist Party, which steered an economic course rather similar in its broad outlines to the Porfiriato in Mexico. Moreover, Peru, like Mexico, had experienced the economic ravages of a recent foreign occupation, which made it equally vulnerable to the penetration of foreign capital. With its economy languishing in ruins from the Chilean occupation, the nation's entrepreneurial class believed that Peru had little choice but to open its doors and seek out the investment capital that was already accumulating in the north.

And if the time to receive foreign capital in the Latin American periphery seemed right to the ruling class, it was equally propitious from the standpoint of the European and North American metropolis where a second industrial revolution was propelling businessmen abroad in search of markets and raw materials. The upshot for Peru was an ever-increasing flow of foreign investment capital between 1890 and 1930. By 1913 British investments in Peru stood at a high-water mark of $166,000,000 – a figure that was soon surpassed by American capital, which rose from a modest $6,000,000 in 1897 to $63,000,000 in 1914, and again to $200,000,000 in 1930.[2] This Anglo-American investment capital gradually carved out the export enclaves in sugar, cotton, copper, oil, and other raw materials which today are familiar features of the Peruvian economic landscape.

As the export complex grew, other sectors of the economy also spurted ahead. During the early regimes of the 'Aristocratic Republic' (1895–1919), banks, factories, and trading houses, in the main foreign-owned or -controlled, proliferated not only in Lima but also in the major coastal commercial centres of Piura, Chiclayo, Trujillo, and Ica. At the same time, funds became available to undertake much-needed urban infra-

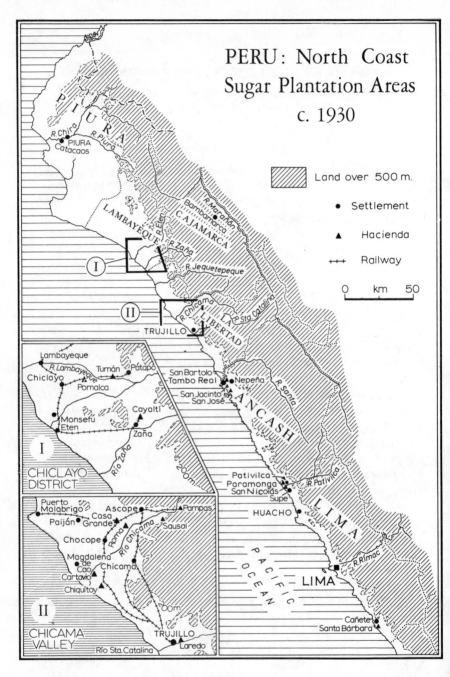

PERU: North Coast Sugar Plantation Areas c. 1930

Land over 500 m.

● Settlement

▲ Hacienda

+++ Railway

0   km   50

PIURA
R.Chira
PIURA
Catacaos
R.Piura
LAMBAYEQUE
R.Eten
R.Zaña
CAJAMARCA
Bambamarca
R.Marañón
R.Jequetepeque
R.Chicama
R.Sta.Catalina
LA LIBERTAD
TRUJILLO
R.Santa
ANCASH
R.Pativilca
Pativilca
Paramonga
San Nicolás
Supe
HUACHO
LIMA
R.Rímac
LIMA
PACIFIC OCEAN
Cañete
Santa Bárbara

I — CHICLAYO DISTRICT

Lambayeque
R.Lambayeque
Tumán
Pátapo
Chiclayo
Pomalca
San Bartolo
Tambo Real
Nepeña
San Jacinto
San José
Cayaltí
Monsefú
Eten
Zaña
Río Zaña
200m.

II — CHICAMA VALLEY

Puerto Malabrigo
Ascope
Pampas
Casa Grande
Paiján
Chocope
Roma
Río Chicama
Sausal
Magdalena de Cao
Chicama
Cartavio
Chiquitoy
300m.
TRUJILLO
CHICAMA VALLEY
Río Sta.Catalina
Laredo

Map 15

structural improvements such as electrification, sewage disposal, and transportation.[3] As in Mexico, these developments signalled the appearance in Peru of modern industrial capitalism, adapted and shaped as it was to fit the traditional export framework which had been the hallmark and destiny of this Andean nation since the colonial days.

Yet while export capitalism began to take root during this period, particularly along the coast, it produced in the process some sharp socioeconomic changes and dislocations which seriously disrupted and altered the traditional fabric of Peruvian society. In the cotton-growing departments of Lima, Piura, and particularly Ica, the introduction of modern methods and machinery set in motion a process of land consolidation which displaced and proletarianized many formerly small, prosperous, and independent farmers. Likewise, in the mining areas of the central and northern Sierra large foreign companies, abundantly wealthy in technological skill and capital, absorbed countless small and medium-sized mining enterprises.[4] Moreover, in both areas a new rural wage proletariat gradually emerged to provide the needed labour for these export industries, a fact that with the passage of time had some major political ramifications. Nowhere was this process of dislocation and change more evident, however, than in the broad, fertile river valleys of the north coast, where an expanding sugar industry was beginning to radically alter the traditional man–land relationships.

The process of land concentration on the north coast

Sugar-planting had been an economic mainstay of coastal agriculture ever since the Spaniards first settled the northern city of Trujillo in the early sixteenth century. Finding the hot, temperate climate of the coast ideal for the growth of sugar cane, the industry took root and flourished throughout much of the colonial period and well into the early years of the Republic. It was not, however, until the economic boom of the 1860s and 1870s that the industry began to cast off its traditional form and take on a modern shape.

Stimulated by rising demand from France and England at a time when the introduction of the steamship opened up the possibilities of low-cost transportation to Western markets, the industry expanded rapidly, particularly during the 1860s. Large amounts of capital generated by the spectacular *guano* boom of that period enabled the industry to increase production and begin the costly construction of a modern exporting infrastructure of railways and port facilities.[5] As early as 1861, the plantations Facalá in the Chicama Valley, Pátapo in Lambayeque, and

Pabur in Piura had introduced the steam engine into their refineries, and already railways on a small scale serviced the Trujillo region as well as the Jequetepeque, Zaña and Lambayeque Valleys to the north. The payment of cash indemnities to planters by the state, in compensation for the manumission of slaves by Ramón Castillo in 1854, served also to shore up a floundering labour market through the massive importation of Chinese indentured labour. At the same time a new group of entrepreneurs, some drawn from the *guano* boom but others consisting of engineers and technicians who had managed many of the old *haciendas*, began to take over the direction of the industry.

A further impulse in this direction was provided by the anti-clerical reaction of the late 1850s. A century after the Jesuit order had been forced by the Crown to abandon the old Lambayeque sugar plantation Tumán in 1767, a new wave of anti-clericalism forced in the Church to give up more of its prime sugar lands of the north coast. Indeed, after 1857 the heart of the Lambayeque, Zaña, and Santa Catalina valleys, which had been in the hands of the convents since the early colonial period, passed into the hands of more dynamic elements in the region. The beneficiaries of this liberal, anti-Church legislation were the brash parvenus of the *guano* boom, whom the old families (in a double allusion to the origins of their fortunes as well as to their social origins) disparagingly dubbed with the sobriquet '*salido del guano*'.[6]

If the flowering of a modern sugar industry took place during the 1860s, it was suddenly and rudely cut short by a series of shocks commencing with the financial panic of 1873. That blow, which was precipitated by the collapse of the *guano* industry, left most coastal planters grossly over-extended and precariously tottering on the edge of financial ruin. The industry struggled along for the next five years, barely remaining solvent, only to be crippled again by the sudden outbreak of the War of the Pacific in 1879. The invading Chilean armies, under the able but ruthless General Lynch, put numerous coastal plantations to the torch, bringing the industry to a virtual standstill by 1883, when peace was finally achieved.

The post-war years were marked by gradual recovery and a resumption in the industry's slow march towards modernization, and by the mid-1890s some major changes could be perceived. Foremost among these was a marked shift in the capital structure of the industry. The pre-war expansion had been largely financed from national sources, primarily funds generated by the *guano* boom. Left virtually bankrupt by the war, the sugar industry, like the Peruvian economy, was in a highly vulnerable position to the penetration of foreign capital. And it was precisely upon the foundations of foreign capital that the industry was rebuilt after the war.

This new capital structure was first reflected in the sharp trend towards consolidation in the landholding system, as most of the medium-sized pre-war *haciendas* were combined and merged into vastly larger and increasingly industrially organized estates. This process of concentration could be traced to the failure of many planters to survive the financial disasters of the war, when domestic sources of capital all but dried up.[7] Their demise was accompanied by the intrusion of a new generation of entrepreneurs, mostly foreigners or nationals backed by foreign capital, who began to rebuild, re-organize, and generally modernize the industry in the post-war decades.

Perhaps the classic example of the displacement of the former planter elite by this intruding group of foreign entrepreneurs, and the concomitant tendency towards concentration and consolidation of the landholding system, occurred in the Trujillo region.[8] There a trio of newcomers headed by the German immigrant Gildemeister began to operate in the nearby Chicama Valley. Something of a Peruvian version of Horatio Alger, Gildemeister had migrated to Peru from Bremen (via Brazil and Chile) in the 1840s and subsequently acquired a fortune in the nitrate industry. Later, foreseeing hard times for the then-burgeoning industry, he disposed of his holdings in Iquique to a British firm for some £1,000,000 sterling and began to invest heavily in land acquisitions in the Chicama Valley. Between 1888 and the turn of the century, a period of general revival and recovery of the post-war economy, Gildemeister acquired eight plantations in the valley, including Casa Grande, which became the nucleus of his growing sugar empire.[9]

Gildemeister's actions were paralleled in the Chicama Valley by the immigrant Larco family and the Grace Company, all of whom contributed markedly to the concentration of land which accelerated rapidly over the next several decades as old plantations and small farms were absorbed and consolidated into larger and more efficient economic units. By the advent of the First World War, sugar-growing was well on its way to becoming a big, corporately organized business in which the small and medium-sized independent producers were increasingly considered to be inefficient and anachronistic. The upshot was a complete transformation in the traditional landholding pattern of the Valley, as virtually all of the old plantations came to be owned by three corporate giants: Casa Grande (Gildemeister, *c.* 4,700 hectares), Roma (Larco, *c.* 4,000 hectares), and Cartavio (Grace, *c.* 1,400 hectares).[10] This process was accelerated when in 1927, in an enormous land transaction which made Casa Grande by far the largest sugar plantation in Peru, the Roma estate was purchased by the Gildemeisters for some 13,000,000 Peruvian *soles*.

Similar tendencies, which saw certain core *haciendas* annexing adjacent and contiguous estates, were occurring in virtually every major sugar-growing valley along the coast. In the smaller adjacent Santa Catalina Valley, for example, the planter José Ignacio Chopitea, beginning with the 570-hectare *hacienda* at Laredo in the 1880s, came to dominate the landholdings of the Valley in 1921, having increased his estate some sixfold to over 3,700 hectares.[11] In the neighbouring department of Lambayeque, estate consolidation was somewhat less violent and precipitous in that the drive towards a sugar monoculture never reached the proportions which it did in La Libertad. Moreover, foreigners did not directly manage and control the process of expansion there to the extent that they did in La Libertad, although foreign capital from certain trading houses (Henry Kendall and Sons, for example, in the case of Cayalti) played as significant a role as in Chicama. Nevertheless, the department's main sugar *haciendas*, Cayaltí, Tumán, and Pomalca, more or less doubled in size between 1900 and 1925, by which time they comprised 3,750, 3,700, and 1,400 hectares respectively.[12] Further to the south, other core *haciendas* such as Tambo Real, San Jacinto, Paramonga, and San Nicolás followed a similar pattern of expansion and annexation, and like their counterparts in Chicama and Lambayeque they came to dominate much of the post-war landholding structure of the north coast.

Mechanization and plant modernization

Along with the concentration of land the industry also began to undergo considerable change in the growing, processing, and marketing of sugar cane during the post-war decades. In the production sector, for example, mechanization, which had occurred on some estates as early as the 1860s, gradually made inroads during the 1890s with more widespread use of the steam plough and a variety of modern cultivators, rakes, and other farm implements. Nevertheless, a leading agriculturalist reported the following reaction of a correspondent for the *Times* newspaper after he had toured the plantations of the north coast in 1894:

[He] expressed his complete surprise at the thoroughly backward state in which he found the area's sugar mills. He went on to say that these *ingenios*, except for a few, had not been altered in over 25 years, despite numerous innovations that had been made during this time in Europe. He concluded that the general agricultural progress realized in the last quarter of a century in other parts of the world has seemingly not reached Peru.[13]

An agricultural census taken in Lambayeque around the turn of the century tended to confirm this view. The ox-drawn plough continued to predominate, as it always had, on the main estates of the department. Two decades later, however, the same plantations were reporting a substantial increase not only in the number of modern farm implements like the Collins rake, but also the widespread use of the Fowler steam plough. Further to the south, in the Huacho Valley, some thirty Fowler steam ploughs were reported in operation in 1925 on one estate.[14]

The pace of mechanization, particularly in the processing sector, seems to have accelerated markedly during the years 1910 to 1920. Modern sugar mills with vastly increased capacities gradually began to replace the antiquated *ingenios*, which in several cases pre-dated the Chilean occupation. The largest and most costly of the new mills was installed at Casa Grande in 1910, with a milling capacity of some 3,000 tons of cane daily, an unheard-of figure for the day. By comparison the relatively modern mill at Tumán in 1905 had a daily capacity of only slightly more than 50 tons. Several other new or renovated mills sprang up on other estates during the sugar boom generated by the First World War, as plantations ploughed back some of their profits into plant modernization and expansion. Such was the case, for example, at Pomalca, where a brand-new steam-driven McNeil mill from England, with a daily capacity of 840 tons, was installed in 1917.[15]

A major consequence of the appearance of these large new mills was the concomitant disappearance of many of the old-fashioned and outdated *ingenios* from the smaller coastal estates. For with the construction of high-capacity, centrally located mills and the simultaneous merging of smaller *haciendas* into the new industrial plantation, old mill equipment quickly fell into obsolescence and was abandoned. This tendency, along with the general concentration within the industry, is graphically illustrated in the sharp drop in the number of coastal sugar mills from sixty-two in 1900 to only thirty-three in 1929.[16] Moreover, the appearance of the new centralized mills had the effect of accelerating the demise of the smaller producers by forcing them to mill their cane at the big *ingenios*, where prices could be controlled and arbitrarily raised.

Milling and marketing were also greatly streamlined by the construction of an extensive transportation infrastructure, ranging from plantation railways and auxiliary cart roads to modern dock and port facilities. Pomalca, which began modestly installing a rail system of only a few kilometres in the late nineteenth century, was perhaps typical of many of the emerging industrial estates. At the turn of the century the plantation boasted thirteen kilometres of fixed track and some 160 Koppel cane-loading cars, while some twenty years later the length of fixed track had tripled and the number of cars had doubled.[17] During the same time the Eten Railway, begun in the 1870s, was extended in order to connect the plantation with the port.

When it came to modern port facilities, the Gildemeisters at Casa Grande proved to be the greatest innovators. In 1916 they successfully petitioned the national government for permission to rehabilitate the nearby port of Malabrigo. When renovation was completed a year later, the port greatly facilitated the trans-shipment of sugar to world markets as well as the importation of general merchandise and machinery for the company's ever-expanding complex of plantations. The new port, along with a modern railway line installed earlier, virtually completed the process of vertical integration, a concept that the Gildemeisters, as well as the Larcos, Aspíllaga Andersons, and others, had assiduously promoted since the turn of the century. One observer, describing the results of this policy in 1917, wrote: 'The [coastal] plantations are now complete units: that is to say, they produce their own cane, process it in their factories, and transport it by their own railways or road system to their own ports for trans-shipment to market. They thus control the production of cane from planting to final sale abroad.'[18]

On the matter of marketing this last statement was true enough, although in need of qualification. Sales and marketing had, in fact, been taken over by the major foreign trading houses and contractors who had provided the capital for plant modernization and consolidation after the war with Chile. During this early period of reorganization virtually every major estate was closely connected with some foreign banking or trading concern – the Aspíllaga Andersons at Cayaltí with Henry Kendall and Sons, the Larcos at Roma with Graham, Rowe and Company, and the Gildemeisters at Casa Grande with Gildemeister and Company in Lima, to name only a few. Each contractor, according to the general practice of trading companies of the day, provided the necessary capital to expand or streamline estate production while acting as brokers and agents for the marketing and transporting of sugar to Liverpool, Genoa, Bremen, or Stockholm.

Significantly, however, some of these houses, foreshadowing the development of the modern corporation, began to take over the production stage of the industry by directly purchasing plantations, thereby not only completing the cycle of vertical integration but also further concentrating the industry in foreign hands. This was the case with the Grace brothers, who had operated in Peru as a trading house since the mid nineteenth century. With the purchase of Cartavio (1892) and later

Paramonga (1927), Grace expanded its heretofore exclusively trading operation into manufacturing and production.[19] The Gildemeisters followed this same pattern when they directly merged Casa Grande in 1908 into their growing commercial empire, which was linked to the family business in Bremen. In contrast, other trading houses such as Kendall and Sons and Graham, Rowe and Company elected to continue operating in the more traditional pattern, leaving the production stage essentially in the hands of their Peruvian clients.[20]

The period of technical and territorial consolidation which was the hallmark of the industry from 1890 to 1920 also revealed a marked tendency towards the constitution of *Sociedades Anónimas*. Prior to the war with Chile, most plantations had been operated by a single entrepreneur or patriarch. After the war and well into the twentieth century, these patriarchal enterprises were increasingly reorganized into family firms, with each member of the patriarch's family receiving a number of shares and votes in the business.[21] The sons and heirs of the patriarch were sent to study agronomy either abroad or at the National School of Agriculture (Escuela Nacional de Agricultura), which was founded in 1901. Returning to the plantation after graduation, they filled the key technical and managerial positions of the business while bringing their newly acquired expertise to bear on the further modernization of their estates.[22] Both the Aspíllaga Andersons at Cayaltí and later the de la Piedras at Pomalca were good examples of this new *modus operandi* in the industry. However, for such a style of organization to succeed, a closely knit family unit was a crucial factor, something which the Larco family in the Chicama Valley was unable to achieve.

In an organizational and technological sense the industry was in an excellent position to exploit the new demands for sugar created by the outbreak of the First World War. Until then sugar production had generally maintained a steady rhythm of expansion, punctuated by occasional oscillations due to over-production and lower prices on the world market. However, with the advent of war in Europe the Peruvian sugar industry, like other raw-material producers throughout Latin America, experienced a new era of boom. From 1914 to 1919, acreage devoted to cane cultivation rose some 20 per cent, exports climbed by one-third (from 177,000 to 272,000 tons), while income and profits soared (from 12,000,000 to 41,000,000 dollars), as the scarcity occasioned by the war caused prices on the world market to soar[23] (see Table 38).

Windfall profits such as these further enabled the major estates to accelerate the process of mechanization and plant modernization. However, the most modern estates (as indicated by per-acre yields in 1918) continued to be located in the Trujillo region, followed at some distance

TABLE 38   *Peruvian sugar exports, 1877–1940*

	Tons (thousands)	Market price (U.S. dollars per lb)	Value (thousands of U.S. dollars)	Value of total exports (thousands of U.S. dollars)	Sugar as a percentage of total exports
1877	47,495	—	—	—	—
1887	39,233	—	2,620	11,956	21.9
1891	37,140	—	4,290	16,431	26.1
1892	59,749	—	7,603	22,561	22.7
1897	105,463	—	4,211	12,897	32.7
1898	105,713	—	4,613	15,128	30.5
1899	103,707	—	5,052	15,363	32.9
1900	112,223	—	7,279	22,485	32.4
1901	114,637	—	5,152	21,594	23.4
1902	117,362	—	6,199	18,520	34.7
1903	127,673	—	5,155	19,289	26.7
1904	131,958	—	5,043	20,333	24.8
1905	134,234	—	9,168	28,787	31.8
1906	136,729	—	7,076	28,480	24.8
1907	110,615	—	4,126	28,723	14.4
1908	124,892	—	5,241	27,395	19.1
1909	125,352	—	5,800	32,464	17.9
1910	122,856	—	6,947	35,371	19.6
1911	125,292	—	7,333	37,110	19.8
1912	149,189	—	7,034	47,193	14.9
1913	142,902	2.16	7,064	45,686	15.5
1914	176,671	2.83	12,466	41,340	23.0
1915	220,258	3.59	12,593	48,737	25.8
1916	239,010	4.78	19,179	79,728	24.0
1917	212,040	5.22	20,555	93,031	23.1
1918	197,988	5.49	21,939	105,256	20.8
1919	272,099	6.65	40,890	132,345	23.1
1920	249,963	11.35	57,228	162,046	35.3
1921	239,356	3.36	17,960	59,978	29.9
1922	274,378	—	18,697	72,155	25.9
1923	282,492	—	28,380	98,439	28.8
1924	265,509	—	21,732	101,713	21.4
1925	208,140	2.56	10,331	87,437	11.8
1926	331,068	—	17,283	89,190	19.3
1927	300,432	2.95	17,146	116,367	14.7
1928	305,970	—	14,552	126,075	11.5
1929	363,380	1.99	12,351	134,032	9.2
1930	338,784	—	12,461	114,689	10.9
1931	330,211	—	11,106	78,967	14.1
1932	325,132	0.75	7,273	49,988	14.5
1933	366,632	0.80	7,894	59,873	12.3

TABLE 38 *continued*

Tons (thousands)	Market price (U.S. dollars per lb).	Value (thousands of U.S. dollars)	Value of total exports (thousands of U.S. dollars)	Sugar as a percentage of total exports
1934 319,959	—	7,461	85,426	8.7
1935 337,537	—	7,207	86,499	8.2
1936 339,700	—	7,063	94,028	7.5
1937 328,094	—	8,944	102,323	8.7
1938 260,182	—	11,891	162,169	7.3
1939 276,574	—	19,479	180,794	10.8
1940 309,094	—	20,729	192,256	10.8

Sources: Computed from *Extracto estadístico del Perú: 1940* (Lima, 1940), pp. 300, 308–9, converted into U.S. dollars at annual exchange rate, except 'Market price' column, which is taken from Gianfranco Bardella, *Setenta y cinco años de vida económica del Perú, 1889–1964* (Lima, 1964), pp. 115, 135.

by those located in the Lambayeque, Zaña, and Pativilca Valleys, with the Santa Catalina and Carabayllo Valleys showing the lowest yields. At the same time the industry became increasingly concentrated in the climatically more suitable north coast, particularly as sugar gave way to cotton in the department of Lima. This drive towards a sugar monoculture in the north, however, also tended to sharply reduce acreage for the production of food staples (down from 22 per cent in 1913 to 19 per cent in 1919), thereby driving up food costs throughout the region and compelling the government to require that each estate devote a minimum percentage of its cultivable land to staple cultivation.

The dispossession of the small sugar producers

The war years also saw the culmination of still another major social process which had begun around the turn of the century. For the tendency towards the concentration of land was not confined in its effects to the pre-war planter elite but also reached down into the ranks of small independent farmers. Traditionally these farmers (*agricultores*), part of a sizeable rural middle class, had cultivated small plots of land in and around the region's urban centres. Providing food staples for the population of the towns and plantations of the area, they constituted a stable and prosperous element of north coast society. However, as the sugar industry was revived and transformed after the war with Chile, this landed group also fell victim to the inexorable drive of the new industrial plantations to gain control of all existing water and land.[24] Indeed land acquisitions became essential not only for the general expansion of their sugar crop but, more importantly, as a source of water and cheap labour, both of which were vital factors in the sugar equation.

The dispossession of small farmers was particularly acute in the Trujillo region, where the process of concentration and consolidation reached extreme proportions. There several small farming communities such as Chocope, Paiján, Magdalena de Cao, Ascope, and others were virtually destroyed by the steady encroachment of the emerging industrial plantations of Casa Grande, Roma, and Cartavio. The same pattern of urban dislocation appears to have been equally severe in other sugar valleys of the coast. For example, the United States Commercial Attaché in Lima, who published a most thorough commercial survey for the coast from extensive personal field trips, wrote in 1925 that the industrial estates of San Nicolás and Paramonga had virtually destroyed the independent life of the adjacent towns of Supe and Pativilca. Likewise, he reported that the village of San Bartolo near the plantation of Tambo Real 'was now completely decadent',[25] and from his description of Nepeña the same process seemed to have occurred in the vicinity of the estates of San Jacinto and San José. A similar fate appears to have afflicted several of the towns and villages near Chiclayo. Thus, a review of the archives of the sugar estate of Cayaltí reveals a long and often bitter conflict, especially acute during the years 1912 to 1915, between the villagers of Zaña and the Aspíllaga Andersons over the plantation's encroachments on to local lands.[26]

This process of urban dislocation produced a classical case of the general proletarianization of a formerly landed sector of north coast society. For, deprived of their lands, the region's small farmers were in many cases forced to seek employment on the area's large sugar plantations. From independent farmers they therefore dropped into the ranks of landless wage-earners, ironically dependent for their existence on those who had usurped their lands. Full of resentment against the emergent sugar companies, they contributed to the creation of an explosive social climate throughout the region, which ultimately found its political expression in the rise of the Aprista movement in the 1930s.[27]

Systems of plantation labour organization

While the expansion of the sugar industry deeply altered the landholding structure of the north coast, it also produced some far-reaching changes in the traditional social fabric of the region. Responding to a critical shortage of labour in the emerging industry, planters began, shortly after the War of the Pacific, to devise some new systems of labour recruitment. Traditionally planters had relied first upon Negro slaves, who were finally emancipated in spite of strong opposition in 1854, and then on Chinese indentured coolies, the supply of which was abruptly cut off in 1874.[28] While some planters continued to press for a renewal of imported indentured labourers from the Orient (indentured Japanese labour still formed one-third of Tumán's labour force in 1900), the new planters generally tended to settle upon a two-track labour system which it was hoped would solve the chronic shortage of estate workers on the coast.

One solution was to try to attract labourers from nearby towns and villages through a free wage system. Since planters were producing an increasingly valuable cash crop for which they received, in the main, hard foreign currencies in return, they could afford to set domestic wages at a relatively attractive rate in comparison with other enterprises and thereby hope to attract a large proportion of the region's potential work force.[29] In addition, the sudden expansion of the industrial estate towards the end of the century, which as has been seen occurred at the expense of nearby farming villages, tended to eliminate or sharply reduce independent farming opportunites and, in the subsequent proletarianization process, to produce a ready-made supply of labour for the industrializing estates.

This appears to have been the case in the towns and villages of Lambayeque, from which most of the sugar estates were drawing at least part of their labour supply by the turn of the century. At both Pomalca and Tumán, for example, an apparently large number of *libres* in a work force of 400 were wage recruits from nearby villages, while Cayaltí drew some of its 600 workers from nearby Zaña. Further to the south, most of the 1,000 inhabitants of the village of Supe cultivated small tracts of land in the adjacent *campiña* and worked on the San Nicolás sugar estate. Similarly, by the 1920s it was reported that the nucleus of the village of Pativilca had been virtually absorbed into the plantation of Paramonga, where most of its inhabitants supplemented their modest farming income with work on the plantation.[30]

The symbiotic relationship between town and plantation over labour, which led to the town's dependence and ultimate demise as an independent entity, did not however solve the labour problem for the expanding plantation. Some wage labourers had always been recruited from the area's villages even before the Chilean occupation, and even though their numbers increased in the post-war years, they were insufficient to fill the void left by Negro slaves or Chinese indentured labour. The only viable alternative was to turn to the large mass of Indians who resided in villages in the nearby Sierra. Although such a solution had been urged for some time, planters had been generally slow to respond to its possibilities. This was in part due to the widely held view that Indian labour was inferior to that of blacks, *cholos*, and orientals. Such an attitude reflected the commonly held racial prejudices of planters and other *costeños* towards the Indian population, a view reinforced by the cultural disparity between essentially westernized slaves or indentured labour and non-western Indians. However, although Indians were not considered good workers, planters nevertheless began to look increasingly towards the Sierra, adopting for recruitment purposes the system of *enganche*.

Although little studied, the *enganche* system appears to have been a modernized version of some more traditional forms of labour recruitment which had been employed both on the coast and in the highlands since colonial times. Its roots in the highlands seem to go back to the post-Conquest Spanish perversion of the Inca *mita* system, in which Indians voluntarily gave their labour at certain times of the year for what they perceived to be the common good of the community. The Spaniards in practice subverted the idea by converting the essentially benevolent *mita* into a vehicle not for the public good but rather for the private gain of the new overlords. Thus, Indians were brutally uprooted and forced into labour in the mines as well as for private agricultural enterprises, thereby becoming thoroughly alienated from their traditional attitudes towards work.

However, if the *enganche* seemed outwardly at least to embody some of the coercive features of the *mita* as practised by the Spaniards, other coastal labour forms, particularly chattel slavery and indenture, also seem to have contributed significantly to its evolution. In many ways, for example, the *enganche* was an outgrowth of indenture, particularly in its emphasis upon the temporary nature of the labourer's work commitment and the possibility of purchasing one's way out of bondage and thereby returning to the status of a freedman. At the same time the debt-peonage features of the *enganche* embodied certain elements of the slave system, in that it could, theoretically at least, immobilize the labourer for long periods of time, even if in practice it rarely did.

In the end, however, the *enganche* tended to mirror the evolving capitalist system of the coast by combining elements of both modern, monetary incentives and more traditional forms of outright coercion in order to lure and prod the Indian out of his isolated and secure mountain redoubt.[31] Depending on the size of the cash advance offered by the *enganchador* or labour contractor, the Indian peasant agreed to come to work for a stipulated period of time ranging from three months to two years, the time it might take to pay back his original debt from his wages. Around the turn of the century wages in Lambayeque ranged from 80 *centavos* to 1 *sol* per day or per task (*tarea*).[32] Until he repaid that debt, with interest, as well as any additional charges contracted at the plantation store, he remained legally bound to the plantation in debt peonage.

This monetary advance and the promise of future wages offered by the *enganchador* was clearly useful and appealing to the peasant who lived within a still limited monetary environment, but who needed cash to purchase seed, tools, and the like. Still, the fact that many early *enganchadores* were local political authorities – including mayors, police officials, or even (as in one known case) a priest – indicated that, early on, the system was based far more on a mix of physical force and moral persuasion and manipulation than on money incentives. Coercion was also readily apparent from the variety of tricks and unsavoury methods used by contractors to induce illiterate peasants to sign contracts which they could not read, as well as from the high number of *braceros* who, once contracted, tried to escape from their new bondage by fleeing the plantation.

Later on, when the peasant had been brought into more active inter-action on the coast with the capitalist system and, conversely, when that system had penetrated and become more diffused in the Sierra after his frequent returns, monetary incentives probably took on a greater significance. In fact, the 1909 law prohibiting local authorities from engaging in the *enganche* may simply have been a confirmation that force was becoming somewhat less necessary, as a money economy became more deeply rooted in the villages of the Sierra where *braceros* were recruited. Indeed, within another decade or so, particularly after better roads began to link the coast with the highlands during the *Oncenio* (1919 to 1930), the money economy had penetrated the Sierra peasant culture to the extent that an increasing number of *libres* were responding directly to the free wage mechanism and voluntarily coming down to work on the plantations. Even then, however, until the world-wide depression of the 1930s effectively ended the labour shortage within the industry, the *enganche* remained a central feature of the plantations' recruiting methods (see Table 39).

Most of the major plantations established working arrangements with contractors who had offices in the nearby Sierra. Cayaltí, for example,

TABLE 39 Number of workers, hours of labour, and wages in the Peruvian sugar industry, 1912–36

	Number of workers				Average hours of work per day		Average wage (without rations) (S/.)		
	Field hands		Ingenio	Total	In the fields	Ingenio	Field hands		Ingenio
	Men	Women	Men				Men	Women	Men
1912	19,296	649	?	19,945	8.8	?	1.25	0.84	?
1913	20,393	549	?	20,942	8.8	?	1.27	0.74	?
1914	21,154	727	?	21,881	9.0	?	1.23	0.82	?
1915	19,782	855	3,796	24,433	9.24	11.30	1.27	0.76	1.46
1916	18,576	999	3,890	23,456	9.22	10.48	1.09	1.06	1.35
1917	18,233	1,053	3,549	22,835	8.30	10.18	1.44	1.13	1.67
1918	18,233	1,229	4,415	25,081	8.14	10.00	1.59	0.99	1.92
1919	19,437	1,824	4,241	27,036	8.33	11.00	1.91	1.13	2.39
1920	20,971	1,120	4,840	28,860	8.8	9.31	1.83	1.00	2.22
1921	22,900	1,071	4,472	27,746	7.20	9.20	1.82	1.04	2.22
1922	22,203	904	4,688	28,938	7.59	9.44	1.75	0.99	2.24
1923	23,346	999	4,636	29,279	7.45	8.39	1.84	1.05	2.35
1924	23,644	795	4,490	30,051	7.45	8.32	1.84	1.12	2.38
1925	24,766	1,313	4,664	30,159	7.56	8.55	1.81	1.05	2.36
1926	24,182	1,173	4,667	28,207	7.57	9.35	1.67	0.98	2.43
1927	22,367	1,030	4,652	29,490	8.0	8.58	1.72	1.04	2.32
1928	23,808	1,044	4,419	30,151	8.16	8.28	1.75	1.09	2.41
1929[a]	24,688	—	—	—	—	—	—	—	—
1930[a]	—	—	—	—	—	—	—	—	—
1931	19,935	530	4,181	24,646	8.0	8.0	1.76	1.01	2.21
1932	19,990	516	4,054	24,560	8.0	8.0	1.50	0.91	1.84
1933	23,408	592	4,294	28,294	8.0	8.0	1.77	0.81	2.02
1934	23,110	601	3,836	27,547	8.0	8.0	1.72	0.82	2.14
1935	22,259	647	3,826	26,732	8.0	8.0	1.78	0.82	2.15
1936	19,898	556	4,006	24,460	8.0	8.0	1.75	0.83	2.18

[a] No figures available.

received most of its *braceros* around the turn of the century from contractors in Bambamarca and Santa Cruz in the province of Hualgayoc in Cajamarca. In addition contractors also recruited in some of the coastal towns such as Monsefú, an independent farming community near Chiclayo which also boasted a substantial home industry in hat-making. Supplementing their meagre income with plantation work, Monsefuanos appeared with some regularity as both *libres* and *enganchados* on the *planillas* of Cayaltí. For their service in delivering *braceros* to the plantations, contractors generally received a commission, usually of 20 to 25 per cent, which was automatically deducted from each *peón's* daily wage, and sometimes (although not in the case of Cayaltí) the concession to operate the plantation store, another potentially lucrative source of income.

As for the *serranos*, they generally contracted on a temporary basis for the planting or harvesting seasons on the coast, a time when their own fields in the highlands could be safely abandoned. On the plantation they were invariably put to work on the most menial field tasks such as cane-cutting or loading, while other more demanding jobs involving the operation of machinery or factory work went to the more experienced and skilled coastal workers, the descendants of slaves, indentured Chinese, or *cholos* recruited from nearby towns. Wage differentials between the two groups tended to fluctuate between 15 and 25 per cent, although field workers generally received a daily food ration in addition to their *jornal*.[33] Each plantation also employed a group of field supervisors called *mayordomos* or *caporales*, whose job was to oversee the various battalions of *braceros* in their field tasks and apply the appropriate sanctions and rewards. In time, particularly as mechanization and specialization progressed, a complex hierarchy, in keeping with the general stratification of society at large, emerged on each plantation.[34]

At the same time, the plantation's social organization underwent vast changes, as increasing specialization, regimentation, and depersonalization replaced an older style of paternalism, which had characterized *hacienda* life in the nineteenth century. This tendency was particularly noticeable in the Trujillo region, where the emergence of the modern, factory-like plantation reached its zenith during the first quarter of the twentieth century. The slower conversion of Lambayeque to this industrial model tended to delay and lessen the social shocks of this transformation, which in time would severely rock the foundations of life in La Libertad.

Moreover, in Lambayeque the very fact that Peruvians rather than foreigners directed the pace of change made the situation there rather different. In the main, the Pardos and the Aspíllaga Andersons tended to cushion the impact of industrialization by applying larger doses of old-fashioned paternalism to plantation operation than their foreign counterparts at Casa Grande and Cartavio. The direct personal intervention of the Aspíllaga Andersons in all aspects of plantation life from the celebration of holidays to attendance at sporting events provided an extra measure of social control which was missing further to the south. To their workers who had been conditioned to respond to the patriarchal structure of highland society or to the smaller, more personal pre-war coastal *hacienda*, native planters like the Aspíllaga Andersons were highly visible and largely accessible authority figures, who continued to act according to time-honoured patriarchal models. At Casa Grande or Cartavio, on the other hand, the worker encountered a more remote and less identifiable authority structure staffed by one or more foreign managers, who were accustomed to a more modern, impersonal, institutionalized paternalism.

The changing work relationships within the new industrial plantation system affected the emerging plantation proletariat in still other ways. While labour violence had by no means been uncharacteristic of plantation life in former times, it became increasingly common in the first decades of the twentieth century, particularly in the Trujillo region. A serious uprising of sugar workers, triggered by the abuses of the *enganche* system, erupted on the estates of the Chicama Valley in 1910. Not dissimilar to the risings of Chinese indentured labour in the 1870s,[35] these disturbances so alarmed and frightened the middle and upper classes of Trujillo that they called upon the authorities to create a permanent rural constabulary in the region to control this potentially dangerous new element of society. The largely spontaneous uprising of 1910, which resulted in widespread looting and loss of life, foreshadowed a period of intense worker unrest in the area. Indeed, by the end of the First World War, organized strikes had become a regular phenomenon in the Chicama Valley, as had government repression.

However, such solutions to the problem of labour unrest could only in the long run be temporary, for by the 1920s the sugar valleys of the north coast had become veritable industrial enclaves, employing, in the case of the Chicama Valley, a work force of over 10,000 persons.[36] Indeed, the 1921 strike in the valley, the bloodiest on record, clearly demonstrated that such a force, when organized, could seriously threaten the existing social and political equilibrium of the region. In fact, this is exactly what happened a decade later, when Trujillo was seized and held by a large force of sugar workers and their alienated middle-sector allies for more than a week, during the so-called Trujillo Revolution of 1932.[37]

The discontent of sugar workers, which was reflected in the union movement after the war, tended to be mirrored in still other sectors of north coast society. Thus, the old merchant class of Trujillo was severely jolted by competition from the company stores, which expanded their operations on several plantations after the war. Stocked with cheaper goods imported directly from abroad, these stores quickly became new commercial focal points in the region, to the detriment of the more established trading interests of the urban bourgeoisie.[38]

A deepening recession in the sugar industry during the 1920s produced still further distress among the region's middle sectors. Caused by steadily falling prices on the world commodities market after 1920 (see Table 38 above) the recession forced companies to further restrict purchases in the cities and to generally retrench their operations. By the late 1920s the economy of the north, closely tied as it was to the sugar industry, was faced with mounting unemployment at all levels of society. A rising tide of discontent and resentment now engulfed the formerly prosperous bourgeoisie of the region, who were joined by the area's already disaffected small farmers and increasingly politicized sugar workers. As hard times intensified, all segments of the community came to question the efficacy of the new sugar order, identifying as their enemy the sugar companies, which they blamed for their economic troubles.[39]

Conclusions

A new sugar order had indeed emerged from the ashes of the now-distant War of the Pacific. Powered by the twin engines of foreign capital and a dynamic new generation of entrepreneurs, the Peruvian sugar industry was rebuilt according to modern specifications and was pulled in a few short decades into the imperial economic framework of the industrializing nations of the northern hemisphere. Old *haciendas* were consolidated, new plant equipment introduced, and a variety of new technology and business methods applied to the industry. In La Libertad this economic revolution went so far as to see production and marketing joined within the same corporate structure, foreshadowing the emergence of the vertically integrated, multinational companies which would dominate Latin America, if not much of the world, in the twentieth century.

At the same time the industry, in the course of its revitalization, dramatically altered the patterns and configurations of north coast life. The drive towards a sugar monoculture resulted in a tendency for the expanding plantations to encroach upon village lands, displacing and proletarianizing large numbers of independent farmers and artisans. In addition to eventually absorbing entire towns and sweeping up their labour force, the new industrial plantations reached up into the villages and Indian communities of the nearby highlands and by means of the *enganche* system recruited thousands of Indians to work on the plantations. Some of these migrant workers remained permanently on the plantation, forming part of a large new proletariat, which in number rivalled its counterpart in Lima. Even the old merchant class, like the former planter elite before it, felt all too painfully the impact of the new economic order. Within a generation the entire order of things had radically changed along the coast, a fact that was to have profound consequences for the future political development of both the region and the nation. For it was within this general milieu of dislocation and change that the Aprista movement burst forth in the early 1930s to become a dominant new force in Peruvian politics for the next four decades.

NOTES

1. I am grateful to Eric Hobsbawm and Juan Martínez Alier for their comments on the original version of this paper. Further research and revision of the paper were made possible by a post-doctoral grant from the Joint Committee on Latin American Studies of the American Social Science Research Council and the American Council of Learned Societies.
2. H. Feis, *Europe: the world's banker 1870–1914* (New Haven, Conn., 1930), p. 23; United States Senate, Committee on Foreign Relations, *United States–Latin American relations* (Washington, 1960), p. 296. British capital declined over the next decade ($125,000,000 in 1925) but still almost matched American investment, which had risen sharply during the *Oncenio*.
3. A major landmark in this investment process was the so-called *Contrato Grace*, which was concluded in 1889 between the Peruvian government and the nation's principal British creditors. According to this agreement Peru's foreign debt was totally re-financed, in return for which the British group assumed direct control and operation of the national railway system. A year later the group formed the Peruvian Corporation Ltd, a holding company charged with the task of operating the nation's railways. In effect, the Grace Contract set the stage for a large-scale expansion of foreign investment in Peru over the next four decades, while further linking the nation's economy to Great Britain. A brief general treatment of the Grace Contract and economic development in Peru during this period can be found in Jesús Chavarria, 'La desaparición del Perú colonial (1870–1919)', *Aportes* XXIII

(January 1972), pp. 131–2 and *passim*. See also 'The Peruvian Corporation Ltd: its origins and history', *West Coast Leader* (Lima), 7 October 1931.

4. Liisa North, 'Origines y crecimiento del Partido Aprista y el cambio socioeconómico en el Perú', *Desarrollo Económico* x, 38 (Buenos Aires, July-September 1970), pp. 191–4.

5. Jonathan V. Levin, *The export economies: their pattern of development in historical perspective* (Cambridge, Mass., 1960), pp. 120–1.

6. Claude Collin Delavaud, *Les régiones côtières du Pérou septentrional* (Lima, 1968), p. 248n. This is an excellent economic geography of the north coast, which contains the best general survey of the evolution of the sugar industry (pp. 236–70 and *Passim*). For a more complete and detailed study, see also Pablo Macera, *Las plantaciónes azucareras en el Perú, 1821–1875* (Lima, 1974).

7. Sugar exports dropped sharply for almost a decade after the outbreak of war, reviving to pre-war levels only during the 1890s: see Table 38 (pp. 238–9).

8. The displacement of the pre-war planter class and the tendencies toward concentration are graphically illustrated by comparing the list of planters in the Chicama Valley in 1876 published in Ernesto Yepes del Castillo, *Perú: 1820–1920, un siglo de desarrollo capitalista* (Lima, 1972) Annex 16, and the modified CIDA table on land concentration published in Peter F. Klarén, *Modernization, dislocation and Aprismo: origins of the Peruvian Aprista Party, 1870–1932* (Austin, Texas, 1973), pp. 17–18.

9. The process of land concentration at Casa Grande can be followed in the various protocols of the Lima notary public Juan Ignacio Berninzón for the years 1877 to 1900, which can be found in the Archivo Nacional del Perú. For subsequent years see the useful though often incomplete Carlos M. Alvarez Beltrán, *El problema social económico en el Valle de Chicama* (Trujillo, 1949), pp. 25–38, as well as Sociedad Agrícola Casa Grande Ltda, *Estatutos* (Lima, 1899), p. 3.

10. The post-war price oscillations on the world sugar market, as well as the general dearth of domestic credit, substantially weakened the financial position of the old planters so that many were forced into bankruptcy in succeeding years. For a discussion of the pattern of consolidation see Klarén, *Modernization*, pp. 3–23.

11. George Vanderghem *et al.*, *Memorias presentados al Ministerio de Fomento del Perú sobre diversos viajes emprendidos en varias regiones de la república* (Lima, 1902), p. 92; and *El Perú centenario* (Buenos Aires, 1922), pp. 99–100.

12. Very useful comparative data on the agrarian structure of Lambayeque can be found in Enrique Espinoza, 'Estadística agro-pecuaria de la república: informe relativo al departamento de Lambayeque', *Boletín del Ministerio de Fomento* III (September 1905), pp. 33–113; and Carlos Bachmann, *Departamento de Lambayeque* (Lima, 1921), particularly pp. 140–209. See also Ricardo A. Miranda, *Monografía general del departamento de Lambayeque* (Chiclayo, 1927).

13. Alejandro Garland, *La industria azucarera* (Lima, 1895), p. 36. Another observer concurred in this judgement, adding that administrative and productive procedures were appallingly inefficient and inadequate on north coast estates (Arthur Rosenfeld, *La industria azucarera del Perú* (Lima, 1926), pp. 11–12).

14. Espinoza, 'Estadística agro-pecuaria', pp. 33–113. See also W. E. Dunn, *Peru: a commercial and industrial handbook* (Washington, 1925), p. 363.

15. Bachmann, *Lambayeque*, p. 149; 'La gran industria azucarera del Perú', *La Industria* (Trujillo), 8 August 1915.

16. Henri Favre, 'El desarrollo y las formas del poder oligárquico en el Perú', in José Matos Mar (ed.), *La oligarquía en el Perú* (Buenos Aires, 1969), p. 81.

17. Espinoza, 'Estadística agro-pecuaria', pp. 33–113; and Bachmann, *Lambayeque*, p. 147.
18. Gerardo Klinge, *La industria azucarera en el Perú* (Lima, 1924), p. 16.
19. For a useful (though company-oriented) account of the Grace corporation in Peru, see Eugene Willard Burgess and Frederick H. Harbison, *Casa Grace in Peru* (Washington, 1954), as well as 'Casa Grace', *Fortune* XII (December 1935), pp. 95–101, 157–64. See also 'Amazing Grace', *NACLA's Latin America and Empire Report*, March 1976.
20. The history of trading companies in Peru remains to be written, although W. M. Matthews has made an excellent start in that direction with his 'Foreign contractors and the Peruvian Government at the onset of the *guano* trade', *Hispanic American Historical Review* LXII, 4 (November 1972), pp. 598–620.
21. Collin Delavaud, *Les régiones côtières*, pp. 256–7.
22. The formation of the *Escuela Nacional de Agricultura* was illustrative of the government's increasing role in accelerating the pace of agricultural modernization during the first decade of the century. Summing up this effort, one contemporary visitor wrote: 'Agriculture is awakening greater interest than ever before in Peru. The government through the Departamento de Fomento, is doing everything possible to encourage its development: the ... Escuela Nacional de Agricultura ... has been most successful as a means of providing practical instruction in this important branch of education ... Many young Peruvians have studied in the United States and Europe, and, on returning home, have put in practice on their *haciendas* the knowledge thus gained. A few have [even] become teachers in the Escuela Nacional ... The Departamento de Fomento [also] distributes free of cost to the agricultural community a great quantity and variety of illustrative literature respecting modern methods of cultivation, irrigation, fertilization of lands, with suggestions as to the best kinds of products to be fostered in certain regions; a bulletin appears monthly filled with useful information and the Escuela de Agricultura publishes a newspaper along the same lines. The government also imports seeds and special plants from other countries and lends aid to the planter in exterminating any diseases that may appear on his lands.' (Marie Robinson Wright, *The old and the new Peru: a story of the ancient inheritance and the modern growth and enterprise of a great nation* (Philadelphia, 1908), p. 308.) Behind this effort by the government stood the Sociedad Nacional Agraria (SNA), which had been founded in 1896 mainly by the nation's sugar planters to further their interests. The widespread adoption of a broad range of new cultivating techniques in the sugar industry, from crop rotation and irrigation methods to the regular application of guano (national demand rose from 112,000 tons in 1900 to 142,000 tons in 1913), all of which led to substantially rising yields, can to a great extent be attributed to the combined efforts of the SNA and the government.
23. Michael Twomey, 'Ensayo sobre la agricultura peruana' (mimeographed), Centro de Investigaciones Sociales, Económicas, Políticas y Antropológicas, La Universidad Católica del Perú (Lima, 1972), p. 26. The drive towards a sugar monoculture along the north coast, as well as the general boom in cotton exports, triggered an inflationary spiral in food costs, which doubled between 1914 and 1920 (Bardella, *Setenta y cinco años de vida económica del Perú*, p. 119). The social effects of this inflation spilled over into the fledgeling labour movement in the country, propelling unionization not only among urban but also among rural workers, particularly in the sugar industry. Despite an estimated 341 per cent increase in income between 1914 and 1919 (see Table 38), planters increased workers' wages during this same

period by only 55 per cent (Table 39). At the same time the national cost of living was doubling.

24. Klarén, *Modernization*, pp. 50–64.

25. Dunn, *Peru*, p. 365.

26. See for example Ricardo Miranda Morante's letter to Cayaltí, 26 February 1938, in the Centro de Documentación Agraria (CDA) in Lima. A former lawyer for the Aspíllaga Andersons, he refers to the violent and often bloody confrontations which took place between Zañeros and local authorities over land disputed with Cayaltí.

27. Klarén, *Modernization*, pp. 50–156.

28. The standard study of Chinese immigration to Peru during this period is Watt Stewart, *Chinese bondage in Peru: a history of the Chinese coolie in Peru, 1849–1874* (Durham, N. C., 1951). On later efforts to import Japanese indentured labour, see Toraje Irie, 'History of Japanese migration to Peru', *Hispanic American Historical Review* XXXI (August 1951), pp. 437–52.

29. Douglas Horton, who is writing his doctoral dissertation on the de la Piedra family agricultural enterprises in Lambayeque, quotes the following conversation which he had with a worker informant on the Pomalca plantation: 'I was born in Catacaos [Piura] in 1890 ... My father had a lot of land, but little by little the wealthy landlords of the valley got it away from him. There were many battles over the irrigation water, and the big landowners always won ... I came to Pomalca in 1913 after working in various *haciendas* and mines including San Rafael [Casma], Vilca Huaca [Huacho], San Nicolás [Supe] and Cerro de Pasco ... In Catacaos the wage rate was sixty *centavos* per day and in Pomalca it was one *sol*; naturally the people came running.' ('Hacienda and co-operatives' (mimeographed), University of Wisconsin Land Tenure Center (Madison, 1974), p. 45.)

30. Espinoza, 'Estadística agro-pecuaria', pp. 33–113, and Dunn, *Peru*, p. 365.

31. Unless otherwise noted, the following discussion of the *enganche* and of plantation social organization is based on the author's recent work in the archives of the Aspíllaga Anderson plantation of Cayaltí, which are now housed in the CDA archives in Lima.

32. Espinoza, 'Estadística agro-pecuaria', pp. 33–113.

33. According to the Aspíllaga Andersons, most *peones* from the Sierra expected and preferred that their wages be paid partly in rations. A typical day's field wages with rations included were broken down in the following way in 1926:

Meat	S/.0.15
Rice (1½ lbs)	0.15
Salt	0.00½
Repayment of original loan (plus interest)	0.50
Wage	0.40
Contractor's fee	0.10
	S/.1.30½

(CDA archives, Ismael Aspíllaga Anderson (Cayaltí) to Ramon Aspíllaga Anderson (Lima), 5 April 1926.)

34. A general breakdown of the 2,300-man work force at Cayaltí in the early 1940s revealed the following general work categories:

Field workers	1,250
Cart drivers	180
Cane cutters	170

Convoyers	50
Mill operators	190
Factory workers	170
Diverse	290

(CDA archives, Administrator General (Cayaltí) to Inspector Regional de Asuntos Sociales (Chiclayo), 29 October 1942 and 30 October 1942.) It is not clear whether the category 'Diverse' included *empleados* or simply various other workers. However, Cayaltí had over 100 *empleados* at about that time (CDA archives, Gerencia Cayaltí (Lima) to Gerente de la Sociedad Nacional Agraria (Lima), 4 October 1945).

35. Violence among the Chinese indentured labourers in the Trujillo region was quite common before the War of the Pacific. One such uprising occurred in 1876 on the *haciendas* Pampas, Sausal, and Chiquitoy in the Chicama Valley, where several hundred indentured labourers rose up and killed their overseers and fled to the canebrakes before being apprehended by the army. The worst uprising, however, occurred in 1870 in the Huacho region, where some 1,200 indentured labourers rioted, resulting in the death of 150 Chinese and sixteen whites, including one *hacendado* murdered at his dinner table (Stewart, *Chinese bondage*, pp. 218–19, 121–3).

36. Projected from the figures given by Carlos Paz Romero, 'Estadística de la industria azucarera–1914', *Anales de la Dirección de Fomento* X–XII (October–December 1915), pp. 1–38.

37. The Trujillo Revolution of 1932 was organized by the fledgeling Partido Aprista Peruano. A general, although partisan, account of the revolution, most notable for its splendid photographs, can be found in Guillermo Thorndike, *El año de la barbarie, Perú, 1932* (Lima, 1969). For a first-hand account of the rise of the labour movement see Joaquín Díaz Ahumada, *Historia de las luchas sindicales en el Valle de Chicama* (Trujillo, 1962). A valuable fictional rendering of the labour movement on the plantations of the Trujillo region can be found in Ciro Alegría's unfinished novel *Lázaro* (Buenos Aires, 1973).

38. Klarén, *Modernization*, pp. 65–83.

39. *Ibid.*, pp. 80–3.

CHAPTER 10

The dynamics of Indian peasant society and migration to coastal plantations in central Peru

HENRI FAVRE

The problems of the transition from one social formation (or mode of production) to another have not yet been seriously tackled.[1] A few attempts have been made to give them some systematic formulation, but they are on too high a level of abstraction to be of much use as guides to empirical research. As far as the concrete evidence available on the passage of traditional societies to capitalism is concerned, for example, it often comes from analyses carried out from a perspective which is too narrowly evolutionist to make generalizations possible. The authors responsible for these studies seem to agree, for the most part, that, as capitalism is a higher social formation, traditional societies are inevitably condemned to break up on contact with it and fall in a passive and mechanistic way, into the moulds established by it.[2] Hence, no doubt, the importance given to the phenomena of destruction and deculturation which arise from these relations, which are certainly real enough, but which cannot be taken as a general rule.

Latin America is a particularly rich field for the study of the many responses which traditional societies of a colonial and seigneurial nature can make to capitalism, which has historically been built up on a broadly agrarian base. These responses from time to time result in some sort of provisional compromise, but they sometimes also result in long-lasting adjustments by which the two social formations come to articulate and consolidate themselves over a period of time, without consequently having to modify their structures. We have shown that the Tzotzil-Tzeltal of Mexico have incorporated seasonal labour on the coffee plantations of Soconusco into their traditional way of life, and that by means of this wage-earning activity this Indian peasant population has kept its communal organization functioning to this day on the high plateau of Chiapas, thereby helping to perpetuate the local colonial system, in which they remain as firmly embedded as ever.[3]

More recently, we have been able to observe in Peru the way in which other highland Indian peasant populations have been led to hire out

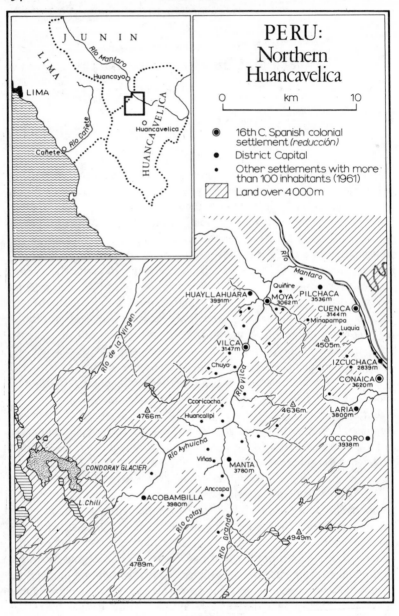

Map 16

their labour power on a seasonal or temporary basis in the developing areas outside the Sierra, in order to continue the pursuit of their own cultural and social goals. In such cases, turning to wage labour constitutes a means of maintaining the traditional order at a time when that order is not longer viable. Wage labour does not, therefore, precipitate any crisis in this social order; on the contrary, it presupposes a preceding crisis which it serves to remedy.

Let us take the case of central Peru, and, more specifically, that region of the central Sierra made up of the northern part of the Department of Huancavelica and the coastal foothills formed by the lower valley of the Río Cañete. In the 1880s, the rural estates of Cañete were affected by the modernization process which extended over the entire Peruvian coast, from north to south, and which had already been under way for several decades. These estates were transformed into cotton plantations, the capitalist exploitation of which requires abundant labour, particularly between the months of March and May, during the cotton-picking (*paña*) season. To satisfy this need for labour, the planters were obliged to turn to the human reserves of the hinterland, as the population of the coast remained relatively low. They organized a system of labour draft (*enganche*), run often by itinerant merchants and sometimes by minor local officials, whose role was to recruit workers amongst the peasants of the Indian communities of Huancavelica by making them an advance payment on their wages. This system is by no means peculiar to the region. But what is perhaps more peculiar to Huancavelica is the fact that *enganche* never became an instrument of coercion or oppression there. It was transformed quite quickly into a simple means of locating, regulating, and channelling the work force, and it then disappeared completely towards the end of the 1910s. In fact, the demand for labour was met very quickly and without any difficulty, for, from the moment that the possibility of seasonal labour in the plantations became known in the population centres or *comunidades* of Huancavelica, the Indians of this region began to pour down the western slopes of the Andes in their hundreds and even thousands, to take part in the *paña* every year on the coast.

What was it that brought about such a rapid adjustment between the supply and demand for employment? Why did the *comunidades* of Huancavelica respond so quickly to the call of the plantations? And, above all, in what way did they interpret and use this wage-earning activity in which they seem to have become involved so willingly? It is to these questions that I should like to supply some tentative answers.[4]

The northern part of the Department of Huancavelica belongs to the territory of a small pre-Inca chieftainship in the central Andes, the Asto, who belong to the Anqara ethnic group. The thirty or so villages or *ayllus* which were established there before the arrival of the Spaniards were perched on rocky peaks, summits and outcrops, almost always at an altitude of more than 3,800 metres. They were given in *encomienda* to Hernando de Villalobos, who handed them on to his son-in-law, Amador de Cabrera, the discoverer of the famous Santa Bárbara mercury mine. These villages were brought together, at the beginning of the second half of the sixteenth century, into four groups situated nearly 1,000 metres lower down, on the temperate alluvial or fluvioglacial terraces along the course of the Mantaro and Vilca rivers. These *comunidades* – Conaica, Cuenca, Vilca, and Moya – carried on functioning for a long time as a single socio-political unit. But the lowering of the status of the chief, which was the main element holding them together, along with the pressures exerted by the nearby *haciendas* and the action of the local colonial administration, brought about a progressive loosening of the links which had kept them together, even if the boundaries of the old chieftainship remained singularly marked on the cultural level.

For the whole of the nineteenth century, and up to the present day, two long-term processes which have acted as essential factors in the social dynamics of these communities have been taking place simultaneously. The first of these phenomena was demographic expansion, which had originated in the previous century but accelerated notably in the years following Independence. We should refer here to the least dubious figures that are available to us. If one is to believe the count made in the region in 1814, the total population of Conaica, Cuenca, Vilca, and Moya at that time came to 5,838. In 1876, according to the results of the first national census to be carried out in Peru, the figure was 6,577. In 1940, the date of the second national census, it had reached 16,972; and in 1961, in the third census, it had risen to 19,972. Certainly the curve that can be drawn on the basis of these figures should be adjusted slightly, taking into account the increasing statistical precision from one census to another. It would then appear less asymptotic than it does, especially as the figures for 1876 seem rather weak, unlike the figures for 1814 and 1961, which may be taken as relatively accurate estimates. At all events, the population of the region appears to have increased more than threefold in less than 150 years.

The second phenomenon, which also had begun to emerge in the course of the eighteenth century, was the emergence and development within the four *comunidades* of an ethnically based social stratification. As early as 1790, the presence of eight non-Indian families is recorded in Vilca, twelve in Cuenca, seventy in Moya, and doubtless as many again in Conaica. They were generally *mestizo* (mixed-blood) families, but also *criollos* (whites born in Peru), and even poor or impoverished Spaniards born in Europe who, driven by need, settled among the Indians, despite the laws covering residential separation of the ethnic components of colonial society decreed and constantly re-issued by the Spanish Crown. The penetration of whites into the *comunidades* of the region increased at the beginning of the nineteenth century, under the impact of the economic crisis brought on at the local level by the ending of mining activities. Several inhabitants of Huancavelica left the steadily declining town to seek new ways of making a living elsewhere; this they found quite naturally in the direct exploitation of the Indians, especially in the years after Independence when the Indians ceased to be protected by Spain's tutelary legislation. Since then, the *comunidad*, which had been an element of the colonial macro-system, became the framework for a colonial micro-system, within which the relations of domination and dependence were again built up.

The newcomers quickly came to monopolize the arable land, beginning with the best – in other words, the irrigated lands – which seem to have come into their hands from about the 1820s onwards in the four *comunidades*. They used the newly created local administrative posts of the Republican regime, such as *gobernador*, *alcalde*, and *juez de paz*, which they contrived to monopolize, to secure legal title to communal property and arbitrarily to deprive members of the *comunidad* of their individual holdings. Moreover, they went in for trading with the Indians, whom they induced to make purchases on credit and to mortgage their houses and their fields. This trading, which in the first instance involved alcohol, and which rested in practice on systematic indebtedness, involved even less risk for the credit-giving merchants because they were at the same time the local representatives of political and judicial authority.

In this way, the Indian population was progressively drawn into dependence on those responsible for fleecing them, whether as *criados* (servants) or, above all, as *peones*. The *criado* was completely integrated into the household of his employer, who, in exchange for absolute control over his labour power and that of his family, provided for his needs and supplied lodging, clothes, and tools, as well as food. Around 1850, the majority of the whites of the region had one or more *criados*, whom they used for their domestic service and for looking after their flocks. On the other hand, the *peón* theoretically remained a free peasant who took care of his own subsistence but who, confined to more and more peripheral and marginal land, often had unwillingly to hire out his labour power, particularly during the busy agricultural seasons such as ploughing, sowing, and harvest, in return for payment in kind or for a derisory amount of cash. Some old men belonging to the dominant families of Moya and Cuenca still recall today the 'good old days' when it was sufficient to throw a ten-*centavo* piece at the feet of the first Indians to come along to obtain all the labour needed to work the fields. If the Indian refused to work, he was thrown in prison and kept there until he agreed to carry out the task for which he had been 'paid'.

This demographic explosion combined with the process of social stratification to have a series of cumulative effects: the pressure of men on the land became all the greater because landed property tended to become concentrated in the hands of a few petty local notables. The consequence was that a growing number of Indians left their villages, climbed further up the mountain, and settled at ever greater altitudes in the hope of opening up land for cultivation, thereby escaping *peón* status and the overall stranglehold of the whites. To be sure, the four original *comunidades* of the region were never totally concentrated in nucleated centres. Throughout the colonial period, administrative and religious documents abound which point out – in order to deplore – the presence of Indians outside the villages, on the high pasture lands, in more or less remote and dispersed *estancias* (hamlets). Moreover, the intimate interconnections between agricultural and pastoral activities have always encouraged that part of the population responsible for looking after the livestock to live temporarily in the grazing areas. The Spanish policy of *reducción* was limited by the requirements of the local economy.

Nevertheless, from the beginning of the nineteenth century, there is evidence of a continuous movement of the population to the higher land, the massive scale of which can be demonstrated by a few figures. In 1814, the villages of Conaica, Cuenca, Vilca, and Moya, created in the sixteenth century in the valleys, still housed 40 per cent of the total population of of the region. In 1940, the population of these villages represented no more than 20 per cent of the total population, and in 1961 it had fallen to only 14 per cent. Between 1814 and 1961, it not only did not increase but sometimes fell quite sharply, as in Cuenca and Moya. This means that the growth in population was drawn up, as it were, on to the higher land. Other more approximate figures, in the sense that details of altitudes are rare and often uncertain, provide further evidence. In 1814, at least three-quarters of the population lived below 3,600 metres. In 1961, the proportion had been almost completely reversed: nearly three-quarters of the inhabitants of the region lived at an altitude of over 3,600 metres. The 4,000-metre threshold had been reached and comfortably passed some years before. Clusters of more than a hundred inhabitants are found today not only on the *puna* or high plateau, but also at the very edge of the tundra, beyond the sites of the old pre-hispanic *ayllus*. This is the case with Yarccapampa, with Incañán, and particularly with Minapampa, on the heights above Cuenca, more than 4,200 metres up, where 150 inhabitants live in a windswept area where the soil is frozen for several weeks of the year, and where the vegetation consists basically of mosses and lichens.

During the first half of the nineteenth century, the movement of the Indian population back to the high ground took place in a completely haphazard way. Family *estancias*, isolated from one another, grew up and multiplied in folds of land relatively protected from the weather, in a chaotic and almost clandestine manner. They consisted of little huts of dry stone, circular or oval in shape, which were reminiscent of the pre-hispanic dwellings whose ruins still stand nearby, and in these huts a couple and their children huddled around a fire of animal dung. The huts were surrounded by enclosures for sheltering a meagre flock of sheep, *llamas*, or *alpacas*, and by tiny, laboriously cleared fields for producing the small quantities of barley and potatoes necessary for subsistence. But production never became sufficient for the *estancias* to completely sever their links with the parent villages upon which they still relied for the supply of certain indispensable agricultural provisions. These provisions continued to be obtained in exchange for looking after the sheep in which the rich farmers of the villages invested the income from their fields.

Still, from the 1850s onwards, some of the *estancias* began to develop through natural demographic growth, whilst others made deliberate attempts to group themselves together into small villages. This gave birth to Manta, Viñas, and Huancallpi, in Vilca; to Pilchaca, then Luquia, in Cuenca; to Laria in Conaica; and to Huayllahuara in Moya, to name but a few. These attempts, which gradually became more general in the last quarter of the century, have a precise political significance. They are evidence of the realization by the Indians of their dependent situation, and also of their determination to escape from this situation. The War of the Pacific (1879–83), which, under the influence of the resistance led by General Cáceres to the Chilean invaders, was transformed from a national into a social conflict, is doubtless not wholly unrelated to the change in outlook which became evident. In any case, from the ending of hostilities, real villages were founded on the edge

of the high plateau or on the high plateau itself. These new villages were
exact replicas of the old ones. They were built on the traditional hispano-
colonial model, which must have seemed like the height of modernity to
people accustomed to the discomfort of the *estancias*. Anybody unaware
of their history might take them for the direct descendants of the *reduc-
ciones* of Viceroy Toledo, so similar are they to them, even in their
archaic features. Straight lines of two-storey houses, built of adobe
bricks or *tapial*, with an outside corridor and a separate kitchen, are
laid out in streets intersecting at right-angles, all clustered around a
central square or rectangular space on which the church and *cabildo*
(local offices) are found.

Once they were organized into villages, the Indians more and more
vigorously challenged the relations which kept them in the orbit of the
old white-dominated *comunidades*. They became more reluctant to
take part in communal activities. They refused to undertake *mayor-
domías* (sponsorship) at festival times, and sometimes had to be compelled
to carry out the *faenas* (voluntary labour) which took place every year
to repair the public buildings, remake the roads, and clean out the irrigation ditches. The saint chosen by them as their patron, and which constituted the principal symbol of their collective identity, provided a
sacred basis for their resistance to the demands of the *comunidad*. Their
supposed deeds, which gave rise to a body of myths of greater or lesser
magnitude, came to justify the displays of dissidence and legitimize their
claims to autonomy. Manipulation of the supernatural still plays a considerable role in the strategies employed by the village to emancipate
itself from the *comunidad*.

In opposition to the *comunidad*, the villages claimed the right to bury
their dead in their own cemetery, to celebrate their feasts in their own
church, and to appoint the authorities of their own *cabildo*. These
pretensions came up against the determined opposition of the dominant
families, for whom recognition of the autonomy of the Indian settlements
on the higher slopes meant loss of control over the labour which they
needed to maintain their economic, social, and even cultural status.
However, satisfaction of these claims depended in the last instance on the
national government and its local representatives. In fact, it was not
enough for the village to build a church for it to become religiously
autonomous; it was not sufficient to built a *cabildo* for it to become
politically independent. It was still necessary to have the church con-
secrated by the bishop of the diocese, and the *cabildo* provided with
authorities recognized by the Prefect of the Department. The conflict
between the *comunidad* and the dissident village was then transferred

to other spheres, though this need not imply that the local struggle became any less bitter. Sometimes it degenerated into a pitched battle, which was immediately presented to the higher authorities as proof of the impossibility of peaceful co-existence.

From the 1910s onwards, the bishopric of Ayacucho, the prefecture of Huancavelica, and the government in Lima began, with the growing strength of the representative system in the country, to take notice of the claims with which they were assailed. Several villages were elevated to the category of sub-parish or annex,[5] which gave them a certain degree of religious and administrative autonomy, and subsequently to that of parish or fully fledged district, which enabled them to run their own affairs. After the seizure of power by Leguía and the promulgation of the Constitution of 1920, it even became possible for them to be recognized juridically as independent *comunidades*. In fact, a notably wide-ranging constitutional disposition partially restored the colonial legislation designed to protect the Indian *comunidades* which had been abolished following Independence. Under the aegis of this provision, which was not resorted to in this region until the 1930s, the dissident villages obtained collective and inalienable ownership of their landed property. That is, their secession, from the moment it was legally sanctioned, *ipso facto* provoked the territorial sub-division of the *comunidad* of origin. In this way, in 1937, Huayllahuara was recognized as a *comunidad* and took from the old *comunidad* of Moya more than a third of its land. The following year, Anccapa, Viñas, Manta, Acobambilla, Ccoricocha, and Chuya were all recognized as *comunidades* within a few months of one another and dismembered the old *comunidad* of Vilca, which retained a mere tenth of its original area.

Some figures may be given as evidence of the importance of this process of decomposition. At the time of Independence, the region was divided for administrative purposes into two districts which grouped together four *comunidades*, two in each. These were the four that had originally been founded in the sixteenth century. At the present time, it is divided into eleven administrative districts, containing seventeen legally recognized *comunidades*. Moreover, it includes forty-five settlements, each of more than a hundred inhabitants, which also aspire to being legally recognized as *comunidades*.

The strategies brought into play by the villages of the Sierra to gain their emancipation, and the means by which these villages relied upon the power of the state in order to free themselves from the relations of domination prevailing within the *comunidades*, merit case studies which cannot be enlarged on here.[6] However, they should not lead us to overlook the parallel attempts made at other levels to make this independence politically viable. They should not disguise the fact that the elevation of a village to the category of district or *comunidad* frequently only came as a more or less tardy recognition of sociological and economic reality. These attempts, which were perhaps less dramatic in their expression but nevertheless produced spectacular results, set out to re-create the communal life of the valleys up on the high plateau.

It became noticeable that the *estancia* or hamlet which became a village gradually stopped taking from and giving wives to the *comunidad* from which it was beginning to detach itself. Its matrimonial exchanges were confined to the neighbouring hamlets until the families which made it up lost all awareness of their common origin, and endogamy thus became possible. Examination of the civil registers enables one to follow step by step the re-structuring and closing of networks of kinship and alliance within the framework of the new village. But, at the same time as it stopped exchanging wives, the breakaway village also ceased to exchange goods and services with the rest of the *comunidad*. It called into question the communal division of labour, particularly by refusing to look after the farmers' animals. Thus, it no longer had access to the agricultural provisions from the valley which its inhabitants used to obtain in return for their work as *peones* or shepherds, and which they had then to produce on the spot, at high altitude, on the plateau.

In this way, the occupation of the high plateau was accompanied by agricultural colonization. Everywhere the grazing lands were cleared on a large scale. In Huayllahuara and in Quiñire, for example, the population undertook important ground preparation work to bring into cultivation certain places where the climatic and pedological conditions were the least unfavourable for the cultivation of cereals. Thanks to a very highly developed specialization with different crop varieties, in accordance with the potentialities of each micro-zone and the characteristics of each micro-climate, agriculture was developed right up to the edge of the tundra. This implies a real technical achievement and demonstrates the remarkable skills of the Andean peasant. At present, potatoes and other tubers are cultivated right up to the foot of the snow-covered peaks. Wheat and barley are sown above 4,000 metres, in old animal enclosures or inside stone paddocks which protect them from the freezing fogs. Even maize manages to yield a harvest at nearly 3,800 metres, in enclosed tree-lined and irrigated fields which surround the dwelling-houses of the village. Certainly, the vegetative cycle is long, as barley only matures at the end of the tenth month after sowing. Yields are low, as the ratio between the quantities sown and harvested does not reach six to one for cereals, even in the best years. Besides, the harvests are very uncertain because of the intensity of the frosts and the frequency of hail. But land is relatively plentiful, and by dint of a considerable amount of hard work subsistence may still be wrested from an unyielding soil. The law of diminishing returns does not operate in a closed economy.

On top of the rigours of the climate, the ill will of men provided a no less difficult and redoubtable obstacle to be overcome. If the *comunidad* scarcely had the means to prevent the political emancipation of its breakaway villages, it could still reduce the scope of that emancipation to the point of making it meaningless, by sabotaging the villages' economic base in various ways. The most common method consisted of deliberately turning animals loose onto the cultivated fields of recently colonized areas just before harvest time, claiming ancient rights of way. Other methods based on an equally twisted interpretation of tradition, or on its perversion pure and simple, were no less effective. Thus, in Moya there was a custom which laid down that in Easter week each family should prepare a soup, the *gloria chupe*, which was consumed on Easter Saturday. Custom allowed poor families to go by night to the richest fields to gather the ingredients they needed to prepare the *gloria chupe*. Today, this custom serves as an excuse for the inhabitants of Moya to go up to the high villages on the night of Good Friday and Easter Saturday to wreck their fields. As these are guarded by their owners, violent confrontations often result, invariably followed by reprisals.

Agricultural colonization of the high plateau lands has brought about profound changes in the landscape, the more so because the high villages have undertaken partial re-forestation on the basis of polylepis and a very hardy variety of eucalyptus, so as to have an on-the-spot supply of essential raw materials for the construction of houses and the manufacture of ploughing implements. Copses, carefully maintained and protected against the depredations of animals, particularly goats, have been formed on stretches of land which until then had been quite bereft of all woodland vegetation. In a similar way, new networks of communications avoiding the valley settlements have been laid out, whilst the traditional roads have deteriorated for want of traffic and maintenance. The entire spatial patterns of the high plateau have changed, not only in their appearance but also in their organization.

The splitting-up of the *comunidades*, the process of which has been briefly outlined above, had three interdependent consequences which have become particularly evident since the second half of the nineteenth century, and which have caused serious social and economic upheaval in the whole region.

First of all, under the impact of this process, the *comunidades* came to control an increasingly restricted vertical 'slice' of the natural environment. The four original *comunidades* of the region had within their territorial boundaries a series of clearly differentiated ecological levels which stretched from 2,800 metres in Conaica and 3,200 metres in Vilca to the summits of the mountains at around 5,000 metres. Their territory thus stretched over almost 2,000 metres, from top to bottom, and included, from the bottom upwards, following the local typology and terminology, a *keshwarr* zone made up of temperate valley lands, a *puna* area made up of the undulating high plateau, and an *orqo* zone of tundra and bare or partially snow-covered high mountainside. At present, these old *comunidades* have lost control of the ecological levels of the *puna* and *orqo* zones, which have been taken over by their breakaway hamlets when they set themselves up as independent *comunidades*. They find themselves confined to the *keshwarr* zone, whilst the new *comunidades* to which they have given birth, and which exercise no control over this zone, are confined to the upper levels. Such a sub-division of the region by altitude is an obstacle to the maintenance of traditional vertical ecological control.

Thus, the *comunidades* tend to have direct access to an increasingly limited range of resources. In fact, each zone, each ecological level, has its own particular products. Maize, wheat, barley, peas, potatoes, *mashwa*, *oka*, *ulluku*, *quinoa*, and pasture for the sheep, *llamas*, and *alpacas* follow each other in order of increasing altitude. By controlling all the ecological levels of the region, the *comunidades* once had direct access to all these products. But from the moment when it only controlled some of these levels, each *comunidad* had access to only a few of the region's products. The economic system thus broke up to the extent that the vertical ecological control on which it was founded was reduced.

Theoretically, the crisis which resulted from the breakdown of the economic system could be overcome by specialization of the communal economies within a framework of exchange between the *comunidades*. In this hypothetical case, the old valley *comunidades* situated in the *keshwarr* zone would devote themselves to the cultivation of maize and cereals, the new *comunidades* founded on the high plateau in the *puna* zone would go in for potato-growing and stock-raising, and they would exchange their surpluses between themselves. By developing the greatest potentials of the ecological levels over which they maintained control, they would continue to exploit, in optimum-yield conditions, the resources of the environment, to all of which they would have access, no longer directly but through barter or the marketplace.

But all this is purely hypothetical, for the *comunidades*, which still perceived exchange as fundamentally unequal, sought above all to be self-sufficient without having to buy, sell, or exchange anything with their neighbours, and they tried to produce everything they needed themselves. The autarky which was held up as the ideal, and which led to an uneconomic exploitation of resources, was more easily restored in the old *comunidades* of the *keshwarr* zone than in the new *comunidades* of the *puna*. The former could sow potatoes on a part of their maize fields, but the latter had more difficulty cultivating maize on potato land, or potatoes on land which was better suited to grazing. Still, none of them could reconstruct, on the exiguous 'slice' to which their ecological control has been reduced, the full potential of traditional production. In particular, grazing, which was formerly so important and so intimately interconnected with agriculture, fell into complete decline. It was no longer practised by the valley *comunidades*, which had lost their pastures, and it was practised less and less by the highland *comunidades*, which converted these pastures into cultivated land.

Finally, the *comunidades*, beginning with those on the high plateau, came to rely more and more on the outside. To regain a self-sufficiency which was increasingly threatened by the region's altitudinal segmentation, they found themselves turning to the wider society. Paradoxically enough, they partly overcame the crisis affecting them and partially succeeded in regaining their stability as autonomous economic units, thanks to the most dynamic and modern sectors of the nation, represented by the centres of capitalist development on the coast.

From the 1890s onwards, when the coastal plantations began to draw upon seasonal labour from the hinterland to pick the cotton crop, many inhabitants of this region hastened down to the coast to take the jobs offered there. They were mainly Indians from the Sierra who were in the process of organizing themselves into hamlets or villages. The wages earned from hiring their labour to the planters made a powerful contribution to the spectacular rise of this high-altitude village organization. They served to finance the building of churches and *cabildos*, which were the symbols of communal identity, and to undertake the often considerable expenses involved in the annual *fiesta* cycle through which the community demonstrated to itself its own cohesion. They also served to finance rural improvement works, the transformation of pastures into fields, and the creation of a *puna* agriculture by the purchase of new varieties and species of seeds which were either hardier or more productive, and in any case better suited to the environment. It is no exaggeration to say that the wages paid by the plantations conditioned, and still condition, the agricultural colonization of the high plateau.

It should be noted above all that wage labour was not seen as a source of income that enabled the acquisition of goods which could no longer be produced directly on account of the reduction in vertical ecological control. It was seen by those who had recourse to it as a source of investments which were channelled into the development of a maximum number of resources in each of the narrow strips to which ecological control was reduced, and into the reconstruction, in each strip, of the whole range of the region's productive potential. Viewed in this light, wage labour could not lead to rapid proletarianization or true incorporation into the market economy. On the contrary, it helped to maintain a traditional autarkic way of life by making it possible in the extreme environment of the high plateau, right up to the snow-line.

It is clear then that the relationship between *comunidades* and plantations through wage labour was of a cumulative kind. On the one hand, work for wages helped to solve, in keeping with traditional cultural values, the crisis resulting from the reduction in vertical ecological control caused by the process of fragmentation of the *comunidades*. But, on the other hand, it helped in a way to perpetuate this crisis by acting as an indirect catalyst of intra-community tensions. Indeed, insofar as it gave dissident hamlets and villages the means to lead a self-sufficient life on the very edge of the biosphere, it stimulated their desire for autonomy and incited them to declare their independence. In fact, without the cash poured in by the plantations in the form of wages, many population clusters would doubtless never have been able to set themselves up as economically viable *comunidades* at the altitudes where they are situated. The entire social dynamic of the region would have been brought to a halt.

NOTES

1. As noted by G. Balandier, *Sens et puissance* (Paris, 1971), p. 27, following L. Althusser and E. Balibar, 'Eléments pour une théorie du passage', in *Lire le capital* (Paris, 1968).

2. Compare the numerous monographs on communities underpinned by a kind of ideology of 'progress', such as two referring to the Andes: Richard Adams, *A community in the Andes: problems and progress in Muquiyauyo* (Seattle, 1959); and Paul Doughty, *Huaylas, an Andean district in search of progress* (Ithaca, New York, 1968).

3. Henri Favre, 'Le travail saisonnier des chamula', in *Cahiers de l'Institut des Hautes Études de l'Amérique Latine* VII (Paris, 1965), pp. 63–134; and, by the same author, *Changement et continuité chez les Mayas du Mexique; contribution à l'étude de la situation coloniale en Amérique Latine* (Paris, 1971).

4. The data presented here have been gathered for the most part within the framework of the Interdisciplinary Research Programme on Andean Peoples, which I directed among the Astos and their Chunku and Laraw neighbours in 1970, 1971,

and 1972. For further details, see the first two volumes of results of this programme – Daniele Lavallee and Michele Julien, *Les villages Asto à l'époque préhispanique* (Lima, 1974); and Henri Favre, *L'occupation et l'organisation de l'espace chez les Asto, du XVIe siècle à nos jours* (Lima, 1977) – to be published by the Institut Français d'Etudes Andines, in Lima.

5. Peru is divided administratively into departments, which are in turn sub-divided into provinces, and these are split up into districts and then annexes.

6. Some case studies can be found in Favre, *L'occupation et l'organisation.*

CHAPTER II

A Colombian coffee estate: Santa Bárbara, Cundinamarca, 1870–1912

MALCOLM DEAS[1]

Cundinamarca was the second region of Colombia to export coffee, following Cúcuta and other parts of Santander, which had been ex- porting since early in the nineteenth century. Cundinamarca was ex- porting noticeable amounts in the late 1860s, and came to export about 10 per cent of the nation's total just before the First World War, the pro- portion thereafter declining. In contrast with Caldas–Antioquia, which became and remains the leading coffee-producing area of the country, estates in Cundinamarca were large, some few having over a million trees. There were few coffee-producing homesteads or smallholdings. The potential coffee land of the department was a frontier for enterprise (and was lyrically described as such by Medardo Rivas in his *Los trabaja- dores de la tierra caliente*, first published in 1899), but it was not frontier land in the colonizing sense. Most of the land had title, and most of the titleholders were able to make it stick. Here the predominant mode of bringing a *finca* into production was to give it out in lots to *arrendatarios*, who would plant out coffee under the owner's or administrator's direc- tion, receiving the young plants from a central nursery. The *arrendatario* would grow his own food crops, but not coffee, and might be moved to work on a new area of the *finca* when his original plants came into pro- duction. The Santander sharecropping system was not employed.[2] This essay will examine in detail the working of a single *finca*, Santa Bárbara in the *municipio* of Sasaima, only one unit in one of the several types of society that coffee has brought into being in Colombia, but one for which a very rich documentation has survived.

Santa Bárbara at its height had some 120,000 trees, on the conven- tional estimate some 100 hectares in coffee, which meant that it was a respectable size, though by no means large for the area.[3] Sasaima was one of the earliest coffee-exporting towns of Cundinamarca, and one of the first to decline, but the archive unfortunately does not cover either the period of the *hacienda*'s foundation or its ultimate collapse. It consists of the correspondence books of the owner Roberto Herrera Restrepo with his administrators, and of his accounts; and the most useful part is the intense and careful correspondence of the administrator Cornelio Rubio,

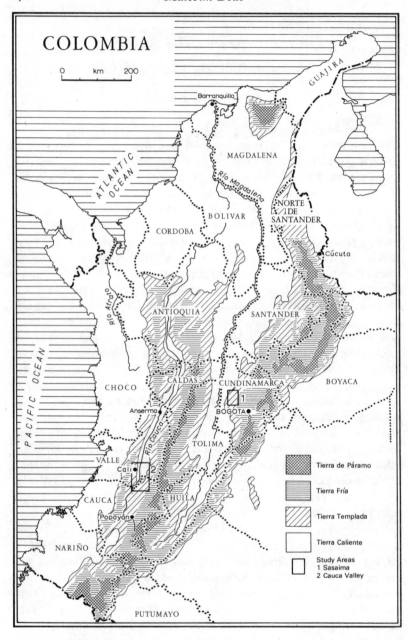

COLOMBIA

0   km   200

GUAJIRA

Barranquilla

ATLANTIC OCEAN

MAGDALENA

Río Magdalena

BOLIVAR

NORTE DE SANTANDER

CORDOBA

Cúcuta

Río Atrato

ANTIOQUIA

SANTANDER

PACIFIC OCEAN

CHOCO

CALDAS

CUNDINAMARCA

BOYACA

Anserma

1

Río Cauca

BOGOTA

TOLIMA

VALLE

Cali

2

CAUCA

HUILA

Popayán

NARIÑO

PUTUMAYO

Tierra de Páramo

Tierra Fría

Tierra Templada

Tierra Caliente

Study Areas
1 Sasaima
2 Cauca Valley

Map 17

from the beginning of 1895 until Roberto Restrepo's death in November 1912.[4] There are many difficulties in using this archive to construct series or even to calculate the owners' real return on their investment. Santa Bárbara certainly did not make their fortune: profit was not constant, it was the subject of innumerable threats and anxieties, and Roberto Herrera certainly worked very hard for it. Cundinamarca coffee may have been relatively 'oligarchic', and its system of production did produce acute tensions in the 1920s, 30s and 40s, especially in the more southerly part of the department, but it long required much care and attention from the owners. High transport costs to the sea and the long-drawn-out expansion of Brazilian production made quality essential, and quality meant continual attention to detail. Some of Roberto Herrera Restrepo's carefulness may have been exceptional, but this attention to detail was likely to be present in all those who faced this difficult market.[5] Though Sasaima was mostly owned by families of *Antioqueño* descent, one cannot attribute special carefulness to them alone. The necessity of paying strict attention to so many aspects of the running of the *hacienda* has left an archive of extraordinary suggestiveness. I have tried where possible to let it speak for itself, placing the date of the letter (where relevant) after the quotations.

Owner and administrator

Roberto Herrera Restrepo was necessarily an absentee. For obvious reasons many Colombian *hacendados* did not live for long periods on isolated *fincas*, or in the small towns (*'villorios'* is one deprecating word for them) like Sasaima. Herrera Restrepo had large family commitments in Bogotá and also ran several other enterprises and estates, which he could not conceivably have handled from Santa Bárbara.[6] The capital was the natural centre for his operations. Many of the essential tasks of running the *finca*, including the occasionally tricky one of finding working capital, had to be carried out there. Herrera Restrepo in Bogotá followed the coffee market and its prospects with the assistance of the circulars received from his London agents, Steibel Brothers, and from others who solicited his coffee from Hamburg and New York. In Bogotá he made his cost-conscious calculations and from time to time experimented with consignments of coffee to other destinations than London, and with speculative dealings in rubber and *tagua* (vegetable ivory). His direction of the *hacienda* was made with the best knowledge he could get of the trends of the market and, as his marginal calculations show, of the position of his *hacienda* in it. He always knew how much his coffee was likely to fetch in

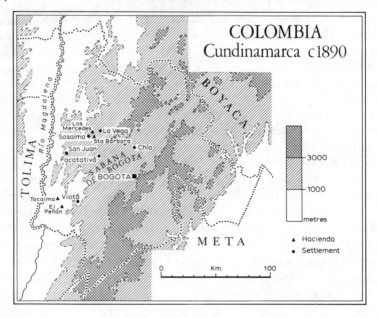

COLOMBIA
Cundinamarca c1890

Map 18

London and how much it was costing to place it there, and for much of the archive's years of low world prices this led him to pessimistic conclusions.

The owner clearly had an intimate knowledge of Santa Bárbara and many of those who worked on it, and of many of the Sasaimeros, and he tried to visit it regularly. He and his family appreciated its beauty, the riding, swimming, and change of climate that it afforded, and the fruit it sent up to Bogotá. Their visits were much appreciated by the administrator, who thought they had a good effect on both morale and morals, but they were not frequent, even though Sasaima could be reached in a day from Bogotá. For most of the time the administrator was alone at the end of the telegraph and the *correo*. This made the personality of the administrator of the utmost importance.

'It is as hard to find a good *mayordomo* as a good horse for a lady' — so wrote one of Herrera Restrepo's friends, recommending him just such a man (Rafael A. Toledo, 7 February 1895). The administrator of a coffee *finca* had to have more qualities than were necessary in the *mayordomo* of a more simple operation, and his relations with his employer would also be different. Cornelio Rubio, the overseer of Santa Bárbara, always began his letters with '*Muy estimado amigo*', whereas lesser *mayor-domos* elsewhere, whose spelling is also much worse, would begin '*Muy estimado patrón*'. Rubio was also better paid than they. He received a bonus on coffee produced, free pasture for twelve head of cattle and a cow, and loans and other attentions to help his own business ventures, which included some dealings in coffee. His correspondence with his employer shows a mutual respect, and a complete trust in Roberto Herrera on Rubio's part. He consults his employer about his marriage and about the plans of other members of his family, and he remembers himself in detail to large numbers of the owner's relations and friends. When members of the family visited the *hacienda* he alone sat at the same table. Like Herrera Restrepo, he was a Liberal, and he comments freely on the general political situation and the policies and prospects of the party. In his employer's interest, but also with a shared puritanism – Roberto Herrera was the brother of the Archbishop of Bogota and a devout Christian – he disapproves of drink, gambling, and fornication and does his best to limit all three at Santa Bárbara: 'You know what Mondays are like.' Though *arrendatarios* are, as we shall see, hard to find, one Aparicio is dismissed for 'staying up all night and gambling... God knows how many of the *peones* have let that rascal get away with their week's wage.' The sale of drink on the *hacienda* was suppressed as a source of trouble, 'fights... stupidities... drink-shop brawlings'. It was the dec-lared and sometimes enforced policy of the *hacienda* that its workers should get properly married. Altogether, the administrator in this part-icular case appears to have identified his own interest totally with those of his employer and, in his own words, to have worked the property as if it had been his own. With such a hawk-eyed accountant and tireless correspondent and demander of correspondence as Herrera Restrepo, it would not have been easy to do otherwise – absence in no way implied neglect. I hope that the nature of the division of labour between owner and administrator will emerge clearly from the quotations that follow.

Although he must have died more than fifty years ago, Cornelio Rubio himself is remembered as an imposing figure who knew the importance of formality and who avoided familiarity with either the *peones* or the people of the town. Returning after an enforced absence during the last civil war, he deplored the relaxation that had set in under his substitute: 'Sinforoso did not oversee the *peones* at all well, as he was altogether too familiar with them and let them waste a sad amount of time.' It is clear that advances in agriculture impose new forms of discipline just as do advances in industry, and a Cundinamarca coffee *finca* required a strong character to enforce them. The various processes of coffee production also demanded the supervision of a person of some formal education. Rubio appears to have made several ingenious adaptations to the machines in use on the *finca*, respectably capitalized as were most of the substantial establishments of Cundinamarca. He also educated his children— he requested textbooks of grammar, arithmetic, geometry, and history, and a box of chalk.

It is difficult to calculate the value of such a man. His salary in 1885 was 80 *pesos* a month (then almost £15), besides his bonuses, board and keep, the free pasture, and the cow. He received increases – he once expressed his loyalty by taking the polite risk of declining one – but like the wages of *peones* and female pickers, the *cosecheras* or *cafeteras*, they probably did not keep pace with the rapid printing of paper money after 1885. His own business ventures do not seem to have prospered. Three months after his employer's death he wrote that he wished to leave the *hacienda*, and the last trace of him in the papers is a letter from Roberto Herrera's son: 'I take note of your letter's explanation of the motives which oblige you to resolve to leave us, a resolution still very painful to all of us, who have always appreciated your worth. As these things are always best made clear by word of mouth, I anxiously await your coming so that we can talk it over.' [25 March 1913] Rubio once signed a letter to Robert Herrera, with sociological precision, 'the humblest of your friends'; perhaps he was too old to transfer the friendship to somebody else. He is a representative of an unstudied class of men whose origin and recruitment remain obscure but who were not the less essential in agriculture innovation. The extension of coffee cultivation created a demand for thousands of such overseers, who had to be persons of some education and who became persons of some standing – a rung on the ladder for those moving upward in society, and a respite for those who might otherwise have moved farther down?

Arrendatarios and other permanent workers

Santa Bárbara supported a blacksmith, a carpenter, and at times skilled builders. This small group does not figure much in the correspondence. Their higher wages can of course be seen in the account books.

The *arrendatarios* and their families formed the largest permanent group on the *hacienda*. I have not been able to establish exactly how many there were at Santa Bárbara, but the correspondence gives the impression that there were not a great many, somewhere between a dozen and a score of families – certainly sufficiently few for many to be mentioned by name in Rubio's letters to Bogotá.[7]

They were allotted *casitas*, simple whitewashed, earth-walled and thatch-roofed little houses, some of which can still be seen among the *fincas de recreo*, the weekend places into which the *hacienda* is now divided. These were the property of the *hacienda*, and the *hacienda* kept them in repair. The administrator was instructed to see that they were kept clean, various diseases, particularly typhoid, being a constant menace. They also received *huertas* where they could grow their own foodcrops and keep pigs and chickens. Though much changed from month to month and from year to year in this troubled time, their normal monthly labour obligation was to produce themselves or a *peón* for '*dos semanas, es decir cada quince días*' – 'two weeks, that is to say every fifteen days'. [Rubio's letter of 22 February 1904] This work was not unpaid, but it was an obligation. In practice it was not fifteen days but the working days of two weeks, and it was an obligation that the administrator had a lot of trouble in exacting.

At times it appears from the letters that Santa Bárbara could neither live with *arrendatarios* nor live without them. Essential as they were in the Cundinamarca system for the first stages of cultivation, and there-after as the nucleus of harvest labour, they were a constant source of difficulty. In the 1920s and 30s the most notorious cause of friction was that they were prohibited from planting coffee themselves – a prohibition which had its origin in the *hacendado*'s desire to prevent theft by being able to claim that all coffee on the *hacienda* was his, and which was rein-forced by changes in the law that might have made him liable to pay an outgoing tenant very expensively for the trees as a *mejora*, or improve-ment. However, this ban is not disputed anywhere in this archive; though it is true that there are no letters from *arrendatarios* in the archive, Cornelio Rubio would have reported any argument over such a ban in his long accounts of his troubles, had such occurred. His preoccupation here was first with finding *arrendatarios*, then with getting them to work.

It was hard to get good men who would stay put. Sasaima was not a new foundation – it dates from the seventeenth century[8] – but it could not satisfy the demand for labour that came with the expansion of coffee. One cannot be sure where the increase came from, but a popula-tion of 3,434 in 1870 had grown to 6,500 by 1884. Some of the *arren-datarios* of Santa Bárbara are described in the administrator's letters as coming from the colder uplands of Cundinamarca and Boyacá; none are said to come from any other part of the country. It is still common to find such migrants or their descendants as permanent workers in this coffee zone, and it would be fair to conclude that that was where most of them came from. The *hacienda* was always on the lookout for suitable families and usually had spare *casitas*, a problem themselves because of rapid dilapidation and the theft of building materials. Rubio reports, writing to a friend in the town of Chía on the Sabana of Bogotá:

peones: I wrote to Marcelo Avendano to see if he, who lives up there and knows the people, could find some families and bring them down, so that we can occupy some of the houses of San Bernardo [the more recently planted upper part of the *finca*] and if possible change some of the bad workers we have got. I think Marcelo will do the job, as I offered him his travelling expenses and something for each family he brings that does establish itself here, as long as they are the best-behaved he knows in the district. [12 October 1909]

Permanent labour was an anxiety as well as harvest labour, and to find it was worth some trouble and expense:

Last Thursday afternoon José returned with a family he had found in Facatativá [a Sabana town], and they are now here working. I gave them the house next to Agustín's, and I have had to give them some help as they arrived, though not clean, cleaned out [*limpios – pero de plata*]. They were living near San Juan, and I knew them some time ago, and they were good people, and I hope they will behave well here too and stay some time. [1 December 1903]

One Boyacense was offered his family's travelling expenses and '$50 for each family he brings me which consists of five or more useful persons'. The *hacienda* did not employ the services of any specialized agents in obtaining labour, preferring more personal and *ad hoc* arrangements. No specialized class of *enganchador* or labour agent seems to have appeared to serve the Cundinamarca coffee estates, which were relatively close to the main source of their labour.

The *arrendatario* was the main source of permanent labour on the *finca*. It is easy to exaggerate the virtues of coffee as a crop that resists neglect. A plantation producing high-quality mild coffee – and that alone was ultimately profitable in Cundinamarca – needs constant attention. It has to be kept weeded and pruned. Not only is the Colombian harvest, cherry by cherry, quite different from the crude slave grabbing and stripping described by Stanley J. Stein in *Vassouras*, but a reading of the manuals written for, and much read in, Colombia will show how much more un-Brazilian care there was besides. A neglected *cafetal* depreciated rapidly in value as its productivity went down, and would-be buyers calculated the costs of getting it back into shape. The *arrendatarios* performed the permanent tasks of the *finca* either in gangs under the administrator's direction, working themselves or providing a *peón* '*cada quince días*', or through informal contracts: an individual *arrenda-*

tario would be paid a certain sum for weeding one or another *tablón* (as the naturally demarcated areas of coffee were called).

There was competition between the *haciendas* for *arrendatarios*, and the upland peasants of the *tierra fría* were not always willing to move permanently into the coffee land, which was rightly considered unhealthy: Santa Bárbara did its best with vaccination, *aguardiente* with quinine, *ácido fénico*, and whitewashing, but this can have had no effect on most of the diseases that flourish with coffee.[9] Whether the lack of deference so much complained of by Rubio had its origin locally or was a matter of migrants emancipated from the stricter social controls of the Sabana one cannot always tell. But in the circumstances of this *hacienda*, the administrator in normal times had few sanctions with which to enforce their labour obligations. *Arrendatarios* were frequently in debt to the *hacienda*, but this gave it no greater control over them, and the debts were kept as low as possible – it was Herrera Restrepo's opinion that indebtedness should be discouraged as the usual end was the loss of both the money and the worker. There is no record in this correspondence of any appeal to outside authority. There was not much to appeal to, and for reasons to be seen later, neither Roberto Herrera nor Rubio were likely to appeal to what existed in Sasaima, as they were unlikely to get much co-operation from their fellow planters and administrators. A few quotations from the very many possible ones that the archive affords will illustrate this constant struggle:

I have had to press the *arrendatarios* quite a bit because, as I did not oblige them to work while the revolution was in progress [the short war of 1895] but let them go and work on other *haciendas*, now they all come back arguing about the terms, and it is just in this busy time that they *have* to work. [22 April 1895]

At the moment we need workers, and one has to be a little indulgent with the *peones* – all the more when one thinks of all the trouble it has taken to get the few *arrendatarios* we have got. [5 May 1896]

It is better to have no *arrendatarios* at all than to have this sort, because you cannot rely on them and every day they make new demands, and if you don't give them everything they want you make yourself the worst sort of enemy. Adrián Murcia usually comes when he's called; and Manuel Rodríguez comes every time, but the poor chap is not much use, and we just have to keep him on because he has always served the *hacienda*, and he is an inoffensive person. Vicente Cárdenas is very good; he comes each time he is called but he is very demanding. [11 March 1899]

Agustín Muñoz is the same one who has been unwilling to be any use at all in this harvest, on the pretext that his wife is ill. For some time he has not come to work himself nor sent either a *cafetera* or a *peón*; in fact he is no use at all, even though his wife's being ill does not stop him going up to the Sabana every week.

Last week he not only did not come to work but took Teófilo Robayo and Francisco García away from us to work his plots. As if that was not enough, he has pastured his animals in the coffee at *puente nuevo* and has ruined the *plátanos* he himself planted with the *peones* the same way.

Things being in this state, given the very bad example he sets to the other *peones*, even going so far as to deny the *hacienda* its right to oblige him to work, I have resolved, and told him so, to give him three months to sell his produce and get out, for to my way of thinking for thousands of reasons this man is a positive inconvenience to the *hacienda*. [28 June 1904] [All the same, he re-appeared and was given further work.]

Exasperation culminated at harvest time. Though it is clear that it was not only then that Herrera Restrepo and Rubio needed the *arrendatarios'* labour, they did see themselves as putting up with their unsatisfactory presence for the rest of the year to ensure a substantial nucleus of workers at this time. It was also the season that offered the *arrendatario* the greatest temptation to avoid his obligations or sell himself dearly:

All the people on the *Hacienda* are now working. I have had to press them a bit, because even with the scarcity of money they rightly complain of, you who know them know how when they understand that the *hacienda* needs them urgently, that is when they make the most conditions [*se hacen rogar más*], so I have had to be a bit strict with them, always using the technique of 'now pulling, now letting go' [*tire y afloje*], with the difference that this time I am thinking of pulling rather more than letting go. [14 April 1900]

This time he could be more exacting, as it was in time of civil war, and the workers were anxious to remain under the relative protection of the *hacienda*. The war did not last:

As for the *peones* it's the same: they all want to argue the terms, and on Mondays one has to go looking for them. All the same, we have to put up with some of them who may be useful to us in the reorganization. Others must either be subjected or else leave. [25 November 1902]

The labour *obligación* on the *arrendatario*'s own *hacienda* was frequently paid at a lower rate than he could get as a harvester elsewhere, or paid insufficiently to be an attractive alternative to working on his own *huerta* or not working at all. Rubio's ethic was not everyone's: 'I have had to have an open struggle with the *arrendatorios*: they are so stupid that one has to make them earn their money by force.' [22 May 1900]

For working elsewhere he threatened those with outstanding obligations with expulsion, with turning them out of their houses and putting the cattle into their plots, though he never appears to have carried out the threat. Roberto Herrera supported him and trusted his judgement:

The conduct of the *arrendatarios* is not surprising because they prefer not to earn anything rather than to serve with the interest they ought in the *hacienda* at this important time [the harvest], for which it puts up with them for the whole year. Your precautions I completely approve, and if necessary you ought to punish the first defaulter by taking his belongings out of his house and locking it up. Push them as much as is necessary because we are quite within right and justice in doing so. I assure you I will support you in helping them in what we can. There is no other system and one just has to go on with the 'now pulling, now letting go' which you know so well how to do. [29 May 1905]

This tension was never resolved on this *hacienda*, nor elsewhere in in Cundinamarca while the *arrendatario* system prevailed.

Harvest, wages, and food.
An abandoned *cafetal* can be cut and weeded back into condition even after some years are past, but a Colombian coffee harvest is as strict in its natural timetable as a crop of bananas. The expansion of coffee cultivation in Cundinamarca brought competition for all available labour at harvest time, and this can be seen most easily in the wages paid. If the *hacienda* did not pay satisfactory wages, most of the much-enlarged harvest labour force would go elsewhere, and the harvest would be threatened. Cornelio Rubio continually reported his efforts and his frequent failures to keep wages down while keeping the number of workers up, an attempt to square the circle: 'I have done everything possible, lowering the wages but at the same time trying to keep the greatest number of workers possible.' [15 January 1900]

His efforts redoubled in the face of the very uncertain prices of the late 1890s and the first decade of this century. He changed the system of payment because there were too many arguments: 'pay-time turns into a frightful argument, an obscene row, to sum it up a riot worthy of a *chicha* shop' – further evidence of lack of deference. He attempted, with little success, to keep workers on the *hacienda* by delaying payment; but this would get the *hacienda* a bad reputation, and workers would not come. He devised very elaborate systems of piece-work and bonuses and prizes (paid out of fines) to get the coffee picked as economically as possible, systems which would make the construction of any wage scale for this mostly migrant labour a very hazardous undertaking, even if they

were not made impossible by the fact that harvest labour was also paid
in part in food, and in food whose price varied wildly from season to
season, from place to place, and from year to year. Payment was usually
by weight picked, but not always. If there was not much coffee to be
picked, the *cosecheros* often preferred a daily wage:

The men from the Sabana who have come down have increased the number of
peones [working on a daily wage], because, as there has not been much coffee
to pick, they have decided not to *sacar costal* [the expression means to take a
sack to fill and be paid by the *arroba*] but to work for the daily wage. [10 May
1898]

Different groups might be working under different systems of payment
at the same time:

To keep around a hundred pickers I had to put the price up to 35 *centavos* the
arroba, trying at the same time to adjust the *peón*'s wage accordingly, because
they did not want to pick by the *arroba* because they did not earn as much as the
wage. As paying them to pick by day costs so much more, because they get now
$1.20 and *miel* and pick two *arrobas*, I think it is much better all things con-
sidered to put the picker's price up to 35 *centavos* the *arroba*. [8 July 1901]

The *arrendatarios* or their substitutes working their *obligación* at a
fixed daily wage were understandably unsatisfactory, though their sloth
still puzzled Rubio: 'I'll never understand these people: they really are
indios. Now they get a good day's wage in the harvest, one still has to
force them and mule-drive them just as if one was asking them to work
for nothing.' [19 August 1902]
Payment had to be made in small notes, which Roberto Herrera sent
down from Bogotá. Small notes were frequently at a premium, in these
inflationary years, and were often hard to obtain. There was no equivalent in this *hacienda* to the *tienda de raya*, the administrator himself
explaining that credit or a token system was impossible: as there was
nothing to buy in the *hacienda*, such a system would be quite unacceptable. The workers all insisted on cash.
These seasonal harvest workers mostly came down from Cundinamarca and Boyacá. They were predominantly, but not all, female, and
as overseer of discipline the *hacienda* appointed a special *mayordomo de
cafeteras*. Santa Bárbara tried to house each family separately in a *casita*,
but there were not always enough to go round. Some *haciendas* had
special buildings for this migrant labour (*cuarteles de peones*), and others
appear to have let it house itself in makeshift huts. Not until after the
Mil Días war of 1899–1903 did the *hacienda* attempt to guarantee its
own supply of migrant harvesters by the system of *enganches*, sending an

agent up to make contracts with *campesinos* of the *tierra fría* and carefully escorting them down – '*cada uno para quitarle los peones al vecino no omite medios*' ('everyone tries to take away his neighbour's labourers'). This met with some resistance in Boyacá, where other *hacendados* naturally regarded this *enganche* itself as just such an intrusion: 'The man commissioned ... to get people in Boyacá could not do anything as the *hacendados* prevented him.' [16 June 1903]

Nor did the system guarantee that the labour remained on the *finca* which had gone to the trouble and expense of collecting it. The *Revista Nacional de Agricultura*, no. 3 (15 May 1906) wrote confidently: 'We trust that the prefects and municipal authorities will lend every support to the owners and administrators of coffee *fincas*, so that workers brought at great expense from distant parts of the republic fulfil their contracts of *enganche*.'

But that confidence was almost certainly misplaced. The prefects and municipal authorities themselves were not always willing or disinterested parties, nor did they have the forces at their disposal to hunt about from *finca* to *finca* for large numbers of unfamiliar Boyacense *cafeteras*. Nor could they have done so effectively in the shortish and urgent time of harvest, when nobody turned workers away:

Hacienda La Victoria has been luring our people away, and I have spoken seriously today about this to the administrator there in a letter, saying this is not the sort of behaviour that should occur in relations between the two *haciendas*, and that if we go on like this, we will end up paying wages worse than we can imagine, and no one will be better off [... *iremos hasta donde no nos imajinamos con los precios de los jornales i no alcanzaremos el fin deseado*]. [12 May 1903]

There were the same troubles with another neighbour, Las Mercedes:

Formerly there was a reciprocal obligation not to receive in one *hacienda* the workers from the other, but now it appears that we are the only ones obliged. I myself in the last harvest, at a time when I most needed people, dismissed ... quite a few *cafeteras* at the behest of the Herreras, and they came that same Saturday to take the wages those *cafeteras* had earned as a fine. We oblige everybody, but it's best to note now that in the next harvest we can take any workers unconditionally. [10 January 1905]

The *enganche* did not account for a very high proportion of the harvest labour on this particular *finca*. Some came down spontaneously, and in 1904 Santa Bárbara records the return of 'four women ... of the ones who came *enganchadas* a year ago'. To attract this spontaneous labour was easier in some years than in others, in some *haciendas* than in others. A bad harvest attracted a disproportionately smaller number of workers –

it was less worth their while under the weight-payment system that all administrators always strove to maintain. Rain could hold up the picking and make it hard to get the pickers out into the trees. A good *finca* had to be laid out so that the pickers could spend the maximum time picking, with as little time as possible lost in carrying the coffee to the collecting point. Santa Bárbara thought itself more attractive than La Victoria as there was less carrying distance: 'Here we collect from them at the foot of each *tablón*.' Such attractiveness of course meant more investment, but small *fincas* on the other hand had to pay a higher rate to harvest workers as they could not offer the same sort of sustained work. This was a predominantly free labour market with some advantages on labour's side. Pickers could compare likely harvests: 'On Sundays I have sent Antonio, Pablo and three *peones* out in different directions to find people. Some came, had a look at the crop, and went away again. In short, the only way to get more pickers was to put up the price per *arroba*.' [25 June 1907]

They would argue about conditions and resist discipline – on one occasion they refused to work under a *mayordomo*'s direction in a certain *tablón*, insisting on picking where they liked. They ceaselessly compared the incomes obtainable from different *haciendas*:

From today in Santa Inés they are offering 30 *centavos* the *arroba*, and they have a lot ready to pick. If that takes people away from us, I don't see what else we can do here except raise the price here too, because if we get fewer people instead of more the coffee will fall, and that is worse than anything. [10 June 1901]

They could weigh the advantages of various systems of payment, not only between piece-work and *jornal* but also between receiving wages wholly in money and partly in kind. In some periods the *hacienda* ran a *cantina* and fed its labour force. It nearly always paid partly in *miel*. On one occasion it especially imported potatoes from the Sabana, and both owner and administrator were very annoyed when they were refused. It appears to be the work force that makes the choice: 'From next Saturday the *peones* will get 15 *pesos* [we are now in the post-*Mil Días* inflation of 1904] because they prefer the *peso* to the food ration.' [22 February 1904] Nevertheless, the *hacienda* always had to concern itself with the availability of cheap food even if it did not provide it directly as part of the wage. In the scarcity that followed the *Mil Días*, it bought what it could for the workers, and it attempted a complete reorganization of its own food production by paying the *arrendatarios* to plant more *plátanos* among the coffee. They were to have the *plátano* harvest 'de pro-

piedad exclusiva'. There was however an ambiguity about this '*propiedad exclusiva*', revealed when the *hacienda* sought to prevent the *arrendatarios* from selling food outside when the *hacienda* itself needed it. The greater the scarcity, the greater the temptation for the *arrendatarios* to do so, and the greater the efforts of the labour-seeking administrator to prevent them. The owner saw the necessity – Roberto Herrera Restrepo wrote as follows to Rubio shortly before his death:

It is quite indispensable that you should maintain respect and authority as my representative in the management of the *hacienda*. You are right in what you say about this, all the more so in the present circumstances in which the *arrendatarios* are furious about the ban on selling the food produced in the *hacienda* outside it, even though they know we are on the eve of the harvest. [22 February 1912]

The *hacienda* was seeking to purchase the *arrendatarios*' surplus at a price it fixed itself (letter from Rubio, 27 May 1901).

As well as *plátanos*, the *hacienda* directed the planting of yucca and maize. It bought *panela* and *miel* continuously and often maize, trying always to get the cheapest, at prices that fluctuated bewilderingly over short distances and short times.

'If we get fewer people the coffee will fall, and that is worse than anything.' In Cundinamarca, coffee did often fall to the ground and was lost.[10]

The instability and variety of methods of payment thus make a real wage scale for harvesting impossible to construct. A similar scale for *arrendatarios* must recognize their role as producers.

Real conditions

Without such scales – and those that exist for Bogotá are of no use – one can still speculate on how well these workers did. The expansion of commercial coffee growing in Cundinamarca did not generally destroy a pre-existing smallholder class, nor did it expel such a group to the margin of operations. The *arrendatario* was settled and often imported by the *finca*. What exactly was there before could be traced from the notarial records – the usual small-scale productions of the *tierra templada*, exchanged at Facatativá for the produce of the *tierra fría*.[11] As I have written above, the archive leaves the impression that most of the *arrendatarios* on Santa Bárbara were not of local origin. They were not displaced locally.

Certainly their condition was sad in the years after the *Mil Días*: the *hacienda* responded to a falling coffee price and to dangerous conditions by cutting its costs to the minimum and so held wages as low as possible, and this was easier in time of war than in peacetime. The disruption of transport in the war sent food prices right up, and the *hacienda* could not compensate:

Even though the people in the *hacienda* have earned quite a lot of money this year, one sees them in a very wretched state. With the dearness and scarcity of food they have only been able to meet the expense of feeding themselves; they have not been able to buy clothes, and there are families which literally have not got any ... so I am writing to beg Señora María in the name of these poor people that if she has any cast-off clothes and is willing she will send me some to share out. [6 August 1901]

Cornelio Rubio thought these old clothes would be the best *gratificación* to offer those who would see the harvest out. The war reduced this entire enterprise to a desperate state that was aggravated and prolonged by the long trough of coffee prices in which the Brazilians widened the world market and changed its tastes. Furthermore, the Sasaima plantations were becoming exhausted, and both its owner and its manager regarded Santa Bárbara with increasing gloom.

The migrant labour did better through the spread of coffee. For the pickers it provided an additional source of income in those years, and if the resistance of Boyacense *hacendados* to *enganche* is taken as an indication, it may even have slowly eased conditions in the uplands. At least it can be said that the additional employment provided complicates the received picture of the years 1885–1910, which is one of an expansion in paper money and falling real wages, a scheme wholly inimical to the interests of the working class. Paper money did favour the coffee exporter, and wages did often lag. But one must also stress that coffee did markedly increase employment, a matter that it would not be impossible to quantify, and at a time when nothing else looked like doing so, after the gradual decline of tobacco and the catastrophic fall of *quina* in the early 1880s. Its influence on the share of wages in the economy might look better than the individual real wage figures for work in coffee, which have yet to be established. It must also have greatly increased the mobility of labour and shattered the customary upland notion of wages. These assertions can be made whatever the course of real wages and are somewhat more important.[12]

The coffee plantations of Cundinamarca arose in a different economic and cultural context from those in the west of the country. They were established by substantial capitalists, men who had perhaps tried before in *quina* or in indigo, who considered that coffee certainly required the scientific and organizational talents of such as themselves if it was to get anywhere. They possessed or obtained full title to the land they employed. There was very little homesteading competition. With the *curso forzoso* of paper money – it was illegal to stipulate in gold or silver – coffee was an attractive investment: Roberto Herrera withdrew from commerce himself with the introduction of paper money, which for all his interests as an exporting *cafetero* he always opposed. The broader view of coffee among these men was, first, that it provided exchange for a desperate country – they all knew intimately the violent consequences of a lack of that. They were the civilizers and coffee the civilizing nexus – it can be seen in Herrera Restrepo's accounts that his coffee earnings paid for his brother's imports of books for the seminary of the Archdiocese. He was a conscientious employer, but he was at least as preoccupied with the wider needs of society – needs served by an example of civilized living such as he tried to give – as he was by the particular needs of his own work force.[13] The *cafeteros'* system of production in Cundinamarca was broadly that of the Sabana taken down the slope, which was natural enough. They were not consciously founding a new social order in the coffee zone and were not to foresee what conflicts were to arise from that simple transplanting of a familiar mode of production after more than half a century had wrought its economic and demographic changes. Many never thought that coffee would last so long: nothing else in Colombia had.

Politics and revolutions

The course of politics cannot be left out of account when one considers how the *hacendado* thought of his property and of his business, or how his subordinates thought of him. Colombia was not a stable country, nor could most *hacendados* in the middle of this instability guarantee the tranquillity of their own properties. The risks were obvious enough in cattle – '*¡Viva la Revolución, muera el ganado!*' ('Long live the Revolution, death to the cattle!') – but they were also present in coffee. The *cafeteros* could not rely on the support either of the national government or of its local agents.[14]

The relations of Santa Bárbara with the nearby town of Sasaima were not harmonious. It was a corrupting influence on the *peones*. It contained merchants who bought stolen coffee. It was the scene of frequent *bochinches*, quarrels which the administrator as far as possible avoided and tried to get his men to avoid. It sometimes had a good priest, to whom the *hacendado*, the Archbishop's brother, paid his tithe, but who did not have very much influence. And Sasaima was a Conservative municipality – it still is, of course: 1,314 Conservative votes to 128 Liberal votes in 1966. For all his fine Bogotá social connections, Roberto Herrera was not a man of much weight in Sasaima. Though at times he was urged to use his connections to get local officials changed, his success was very limited.

He urged his administrator to take care: 'Look after the *Alcalde* and the Secretary if they go to the *hacienda*; give them some of the brandy from the cupboard.' [25 March 1889] His letters to the *alcaldes* are flattering and correct, but from the few there are one deduces that he watched the local political scene with unrelieved apprehension.

This apprehension was fully justified in time of revolution. With the approach of trouble Roberto Herrera would arrange some simple telegraphic code to warn his *mayordomos* to be ready to avoid as far as possible the recruiting of beasts and men: '*Venda béstias*' or '*Mande cacao*'. They would be told to pay the *exención militar*, for themselves and for as many men as possible. The *hacienda* would become a place of refuge for Liberals who did not want to fight: both Roberto Herrera and his agent disapproved of the bellicose wing of the Liberal Party, led by General Rafael Uribe Uribe, as did most Bogotá Liberals. Herrera himself would get his cattle 'denounced' by a friendly dealer – cattle slaughter in time of war became a government monopoly – and would send down as many useful certificates of exemption as he could obtain in the capital, though these were often disregarded by local Conservative authorities and by government soldiers in the field. Knowing that he would have difficulty in getting his coffee out, he would give orders to cut all possible costs and carry out as little work as possible. *Peones* could be persuaded to work for less in return for enjoying the protection of the *hacienda*: 'Taking very great care that they don't catch the *peones*, I have been able to keep up the work as before and have reduced the wages as follows: the *peones* who got 50 *centavos*, I pay them 30; those who got 45 *centavos*, 25 ...' [1 March 1895] In return for the protection of the *hacienda* they hoped work would continue – but *haciendas* still competed to protect. Coffee would be piled up in all the available *hacienda* buildings, the living rooms of the main house included, to wait for peace.

Recruiting was severe and violent, and the Sasaima authorities logically preferred to start on the Liberal *haciendas* – 'with the *alcaldes* we have here there are no guarantees or safe-conducts.' [6 March 1900] Matters would get much worse in the *Mil Días*, but even in the comparative peace of 1898 there were alarms:

Today I have been told that the *alcalde* of Sasaima and Colonel García . . . have agreed together not to go to the trouble of going out or sending out commissions to recruit, but that from tomorrow they will send out notes to owners or administrators of plantations ordering that each send in so many recruits from his workers. This would not surprise me at all, but it's clear too that they will do this in order to exact fines, for they must understand that, with very few exceptions, nobody will obey. For my part, if they ask me, I prefer a thousand times that they take me into Sasaima or fine me than to hand over the *peones* bound hand and foot, who look on their *patrón* as their protector. If it is going to come to that, I am writing to tell you my way of thinking. [16 March 1898]

On 22 March 1898 one hundred recruits from the Sasaima district were sent down to Villeta on the Honda road, 'all volunteers, each one with a rope round his neck'.

During wars the administrator would hide as many mules and horses as he could, and keep spies posted to warn of the approach of recruiting *comisiones*: 'I have spies posted all over the place, and the *peones* hide until the commissions have gone by.' [29 July 1901] He did his best, keeping his men away from the roads, and using only women as messengers, but with the full struggle of the *Mil Días* the government's methods became increasingly drastic. 'It is no good replacing the gates and chains as the soldiers break them repeatedly.'

Here we have had great alarms since last Thursday, because a Bogotá battalion came down and they spread out through all the *haciendas* to recruit in the most atrocious manner. From here they took the following . . . [altogether the *hacienda* lost seven men]. This lot was inexorable; they did not respect age, class, exemptions, or anything . . . from the *haciendas* on the Namay side they brought *peones*, administrators, and anyone they found. [13 March 1900]

This battalion had a target of 400 men and said it would go on until it was reached. One *peón* of Santa Bárbara was shot dead while trying to run away.

Shortly afterwards local antagonisms made the situation even worse, as recruiting fell into the hands of a local Conservative from Sasaima, Don Eliseo García:

He abused and recruited everybody, and took a delight in contributing so efficiently to the tormenting of his own *pueblo*. They say he has said that his greatest satisfaction will be to see this year that the *haciendas* of the rich lose their harvests. Everyone hates him now. He asked Contreras for a commission last Sunday, to go and take recruits from La Vega [a predominantly Liberal *municipio* to the northeast of Sasaima], and he went and shut in the Plaza, and as it was market day he brought back ninety-six recruits, *gente decente* [respectable people] and *peones*. [14 March 1900]

It was very hard to hide anything from Don Eliseo as he was a local man, a *cazador* (a huntsman), who knew the whole area intimately: 'War lends itself very well to helping the rabble do its worst beneath the protection of the chiefs' – '*la guerra se presta muy bien para que la canalla haga su agosto, mucho más a la sombra de los magnates*' – a constant theme of Colombian politics. The *agosto* included not only the direct extortion of recruiting and taking animals – 'No muleteer wants to go out on the road as he will lose his mules – if the guerrillas don't take them then the government will' – but also the levy on the disaffected, what peaceful Liberals paid for not going to war, and a number of local rackets. The same Eliseo García who wished to ruin the harvests of the rich got his hands on the mules and offered for high prices to take coffee down to the Honda. Conservative generals also controlled all the steamers on the Río Magdalena. Added to all these troubles was the risk of epidemic, as the usual precautions of vaccination were now impossible, and diseased troops from other climates camped on the *hacienda*.

Liberal rebels presented a different danger – the period from 1885 is one of Conservative hegemony, and 1885, 1895, 1899–1903 (the *Mil Días* or Thousand Days) are all Liberal risings. Herrera Restrepo remained a staunch Liberal, always opposed to the Conservative *Regeneración*, even naming one of his mules after it, but he was an out-and-out *pacífico*, and the rules for his men's behaviour he made out clearly in 1885. Those in the *hacienda* were not to compromise themselves. Marauding Liberals were to be told that the property belonged to a Liberal, Conservatives were to be shown as many proofs of good behaviour as possible and told that the property belonged to a brother of the Archbishop, who was naturally a Conservative. These instructions were followed. In September 1900 Antioqueño and Caucano troops visited the cattle *hacienda* of El Peñon and asked if the *mayordomo* and the owner were Liberals: 'and as I could not deny them the information,' wrote the *mayordomo*, 'I spoke to them quite frankly and said that it was the property of the Archbishop and of one of his brothers who was a Liberal.' [22 September 1900]

There were Liberal guerrillas in the Sasaima area in 1895, and in the *Mil Días* the *pueblo* was briefly taken by Liberal forces. However pacific the resolves of Herrera Restrepo's people at the beginning of the war (and they certainly did regard it as a foolhardy revolution), neutrality was very hard to maintain in the face of government provocation. There were not only the *contribuciones* – 'What they punish in us *pacíficos* is the *picardía* [knavery] of not taking part in the War' – but also the news of what was happening to their relations in other parts of the country.

Cornelio Rubio had an uncle and two brothers in arms in Tolima, and his family there was persecuted:

This sort of proceeding only corrupts one with politics, even a person who has never wanted to be involved. How can one look on this sort of thing indifferently? . . . I say with all sincerity to you now that for my part I am sorry that I have not the freedom to take part myself were the circumstances to be right. I'm now as much in favour of this war as anyone, I have great faith in it. If the right opportunity presents itself, I repeat, the only course will be for my family to support the war; they have been outraged, they have been ruined without mercy. Of course I don't say this in a spirit of vengeance against certain determined persons, though they would deserve it, but in general, to give our cause some support . . . [3 and 23 January 1900]

Rubio was very anxious that the *hacienda* should not be compromised by any of its men leaving for the Liberal guerrillas, particularly as some of those in the district had a very evil reputation '*por sus malos procedimientos*'. All the same, some did take up arms. Towards the end of the war Rubio was convinced that the local Conservatives were determined to rid the district of Liberals once and for all. 'One must wait to see if the Sasaimeros will let me go back there,' he wrote from a temporary refuge in Facatativá, 'as I have heard from good sources that they propose to get rid of us few Liberals who live there, by driving us by every possible means to despair.' [16 October 1901]

The passions of the Conservatives went beyond the interests of coffee. The government imposed a heavy emergency tax on coffee exports, which was duly posted in Sasaima:

We have already seen the decree with which they have decided to favour the only industry which seemed to give us all some hope. In these parts as you would suppose there have been many people who approve it unconditionally, even *cafeteros*. They only take account of where the decree comes from and then it's good, fair and just for them whatever it contains. [7 May 1900]

This sectarian fervour perhaps had a further explanation, and Rubio wrote again a fortnight later: 'Among those who gave the Government's decree on coffee such a good reception there are people who surprise one by being so blinded and carried away by political passion. It must be that they have the agreeable (for them) expectation that this abominable decree will only be applied to the government's enemies.' [21 May 1900] 'God alone knows what we shall see next' – '*Pues sólo Díos sabe lo que hemos de ver . . .*' [1 June 1900]

The war's effects on production are obvious enough, and the war was not followed by a definitive peace. There were plenty of other alarms before the archive closes, and in all these the *hacienda* feared for its labour force. Disturbances in public order, *cuadrillas de malhechores* on the roads, would prevent pickers coming down for the harvest. Recruiting might start again. Owner and administrator prayed for peace, that the laborious might be allowed to work, but they could take few precautions. In 1906 Roberto Herrera sent Rubio a revolver with twelve cartridges, in 1912 two Gras rifles. His instructions on national politics at election times were clearly set out as follows:

You should make enquiries and give your vote to persons who can be recognized as being of good judgement and good position, and who will therefore come to Congress to work not for this party or that but for the interests of the whole country. That is the tendency of everyone who sees the necessity that we get on the right road to remedy the evils that beset us. My opinion is that you should give your vote to the candidate who appears to you the most respectable of those you have here and otherwise take no active part. [to the *mayordomo* of El Peñon, 24 May 1909]

Rubio had some influence over the vote of Santa Bárbara's *arrendatarios*, but not enough to have any significant impact on election results. A number of anxious letters over roads, and on the tax valuation of the *hacienda*, likewise show little influence over the local government.

'I would today very willingly exchange the *hacienda* for the 25,000 gold *pesos* which they have fixed in the valuation. We proprietors are the mere administrators for the government, and with no salary. Such a load of contributions can't be borne, especially in coffee which is a ruined business. The worst is that it is an evil with no remedy. [13 November 1905]

Or, as Rubio put it, 'One is left as an *arrendatario* paying an extraordinary rent' – '*uno queda como arrendatario pagando un arriendo extraordinario*'. This was because Santa Bárbara did not recover from the war.

The decline of Santa Bárbara

Señor *Alcalde* of the *municipio* of Sasaima. I, Cornelio Rubio, being over 21, etc., etc., respectfully solicit from you the following: That you will summon to your office Señores Francisco Zapata, Felix Basurto, and Campo Elías Rubio ... so that under oath and according to the other legal requirements they may declare on the following points:

1st, Their age, etc., etc.

2nd, If they know the *hacienda* called Santa Bárbara in this *municipio*, property of Señor Don Roberto Herrera Restrepo.

3rd, If they know and are aware that this said *hacienda* has not had and has no other source of production besides plantations of coffee.

4th, If they know and are aware that this said *hacienda* finds itself in a lamentably deteriorated state owing to its absolute and complete abandon during three years of war, and since then to the scarcity of labour.

5th, If they know that the *cafetales* of Santa Bárbara are today reduced to less than the third part of what they were before, owing to the reasons aforementioned and to the exhaustion of the lands where they were planted, and that to this same proportion of one-third their production has been reduced.

6th, That they say also if they are aware that the present price of coffee is in complete disaccord with the expenses of production of coffee for export or for sale within the country; and

7th, That they say without prejudice to the best of their understanding whether they believe that the valuation which has just been fixed in the new *catastro* of 25,000 gold *pesos* is fair or exaggerated, and if the last, that they say how much they think said *hacienda* can be worth.

> Cornelio Rubio
> Sasaima, 3 April 1909.

These plantations are now very old and consequently have age and the exhaustion of the land against them. The plantations of Santa Bárbara represent scarcely a third part, more or less, of what they were before. [4 April 1909]

Writing thus to the *Junta de Catastro* at Facatativá, Roberto Herrera reckoned even 20,000 gold *pesos* too high.

These documents asking for a reduction in the tax assessment naturally present a dark picture, but there is much other evidence to support it.

First, there was the unsteady but finally dramatic decline in the quantity of coffee produced by the *hacienda* (see Table 40). As the *finca* became less productive the cost of harvesting rose, and they remembered the good old days when they could pick in two days as much as they could now pick in a week. The quality also declined, and the list of the London agents' adjectives of criticism grew longer: *pálido, gris, defectuoso, pequeño, duro, mediano verdoso, deslucido, moteado, algo pequeño* (pale, grey, defective, small, hard, rather green, dull, spotty, rather small) – Santa Bárbara was an aged plantation, not much could be done about it, and the mediocre prices prevailing gave little incentive. Herrera Restrepo did experiment with other types of coffee; he sent soil samples for analysis in Germany, and he planted peas impregnated with 'nitro-bacterine', a patent English fertilizer, among his flagging trees. None of this appears to have done much good.

'The growing of coffee can sustain itself in present circumstances, but to create a new plantation would be a folly today.' [Alberto Plot to Roberto Herrera, from Girardot, 18 November 1905] At best, such a *finca* could tick over. The outlook for Cundinamarca coffee in the first

TABLE 40   *Hacienda Santa Bárbara: coffee exports, 1886–1907*
            (62-kg sacks)

1886	528
1887	587
1888	405
1889	450
1890	366
1891	288
1892	500
1893	595
1894	713
1895	1,065
1896	1,564
1897	707
1898	2,397
1899	674
1900–3	{ Very scant exports owing to civil war
1904	1,289
1905	596
1906	1,100
1907	138

decade of this century was pessimistic. Was there sound reason to think that coffee would have a course so different from tobacco, from indigo, from quinine? Not in the opinion of the American consul in Bogotá in 1903: 'A study of the industries of Colombia, past and present, impresses one with the fact that without an exception they have all risen to a height from which much was expected, and that when just approaching the zenith, for some cause such as war, overproduction or the like ... they have begun to decline.'[15]

Roberto Herrera became increasingly indebted to his London agent – at the close of 1907 he owed £3,398 2s 4d. In that same year he tried to sell the *hacienda,* but his correspondent predictably declined the offer: *'el negocio del café en mala situación'* – 'the coffee business is in a bad state'. [Lorenzo Cuellar to Roberto Herrera from Buenos Aires, 14 August 1907] The closing years of the archive show that Herrera Restrepo paid off the coffee debt with letters bought on the proceeds of his other enterprises. He continued to deal in cattle and expanded his cattle operations, but he also showed signs of wanting to withdraw from agriculture altogether. He might have welcomed an agrarian reform, as other landlords similarly placed perhaps did in the 1930s and have done since. His successors eventually planned to sell the *hacienda* in lots for *fincas de recreo*, and it is underneath these not very agricultural establishments that the ghost of the old enterprise can now be faintly seen.

The social problems which coffee eventually brought to some regions of Cundinamarca, and which issued in relatively spectacular conflicts in the late 1920s and early 1930s, have received some attention. These once pioneering, risky, and even patriotic ventures had by then come to look greedy and oligarchic and oppressive. Conflicts within them similar to those I have described, in some famous cases combined with disputes over the title to the land, were so intensified by the Depression that government intervention was required to resolve them. Sasaima by then had ceased to be a coffee-producing *municipio* of leading importance, though it still had nearly two million trees about 1930, compared with the leading *municipio* of the Department, Viotá, which had five million. One of the earliest parts of Cundinamarca to produce coffee, Sasaima was one of the earliest to decline, for sub-division has already gone much further there than in the rest of the area. Viotá's five million trees were said to be in thirty plantations, Sasaima's two million in a thousand. This *parcelización* is probably a sign of marginality.[16] When General Uribe Uribe foresaw the end of the trough and in 1908 raised the cry '¡*Colombianos, a sembrar café!*', this estate was unable to make an enthusiastic response.

Santa Bárbara, 1870–1912

Roberto Herrera's accounts put the capital value of the *hacienda* each year as its original price plus the cost of physical improvements. In the inflationary conditions of Colombia, calculations of profit made on that base are not very realistic, and it would also be necessary to make some allowance for the *hacienda*'s eventual exhaustion.[17] There were certainly substantial earnings, but the long-awaited high years of the 1890s were not something out of fable. The proceeds of Santa Bárbara coffee sold in London, with cost of shipping from Barranquilla, insurance, and agent's fees deducted, averaged £3,640 between 1886 and 1899, with a high point of £7,976 in 1896, and the worst year (1891) yielding only £1,576. *Hacienda* costs and the principal item of wages, and the heavy local transport expenses to the Río Magdalena and down it to Barranquilla, must be subtracted to give some approximation of the real profit. This should ideally be done on a harvest basis, and because of the time-lag between coffee leaving the *hacienda* and being sold in London, the

TABLE 41   Hacienda Santa Bárbara: proceeds of sales of coffee in London, 1886–99 (£ sterling)

1886	2,240
1887	3,460
1888	2,337
1889	2,738
1890	2,049
1891	1,576
1892	2,829
1893	3,266
1894	3,192
1895	5,728
1896	7,976
1897	3,247
1898	7,369
1899	2,128

Sources: Santa Bárbara *hacienda* archives, volume *Cuentas de ventas de café*; the figure for 1886 is taken from the account book 'Santa Bárbara'.

accounts calculate profit on estimates of future sales that were not always fulfilled. In 1886 proceeds of coffee sold in London were £2,240, and Herrera Restrepo calculated his profit on the *hacienda* at 7,914 *pesos*, which translated again into sterling at that year's premiums would give around £1,600 (see Table 41). Those proportions may not have been maintained in the competition of the closing years of the century, which brought higher wage bills and higher transport costs. The war made all calculations impossible, and for some time after it local costs remained exceptionally high. Their rise was held by the American consul to be a greater threat to the industry in Colombia than the still depressed world price. He concluded,

I know that owners of plantations are extremely anxious to get rid of their estates or lease them for long periods on very liberal terms, and in some cases asking no rent whatever, but leasing them on the sole condition that they be returned at the expirations of the lease in the same condition as when received.[18]

Coffee has had its cycles in Colombia and survived them. But not every district, not every *cafetal* nor every *cafetero*, has done so. As Lord Salisbury noted in one despatch from Colombia, risk capital does imply an element of risk, and this existed as much for the native as for those expatriates Lord Salisbury was not very anxious to protect. There were the hazards – of the market, of labour, of the seasons, and of the land –

that no agriculture can escape. There were the additional hazards of experiment where the entrepreneur had few precedents and fewer scientific resources at his command. And no agricultural enterprise exists in an economist's vacuum: there were also present here other risks and difficulties that must have their place in the agrarian history of nineteenth-century Latin America.

NOTES

1. I must thank the following for their comments on this essay: J. León Helguera, Pierre Gilhodes, Roger Brew, Charles Bergquist, Marco Palacios, and Donald Winters. The most interesting parts of this paper are taken from the *archivo* of Roberto Herrera Restrepo, and I am deeply grateful to the late Dr José Umaña and to Sra María Carrizosa de Umaña for their generosity in letting me use the archive, for their many kindnesses besides, and for their help on many points of difficulty.

2. For some details of the Santander sharecropping system and some hint of the different historical antecedents and demographic circumstances of coffee in Santander, see Mario Galán Gómez, *Geografía económica de Colombia*, Vol. 8, *Santander* (Bogotá, 1947), especially chapters 21 and 28; and Virginia Gutiérrez de Pineda, *Familia y cultura en Colombia* (Bogotá, 1968), pp. 120ff. A full description of the varieties of organization compatible with coffee in Colombia, and of the reasons for their emergence, has yet to be attempted.

3. Calculating from its production (see Table 40), it appears to have had some 60,000 trees in production in the 1880s, and to have engaged in extensive new plantings in the early 1890s: production rose steadily from 1894 to 1898. These calculations are fairly crude, being made on the basis of a yield of half a kilo per tree. The figure of 60,000 trees for 1880 is confirmed by *El Agricultor*, no. 18 (Bogotá, 1 November 1880).

4. The archive consists of thirty-eight volumes, of which eighteen are of correspondence received and twenty are account-books; of the latter, three are of particular interest: *Cuentas de ventas de café, 1880–99, Cuentas de importaciones, 1874–1901*, and one small account-book for the *hacienda* of Santa Bárbara, covering the years 1883–9.

   There is a privately printed memorial to Roberto Herrera Restrepo, 1848–1912, entitled *Roberto Herrera Restrepo, 1848–1948* (Bogotá, 1948); and further details of his family's history and antecedents can be found in Monseñor José Restrepo Posada's essay on Roberto Herrera's brother Bernardo Herrera Restrepo, the Archbishop of Bogotá, published in *La Iglesia*, Anno XXXIX, nos. 654–7 (September–December 1945).

5. Sasaima coffee was exceptionally fine, and until the end of the 1890s Herrera Restrepo's *marca* ЯHR sold at a distinct premium above the general level of Colombian prices in the London market, which kept him loyal to it. This advantage had disappeared by the late 1890s.

6. The best-documented enterprise in the archive, apart from the Santa Bárbara, is the cattle ranch of El Peñon, near Tocaima. But there are also details of the 'Compañía de Colombia', a very large but not very successful cattle, *quina*, and rubber enterprise situated between Neiva and the *llanos*, in which he inherited his father's share; and also of renting dairy land on the Sabana, and of other activities

besides. See Gabino Charry G., *Frutos de mi tierra: geografía histórica del departamento del Huila* (Neiva, 1924), pp. 37ff.

7. A contemporary estimate of the number of families permanently needed was one family of five persons per 5,000 trees. This would place the need for permanent labour on Santa Bárbara, at its greatest extent, at some twenty-four families.

8. Various authorities give various years; Roberto Velandia, *Historia geopolítica de Cundinamarca* (Bogotá, 1971), p. 392, argues for 1620.

9. There is an excellent contemporary description of these, based on the observations of the author in the *Hacienda* Ceilán, Viotá, Cundinamarca, in Ramon V. Lanao, 'Endemias del clima del café' (unpublished thesis, Bogotá, 1891). The list includes *sabañones* (fungoid rot of hands and feet), dysentery, worms (a good purge always brings them out 'by platoons'), various other parasitic infections, and, most widespread and most damaging, anaemia, '*la enfermedad constitucional de casi todos los jornaleros*' – 'the occupational disease of nearly all the labourers'. The remarks on the relation of anaemia to loss of appetite and the sufferers' consequent lethargy and irritability are very acute for the time and suggest that not all Rubio's difficulties in getting his men to work were problems of incentives.

10. The British Vice-Consul in Bogotá reckoned that labour shortage meant that half the coffee was being lost at the end of the *Mil Días* War in 1903: see Spencer S. Dickson, *Report on the present state of the coffee trade in Colombia*, Parliamentary Papers, 1904, *Accounts and Papers* vol. XCVI, Cd. 1767–2, Diplomatic and Consular Miscellaneous Series no. 598.

11. Writing in 1763, Basilio Vicente de Oviedo described Sasaima as a small, predominantly *mestizo* settlement, producing small quantities of tobacco, cotton, yucca, plantains, maize, sugar-cane '*y demás frutas de tierra caliente*'. See his *Cualidades y riquezas del nuevo reino de Granada*, ed. Luis Augusto Cuervo, Biblioteca de Historia Nacional XLV (Bogotá, 1930), p. 267.

12. For a recent discussion of this question, see Miguel Urrutia Montoya, 'El sector externo y la distribución de ingresos en Colombia en el siglo XIX', *Revista del Banco de la República* (Bogotá), November 1972, pp. 1–14. See also General Rafael Uribe Uribe, 'Estudio sobre los salarios', in his *Discursos Parlamentarios, Congreso Nacional de 1896*, 2nd edn (Bogotá, 1897), pp. 231–7: he estimated that paper money in the previous decade had reduced wages in real terms by a third. A crude guess made publicly at the time is perhaps worth more than some later elaborations, and paper money on the unprecedented scale of the late 1890s and the *Mil Días* brought, in Vice-Consul Dickson's words, 'financial chaos ... ultimately ... to everyone's disadvantage'. General Uribe Uribe also reckoned that one-fourth of all Colombians were 'directly' involved with coffee. A more particular later estimate for Cundinamarca in 1906 reckoned that 750 plantations employed some 12,000 permanent workers and 100,000 harvesters on forty-six million trees: see Luis Mejía Montoya in *Revista Nacional de Agricultura*, no. 8 (31 July 1906). Diego Monsalve, *Colombia cafetera* (Barcelona, 1927) gives 2,817 plantations and fifty-three million trees for Cundinamarca. On the early history of paper money, see Guillermo Torres García, *Historia de la moneda en Colombia* (Bogotá, 1945), chapters 8 and 9.

13. Though offered the Ministries of Hacienda and the Treasury, Herrera Restrepo refused public office on principle, especially after the *Regeneración* movement came to power in 1885. The reputation for rectitude, hard work, and public spirit shown in *Roberto Herrera Restrepo, 1848–1948* is amply confirmed in the archive.

As all Latin American exports are reputedly followed by wild extravagance in the exporters, it is worth noting that there is no evidence for that here. Roberto Herrera and his family lived and celebrated the *rites de passage* at the accepted gentlemanly level of the cosmopolitan years before 1914. To such as he, coffee's success or failure meant nothing less than membership in, or exclusion from, civilization. To use a word much used at the time, it was what stood in the way of Colombia's becoming a nation of Kaffirs. Colombia's international reputation was indeed appalling: remember the interior of the 'Republic of Costaguana' in Joseph Conrad's *Nostromo*, the man Pedro in *Victory*. It should also be remembered that Bogotá was an expensive place to lead a civilized and civilizing life: the first was very much cheaper for Colombians abroad.

14. On government policy towards coffee in the 1890s, see Uribe Uribe's speeches 'Gravamen del café', in *Estudios sobre café* (Bogotá, 1952), pp. 187–223. Many of Uribe Uribe's observations in them are borne out by the Herrera Restrepo archive. As well as for its tax on coffee exports, Uribe Uribe attacked the government for making the scarcity of labour worse by keeping 8,000 men under arms. Losses in civil war had their effect, too, which he does not mention. The coffee growers' difficulties with the government after the *Mil Días* War can be seen in the appropriate numbers of the *Revista Nacional de Agricultura*.

15. See the useful despatch from Mr Snyder to the Department of State, 'Present state of the coffee trade', 21 August 1903 (U.S. National Archives microfilm: Despatches from U.S. Consuls in Bogotá, roll 3, no. 21*bis*).

16. Figures from Monsalve, *Colombia cafetera*, p. 426. The best sources for the conflicts of the 1920s and 1930s are still the appropriate numbers of the *Boletín de la Oficina Nacional de Trabajo* of the *Ministerio de Industrias*, and the various *Memorias* of the department of Cundinamarca.

17. Calculations without allowance have been made from Roberto Herrera's books by Dario Bustamente Roldán in his 'Efectos económicos del papel moneda durante la Regeneración' (unpublished thesis, Universidad de los Andes, Bogotá, 1970). From the mid-1880s they ran at about 20 per cent, rising to 66 per cent, 72 per cent, and 65 per cent for 1895, 1896, and 1897 respectively. (See Roldán's *cuadro* III. His estimates end in 1899.)

18. Mr Snyder to Department of State, 22 August 1905 (U.S. National Archives microfilm: Despatches from U.S. Consuls in Bogotá, roll 4).

BIBLIOGRAPHICAL NOTE

For the wider context of Cundinamarca coffee, the best work remains Robert Carlyle Beyer, 'The Colombian coffee industry: origins and major trends, 1740–1940' (unpublished Ph.D. dissertation, University of Minnesota, 1947): this study also contains an excellent bibliography. Another indispensable book is Diego Monsalve's magnificent *Colombia cafetera* (Barcelona, 1927). An able sketch of the industry at the turn of the century is Vice-Consul Spencer S. Dickson's *Report on the present state of the coffee trade in Colombia*, Parliamentary Papers, 1904, *Accounts and Papers* vol. XCVI, Cd. 1767–2, Diplomatic and Consular Miscellaneous Series no. 598. See also Phanor J. Eder, *Colombia* (London, 1913), chapter 10; and Augusto Ramos, *O café no Brasil e no estrangeiro* (Rio de Janeiro, 1923), pp. 339–41, for near-contemporary estimates of the situation of Colombian production. General Rafael Uribe Uribe, *Estudios sobre café*, Banco de la República, Archivo de la Economía Nacional no. 6 (Bogotá, 1952) is a still-valuable collection of his later articles.

On Sasaima in particular, see Medardo Rivas, *Los trabajadores de la tierra caliente*, 2nd edn (Bogotá, 1946), chapter 15, 'El café', pp. 310–11; and the same author's *Viajes por Colombia, Francia, Inglaterra* (vol. 2 of his *Obras completas*, 2 vols., Bogotá, 1885), pp. 1off. Here he specifically praises coffee as a better employer than sugar or cattle. See also Salvador Camacho Roldán, *Notas de viaje (Colombia y Estados Unidos de América)*, 4th edn (Paris and Bogotá, 1905), pp. 29–30.

There is a good descriptive account of coffee installations in Viotá, similar to Sasaima's though on a somewhat larger scale, in O. Fuhrmann and Eugene Mayor, *Voyage d'exploration scientifique en Colombie* (Tome v of *Memoire de la Societé des Sciences Naturelles de Neuchâtel*, 2 vols. (Neuchâtel, 1911), vol. 1, pp. 101–10. The early manuals on coffee cultivation used in Colombia are conveniently collected in José Manuel Restrepo *et al.*, *Memorias sobre el cultivo del café*, Banco de la República, Archivo de la Economía Nacional no. 5 (Bogotá, 1952).

PART III

The development of commercial agriculture using European immigrant labour

In so far as its starting point for the analysis of the process of agrarian change is the demise of the slave plantation system, Thomas H. Holloway's essay on labour organization in the Brazilian coffee industry provides certain points of contact with the papers included in Part IV. However, in this particular case the social and economic changes resulting from the large-scale immigration of European labour were so massive and far-reaching that they render any discussion of the changing status of the slaves themselves of minimal interest compared with the examples studied in the final section. Whereas in the case of northeast Brazil's sugar cane industry an uncertain future for the commodity's markets meant that the decline and abolition of slavery was not accompanied by a relative shortage of labour (see the papers by Peter L. Eisenberg and Jaime Reis in Part IV), in the São Paulo region the decline of slavery occurred precisely at the time when great new opportunities were opening up for the cultivation and export of coffee. The coffee planters could never have taken full advantage of these new possibilities if they had tried to rely on local Negro labour; it is doubtful if even inter-regional transfers of ex-slaves would have supplied the quantity of manpower required. Instead, by encouraging the immigration of vast numbers of European labourers (mainly Italians) they totally transformed the social structure of the state of São Paulo. Consequently, for our present purposes, the principal theoretical interest of Holloway's paper lies in the comparison that can be made with other types of commercial agriculture which used European immigrant labour, such as the cereal-growing industry of the Argentine *pampas*, described in the paper by Ezequiel Gallo.

Holloway first considers the system of sharecropping, using European immigrants, which certain planters adopted in their attempts to solve the problem of the transition from slave labour. However, the planters soon discovered that the element of coercion embodied in this sharecropping system was self-defeating, since it discouraged further immigration. Inevitably they gradually came first to accept and then to rely completely on free labour, although, as Holloway explains, the particular form which this took in the context of the São Paulo coffee industry departed fairly radically from both the rural proletarian model and tenant farming. The *colono* contract involved a complex mixture of day-wages, piece-rate payments, payments in kind, and the usufruct of land. Possibly the last of these was the main attraction for immigrant labour, and the availability of valley-bottom lands which were unsuitable for coffee within the plantation system enabled the planters to offer this inducement to immigrant labourers without reducing the amount of land available for coffee-growing.

Holloway shows that considerable numbers of ex-*colonos* experienced both geographical and social mobility. The former gave a substantial boost to the latter, for by moving west to the agricultural frontier many immigrants were able to establish themselves as small planters in their own right. Nevertheless, the existence of a powerful landowning class in the coffee-growing region set certain definite limits on the ability of immigrant rural labourers to establish themselves as independent peasant–farmers: limitations which, at least at first, were much less evident in the case of the cereal-growing areas of the Argentine *pampas*.

Ezequiel Gallo's paper on cereal-growing in the province of Santa Fe argues that the choice of crop itself played a central role in determining the future social and economic structure of the area, although he also emphasizes that, since this was an area of new settlement, it was completely free from the historically influential social and economic structures and relationships established by, and embodied in, a pre-existing and more archaic mode of production. To this extent the cereal-growing areas of the Argentine *pampas* must be sharply distinguished from the older cereal-growing areas of Latin America, such as Chile or Mexico (see the papers by Bauer, Kay, Brading, and Bazant in Part I). In contrast to the case of Brazilian coffee, in Santa Fe, at least during the period which Gallo analyses, there was practically no landlord control over the land, and great numbers of European immigrants (again, mainly Italian) were able to establish themselves very rapidly as independent farmers through the system of agricultural colonies favoured by the provincial authorities. By using a wide variety of census data Gallo underlines the difference between the cereal-growing area of Santa Fe and the sheep-raising zone, and stresses that the characteristic and principal form of agricultural enterprise in the cereal region was the small or medium-sized farm in which the greater part of the agricultural work was carried out by family labour. Even in this case, however, wage labour played an important role at harvest time, when large numbers of seasonal migrant workers were required. Gallo argues that between them the absence of a pre-existing landlord class and the special pattern of land settlement permitted the evolution of a rather more egalitarian class structure than that typically found in most other parts of Latin America.

CHAPTER 12

The coffee *colono* of São Paulo, Brazil: migration and mobility, 1880–1930

THOMAS H. HOLLOWAY[1]

The period from the 1880s to the 1920s was the 'Golden Age' of coffee in western São Paulo. Santos, São Paulo's only major port, had replaced Rio de Janeiro as the world's most important coffee export centre by 1894. Santos' share of the world coffee market rose from less than 25 per cent in the late 1880s to 50 per cent by the first years of the twentieth century, and it continued to supply more than half the world's coffee until after the First World War. In absolute terms the annual production of the Santos coffee zone increased from an average of under two million bags during the last years of slavery to more than eight million bags in the first five years of this century, and continued at high levels thereafter.[2] The transition from slave to free labour, the rapid expansion of coffee cultivation, and massive European immigration into São Paulo characterize the period here under examination – the four decades from the decline of slavery in the 1880s to the Great Depression.

The geographical area being considered is the coffee region which exported its production through the port of Santos – that is, the interior plateau west and north of the city of São Paulo. The section of the Paraíba River Valley in eastern São Paulo, together with the coffee areas of southern Minas Gerais and Rio de Janeiro state, exported through the port of Rio de Janeiro. The coffee boom in the Paraíba Valley preceded that of the western plateau and was characterized by the slave labour system. By the late 1880s production in the Paraíba area had gone into a marked decline from which it never recovered.[3] In the 1890s over 90 per cent of São Paulo's coffee exports came from the western plateau area tributary to the port of Santos, and by the second decade of this century the Santos zone accounted for more than 98 per cent of the state's coffee exports.[4]

The São Paulo plateau forms a distinct geographical and chronological unit in the history of coffee in Brazil, and in many ways the economic system which developed there from the decline of slavery to the Great Depression may be considered a distinct unit as well. During that period a unique form of agricultural labour organization was used in São Paulo which can only be subsumed under the label '*colono* contract'.[5] It formed

Map 19

the specific economic framework under which hundreds of thousands of
people laboured for half a century to produce more than 300,000,000
sixty-kilogramme bags of coffee, nearly one-half the total produced in
the world in that period. After discussing immigrant mobility in rural
São Paulo generally, this paper will describe the development of the
particular form of work organization which replaced slavery in the coffee
plantations, and present evidence of upward mobility on the part of
immigrant workers in the rural areas.

Immigration and the rural labour force

The coffee *colonos* were predominantly first-generation European immigrants. On an 1886 population base of some 1,250,000, roughly 2,750,000
immigrants entered São Paulo from that year to the early 1930s. More
than a million of the total were Italians, primarily from northern Italy.
Portuguese and Spanish made up about half a million each, with Germans,
Eastern Europeans, Syrio-Lebanese, and later Japanese constituting the
remainder. These workers were largely peasants or agricultural labourers
pushed into emigration by political changes, poor economic conditions,
and population pressure in their countries of origin. Some individuals

began as itinerant peddlers and eventually made a successful entry into the commercial and industrial elite. But as a group the immigrants brought little capital or entrepreneurial expertise. While foreigners also dominated the urban labour market, the industrial labour force remained small relative to the number of workers occupied in coffee production.[6]

Attracted by coffee, the immigrants came supplied only with the strength of their hands and went to work on the plantations. By the time of the 1905 agricultural census in São Paulo, 65 per cent of the rural workers of all types in the western plateau were foreign-born (221,000 of a total 338,000), and in those *municipios* where coffee cultivation was the most highly concentrated, immigrants made up as much as 90 per cent of the rural labour force. When the larger coffee plantations are singled out for closer analysis, the proportion of foreign workers is higher still. Of all the foreign-born agricultural workers in the state, 98 per cent were located in the western plateau region.[7]

The outstanding characteristic of the coffee *colono* was movement. The first and most universal manifestation of this was the uprooting and transfer to the New World. Once the immigrants reached São Paulo, mobility took many forms, and it did not always imply social or economic improvement. There was migration from plantation to plantation in the coffee zone, towards the coffee frontier in the west, to regional urban centres, and to the state's capital city; and many immigrants eventually returned to their homelands. Relatively less important but still significant was migration to other parts of Brazil and to Argentina. Whenever a coffee *colono* moved he left a place to be taken by another, in a cycle which was often repeated. However, it would be an exaggeration to convey an image of a seething mass of humanity constantly on the move, and there were cases of *colonos* remaining for much of their productive life on a single plantation. The historical record reveals little regarding individual career patterns and rates of migration within this economic system. It is possible, nevertheless, to give a gross indication of the extent of the turnover of the labour force in rural São Paulo.

Extrapolating from the number of coffee trees in production and the average number of trees each *colono* cared for, about 100,000 workers were needed in the coffee industry of western São Paulo around 1890, rising steadily to some 400,000 workers before 1910. The necessary coffee labour force remained between some 375,000 and 425,000 at any given time during the 1920s.[8] These estimates of labour needs contrast with the summary data in Table 42 on total foreign immigration into the port of Santos.

Not all immigrants went directly into the plantation labour pool. These

TABLE 42   *Total immigration into Santos, 1886–1935*

1886–95	621,000
1896–05	504,000
1906–15	557,000
1916–25	408,000
1926–35	695,000
Total	2,785,000

Source: *Boletim da Directoria de Terras, Colonização e Immigração,*
no. 1 (October 1937), p. 46.

totals include children too young to work, women not active in the labour
force, and those immigrants who entered the urban areas. Even after
allowances are made for such groups, however, it seems apparent that if
the existing plantation labour force had been relatively stable a large
proportion of the new immigrants would have faced unemployment. Yet
lack of employment opportunities in the coffee zone was not one of the
many criticisms which consular officials, foreign observers, and immigrants themselves directed at conditions in São Paulo. The planters,
for their part, consistently complained of labour shortages of greater or
lesser severity, and labour scarcity was the rationale for continued
government immigration subsidies.

The principal labour-contracting agency throughout this period was
the immigrant hostel in the city of São Paulo, built by the Provincial
Government in 1886–7 and administered by the state Department of
Agriculture. More than half the newly arrived immigrants through
Santos spent their first days in the hostel, where they contracted for
jobs on the western plantations. Workers in the capital city who wished
to go to work in coffee could enter the hostel and use the labour exchange
in the same way as the new arrivals. While it was not the only means of
arranging for work on the plantations, especially for those already in the
coffee zone who wanted to change employers, the hostel was especially
important for recent immigrants. Table 43 summarizes data on immigration into São Paulo, movement through the hostel, and those passing
through the hostel who took work in the western coffee zone, for the
period 1901 to 1920. Nearly a million immigrants had already entered
São Paulo between 1886 and 1900, and the total labour needs of the
coffee industry increased only slowly after about 1906–7. Therefore
the data in Table 43 would seem to indicate a considerable degree of
geographical mobility of the rural labour force in the western coffee

TABLE 43   *Santos immigration and São Paulo immigrant hostel movement, 1901–5*
to 1916–20 (thousands of persons)

Years	A Total immigration into Santos	B Total hostel movement	C B as % of A	D Persons leaving hostel for work in western coffee zone	E D as % of B
1901–5	206	141	68	130	92
1906–10	200	145	73	128	88
1911–15	356	260	73	216	83
1916–20	129	120	93	109	91
Total	891	666	75	583	88

Sources: Col. A: same as Table 42. Cols. B and D: São Paulo (State), *Anuario estatístico
de Estado de São Paulo*, various years.

zone, as newly arrived immigrants moved in to take the place of workers
moving out.

I turn now to a consideration of the system of labour organization
under which these immigrants worked in the plantations of São Paulo –
the system which made it possible for the coffee planters to attract and
maintain a labour force during the transition from slaves to free labour
and the rapid expansion of the coffee industry. To understand the workings of the *colono* contract it is important to examine its origins and
evolution, starting in the mid nineteenth century.

Early experiments with free labour

Beginning in 1847 and continuing into the 1850s, several planters in
western São Paulo attempted to replace their slaves with free European
immigrants under *parceria*, or sharecropping. Senator Nicolau Vergueiro
most actively promoted this early programme, and the revolt of the
Swiss sharecroppers on his plantation in 1857 brought to light the defects
of the system.[9] Hard economic realities rather than a humanitarian
interest in the end of slavery motivated Vergueiro and his fellow planters.
The attempts to use free labour took place in the frontier zone where
commercial coffee cultivation was being introduced for the first time.
The continued expansion of coffee in western São Paulo depended on the
availability of manpower, and by 1851 the British and Brazilian governments had effectively stopped the transatlantic slave trade. The planters
on the frontier had to depend on inter-regional slave transfers to fill

their expanding labour needs. Some landowners were thus receptive to the idea of experimenting with free labour.

In mid-nineteenth-century Brazil, one of the basic problems to be solved in such experiments was how to compensate workers for their labour and how much to pay. The maintenance of an adequate labour force on the one hand, and the continued profitability of the plantation on the other, depended on the adequate solution of those problems. Slaves did nearly all the plantation work in the coffee zone. Non-slave labourers were the relatively unimportant group of *agregados* (tenants allowed usufruct of marginal estate lands for occasional labour services) who, in their relationship with the landowners, resembled informal retainers more nearly than salaried employees. Independent workers hired for a daily wage, called *camaradas*, were also insignificant on the coffee plantations. In such a situation any plan envisaging money payments to workers was an innovation involving some degree of uncertainty. The planters had only a rough idea of what the total coffee yield would be or what the market would be like a year hence. Sharecropping forced the landowner to forgo some of the potential income which was exclusively his under slavery, yet it prevented the remote but frightening possibility that wages might absorb more than the revenue from the crop.

In the early sharecropping system the planters paid the transportation costs of the immigrants from Europe and advanced sufficient funds to tide the new arrivals over until they could harvest food on their own plots of plantation land. Each family was to receive half the profits from the sale of the coffee crop from the trees under his care, as well as half the production of the food plots in excess of subsistence needs, and a place to live. Under ideal conditions it would take several years to repay the debt to the landlord, making the sharecropper the effective equivalent of an indentured servant or a slave intent on buying his own freedom.[10] This was one of several reasons for the failure of these experiments. The problem of the initial debt was not removed until the mid-1880s when the provincial and Imperial governments began to subsidize European immigration into São Paulo.

In this forerunner to the *colono* system, the money income of the worker depended on the productivity of the trees under his care and on the prevailing coffee prices in the Santos market. Under *parceria* the worker shared any loss equally with the landowner. But the sharecropper or *parceiro* rarely rose much above the subsistence level, and to him a killing frost or a bad turn of the coffee market threatened not simply the loss of a capital investment, but the loss of all monetary income. In addition to being at the mercy of nature and the coffee market, the worker was open to fraud after the crop was turned over to the landowner. Senator Vergueiro's son José reported that sharecropping had failed largely because of the workers' mistrust. The sharecroppers were 'always suspicious, and thus convinced that the landowner wanted to cheat in operations such as weighing, shipping, selling, etc. . . . any of his production'.[11]

Throughout this early period of institutional evolution the number of free workers remained small relative to the slave labour force. After the revolt of the sharecroppers in 1857, Vergueiro's *fazenda* and some others returned to the use of slaves. The number of plantations with free labour 'colonies' reportedly fell from twenty-nine in 1860 to thirteen in 1870.[12] In 1884 an estimated 1,000 free families were working on São Paulo coffee plantations under a variety of forms of payment.[13] Slavery continued to be more economical for planters than recruiting, transporting, and paying immigrants, and sufficient slave labour was available until 1887. Free workers did not take on significant numerical importance in the coffee industry until the transition period from 1886 to 1888.[14]

For the Paulista slavocrats one of the important lessons of the early free labour experiments was that positive incentives had to replace coercion as the dynamic of the labour system. Considering the debt burden and the uncertain income of the sharecropper, economic incentives did not counterbalance the system's negative aspects. At the level of the individual planter's attitudes, the appeal of the coercive approach to labour relations lingered even after the abolition of slavery. Some planters probably found coercion effective in the short run, especially in isolated areas and with newly arrived immigrants not yet oriented to general conditions in São Paulo. But a consciously developed system of negative sanctions was never institutionalized, and the state did not exercise its police powers in support of such a system. The goal of the coffee capitalist was not to maintain a system of subjugated labour, but rather to produce his crop and make a profit. The São Paulo planters were continually able to achieve their objective, through such crises as the abolition of slavery and world coffee market slumps, by developing a system of positive incentives at the institutional level which replaced the coercive foundations of the dying slave regime.

After 1860 the sharecropping system was changed in several ways. Rather than a percentage division of the proceeds from the sale of the crop, some plantations began to pay each worker a fixed piece-rate for each volume unit of coffee harvested from the trees under his care. In addition, the landowner gave up the right to one-half of the food crops

Thomas H. Holloway

the worker grew on *fazenda* land. An official investigation indicated
that the only apparent advantage in this change from sharecropping to
piecework was to diminish the degree of uncertainty under which the
immigrants laboured.[15]

Under the original sharecropping plan, landowner and labourer
shared all the risks involved in coffee production. Under the piece-
work contract such risks were divided, with some falling on the landowner and others on the worker. The planter's labour costs per unit
of production were now relatively fixed, regardless of how abundant or
sparse the yield per tree or unit of land. On the other hand, he assumed
the risks involving coffee market and exchange rate fluctuations. The
worker was freed from short-term market changes, and the possibility
of fraud in the processing and shipping stages was diminished, but the
piece-rate did not give the labourer a contractually fixed money income.
He was left with those risks involving frosts, drought, and the delicate
nature of the coffee shrub. A frost in 1887, for example, caused the
production of the western plateau of São Paulo to fall 36 per cent below
the 1881–90 average. Such frosts usually affected some local zones
more severely than others. If a piece-rate worker happened to be in a
severely affected zone, his money wages for the year could conceivably
have dropped to near zero.

The colono contract system

At the same time that the piece-work system was generally replacing
sharecropping in the 1860s and 1870s, some free labour plantations
in São Paulo went one step further in reducing the workers' uncertainty.
They separated the pay for the annual cultivation of the coffee groves
from the harvest piece-rate.[16] This was the final step in the evolution
from sharecropping to the *colono* contract. With the wage for the care
of the trees now independent of the harvest, the worker was no longer
dependent entirely on the vagaries of natural fluctuations. The *colono*'s
share of the risks of the coffee industry was reduced somewhat and his
money income made more stable, while still allowing flexibility based on
individual initiative and varying family composition. At the harvest the
plantation overseers mobilized the entire labour force to pick the groves
at the most appropriate stage of maturity and in the shortest possible
time, making the most effective use of the available manpower and
transport facilities.

The landowner assumed the degree of risk which the *colono* lost with
the separation of cultivation from harvest payments. The *fazendeiro*'s

costs for the newly established category of cultivation wage no longer depended on productivity per tree. The total number of coffee trees on the plantation, rather than the size of the crop, determined the cost of cultivation. As was not the case under sharecropping, there was now the possibility that if a crop were small, due to frost damage, for example, wages could exceed the total revenue from its sale. But by the 1880s the expansion of the railway system had lowered the risk and the cost of transporting coffee and had given planters better knowledge of market conditions. Many planters either had experimented with free labour or knew a neighbour who had. A general familiarity had developed regarding how various rates of payment would affect production costs and profit margins.

Continuation of the separate harvest payments, now at a lower rate, still cushioned the planter somewhat from the effects of a small yield. In those years when each tree bore relatively little coffee, the total man-hours needed for the harvest fell only slightly. The *colono* would have to spend nearly the same amount of time harvesting each tree as in years of abundant yield, with less return per day of work. The harvest portion of the planter's total wage bill remained fixed per unit of coffee produced. Another advantage for the *fazendeiro* was that the *colono*'s money income depended largely on maximum use of his own labour and that of his family in both harvest and cultivation. The landowners could normally be assured that the incentives built into this piece-work and task system would extract the full potential from the existing manpower pool on each plantation.

By the 1880s, before the final abolition of slavery, this type of mixed contract became standard in western São Paulo. After 1888 it was adopted nearly universally in the plateau area. There were variations in its details from region to region and over time, in response to changes in the local labour market, the world coffee market, and natural conditions, but the essential provisions of the *colono* contract were as follows: Each *colono* family contracted to keep a certain number of coffee plants free of weeds through the year, ranging from a minimum of 2,000 if only one worker were available to as many as 15,000 if there were several children of working age. Contemporary economic studies of coffee calculated an average of some 5,000 plants per family.[17] Cultivation wages varied considerably from area to area within the coffee zone and over time and were calculated in proportion to other forms of income. *Colonos* might be given the use of more land for food crops, for example, but receive lower cultivation wages than on a neighbouring plantation where less free land was provided. Because of these factors, generalizations about wage rates over large areas or for long periods are difficult to make. To give a rough indication of wage levels: annual cultivation payments ranged from around 50 *milreis* per thousand plants in the mid-1880s to some 80 to 100 *milreis* by the late 1890s, dropping somewhat in the crisis ot the first decade of this century, and later regaining and surpassing former levels in the inflation of the 1920s.[18]

The annual cultivation wages made up approximately half the *colono* family's money income. The other half came from harvest piece-work, paid at a rate of some 400 to 500 *reis* per fifty-litre *alqueire* of coffee berries picked, winnowed, and delivered at the cart road alongside the grove. Unlike the income from cultivation, the harvest portion of the *colono*'s income fluctuated considerably. If the trees were heavily loaded one man could pick as many as eight *alqueires* per day, or as few as three or four *alqueires* if the crop was sparse. If harvest workers happened to be abundant in relation to the size of the crop, each *colono*'s total income from the harvest would drop. A much less significant source of money income came from miscellaneous day labour around the *fazenda*, paid at a rate of some 2 to 3 *milreis* per day up to the third decade of this century.

Very important parts of the *colono* contract were a house, permission to plant subsistence crops either between the rows of coffee or in separate plots, and pasture for domestic animals. Variations in the adequacy and quality of such non-monetary provisions encouraged geographical mobility and were frequently the subject of controversy. But *fazendeiros* knew they could not eliminate these incentives, and workers knew they could expect to obtain them. It should be reiterated that the coffee *colono* paid no rent, in either money, products, or labour, in return for these perquisites, nor did he compensate the landowner through loyalty or occasional services as in a patron–client relationship. The house, plot, and pasture were considered separate from and in addition to the money payments for cultivation and harvest. Land was a relatively abundant resource in the coffee complex of São Paulo, and the plots alloted to *colonos* were usually in valley bottoms where coffee did poorly. By using his land in this way the landowner could offer these incentives to the workers and keep his monetary wage bill lower than it otherwise might have been.

The most important variation of the *colono* contract was the system used to open new coffee groves. In São Paulo new groves were planted only in virgin forest, where the soil was most fertile. Landowners brought in migrant gangs of native Brazilian workers to chop down the largest trees and burn off the surface vegetation. After clearing and burning, the land was put in the care of an immigrant worker known as a *formador* under a system known as the *contrato de formação*, which can be loosely translated as the 'development contract'. The *formador* agreed to plant the contracted area and care for the young plants for four to six years, keeping the ground free of weeds and replanting any dead seedlings. The young bushes began to bear in small quantities in the fourth year of growth. From the fourth to the sixth year, depending on the length of the contract, the *formador* kept the proceeds from the sale of these crops. At the end of the period the *formador* turned the producing groves over to the *fazendeiro*, who then contracted their care to *colonos* under the standard annual contract. During the boom of the late 1880s and early 1890s the landowner paid the *formador* a small sum per plant at the end of the development period, but after 1896 the declining rate of coffee expansion, low prices, and the competition among workers to assume development contracts combined to eventually eliminate such payments.

The *contrato de formação* thus enabled the landowner to open new coffee groves and provide for their care through the initial unproductive years at a low cost. For the worker the most important part of the contract was the permission to use the space between the rows of coffee seedlings for growing corn and beans. In keeping the young coffee free of weeds he simultaneously cultivated his own food crops. These subsistence products were primarily for sale in local markets, since the consumption of the *formador* was a small fraction of the total yield. The *formador* family often augmented its income by working during the harvest in the producing groves of the plantation, alongside the regular *colonos*.[19] Especially among those workers who had been in São Paulo for a time and were familiar with local cultivation practices, climatic conditions, and markets, becoming a *formador* held the possibility of accumulating considerable savings in a relatively short period.

The *contrato de formação* differed from the *colono* contract mainly in its duration and in the different proportion of cultivation wage and food crop provisions in the total income 'package'. The *colono* was limited in the amount of food he could produce on *fazenda* land, but received a money wage for the annual cultivation of mature coffee trees. Relatively more of the income of the *formador* came from the sale of cash crops, but he received little or no payment for weeding coffee. Another difference was that the *formador* lived in an isolated shack but was free from the direct control of an administrator. The *colono* lived in a permanent house near other *colono* families and was under closer supervision from the plantation headquarters.

After the crisis of overproduction and low prices around the turn of the century had shaken the Paulista planters out of their complacency in such matters, the *colono* contract system came under frequent attack. Experts in agricultural economics argued that it had served a valuable purpose in easing the transition to free labour but that the system of work organization should be altered in response to the worsening economic position of the coffee industry. Others advocated the adoption of a renting pattern, or a return to sharecropping.[20] But continued competition among planters for an ample but mobile labour force limited the possibilities of change in spite of such efforts. The *colono* contract remained in general use in the São Paulo plateau until, in the 1930s, the collapse of the world economy changed the general conditions which had prevailed for the previous half-century. The *colono* contract should not be confused with tenant farming, renting, or sharecropping. Moreover it was not a wage system, in the sense of a unit of pay per unit of time worked. It was a unique combination of annual wage, piece-work harvest payments, daily wages, and the non-money perquisites of housing and usufruct of plantation land for food crops and domestic animals, adapted to the São Paulo coffee industry as it developed after 1880.

Upward mobility of immigrants

In attempting to evaluate the immigrant experience in the São Paulo coffee industry, it is difficult to separate the harsh realities of day-to-day plantation life from the longer-range prospects for capital accumulation and social and economic improvement. Even in the best of times, the work of a coffee *colono* was menial drudgery. Planters maintained strict control over the workers' daily routine. Medical care was lacking or prohibitively expensive; schools for *colono* children were practically non-existent. In worse conditions, *colonos* lost back wages when marginal plantations declared bankruptcy; they were charged exorbitant prices in the plantation store for salt, oil, kerosene, and other needs; or they suffered physical punishment. The *colonos* were hired so that their labour power could be exploited, and for many the experience on the plantations was a negative one. The tales of misery are there to be told along with the success stories. The negative aspects of *colono* life were revealed mainly by consular officials sent to investigate conditions in São Paulo.[21] But at the same time that they described the abuses which workers suffered in the coffee zones, the Italian visitors reported that many of their countrymen ate well, accumulated savings, and became independent farmers.[22] There is clear evidence that many first-generation immigrant coffee workers achieved a notable degree of upward economic mobility.

The two principal sources of information on the upward mobility of former coffee *colonos* might be classified as descriptive and quantitative. An example of the first type is the story of the Marchetti family, Italians who arrived in São Paulo in 1888 and worked as *colonos* near the town of Jaú until 1895, and in those seven years saved the sum of 12,000 *milreis*. The family was made up of the parents, three sons, and one daughter, all of whom were able to contribute to the family labour pool, and they were *colonos* during the height of the coffee boom. With 8,000 *milreis* of their savings the family bought over 70 hectares of virgin forest land on a large plantation being broken up by heirs of the former owner. The going was hard at first, but by 1898 they were beginning to prosper, with 24 hectares of corn from which they expected to harvest more than a hundred cartloads of grain, plots of potatoes and other subsistence products, eighty hogs, and a flock of laying hens. As soon as their coffee groves began to bear, their cash income would increase substantially.[23]

Such individual career patterns are informative regarding the preconditions and mechanisms of upward mobility, but there is little way of determining how representative such a story might be. In the absence of primary research at the local level, one alternative is to analyse the available data on landholding by nationality on a regional and state-wide basis. It should be pointed out that in the present context the change from coffee *colono* to independent farmer is taken as evidence of upward mobility. Other indicators might be the move into towns and cities to enter petty commerce or artisan occupations, or return to the country of origin with capital accumulated in São Paulo. For several reasons, our attention here will concentrate on the move to the status of landholder.

First, most immigrants who became independent farmers probably began in São Paulo as coffee *colonos*. Coffee plantation work was virtually the only rural employment available, and those who achieved some success in urban pursuits were less likely to have then turned to farming. Contemporary observers recognized that the immigrants to São Paulo were practically indigent at the time of their arrival.[24] If such were the case, then the capital necessary for purchasing a farm or establishing one in the virgin territory along the frontier must logically have been accumulated while working as a coffee *colono*. Furthermore, land ownership, and especially coffee planting, was the economic sector traditionally dominated by the native Brazilian elite. Thus ex-*colono* entrance into those sectors might presumably be an especially significant indication of

TABLE 44   *São Paulo: rural properties in the western plateau, by country of origin*
of owner, 1905

Country	No. of properties	% of total	Total value (thousands of *milreis*)	Average value per property (thousands of *milreis*).
Brazil	24,478	78	802,747	32.8
Italy	4,494	14	44,365	9.9
Spain	348	1	2,825	8.1
Portugal	1,141	4	28,340	24.8
Other	857	3	51,112	59.6
Total	31,318	100	929,389	29.7

Source: Calculated from São Paulo (State), Secretaria de Agricultura, *Estatística agrícola.*
e zootécnica, 1904–05, 5 vols. (São Paulo, 1906–10).

upward mobility. The first state-wide survey to include land ownership
by national origin of owner took place in 1905. The pertinent data from
that census for the western plateau of São Paulo are summarized in
Table 44.

This table shows that less than twenty years after the beginning of
mass immigration to São Paulo, Italians had made considerable inroads
as rural property-owners, although the average value reported for their
farms was much lower than the average for Brazilian-owned plantations.
Examining local units in more detail, we find that in thirty-four of the
ninety-seven *municipios* in the western plateau, as of 1905, non-
Brazilians owned more than 30 per cent of all properties counted.
Table 44 also shows that by 1905 Spanish immigrants, who had arrived
in relatively small numbers up to that time, had not become important
as a landholding group. The data for Portuguese and 'other' nationality
groups include the properties held by foreign investment interests and
urban capitalists, along with ex-*colono* farmers of Portuguese, German,
and Austrian origin. Foreign capitalists owned very few of the total
number of properties (British firms held just twelve in the plateau region
in 1905); but those few were among the largest individual units, with
more than a million coffee trees per plantation.

Whereas Table 44 includes only the western plateau region of the
state, where 55 per cent of the total of 57,184 rural properties were
located in 1905, Table 45 summarizes data on landholding by nationality
in 1920 for all of São Paulo, including the stagnant areas in the Paraíba
Valley and southwest of the capital city. Table 45 shows that by 1920

TABLE 45 *São Paulo: land ownership by country of origin of owner, 1920*

Country	No. of properties	% of total	Area (hectares)	Average area per property (hectares)	Value (thousands of milreis)	Average value per property (thousands of milreis)
Brazil	54,245	71	9,824,482	181	1,834,402	33.8
Italy	11,825	15	916,487	78	257,547	21.8
Spain	3,530	5	208,418	59	53,209	15.1
Portugal	3,875	5	437,308	113	121,299	31.3
Other	2,835	4	352,245	124	71,087	25.1
Total	76,310	100	11,738,940	154	2,337,544	30.6

Note: In addition to the total shown, owners of unknown or multiple nationalities and governmental agencies owned a total of 4,611 properties in São Paulo.

Source: Brazil, Directoria Geral de Estatística, *Recenseamento realizado em 1 de Setembro de 1920*, vol. III: 2 (Rio de Janeiro, 1924), p. XXXV.

Italian, Spanish, and Portuguese – the three largest immigrant groups – together owned 25 per cent of the rural properties recorded in the state. Although the average value of foreign-owned farms remained relatively lower than for those owned by Brazilians, the Italians and Spanish had noticeably reduced the gap in this regard between 1905 and 1920.

The published version of the 1920 Brazilian census does not include a nationality breakdown of landowners at the *municipio* level, making it impossible to discriminate the data in Table 45 by regions within the state. *Municipio* data were published, however, separating 'foreign-born' from native Brazilian landowners, and they illustrate the concentration of non-Brazilian property-owners in the coffee zone. Of the 76,310 properties in the total shown in Table 45, 50,054 were located in the *municipios* of the western plateau. Of the 22,065 foreign-owned properties in Table 45, 19,540 (89 per cent) were in the western plateau. Those 19,540 foreign-owned properties made up 39 per cent of the 50,054 properties in the western-plateau *municipios*. In contrast, only 30,514 Brazilian-owned properties (56 per cent of the 54,245 shown in Table 45) were located in the western plateau.[25] Again, this high proportion of non-Brazilian land ownership does not reflect a significant incursion of foreign capital interests, since British, French, North American, and multinational firms represented only a small proportion of the total number of property-owners.

In 1923 the São Paulo Department of Agriculture surveyed the coffee-producing *municipios* of the state to determine the extent of foreign ownership in São Paulo's most important economic sector. Table 46 presents data from that survey for the western plateau region of the state, where 93 per cent of the coffee farms and 96 per cent of the trees producing in 1923 were concentrated.

Whereas Tables 44 and 45 include data on all rural properties, Table 46 is concerned only with coffee-producing farms. It shows that the immigrants who went to São Paulo to work in the plantation labour force assumed a significant position as landowners and producers themselves. The over 12,000 coffee farms belonging to Italians, Spanish, and Portuguese comprised 40 per cent of the coffee plantations surveyed in the western plateau and contained 25 per cent of the producing trees. These regional averages tend to mask the even more impressive position of immigrants in many local areas. In 50 of the 120 *municipios* surveyed in the western plateau, the foreign-born owned 50 per cent or more of the coffee farms. Again, the average Brazilian-owned coffee plantation was much larger than the average size of those owned by first generation immigrants, but the latter had made considerable progress. It should also

TABLE 46   *São Paulo: coffee ownership in the western plateau, by country of origin of owner, 1923*

Country	No. of coffee farms	Percentage of total	No. of coffee trees (thousands)	Percentage of total	Average no. of trees per farm (thousands)
Brazil	17,112	57%	530,093	69%	31
Italy	9,631	32%	139,925	18%	15
Spain	1,123	4%	20,401	3%	18
Portugal	1,282	4%	28,340	4%	22
Other	943	3%	44,081	6%	47
Total	30,091	100%	762,840	100%	25

Note: These data are from *municipio* tax records. Five of the 126 *municipios* in the plateau region in 1923 evidently did not tax coffee trees and are not included in these totals. Other sources indicate that the five missing *municipios* contained some 23,346 trees, less than 3 per cent of the approximately 786.2 million coffee trees in production in the western plateau as of 1923.

Source: Calculated from *Boletim do Departamento Estadual do Trabalho* (São Paulo), nos. 50–1 (1st and 2nd quarters, 1924), pp. 23–8.

be noted that while very few immigrants became naturalized Brazilian citizens, by the time of the 1920 census and the 1923 coffee survey an indeterminate number of the Brazilian-owned farms were probably held by the children of immigrants born in Brazil after the beginning of mass immigration in the 1880s.[26] It is impossible to trace such inter-generational mobility with the data at hand.

The colono labour system and upward mobility

Several factors should be emphasized in discussing the relationship between work as coffee *colonos* and the eventual upward mobility of immigrants in São Paulo. First, the workers were geographically mobile. They had no cultural or family ties to hold them to a given locality, and the planters failed to devise an effective means of restricting the workers' movement beyond the standard one-year contract. Thus the immigrants were able to move to those areas and occupations where their own self-interest could best be fulfilled. The planters, in competition with each other for workers, continued to offer a pattern of incentives sufficient to attract a potentially scarce labour force. Second, the *colono* contract put a premium on family co-operation in the allocation of labour resources and the accumulation of capital. Large families without small children could contract for the care of more coffee trees, pick more *alqueires* during the harvest, and cultivate more food crops for consumption and sale. The incomes of family members were invariably pooled and controlled by the family head. Third, the non-monetary incentives of the *colono* contract cushioned the worker from fluctuations in the local wage–price structure. Under normal conditions food and shelter – the basic means of subsistence – were not directly related to the money wages, indebtedness, or savings of the *colono* family. And to the extent that coffee *colonos* were producers of foodstuffs for local markets, they would monetarily benefit from a rise in the prices of corn and beans. The Italian Consul in São Paulo reported in 1901 that *colonos* under ideal conditions could live off their harvest wages and income from the sale of chickens, hogs, corn, beans, etc., saving the wages they received from the annual cultivation of the plants. He went on to say, however, that conditions were often far from that ideal.[27]

These specific aspects of the system of labour organization made it possible under certain conditions for immigrant workers to accumulate capital. But a significant number of *colonos* still could not have become independent farmers without the expanding regional economy of São Paulo and the continued availability of fertile land. The entire western half of the state was unexplored virgin forest until the westward encroachment of the coffee frontier. Until well into this century, illegal or extra-legal usurpation of the public domain was a common method of acquiring land, both for large commercially oriented plantations and for smaller family farms. Actual cultivation was the only reasonably sure way to maintain effective control over claims. The first cadastral survey of São Paulo was not begun until 1916, and the state government soon gave it up as an impossible task in the face of opposition from small-scale squatters and large landholders with dubious titles.[28]

The abundant supply of land was closely related to the continued existence of the *colono* contract form of labour organization and the ability of the former coffee workers to become farmers. With little demographic or economic pressure to change familiar patterns, land was used extensively rather than intensively. The allocation of plantation land for the usufruct of the workers made it possible for the planter to supplement monetary wage outlays, and it provided necessities which the *colono* would otherwise have had to purchase. Since arable land was available and relatively inexpensive, it remained within reach of the fortunate *colono* family with savings to invest.

The upward mobility of immigrant workers in rural São Paulo was far from universal. Only a small proportion of all immigrants became landowners, although landholding is only one of several possible indicators of upward mobility. Those who were able to take advantage of the *colono* contract system to accumulate savings and become independent farmers did so only after several years of toil and a low level of ongoing consumption. Nevertheless, such mobility was an important aspect of the historical development of São Paulo. It is especially significant in relative terms, seen as an increasing proportion of the total landholding group in the state. With the large-scale influx from Europe beginning only after 1886, first-generation immigrants owned more than 15 per cent of the rural property units in the western plateau by 1905, more than 25 per cent of the farms in the entire state by 1920, and more than 40 per cent of the coffee farms in the western plateau by 1923. In spite of the unenviable daily existence of many coffee workers, the concrete examples of success were apparent for all to see. By working on the plantations of São Paulo, a considerable number of immigrants were able to realize what one Italian official described as 'the dream of the peasant, to work his own farm ...'[29]

NOTES

1. I wish to thank the Foreign Area Fellowship Program for financial assistance which made this study possible in Brazil and at the University of Wisconsin, Madison.
2. Brazil, Departamento Nacional do Café, *Anuário estatístico, 1938*, 5th edn, revised (Rio de Janeiro, 1938), facing p. 264.
3. The classic monograph on the Paraíba Valley coffee era is Stanley Stein, *Vassouras, a Brazilian coffee county, 1850–1890* (Cambridge, Mass., 1957).
4. São Paulo (State), Secretaria da Fazenda, *Relatório*, various years.
5. Much confusion has resulted from the multiplicity of terms used to designate types of agricultural workers and systems of labour organization in Latin America. '*Colono*' is one of the more common of such terms. In Brazil it has been applied variously to immigrant farm labourers in general, inhabitants of semi-autonomous colonies of small farmers, and plantation workers under the arrangement discussed here. On the other hand, the specific pattern of labour organization most commonly called the *contrato de colono* or *colonato* has been confused with sharecropping (*parceria*), wage labour (*trabalho assalariado*), and the task-rate jobbing contract (*empreitada*). In the present paper the term '*colono*' refers only to coffee workers remunerated under the *colono* contract system.
6. According to a contemporary survey, there were 22,355 workers employed in industrial establishments in the state of São Paulo in 1907. By 1920 the corresponding figure was 84,000 (Azis Simão, *Sindicato e estado* (São Paulo, 1966), p. 43). In contrast, the 1905 agricultural census counted 415,476 rural workers in the state (São Paulo (State), Secretaria de Agricultura, *Relatório*, 1907, pp. 46–7). Warren Dean has studied the role of immigrant entrepreneurs in *The industrialization of São Paulo, 1880–1945* (Austin, Texas and London, 1969).

7. São Paulo (State), Secretaria de Agricultura, *Estatística agrícola e zootécnica, 1904–05*, 5 vols. (São Paulo, 1906–10), *passim*. The *municipios* making up the western plateau region have been adapted from Sérgio Milliet, *Roteiro do café e outros ensáios*, 3rd edn, revised (São Paulo, 1941), pp. 10–12.

8. These estimates are calculated at a rate of 2,000 coffee plants per worker, the minimum average adult work load frequently cited in contemporary analyses of coffee economic problems. For a more detailed discussion of coffee labour needs see Thomas H. Holloway, 'Condições do mercado de trabalho e organização do trabalho nas plantações da economia cafeeira de São Paulo, 1885–1915', *Estudos Econômicos* II, 6 (São Paulo, 1972), pp. 145–77.

9. The Swiss schoolteacher of the colony reported this incident and criticized the sharecropping programme in Thomas Davatz, *Memórias de um colono no Brasil*, transl. Sérgio Buarque de Holanda (São Paulo, 1941).

10. Pierre Denis, *Brazil*, transl. Bernard Miall (New York, 1911), p. 186. Details on the living conditions of the sharecroppers are in Emília Viotti da Costa, *Da senzala à colônia* (São Paulo, 1966), pp. 78–109.

11. José Vergueiro, *Memorial acerca de colonisação e cultivo de café apresentado ao Ministro de Agricultura* (Campinas, 1874), p. 5.

12. Sérgio Buarque de Holanda, 'As colônias de parceria', in Sérgio Buarque de Holanda (ed.), *História geral da civilização brasileira*, Tome II, vol. 3 (São Paulo, 1969), p. 257.

13. C. F. Van Delden Laerne, *Brazil and Java* (London, 1885), p. 139.

14. On the abolition of slavery see Robert Conrad, *The destruction of Brazilian slavery, 1850–1888* (Berkeley, Calif., 1972); and Robert Toplin, *The abolition of slavery in Brazil* (New York, 1972).

15. João Pedro Carvalho de Morais, *Relatório apresentado ao Ministro de Agricultura* (Rio de Janeiro, 1870), *passim*.

16. Van Delden Laerne, *Brazil and Java*, p. 140.

17. See, for example, São Paulo (State), Secretaria de Agricultura, *Relatório*, 1896, p. 56.

18. Prior to 1912 wage reports can be found sporadically in the annual *Relatórios* of the São Paulo Secretary of Agriculture, Italian consular reports, and travel literature. Beginning in 1912 the quarterly reports by *municipio*, in the *Boletim do Departmento Estadual do Trabalho* (São Paulo), provide a more systematic basis for analysis.

19. Discussions of the relative advantages of the *formação* contract are found in Silvio Coletti, 'Lo stato di S. Paolo e l'emigrazione italiana', *Bollettino dell'Emigrazione*, 1908, no. 15, pp. 4–5; and in Denis, *Brazil*, pp. 241–3.

20. See, for example, Luiz Pereira Barreto, 'A colonisação', *Revista Agrícola*, 1901, pp. 260–4; and Germano Vert, 'O café barato', *Revista Agrícola*, 1902, pp. 125–8. The coffee crisis of the early twentieth century is analysed in Thomas H. Holloway, 'The Brazilian coffee industry and the first valorization scheme of 1906–07' (unpublished M.A. thesis, University of Wisconsin, 1971).

21. Michael Hall has made extensive use of Italian consular reports as evidence for the miserable condition of immigrant coffee workers in São Paulo in 'The origins of mass immigration in Brazil, 1871–1914' (unpublished Ph.D. dissertation, Columbia University, 1969).

22. See Filippo Ugolotti, *Italia e Italiani in Brasile, note e appunti* (São Paulo, 1897), p. 101; and for a summary of the possibilities and drawbacks of *colono* work from

several consular reports, see Antonio Franceschini, *L'emigrazione italiana nell'America del Sud* (Rome, 1908), pp. 483–9.

23. A. Gomes Carmo, 'Uma família de antigos colonos italianos', *Revista Agrícola*, 1898, pp. 113–16.
24. Ugolotti, *Italia e Italiani*, pp. 16, 91; Silvio Coletti, 'Lo stato di S. Paolo e l'emigrazione italiana', in *Emigrazione e Colonie*, vol. 3: *America* (Rome, 1908), p. 374; and Robert Foerster, *The Italian emigration of our times* (Cambridge, Mass., 1919), p. 316.
25. José Francisco de Camargo, *Crescimento da população do Estado de São Paulo e seus aspectos econômicos*, 3 vols. (São Paulo, 1951), vol. 3, pp. 117, 125.
26. Between 1889 and 1907 a total of 4,663 persons became naturalized Brazilian citizens (*Brazilian year book, 1909* (Rio de Janeiro, n.d.), p. 37). That figure is less than 0.3 per cent of the 1,740,833 immigrants recorded as entering all of Brazil in the same period (Arthur H. Neiva, 'Ligeiras notas a respeito do quadro de imigração no Brasil a partir de 1820', *Boletim Geográfico* VIII, 91 (October 1950), p. 850). The naturalization provision of the Republican constitution of 1891, by which foreigners in Brazil on 15 November 1889 automatically became citizens unless they declared otherwise, became a dead letter for all practical purposes.
27. Attilio Monaco, 'L'emigrazione italiana nello stato di San Paolo del Brasile', *Bollettino dell'Emigrazione*, 1902, no. 8, p. 47. See the similar comments in 1922 by André Betim Paes Leme, 'A fixação de um salário minimo', *Revista dos Fazendeiros* V, 56 (15 February 1922), unpaginated.
28. São Paulo (State), Secretaria de Agricultura, *Relatório*, 1915–16, pp. 283–2; ibid., 1917, p. 211.
29. Adolfo Rossi, 'Condizioni dei coloni italiani nello stato di San Paolo (Brasile)', *Bollettino dell'Emigrazione*, 1902, no. 7, p. 32. Rossi toured São Paulo in the depths of the coffee crisis and submitted one of the most critical of the Italian consular reports, yet he repeatedly found evidence of material well-being and capital accumulation on the part of *colonos*: see pp. 28–31, 41, and *passim*.

CHAPTER 13

The cereal boom and changes in the social and political structure of Santa Fe, Argentina, 1870–95

EZEQUIEL GALLO

The humid *pampa* of Argentina displays a series of social and economic characteristics that clearly mark it off from other rural areas of Latin America. Relatively speaking, the *pampa* farm or ranch (*empresa rural*) has a very high technical level by the standards of the rest of the continent. Its system of social stratification is notably more flexible and diverse than is to be found in the other Latin American republics. At the same time, the existence of a very favourable relationship between the amount of cultivable land and the size of the population means that the Argentine *pampas* have some features in common with the temperate grasslands of the western United States, Canada, Australia, and New Zealand.

These particular features of the *pampa* region are certainly not of recent origin – on the contrary, many of them have been present at least since the time Argentina became independent. The causes of this situation were naturally very various. Here I shall confine myself to dealing with three of the most important factors. Firstly, millions of hectares of highly fertile natural pasture land were available in the mid nineteenth century for agricultural development. Secondly, these territories were thinly populated both before and after the Conquest. Moreover, at the beginning of the nineteenth century most of the *pampa* was practically unexploited, being occupied only by roaming herds of wild cattle and a few tribes of nomadic Indians. The agricultural colonization of this immense frontier of fertile land kept land prices comparatively low throughout most of the nineteenth century, and this enabled various social groups, most of them immigrants, who had grown rich in urban or rural commerce, to acquire a stake in it. As a consequence, in the *pampa* region there were no pre-existing patterns of agricultural organization and labour that might have been incompatible with the introduction of modern organizational methods and techniques. Similarly, the introduction of wage labour coincided with the emergence of the modern rural business enterprise, whilst the chronic shortage of labour gave the working people of the region a degree of independence and negotiating power without parallel in the other rural areas of Latin America. Finally, the incorporation of the region into the world market took place at an early stage and was stimulated throughout most of the nineteenth century by a growing demand for its food products, arising from the rapid expansion of European industry.

Consequently, *pampa* agriculture was immersed in the capitalist mode of production and was closely tied to the world market from a very early stage. Of course, a more detailed and painstaking examination would produce a much more complex and subtle picture of the historical evolution of the region than the one outlined above. Among other things, it would show that the present characteristics of the region have been strongly influenced by the specific features of the various economic activities that have followed each other in the course of time. The change from the traditional colonial *estancia* producing mainly cow hides to the more complex and sophisticated salt-beef operation; the gradual replacement of the latter by the introduction of sheep-rearing in the middle of the nineteenth century; the spectacular expansion of cereal cultivation from the 1870s onwards; and finally the combination of agriculture and stock-raising which characterizes the present-day *estancia*, and which led to the installation of the great freezing plants – all these stages altered not only the patterns of social and economic organization but also the physical appearance of the great plains of the *pampas*. The great flat expanses, broken here and there by low, gently rolling hills, covered in many places by ponds and marshes and areas of coarse grasses that at the beginning of the nineteenth century could only support wild cattle, slowly gave way to *estancias* with wire fencing, alfalfa, and herds of improved stock, and to rolling farmland under many varieties of cereals and maize. This situation was well established on the *pampas* by the beginning of the twentieth century.[1]

As I have said, all these activities left their stamp on the present-day landscape of the region and contributed in varying degrees to the growing occupational differentiation of the rural labour force and to an increasing flexibility in the social structure. Nevertheless, few factors had such a powerful and decisive impact as the introduction of cereal-growing, especially wheat, in the second half of the nineteenth century. The contribution of this new activity can be summed up under the following headings. Firstly, since it required a much higher intensity of labour use than ranching operations, it was of crucial importance in populating the region. The origins of the great human migrations from Europe to Argentina were intimately linked with the advance of the cereal frontier. Secondly, cereal-growing estates, by stimulating the establishment in the countryside of a series of related economic activities in industry, commerce and transport, contributed markedly to the diversification of the economic life of the region, and at the same time gave a powerful impetus to the creation of hundreds of small urban centres. Finally, the emergence of an important middle-class sector – composed of farmers, merchants, transport operators, and manufacturers – in the rural areas seems to have been closely linked to the introduction of cereal crops. As I shall try to show presently, the emergence of this new rural infrastructure also produced significant, though less spectacular, changes in the political character of the region.

That cereal cultivation has such an impact on rural society as a whole has been pointed out, in other contexts, by several authors. In an article published in 1956, Robert Baldwin suggested that the economic development of certain areas and their patterns of social stratification were determined by the production function (the way in which capital, land, and labour are combined) and by the technology of the dominant economic activity in the region.[2] To illustrate the problem, Baldwin compared a region dominated by a plantation economy with a region where the main activity was wheat-growing. Because of its particular characteristics, the wheat-growing operation had, in his opinion, stronger forward and backward linkages than the plantation, thus resulting in greater economic diversification within its area of influence. At the same time, the production function of the wheat-growing operation introduced another element of differentiation, inasmuch as it created a more egalitarian income distribution, with the consequent benefits to the economy and social structure of the region. Douglass North summed up Baldwin's ideas in the following way:

If the export commodity is a 'plantation' type commodity which is relatively labour intensive and in which there are significant increasing returns to scale, then the development will be in marked contrast to one in which the export commodity may be produced most efficiently on a family-size farm with relatively less absolute amounts of labour required. In the first case there will tend to result an extremely unequal distribution of income with the bulk of the population devoting most of their income to foodstuffs and simple necessities (much of which may be self-sufficient production). At the other end of the income scale, the plantation owners will tend to spend most of their income upon luxury consumption goods which will be imported. In short, there will be little encouragement of residentiary types of economic activity. With the more equitable distributon of incomes, there is a demand for a broad range of goods and services, part of which will be residentiary, thus inducing investment in other types

of economic activities. There will tend to develop trading centres to provide a
wide variety of such goods and services, in contrast to the plantation economy
which will merely develop a few urban areas devoted to the export of the staple
commodity and the distribution of imports.[3]

Baldwin's analysis tied in quite smoothly with the propositions arising
from the so-called 'staple theory', which originated among Canadian
economic historians, and which emphasizes the strategic importance of
export products in some regions. The resultant model was widely applied
in a number of works analysing the economic growth of regions referred
to by R. Nurkse as 'of recent settlement', such as Canada, Australia,
New Zealand, the western United States, and Argentina.[4] It is important
to point out, however, that the type of analysis proposed was applicable
specifically to regions which in the nineteenth century specialized in
agricultural activities without the need to overcome obstacles provided
by pre-existing institutions or strongly embedded traditions of rural
labour. In this sense, this type of approach is of dubious applicability
to the evolution of older cereal-producing regions like Russia, India, or
(in the case of Latin America) Chile.[5]

Although the literature on the subject is enormous, there are few
detailed analyses of the impact of cereal-growing operations on rural
society compared with alternative agricultural activities. This paper will
attempt to illustrate the problem with reference to the province of
Santa Fe during the boom period of wheat production, from 1870 to
1895. After a brief description of the main characteristics of the cereal
boom, a comparison is made between the three major regions of the
province: the predominantly cereal-producing districts, the other rural
areas, and the two large provincial urban centres of Rosario and Santa
Fe. Finally, the paper will attempt a more detailed analysis by comparing
a group of typical wheat-producing districts with those areas where
sheep-ranching continued to be the predominant activity even after the
great expansion of cereal cultivation.

Cereal expansion in Santa Fe between 1870 and 1895[6]

The expansion of cereal production in Santa Fe between 1870 and 1895
can only be described as spectacular. A few figures are enough to illustrate
this statement. During the twenty-five years under examination more
than 300 agricultural colonies were founded, and these constituted the
main nuclei around which the subsequent development of the province's
agriculture revolved. In 1872 the area sown with cereals and flax reached

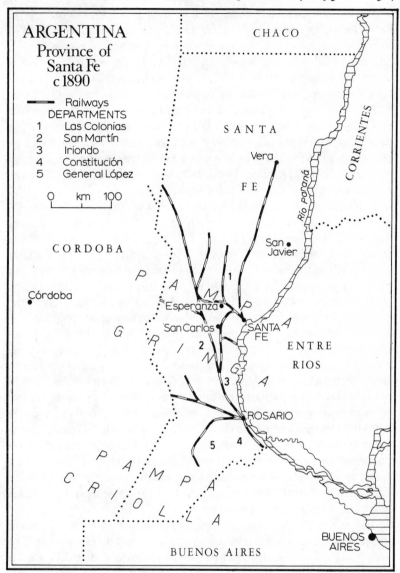

ARGENTINA
Province of
Santa Fe
c 1890

Railways
DEPARTMENTS
1   Las Colonias
2   San Martín
3   Iriondo
4   Constitución
5   General López

0   km   100

CHACO

SANTA

Vera

FE

San Javier

CORRIENTES

Río Paraná

CORDOBA

Córdoba

PAMPA

Esperanza

San Carlos

SANTA FE

GRINGA

ENTRE RIOS

ROSARIO

5   4

PAMPA

CRIOLLA

BUENOS AIRES

BUENOS AIRES

Map 20

62,500 hectares; in 1895 there were more than 1,600,000 hectares in Santa Fe under those crops. As far as wheat – the main cereal crop in Santa Fe – is concerned, the figures show 21,000 hectares sown in 1872 and more than one million in 1895. By the latter year, Santa Fe was producing rather more than 50 per cent of Argentina's wheat, and the country had become the second largest exporter of wheat in the world.

This spectacular expansion of the area under cultivation took place at a time when other sectors of the provincial economy were making equally rapid strides. The railway network, which was less than 110 kilometres in 1870, had grown to 3,000 kilometres in 1895. In the same way, the number of industrial workshops increased fifteenfold, whilst the population increased far less than fivefold.

The same picture is found from an analysis of demographic and social indicators of development. The population of the province rose from 89,000 in 1869 to 397,000 in 1895. This rapid increase was mainly due to the massive influx of European immigrants, particularly Italians, and, on a smaller scale, to the arrival of internal migrants from other parts of Argentina. The growth in population was accompanied by other changes which substantially altered the social physiognomy of the province. In 1869, Santa Fe had only two urban centres of any size, Rosario and Santa Fe, whilst the rural areas could claim only four centres with barely more than 500 inhabitants each. No 'urban' centre in rural Santa Fe had as many as 2,000 inhabitants. By 1895, apart from the two large cities (whose population, especially that of Rosario, had grown considerably) there were in the rural areas of Santa Fe fifty-six centres of more than 500 inhabitants, and six of them had more than 2,000. In 1869 the material and educational conditions in which the inhabitants of Santa Fe spent their lives were very poor. According to census figures published in that year, 72 per cent of the inhabitants of the province could neither read nor write, and 78 per cent of the people lived in flimsy mud and straw huts known as *ranchos*. By 1895 these figures had fallen to 47 and 35 per cent respectively.

This notable improvement in the living conditions of the population of the province was accompanied by a no less marked diversification of its social and occupational structure, the main feature of which was the expansion of the middle sectors of the region. A conservative estimate of the none-too-reliable census data that we have shows that the middle sectors of Santa Fe rose from 12 per cent of the economically active population in 1869 to 30 per cent in 1895.[7]

It is consequently possible to establish a very striking parallel between the expansion of cereals and the economic and social growth of Santa Fe during the last third of the nineteenth century. This parallel does not permit us, however, to establish causal connections between the two ,phenomena, particularly because even before the cereal boom began there were already two growth areas in Santa Fe which continued to expand throughout the period in question – the commercial growth of the city of Rosario, which since the 1850s had become the main commercial nexus between Buenos Aires and the interior provinces, and the rapid development of the sheep-rearing industry from the 1860s onwards. Moreover, in the mid-1880s the growing and processing of sugar cane began to develop quite vigorously. This phenomenon, however, was much less important than those already referred to and, besides, was confined to a small group of districts in the northern department of San Javier. In the following analysis we shall consider the different ways in which the three regions into which we have divided the province – the cereal zone, the non-cereal rural areas, and the two large urban areas – have evolved. It is important to remember here that we are not comparing types of enterprise as such, but the regions in which these enterprises were principally established.

The three regions of Santa Fe

Table 47 gives population figures for Santa Fe between 1869 and 1887. These figures show quite clearly that the cereal region made the greatest contribution to the rapid population growth of the province between 1869 and 1887. This applies both to the cities and to the other rural regions. The difference in population growth between cereal and non-

TABLE 47   *Santa Fe: population by region, 1869 and 1887*

Regions	1869		1887	
	Population	Percentage of total	Population	Percentage of total
Urban (Rosario, Santa Fe)	33,839	37.9%	66,013	29.9%
Cereal region	10,000	11.2%	95,965	43.6%
Non-cereal rural areas	45,279	50.9%	58,354	26.5%
Total	89,118	100.0%	220,332	100.0%

Sources: *Primer censo nacional* (Buenos Aires, 1869), pp. 110–11; *Primer censo provincial*, 4 vols. (Santa Fe, 1887), vol. 2, pp. 1–2.

cereal areas is particularly notable, partly because of the greater sub-division of rural property brought about by the introduction of cereal growing.

These statistics suggest, therefore, that the majority of European immigrants moved into the cereal region. In fact, of the 84,215 foreigners living in Santa Fe in 1887 (making up 38.3 per cent of the total popula-tion), 59.3 per cent were settled in the cereal region, 30.2 per cent lived in the two cities, and only 10.5 per cent were resident in the rural zones where ranching or plantations were predominant.

The situation was quite the reverse as far as migrants from other Argentina provinces were concerned. Their contribution was, of course, much less than that of the European migrants (in 1887 there were about 35,000, compared with almost 85,000, foreigners). Of the internal migrants, 43 per cent lived in the non-cereal rural areas, 30 per cent in the large cities, and the remaining 28 per cent in the cereal region. In 1887, then, the population distribution of Santa Fe by place of origin of its inhabitants was as presented in Table 48. These figures show, among other things, the markedly cosmopolitan nature of the popula-tion of Santa Fe, which becomes even more striking if it is borne in mind that a considerable proportion of the inhabitants actually born in Santa Fe were the children of European and internal migrants settled in the province.[8] At the same time, the figures show the marked contrast between the cereal region, with 52 per cent foreigners, and the rest of the rural areas, where only 15 per cent of the inhabitants had been born outside the country. These differences are reflected in popular literature in the very expressive terms *'pampa criolla'* and *'pampa gringa'* with which the cattle country was distinguished from the strictly agri-cultural areas.

TABLE 48   *Sante Fe: places of origin of inhabitants, 1887*

Place of birth	Regions (per cent)		
	Large cities	Cereal region	Non-cereal rural areas
Province of Santa Fe	42%	37%	59%
Other provinces	19%	11%	26%
Foreigners	39%	52%	15%
Total	100%	100%	100%

Source: Primer censo provincial, vol. 2, pp. 6–8, 16–17.

The impact caused by the introduction of cereal-growing may also be seen with reference to the spectacular growth of the small rural towns. Of the sixty-two centres classified by the 1895 census as having more than 500 inhabitants, fifty-five were located in the cereal zone; of the six which had passed the 2,000 mark, five were in the agricultural colonization zone. The connection between the formation of agricultural colonies and the foundation of rural towns or villages becomes clear when it is borne in mind that in the great majority of cases the founders of the villages were the same entrepreneurs who had set up the agricultural colonies.

The figures on the quality of housing found in the 1895 census show a similar picture to the one noted above. The proportion of low-quality housing (*ranchos*) varied in the cereal zone from a maximum of 35 per cent in the department of Iriondo to a minimum of 20 per cent in the department of San Martín. In the other rural areas it ranged between 51 per cent in the department of Constitución and a maximum of 87 per cent in the northern department of Vera. Around 1895, then, things were a lot better in the cereal area, judging by one of the few available indicators for measuring the material living conditions of the rural inhabitants of Santa Fe.

The picture was much the same with respect to education. The most detailed figures of the 1887 provincial census (if we took the 1895 national census the proportions would be reduced) show that the illiteracy rate in the population over six years of age was 36 per cent in the large cities, 50 per cent in the agricultural colonies, and 64 per cent in the other rural areas. It is interesting to note that in Esperanza and San Carlos, the two oldest agricultural districts or colonies in the province, the illiteracy rates of 28 and 30 per cent were lower than those in the cities of Rosario and Santa Fe, where 35 and 37 per cent of the population respectively could neither read nor write.

It is more difficult to establish differences in social and occupational structures between the regions into which we have divided the province. In an earlier work I used for this purpose a survey sample carried out on the basis of occupational figures published in the national censuses of 1869 and 1895. Unfortunately, the characteristics of the sample do not permit a breakdown of the data at departmental, much less at district, level. These figures only enable us to piece together a general view of the whole province. In this picture, as I have pointed out, the outstanding feature was the very significant increase in the Santa Fe middle sectors. To what extent this increase was more pronounced in the cereal region is difficult to determine. There are, however, some indications that this was

TABLE 49   *Santa Fe: social and occupational structure, 1887*

Region	Categories (per cent)				
	Employers	Clerks	Artisans	Labourers	Total
Large cities	27.2%	10.3%	16.7%	45.8%	100.0%
Cereal region	38.9%	5.4%	4.2%	51.5%	100.0%
Non-cereal rural areas	28.5%	4.8%	2.8%	63.9%	100.0%

Source: *Primer censo provincial*, vol. 1, pp. 93–4.

the case, such as the very substantial increase in the number of independent farmers, who rose from about 1,000 to 1869 to almost 20,000 in 1895. The 1887 census gives another series of data at the district level which seem to confirm this impression. The census authorities asked people to place themselves in one of four social and occupational categories – employer, clerk, artisan, or labourer. Naturally, given the nature of other information and the lack of precision in the two intermediate categories, the results – shown in Table 49 – must be interpreted with extreme caution. Nevertheless, it is interesting to see how the people of Santa Fe placed themselves in the different categories suggested to them by the census authorities.[9]

Despite their lack of precision, these statistics do provide another piece of evidence in support of the argument developed in this essay: that the degree of social diversification and modernization was appreciably higher in the cereal region than in the rest of the countryside. These figures are also in agreement with the observations of visitors to the province at the time. All of them stressed the contrast between the areas of agricultural colonization and the rest of the *pampas* – and the contrast not only with other parts of Argentina but with areas of the Old World whence the immigrants had come. It is enough to quote one of these authors, the well-known Italian writer Edmundo D'Amicis, who made the following observation after travelling through the Santa Fe cereal zone: 'There [in Santa Fe], as tillers of the land, as inhabitants of a region virtually created by themselves, the Italians have no other social class above them: here [in Italy], on the other hand, they feel the entire weight of the hierarchical structure of a traditional society on their backs.'[10]

Differences between cereal and sheep-raising areas

In order to give greater precision to the comparison between the different regions, it is appropriate to compare the impact of cereal production with that of the wool-producing sheep ranches in their own areas of influence. I have chosen sheep-raising because it was the predominant activity in the *pampa* of Santa Fe before cereal cultivation was introduced. It should be borne in mind that the spread of wool production had only taken place in Santa Fe in the decade preceding the massive introduction of wheat in the 1870s; however, many of the wool areas had been settled long before the wheat areas. In this respect, the cereal area always had more clear-cut frontier features, although this aspect was not completely absent in some wool-producing districts in the far south of the province. Furthermore, it should be pointed out that during the period under examination there was no replacement of one activity by the other; instead, broadly speaking, they developed in separate areas: wool production in the south of the province and cereal cultivation in the districts and departments of the central region.[11]

Once that has been said, it is convenient to give a brief description of the main features of both activities. The sheep ranch was a very modern undertaking for its time and was an important influence in changing the social composition of the *pampa* region. It was generally smaller than the ranches devoted to producing very low-quality cattle, and it brought a significant widening of entrepreneurial functions into the rural areas. In the first stage of the expansion of sheep-breeding this tendency was accentuated by the widespread practice of having flocks of about 500 sheep raised by *arrendatarios* (tenants). At the same time, the breeding of sheep brought a greater division of labour within the ranch, in part because this was required by the more sophisticated techniques used, but also because of the peculiarities of the operation itself, such as the series of new activities arising from the shearing of the sheep on the ranch. All these innovations led some authors to believe that the peopling of the rural areas from the 1850s onwards was closely tied to the expansion of sheep ranches.[12]

But in spite of these changes, the influence of the sheep ranches on the surrounding region was not as spectacular as the subsequent impact of the cereal farms. The greatest difference between the two activities arose basically from the size of the operation. It is difficult to speak of the average size of the sheep ranches in Santa Fe because of the very great variations existing between the various wool-producing districts. In general terms, however, it can be said that they ranged between 2,000 and 10,000 hectares, with several cases comfortably exceeding the latter figure, such as the properties of Diego de Alvear, in the department of General López, which were well over 100,000 hectares. These figures make a spectacular contrast with the cereal zone, where farms varied between 33 and 150 hectares, with a few cases of up to 600 hectares.

It is clear that these differences led to a greater diffusion of rural property and of entrepreneurial functions at the same time as they led to denser settlement with more even income distribution in the cereal zone. It should be emphasized here that both activities were characterized by the intensive use of labour only at certain times of the year such as shearing and harvesting. Both types of enterprise used relatively little permanent labour, and in the case of cereal operations it was quite usual for most of the regular tasks to be performed by members of the farmer's family. A sheep ranch of about 5,000 hectares did not employ more than ten permanent labourers, whilst a cereal farm of 100 hectares had one or two wage labourers at the most, and sometimes not even that. But the greater use of labour by the sheep operation was more than compensated for by the much larger number of cereal farms and their much greater reliance on the use of family labour.[13]

These were not, however, the only differences between the two types of operation. Because of the technical characteristics of both enterprises, the cereal farm used a much larger quantity of agricultural tools and machinery (such as ploughs, harvesters, and threshers) per hectare, and this had a positive effect on the industrial development of the region. Flour-milling needed time but not a great deal of capital, and for this reason many immigrants set up mills near their farms (*chacras*). Wool-processing, on the other hand, was carried on outside the region and even more outside the country. Another important factor was that transport requirements were much more intense in the wheat region. It is clear from Map 20 above that the railway network was considerably larger in the cereal zone, with the consequent installation of repair workshops and complementary activities.

In Table 50 I have tried to highlight these differences by comparing a group of typical cereal districts with others where wool production was predominant. For this purpose I have extracted from the 1887 census the nine agricultural districts with the greatest proportion of land given over to cereal production. All are in the same region and form part of the department of Las Colonias. To contrast with this I have taken eight typical wool-producing districts, in the departments of Constitución and General López, all of which had only a very small part of their land under cultivation – a proportion which varied from a maximum of 3.5 per cent to a minimum of 0.1 per cent.

The comparison may, of course, be affected by some variables which have not been considered here. It is important to draw attention to one of these: the wool districts were areas of older settlement, almost all of which were populated and exploited from the beginning of the nineteenth century and even before.[14] The agricultural districts, on the other

TABLE 50   *Santa Fe: social and occupational structure of the wheat- and wool-producing regions, 1887*

	Cereal region	Wool region
Population per square km	8.7	3.8
Foreigners	55.1%	10.6%
Internal migrants	4.2%	22.6%
Illiterates	32.0%	62.0%
Ranchos	49.2%	54.5%
Occupational structure:		
Employers	42.9%	33.0%
Clerks	8.0%	6.8%
Artisans	7.0%	0.9%
Labourers	42.1%	59.3%

Source: Primer censo provincial, vols. 1 and 2, *passim.*

hand, were settled between 1856 and 1875. It should be noted, however, that the majority of these districts were among the first agricultural colonies to be established in Santa Fe. Having made this observation, we can now look at some of the differences between the two regions. The figures in Table 50 confirm some remarks made earlier: as was to be expected, the greater sub-division of rural property in the cereal region resulted in a higher density of population. The cereal region also attracted a substantially higher number of foreign immigrants, but it drew relatively few migrants from other Argentine provinces.

The figures for education in particular, and to a lesser extent those for housing, also confirm the tendency noted previously. But for this latter point it is important to make two qualifications: firstly, the cereal area was affected by the influx of a very large number of new inhabitants who had settled there not long before 1887. These people, when they arrived, put up very temporary dwellings, which were only replaced by better-quality ones in the course of time. In this sense the longer-established settlement of the wool region must have helped make the difference less marked. Secondly, the great boom in Santa Fe between 1887 and 1893 was reflected in a noticeable improvement in the quality of the housing. Even though the census of 1895 does not have figures for the district level, those it gives for the departments bear this out. In the department of Las Colonias, where the nine agricultural districts under examination were located, the proportion of low-quality *ranchos* had fallen to 32 per cent (as against 49.2 per cent in Table 50). The same thing happened in the department of Constitución, where most of the wool-producing districts were to be found. There the proportion had fallen to 41.2 per cent, as against the 54.5 per cent given for the eight wool districts in 1887. The fall was also marked, though less than in the cereal regions. It should be pointed out, however, that a not insignificant amount of land in the wool areas began to switch to cereal production between 1887 and 1895.

Finally, the variations noted in the social and occupational data are also significant, particularly those in the two extreme categories of employers and labourers, although the difference in those referring to the proportion of artisans would seem to indicate a greater degree of industrial development in the cereal region. This finding is confirmed by other figures from the same provincial census, which show that while in the cereal districts there was an industrial establishment or workshop for every sixty-three inhabitants, in the wool-producing area it was one for every 1,201 inhabitants. The workshops, as may be imagined, were very small-scale; but even on this level the cereal region easily outstripped the wool area. While in the former the average capital investment per establishment was 4,559 *pesos*, in the latter it only reached the paltry figure of 285 *pesos*. The same can be said with regard to the number of commercial establishments, although in this case the differences were not so marked. In the cereal districts there was a business for every seventy-four inhabitants; in the wool area, one for every 153. The average capital per establishment was 8,208 *pesos* in the cereal region and 3,291 in the wool districts.

The political scene

I think the data assembled so far show quite clearly that the degree of diversification and social and economic progress was much greater in the areas affected by the introduction of cereal-growing. With regard to the *pampas* as a whole, which had previously been dominated by extensive cattle-raising estates, the introduction of cereal cultivation brought a very considerable change in the scale of operations. It is interesting to see if this is also the case in the field of political institutions.

This is not so easy to determine, however, since Santa Fe politics were not autonomous and were heavily influenced by decisions emanating from the central authorities. Current practice also made it difficult for new forms of political expression to emerge peacefully. The system in force in Argentina before the introduction of the compulsory secret ballot in 1912 was characterized by very low electoral participation, with rarely more than a 20-per-cent turnout of those entitled to vote, and furthermore a large majority of those who took part in the voting did so under the influence of the local bosses (*caudillos*). The *caudillo* system was particularly strong in the rural areas, where, through a complex system of reciprocal right and obligations, the local chiefs could ensure the support of a considerable number of the labourers working on their cattle ranches. It is interesting to analyse what was involved in this system of mutual favours. The influence of a rural *caudillo* in any region was based on the personal services he could distribute among his followers. These favours were of various kinds, such as finding employment for them or simply giving them either money or goods for their own use. Of no less importance was the influence the *caudillo* could exert over the local authorities, to make sure they overlooked the crimes which his followers were liable to commit at that time against the property of the rural population.[15] This varied range of favours was repaid with the unconditional loyalty of his followers, a loyalty which might even involve loss of life in that time of violent political confrontation. What really distinguished this system of political relations, however, was the fact that the ties binding the leader to his followers were strictly personal in character and were not based on a consideration of the social and occupational interests of the *caudillo*'s followers.

This peculiar political system rested, as we have seen, on low electoral participation and a marked dominance of the rural areas over the towns, where the *caudillo*'s influence was less pronounced. There is not much doubt about the solidity of the prevailing system, and its beneficiaries had few qualms about resorting to electoral fraud and violence if the opposition at the time seemed to threaten the stability of that system – hence the frequency of the civilian and military revolts and uprisings that were such a common feature of this period.

As though these obstacles were not enough, the majority of the farmers of Santa Fe were foreigners and consequently had no voting rights. This problem could have been overcome by taking out Argentine citizenship, but the nature of the prevailing legislation, which made few discriminations against foreigners, meant that there were few material advantages to be had from doing so. Nor was the administrative process involved in obtaining the appropriate documents an easy one, particularly in the rural areas. For these and perhaps other reasons, the number of foreigners who adopted Argentine citizenship was very small. On the face of it, this could be taken as an indication of the political passiveness of the farmers, who would not seem to have been very different in this respect from the rather inactive Argentine citizens. At the same time, in the cereal zones a sort of political *caudillo* emerged, similar to the ones who had operated for so long in the cattle regions. It is interesting to note that many of these *caudillos* were foreign immigrants who thereby became integrated into the existing institutional system.

All these factors must, of course, be taken into account when analysing the political behaviour of the inhabitants of the cereal area. But, at the same time, it is as well to bear in mind that the political and institutional setup at the time was much more complex than the above facts suggest. Because there were also many other events which indicate a rather active and original political participation by the population of the cereal area, these should be analysed briefly here.

It has already been noted that armed revolt was one of the few means available to the opposition to impose its ideas. It is obvious that it was not necessary to have citizenship in order to have recourse to this means. In this period there were six such revolts in Santa Fe (1871, 1877, and 1879, and three in 1893); in four of these the farmers played a very active part. The part played by the people of the agricultural colonies in the events of 1893 was of particular importance, as they came to form the central nucleus of opposition to the conservative regime and were the chief bulwark of a new political grouping – the Unión Cívica Radical – which would come to play a very significant role in national politics.

But over and above these occasional forays into the political life of the province, the period under examination saw very active participation by the farmers in political problems at the municipal level. During the very turbulent years of the 1870s and the 1890s the newspapers carried accounts of innumerable conflicts and incidents between the people and the local authorities. It is precisely at the local level that the Santa Fe settlers introduced forms of political action and institutions, such as an autonomous and relatively representative municipal system, that had hitherto been practically unheard of on the *pampas*.

The municipal system had its good and bad points and obvious limitations, given the features of the prevailing institutional system. But during the period from 1870 to 1895 there was always some agricultural village where some kind of autonomous municipal government was in force. Such an institution was something of a novelty in the *pampa* region and was distinguished by certain features which in terms of current political practice were significant innovations. First of all, the municipal elections held in the agricultural colonies recorded a much higher degree of popular participation than those held in the other rural districts, or for that matter in the large cities of the province. Secondly, these municipal elections were, in many cases, genuinely competitive affairs between different lists of candidates bidding for local power. This is in marked contrast to what happened in the cattle zones, where only the official list of candidates was presented with monotonous regularity. Thirdly, until 1890 foreigners could vote and stand for office in these elections.

It was precisely the suspension of the municipal rights of foreigners which was one of the main causes of the rural protest movements of 1893. Already in 1891 the settlers had presented their demands in clear and summary form:

We demand the vote in municipal elections because: (1) the municipal government is not a political body but an administrative entity which must necessarily be popular and democratic . . . (2) we are taxpayers and residents of the municipal district; (3) if we take an active part and have duties in municipal life we must also have rights; (4) foreigners were the founders of the agricultural colonies . . .[16]

The farmers took up arms for these same political principles in 1893. When the armed struggle was over, the farmers contested the provincial elections of 1894 with a programme which once again asserted their right to an autonomous and representative municipal life:

Greater popular participation in public affairs. Reduction of excessive taxation. Cuts in the present extravagant budget. Justices of the peace to be directly elected by the people of the neighbourhood and to have clearly defined and purely judicial functions . . . Creation of autonomous municipal governments in the main towns and colonies. Banking reform – members of the board to be elected by shareholders. Franchise and full liberty for the press and political parties.[17]

These kinds of demands were unprecedented in the *pampa* region of Argentina, and I would even contend that it was the first time that a clearly defined socio-occupational group (in this case the farmers) had devised a political platform of this nature, emphasizing the situation of an entire social group, which could not be dealt with, as it has been before, through the distribution of personal favours. It is consequently hard to deny that in the cereal zone there emerged institutional forms which, although they were limited and restricted, were new in the context of rural Argentina.

It is not my intention to demonstrate conclusively that there was a clear causal relationship between the introduction of cereal-growing and the social and institutional changes dealt with above. The type of information assembled and the way it has been analysed would not permit such a conclusion to be drawn. I do believe, however, that the material presented here strongly suggests the possibility that the degree of social progress and diversification achieved in Santa Fe was closely bound up with the very specific characteristics of cereal-growing operations. The same can be said with regard to the more modest and limited changes observed in the political life of the province. But in both instances, and especially in the latter, more detailed research is needed in other areas in order to eliminate the possibility that the Santa Fe phenomenon was affected by other kinds of variables than those considered here. Only in this way can we be sure that our case study is representative of the wider society. Meanwhile it is possible to suggest that the type of social structure that emerged on the humid *pampa*, and which gave the region very peculiar characteristics in the context of rural Argentina and indeed of Latin America, was in large measure related to the spectacular expansion of cereal production which began in the 1870s.

NOTES

1. There is an extensive bibliography on the economic development of the *pampas*. The following are useful works of reference: M. A. Cárcano, *Evolución histórica del régimen de la tierra pública* (Buenos Aires, 1917); A. Montoya, *Historia de los saladeros argentinos* (Buenos Aires, 1956); H. Giberti, *Historia económica de la ganadería argentina*, 2nd edn (Buenos Aires, 1961); J. Scobie, *Revolution on the pampas: a social history of Argentine wheat, 1860–1910* (Austin, Texas, 1964); R. Cortés Conde, 'Patrones de asentamiento y explotación agropecuaria en los nuevos territorios argentinos', in A. Jara (ed.), *Tierras nuevas* (Mexico, 1969), pp. 105–20; T. Halperín Donghi, 'La expansión ganadera en la campaña de Buenos Aires', *Desarrollo Económico* III, 1–2 (Buenos Aires, 1963), pp. 57–110.

2. R. Baldwin, 'Patterns of development in newly settled regions', *Manchester School of Economic and Social Studies* XXIX (1956), pp. 161–79.

3. D. North, 'Agriculture in regional economic growth', *Journal of Farm Economics* LI, 5 (1959), pp. 943–54.

4. R. Nurkse, *Patterns of trade and development* (Oxford, 1962).

5. The bibliography is very large. The following may be consulted: D. North, *The economic growth of the United States: 1790–1860* (New York, 1966); M. Watkins, 'A staple theory of economic growth', *Canadian Journal of Economics and Political Science* XXIX (1963), pp. 141–58; M. W. McCarthy, 'The staple approach in Australian economic history', *Business Archives and History* IV (1964), pp. 1–22; G. W. Bertram, 'Economic growth in Canadian history: the staple theory and the take-off hypothesis', *Canadian Journal of Economics and Political Science* XXIX (1963) pp. 159–84.

   For the Argentine case, see Ezequiel Gallo, 'Agrarian expansion and industrial development in Argentina, 1880–1930', *St Antony's Papers* (Oxford, 1971), pp. 45–61; and Lucio Geller, 'El crecimiento industrial argentino y la teoría del bien primario exportable', *El Trimestre Económico* XXXVI (Mexico, 1970), pp. 763–811. For the case of plantation economies, see G. L. Beckford, 'The economics of agricultural resource use and development in plantation economies', *Social and Economic Studies* XVIII (Jamaica, 1969), pp. 321–47 (reprinted in H. Bernstein (ed.), *Underdevelopment and development: the third world today* (London, 1973), pp. 115–151). An interesting attempt to link these problems with forms of political action can be found in A. L. Stinchcombe, 'Agricultural enterprise and rural class relations', *American Journal of Sociology* LXVII (1961–2), pp. 165–76 (reprinted in J. L. Finkle and R. W. Gable (eds.), *Political development and social change* (New York, 1971)).

6. If there is no indication to the contrary, the data in this section are taken from my 'Agricultural colonization and society in Argentina: the province of Santa Fe, 1870–1895' (unpublished D. Phil. thesis, University of Oxford, 1970). The census data were abstracted from the national censuses of 1869 and 1895 and the provincial census of 1887. Data were also used from the work directed by A. Lattes and Jorge Somoza, as analysed by Ruth Sautu: see 'Muestra de los censos nacionales de 1869 y 1895', *Documento de Trabajo* 48, Instituto Torcuato di Tella (Buenos Aires, 1967).

    It is important to make clear that after 1895 the characteristics of the *pampa* region changed significantly. The rearing of purebred cattle replaced sheep, which were displaced towards the territories of southern Argentina. The most important change in arable farming was the appearance of tenancy as the principal form of land tenure. Although renting did exist in the period dealt with in this article, it was only from 1895 onwards that it took on the dominant role that it was to maintain until the 1950s. In Santa Fe, the southern part of the province, which previously had been devoted to sheep-rearing, was worked by tenants. The central region, on the other hand, retained the features described in this article. For the emergence of tenancy, see Gallo, 'Agricultural colonization' (1970), and R. Cortés Conde, 'Cambios históricos en la estructura de la producción agropecuaria', *Desarrollo Económico* XX (Buenos Aires, 1966), pp. 493–509.

7. The way in which the census data were presented does not enable the population to be classified into very precise socio-economic groups. In this case, those farmers who owned or rented land using wage labour were regarded as belonging to the middle sectors. Also in this category were merchants and industrialists, teachers, professional people, and public officials.

8. The Italian consul calculated that of the 135,785 inhabitants recorded as Argentines in the 1887 census, 40 per cent were the children of foreign immigrants. See the report of Vice-Consul Carlo Nagar in *Emigrazione e colonie* (Rome, 1893).

9. It should be emphasized here that when one speaks of, for example, the cereal region, this refers not solely to estates involved in cereal cultivation but rather to the region as a whole where these crops predominated. Consequently, the category of 'cereal region' includes the cities and towns located therein. The percentage of workers, therefore, includes not only agricultural labourers (a minority in this category) but also workers in the factories in the cities, and especially those engaged in railway construction.

10. E. D'Amicis, *In America* (Rome, 1897), pp. 102–3; Gallo, 'Agricultural colonization' (1970) may also be consulted for further examples.

11. For the reasons why agricultural entrepreneurs chose one activity or the other, see Ezequiel Gallo, 'Ocupación de tierras y colonización agrícola en Santa Fe', in A. Jara (ed.), *Tierras nuevas* (Mexico, 1969), pp. 92–104.

12. For the sheep *estancias*, see the works of Giberti and Montoya cited in note 1 above. Also useful are H. Gibson, *The history and present state of the sheepbreeding industry in the Argentine republic* (Buenos Aires, 1893); E. Zeballos, *Descripción amena de la república argentina*, 3 vols. (Buenos Aires, 1881–8), especially vol. 3, *A través de las*

Cabañas (1888); Thomas J. Hutchinson, *Buenos Ayres and Argentine gleanings* (London, 1865). I should like to acknowledge here the information provided by Ernesto Laclau, who is completing his doctoral dissertation on this subject.

13. See Gallo, 'Agrarian expansion', and Scobie, *Revolution on the pampas*. The following may also be consulted: Carl Taylor, *Rural life in Argentina* (Baton Rouge, Louisiana, 1948); F. Molinas, *La colonización argentina y las industrias agropecuarias* (Buenos Aires, 1910); R. Campolleti, *La chacra argentina* (Buenos Aires, 1914); and H. Miatello, *La agricultura y la ganadería en la República Argentina* (Buenos Aires, 1916).

14. The first sheep *estancias* had been set up in this region in the early 1860s. But the region, or part of it, was already populated at that time, and there were already a number of cattle *estancias*. Also, some of the districts were on the much-used route from Buenos Aires to the interior provinces. This situation was in marked contrast to that of the cereal districts located in a typical frontier zone which was completely unpopulated before the spread of cereal cultivation.

15. An example of this situation, from the many that could be given, comes from a public official: 'I tried to find out what deficiencies there were, and the first thing that took my notice was the continuous misdeeds of some magistrates ... and the audacity with which a band of outlaws had taken control of the agricultural colonies under the more or less direct protection of said magistrates.' 'Informe del jefe político del departamento de Castellanos', in Archivo de la provincia de Santa Fe: Archivo de gobierno, tomo 175, legajo 2 (1892).

16. *La Unión* (Esperanza), 15 November 1891. It is interesting to note here, as evidence of the intense political activity at the local level, that in the 1860s there were already two political journals in the agricultural colonies (*El Colono del Oeste* and *El Serrucho*). For this period, see Ezequiel Gallo, 'Conflitti socio-politici nelle colonie agricole di Santa Fe, 1870–80', in *Quaderni Storici* XXV (Ancona, 1974), pp. 160–92.

17. *La Unión* (Esperanza), 19 November 1893. For these events, see Ezequiel Gallo, *Colonos en armas: las revoluciones radicales en la provincia de Santa Fe* (Buenos Aires, 1974).

PART IV

The transition from slave plantation to capitalist plantation

The decline and eventual abolition of slavery in northeast Brazil and the subsequent technological changes in the sugar industry are discussed by Jaime Reis and Peter Eisenberg in the first two papers of this section. Both make clear the extent to which almost all the agricultural land in this region was controlled by the planter oligarchy, thereby leaving the ex-slaves and other classes of free labourers few opportunities to escape from work on the plantations, which remained virtually their only source of income and employment. Moreover, ecological conditions discouraged the ex-slaves from migrating in large numbers away from the coastal sugar zone into the interior, for the arid backlands of the sertão already carried a surplus population which, unable to eke out more than bare living from the region's meagre and uncertain resources, was itself actually seeking to migrate (albeit seasonally) towards the sugar cane areas. Eisenberg's paper contains a broad general analysis of the economic factors affecting the Brazilian sugar industry in this period of crisis and change, and some useful comparisons are made with the Cuban sugar cane industry. In contrast, Reis's paper presents a more detailed study of the social relations of production within the changing plantation system, with particular reference to the slow but steady transition from the use of slaves to *moradores* as the major source of agricultural labour.

Whereas in northeast Brazil the process of agrarian change seems to have been relatively smooth and untraumatic (at least from the point of view of the landowners), Michael Taussig shows that in the Cauca Valley of Colombia the elimination of Negro slavery initially resulted in a very considerable degree of economic and social disruption in the plantation system. In some areas there even developed for a time, a sort of 'outlaw' black peasantry squatting on the heavily forested margins of *hacienda* lands or on free or *indiviso* lands along the river banks or on the savannahs. This posed great problems for the large landowners who tried continually, but often with only limited or temporary success,

343

to reassert their former social and economic dominance and control over these groups. Later, however, the opening-up of communications and trade with the Pacific coast, the growth in population, and the renewed tendency towards land monopolization by a small number of corporate landed enterprises brought about the gradual but remorseless proletarianization of the peasantry. Nevertheless, the attitude of the rural labourers towards work in the sugar plantations remained highly antagonistic; only dire poverty, or the threat of it, forced them to cut cane, and wherever possible they sought other ways of making a livelihood. In conclusion, Taussig describes the ideological outlook of this rural semi-proletariat and suggests that the values and belief systems which have been thus developed, and which would probably be described as 'anomic' or 'deviant' by certain schools of sociological thought brought up in the western tradition, are in reality logically and inextricably linked with the deprivations of the rural labourer's living and working conditions.

Strictly speaking, any discussion of the agrarian societies of the British West Indies lies outside the scope of this book. However, many of the general theoretical problems relating to this particular section have also been examined by economists and sociologists studying the social and economic problems of the West Indies. It was therefore decided to include at least one paper which analyses how the transition process from slavery to wage labour had worked itself out in this area. Brian Blouet's paper, which discusses the consequences of emancipation in Trinidad, provides a further example of the close interactions between (on the one hand) local ecology, the demographic profile of the time, and the specific man—land relationship as expressed by the prevailing land tenure system, and (on the other hand) the particular form of transition to free wage labour. Unlike, for example, the densely populated northeast of Brazil or the Leeward Islands, the existence in Trinidad of relatively empty Crown lands, and, for a time at least, an open agricultural frontier, gave the ex-slaves all the opportunity and incentive they needed to abandon the plantation system and to establish themselves as independent peasant farmers. However, as Blouet points out, many ex-slaves settled on small plots of land around the periphery of the plantations and began to work on a seasonal basis in the sugar cane harvest. To a certain extent these semi-proletarians were able to strike a balance between their own peasant or subsistence farming activities and seasonal wage labour in the plantations which, taken together, were capable of providing them with an adequate livelihood. Certainly the plantation owners complained about the recalcitrance of their ex-slaves in refusing to work for anything less than a wage which – perhaps inevitably, given their historical experience – the planters regarded as exceptionally high. In other words, when the plantation owners complained of a labour shortage they were really complaining about the relative cost of labour power, a problem which they began to resolve during the second half of the nineteenth century by the importation of large numbers of indentured labourers from India.

CHAPTER 14

The consequences of modernization for Brazil's sugar plantations in the nineteenth century

PETER L. EISENBERG[1]

In the late nineteenth century, two crises disturbed the Brazilian sugar economy. A serious market crisis arose when European beet sugar usurped traditional cane sugar markets. A serious social crisis arose within Brazil when the Imperial government moved to abolish slavery. This study examines the sugar planters' means of dealing with these crises, why they failed in comparison with Cuban sugar planters, and how they nevertheless succeeded in preserving their social position. It also speculates on how the market crisis might have been overcome and how the social crisis might have been handled differently.

The Brazilian planters attempted capital improvements and re-organization of production to cope with the market crisis, but they failed. The only real solution would have been integration into a northern-hemisphere market via recolonization, but that would have entailed heavy political costs. The planters coped better with the social crisis. They succeeded in transferring the losses suffered in export markets to the plantation work force in the form of depressed wages and poor working conditions. Their efforts, aided with government subsidies, perpetuated their dominance in Brazil's sugar areas. Thus 'modernization', understood as technological advance and the abolition of forced labour, failed to produce general changes.[2]

The economic crisis

The market crisis affected all cane sugar producers, who had lost about one-half of the world market by the end of the century (Table 51). The shift away from cane sugar consumption did not reflect changing tastes, for cane sugar and beet sugar were good substitutes. In fact, the volume of world cane sugar production increased fivefold during the latter part of the nineteenth century. Nor did the shift indicate that demand was declining, for average annual per capita consumption in England rose from fifteen pounds in the early 1800s to seventy-two pounds by the late

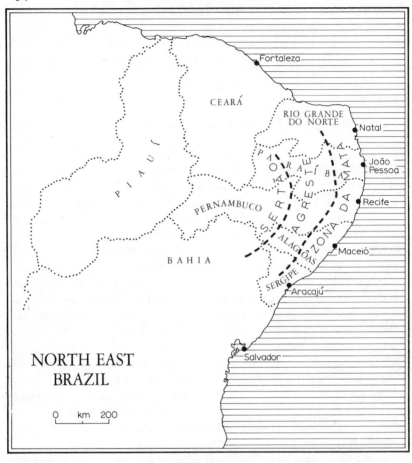

Map 21

1880s.[3] Such accelerating consumption should have benefited suppliers. In general, it did – but not Brazil.

The crisis first manifested itself in falling prices in the early years of the century (Table 51). Brazil's sugar export revenues began slipping seriously in the 1870s. Although export volumes continued to grow, and the trade recovered briefly in the 1880s and early 1890s, in subsequent years Brazil suffered disastrous falls in both revenues and volumes.[4] While the competition from beet sugar affected all cane sugar producers, and the absolute volume of cane sugar exports from Martinique, Guadeloupe, and Mauritius also fell, the decline was not generic. Cuba's

TABLE 51 *Sugar prices and values, 1841–5 to 1906–10*

Years	Average world production (tons)	Beet cane and beet (%)	Average Brazilian exports (tons)	Average Cuban exports (tons)	Average raw price (per cwt., c.i.f. London)	Average Brazilian exports (£ per ton)
1841–5	959,078	5.1%	87,979	143,612	36s 0d	£14.5
1846–50	1,146,281	9.3%	112,830	208,598	26s 2d	14.3
1851–5	1,433,105	13.7%	127,874	320,722	21s 10d	15.9
1856–60	1,676,492	21.3%	98,864	394,200	26s 7d	20.9
1861–5	1,912,388	25.9%	113,551	534,600	22s 2d	17.1
1866–70	2,414,270	32.0%	109,001	682,000	22s 5d	15.4
1871–5	3,003,043	40.0%	169,337	682,000	23s 0d	13.7
1876–80	3,320,512	44.2%	167,761	568,600	21s 1d	14.4
1881–5	4,333,972	51.2%	238,074	505,215	17s 5d	10.5
1886–90	5,572,260	56.5%	147,274	621,696	13s 1d	11.3
1891–5	7,243,020	52.0%	153,333	933,470	12s 6d	14.5
1896–1900	8,174,820	61.0%	113,908	272,427	10s 4d	11.8
1901–5	10,414,020	50.0%	78,284	943,212	9s 4d	9.4
1906–10	12,831,200	49.3%	51,338	1,393,898	9s 10d	9.7

Sources: Noël Deerr, *The history of sugar*, 2 vols. (London, 1949–50), vol. 1, p. 131; vol. 2, pp. 490–1, 531. 'O açúcar na vida econômica do Brasil', *Annuário Açucareiro para 1938* (Rio de Janeiro, 1939), pp. 233–6. Cuban Economic Research Project, *A study on Cuba* (Coral Gables, Florida, 1965), p. 83.

successful experience demonstrates that Brazil suffered from more specific disadvantages. To understand these difficulties, therefore, I shall briefly compare the Cuban sugar economy with that of Pernambuco, the northeast province which led Brazil's sugar exports throughout the later nineteenth century.

A glance at a map suggests immediately that Cuba's principal advantage over Brazil, as far as selling sugar to large consumer markets was concerned, was its proximity to the United States. Certainly the island's location allowed lower transportation costs to the United States than those charged on sugar shipped from Brazil or virtually any other foreign supplier. As ocean transport costs steadily declined in the nineteenth century, however, owing to steam engines and other advances, Cuba's advantage over Brazil in this regard became less crucial.[5] But Brazil still failed to gain permanent access to the rich North American market. In the 1880s, when Cuba was recovering from the destruction and indebtedness of the Ten Years War (1868–78), Cuban exports declined, and Brazil tripled her sugar shipments to the United States. The success raised hopes of replacing lost European markets. Optimism swelled when the United States promulgated the McKinley tariff in 1890, which like the British Sugar Act of 1846 reduced charges on raw sugar and molasses. Just as Brazil had gained easier access to the English market after 1846, so sugar exporters hoped for similar access to the North American market after 1890. In 1891 the United States signed a reciprocal trade agreement with Brazil; but all hopes were dashed when, in the same year, the United States signed the Foster–Canovas treaty with Spain, which extended the same favours to Cuba and Puerto Rico. After those islands separated from Spain in the late 1890s, the United States signed new reciprocal trade treaties which ratified their status as sugar colonies of the North Americans.[6]

Geographical proximity gave Cuba a favoured position, and colonial preference agreements formalized the relationship. But these factors alone do not explain Cuba's access to the United States market and Brazil's exclusion. Economic considerations, such as the supply of the crucial productive factors of land and capital, are also important.

Sidney Mintz has pointed to soil fertility as the determining factor in the sequential rise of sugar colonies in the Caribbean.[7] Many writers have commented on the excellence of Cuban soils for growing sugar, and this great fertility certainly contributed to Cuba's high yields and her comparative advantage *vis-à-vis* Brazil.[8] New Cuban cane lands produced as much as 119 tons of cane per hectare, and median lands in the 1870s yielded nearly 70 tons per hectare, whereas reported yields in Pernambuco never exceeded 60 tons per hectare.[9] As a result, Cuba could produce over 1.2 tons of sugar per hectare in the 1890s, when Brazilian cane fields and mills were yielding no more than 0.24 tons per hectare.[10]

While good land was abundant in Cuba, labour was relatively scarce. Unlike Brazil, which had exported sugar since the sixteenth century, Cuba only entered large-scale sugar production in the early nineteenth century, when Haitian production declined following the slave and independence revolts beginning in 1791. In the eighteenth century, Cuba had exported principally tobacco, but the volume of this activity never reached such proportions as to cause massive importations of African slaves. As a result, when Cuba really began to produce sugar, slaves were scarce and expensive.[11] The rapid expansion of Cuban sugar production outstripped the importation of African slaves, and by the 1840s the Cubans were contracting Chinese coolie labour for the plantations.[12]

In Brazil's sugar areas, on the other hand, labour abounded. Whereas Cuba had fewer than 300,000 slaves in 1871, Brazil registered 1,500,000 in 1873. Of course, Brazil's slaves did not all work in sugar production;

but in Pernambuco, Alagoas, Sergipe, and Bahia, the principal sugar-exporting provinces, there were over 300,000 slaves.[13] Even when Brazil's sugar area converted from slave to free labour, the number of native workers more than met the industry's demand, and real wages actually declined after 1870.[14] Comparable wage data for Cuba are not available, but it seems clear that the labour-scarcity situation persisted in the late nineteenth century. Cuban workers began organizing as early as the 1850s, and strikes occurred after the 1860s, at least thirty years before comparable labour organization and activity in Pernambuco.[15]

If labour was scarce in Cuba, capital was not. Spanish, Spanish American, and Cuban capitalists financed the early sugar plantations at monthly rates starting around 1.5 per cent. Attracted by the island's proximity and economic prospects, United States capitalists also played a growing role in financing the plantations. In cases of default, as for example during the Ten Years War, the foreign capitalists became plantation-owners both by necessity and by choice. The growing United States interest can also be deduced from the annexationist propaganda of the 1840s to the 1870s.[16]

The fortunate combination of fertile land, scarce labour, and available capital allowed Cuba to lead the world in modernizing its cane sugar industry. By the 1860s, 70 per cent of Cuba's 1,350 mills used steam engines, in comparison with only 2 per cent of Pernambucan mills; as late as 1914 only one-third of Pernambuco's mills used steam power.[17]

But modernization meant more than just steam engines and multiple-effect vacuum pans. The growing size of sugar mills encouraged division of labour between the agricultural cane-growing sector and the industrial sugar-making sector, because the mills simply needed more cane than any one plantation could supply. Moreover, if independent planters supplied the cane, millers could concentrate attention and investments in expensive machinery. In Cuba, this reorganization of production replaced the traditional *ingenios* with large-capacity mills called *centrales*. The cane suppliers, known as *colonos*, included two categories: the independent grower, who formerly may have operated a mill but now only grew cane on his own land; and the dependent grower on *central* land. The Cubans experimented initially with contracted cane prices, but this system proved disastrous when sugar prices fell unexpectedly. The Cuban *central* owners then paid for cane on the basis of the current sugar price, and the system succeeded. United States investors' growing interest in Cuba provided much of the capital necessary to transform or create *centrales*. The Ten Years War and the Wars of Independence

(1895–98) destroyed many older mills and thereby sped the disappearance of the traditional *ingenio*. By the early twentieth century, 170 to 180 *centrales* completely monopolized Cuban production.[18]

In Brazil, due to different relative factor costs, fewer stimuli induced modernization. The British appear to many writers to have played a role similar to that of the North Americans in Cuba; but the appearance is deceptive. Brazilian correspondents borrowed capital from British commercial banks in Recife and then made short-term loans, at 1.5 per cent monthly or more, to the planters to cover operating expenses. But Brazil's comparative disadvantages in sugar production did not attract the same quantity of foreign capital as did Cuba. To effect the transformation of traditional *engenhos* to *centrales*, or *engenhos centrais*, considerable government aid was necessary.[19]

Official aid became available in the 1880s and 1890s and was essential for modernization. At first, the Imperial government guaranteed a profit of 7 per cent to companies building *engenhos centrais*. These mills owned no cane fields and bought their raw material from independent growers, known as *fornecedores*. But two difficulties plagued the subsidized *centrais*. Firstly, many of the foreign concessionaires perpetrated frauds by speculating with their concessions and inflating costs, acts suggesting they had little interest or faith in Brazil's sugar export markets. Secondly, the mills which reached completion had trouble in organizing a regular cane supply. Cane-growers maintained their own mills and refused to send cane if they did not like prices or conditions; they also felt they were being reduced to the status of *lavradores* or sharecroppers, and they resented it. No exogenous forces such as wartime destruction obliged the traditional mill-owners, *senhores de engenho*, to collaborate with the new *engenhos centrais*.

The Brazilians overcame these difficulties by relying almost exclusively on generous official loans to native entrepreneurs; the new Republic founded in 1889 allowed the states to collect export taxes, and in Pernambuco these taxes were returned to the planters in the form of long-term low-interest mortgages. Moreover, the new modern mills, now called *usinas*, not only bought cane from independent growers but also owned their own cane lands to ensure steady supply and independence from the still-powerful *senhores de engenho*. Thus the *usina* re-created to a large extent the productive organization of the traditional *engenho*, only on a larger scale.[20]

By 1910, some sixty modern mills were operating in Pernambuco, of which two-thirds had received subsidies. But another 2,000 traditional *engenhos* continued to supply local demand for crude sugar (*rapadura*) and cheap rum (*cachaça*).[21] Thus, while government aid permitted modernization of a small proportion of the mills, the transformation and reorganization were never completed.[22]

Even within Brazil, where domestic demand might have partly compensated for loss of foreign markets, distance and domestic competition limited the northeastern sugar industry's marketing possibilities. The Pernambuco sugar exporters attempted in the first decade of the twentieth century to cartelize the national market. Their attempts failed because the most populous consumer areas of Minas Gerais, Rio de Janeiro, and São Paulo had had their own local sugar industries since the colonial period, and those industries were reluctant to join the northeastern cartel. The refiners in those areas, moreover, enjoying a near-monopsony due to the export crisis, played producers off against each other and frustrated the cartel's efforts.[23]

Nathaniel Leff has recently argued that in Brazil the sugar-producing areas' difficulties were further aggravated by the presence of the coffee economy. Since arbitrage in principal ports kept the reigning foreign-exchange rate about the same for both sugar and coffee areas, the flourishing coffee economy's high export earnings maintained the national exchange rate for Brazilian *milreis* above the level it otherwise would have found if it were only a function of the more slowly growing sugar earnings. Given the general decline of the value of Brazilian currency, the exchange rate fell more slowly than would have happened without the buoying effects of coffee's earnings. Thus sugar exporters receiving foreign currency would have been able to buy more *milreis* and thereby cushion the export decline.[24] Such revenue effects would only have been clearly positive, however, if the inflation did not affect domestic prices for exporters and if their import demand were low. Sugar exporters could have escaped the effects of a more acute domestic inflation, for market imperfections such as poor communications and the working class's lack of bargaining power would have arrested the spiral's climb. But the need to import expensive capital equipment for modernization would have eaten into these short-run revenue gains. Those gains would not have been sufficient to stimulate the growth of a local capital goods industry, as Celso Furtado has suggested, and thereby reduce the dependence on foreign imports, for even in São Paulo – where economic conditions were much more propitious – such an industry did not appear until the 1930s. Previous efforts in that direction had depended far more upon protective tariff legislation and trade treaties than upon exchange rates.[25]

The sugar export market difficulties led to regional income differences within Brazil, and many Pernambucans blamed their problems on political discrimination. But political discrimination was a consequence, not a cause, of Pernambuco's difficulties. Pernambuco received larger Imperial subsidies for the building of *centrais* than any other province. The European immigration and early industrialization which Rio de Janeiro and São Paulo enjoyed resulted from the strength of those areas' coffee economies far more than from any Imperial subsidies (Table 52). In the Republic, moreover, when northeasterners in general disappeared from the top levels of the executive, charges of regional discrimination continued but with no greater justification. State budgets in both the northeast and the centre-south funded the principal economic development programmes, such as *usinas* and immigration; Pernambuco could hardly blame São Paulo for not spending its revenues outside the state.[26] Even in the twentieth century, when federal agencies such as the Superintendência para o Desenvolvimento do Nordeste (SUDENE), the Banco do Nordeste, and the income tax bureau encourage industrial investment in the northeast, the meagre results provoke continued complaints about the growing gap between the northeastern economy and that of the centre-south.[27] But the basic fault, to paraphrase Cassius to Brutus, lay not in São Paulo but in the northeast itself. Internal colonization may have aggravated the differences between the areas – for example, by

TABLE 52   *Brazilian export earnings, 1841–5 to 1906–10* (thousands of £)

	Average sugar earnings	Average coffee earnings
1841–5	1,265	2,058
1846–50	1,651	2,473
1851–5	1,882	4,113
1856–60	2,445	5,635
1861–5	1,944	6,863
1866–70	1,718	6,737
1871–5	2,353	10,488
1876–80	2,355	12,103
1881–5	2,646	11,359
1886–90	1,537	14,381
1891–5	2,182	20,914
1896–1900	1,289	16,669
1901–5	637	20,952
1906–10	480	27,877

Sources: 'O açúcar na vida econômica do Brasil', pp. 233–6; Affonso de Taunay, *Pequena história do café no Brasil (1717–1937)* (Rio de Janeiro, 1945), pp. 547–9.

depriving northeasterners of influence in national government, as Andre Gunder Frank has written[28] – but the difference derived mainly from the contrasting positions of Brazilian coffee and Brazilian sugar in the world markets.

If my analysis is correct, the only possible solutions to Pernambuco's sugar market crisis were integration into a northern hemisphere market via recolonization; new use of the productive resources employed in sugar; or continuation with the maintenance of the status quo and transferral of the cost to other groups in Brazilian society.

Had the northeast seceded from the rest of Brazil – an event whose possible consequences Leff speculates on, and which was in fact actually attempted in 1824 – the sugar exporters undoubtedly would have experienced a faster fall in the exchange rate and short-run revenue gains. Secession would have freed the northeast from the pernicious effects of the centre-south's regional preponderance. It may also have inhibited labour mobility and thereby lowered the cost of labour, whether slave or free. Moreover, it would definitely have ended the southward drain of capital in the form of Imperial taxes, and facilitated local subsidies for modernization. But none of these changes would have restored Pernambuco's export markets, and the small local population could not have absorbed the area's production.[29]

Only if the independent sugar-producing region joined the formal British Empire or the informal United States empire might it have fared better in the international market. If the independent northeast could have offered especially favourable conditions to attract foreign capital, the home country subsequently might have made preferential trading arrangements to guarantee markets to the colony. Of course such neo-colonialism would have entailed high political costs in terms of loss of sovereignty, such as Cuba experienced in the first half of the twentieth-century; nevertheless, the sugar exporters would have had improved earnings.[30]

A land reform which redistributed resources employed in sugar production would not have salvaged the private economy, for no other single export crop was as lucrative as sugar in Pernambuco. At times cotton drew investments from sugar areas, but cotton's position on Brazil's export list depended upon the temporary absence of leading world producers from the international market. Once those producers returned, as after the United States War of Independence, the Napoleonic Wars, and the United States Civil War, Brazil was displaced from world cotton markets.[31] Tobacco had been grown near the sugar zone in Bahia's Recôncavo, but as an export crop it was never as rewarding as sugar.

Cattle-raising had traditionally enlivened the economy in Pernambuco's backlands, but that area lacked good pasturage and a permanent water supply, while Minas Gerais and Rio Grande do Sul, nearer the populous centre-south and rich in cattle- and dairy-farming, dominated the national market.[32] Finally, coffee, cocoa, and natural rubber became important exports in the latter part of the nineteenth century, but the climates and soils required to grow these crops were not to be found in Pernambuco. In the absence of any alternative export activity yielding returns equal to those of sugar, therefore, the planters' concentration on sugar is understandable.[33]

Since neither regional independence nor different utilization of land were real possibilities, it is not surprising that the planters chose to meet the export crisis with technological modernization. The government subsidies built a protected competitive position for the *usina*-owners and encouraged investments in plantations. The failure to cartelize the national market prevented the planters from recovering losses through higher prices to domestic consumers. The planters were able, however, to pass the costs of falling export markets to the free workers in the form of depressed wages, poor conditions, and insecure job tenure.

The social crisis

As world sugar competition created a crisis in Brazil's export markets in the later nineteenth century, the abolition of slavery, begun with the ending of the African trade in 1850, created a social crisis at home. The timing of abolition resulted mostly from political considerations and not fluctuations in export earnings; but it directly affected production costs and the organization of the sugar industry's labour force. Various regions of Brazil reacted differently to abolition, depending upon the value and need for slave labour.[34]

In Pernambuco the planters' monopoly of land in the sugar zone, together with sugar's continued comparative advantage within the province, gave the planters economic and political supremacy. This power enabled them to convert from slave to free labour with a minimum of inconvenience and thereby to pass much of the cost of the export crisis to the free workers, who had virtually no bargaining power at all.

The number of mills actually increased in the latter years of the nineteenth century. If it was not a product of sugar's comparative advantage, one might ascribe the new investment to non-economic motives such as prestige and political influence associated with large land holdings. Some planters in fact may have acquired land for such reasons, for the absence of land taxes or other carrying charges left landholding virtually costless. But the sugar oligarchy's positive pressures for modernization showed that they were fully capable of pursuing their economic self-interest. Sugar remained the preferred investment; and new mills made money.

While the planters worked only very small portions of their estates, the size of their holdings effectively excluded the development of a small-farmer class which might have challenged their supremacy. Planters monopolized local political office, where their power reflected their monopoly of the means of production. To be sure, planters differed among themselves and fought out these differences in the Imperial political parties of Liberals and Conservatives, and also in and out of the courts, but these conflicts never spread far enough to endanger their class supremacy. Even when popular elements and urban groups entered the fray, the planters continued to participate on both sides, and the defeat of individuals never signified the plantocracy's defeat. Thus the political supremacy enjoyed since the early colonial period continued into the twentieth century. Office did not always entail power, but in rural Pernambuco, at least, the planters both reigned and ruled.[35]

This power enabled the planters to benefit from the transition from slave to free labour. After 1850 the outlawed African slave trade effectively stopped. But the flourishing coffee industry in the centre-south still relied on slave labour, and its demand forced prices to climb rapidly. These rising prices, in conjunction with the relatively sluggish sugar export trade, made slave labour in sugar less and less profitable. Even without working out formulae for capitalization of future income streams realizable through the use of slave or free labour, it is clear that prevailing interest rates and sugar's uncertain markets would have obliged planters to discount heavily future earnings from slave labour.

In fact, the planters had converted from predominantly slave to predominantly free labour by 1872, when the first general census in Imperial Brazil showed a preponderance of free agricultural workers in all Pernambuco's sugar *municipios*.[36] The conversion to free labour proceeded in several ways. Coffee's demand for slaves led to an inter-provincial slave trade which drained slaves from the northeastern sugar areas to the centre-south. Other Pernambuco slaves simply died. A fair number were emancipated prior to final abolition in 1888, through legal measures, private philanthropy, and perhaps even manumission.[37]

Declining profitability accounts for the sugar planters' quick conversion to free labour. The planters simply could not afford to purchase slave labour. Nor did they attempt to breed their own slaves. In United

States history, the imputation of such an industry has been based on demographic data and contemporary testimony. While some scattered references to such activities in the coffee areas of Brazil do exist, the data do not support a similar imputation in Pernambuco.[38] Three indicators for Pernambuco imply the existence of a slave-breeding industry, but when other factors are considered the case is not very convincing. Firstly, decreasing male-to-female ratios suggest a growing interest in women for breeding purposes. However, this trend is better explained by the fact that after 1850 the absence of sex-selective African imports and the trading south of prime males allowed the sex ratio to return to natural proportions.[39] Secondly, the median age of slaves in Pernambuco increased between the 1872 and 1887 counts. This change probably reflects the northeast's selling young adults to the centre-south; but they were not necessarily slaves bred for that purpose. Moreover, in 1871 the law freed *ingenuos,* children born of slave mothers, thereby outlawing slave-breeding.[40] Finally, the increasing child-to-woman ratio of slave children per thousand slave women of child-bearing age might also reflect deliberate breeding. More likely, however, the increase corresponds only to the trend in the general population, along with improved recording.[41]

The preference for free labour over slave labour also derived from the need to employ willing workers in the new technology, which usually entailed complicated machinery. The masters refused to invest in the slaves' education to enable them to operate this machinery, for they feared to trust slaves with such expensive equipment since sabotage was a common form of slave resistance to onerous conditions.[42]

The northeastern planters clearly treated slaves as labour inputs. Thus assertions that planters in the aggregate treated slaves as members of an extended family, or as a quasi-feudal lower estate, do not apply in Pernambuco. Gilberto Freyre more than anyone else has elaborated the view that the slave-owners' paternalistic affections for their slaves, and in particular their promiscuity with female domestics, softened slavery.[43] Since planters often freed their illegitimate children, the conversion to free labour may have resulted more from humanitarian motives. No matter how widely such attitudes were shared, however, the natural increase of mulattoes never met the demand for labour, and over half the Pernambuco labour force had to be imported from Africa before 1850. Moreover, in the period between 1850 and 1888, only 10 per cent of the slave population became free workers in Pernambuco. Masters on the whole were probably indifferent as to whether their work force contained ex-slaves or people born free. When they freed slaves with the qualification that they continue working on the plantations, they were guaranteeing their labour supply as much as protecting the extended family.

By the same token, masters were willing to forgo the social prestige and power based on slave-ownership.[44] While they may traditionally have considered their slaves primarily as a lower estate in a quasi-feudal society, after 1850 the social value of slavery fast receded into the background, and the planters replaced slaves with client populations of squatters, wage workers, and sharecroppers, groups which were nearly as subservient. Thus the planters protected their status while abandoning the slave estate.

My emphasis on economically motivated gradual abolition in Pernambuco disputes Robert B. Toplin's assertion that slavery in Brazil was only abolished after increased abolitionist activity and violence by slaves themselves. Toplin accepts at face value the official slave population estimates of the late 1870s and early 1880s, which did not represent new counts but only deductions of reported slave deaths and legal exits from the 1873 slave register.[45] Counting as slaves the 27,000 *ingenuos* living in Pernambuco after 1871, as Toplin does, might more accurately reflect social reality but certainly not the economic importance of slavery, for the oldest of these children would barely have reached working age by 1888, the date of final abolition.[46] While Toplin documents well the frequency of mass escapes in São Paulo, there simply is no evidence that some 31,000 slaves fled their owners in Pernambuco between 1885 and 1887; evidence of mass flights does exist for early 1888, but it is not pertinent.[47]

Slavery became so unprofitable that certain particularly poor northern provinces, such as Ceará and Amazonas, actually abolished it in the early 1880s, several years before national abolition. Others areas like Pernambuco were phasing the institution out in practice if not in law. Thus where economic activities using slave labour enjoyed strong markets, as in Brazil's centre-south or the United States cotton states, slavery remained profitable, and violence became necessary to abolish it. Where such activities did not boom, once the international traffic stopped slavery more quickly became a liability, and the slave-owners themselves took initiatives to substitute free labour.[48]

If the slave-owners treated their slaves as productive factors, whose cost determined whether they or free workers would be used, then clearly capitalist production used slave labour. As Mintz has written, 'The slave population, producing some basic commodity for the mother country, was a special, emergent capitalist form of industrial organization.'[49]

If one denies that capitalism could use slave labour, then he may exaggerate the importance of the transition to free labour. Thus Genovese, for whom capitalism is 'the mode of production characterized by wage labour and the separation of the labour force from the means of production – that is ... labour power itself has become a commodity', sees in Brazil's northeast a transition from slavery to seigneurialism with capitalist elements represented by the increasing importance of wage and salary workers.[50] But slave labour had long been a commodity in Brazil, and the transition to free labour in Pernambuco did not entail major changes in the relationship between the workers and the means of production nor, for that matter, between the workers and the distribution of production. Rural wages yielded little more claim on land, capital, or the fruits of these productive factors than had the subsistence rations of slaves. At best, free workers gained a greater claim over their own labour power in the sense that they could refuse to sell it; but eventually they would face the alternatives of stealing or starvation. An examination of free labour conditions in Pernambuco after 1850 makes it clear that abolition in the long run meant little.[51]

Free labour on the sugar plantations entailed wage and salary work, squatting, and sharecropping. Wage labour and squatting were probably the commonest forms of employment, especially for ex-slaves since these modes required little or no capital equipment. Wages in the sugar zone increased in the later 1860s and early 1870s, owing to increased demand by local railway-builders and cotton-planters. But by the last quarter of the century the growing proportion of free labour, and the deteriorating export position, placed strong downward pressure on wages. At the same time prices of basic foods such as manioc flour, beans, and jerked meat rose, with the result that real income fell even faster than wages. While some workers may have grown their own manioc and beans on squatters' plots, few kept cattle for meat. Those who depended exclusively on wages, moreover, bought all staples and suffered acutely from the fall in real purchasing power. Sharecropping, on the other hand, demanded at least tools and draft animals. But the success story of José Marreira, who in José Lins do Rego's novel *Banguê* rose from *lavrador* to *senhor de engenho*, was atypical. Relative to the rural work force, only a few individuals were sharecroppers, and only a tiny fraction of these accumulated the capital necessary for land-owning.[52]

None of these labour modes entailed much bargaining power. Planters could hire and fire wage workers and squatters at will in Pernambuco's labour-abundant economy, and frequently they made demeaning social or political demands which could not be refused. Even sharecroppers, who by virtue of their moderate capital holdings qualified as a kind of rural middle class, could be dispensed with literally overnight, for the planters' monopoly on land meant there were always plenty of landless workers willing to grow cane for a share of the sugar produced.[53]

All forms of free employment entailed the basic liberty to leave the job, a right denied to slaves; but this freedom should not be exaggerated. The free worker did not find alternative employments in the northeast, as did ex-slaves in some Caribbean plantation societies after abolition.[54] Census data do not indicate any redistribution of the free coloured population toward Pernambuco's west, where they might have entered subsistence crop farming, given the greater availability of land and the smaller population; nor did workers move out of the rural areas into the capital, Recife. Census data do show a much faster rate of native population growth in Brazil's centre-south provinces than in the northeast. This growth may reflect superior economic conditions making for higher natural demographic increase, or it may indicate the migration south of northeastern workers, and thereby a much higher degree of labour mobility than is presently thought.[55] The source of this growth awaits further study; in any event, most ex-slaves stayed in Pernambuco and in the sugar zone.[56]

The lack of jobs and the unattractiveness of free labour conditions on plantations led to constant vagabondage. The vagabonds took jobs only infrequently, and the rest of the time they lived off the land. Since the sugar planters virtually monopolized the land, in effect the vagabonds lived by stealing. Even when ex-slaves took jobs, their previous work experience had left a bitter taste and predisposed them to value leisure highly. Hence their supply curve bent backward, and they 'bought' leisure by sacrificing steady employment. Even in the centre-south, where general economic conditions far surpassed those prevailing in Pernambuco, vagabondage occurred. Thus the superabundant work force allowed sugar planters to reject many workers; but the poor working conditions also led many workers to reject steady employment on the plantations.[57]

Some Pernambucans thought to improve the quality of rural labour by encouraging European immigration; but European immigrants found little reason to settle in Pernambuco. The hot climate in the sugar zone, the scarcity of land, and principally the unfavourable economic conditions in the sugar industry all discouraged immigrants. Slavery and discriminatory civil legislation did not particularly keep Europeans out of Pernambuco any more than São Paulo. But the booming coffee

economy permitted the subsidizing of hundreds of thousands of Europeans, and these newcomers took the chance of settling there because
they could hope to improve their lot in the growing economy. The immigrants began working in coffee, but they soon moved into other occupations, accumulated capital, and frequently played important roles in
the centre-south's industrialization. The absence of such an economically
active group in Pernambuco may have debilitated that region, but we
should not forget that the immigrants' activity was probably more a
function of the vigour of the coffee economy than of their inherent
talents.[58]

Just as a different government might have cushioned or avoided the
export market crisis, so too a different government might have acted
more positively to ease the transition from slave to free labour. The
government saw fit to offer compensation through emancipation funds to
slave owners before 1888. While it refused to indemnify for final abolition, the government made no attempt to aid the ex-slaves. In the United
States, a coalition of moderate and radical reconstructionists in Congress
overrode President Andrew Johnson's veto and created a Freedmen's
Bureau. Radicals advocated the distribution of vacant and war-con-
fiscated lands, which led to the slogan '40 acres and a mule'; but the
Bureau lasted only a year, and little reform occurred.[59] In Brazil, abolition did not occur amidst the destruction of a Civil War, and the Brazilian government could completely ignore the ex-slaves after 1888. This
neglect left the freedmen on northeastern plantations as before; in the
centre-south, it meant that as 'whiter' and possibly better-educated
European immigrants won the better jobs, freedmen remained at the
bottom of society.[60]

Even a successful Freedmen's Bureau in Brazil, however, would not
have guaranteed the improvement of the workers' welfare without
massive government support. A broader reform, backing worker organization for greater bargaining power, might have yielded short-run
benefits; but in the end plantation worker unions would only be dividing
the shrinking sugar revenues more evenly, without making long-term
provision for their general welfare. Moreover, they would have remained
subject to the planters' influence in local government.[61]

A more thoroughgoing land reform, which not only redistributed
land but also changed the basic crops cultivated, might have yielded
a more equitable distribution of income and raised workers' welfare;
but it was not politically feasible. A government less subject to planter
control might have turned to land reform combined with diversification
to avoid the income effects of sugar's stagnation. A Pernambuco growing

a wider variety of export crops, such as sugar, cotton, and tobacco, as well as food for regional consumption, would have remained relatively immune to violent changes in any one commodity market, while at the same time it might have met importers' needs for foreign exchange. More marginal lands could have been used for livestock, poultry, or vegetables, improving the general nutritional level. The government might have supplied the substantial credit entailed in such a land reform in the form of many small loans, instead of the few large subsidies granted to the *usineiros*, who after all defaulted on these loans anyway.[62] The land required could have been taken from the planters, thereby increasing either the number of landholdings without creating *minifundia* or else the number of landholders through co-operative or collective arrangements. A short-term reduction in gross regional product probably would have resulted, but that product would have been more equitably distributed. Such reform in nineteenth-century Brazil of course was unrealistic, although not unheard-of, as the writings of Antonio Pedro Figueiredo in 1848 and 1849 testify.[63]

If this study emphasizes one theme, it is that modernization involving capital improvements and reorganization, and the abolition of forced labour, did not always bring either economic or social change for the better. Brazil's northeastern sugar regions made certain necessary adjustments in the last quarter of the nineteenth century, but these only served to soften the impact of unfavourable foreign markets on the planter class and preserve the traditional economic and social structure. Where other planter groups enjoyed a more successful experience in this period, as in Cuba and São Paulo, the principal factor governing their successes was the strength of their export markets.

The only alternatives to stagnation for Pernambuco entailed recolonization or radical structural reform; in both cases the costs would have been borne by the planters. With a land reform, the region's product might have suffered in the short run, but in the long run the majority of the population might have benefited. The planters remained dominant politically and followed their clear economic self-interest. But the market, in conjunction with unavoidable political distortions, precluded a socially efficient pattern of development.

Brazil is far from being the only colonial or semi-colonial area in which modernization has preserved the traditional structure. It was no accident that Cuba, one of the most advanced sugar colonies in the western hemisphere, in terms both of technology and of the development of labour organizations, was also the first to experience a successful socialist revolution. No amount of capital investment or revision of labour modes in capitalist agricultural export economies can yield social benefits unless the changes increase workers' control and participation in production. Cuba began a revolution in 1959. Pernambuco went through several adjustments in the last quarter of the nineteenth century, but it still awaits a more general beneficial modernization.[64]

NOTES

1. I am grateful to colleagues at Rutgers – Michael Adas, Samuel Baily, Tilden Edelstein, Karl Hardach, David Ringrose, and Traien Stoianovich – for suggestions in the preparation and revision of this study. This study was originally published by the University of California Press and is reprinted by permission of The Regents of the University of California.

2. Modernization has been defined as 'the development of industrial systems based on high levels of technology, on growing specialization of economic roles, and of units of economic activity – production, consumption, and marketing – and on the growth of the scope and complexity of the major markets, the markets for goods, labor and money' (S. N. Eisenstadt, *Modernization: protest and change* (Englewood Cliffs, N.J., 1966), pp. 3–4).

3. Hermann Paasche, *Zuckerindustrie und Zuckerhandel der Welt* (Jena, 1891), pp. 411–12. I have averaged consumption data for 1801–5 and 1886–90.

4. The First World War interrupted European beet sugar production and thereby stimulated all cane sugar producers. After the war, however, cane sugar producers in the western hemisphere underwent a recession. While Cuba recovered in the later 1920s, Brazil did not, and by the 1930s the Brazilian sugar industry was becoming more and more dependent on government aid. See Cuban Economic Research Project, *A study on Cuba*, p. 235; A. José Barbosa Lima Sobrinho, *Problemas econômicos e sociais da lavoura canavieira*, 2nd edn (Rio de Janeiro, 1943), p. 33; Paul Singer, *Desenvolvimento econômico e evolução urbana* (São Paulo, 1968), pp. 342–5.

5. Douglass C. North, *Growth and welfare in the United States* (Englewood Cliffs, N. J., 1966), pp. 109–10. North shows that the index of U.S. export freight rates, presumably roughly proportional to rates charged on ships bound to the U.S., fell by 75 per cent between 1815 and 1850, and again by nearly 50 per cent between 1897 and 1908.

6. Eduardo Prado, *A illusão americana*, 3rd edn (São Paulo, 1961; first published 1893), pp. 149–51, expressed the Brazilians' bitterness against the U.S.A. Hugh Thomas, *Cuba: the pursuit of freedom* (New York, 1971), pp. 288–9, 290–1, 457, reviews the agreements of the 1890s; and Cuban Economic Research Project, *A study on Cuba*, pp. 218–19, summarizes the Reciprocity Treaty of 1902. The causes for the decline of Cuban production in the early 1880s deserve further investigation.

7. Sidney W. Mintz. 'Labor and sugar in Puerto Rico and Jamaica, 1800–1850', *Comparative Studies in Society and History* I, 3 (March 1959), pp. 273–80; reprinted in Laura Foner and Eugene D. Genovese (eds.), *Slavery in the New World* (Englewood Cliffs, N.J., 1969), pp. 170–7.

8. See, for example, Robert P. Porter, *Industrial Cuba* (New York, 1899), p. 282.

9. Manuel Moreno Fraginals, *El ingenio* (Havana, 1964), pp. 94–6. I assume the Cuban *caballería* of 33.3 acres equalled 13.5 hectares, after Roland T. Ely, *Cuando*

reinaba su majestad el azúcar (Buenos Aires, 1963), p. 438. For Pernambuco yields, see Henri Raffard, *O centro da indústria e commércio de assucar no Rio de Janeiro* (Rio de Janeiro, 1892), p. 112; Paul Walle, *Au Brésil du río São Francisco à l'Amazone* (Paris, 1912), p. 164; Manoel Antônio dos Santos Dias Filho, 'Industria assucareira', *Boletim do Ministério da Agricultura, Indústria e Commercio*, Anno I, 5 (Rio de Janeiro, 1913), p. 60.

10. Porter, *Industrial Cuba*, pp. 281–2; 'O açúcar na vida econômica do Brasil', pp. 233–5. In deducing the Brazilian area under cultivation, I assume yields of 60 tons per hectare, and no more than 8 per cent sugar extracted from cane. Probably median extraction yields were much lower, which would increase the total area under cultivation and aggravate the discrepancy with Cuba. Directoria Geral de Estatistica, *Indústria assucareira, usinas e engenhos centraes* (Rio de Janeiro, 1910), p. 3, gives average extraction for modernized Pernambuco mills as 7.5 per cent.

11. Franklin W. Knight, *Slave society in Cuba during the nineteenth century* (Madison, Wisconsin, 1970), pp. 4–6, 29.

12. Duvon Clough Corbitt, *A study of the Chinese in Cuba, 1847–1947* (Wilmore, Kentucky, 1971), pp. 1–26.

13. Knight, *Slave society in Cuba*, p. 63; Robert Brent Toplin, *The abolition of slavery in Brazil* (New York, 1972), p. 268.

14. Peter L. Eisenberg, *The sugar industry of Pernambuco, 1840–1910: modernization without change* (Berkeley, 1974), Table 32, p. 190.

15. Philip S. Foner, *A history of Cuba and its relations with the United States*, 2 vols. (New York, 1962–3), vol. 2, pp. 136–48. 'Liga Operaria Pernambucana', *Diario de Pernambuco* (Recife), 26 July 1890. Júlio Pires Ferreira, *Almanack de Pernambuco para o anno 1899–1909* (Recife, 1900–10) mentions important strikes in the section 'Cronologia.'

16. See Ely, *Cuando reinaba su majestad el azúcar*, pp. 238–415 for descriptions of capitalists who financed Cuban sugar; and Thomas, *Cuba*, p. 271 for interest rates. On U.S. capital and annexationists, see Leland Jenks, *Our Cuban colony* (New York, 1928), pp. 33–5, and Thomas, *Cuba*, pp. 207, 263, 271–5.

17. Deerr, *The history of sugar*, vol. 1, p. 130. Ramón de la Sagra, *Cuba 1860* (Havana, 1963), p. 138. Cuban Economic Research Project, *A study on Cuba*, pp. 89–90. *Relatório que à Assembléa Legislativa Provincial de Pernambuco appresentou no dia da abertura da sessão ordinaria de 1857 o Exmo Sr Conselheiro Sérgio Teixeira de Macedo* (Recife, 1857), p. 75. Gaspar Peres and Apollonio Peres, *A industria assucareira em Pernambuco* (Recife, 1915), pp. 32–3.

18. Jenks, *Our Cuban colony*, pp. 31–3. Thomas, *Cuba*, pp. 276–7. Cuban Economic Research Project, *A study on Cuba*, pp. 92, 96, 235.

19. Eugene D. Genovese believes that the foreigners in Brazil, as in Cuba, were major sources of capital for modernization (*The world the slaveholders made* (New York, 1969), p. 91). See also Richard Graham, *Britain and the onset of modernization in Brazil* (Cambridge, 1968), pp. 149–50; and D. C. M. Platt, *Latin America and British Trade, 1806–1914* (London, 1972), p. 284.

20. For a detailed review of official aid to Pernambucan *engenhos centrais* and *usinas*, see Eisenberg, *The sugar industry of Pernambuco*, chapters 4 and 5, pp. 63–118.

21. Peres and Peres, *A industria assucareira em Pernambuco*, pp. 32–3.

22. Some contemporary observers believed that Brazilian sugar was inferior in quality. I am not sure to what extent this was the case, nor, if it is true, to what extent the inferiority could be ascribed to lack of capital investments to improve cane cultivation and manufacturing techniques. For a sample criticism of Pernambuco sugar,

see A. F. Howard, 'Report for the year 1896 on the trade etc. of the consular district of Pernambuco', Great Britain, *Parliamentary Papers*, 1897 House of Commons by Command, vol. 79, *Accounts and Papers*, vol. 28, p. 10.

23. Miguel Costa Filho, *A cana-de-açúcar em Minas Gerais* (Rio de Janeiro, 1963); Gileno Dé Carli, *Evolução do problema canavieiro fluminense* (Rio de Janeiro, 1942); and Maria Teresa Schorer Petrone, *A lavoura canavieira em São Paulo* (São Paulo, 1968) are standard introductions. On the cartel's failure, see Luis Correia de Britto, 'Colligação assucareira', *Boletim da União dos Sindicatos Agricolas de Pernambuco* III, 3 (Recife, March 1909) pp. 175–201.

24. Nathaniel Leff, 'Economic development and regional inequality: origin of the Brazilian case', *Quarterly Journal of Economics* LXXXVI (May 1972), pp. 258–9.

25. Nathaniel Leff, *The Brazilian capital goods industry* (Cambridge, Mass., 1968), pp. 8–40. Celso Furtado, *The economic growth of Brazil* (Berkeley, Calif., 1963; first published in Portuguese in 1959), p. 224.

26. For an analysis of *central* mill subsidies, see José Honório Rodrigues, 'A revolução industrial açucareira: os engenhos centrais', *Brasil Açucareiro* XXVII, 2–4 (Rio de Janeiro, February–April 1946), pp. 179–82, 229–33, 392–7. Complaints about regional discrimination first appeared in the Sociedade Auxiliadora da Agricultura de Pernambuco, *Trabalhos do Congresso Agrícola do Recife em outubro de 1878* (Recife, 1879), *passim*. For continued complaints see S. B., 'Bancos agricolas', *O Brazil Agricola* (Recife), Ano II (31 January 1881), pp. 76–7; 'O norte e o governo', *Jornal do Recife*, 27 June 1888; 'São Paulo e o norte', *Journal do Recife*, 6 April 1890.

27. For an early and optimistic study of such programmes, see Stefan H. Robock, *Brazil's developing northeast: a study of regional planning and foreign aid* (Washington, 1963). For a later and more pessimistic account, see Alberto Tamer, *O mesmo nordeste* (São Paulo, 1968).

28. Andre Gunder Frank, *Capitalism and underdevelopment in Latin America: historical studies of Chile and Brazil* (New York, 1967), p. 170.

29. Leff, 'Economic development and regional inequality', p. 259. On the 1824 revolt, see Amaro Quintas, 'A agitação republicana no nordeste', in Sérgio Buarque de Holanda (ed.), *História geral da civilização brasileira*, 7 vols. (São Paulo, 1963–72), vol. 3, pp. 207–37, especially pp. 227–37.

30. Nathaniel Leff has considered the advantages of neo-colonialism for Brazil: 'Economic retardation in nineteenth-century Brazil', *Economic History Review* (Second Series) XXV, 3 (August 1972), p. 505.

31. Furtado, *The economic growth of Brazil*, pp. 99, 138.

32. Caio Prado Júnior, *Formação do Brasil contemporâneo*, 7th edn (São Paulo, 1963; first published 1942), pp. 185–6.

33. Virgilio Noya Pinto, 'Balanço das transformações econômicas no século XIX', in Carlos Guilherme Mota (ed.), *Brasil em perspectiva* (São Paulo, 1968), pp. 135, 139, reports relative values of Brazil's exports.

34. For a good introduction, see Robert Conrad, *The destruction of Brazilian slavery, 1850–1888* (Berkeley, Calif., 1972), especially pp. 47–69, 170–82, 199–209.

35. On land holdings and the political power of the sugar planters, see Eisenberg, *The sugar industry of Pernambuco*, chapter 6, pp. 121–45.

36. *Recenseamento da população do Império do Brasil a que se procedeu no dia 1 de agosto de 1872. Quadros Estatísticos*, 23 vols. (Rio de Janeiro, 1873–6), vol. 13, pp. 1–114.

37. Peter L. Eisenberg, 'Abolishing slavery: the process on Pernambuco's sugar planta-

tions', *Hispanic American Historical Review* LII, 4 (November 1972), pp. 580–97. Except where noted the following remarks on slavery and free labour are based on that article.

38. See Toplin, *The abolition of slavery in Brazil*, p. 19, for evidence that breeding occurred. The standard statement of slave-breeding in the U.S. is Alfred H. Conrad and John H. Meyer, 'The economics of slavery in the ante-bellum south', *Journal of Political Economy* LXVI (April 1958), pp. 95–122; reprinted in Robert William Fogel and Stanley L. Engerman (eds.), *The reinterpretation of American economic history* (New York, 1971).

39. Conrad, *The destruction of Brazilian slavery*, pp. 62–3.

40. Average slave age in Pernambuco rose from 24.7 to 32.6 years. *Recenseamento . . . 1872*, vol. 13, p. 217. *Relatório . . . Ministro . . . Agricultura, Commercio e Obras Publicas, Rodrigo Augusto da Silva* (Rio de Janeiro, 1888), p. 24.

41. For Pernambuco's vital indicators, see Eisenberg, 'Abolishing slavery', Table 2, p. 594.

42. Caio Prado Júnior, *Historia econômica do Brasil*, 11th edn (São Paulo, 1969; first published 1945), p. 90. Mircea Buescu and Vicente Tapajós, *História de desenvolvimento econômico do Brasil* (Rio de Janeiro, n.d.), p. 153.

43. See, for example, Gilberto Freyre, *New worlds in the tropics: the culture of modern Brazil* (New York, 1945), pp. 200–2.

44. For a recent example of this Weberian analysis, see Florestan Fernandes, *Comunidade e sociedade no Brasil* (São Paulo, 1972), pp. 309–14, 399–404; and Toplin, *The abolition of slavery in Brazil*, p. 13. Elsewhere in Brazil, planters allegedly kept slaves from force of habit, despite declining profitability (Stanley J. Stein, *Vassouras: a Brazilian coffee county, 1850–1900* (Cambridge, Mass., 1957), pp. 229–30). Eugene D. Genovese has maintained that planters owned slaves in the American south for a variety of non-economic reasons (*The political economy of slavery* (New York, 1961), pp. 30, 50 and *passim*).

45. The estimates listed 72,000 slaves in 1885 and 41,000 in 1887 (Conrad, *The destruction of Brazilian slavery*, p. 292). Toplin himself casts doubt on the reliability of the statistics (*The abolition of slavery in Brazil*, pp. 108–9).

46. *Relatório com que o Exmo 1° vice-presidente Dr Ignacio Joaquim de Souza Leão passou a administração da provincia em 16 de Abril de 1888 ao Exmo Presidente Desembargador Joaquim José de Oliveira Andrade* (Recife, 1888), p. 19.

47. Toplin, *The abolition of slavery in Brazil*, pp. 20–4, 223.

48. On the profitability of slavery in the U.S. cotton south, see Robert William Fogel and Stanley L. Engerman, 'The economics of slavery', in their *The reinterpretation of American economic history*, pp. 311–41.

49. Sidney W. Mintz, 'Review of Stanley M. Elkins' *Slavery*', *American Anthropologist* LXIII (June 1961), pp. 579–87; reprinted as 'Slavery and emergent capitalism', in Foner and Genovese (eds.), *Slavery in the New World*, pp. 27–37.

50. Genovese, *The world the slaveholders made*, pp. 16, 90–1. Both Marx and Engels considered slave labour to be distinct as a mode of production and a form of exploitation, along with serf labour and wage labour: Karl Marx, *Capital*, trans. Samuel Moore and Edward Aveling, ed. Frederick Engels (New York, 1906), p. 591; Engels, 'The origin of the family, private property and the State', in Marx and Engels, *Selected Works*, 2 vols. (Moscow, 1958), vol. 2, p. 324.

51. Gilberto Freyre affirms that the workers had been better off as slaves (preface to Júlio Bello, *Memórias de um senhor de engenho* (Rio de Janeiro, 1938), p. x). Freyre is

not alone in this view: see Manuel Diegues Júnior, 'O banguê em Pernambuco no século XIX', *Revista do Archivo Público*, Anos VII–X, nos. 9–12 (Recife, 1952–6), pp. 17, 29. But the fact that Pernambuco's free coloured population succeeded in reproducing itself and increasing in numbers indicates that freedom was preferable to slavery. Nevertheless, there were few differences in working conditions. In this respect, I agree with the conclusions of J. R. Russell-Wood, 'Colonial Brazil', in David W. Cohen and Jack P. Greene (eds.), *Neither slave nor free* (Baltimore, 1972), p. 132.

52. José Lins do Rego, *Banguê* (Rio de Janeiro, 1934). For contemporary planter exaltations of sharecropper upward mobility, see Antonio Venâncio Cavalcante de Albuquerque, 'A agricultura ou a questão da atualidade', *Diario de Pernambuco*, 5 April 1877; and Ceresiades, 'A agricultura em Pernambuco, IV', *Diario de Pernambuco*, 22 June 1878. For a sceptical view, see L. B., 'Banco agricola', *O Brazil Agricola*, Anno II (15 November 1880), p. 38. The resentment of the *senhores de engenho* over their demotion to the status of cane suppliers to the *central* mills is good evidence that sharecropping was not always so rewarding.

53. For a concise summary of free labour modes in nineteenth-century Pernambuco, see Manuel Correia de Andrade, *A terra e o homem do nordeste*, 2nd edn (São Paulo, 1964; first published 1963), pp. 93–4, 119–20.

54. Gwendolyn Midlo Hall, *Social control in slave plantation societies: a comparison of St Domingue and Cuba* (Baltimore, 1971), pp. 120–1; J. H. Parry and P. M. Sherlock, *A short history of the West Indies*, 3rd edn (London, 1971; first published 1956), pp. 195–6.

55. Nathaniel Leff argues that transport costs prevented such labour mobility ('Economic development and regional inequality', p. 254–6).

56. To trace free worker movements, compare the *Recenseamento da população . . . 1872*, vol. 13, p. 214, with Directoria Geral da Estatística, *Sexo, raça e estado civil, nacionalidade, filiação, culto e analphabetismo da população recenseada em 31 de dezembro de 1890* (Rio de Janeiro, 1898), pp. 94–9.

57. Toplin, *The abolition of slavery in Brazil*, pp. 259–61, suggests the scope of post-abolition vagabondage. In Pernambuco, part of the vagabondage may really have been seasonal unemployment. The sugar industry's peak labour demand occurred in the harvest months, September to January; during the planting and cultivating months the plantations needed less labour, and the unemployed workers may have appeared to be vagabonds.

58. Warren Dean, *The industrialization of São Paulo* (Austin, Texas, 1969) chapter 4; Peter L. Eisenberg, 'Falta de imigrantes, um aspecto de atraso nordestino', *Revista de História* XCIV (São Paulo, January–March 1973) pp. 583–601; Peter L. Eisenberg and Michael M. Hall, 'Labor supply and immigration: a comparison of Pernambuco and São Paulo', paper presented at the Fourth Annual Meeting of the Latin American Studies Association, Madison, Wisconsin, May 1973.

59. Kenneth M. Stampp, *The era of reconstruction, 1865–1877* (New York, 1965), pp. 112, 125–35.

60. For an introduction to the plight of the Brazilian Negro after abolition, particularly in São Paulo, see Florestan Fernandes, *The Negro in Brazilian society* (New York, 1969; first published 1965), pp. 1–20. For an opposite view, see Herbert Klein, 'Nineteenth-century Brazil', in Cohen and Greene (eds.), *Neither slave nor free*, p. 332.

61. On the tentative efforts of peasant leagues to fight the planters in the 1960s, see Lêda Barreto, *Julião – nordeste – revolução* (Rio de Janeiro, 1963), and Cynthia N. Hewitt, 'The peasant movement of Pernambuco, Brazil: 1961–64' in Henry A. Landsberger (ed.), *Latin American peasant movements* (Ithaca, N. Y., 1969), pp. 374–98. In 1964 the *coup d'état* by a military group hostile to labour mobilization crushed the peasant leagues.

62. *Mensagem do Exmo Sr Dr Herculano Bandeira de Mello, Governador do Estado, lida por occasião da installação da 2ᵃ sessão ordinária da 7ᵃ legislatura do Congresso Legislativo do Estado ao 6 de Março de 1911* (Recife, 1911).

63. 'Colonisação', *O Progresso* (Recife, 1950; first published 1848–9), Tomo II, pp. 634ff.

64. For recent testimony that the situation described for the late nineteenth century has not basically changed, see Marvine Howe, 'Brazil peasants find their plight worsens', *New York Times*, 27 November 1972, p. 12.

CHAPTER 15

From *banguê* to *usina*: social aspects of growth and modernization in the sugar industry of Pernambuco, Brazil, 1850–1920

JAIME REIS[1]

During the 1930s, the hostility between the central mill-owners of Pernambuco and their independent cane suppliers, which had been growing since the late nineteenth century, finally reached an acute stage. An outgrowth of this was a body of literature produced by a vigorous school of local writers, who sought to assess the impact on their society of the sugar economy's development over previous decades. Their main argument concerned the excessively high social cost of modernization and the urgent need to halt the destruction of the traditional fabric of the community which it was bringing about.[2]

According to these defenders of the old order, a serious loss was entailed by the growth of the central mills, or *usinas*, because in the process they were swallowing up the smaller, old-fashioned plantations, known as *banguês*. This had the result of gradually uprooting the centuries-old class of planters who had presided from the beginning over the nation's destiny and who embodied all that was best in its character. Of no less importance, the *usinas* were accused of producing a deterioration both in labour relations and in the standard of living of the rural population. The rural labourer, it was claimed, had become a pariah of the *usina*. Finally, the critique that attempted to vindicate the old *engenhos* found itself obliged in turn to defend the slave labour system with which they had been identified from the earliest times. Here it was the familiar argument that plantation slaves were often materially better off than their free counterparts locally, or than the proletariat of contemporary industrialized societies.[3]

The modernization and growth of an agricultural economy often brings in its train much hardship for the population involved. Frequently, the change is characterized by a redistribution and more intensive utilization of both human and natural resources. Formerly fallow or under-utilized lands are brought under cash crop cultivation or converted into pastures; the subsistence sector is forced to shrink to make way for the expansion of commercial agriculture; and traditional communities and their way of life are destroyed, or at best severely mutilated. Often this means that large numbers are displaced, stripped of their land, or employed in new forms of labour organization under unprecedentedly harsh conditions. In some circumstances, however, the development of an agricultural economy can take place without its being at all clear that the population involved has suffered any of these kinds of resultant hardship.

The sugar belt of Pernambuco between 1850 and 1920 would appear to be a case in point. During this period it experienced an expansion of production, the abolition of slavery, and a technological revolution in sugar manufacturing. Yet, as will emerge in the following pages, this failed to produce the social traumas usually associated with such events.

I shall not be dealing here in any detail with the growth and modernization of the sugar industry *per se*, a subject which has already received a good measure of scholarly attention.[4] Nor will I be concerned with the much-publicized impact of these changes on elite groups, the *senhores de engenho* foremost among them. Rather the emphasis will focus on how the evolution of the sugar economy affected those who worked in it but had no say in how it was shaped – the majority, in fact, of the rural population. Any attempt of this sort – that is, to estimate the welfare of a group of people over time – is always a thorny problem. In this instance, three areas have been selected for consideration, not only on the grounds that they appear to be central to the issue at hand but also because they provided the ammunition for the attacks mentioned above on the *usina*'s role in Pernambuco. These areas are the stability of the social structure of the sugar zone, so far as the poorer elements of society were concerned; their material circumstances; and, finally, the nature of their relations with the plantation owners. Before proceeding to the examination of these three aspects, however, a brief account of the region's economic history during this period is called for.

The *usinas* first made their appearance in the *zona da mata* (the tropical forest zone) of Pernambuco in the 1880s but only properly took root there in the following decade. During the preceding half-century sugar production had grown rapidly, rising from 50,000 to almost 150,000 tons a year. Since the technology used had changed very little in the meantime, the increase must be ascribed almost entirely to the expansion both of the geographic frontier of the sugar zone and of the number of plantations, which rose from approximately 700 to 1,800 during this time. The development of the railways after 1857, by enabling producers to overcome the age-old problem of transportation, contributed substantially to the occupation and exploitation of land further and further from the coast and the commercial centre of Recife. Other factors of growth were the easy credit policies of the government in the 1850s; the capital accumulated during the short cotton boom of the 1860s, which was later invested in sugar; and the demographic expansion, which afforded the plantations the abundant labour they needed and enabled them to overcome some of the problems raised by the abolition of slavery.

During the next two or three decades, the modernized part of the sugar economy expanded slowly. In spite of substantial government aid for the installation of central sugar mills, it was not until the end of the First World War that they became the dominant element in the processing of cane. By this time, sixty *usinas* produced more than half the sugar in Pernambuco. In the meantime the number of *banguês* had fallen from 1,800 in 1888 to 900 in the early 1920s.

With their higher sugar cane ratio and their labour-saving technology, the *usinas* were a distinct improvement over the *banguês*. Even so, they were not the great success that had been expected, and in particular they failed to place the sugar sector on a competitive footing in international markets, at a time when the world supply of sugar was increasing much faster than the demand, and consequently prices were plummeting. Insufficient capital, poor management, a shortage of skilled workers, and topographical obstacles to large-scale factories all conspired to this end. Increasingly Pernambuco was obliged to sell in the domestic market where tariff barriers protected its relative inefficiency but where it had also to allow room for other Brazilian producers. The result was that in spite of modernization output stagnated, between 1890 and 1920, at around two million bags a year.[5]

The new industrial system brought no change in the economy's perennial features of monoculture and *latifundia* landholding. Indeed, the second of these was reinforced, thanks to the gradual process of land acquisition undertaken by the *usinas*, since by 1920 forty-one of them had absorbed over four hundred *engenhos*. Nor did the change in ownership produce improved cultivation methods, which continued to rely entirely on the time-hallowed slash-and-burn techniques and on the universal use of the hoe and the billhook as the sole implements for field work. Low yields and a relatively heavy expenditure of labour remained therefore the norm in the production of cane. Altogether it was a difficult period for every type of producer, whether it be an *usineiro*, a *banguêseiro*, or merely a cane supplier; and at best profits were meagre, so that a cheap and abundant labour force became more than ever an essential requirement for the sugar plantations of Pernambuco.[6]

The social structure of the sugar zone

Although the economy was still founded on slave labour, by the middle of the nineteenth century the majority of the rural population consisted of free men of all racial types, descended variously from indigenous groups, Portuguese settlers, and African slaves; 3 or 4 per cent were actually ex-slaves, but in the lower ranks of society this appears to have been a distinction of little importance. Except for the small and inbred group composed of planters, who together monopolized the ownership of the whole of the forest zone, the free population was landless. For the most part it consisted of *moradores*, or squatters on plantation lands, something that the French traveller Tollenare had already observed in the early 1800s, when he estimated that nineteen-twentieths of the free inhabitants of the *zona da mata* lived in this way.[7] Given the system of land tenure, there was little else they could do.

Moradores were not only landless; they were virtually destitute in every other way as well. With the consent of a *senhor de engenho*, they could build a hut, raise subsistence crops, and hunt and fish on his estate. Equally important, the *senhor* would protect them in any disputes they might have with the authorities or with the retainers of other plantations. The *morador* had no rights of occupancy whatsoever and could be evicted at a moment's notice. But he was also free to move, and, in spite of the displeasure or inconvenience he might cause thereby, he frequently did so, to the point of his being commonly described as nomadic and root-less, incapable of settling anywhere for any length of time.

Prior to the 1850s, the burden of duties was hardly exacting. A squat-ter paid little or no rent and did not have to share his crops with the landowner, providing he raised only enough for himself and his family. All that was expected was faithful obedience to the *senhor* and the per-formance of such personal services as he might require from time to time. From the planter's point of view, his *moradores* supplied him with guardians for the more remote parcels of his land, henchmen for his private militia, and supporters in his electoral struggles. Indeed, the prestige of a *senhor de engenho* was measured not only by the size of his slave-holding or the amount of sugar he made, but also by the number of his *moradores*, which helps to explain why squatting was tolerated on such a scale.[8]

After mid-century, the simultaneous decline in the slave population and growth of sugar production obliged planters to turn to the free population to meet their growing demand for workers. The conversion from slave to free labour, culminating with abolition in 1888, caused hardly any of the problems anticipated.[9] Despite its much-advertised reluctance to engage in heavy manual work, the rural proletariat of *moradores* was not in a position to resist the pressures for incorporation into the work force of the plantations. The overwhelming control of a planter over his resident free labour force had its foundations in a variety of circumstances: the immense social distance which separated them and the associated habits of obedience of the humble *vis-à-vis* the mighty; the informal police and judicial powers enjoyed by landlords over their squatters; and the ultimate sanction of expulsion, a not unusual occurrence which inevitably raised for the *morador* the immediate problem of finding another plantation where, after all, similar conditions were likely to prevail. A few could avoid these constraints, but the interstices of the plantation system were much too narrow to allow for a large number of so-called vagrants to live off the land without answering to anybody. As one observer noted, 'the land has masters, and they have the power to stop strangers from using it'.[10] Vagrants existed, of course, but significantly they never failed to be roundly denounced by most people of substance, and it seems likely that most of them were *moradores* in transit from *engenho* to *engenho* rather than vagabonds in the true sense of the word.

Important changes were thus occurring in the pattern of life of the free population but, it should be stressed, entirely as a result of pre-existing relations of dependence and not because such relations were newly created in order to secure a labour force to replace the slaves. The extra-economic duties remained: *moradores* went on guarding property limits, fighting at the hustings, serving as bodyguards, and so on. In addition they were now also expected to put in some work in the cane fields, in transport duties, or in the mill, often alongside the slaves and even under the supervision of an overseer armed with a whip. A further consequence was their inclusion in a monetarized system of rewards. Whether a *morador* or an outsider, the free plantation worker was paid a daily wage for his work, usually *a seco* – that is, without the provision of meals, clothing, or medical attention. Piece-work was rare, except perhaps in cane-cutting and in transporting the harvested crop from the field to the mill; and the worker received his due at the end of each week, although inevitably there were complaints that some employers were less than punctual with their payments.[11]

It has recently been claimed that such was the hold of the landlords over the landless during this period that squatters were gradually made to work in place of the slaves, but merely in return for the permission to squat and without any additional payment in cash or its equivalents.[12]

No doubt the *senhores de engenho* of the late nineteenth century would have greatly relished an arrangement of this kind, and at first sight it may seem surprising that they did not secure it. But no evidence has yet been found or adduced to support this view, while there is a great deal that contradicts it. Indeed, in the often-furious debate of the 1880s over replacing slave labour, it was always made abundantly clear that it was wage labour that was being considered as the alternative. Similarly, the detailed estimates made by various experts of what it cost to operate a plantation without slaves were always calculated on the basis of wage-earning day labour. Writing in 1888, one of them described a *morador* as deriving his livelihood from 'the crops he raises on someone else's land, to which is added the income from a few days of work, at a daily rate of between 560 and 640 *reis*'.[13] What was lacking in the forest zone in order to secure this more ruthless use of free labour was either an immobile labour force or, in the absence of this, the complete collusion of employees in matters of employment, with the closing of all alternatives to plantation work, including the exit from the sugar zone. But none of these conditions obtained. It appeared impossible for the *senhores de engenho* to act as a coherent group for any length of time, even on a small scale. At the same time, their free workers could and did leave their places of residence without the slightest difficulty and were equally capable of leaving the forest zone altogether, should the conditions there become unbearable.

The association with cash crop production did not mean, however, a reduction of plantation hands to the status of wage labour pure and simple. There was no reason for planters to attempt this, while a good many circumstances demanded that their labourers remain as *moradores*. To begin with, in spite of the expansion of cane acreage, there continued to be that 'overplus' of land which according to Henry Koster gave 'room for the habitations of free people in the lower ranks of life'.[14] In the second place, planters still needed to keep hold of a well-proven lever to control the landless element, from whom they must exact services and obedience. Lastly, land was a convenient and inexpensive way of paying free workers who might otherwise starve, steal, or require higher wages. The lower rates of pay and the occasional nature of their employment kept money incomes far below the level at which a family, if it had to, could buy everything it needed. In 1879, for example, when wages were about 640 *reis* per day, the weekly cost of feeding an adult was estimated at 2$000 *reis*. On this basis it would have been impossible to keep a family of five, even assuming year-round full employment for one of its members.[15]

The post-emancipation development of the *usinas* similarly failed to generate pressures for social change, and the pattern of labour relations of the forest zone was therefore left more or less intact. In part, this was caused by the coincidence of technological modernization with a stagnant level of sugar output. Given that the economy remained monocultural, the demand for labour inevitably declined. The extent to which the labour market was affected can be gleaned from a comparison of the labour productivity of *banguês* and *usinas* respectively. The latter's advantage began with substantial savings in the actual processing of cane into sugar. In the early twentieth century this amounted to over 50 per cent, since the most optimistic estimates put the industrial labour costs for producing a ton of sugar in a *banguê* mill at 8.8 man-days, whereas on average the *usinas* needed only 3.6 man-days. But the greatest impact of modernization stemmed from the fact that the new factories could obtain the same amount of sugar from a much smaller quantity of cane. This entailed a saving of one-third on the amount of field labour per ton of sugar produced, and a similar saving in the amount of cane land required. The overall result was that while an *usina* required only about 64 man-days per ton of sugar, a *banguê* took 100 man-days to produce the same amount.[16]

The second factor was demographic. While employment opportunities contracted, the population of the plantations expanded – between 1890 and 1920, it went from 590,000 to 880,000 – and with it, naturally, the labour force. Furthermore, there was apparently no serious threat to the supply of labour arising from migrations out of the region, at least as long as living conditions did not suffer drastically. None of the neighbouring areas of the forest zone was sufficiently attractive to draw away its population. North and south, the sugar belt extended into the adjacent states of Paraíba and Alagoas, while to the west the arid hinterland, or *sertão*, offered only the most precarious of living conditions.

The *sertão* acted not only as a barrier to outward migration but also as an additional source of labour, since it supplied every year a stream of migrants who travelled down to the coast for a few months to serve on the plantations. It was an entirely spontaneous phenomenon induced by the extreme penury prevalent in the *sertão*, which encouraged these so-called *corumbás* to go and seek elsewhere a supplement to their meagre incomes. From the planters' point of view the virtues of this situation were manifold. It had obviously the effect of depressing wages and of assuring the planters of an even larger work force than their *moradores* alone provided. But, more important, it was the answer to the problem of the pronounced seasonality of the labour demand which is characteristic of all sugar economies. The *corumbás* stayed on the coast between October and March, precisely the sugar harvest months when they were most needed, thanks to the coincidence of this period with the slack season in the *sertão*.[17]

From the plantation-dweller's point of view, the spread of large-scale sugar factories after 1890 made very little difference to his way of life. The sugar industry now relied entirely on wage labour, which consisted of *moradores* and *corumbás*; but this did not in the least impinge on the former's subsistence activities, which were in a sense the core of their way of life. Although they were apt to devour *engenhos*, the *usinas* were modest in their consumption of agricultural land. In 1920, only three districts of the *zona da mata* had more than 10 per cent of their surface under cash crop cultivation. Obviously, there was no reason to drive squatters off and reduce them to a condition of exclusive wage-earning. On the contrary, there was every advantage in maintaining a status quo which made it possible to remunerate the labour force at below subsistence wage rates.[18] Moreover, the abundance of unskilled labour to be found on the plantations themselves precluded the need for planters to compel their *moradores* to provide labour services for long periods, which might otherwise have prevented them from taking proper care of their subsistence plots.

Similarly, employers did not have to resort to any but the voluntary methods of labour recruitment which they had depended on prior to the 1890s. Vagrancy laws, though on the books, were never systematically enforced, and no evidence has been found for any form of debt peonage, unlike the systems of labour coercion then being employed in the rubber zones of the Amazon basin. The *barracão*, or plantation store, which began to spread in the late nineteenth century to cater for the growing wage-labour force, was not an instrument for creating debt-bound labourers but, by all accounts, an additional source of income for the planters who kept them. It also frequently helped to solve the latter's liquidity problems by enabling them to pay their workers with slips rather than cash.[19] Similarly, no efforts were made to attract labour from the *sertão* or to retain it on the coast against its will by some form of *enganche*. Since there was an ample supply of labour, harsh methods of recruitment were ill-advised because they were not only unnecessary but also costly. The rural population was therefore left with the traditional freedom of movement which was an integral part of its way of life.[20]

Although the preceding remarks cover the overwhelming majority of the landless rural population, the performance of certain small but signi-

ficant groups within it must be examined separately. Among these the
lavradores, or sharecroppers, stood apart by virtue of their relative wealth
and social status. As a rule they owned a few slaves and some tools and
animals, and they contracted to raise cane on a half-share basis with a
senhor de engenho whose mill they were obliged to use. In spite of their
higher social position, their tenure was no more secure than that of the
humblest *morador*. Heterogeneity was one of the hallmarks of this group,
as can be seen from the remark of an English observer in the 1840s that
'there are *lavradores* of all grades, in colour and respectability; some
plant very extensively their plantations, producing as much as fifty tons
of sugar yearly, while others produce no more than one or two tons'.[21]
Similarly, some were more 'gentlemanly' than others. A *morador* who was
lucky and diligent and who enjoyed the protection of a kind master
might ascend to this station. At the same time, a member of the sugar
elite who could not afford to own or rent a whole *engenho* might engage
himself as a sharecropper, and a ruined *senhor de engenho* might be forced
to become a *lavrador*.

The expansion of the sugar economy prior to abolition did not affect
sharecroppers adversely, and as a group they held on to their share of
about half the cane raised on Pernambuco's estates. It seems likely that
their numbers increased during this period, particularly if we assume
that over time their average individual output remained constant. The
wide favour enjoyed by the sharecropping regime stemmed from the fact
that for a sugar planter it offered many advantages. By contributing (in
effect) to the *engenho*'s stock of slaves, the *lavradores* afforded him a
simple way of achieving a larger output of sugar than would have been
possible on his resources alone. In the second place, as they grew cane
entirely on their own account, part of the overall risk involved in sugar
production was shouldered by them rather than by the *senhor de engenho*.
This was particularly useful as cane cultivation is by far the most aleatory
part of the entire process. Finally, the cane they supplied to the mill
came out at a lower cost to the planter than that which he himself raised.
According to an estimate made in 1885, for example, the planter's cane
cost him 14 per cent more than that supplied by his *lavradores*.[22]

Although the uncompensated abolition of slavery destroyed most of
their wealth as well as their ability to provide labour through their slaves,
much of the usefulness of the *lavradores* still remained. With the *usina*,
too, after 1890 their great value lay in the fact that they spread the landowner's risks while in the end producing cheaper cane, and that at the
same time, having no legal tenure, they could be evicted without the
slightest trouble. These reasons continued to be so powerful that the

senhores de engenho who no longer ground cane themselves but supplied the *usinas*, which left them with much less to do, still had half their cane produced by *lavradores*.[23]

As they acquired land, the *usinas* found no reason to do away with the sharecroppers who were there already; rather, they often entrusted all of their cane lands to *lavradores*, who were thus left unscathed by the progress of modernization. Indeed, their position changed so little that an account given by Gileno Dé Carli of the *lavradores* in 1940 used a description first published in 1878 to stress this continuity.[24] And if we continue to accept the assumption that the average output per *lavrador* remained stable in the early twentieth century, we may conclude that the number of sharecroppers stayed roughly constant between 1890 and 1920.

The stagnation of agricultural methods helped to some extent, too, in preserving this group. If the *usinas* had invested heavily in irrigation and drainage or had brought in widespread mechanization and soil fertilization, it is conceivable that they would also have eliminated the sharecroppers, who would be less in a position to contribute to a modernized agriculture. But since this did not happen, one may ask why sharecropping did not expand to take up a larger share of the production of cane, in the absence of such innovations. There are two possible answers to this. One is that planters, particularly in the case of *banguês*, wished to retain some personal control over the cash-cropping on their estates, possibly for reasons of personal prestige — and here it should be remembered that even in 1920 they were still largely resident landowners. The other is that the distribution of wealth in the society of the forest zone was such that within the landless population the number of people who were willing and had the resources for sharecropping was very limited.

The apparent stability of this group is not inconsistent with the possibility of a high rate of turnover for its members. The latter seems likely, in fact, owing to the heavy risks associated with this type of enterprise and to the small margin of profit allowed by the landowners. Such ups and downs, however, would not be crucially related to any of the effects of growth and modernization but would be inherent in the perennial features of the sharecropping system of the forest zone. Whatever the turnover, the persistence of the *lavradores* as a group is important not only because it is a facet of the prevailing stability of the *zona da mata*, but also because in an eminently static society it stood for the only aspirations to mobility that a striving *morador* could realistically entertain.

In contrast, the *almocreves*, or pack-horse drivers, who formerly conducted most of the carrying trade between the plantations and Recife, were the great victims of this period. This was another small group, estimated in 1878 at 20,000; and though socially not as grand as the *lavradores*, they were definitely still a cut above ordinary plantation hands. The *almocreves* had a poor reputation, however. Their mobile way of life was peculiarly well suited to crime, and to horse-thieving in particular. In their spare time they were alleged to give themselves over to 'gaming and drunkenness, to dances and debauchery, all of which gave rise eventually to the fights and affrays which fill our criminal statistics'.[25]

As a rule, the *almocrêve* owned a horse, a gun, and perhaps even a slave. While the *almocreves* were familiar with the delights of urban life, their trade gave them an excellent chance to make some money on the side, and they might become sharecroppers one day. Best of all, they were free from having to work in the cane fields with the hoe. But they could not compete in speed or freight charges with the developing railways, and by 1883 only 8.5 per cent of all the sugar arriving in Recife came with the *almocreves*, though they were still left with the carriage from the *engenhos* to the loading points on the railways. A few years later, the British consul remarked that the extension of the railways had 'deprived them of their occupation in animal transport and many of them were thus compelled to turn their attentions to agriculture'.[26]

A similar case was that of the relatively better-off skilled and semi-skilled workers who operated the mills of the old *banguês*. During the period of economic expansion, between 1850 and 1880, they were obviously much in demand, since there was a sharply increasing number of *engenhos* in competition for their services. Once this expansion came to an end and – worse still – once the process of industrial concentration got under way, they began inevitably to be displaced from their occupations.[27] A minority within this minority had particular cause to complain of a demotion in social and economic terms. Clearly, most of the sugar-masters of the 900 *banguês* which ceased to grind cane prior to 1920 were unable to become sugar-masters elsewhere. They were obliged to become wage rather than salaried workers; and they lost the prestige which was commonly associated with such a skilled and crucial task as supervising the workings of a sugar mill.

For most other skilled workers, the *usina* proved to be a mixed curse because it also generated a formerly non-existent demand for factory operatives, work for which their experience qualified them particularly well. By 1920 there were more than 7,000 industrial *usina* workers in Pernambuco, and it is worth noting that their position within plantation society appears to have differed relatively little, in general, from that of

their predecessors. Like them, they enjoyed the usual privileges of plantation labourers while at the same time receiving a somewhat higher rate
of pay than field hands (usually 25 per cent more).[28] Naturally, their
employment was seasonal; but as long as the harvest lasted it was probably more secure than that of the average cane worker.

Thus between 1850 and 1920 there was little change wrought in the
pattern of life of the rural working class, with the exception of insignifi-
cantly small sections of it. There were none of the dislocations commonly
associated with the development of commercial agriculture, and it is
interesting that the establishment of modern forms of production coincided with the period of greatest stability in this respect, from 1890 to
1920. The transition to free labour under conditions of economic expansion did lead to some alterations in the situation of plantation-dwellers,
but always within the traditional framework of social relations. Later,
when a sharp break with the past did occur, in the 1930s and still more
after 1945, it came as a result of the expansion of sugar exports, which
created in turn a demand for more cane land rather than simply because
of modernized technology. It took the form, naturally, of eradicating
squatting and forcibly converting the *moradores* simply to wage labour.

The material welfare of the rural population

The stability of social forms which obtained prior to 1920 does not imply,
however, an absence of changes in the material welfare of the rural
population. The next step, therefore, must be to ascertain whether and to
what extent conditions varied in this respect, and in what way the evolution of the economy contributed to this. The most important element
here is obviously the general standard of consumption of the rural proletariat and its measurement over time. A suggestive approach to the
problem emerges when we consider what might be called the domestic
economy of plantation labourers between 1850 and 1920.

Prior to the 1850s, practically all unskilled plantation labour was performed by slaves. Squatters were rarely employed as wage labourers and
then only in tasks not directly connected with sugar production, such
as mason's work and carpentry. The result was that they lived largely on
what they could produce by themselves in the way of food, which left
them with a diet consisting entirely of manioc and beans, to which might
be added the occasional fish or game. The amounts consumed probably
varied little. There is no indication of restrictions being placed on the
size of subsistence plots, so that presumably squatters were able to raise
as much as required for their personal family needs. Anything beyond

this had to be bought with cash, and this might exceptionally be done by selling the surplus of a good crop of manioc or beans, or by manufacturing cotton bags for sugar as a cottage industry. But as a rule they lived divorced from the world of commercial exchange, and the emptiness of their huts and the simplicity of their diets attested to this.[29]

In the latter part of the century, the employment of *moradores* on the plantations meant that an increasing sum of money was to be earned, and this could be used to purchase goods regularly which had hitherto been more or less unavailable: jerked beef and salted codfish, which Joaquim Nabuco once described as luxuries on the table of a labourer, and clothing, tools, household utensils, and trinkets.[30] At the same time, a family was still able to raise enough in the way of beans and manioc to provide the bulk of its dietary needs.

The newly acquired burden of plantation work was not so great as to prevent the continuation of traditional subsistence agriculture, and nature being bounteous in the forest zone, the task of raising basic foodstuffs consumed relatively little time and effort. It follows from this that any increase in per capita cash income amounted to a net improvement, while a reduction gave the measure of the deterioration in the standard of living of plantation workers. Thus, thanks to the simple structure of the domestic economy it is relatively easy to obtain a rough index of how material conditions changed over time.

To calculate the per capita cash income of the free population of the sugar belt, the first step is to establish the aggregate income coming from plantation work, supposed to be the only significant source of income available in the area. This is done by multiplying the current average wage by the number of man-days of free labour needed by the sugar economy in a given season. The second of these figures is obtained from the year's total output of sugar on the basis that the production of one ton of sugar would require an average of 100 man-days. The immediate result of these calculations points to the conclusion that during the period from 1850 to 1890 there was overall a marked improvement in the standard of living of the landless population of the *zona da mata*, expressed through a rise in per capita cash income. Thus, during the 1840s, when virtually all the work was done by slaves, this income would have been next to nil; but the early 1870s, with about half the sugar output of Pernambuco being produced by free hands, it has risen to approximately 12$900; and in 1890, it had reached about 17$800.[31]

In order to construct this index of consumption standards, it has been necessary to make certain assumptions which must now be examined. As with all per capita quantifications, the first question to be asked is whether these figures present a realistic impression of what working people on the whole were getting in the *zona da mata*. The hypothesized uniform distribution of cash income throughout the region is not hard to accept if we consider that a remarkably uneven one would have been unlikely in the long run because of the high mobility of the labour force. A peculiarly lopsided distribution of work and cash income within a single plantation would have been equally improbable, since it was in a planter's best interests to spread these benefits evenly rather than to foster the growth of a wealthier and more independent group among his *moradores*.

A less easily discarded assumption is the notion that a cash income was solely to be obtained from working on a sugar plantation. This quite clearly does not tally with reality, since there were other forms of wage-earning in the sugar belt, as for example in public works or in the construction of railways and *usinas*. Some squatters also made money by growing food crops for sale. On the other hand, over the years these activities could be seen as either sporadic or insignificant by comparison with sugar production which dwarfed everything else in the area. Another difficulty lies in the fact that not all plantation work was done by *moradores*. Some of it was performed by *corumbás*, who siphoned off an unknown share of this total cash income, and in years when the *sertão* was afflicted by drought this could represent a considerable proportion.[32] With the exclusion of these anomalous periods, however, one could argue that the loss of income to migrants from outside the area, even if not small, might still be assumed to represent a fairly constant fraction of the whole. Although our results would be higher than the actual per capita cash income of the resident population, they would remain nevertheless as an acceptable index because the actual and the computed figures would be constantly proportional to each other. It could be added that the alternative sources of cash earnings already mentioned would offset, wholly or in part, the deductions which ought to be made on the migrant workers' account.

The strongest objection is to the omission of the real value of the income estimates made above. To establish a perfectly accurate cost-of-living index for the sugar workers of the forest zone is an almost impossible exercise. A rough one is provided, however, by the price of jerked beef, a commodity which had become a basic part of the working man's diet by the end of the nineteenth century, and his only source of protein. It is also fair to suppose that it was by far the largest and most frequent item of expenditure. Most other goods such as clothing or utensils were prohibitively expensive, whether imported or manufactured locally, and would only be bought very occasionally; and the equally high cost of jerked beef meant that most of the money earned by plantation workers had to be spent on food. A cost-of-living index drawn up for an urban population – say, that of Recife – would be inappropriate, because it would include the price of common foodstuffs such as beans and manioc which squatters did not have to buy.

With the help of this crude yardstick – that is, the amount of jerked beef per capita that plantation dwellers could afford – we can trace the impact of economic growth and modernization in terms of the rural population's material welfare. The first point to emerge is that the decades between 1850 and 1890 were not a period of unbroken improvement after all. Between 1872 and 1890 there was already a fall in the level of consumption, and this means that free plantation labour began to experience a deterioration in living conditions well in advance of the advent of modern sugar mills (see Table 53, columns 6 and 7). If the analysis is taken beyond this date, to 1920, it may be noted not only

TABLE 53   *Pernambuco: sugar production, income, and cost of living, 1872–1920*

	(1) Sugar output (tons)	(2) Labour input (millions of man-days)	(3) Nominal wages (*milreis* per day)	(4) Aggregate income (millions *milreis*)	(5) Population (thousands)	(6) Per capita income (*milreis*)	(7) Price jerked beef (*milreis* per kg)
1872	94,500	4.9[a]	1$000	4.9	380[b]	12$900	$400
1890	145,000	15.0	$700	10.5	590	17$800	$800
1900	127,000[c]	11.6	$800	9.3	660	14$100	1$200
1920	180,000[d]	14.4	1$500	21.6	881	24$500	2$500

[a] Not including slave labour. This is based on an estimate of free labourers being responsible for about half the production (Galloway, 'Sugar industry', pp. 298–9).
[b] Not including slaves.
[c] Assuming one-quarter of total output produced by *usinas* (Davino Pontual, 'Organisação agricola', *Boletim da União dos Sindicatos* 1 (1907), pp. 120–64).
[d] Assuming one-half of total output produced by *usinas* (*Annuario estatistico (1927)*, pp. 324–9).
Sources: Sugar output: J. H. Galloway, 'The last years of slavery', p. 603; *Relatório da Associação Commercial Beneficente de Pernambuco* (various years). Wages: Eisenberg, 'Abolishing slavery', Table 7, p. 589; Brazil, Ministerio da Agricultura, Industria e Commercio, *Salários de trabalhadores rurais*, p. 350; 'Agricultura', *Diario de Pernambuco*, 11 January 1902. Population: *Recenseamento da Populacão ... 1872*, vol. 13; Brazil, *Recenseamento (1920)*, vol. 4, 'Populacão'. Figures for 1890 and 1900 were obtained by interpolation rather than from the census results for those years, because the latter was notoriously unreliable. Jerked beef prices: *Diario de Pernambuco; Revista Agricola e Commercial; Jornal do Commercio (Recife)*.

that the deterioration continued, but also that the sharpest drop occurred between 1890 and 1900, when the *usinas* appeared and were spreading rapidly. The decline gives the appearance of having slowed down considerably in the following two decades, although in the meantime the progress of modernization proceeded unabated. The truth of the matter is, however, otherwise. The early 1900s, prior to the First World War, were worse than is suggested by the figures for 1920 – a point of reference chosen simply because it was a census year. In fact the international conflict did much to temporarily buoy up the sugar economy, thereby raising the real income of the labour force above the level of recent years.

On this evidence, a causal connection between the long-run decline in the consumption standards of sugar workers and the modernization of the economy becomes more than plausible. The exact nature of this link is brought out by the results in columns 1 and 2 of Table 53, which indicate that the responsibility of the *usinas* lay first of all in their failure to promote the expansion of output, and secondly in the fact that they brought labour-saving innovations to what was practically the only source of monetary activity in a region suffering from economic stagnation.

But other circumstances contributed to this evolution too. Thus, further examination of Table 53 suggests that an ample labour force and falling sugar prices depressed the level of wages, while the demographic expansion meant that the declining income had to be spread ever more thinly (columns 3 and 5). Moreover, the rise in the cost of living which was an important factor was the result of circumstances connected only in the remotest fashion to the vicissitudes of the sugar economy (column 7). All of these factors were the result of secular trends which anteceded the modernization of the sugar industry and were not substantially altered by it.

Contrary to what has been asserted elsewhere, the social impact of these changes bears little resemblance to that caused by the economic expansion of the sugar sector in the post-1945 period.[33] The former period included neither the expulsion of a large segment of the rural population nor the strong expansion of local consumer demand which characterized the latter. Rather, in the earlier process which is being considered here, the rural proletariat tended to drift back towards the reliance on subsistence agriculture from which it had just recently started to move away. The licence to squat was increasingly becoming the best way of maintaining a labour force to which planters could not afford to pay year-round subsistence wages, and less a means of exacting from a free population the reluctant performance of plantation duties.

However, the question of material welfare cannot be reduced to the mere determination of consumption standards. Although in this respect there were improvements after 1850, it must be said that in one other way, at least, the development of commercial agriculture was not to the advantage of the squatting population. The most obvious new hardship was the notoriously heavy work involved in cane cultivation and sugar manufacture, which squatters proverbially disliked and avoided. Most employers believed that natural indolence was the simple cause of this aversion and that little harm was done to their dependents by requiring these additional services from them. But the consideration of alternative and equally plausible explanations suggests that the heavier complement of work which became the lot of the average *morador* truly represented a loss for him.

Prior to abolition, and possibly afterwards too, the status of manual labour in a slave society was doubtless part of the disincentive to service on the plantation. In the second place it should be noted that the poor physical condition of most of the *moradores*, consequent upon a deficient diet, rampant disease, and inadequate shelter and clothing, was equally responsible for their reluctance. In 1882, a technical report on the sugar economy noted that 'nobody denies that heavy manual labour is the great worry of all planters, and that our workers avoid it as being beyond their strength'.[34] A third reason was the unpunctual payment of wages and the exorbitant conditions often imposed on sugar workers by their employers. Lastly, we must remember that the increasing involvement in the life of the plantation also cost the *morador* a certain degree of independence, as the result of having to submit to the stricter work discipline required by the operation of the *engenho*.

Nevertheless, the point must be kept in perspective. The amount of labour that on average a *morador* might have to perform was probably never enormous. A rough estimate for a peak harvest month – December 1893 – is that about 50,000 men a day would have been needed to harvest and process the cane, at a time when the total population already exceeded half a million.[35] Even allowing for the fact that the sowing and weeding of cane were going on concurrently, it seems clear that for most of the year only a fraction of the adult population would have to come forward to do the work of the plantations. Furthermore, from the end of the nineteenth century, the reserve army of labour was increasing much faster than employment and therefore the individual burden of labour would be shrinking constantly thereafter.

The fate of the plantation slave in the context of an expanding economy can also be examined within the framework of analysis adopted here. It would be idle to pretend that a proper and exhaustive treatment could be made to fit into the short compass of this article, but some useful points can nevertheless be made. In the last decades before abolition, the regime of slave labour retained its perennial features of harsh discipline, grossly inadequate living conditions and excessive exertion. In general, the slave was still treated as an economic input rather than as a human being. One may speculate that owing to the stepping-up of economic activity, the dwindling size of the slave force would lead to a more intensive use of chattel labour. As de Mornay had noted at mid-century, 'the greater number of *engenhos* are very deficient in slaves, and the consequence is that much work, not of immediate necessity for the production of a larger quantity of sugar, is left undone, or very badly done, or else the slaves are very much overworked'.[36] Against this it could be argued that slave prices rose sharply after the close of the slave trade in 1850, and this would presumably encourage owners to place a higher value on their slaves' lives and welfare. The opportunity for adding free workers to the existing labour force as required would also make it less important to drive slaves harder than before. The pressure of the abolitionist campaign between 1880 and 1888 and the not unconnected increase in the numbers of slaves who ran away would be a further influence in the direction of better conditions.

The fact that slaves had a higher mortality rate than free men casts considerable doubt on the notion that the former were treated in such a way as to be altogether better off than the latter.[37] Aside from the considerable though unquantifiable value of freedom, the slave was at a disadvantage because he had to put in a much greater amount of work than the *morador*, who was not tied up all the year round with plantation labour. Discipline and punishment lend themselves equally badly to measurement, but it is undeniable that here again the slave was worse off by far. Purely in terms of consumption standards, however, it seems that the lot of the 60,000-odd plantation slaves was better, on average, than that of the *moradores*. Housing, clothing, and medical attention were so deficient in either case as to make little difference. Both slaves and free men were able to get a reasonably abundant supply of locally grown foodstuffs, the former because the fairly prolonged slack season in sugar production left enough time for this. The main difference was in the consumption of imported foodstuffs. The typical *engenho* slave's allowance of jerked beef – between 50 and 80 kg a year – was larger than the amount a free worker could ever hope to purchase with his cash earnings. In the 1870s, for example, 50 kg of jerked beef would have cost about 20$000 *reis*, at a time when the per capita income of squatters was half that amount. Moreover, the annual maintenance cost of a slave during this period was estimated at between 36$500 and 73$500, a sum far in excess of the ordinary free man's income.[38]

The minorities within the landless labour force of the plantations had a domestic economy similar to that of the *moradores*, but otherwise the evidence is so scarce that only a few remarks can be made on this score. By the end of the period we are studying, the *lavrador*, for example, was probably worse off than he had been in the 1850s. Since his output of cane was constant and the sharecropping system remained firmly on a basis of half shares with the landowner, his income, measured in bags of sugar, remained also roughly the same. In real terms, however, it did not. A deterioration can be observed if we compare the 1870s with the first decades of this century: the price of jerked beef tripled, while that of sugar fell slightly.[39] But the precise extent of this loss is hard to determine, because after abolition *lavradores* were employing an unknown amount of wage labour, and in the absence of information on the structure of production of sharecropping units it is impossible to know how much of it was passed on to their unskilled workers.

For the skilled mill-workers of the *banguês* the situation is clearer. There were no secular changes in the length of the harvest, and so the number of days they worked varied little from year to year. The same could not be said of their real wages, which obviously declined considerably during the half-century, as shown in Table 54. Sugar-masters were better off than boilermen because they were relatively harder to come by; but both categories fared badly, considering the rise in the cost of living for rural workers.

Similar reasoning leads to the conclusion that the factory operatives of the *usinas* also suffered in their standard of living, but less so than the unskilled labour force. Because it was in the employer's interest to keep a stable work force in the factory, their employment was fairly well assured for the duration of the *safra*. In this, they were better off than field hands, who, in addition to facing a contracting market for their

TABLE 54   *Pernambuco: daily wages for skilled workers in banguês, 1876 and 1905*

	1876	1905
Sugar-master	2$000–3$000	3$000
Boilerman	1$500	$900

Sources: 1876: Henrique Augusto Milet, *Os quebrakilos e a crise da lavoura* (Recife, 1876), p. 7. 1905: 'Custo da producção do assucar', *Relatório da Associação Commercial Beneficente de Pernambuco* (Recife, 1906), p. lxxxiv.

services, were much more dispensable because they were more easily replaced. On the other hand, they enjoyed no special advantage when it came to the real value of wage rates, since these were roughly in proportion to those earned by unskilled labourers. Besides the higher pay and steadier employment, *usina* operatives also benefited in the type of work they did. To perform relatively light duties in a modern factory under shelter was much better than labouring in the fields, exposed to the sun and rain, or in an overheated and often dangerous *banguê* mill. Not unexpectedly, a government inspector found in 1895 that 'other things being equal, men would rather work in any *usina*, no matter how distant, than in the best *banguê*, this being a problem at present for many *senhores de engenho*'.[40]

Since there was a discernible fall in material conditions during the period from 1872 to 1920, it is puzzling at first sight to find that, of the handful of observers who troubled to report on these matters, nobody ever gave any hint of a change. Whether in 1880, when they were described as 'poor and hungry, ragged and barefooted, ignorant and stupid, idle and corrupted', or in 1920, when they were portrayed as 'miserable serfs, chained to the soil by the shackles of poverty, ignorance, and hunger', the same dismal picture of the rural proletariat is always conveyed.[41] A brief sketch of the abject and miserable existence of plantation workers not only provides a suitable backdrop for the present discussion but also explains this contradiction between appearance and reality.

The plantation-worker lived through this period crammed into a squalid mud hut with his family or, if a bachelor, in a stable or old slave quarters. Hygiene and comfort were non-existent; furniture and utensils were minimal. Even during the better times, malnutrition plagued the average plantation resident who got none of the important vitamins from his diet of beans, manioc, and jerked beef or salted codfish, and whose intake of proteins and fats was far below the requirements for a normal, healthy existence. The incidence of disease was appalling, a consequence of the environment and of the combination of poverty, ignorance, and a total lack of health assistance. Apart from endemic smallpox, bubonic plague, and yellow fever, the vigour of the population was severely undermined by such debilitating conditions as malaria (40 per cent of the population), ankylostomiasis (70 per cent), and verminosis (100 per cent). A massive illiteracy rate completes this picture.[42] Seen in this light, the ups and downs of the living standard appear like the proverbial drop of water in an ocean of hardship.

Labour relations on the sugar plantations

The accepted view of the labour relations of sugar plantations, the last question to be examined here, is that under the regime of the *banguê* cordiality and mutual dependence were their essential characteristics. The squatter demonstrated this through his loyalty and devotion to his master's interests, the planter by caring for his dependents almost as if they were a part of his extended family. When in need, the poor could count on a word of comfort, on a loan or a drop of medicine; when caught in misdeed they could be equally certain of receiving the right punishment and did not particularly resent it. With the *usina*, however, this happy state of affairs had to end. Modernization was prompted by a desire to maximize profits, and this was incompatible with the aristocratic values which were prevalent among the planters who owned *banguês* and which provided the foundation for their patriarchalism.

Our purpose here is not to deny this antithesis but rather to suggest that if placed in the proper context it loses much of its strength. In drawing a comparison with the *banguês* for the period up to 1920, the *usina* does not fare nearly so badly as its critics contended.

To begin with, there is an opposite side to the paternalist tradition in labour relations, which must also be noted. By custom, every landowner was the informal but nevertheless enormously powerful judicial, legislative, and executive authority within his territorial domain. What rendered this unpleasant from the squatter's point of view was the frequently arbitrary and brutal manner in which public order was thus maintained, owing to the absence of practical limits to this private power and to the habits contracted by *senhores de engenho* over centuries in dealing with slaves. Corporal punishment of disobedient retainers was and had always been 'a method of discipline used by all planters, in the absence of proper laws to organize agricultural labour', as one of them publicly declared in 1918.[43] Violent expulsions of squatters, accompanied by the burning of their crops and dwellings, on the mere whim of the landowner, were neither impossible nor infrequent. The Recife press of the time provides an immense repository of reported incidents that attest to this darker side of the paternalism of planters.

It comes as no surprise, then, that a flattering conception of labour relations in the forest zone is quite modern and enjoyed little currency prior to the 1920s, when its first formulations began to appear. The prevalent view, in fact, seems to have been the very reverse of this.

Whenever, for example, the question of European immigration to Pernambuco was discussed, one of the strongest objections raised was always that foreign workers would not settle there because they would not tolerate the brutal treatment dispensed by the local *senhores de engenho* to slaves and free workers alike. As late as 1918, the historian Oliveira Lima wrote of the planters, with whom he was closely connected by personal ties: 'We have inherited from the slave era an unintentional though nevertheless revealing disregard for the social and economic betterment of the people whom we have got used to considering our inferiors.'[44]

Just as the paternalist side of planter–squatter relations has been claimed to be changing with the evolution of the sugar economy, so too its converse was not immune from the same influences. The economic decline of sugar, in conjunction with the development of the state and of modern communications, presumably weakened the virtually unlimited power of the landlord over his dependents and curbed the excesses that such a distribution of power inevitably engendered. On the other hand, a higher population density and unceasing deforestation counterbalanced this by narrowing the physical distance between planter and squatter and making the latter ever more accessible to the former's power. The establishment of new *engenhos* by sub-division of the pre-existing ones, between 1850 and 1880, further reinforced this trend. Similarly, the advent of the federal republic in 1889 heralded an era of weakness for constituted authority and therefore of greater licence for the landed magnates of rural Brazil.

The net result of all these factors together is not clear. By 1920, the planter was no longer the omnipotent despot of colonial days; but then the situation of the typical plantation dweller had equally changed a great deal too since the early 1800s, when Tollenare observed him living in a clearing in the primeval forest, more or less ignored and untroubled by a remote *senhor de engenho*.[45] A tentative conclusion is that in this respect the squatter population experienced nothing startling in the way of either an improvement or a deterioration.

The *usinas* made relatively little difference to the situation. To begin with, if paternalism is cast as a form of behaviour peculiar to an old-established elite, then it must be stressed that the new factories were created for the most part by members of the traditional plantocracy. Moreover, where an *usina* bought up a *banguê*, it often left its former owner in charge, on a rental basis.[46] In the second place, the approach of *usina* management to the question of internal order did not differ from that of the old days. The methods of discipline they used with the labour force remained consistent with the brutal practices hallowed by a tradition of four centuries.

In an area of acute and widespread poverty, however, it is the field of effective material assistance to workers which provides the acid test. As regards the great mass of plantation labourers, there is little to distinguish the negligent performance of the *usinas* from that of the *banguês*. In health, for example, owing to the scale of its operations, the former may have lacked the medicine chest of the archetypal *senhor de engenho*. But this was obviously not even remotely a solution for the health problems of Pernambuco's sugar workers. What was needed was concerted government-backed and government-financed action to eradicate disease. It is revealing, then, that when the opportunity for a broad prophylactic scheme presented itself in 1920 the vast majority of *municipios*, all of which were controlled by agrarian interests, rejected it owing to the 'indifference with which public health is treated, many people asserting that such measures are not important and that these diseases do not even exist'.[47] With education it was the same. Any departure from the norm of neglect was generally received with amazement. 'Would that all *usineiros* and landowners followed the examples set by Baron Suassuna and Colonel Santos Dias!' exclaimed a reporter, referring to the exceptional fact that these two gentlemen maintained schools on their estates.[48]

By the end of the First World War, many *usinas* were introducing some social services – cheap housing, schools, medical aid – for their factory workers, and to this extent modernization proved to be beneficial.[49] Yet since the agricultural labour force which formed the bulk of the population was bypassed, the impact of the *usinas* in this way was slight. The *banguês*, on the other hand, were not even capable of such limited efforts, assuming they had wanted to make them. They lacked the large and concentrated industrial labour force and the more substantial profits which enabled the *usinas* to carry out these ventures with success. And unlike the *usinas*, they did not have to try to solve the problems of ensuring the stability of a large labour force and of warding off the nascent peril of anarcho-syndicalism, through the improvement of the living conditions of their operatives.

The first stage of industrial modernization of the sugar economy, between 1890 and 1920, had a negative impact on social conditions, but this was altogether very limited in extent. For this period at least, it is indeed more useful to draw parallels than to try to contrast these two types of plantation organization. Our concluding remarks here will therefore be to substantiate the alternative view that the *usina* prolonged and reinforced the social complex built up under the *banguê* and entailed similarly heavy social costs.

Having already seen what the material circumstances of the plantation work force were, the question which must be asked is why, in view of the abundance of unused land and the availability of spare time that under-employment made possible, the squatters were unable to improve their lot in life. Some squatters always did some business by selling foodstuffs, but the market was limited by the predominance of a rural self-subsisting population and the large-scale importation of food to feed Recife. The diversification of commercial agriculture would have been a far better solution, though one that required the capital and knowledge that only the elite could furnish. Yet obviously there was no interest in this on the part of a group which already had a considerable investment of funds, expertise, and social prestige in sugar production and which did not want any rival economic activities to upset its existing financial and labour arrangements. In this light, the implantation of the *usinas* could only serve to further prevent the sort of economic change which might have been socially beneficial. Since they represented an even heavier investment in sugar production, they strengthened the logic of the resistance to any departure from the nefarious condition of monoculture.

But the major obstacles to improvement are also to be found within the plantation structure itself, and here the *usina* merely reproduced what had long obtained under the *banguê*. The *moradores* were not interested in change, on the one hand because of the mental and physical apathy that handicapped them as a result of ill-health, undernourishment, and the deeply ingrained habit of poverty, and on the other hand because it was pointless to raise cash crops when one could be evicted at a moment's notice and lose all the fruits of one's effort. The beginning of the solution for this would have been a class of smallholders, built perhaps round the *lavradores* or relatively prosperous European immigrants who could have afforded to buy a plot of land. But this the planters would never countenance, although it was discussed at length. They feared too much the presence in their midst of an element which would disrupt the balance of labour relations and weaken the social control afforded by the 'exclusivism' of the great sugar estates. In fact, even though the critics sometimes pointed out that a healthier and wealthier worker might enhance productivity, they appeared to prefer him as he was: docile, poor, and under-employed.[50]

It is perhaps idle to condemn the social impact of modernization in Pernambuco, if we consider that without it the sugar industry would probably not have survived during the twentieth century. Indeed, given the price trends in the sugar market and the region's demography, it might have been better if modernization had been altogether a more thoroughgoing process. Larger and more successful *usinas* would have meant greater output, more employment, higher productivity, and an improvement in per capita income. There was certainly plenty of free land to permit this expansion. Moreover, a faster rate of growth would have led to a stronger consumer demand for foodstuffs and manufactures and eventually to the diversification of the economy, at a time when in industrial terms the northeast of Brazil was not yet hopelessly behind the centre-south.

The price of this improvement, however, would have been a heavy one. The wider swathe cut by a more intense modernization of the economy would have entailed the erosion or even the obliteration of the sector of subsistence agriculture which was still the plantation dwellers' last line of defence against economic adversity. It would have also put an end to the way of life of the *moradores* by forcing them to become wage labourers and no more.

The critics of the 1930s would perhaps have argued, on the other hand, against any presence of the *usina* whatsoever, although to do so they would have had to forget that the *banguê* simply could no longer compete in any market. The sugar economy would have collapsed; and in the process even greater hardships than those associated with modernization would have been visited on the rural proletariat. Considered optimistically, the ruin of the sugar planters might have paved the way for a peasant economy of a polycultural nature. But it is no less likely that the demise of the social and economic elite should have made the region attractive to outside investors. The result might well have been a new and more dynamic export agricultural sector rising phoenix-like from the ashes of the sugar plantations, to inaugurate an era of greater dislocation and even harsher exploitation.

NOTES

1. I am grateful to Liz Dunbar and Simon Mitchell for their comments on this text. At an earlier stage of research David Denslow's advice was invaluable.
2. Outstanding examples are Gilberto Freyre, *Nordeste: aspectos da influência da canna sobre a vida e a paisagem do nordeste do Brasil* (Rio de Janeiro, 1937; Júlio Bello, *Memórias de um senhor de engenho* (Rio de Janeiro, 1938); R. Fernandes e Silva, *A velha questão do fornecimento de cannas em Pernambuco* (Recife, 1928). For the same view in fiction, see José Lins do Rego's novels, particularly *Banguê*, *Fogo Morto*, and *Usina*, written during the 1930s and 1940s.
3. '*Banguê*' and '*engenho*' are used here synonymously to describe sugar plantations

which had retained the forms and scale of the colonial period, albeit with some innovations such as steam power or the use of bagass as fuel. Similarly *'banguêseiro'* and *'senhor de engenho'* are also used interchangeably. The *usina* was a larger-scale plantation, usually owning the land of several *engenhos*, to which its factory was connected by an internal railway. The factory was generally on a far larger scale than that of a *banguê* and incorporated such devices as turbines and vacuum pans. See the appropriate entries in Bernardino José de Souza, *Dicionário da terra e da gente do Brasil* (São Paulo, 1961).

4. J. H. Galloway, 'The sugar industry of Pernambuco during the nineteenth century', *Annals of the Association of American Geographers* LVIII (1968), pp. 285–303; Peter L. Eisenberg, *The sugar industry of Pernambuco: modernization without change* (Berkeley, Calif., 1974). See also the unpublished research of David Denslow of the University of Florida.

5. For figures and comments, see the *Relatório da Associação Commercial Beneficente de Pernambuco* for several years; also Gaspar Peres and Apollonio Peres, *A industria assucareira em Pernambuco* (Recife, 1915); and *Annuario Estatístico de Pernambuco* (Recife, 1927), pp. 324–9.

6. Gileno Dé Carli, *O processo histórico da usina em Pernambuco* (Rio de Janeiro, 1942), p. 31. *Relatório da Associação Commercial*, 1906, pp. lxxxiii–lxxxvii.

7. José Bernardo Fernandes da Gama, *Memórias históricas da província de Pernambuco precedidas de um ensaio topografico-histórico*, 2 vols. (Pernambuco, 1844), vol. I, p. 43. The classic account of *moradores* is in L. F. de Tollenare, *Notas dominicais tomadas durante uma viagem em Portugal e no Brasil em 1816, 1817 e 1818* (Salvador, 1956), pp. 53, 95–7.

8. Tobias Barreto, *Discursos* (Pernambuco, 1887), p. 90.

9. For a detailed treatment, see J. H. Galloway, 'The last years of slavery on the sugar plantations of northeastern Brazil', *Hispanic American Historical Review* LI (1971), pp. 586–605; Peter L. Eisenberg, 'Abolishing slavery: The process on Pernambuco's sugar plantations', *Hispanic American Historical Review* LII, 4 (November 1972), pp. 580–97.

10. 'Bancos agricolas – I', *O Brazil Agricola, Industrial, Commercial, Literário e Noticioso*, 15 November 1880.

11. António Pereira Simões, 'Parecer', *A Tribuna*, 7 December 1882.

12. Galloway, 'Last years of slavery', p. 601. This is not to deny that later they should have suffered this fate: see Francisco Julião, *Cambão – the yoke: The hidden face of Brazil*, transl. John Butt (London, 1972), Part I.

13. Henrique Augusto Milet, letter in *Diario de Pernambuco*, 17 May 1888. For examples of these estimates, see Presciano de Accioli Lins, 'Despezas de algumas experiências feitas neste engenho', *Jornal do Recife*, 10 May 1876; 'Cultura da canna e fabrico do assucar na província de Pernambuco', *Revista Agricola e Commercial*, 20 August 1876; 'Agricultura', *Jornal do Recife*, 14 January 1885.

14. Henry Koster, *Travels in Brazil* (London, 1816), p. 360.

15. Comissão Central de Socorro to President of Pernambuco, 21 July 1879, Arquivo do Departamento de Obras e Serviço de Fiscalização de Pernambuco: documentos diversos, B/20/1. For wage rates, see Eisenberg, 'Abolishing slavery', Table 7, p. 589.

16. Apollonio Peres, 'O estado de Pernambuco', *Boletim da União dos Sindicatos Agricolas de Pernambuco* IV (1910), pp. 683–95; *Annuario estatístico* (1927), pp. 324–9.

17. Júlio Bello, *Memórias*, p. 134.

18. Peres and Peres, *Industria assucareira*, p. 45. For figures on land holdings and utilization, see Brazil, Directoria Geral de Estatística, *Recenseamento do Brazil realizado em 1 de setembro de 1920*, 5 vols. (Rio de Janeiro, 1922–30), vol. 3: *Agricultura*.

19. Gaspar Peres, 'Pequena propriedade', *Trabalhos da conferência assucareira do Recife (2ª do Brazil) reunida em 14 de março de 1905* (Recife, 1905), p. 100.

20. For a detailed account of labour conditions around 1920, see Brazil, Ministerio da Agricultura, Industria e Commercio, *Salários de trabalhadores rurais* (Rio de Janeiro, 1924), pp. 347–9.

21. Cited in John MacGregor, *Commercial statistics*, 5 vols. (London 1844–50), vol. 4 (1848), part 21, p. 88. For further description and sources on *lavradores*, see Galloway, 'Sugar industry', p. 291.

22. 'Agricultura', *Jornal do Recife*, 14 January 1885.

23. Dé Carli, *Processo histórico*, pp. 46–8.

24. Ibid., pp. 48–50.

25. *O commercio e a lavoura de Pernambuco e suas relações com a renda pública* (Recife, 1862), p. 53.

26. Cohen to Salisbury, Pernambuco, 14 August 1889, House of Commons, *Accounts and Papers*, 1890, vol. 74, p. 118.

27. Gaspar Peres, 'Pequena propriedade', pp. 97–102.

28. Peres and Peres, *Industria assucareira*, p. 45. Francisco do Rego Barros to President of Pernambuco, 14 February 1887, Arquivo Público Estadual de Pernambuco: engenhos centrais.

29. Tollenare, *Notas dominicais*, pp. 95–6.

30. Joaquim Nabuco, *O abolicionismo* (São Paulo and Rio de Janeiro, 1938), p. 162.

31. See sources for Table 53.

32. A figure of 45 per cent of the labour force at peak periods has been suggested (Einsenberg, 'Abolishing slavery', p. 589).

33. Paul Singer, *Desenvolvimento econômico e evolução urbana* (São Paulo, 1968), p. 309. At the same time, my findings support Singer's remarks concerning the lack of purchasing power in Recife's hinterland as a factor in its slow industrial development (see *Desenvolvimento*, p. 317).

34. José Manuel de Barros Wanderley, 'Parecer do relator da commissão de economia social', *A Tribuna*, 31 August 1882.

35. The monthly output of sugar may be taken as roughly equivalent to the quantity transacted in the Recife market. Figures for this are given by the *Diario de Pernambuco*. For the labour requirements of the *safra*, see the estimates in Henrique Augusto Milet, *Os quebrakilos e a crise da lavoura* (Recife, 1876), p. 5

36. MacGregor, *Commercial statistics*, vol. 4, part 21, p. 89.

37. Eisenberg, 'Abolishing slavery', p. 582.

38. Tollenare, *Notas dominicais*, p. 74. For the cost of slave maintenance, see 'A propósito do congresso da lavoura', *A Tribuna*, 26 August 1884; 'Engenho Matto Grosso', *Diario de Pernambuco*, 31 October 1888.

39. Sources for sugar prices are the *Diario de Pernambuco*, the *Relatórios da Associação Commercial*, and occasionally the British consular reports printed in the House of Commons, *Accounts and Papers*.

40. J. A. de Almeida Prado to President of Pernambuco, 18 December 1895, Arquivo do Departamento de Obras e Serviço de Fiscalização de Pernambuco: Usinas, B/3/21.

396 *Jaime Reis*

41. 'Bancos agricolas – I', *Brazil Agricola*, 15 November 1880; Inacio de Barros Barreto, 'O papel da lavoura na vida econômica, social e politica de Pernambuco', in 2° *Congresso dos Prefeitos de Pernambuco: Anais* (Recife, 1918), p. 126.
42. On living conditions in general, see José Maria Bello, *Memórias* (Rio de Janeiro, 1958), p. 16. For health conditions, a well-documented description is found in Octavio de Freitas, 'As moléstias dos trabalhadores do campo', *Boletim da União dos Sindicatos* VII (1913), pp. 585–91. The problems of nutrition are discussed in Josue de Castro, *A alimentação brasileira à luz da geografia humana* (Porto Alegre, 1937).
43. 'O caso Siqueira Netto', *Diario de Pernambuco*, 1 June 1918.
44. Oliveira Lima, 'As condições sociais do interior', *Diario de Pernambuco*, 10 February 1918.
45. Tollenare, *Notas dominicais*, p. 53. For the forest cover and problem of deforestation of the early twentieth century, see *Relatório apresentado ao Excellentíssimo Sr Dr Vicente de Andrade Bezerra, Secretario do Estado, pelo Engenheiro Dr José Apolinario de Oliveira, Director de Obras Publicas* (Pernambuco, 1917), pp. 24–7.
46. Dé Carli, *Processo histórico*, p. 24.
47. 'Topicos', *Jornal do Comercio* (Recife), 6 October 1920.
48. Samuel Campello, *Escada e jaboatão: memória apresentada ao VI° Congresso de Geografia* (Recife, 1919), p. 15.
49. *Estado de Pernambuco: obra de propaganda geral* (Rio de Janeiro, 1922), p. 134.
50. Oliveira Lima, 'Condições sociais'.

CHAPTER 16

The evolution of rural wage labour in the Cauca Valley of Colombia, 1700–1970

MICHAEL TAUSSIG[1]

The paradox suggested by the term 'Andean tropics' is indicative of the singularity of landlord–peasant relationships as they have evolved over the past four centuries in the Andean drainage basin of the Río Cauca, as in the whole of Colombia. This country was the chief gold producer of the Spanish American empire and had the highest Afro-American population of the Spanish American mainland. Its social and economic history has been firmly etched by the early numerical ascendancy of free 'mixed bloods' and the political and property relationships they represented. Nineteenth-century Colombia was unique, even for Latin America, in the diversity of its regionalism, factionalism, and *caudillismo*. Added to this, the fanatical separation of the entire society into two monopolistic political parties, not dissimilar to religious war machines, has from 1840 until very recently set it apart from the other Latin American republics.

Its composite character brought together all the features that were found separately in the other Latin American colonies. Its topography owes everything to the splayed backbone and dissected valleys of the Andes; yet African slaves, not Andean Indians, formed the basis of its wealth. But in contrast to the other slave colonies, it was not the intensive cultivation of tropical crops on large-scale plantations conveniently located near the coast that made the slaves necessary: rather, it was an economy based on mobile, scattered, and small-scale alluvial gold-mining camps. In short, it was both Caribbean and Andean in its component elements, but unique in its synthesis.

Forming an intermediate cultural area between the 'high' cultures of Mesoamerica to the north and the Inca empire to the south, Colombia's mosaic of chiefdoms and incipient indigenous states had quickly succumbed through war and flight to the *conquistadores*, who could find no firm aboriginal authority through which to channel their demands, as they did with the Aztecs and the Incas. With the exception of a few highland areas, conquest and colonization largely meant genocide, on a scale equalled only in the Caribbean colonies such as Hispaniola.[2] Thus deprived of a labour force, the colony was facing severe difficulties by the end of the sixteenth century, and recourse was made to African slaves, who by 1600 were entering the Caribbean entrepôt of Cartagena at the rate of around a thousand a year. The slave system itself displayed many contradictions. The intensity of exploitation in the mining areas was high, yet it was extremely difficult to enforce that exploitation. The colony was vast and generally poor. Except for a handful of tiny cities and occasional areas of dense settlement, it was impossible to effectively police the slaves through brute force and penal conditions. Slaves fresh from Africa, known as '*bozales*' ('muzzled'), were much preferred for their ease of socialization compared with *ladinos*, who were considered craftier, far wiser in the ways of the colony, and much more likely to escape and cause problems. Lacking a strong military establishment, the masters adopted a policy of personal intervention into the innermost regions of the slaves' social structure and spiritual space, involving minute and constant paternalistic direction of sexual and family life. The ideology of white supremacy was hammered home through Christian ritual and state norms which further encouraged servility. The effectiveness of these policies can be seen in the number of slave rebellions which were unsuccessful through over-caution and the blacks' exaggeration of the whites' forces.

Manumission was generally held out to the slave as a reward for good behaviour and as a means of alleviating social tension and reducing the temptation to make an easy escape into the enormous hinterlands. By the last quarter of the eighteenth century the ratio of 'free blacks' (*libres*) to slaves was about eight to one, and in the words of one of the foremost students of the institution in Colombia, slavery had become something of an apprenticeship.[3] But if it was an apprenticeship designed to equip and induce the slave to participate later in the society as a free person, it failed dismally. Whether manumitted, runaway, or born free, the black usually refused, and was able to refuse, to enter the mainstream of the economy as a wage labourer or tenant farmer, which were the only conditions acceptable to the labour-starved landlord and mine-owning class. This situation was sustained until well into the twentieth century, when rural proletarianization eventually occurred on a massive scale.

The Indian element of the population passed through a succession, as confusing as it was rapid, of slavery, *encomienda*, *reducción*, *mita*, and *concertaje*; institutions which – though monumentally engraved on the social configuration of Mexico and Peru – found little footing in most of Colombia, especially in the lowland areas, even though *encomiendas* continued to be granted until the early eighteenth century. Diminished as it was, Indian labour played a crucial role which is usually overlooked.

Indians provided and maintained most of the social infrastructure of roads, bridges, wayside houses and other public works, even in the low-lying valleys. Owners of African slaves were most reluctant to have their precious *piezas* serving gratis on public works. In addition, a continuous effort was made in many areas to establish and support an ethnic division of labour whereby Indians would provide food crops for slave mining gangs, thus allowing the slave-owners to get the most out of their bought labour force, at the state's expense, so to speak. With the steady diminution in the Indian population, and the associated trend towards their being driven off their communal lands into debt peonage, this convenient pool of state-run labour was lost, with many negative consequences for the transport system and basic food supply.

With the transfer of gold production to capital-intensive foreign companies, as a consequence of the phased abolition of slavery which began early in the nineteenth century, the Colombian economy underwent a radical re-orientation towards the export of tropical cultigens such as tobacco, quinine, and indigo from the lowland valleys and rain forests. This possibility was created by burgeoning European markets and the greatly reduced costs in oceanic transport occurring around that time. This greatly accelerated the process of the regionalization of the country, converting it into a handful of quasi-satellites, with each region pointed towards the nearest coastal outlet, and each more closely connected to the exterior than to the others.

This state of affairs was sustained, if not accentuated, by the railways, which were constructed for the transport of coffee in the late nineteenth and early twentieth centuries. This phase of the commercial development of the lowlands was also acutely affected by lack of labour. Tobacco, for example, the leading crop in the Magdalena Valley around the mid nineteenth century, depended heavily on Indian migrants forced off their alienated communal lands in the eastern highlands to work as share-croppers, tenant farmers, and day labourers. Their powerlessness during the period of government monopoly of this crop remained unchanged when it passed into private hands, accompanied by stringent vagrancy laws which practically allowed landowners to enserf the terrorized rural proletariat.

Coffee, which became the mainstay of the national economy from the late nineteenth century onwards, owed as much (if not more) to free *mestizo* peasant smallholders along the temperate mountain slopes as it did to plantations worked by *peones*. Where there were *peones*, as along the western slopes of the Eastern Cordillera, they were able to exert powerful political leverage when national circumstances were favourable.

Behind these patterns of forced labour on the valley bottoms and small freeholders on the hill-slopes lay the fact that labour was as excessively scarce as land was abundant. The inclination of the peasantry, if given half a chance, was towards independent production on self-secured plots, preferably on the slopes where marked ecological diversity due to variations in altitude allowed them to practice within a small area a balanced agriculture of inter-planted corn, plantains, beans, and sugar cane, as well as the strictly commercial crop of coffee. The sensitivity of the ratio of subsistence production to commercial production, a crucial factor in determining peasant independence, became clearly recognized – as the Antioqueño folk aphorism, 'bought corn does not fatten', bears witness.

The Cauca Valley

The Cauca Valley, which is far more isolated from the exterior than the Magdalena, and on which this discussion will now focus, suffered a virtual eclipse during the nineteenth century as a result of the new international framework into which Colombia entered. This immensely fertile alluvial valley, running some 200 km north to south, and 15 km wide, lies enclosed by two of the three chains of the Andes which break central Colombia up into precipitous longitudinal strips. The river which drains it – the Cauca – has no clear run to the sea, and the western chain or cordillera of the Andes kept it virtually landlocked until 1914.

This Valley had been the centre and breadbasket of the slavocracy which ruled over most of western Colombia until well into the nineteenth century. By the eighteenth century a small number of intermarrying families had upwards of 1,000 slaves each, employed in Valley plantations and in mines both in the Valley and across the Western Cordillera in the rain forests of the Pacific coast. The rise of the slave regime in the seventeenth century, subsequent to the extraordinary decline in the Indian population, meant important changes in the nature of the society. Slaves were not just slotted into another *casta* category, leaving the colonial structure intact; slavery meant the emergence of a private sector within the colonial mercantilistic economy. The buying and selling of labour put a premium on, and gave a boost to, the merchant class as the only group strategically placed to mobilize liquid capital and maintain the trade web necessary for continual imports of human cargoes. This commercial aristocracy fused with the descendants of the *conquistadores* to control a giant complex of ranching and mining, together with an intricate network of regional and inter-regional trade and credit, sewing together vast areas of scattered settlement and far-flung cities. Their mines not

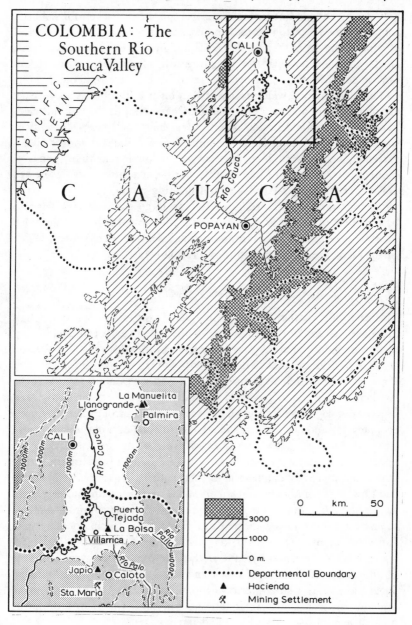

COLOMBIA: The
Southern Río
Cauca Valley

PACIFIC OCEAN

C   A   U   C   A

Río Cauca

POPAYAN ⊙

CALI ⊙

Inset map:

La Manuelita ▲
Llanogrande ▲
Palmira ○

CALI ⊙

Río Cauca

Puerto Tejada ○
La Bolsa ▲
Villarrica

Japio ▲ ○ Caloto
Sta. Maria

Río Palo

Legend:

▨	3000
▨	1000
	0 m.

0   km.   50

•••••••• Departmental Boundary
▲ Hacienda
⚒ Mining Settlement

Map 22

only produced gold but served as captive consumer markets for salt beef, Indian-produced cotton goods, tobacco, sugar products, and liquor, most of which came from their Valley holdings, and which the slaves bought, legally or illegally, with the private earnings from the occasional free mining activities that their owners found it necessary to allow them.

The plentiful and widespread distribution of gold deposits encouraged the formation of a class of small slave-owners who, not having sufficient hands to work lode deposits, concentrated their small gangs of twenty or so slaves along the river banks, panning for gold. Rainfall in this area is extremely heavy throughout the year with a double maximum, and consequently some three to four months of production were lost or slowed down every year by the swollen and flooding rivers. Lacking the complementary and diverse resources of the large slave-owners, yet also basing their economy on a large capital investment in slaves, the small owners were often forced into usurious debt or bankruptcy, which further enhanced the position of the ruling clans.

The slave hacienda

One such clan was the Arboleda family, which rose to prominence through the slave system at the beginning of the seventeenth century, having shifted its gangs from the Anserma region in the north of the Valley on account of Indian raids. They settled down in the region's capital of Popayán and put the slaves to work in the gold-rich Caloto area along the southern rim of the Valley floor. This quickly became the richest worked source of gold in the Valley, and it was the main prop to the province's economy throughout the seventeenth century and part of the eighteenth. The Arboledas forged affinal links with the rising merchant class, intensified their mining in Caloto as part of the Santa María mining settlement, and in 1688 bought a large neighbouring *hacienda*, La Bolsa. In addition to all this, they were amongst the first to expand mining on to the Pacific coast, in the late seventeenth century. In 1777, profiting from their close connections with the Church and the expulsion of the Jesuits from the colony, they bought for 70,000 pesos an additional *hacienda*, which had belonged to the Jesuits, in the Caloto area. This was Japio, tens of thousands of hectares of valley and slope land, used for cultivating sugar cane and raising livestock with slave labour. Thus they welded together the rich gold placers and mines of Santa María with the sugar and cattle *haciendas* of La Bolsa and Japio.

The owners were generally absentees, preferring to live in the temperate and more comfortable climate of the region's capital, Popayán (70 km to the south of the Valley rim), which was the centre of state power, the site of the royal smelter, and the place through which trade with Bogotá, Quito, and the Caribbean coast was co-ordinated. The day-to-day management of their holdings they left to resident administrators, who received copious written instructions and who were allowed 5 to 10 per cent of the production.

One such set of instructions to the mining administrator in Santa María (in which the Arboledas had over 250 slaves by 1820), in 1753, provided for a salary of 10 per cent of the gold extracted, some staple foods, and three black servants. One-third of the instructions deal minutely with the details of, and need for, religious instruction. Children had to be taught prayer each morning and adolescents each night, while adults were to be instructed in Christian worship twice a week and on all holy days, apart from prayer and singing each evening. Great care was to be taken with the sick slaves, and if medicines were not available they were to be bought at the mine's expense. In the case of impending death, a priest had to be notified so that confession and the last sacraments could be administered. In addition, a *negro racional* who knew how to 'help die well' should be made available. If no priest was to be found, the administrator should substitute as best he could and collect all the slaves into the sick bay to pray and entrust the dying to God's care.

A priest had to baptize the new-born, and care had to be taken that the mothers did not drown their babies, as had happened on many occasions. The mothers were to be given three months off work, an extra ration of clothing, and a specially nutritious diet for the first forty days (a general custom and one still practised today when such foods are available).

Despite the emphasis here on the Church, the role of formal Christianity in the colony as a whole, and amongst the Afro-American segment in particular, was more indirect than the manifest organizational framework might suggest. Its ideological function was to serve as a node around which folk mysticism and official doctrine met and congealed. The basic categories of the sacred and the supernatural were rooted in the mysticism of everyday life, drawing together the folk beliefs of medieval Catholicism with black and Indian cosmologies. The Church *per se* was but a single moment in this field of forces and was often organizationally weak and corrupt.[4]

The administrator was personally to give the slaves their weekly ration each Sunday, consisting of one-fifth of a bushel of corn, two dozen plantains and $12\frac{1}{2}$ lb of meat (an amount that the average lower-class Colombian today would be lucky to get every two months). Once a month, half a pound of salt was added. All this applied only to adult workers: children and those not working received half these amounts. The slave *capitanes* received 1 lb of salt, and the white *mayordomo* 2 lb. These rations were considerably in excess of those recorded in other mining areas outside the Valley.[5]

Special vigilance was demanded against theft of both food and gold. The mining areas had to be patrolled on *fiesta* days, and a permanent guard had to be mounted whenever fresh lodes were opened up. Nightly patrols were mandatory, and a curfew was always imposed after evening prayers, when the slaves were meant to retire to their huts and the gates of the camp were locked until morning. No slave could leave the customary areas without special permission, even on *fiesta* days, and they were to be punished for drinking liquor. Tight restrictions were enforced against wandering traders who tried to sell liquor, and no slave was to be allowed to go to the nearby town because of the 'sins they would be tempted into'. The maximum punishment that could be inflicted was twenty-five lashes, and these had to be spaced out at something like three, six, or nine a day until completed, 'always with charity because an excess is bad.'

With regard to the *haciendas*,[6] our records begin with Japio in 1774, three years before it became part of the Arboleda empire and when it was under government supervision following its confiscation from the Jesuits. Its sister *hacienda*, Llanogrande, situated well to the north and also part of the Jesuit domain, was turning out annual profits, from sales of cattle to markets as far away as Quito, of around 4,500 to 9,000 *pesos* in the mid eighteenth century when it had some ninety slaves.[7] Japio in 1774 had 127 slaves – by far the most costly item in its inventory – supplying all its manual labour. These slaves were mainly used in the cultivation of its 22 hectares of sugar cane and in the grinding of the cane to produce sugar syrup (*miel*). The peculiar and extremely favourable climatic conditions of this Valley are such that sugar cane, while it takes fifteen to eighteen months to mature, can be grown and harvested all the year round. Hence there is no *zafra*, as in most sugar-producing areas; labour can be uniformly used throughout the year, and so there is the possibility of avoiding the social problems of a large unemployed work force during the slack period. The state of Japio's cane fields showed that the system of year-round planting and harvesting was in operation; at the time of the 1774 inventory, 8 hectares were ready for harvest, 4 were about three-quarters mature, 4 were at the six-months stage, 3 were sprouting, and 1 had just been sown. There was one wooden two-piece mill for grinding cane, together with a small furnace and heavy bronze pots for thickening the syrup, as well as inverted cone moulds for preparing a crude sugar. Only twenty-four light spades and four machetes were listed amongst the tools, a surprisingly small number but one which was confirmed in later records.[8] There were some two thousand head of cattle, almost one hundred bullocks for ploughing, mules to transport cane and firewood to the mill, forty horses to turn the mill, and plantings of corn and plantain sufficient to make the *hacienda* self-sufficient. In addition, slaves had their own provisioning grounds, which were considered indispensable, as otherwise maintenance costs would have been excessive.

Of the 127 slaves only some fifty were workable, comprising men, women, and children above twelve years of age. Something like 200 steers a year were killed at weekly intervals to provide the *hacienda*'s meat ration, leather, and tallow, yet still on frequent occasions some 25–50 lb of meat had to be bought from the nearby town of Quilichao some 8 kms away. Tallow was crucial for greasing the mill's moving parts and for the making of soap and candles, a good proportion of which were destined for the *hacienda* chapel, which kept them burning every night.[9] Hides were essential for harnesses, beds, and pack bags.[10] Only specially privileged slaves received tallow and leather; 10 lb of tobacco was consumed annually by each adult slave.

The *hacienda* was thus essentially a self-contained unit. It was also its own ceremonial centre, containing its own chapel, as did all the Valley *haciendas*. Besides this, it was also the centre of the parish of Our Lady of Loreto (just as the nearby mining settlement of Santa María was also a parish centre). The meticulous list of religious ornaments runs into several pages. The chapel itself was of brick and tile, in contrast to the other buildings of adobe and palm thatch. Pride of place was given to the figure of Our Lady of Loreto, complete with silver crown, with the Holy Child in her arms, also crowned. Her shimmering wardrobe included petticoats of glacé silk, two necklaces of gold and one of coral, a brooch of twenty-nine emeralds, bracelets of coral, and other jewels. Rich brocades and other bejewelled saints completed the stunning spectacle, which was presided over by a visiting priest with a stipend of 50 *pesos* a year. Chapel and trappings amounted to 15 per cent of the *hacienda*'s total value.

Except for an increase in the number of cattle and a slight decrease in the number of slaves, the *hacienda* was much the same when the Arboledas acquired possession three years later. But it came to signify much more, as it now acquired a direct role in feeding the mines. By 1789, the *hacienda* cost 744 *pesos* in annual maintenance (as compared with 600 *pesos* in the mid-1770s), and money received from the sale of agricultural products was at least 2,344 *pesos*. This gave them an annual profit of 1,600 *pesos*, which was a paltry 2 per cent on their original investment but was not unreasonable when compared with colonial interest rates, which were always very low.

As far as the mines are concerned, no accounts are to hand. However, it is possible to estimate a profit of at least 160 *pesos* per slave per year.[11] Since by 1819 the Arboledas had 204 adult slaves mining in the Caloto area of Santa María, their annual income from this activity in this area alone must have been in the region of 25,000 to 30,000 *pesos*, and probably at least double that if the coastal mines are included. This was a colossal figure for the time, and one totally dependent on slaves and the intricate combinations by which they were worked. Considering that the founder of the family, Jacinto de Arboleda, left in his will in 1695 a total of 26,512 *pesos*, comprising only forty-seven slaves,[12] and that by 1830 Sergio and Julio Arboleda had some 1,400 slaves, with profits of the above order, one can see what kind of progress had been made.

But these and similar figures, although helpful up to a point and extremely hard to come by, need to be placed in context before they can be meaningfully interpreted. In the first place, a substantial proportion of the production was never exchanged for cash but went direct to the mines. More importantly, one has to consider the whole framework of economic institutions at the time. Banks did not exist; capital was in short supply outside the religious orders. The free market, as it came to be understood in nineteenth-century Europe, was barely developed. In its place existed small local markets (owing as much to custom and social obligation as to commodity speculation) and long-distance trade heavily dependent on personal trust and connections. Enveloping all of these was an elaborate system of state controls – taxes, monopoly contracts, and price-fixing and wage regulations – all aimed at preserving a social structure of hierarchically arranged castes, each with a separate legal status, virtual endogamy, residence rules, and task specialization. This was a far cry from the 'free economy' and society of 'equals' with which the capitalist market society was associated; accordingly, the social implications of economic indices and material factors have to be interpreted in a manner for which classical and marginalist economic doctrine make little, if any, allowance. Conversely, the economy itself has to be seen as an aspect of these social relationships, rather than as an autonomous sub-system tending to predominate over the other levels of society. This would seem to be true not only for the colonial period but also, to a large extent, for most of the nineteenth century, when, despite the rise of liberal ideology and class formations in place of rigid castes, the Valley's economic structure remained heavily based on subsistence activities.

What of the slave social structure? At least for the *haciendas*, if not for the mining settlement, the birth rate was far in excess of the death rate by the last quarter of the eighteenth century. The data are inadequate, but a birth rate of the order of forty-two per thousand and a death rate as low as twenty-five per thousand are suggested. This probably exaggerates the reality but nevertheless indicates a substantial population growth rate at this time, with all the implications that had for the vitality of the slave system and the reduced need for new acquisitions.[13]

Church marriage and legitimate birth were the norm, slaves being the same in this respect as the whites. The ratio of males to females was roughly one to one, although the males married later than the females and seem to have had a shorter life expectancy. In the *haciendas*, almost the entire population was arranged in separate huts in complete nuclear family form in 1767, but by the end of the century the female-headed, denuded nuclear family constituted a fifth to a quarter of the population. In the mines, by 1819, 'matrifocality' was a distinct feature, with female-headed households accounting for a third of the population, owing to the later age of marriage for males and a preponderance (by 14 per cent) of adult females over adult males. This could be taken to confirm the common assertion that life was much harsher in the mines, but it could equally well be due to the dislocating effects of the Wars of Independence.

The tendency to emphasize matrilineal descent over patrilineal was obvious in administrative matters, as the state regarded the mother–child dyad as more certain and reliable than paternal links, a principle it used against Indians and blacks.[14] In 1821, the law of free birth by which all slave offspring born after that date were formally free yet had to serve the masters of their mothers until eighteen years of age was a double reflection of this tendency by the state and the wider society to encourage the matrilineal principle amongst the slaves and lower *castas*.

At the same time, however, administrators and owners showed a common concern over 'licentiousness' and repressed consensual unions. Slaves in free unions were sold in preference to those who were legally married. From the master's point of view, there was very little in the way of formal status differentiation amongst the slaves, apart from one or perhaps two *capitanes* for upwards of a hundred slaves.

An undoubtedly powerful influence in the area came from the illegal cultivation of contraband tobacco by 'free' black peasants, either legally manumitted or runaway. Situated along the river Palo at the northern periphery of the Arboledas' *hacienda*, in the zone that today roughly corresponds to the *municipio* of Puerto Tejada, these blacks had been growing vast quantities of high-quality tobacco since the last quarter of the eighteenth century. 'Living outside of the social conventions and legal provisions of the time', these people produced around one-twelfth of the entire Valley crop, at least up till 1850.[15] Most of the tobacco was grown clandestinely. The selling price was higher, and police rarely dared enter the area which included a well-defined *palenque* of escaped slaves. This activity was associated with the growth of armed bands of *contrabandistas* in perpetual conflict with the state.

Thus a large number of 'outlaw' cash-cropping black peasants existed on the very edge of the Arboledas' slave *hacienda*, during the last half-century of slavery, and constituted a type of internal 'republic' or state within the state, cut off from the rest of society except for the illegal cash and crop transfers of tobacco upon which so much of their autonomy depended.

The presence of such a large group of militant, powerful, and *de facto* free black peasants was undoubtedly of great importance in shaping events following abolition, providing *all* the blacks with some political leverage in their conflict with the large landowners.

However, the general picture of the slave *hacienda* itself was one of a very 'tight' and controlled social organization, at least externally, and one which began to fragment only in the early nineteenth century, when political pressures for abolition mounted, and when male slaves were recruited to fight in the Wars of Independence. Bolívar himself was a firm advocate of the latter, mainly on the grounds that if blacks did not fight and die, then the future of the society would be endangered by a black majority enjoying the fruits of freedom won at the cost of heavy white casualties.[16]

As for the political relationship between master and slave, it appears that the Arboledas had no serious problems until eight years before abolition. The colony had been founded on war, slavery, and continual rebellion. In western Colombia, Indians like the Pijao and many smaller groups had preferred to fight and die, and the first experiments with African slaves were only slightly more successful.[17] Slave rebellions and escapes were common in the sixteenth century and reappeared in the late eighteenth as a major social factor alongside the growing restlessness of free blacks and a general wave of discontent in the colony as a whole. In the Valley, plots were uncovered for regional revolts, some of which included alliances with Indians, and there is a suggestion that secret black societies or slave *cabildos*, common enough along the Caribbean coast, even existed in some of the Cauca Valley *haciendas*.[18]

Although the Caloto area seems to have been free of such outbreaks, one small uprising has been recorded for 1761, when a mine-owner and his son were killed by their rebellious gang, which was quickly rounded up by the local mayor and thirty well-armed men.[19] In 1843, slaves from Japio and La Bolsa joined the rebel army of General Obando, which was sweeping western Colombia with the promise of general abolition, and sacked these two *haciendas*. Their reward for this was to incur such wrath, fear, and business-like calculation on the part of their masters, who clearly saw the writing on the wall, that 99 adult and 113 child slaves were sold to Peru for 31,410 *pesos* where slavery was still secure and demand high.[20]

Whatever relative peace the Arboledas appear to have enjoyed for most of the slave era, the memories bequeathed by that experience still indicate unremitting bitterness. It is commonly held by blacks native to the region that the interior walls of the still-existing *haciendas* are permanently blotched by the blood of the tortured and whipped slaves which no amount of whitewashing can long conceal, and at midnight on Good Friday people will claim they can hear the clatter of a mule carrying the last slave-owner, endlessly seeking absolution for his sins.

Manumission, laissez-faire, and regional disarticulation

The Arboledas, in common with all the large slave-owners, resisted the manumission laws of the nineteenth century and contested abolition by an unsuccessful civil war in 1851. Nevertheless, the alacrity with which they picked up the reins of freedom and harnessed the freed blacks to their mills and fields was little short of astonishing, especially given the resistance of their former slaves and their opportunities to back it up. The Arboledas' relative success in this matter, as with their immunity from slave revolts compared with the rest of the colony, must have been due in good part to the size and density of their holdings and to their geographical position between two closely connected major cities, Cali and Popayán. The region was densely settled in relation to most other parts of the country, and state aid was more forthcoming. Moreover, the Arboledas had prepared contingency plans for general abolition – a policy which was unconsciously encouraged by the national government's vacillation and slowness. By the time of abolition in 1851, the *Hacienda* Japio, and its sub-division Quintero, had prepared for the transition by institutionalizing a new category of workers, the *concertados*: blacks who, in return for a small plot of a few hectares, worked a certain number of days on the *hacienda*. Just before abolition some 40 per cent of the adult slaves had been put in this position. The general predicament that the large landowners faced was well put by a neighbouring slave-owner, Joaquín Mosquera, who wrote in 1852:

Up till now the general abolition has not produced any serious commotion; but I do see alarming difficulties because agitators have been advising the blacks neither to make work contracts with their former masters, nor to leave their lands, but to take them over. I know that Señor Arboleda has offered his 3 *reales* a day to continue working on his sugar cane *haciendas*, but none has taken up his generous offer.

Three months later he added that he had just made a tour of inspection of his mines in the Caloto area, which, owing to abolition, resembled a town destroyed by an earthquake. He spent two weeks bargaining with the ex-slaves over the re-arranging of the mines, most of which he rented out 'at vile prices' to local white merchants and the blacks, who paid him up to 1 *peso* a month. The huts and plantain groves were divided up between the ex-slaves, by families, and distributed free of charge. The pastures were rented at the rate of 2 *reales* per head of cattle. The blacks, he wrote, 'are now the owners of my properties, leaving me only a kind of dominion, allowing me but one-fifth of my previous income.'[21]

In 1853, the Arboledas began a refinement on the *concertaje* system in an attempt to both hold labour and expand production without resorting to the tenant production policy which Joaquín Mosquera had opted for. Three hundred and thirty hectares of virgin forest were divided up amongst most of the ex-slaves of Quintero, who were also provided with 'bread, clothing, and a roof'. The holdings consisted of two parts: one for a village site, and the other for cultivation, both for themselves and for the plantings of the *hacienda*. Their task was to clear the jungle and pay off their rent dues, known as *terrajes*, with five to ten days' labour each month for the *hacienda*, which together with Japio had 50 hectares of sugar cane, 20 hectares of plantains, and 21 hectares of cocoa trees. The owners attempted to control all activities closely. Public gatherings were restricted, and even work on the private plots was monitored. Lacking other means of coercion, they developed a patronage system whereby a finely graded hierarchy of latent status differences was accentuated and formalized. However, even though the owners scored considerable successes, their hegemony was far from intact. Years later, looking back on this transition period, the owner wrote that anarchy reigned, and so great was the 'horror that permeated those woods, that nobody dared to enter them in claim of *terrajes*'. An administrator was unsuccessfully contracted to 'enforce morality', and a belligerent neighbour himself volunteered to police the region in return for money rents (which were infinitely smaller than the cash equivalent of labour dues) but was assassinated in the attempt.

The blacks' resistance was ably reinforced by the frequent national political convulsions which tore the country apart, nowhere more than in the Cauca Valley. This region was fiercely divided between rival elites scrambling for state power. It was permeated more than any other part of the republic by the class presence of the hostile new yeomanry, imprinted with the antagonisms of centuries of slavery and now squeezed by the political rivalries of the whites and the pressures of a subsiding economy. It was in this process of economic contraction that the estate-owners strove to commercialize their holdings and recover their earlier status – a hope as premature as it was desperate, given the Valley's isolation from new markets and new means of turning land into cash.

As the republic entered the lists of free trade, liberalism, and tropical exports, regions were disarticulated from one another and inter-regional commerce shrank. The owner of Japio noted in 1857 that the economy of the country, and particularly of the Cauca region, was in bad straits and, in his opinion, far worse than in the eighteenth century. Everything was in ruin: public buildings, bridges, churches, and private houses. The countryside was covered with the debris of run-down *haciendas*, and it was now impossible to find artisans for reconstruction. And 'if we look to the mountains enclosing the Valley, the roads are completely abandoned, covered by jungle and inhabited by reptiles, mute but eloquent witnesses to the decadence of internale commerce'.[22] On the other hand, 'if we have lost our internal trade, we have gained an external one. Today foreign imports are six times as great as before.'[23]

The cultural fabric sewn by state and Church in the earlier mercantilist society also disintegrated. From the earliest days of the colony, and especially since the Jesuits ran it, the *hacienda* had been its own centre of religious contemplation, glory, and submission. Japio was itself an official part of the national ecclesiastical administration, but as the larger society ruptured, so did the integrating function of its religious ideology, leaving the *hacienda* as far from God as it was from labour and foreign markets. This was brought out in the disputes between the Church and the *hacienda* in 1858. The owner contested the right of the former to keep charging him dues, claiming that since the slaves were now free and could earn wages, he could relinquish that responsibility. Furthermore he stated that when there had been slavery there was some benefit to be gained from the Church, but:

Today the other landowners, as much as myself, only receive damages. The priests only come to the *hacienda* chapel to celebrate the *fiestas* of the Saints, and the blacks only to attend as a pretext to enjoy themselves in situations quite unfavourable to morality and to agricultural work. This is why there are no *peones* to do the work, why vagrancy increases, why fights multiply with the liberal use of liquor, and why assaults, robberies, and other attacks on private property grow every day more common.

The chaplain's acerbic reply was most revealing. He alleged that until the time of abolition the parish priests were forced by the owners to give a monthly mass, and that he had complied with this duty until it became impossible for lack of worshippers. The slaves, having then no free time, had to spend their Sundays working on their own provision grounds. Moreover, all the sacred ornaments belonging to the chapel were deposited in the owner's house. As for the Church *fiestas*, these were not the cause of fighting and immorality, because there were very few *fiestas*; it was rather the owner who was to blame, for insisting on selling liquor to all and sundry without scruple so long as he received money. He concluded by sounding a note from a lost era when man and nature were viewed as part of the same inalienable cosmos and not just as commodities for the market: 'From our point of view,' he wrote, 'the payment of Church dues falls on the spontaneous fruits of the earth and on the people who gain from its cultivation.' His point of view was not shared, and the chapel fell largely into disuse.

The cleavages in the local society were further aggravated by the fact that the blacks and the estate-owner took up entrenched positions on opposite sides of the political fence formed by the division between the Liberal and Conservative parties. It was the Liberals who had dealt slavery its final blow, and it was to them that the blacks lent their fervent support.

By the late 1850s, despite the anarchy of labour, the *hacienda* was producing about 90,000 lb of molasses a year, as compared with 2,500 lb in 1789 and 78,000 in 1838. Outweighing by far the significance of this increase was the secondary (and, relatively speaking, capital-intensive) elaboration of this raw material into brandy. This had begun in 1851 as a switch in resource allocation to offset the threatened decline in labour and field production, and it was probably the chief factor accounting for the economic viability of the *hacienda* in the post-abolition era.

Other *haciendas* relied largely on tenant farming and income from rents. This system seems to have been the norm for much of Colombia during the second half of the nineteenth century, but it was far more significant, or effective, in the densely settled highlands than in the valleys. The enormous and impoverished *Hacienda* La Paila in the northern part of the Cauca Valley relied on charging tenants between 1.6 and 3.2 *pesos* per year for plots of between one-half and two acres, as well as their labour services on the *hacienda*. (These annual money rents, similar to Japio's, could be paid by a mere five to thirty days of wage labour.) In the 1850s, despite La Paila's gigantic size, its income amounted to no more than the average U.S. farmer's, because of high wages and the scarcity of labourers. Only cattle-raising could give greater profits. In the eastern highlands, where Indian communal tenure had been destroyed, income from rents was a very important and profitable source of income; one *hacienda*, for example, is recorded as obtaining in the 1840s an annual income from money rents in excess of its buying price.[24]

Despite his unflagging and misplaced optimism concerning the *terrajeros*, the owner of Japio found it necessary to extract labour through a system of contracting and sub-contracting. A medley of cash contracts was established, with all categories of tenants and outsiders working alongside a labour aristocracy of resident whites. In the instructions to his administrator, in 1857, the owner urged the procurement of honest white *peones* (*peones blancos formales*) from central Colombia to serve as a resident labour force. Once proven, they should be contracted for three years and given a regular salary, a hut, and a small plot. They should not be charged a rent but were expected to work on the *hacienda* when required and could not work for anybody else without the owner's personal permission. The black *terrajeros* were obliged to work when called upon to do so. If they did not work well they were to be thrown off their plots, and under no circumstances were they to be employed in the harvest of food crops like rice. This measure was dictated by the inability to control theft and the desire to keep tenants as dependent on the *hacienda* as possible. Black women were to be employed for weeding, and if the administrator took the trouble to consult a trustee black, he should be able to lower the prevailing wage rate for this. All work was to be paid at piece-rates.

Money rents should be collected every two months, and those who did not pay should be deprived of their land. Great care was necessary to ensure that the blacks did not steal firewood and damage the woods, and this could be achieved by paying informants (*agregados honrados*) to act as spies.

The cash *terrajes* (rents) amounted to a mere 326 *pesos* a year, from some 180 small tenants. The owner reserved all rights to firewood, would not pay for improvements to land, and would not allow the tenants to work for anyone else so long as they were required by the *hacienda*. Payment of labour dues was incumbent on the entire household, not just its head. A further source of income, continuing the trend towards sub-division and sub-contracting, was to rent out large areas of land to other landowners, who established the *terrajero* system in their turn.

Through the planting of perennials like cocoa and the fencing-in of savannah, an attempt was being made to hem in the restless peasantry. Especially reliable tenants were to be chosen in order to facilitate rent-collecting, and these were to be excused from paying or serving as much as the rest. As salary, the administrator was to receive 6 *pesos* a month plus 5 per cent of the sales of sugar and molasses, 3 per cent of brandy sales, 5 per cent of brick sales, and 10 per cent of the *terrajes* payable in cash.

Thus the monolithic and tightly centred slave *hacienda* was replaced by an encysted series of concentric spheres of authority with a great variety of distinct yet overlapping relationships with the central power. Large renters, resident white *peones*, rent workers, free contract workers, and small tenants were thereby structurally placed in a network of rivalries to one another, in an attempt to bind them to the *hacienda* and make the best of the owner's insecure grip over his enormous and sparsely occupied state.

Slaves had constituted just over one-half of the value of the *hacienda*'s total inventory. Free wage labour now constituted one-half of the *hacienda*'s annual running costs of around 500 *pesos*. Even so, the labour bill represented only 15 per cent of the annual 1,500 *pesos* of profits accruing at this time.

By the mid-1860s, the *hacienda* was doing even better. Annual rents, including those from small landlords but excluding labour services, amounted to 1,700 *pesos*, and annual profits, based essentially on sales of brandy and cocoa to strictly local markets, were around 25,000 *pesos*. However, this was neither a steady nor an assured income since the *hacienda* was several times overrun and confiscated during the civil wars, in which the owner played a prominent, and invariably costly, losing role. Following each defeat and temporary appropriation of the *hacienda*, tenants and squatters would penetrate and enlarge their holdings at the estate's expense, only to be pushed back when national conditions were once again favourable to the owner's return.

As an illustration of this oscillating pattern we can review the situa-tion in 1871, when the owner, once again in more or less secure posses-sion, instructed his administrator to take a census of the squatters and expel those who were not bona fide *terrajeros* or were not forthcoming with their rent, noting that there were many people illegally occupying his land. He recommended that the expulsion should be done very cautiously. Prior notice should be given, which, if not obeyed, should be followed by the destruction of the squatter's house and the filing of a complaint with the local magistrate or mayor. It would not be prudent, he wrote, to expel all the refractory tenants simultaneously; rather, they should be dislodged one at a time. The policy of renting out large areas of land to *arrendatarios*, with their own *terrajeros*, was still in existence as a means of occupying more land, facilitating social control, and diluting authority. It was wise to make an inspection of the tenants once or twice a year with a magistrate or the mayor, at the *hacienda*'s expense, and to contract a rent collector to take care of the arrears, allowing him 25 to 40 per cent of what was collected, according to the difficulties involved. All squatters on pasture land had to be expelled by destroying their habitations, and all clearing of land for the sowing of corn by tenants had to be stopped.

A new factor gradually arose in this unstable situation, as soil exhaustion in the cane fields began to set in. Since the 1850s, only one ratoon was being harvested, and by 1871 fertilizer made out of the dried cane fibre (*bagazo*) had to be applied. While the lands of the more thickly wooded and lower-lying sub-division of Quintero were far more suitable for cane cultivation, it was there that tenants and squatters were most fractious. 'Quintero demands more care than Japio,' the owner wrote, 'because there everything is in disorder, and it is now habitual that there is no respect for private property.'

By the 1870s profits were well down, and they remained so until the demise of the family and the beginning of a new era in the early twentieth century. The capital infrastructure had remained virtually unchanged since the early 1850s, with the mill of stone rollers driven by animal traction and the primitive distillery remaining the same. Despite the *hacienda*'s notable success in relation to most other Valley *haciendas* over the same period, it eventually met the same fate as other large-scale commercial landholdings. The pressures of intermittent but frequent civil wars, a refractory tenant work force, and the restricted nature of the market created insuperable obstacles for an inappropriate mode of production which was based on the quite contrary principles of political stability backed by a strong state, *latifundia*, a large, docile landless work force, and a flourishing market.

The Valley — which in colonial times had formed the centre of the gold-exporting economy — now found itself on the very margin of the commercial world, as the national domain was divided into selectively discriminated dependencies by the world market. The landed class, in its attempts to develop a plantation agriculture, converting slaves into

tenant workers, not only had to bear the staggeringly high costs of transportation across the Andes, exacerbated by the state's manipulation of
road taxes, but also had to contend with the hostile political reaction
that its policies inevitably provoked amongst its supposed work force.
The large landlords were truly caught in the vice of a contradictory
transition period between two modes of production, which they tried to
resolve through neo-feudal exactions diluted by elements of free contract
labour, both of which were inevitably unsatisfactory. The former were
virtually impossible to maintain, as land was abundant and the culture of
servility had been transcended; the latter was too expensive, given the
bottleneck to exports and any sort of market formation.

It was these contradictory and antagonistic forces which made the
Valley into a battlefield of economic stagnation and contending socio-
economic formations. The tendency towards a semi-subsistence yeomanry,
on the one hand, was arrested by the sluggish and fitful maturation of a
capitalist export agriculture based on large estates, on the other. And
the latter was riveted into near-paralysis by internal disputes deriving
from its incomplete control over the means of production.

One eyewitness after another described the general ruin and the
tantalizing promise of the Valley during this period. It was commonly
agreed that the problem lay in finding an outlet to the sea and in over-
coming the laziness of the lower classes. Nineteenth-century geographical determinism and invidious psychologizing reinforced one
another, for the astonishing fertility of the soil meant that 'to eat one
does not have to work', and from this simple circumstance derived the
fact that 'people excuse themselves from serving others, and this spirit
of social equality that predominates amongst the poor drowns and
tortures the aristocratic pretensions of the old mining feudocracy'.[25]

'When a road is opened to the sea', continued the same author wist-
fully,

agriculture development will be vigorously unleashed throughout the Valley,
producing massively for the external market ... Cali will become the emporium
of commerce in the south of the Union, changing the face of the Valley completely, multiplying the *haciendas*, and shifting livestock to the mountain-
sides ... eliminating all the shacks and replacing them by rural businesses...
profits will change completely, reaching down as far as the most miserable
hovel, and those who today, whether through abandonment or ignorance, prefer
a life of idleness to the zeal of production will change their ideas once they
see the most active and intelligent amongst them accumulating riches ... to
achieve this happy future all that is necessary is that the idle hands which exist
today stop being idle, and that social harmony, the best guarantee of work and
business, be allowed to prevail.[26]

But what was necessary was far from possible. Freed blacks continued to seek refuge along the fertile, raised river banks, planting their staples of plantain and corn and a few commercial crops like tobacco and cocoa. Their plots stretched in irregular ribbons along the rivers, simulating with inter-planted crops the dense growth that had been there initially. Fishing and panning for gold were supplementary activities,[27] as was the occasional raising of livestock on the 'common lands' and *indivisos* of open savannah. These black peasants were in many senses outlaws, free peasants and foresters living by their wits and armed strength rather than by any legal guarantees to land and citizenship rights. 'In the woods that enclose the Cauca Valley,' wrote a German traveller in 1880,

vegetate many blacks whom one could equate with the maroons of the West Indies. Whether because of crimes that were too grave even for the liberal Caucan justice, or because of the simple desire to return to a savage state typical of their race, what is certain is that they search for solitude in the woods, where they regress once again slowly to the customs of their African birthplace, as one commonly sees in the interior of Haiti. These people are tremendously dangerous, especially in times of revolution, when they get together in gangs and enter the struggle as valiant fighters in the service of whatever hero of liberty promises them booty.[28]

The open grassland or 'common lands', as they were referred to by the peasantry, were more like no-man's-lands and were in some ways the functional equivalent of the truly communal lands that highland Indians had held, but they differed from them in highly significant ways. Whereas the highland Indians had had government sanction for this type of holding, which involved community councils and formal internal controls, the commons of the Cauca Valley lowlands in the second half of the nineteenth century were, if anything, negatively sanctioned by the state and informally controlled. For it was in the very nature of this Valley society that informal, underground controls would be the dominant modality of social organization, and this was as true for the regulation of peasant land as it was for all aspects of their social structure up to the present day. Pursued by a hostile gentry, denied any representation in the formal hierarchies of government, lacking security of land tenure, denied the possibility of any representative village structure in the official scheme of administration, the black peasants matched the former Indian communities point for point, but in an inverse relationship. There were no black institutions that meant anything in the official law-books, yet blacks were discriminated against and regarded as a distinct cultural group from the whites. Their social organization was, so to speak, created out of a series of flitting shadows,[29] built (like the infrastructure of guerrillas) out of invisible supports and quickly dispersable elements, and capable of endless permutations and combinations, as their kinship structure still certifies.

Were there any other remedies open to the upper class? Apart from the solutions tried by the Arboledas there were two others, as distinct from one another as the past and future epochs they respectively represented. One was to propound and apply vagrancy laws. Police were given wide powers to arrest so-called vagrants and force them to work on *haciendas*, and, as one student of these matters has written, 'the plains of the Cauca were turned into lands of brigandage and fear'.[30] Such measures to contain ex-slaves were notorious in Venezuela (which had been under the same jurisdiction as Colombia), and the clear purpose of these laws was to keep the *peón* or day-labourer on the land under supervision.[31] Vagrancy was an important concern of the state from the 1850s onwards, as government reports attest.[32] But the state, suffering from severe structural weaknesses, was unable to achieve the ends so desired by the entrepreneurial class. In 1874, for example, town officials of Palmira, the most important rural town in the Valley, received a complaint from the heads of the tobacco industry. The decadence of this industry, they complained, was due to lack of manual labour – not just the lack, however, but also its reluctance. To overcome this, stronger laws favouring the employing class were essential to compel recalcitrant workers into disciplined activity. 'What is necessary,' they urged, 'are means that are coercive, prompt, efficacious, and secure.'[33]

The other attempted remedy, vastly different in its subtlety and understanding of modern economic forces, was effected mainly by European and North American merchants, who formed a rising commercial class in the Valley from 1860 onwards. These were in fact intermediaries organized for the buying of export crops from smallholders – crops which then trickled over the rough trails and rivers to the coast. Given the uncertainties of the Valley's politics, the reluctance of smallholders to work for wages, and the fluctuations in the world market, this policy made sound sense. The type of intermediary most likely to succeed was the one who had sources of foreign credit and good market information. Such was the founder of the Eder family fortune, Santiago Eder, who, as a U.S. citizen and Consul, with close relatives in commercial houses in London, New York, Panama, and Guayaquil, established himself in the southern part of the Valley in the early 1860s. With the impetus from his successful dealings in foreign trade, he was slowly able to climb ahead of his Colombian rivals (such as the Arboledas), whose incapacity to engage in foreign commerce meant a decline in all components of their wealth. As the latter type of family – rooted in slavery, lacking capital, and locked in the internecine political conflicts of the day – spent their energies and money, so entrepreneurs like Eder managed to acquire enormous land holdings to reinforce their trading activities. Eventually, with the opening of a route to the sea, they came to control the Valley's economy. The fact that Eder himself, as Consul and U.S. businessman, had to be backed up by a U.S. warship on one occasion when both due respect and debt payments were in default was only the most outstanding and obvious outward sign of the international political connections which were behind the new ways of making money from land.

By the mid-1860s, the perilous Río Dagua route across the western Andes had been sufficiently improved to allow a substantial increase in trade with the exterior,[34] so that by 1876 the value of trade was of the order of 2,000,000 *pesos*, as compared with 85,000 *pesos* in the mid-nineteenth century.[35] Santiago Eder, who would have had no success without the financial aid of his kinsmen in the business houses of Europe and the U.S.A.,[36] was one of the prime movers behind this route and the subsequent improvements which allowed him to weave together a network of foreign and domestic commerce. With the aid of tobacco bought from surrounding black smallholders,[37] which he exported to Panama and London, he gradually underwrote a large sugar plantation. He profitably rode the successive export booms in indigo, quinine, rubber, and coffee, and he imported cotton goods, luxury foods, wheat flours, wood, sewing-machines, matches, kerosene, ploughs, and even machetes from western Europe and the U.S.A. As one of his descendants writing in the twentieth century observed, Eder understood that indigo, for example, was going to be a boom of very short duration, and thus he kept well supplied with information as to the state of the international market through his overseas contacts, not to mention sharp injections of capital when and where they were necessary.[38]

By the late 1860s he had over a thousand hectares of choice Valley land, was the first or second person in the Valley to construct a hydraulically powered sugar mill, and was already producing 95,000 pounds of crude sugar at a time when the Arboledas' Japio, at the peak of its productive career, was grinding 90,000 pounds of molasses.

Coffee, which ultimately proved to be far less successful on the Valley floor than on the temperate slopes, excited Eder's interest in 1865, and during a trip to London he formed the Palmyra Coffee Plantation Co., in which he, one of his brothers living in London, and the City firm of Vogl Brothers held the shares. With this capital formation he was able to plant extensively alongside his other holdings. Orders of around £2,000 for tobacco were regularly placed with him by London and German buyers, often in the form of standing credits, a type and amount of financing which was also made available to him by Manchester cotton firms for imports. In 1878, for example, his profits on the sales of imports alone were slightly over 10,000 *pesos*.

Land and property accrued through other means as well. When other businessmen, unlike him, failed to play the market swings correctly and went bankrupt, he was able to acquire their holdings, since their foreign creditors had no interest in taking them over directly themselves. Also, being a foreigner, he was not liable to have his property confiscated during the civil wars. In fact, this meant that Colombians would entrust their holdings to him.

By 1874, when the manager of Japio was forlornly recommending a new mill, the 'Victor', from the U.S.A., Eder's plantation La Manuelita was installing a 'Louisiana No. 1' mill and was not only producing the highest-grade sugar but, by 1881, was the biggest producer in the Valley, with around 550,000 lb a year, part of which found its way to foreign ports.

Writing to the U.S. Secretary of State in 1868, in keeping with his duties as Consul and in pursuit of his incessant requests for aid, Eder described the Valley in glowing terms as a natural paradise of physical resources whose exploitation only awaited U.S. interest. The local whites, who formed but a sixth of the (predominantly black) population, saw U.S. intervention as the only solution to the endless civil disturbances which racked the Valley.[39] The 1876 outbreak – ostensibly, like all the rest, a civil war between Conservatives and Liberals – did great damage to the city of Cali and was described by Eder in terms which leave little doubt as to its basis in class conflict, albeit one that was crucially dramatized by religious doctrine and confusingly channelled by the *Realpolitik* of formal party alliances. The 20,000 inhabitants of the city, he wrote, included a vagabond population of some 16,000, made up of Negroes and *mestizos* imbued with intensely communistic doctrines. The remainder were principally of Spanish origin and, unlike the rabble, belonged to the Conservative party. The leader of the rebel vagabonds was described as a communist visionary, a mystic lunatic, and an assassin, driven by the maxims of the French Revolution and the Colombian Democratic Clubs founded in the 1840s. This leader obviously represented a powerful populist movement with chiliastic overtones, searching for glory and the end to all *Godos* (Conservatives), who were to be swept out of the city in a flood of vengeance and destruction to Conservative and

Liberal property alike – a lack of discrimination which drove the Liberal government to swift retaliation. In the last analysis, class interests pre-dominated over party ones, as had always been the case.

The extremely complex relationship amongst religion, party, race, and class, naturally found expression on the *haciendas* as well. In the mid-1870s, Japio's owner received a letter from his son, then managing the property:

In the last session of the local Democratic Club, mainly attended by blacks, they were saying that the aim of the Conservatives is to make a new revolution in order to re-enslave all the blacks. The Conservatives are believed to be saying, 'Slavery or the gallows for all blacks!' What is more, the blacks state that the Conservatives are not true believers but feign Catholicism in order to deceive; the only true Catholics are the Liberals.

All this was accompanied by the most alarming threats of death to the Arboledas.

Again in 1879 there was deep unrest in the forests around Japio. The slightest hint could panic people into believing that slavery was to be reinstated, and on this occasion, on account of the owner's attempts to lay in stores of rice and plantain flour, it was held that a massive round-up and sale of blacks to the exterior was imminent, as it had been previously.

Throughout the last quarter of the nineteenth century the peasantry was armed and fighting for one local Liberal machine or another. The owner of Japio had almost given up hope of ever regaining control; re-peated attempts were made to let large areas of land and live off the rent, and by 1882 the family was eager to sell out altogether. Production of brandy, their mainstay, was unreliable and intermittent. In addition to armed resistance, it was difficult to control even that fraction of the population which did frequently work on the *hacienda*. In July 1882, for instance, all the workers held a week-long *fiesta*, drinking, horse-racing, and bullfighting their time away, much to the administrator's fury: 'We mill weekly when there is no *fiesta* and when the blacks don't have to lie down' was his bitter comment.

The new rural economy

The twentieth century ushered in profound changes. The conflict be-tween the two previously existing modes of production – that based on a subsistence yeomanry on the one side, and a latent rural capitalism on the other – was settled in favour of the latter. Analytically we can point to four major factors accounting for this:

(1) Political unification of the upper class and consolidation of the nation-state.
(2) A massive increase in foreign (U.S.) investment.
(3) The opening of the Valley to international commerce by rail and sea.
(4) Demographic changes; a sharp increase in the local rural population (placing pressure on land) and in the cities (increasing the consumer market for agricultural products).

In 1901, with the shattering *Mil Días* War and its severe dislocation of local political machines, the growing tendency towards national central-ization of the state and the consolidation of regional and factional elites into one unified class was greatly accelerated. The regionalization of the country into semi-autonomous exporting or subsistence enclaves re-mained, thereby supporting regional elites, but the need for national integration at the political and financial levels transcended the finer geographical divisions, if only to produce a secondary overlay of sub-sidiary connections to maintain the export orientation. A reciprocal historical movement was triggered off whereby foreign investment increased as state power and local capitalist hegemony increased. Between 1913 and 1930 foreign money poured into the country at un-precedented rates, greater than for any other Latin American re-public over the same period. U.S. private investments, mainly in public works and services, amounted to $280,000,000. Radical fiscal reforms, devised by U.S. advisers, established an efficient national banking structure for the first time. Land was now felt to be scarce, also for the first time, as population pressure began to have political consequences. The political arrangement of land holdings, concentrated in a small elite, was forcing peasants into new ways of existence and new market relations. Land values increased in response to swelling urban food de-mand. An intricate and lengthy series of disputes over the 'common lands', *baldíos*, and *indivisos* terminated in the opening decades of the century to the detriment of the peasants, as cattlemen, inspired by rising beef prices, wanted more land and no longer had to pacify labour in what was quickly becoming a society with a surplus of workers.

Of colossal importance to the Cauca Valley, given the presence for the first time of land pressure, was the simultaneous opening of the Panama Canal and of a railway from the Valley to the Pacific Ocean. The com-mercial potential of the Valley, so tantalizingly promised for decades, could now be realized, and agriculture could be transformed from a plaything of 'sun and rain', as it had been called, into a rational business.

The fate of the peasantry is most graphically revealed when we turn to the south of the Valley, where the peasant population was largest and densest.

According to official statistics the population of the Caloto area (today's) Norte del Cauca region) had remained at around 20,000 throughout the second half of the nineteenth century. But by 1918 it was about 30,000, and it had reached 66,000 by 1950. As for the nearby city of Cali, the provincial capital, its population of around 12,500 had grown to 25,000 by 1905, and by 1938 it had 88,366 inhabitants.

By the early twentieth century, Japio and its immediate surroundings had changed ownership. A large part had gone via daughter marriage to the up-and-coming Holguín family, with wealthy industrial and rural interests, which provided Colombia with two presidents. Smaller parts of the holdings went to middle-class entrepreneurs, who turned to cattle-raising and cocoa production. The peasantry was put on the defensive as myriad land claims by wealthy businessmen descended on them. 'We are the government, and our fences are our titles' was the landlords' reply to anguished peasants who stubbornly retained faith in the law, as fences were driven through their plots, evicting tenants and squatters indiscriminately. The process started slowly around 1910, with the smaller landlords taking the initiative. These were men who lived close to the peasants but were not of them – men who understood them and knew how to manipulate them, insinuating themselves into the peasant labyrinth. They converted the free peasant 'squatters' first into *concertados* with tiny and insufficient plots in return for labour services, and then in the late 1920s into fully fledged wage-earning rural proletarians without any land, lumped into new villages such as Villarrica. As prospects quickened, the Arboledas' affinal descendants of the Holguín family returned in 1913, after many years' absence, in order 'to dominate the blacks and expand their *hacienda*', in the words of one of their old *mayordomos*. They were able to roll back hundreds of free peasant families, force through fences and pastures, and claim increased ground rents from those who remained. Threats of armed conflict arose but were cooled by the arbitration of one of the most important black leaders in the area, regarded as a bandit by the landed class, and as a charmed person with magical powers by the peasantry. Such leaders rose to fame in the *Mil Días* War as colonels and generals of local guerrillas, and they were said to have large but hidden *fincas* (farms) with 'many wives'. Local legend has it that they could transform themselves into animals and plants and were immune to bullets. Similar dispossession occurred to the northeast of the Río Paila, where the Eders forcefully and success-

424

Michael Taussig

fully contested peasant claims to a giant *indiviso*, on which one of the biggest sugar plantations in Colombia now stands.

The ambivalence involved in struggles led by bandit chiefs was largely eliminated in the 1920s, as peasants formed defensive but militant *sindicatos*, a wave of which spread all over Colombia in the second and third decades of the century. They also began to commercialize their own agriculture, spending a greater proportion of their time and land on marketable crops such as cocoa and coffee. This was in response to the new monetary demands by the landlords, who were determined to make up in rent for what they could not lay their hands on by evicting their tenants, and to the more subtle but equally effective pressures of incoming commercial middlemen, representing large trading houses with tentacles stretching from as far away as the capital or the northern hemisphere.

A part-time resident of the Valley, descendant of the Eder family, has left us a description of rural commerce at this time. The bulk of the country's business was done by general stores, which functioned as exporters and importers, wholesalers and retailers. Foreign trade worked through commission houses for American and European firms. Even a large part of the gold and silver went through the same companies. As for coffee, the larger planters shipped direct to the commission merchants, to whom they were often indebted for advances. The smaller ones sold to the general stores, which financed the purchases with sixty- and ninety-day drafts on the commission houses. Local dealers had agents, who scoured the countryside. These local dealers may have been independent but more often were in very close relationship to, if not actually the purchasing agents of, the foreign houses, many of which also owned a number of plantations which they had taken over as debt securities.[40]

By the second decade of the century, the extreme southern region's commercial and population centre had shifted to 'black territory', in the depths of the dark jungle (*monte oscuro*), as it was called by outsiders. Here, the blacks slowly evolved a flourishing market at the junction of two tributaries of the Río Cauca, linked to the city of Cali by the river system. By the late 1920s this centre, called Puerto Tejada, had become part of the road network, which allowed for a freer and more varied movement of goods, and also took a good deal of the transport business away from blacks, who had previously monopolized the riverine transport. Above all, it signified the region's commercial coming of age. As peasants turned more and more to cash crops, they became involved in a vicious circle whereby dependence on money to the detriment of the 'natural economy' and local self-sufficiency led to their selling most of what they produced and buying most of what they consumed. The crop they chiefly relied on was cocoa, which did superbly well under local conditions, required very little labour (far less than coffee), was what they had been used to since slavery, had a high selling price, and, what is more, could not easily be removed by landlord predators greedy for cattle and sugar lands. As peasant *sindicatos* gathered temporary strength, and a mild agrarian reform was activated in the mid-1930s in response to growing rural violence throughout the country, so tree crops like cocoa also acquired a legal importance, as they represented improvements for which any landlord bent on appropriation would have to pay compensation. These plantings were initiated by the peasantry without any capital overhead costs; they emerged slowly and naturally out of their diverse holdings in steady proportion to the decrease in subsistence agriculture on which they lived while waiting the five or so years the cocoa needed to mature. This became impossible later on, when holdings became too small to achieve this balance, and cacao planting after that date meant getting into debt during the period of waiting.

The middlemen who flocked to the area acquired complete political and economic control over the Puerto Tejada area. They were white, generally from Antioquía, and mostly members of the Conservative party. By the late 1930s, land pressure was acute. The sugar industry in particular, and large-scale agriculture in general, was on a very firm footing, institutionalized into the social fabric by stable financial arrangements and powerful landlords' associations welded together by a common fear of the peasantry and the need to control marketing and infrastructural development. Technological advances, with new and improved varieties of cane, other crops, and livestock (*cebú*), began with the Chardon mission and the opening of the Palmira agricultural school in the early 1930s. A local black schoolteacher wrote in 1945, in an appeal to the government:

For a long time now many people have been forced off the land here. Most people have only two to ten acres and nearly all grow cocoa exclusively. Most of the peasants are illiterate and only know how to work their plots. During the first decades things went well because the soil was so rich and there were no plagues. But now there are too many people. *Minifundia* and mono-production have emerged with all their dreadful consequences. The occupants of each plot doubled and tripled in a short time, and the plots became smaller. In the past fifteen years the situation has changed threateningly. Today, each crop gets smaller and smaller, and the harvest is preceded by a long wait; thousands of physically active people are forced into idleness . . . usury increases, stealing increases, life is now a pendulum oscillating between misery and forlorn hopes. The peasants of Puerto Tejada are suffering a situation without parallel. It is obvious that it is not possible to limit this process, yet neither is it possible to diminish the danger of this situation as more and more people are deprived of their patrimony.'

In 1948, with the assassination of Gaitán, the populist leader of the Liberal party, a frustrated social revolution which had been brewing since the 1920s broke out all over Colombia. The predominance of the old party hatreds and ideology, together with the failure of any of the political organizations to assert overall control, resulted in a ceaseless *Violencia* which coursed through the countryside for more than ten years, turning peasant against peasant according to party allegiance and territoriality, and resulting in the death of over 200,000 people. Patron—client hierarchies became bandit groups, often detaching themselves from their urban *patrones*; various species of *mafioso* sprang up, and some communist guerrillas emerged as well.

One effect of this was to drive peasants off the land, as the dangers of rural isolation and landlord opposition to antiquated forms of tenure in developing regions were allowed full scope. In the Puerto Tejada area, the blacks, unlike practically any other rural area in the country, reacted to Gaitán's murder with a spontaneous uprising in which the stores and bars of the white elite were sacked and an anarchic rebellion, more a revelry than a concerted political assault, took place. It died away as quickly as it had begun, thanks to aerial machine gunning and the arrival of government troops who sustained martial law and Conservative party rule for the next ten years. This was not lost on some local landlords, who began to appropriate what was left of the peasants' lands by force and 'offers they could not refuse'. To these were added hired bandits, flooding, blocking of access, and finally, in the early fifties, aerial spraying of herbicides which killed the shade trees of the cocoa plantings and, later, much of the cocoa itself.

There was a sudden drop in the cocoa production of this region commencing between 1950 and 1953, so that by 1958 the basis of the peasant economy had suffered an 80 per cent decline. It was no coincidence that this was when two new sugar plantations were set up. An analysis of two of the four local land registry offices shows that the owner of these two plantations 'bought' 270 separate parcels of land between 1950 and 1969 and, with hardly an exception, these were all peasant plots acquired through extortion.[41]

The township itself was changed from a service and marketing centre into a rural slum, little more than a barracks and dormitory for landless sugar cane workers. To the steady stream of the locally dispossessed was added in the 1960s the flood of black migrants from the Pacific coast, fresh from a subsistence culture and, at first, eager for wage work in the cane fields which the locals despised. In the fourteen years between 1951 and 1964, the town's population almost doubled, and migrants came to constitute almost one-third of the population. Most of the land was under sugar cane, and only one-fifth of the area's population actually lived in the countryside. The sugar growers' association estimated that half of their work force was made up of migrants, with the other half made up of people displaced by the expansion of their plantations. Sugar production in the Valley as a whole from 1950 onwards increased at an annual rate of about 10 per cent.[42]

During the first thirty years of major 'take-off', the plantations and their associated mills had concentrated ever-increasing amounts of land and labour into unified corporate monoliths, owning all the cane land and allowing workers to form unions as part of the national trade-union movement which had begun in the 1930s. This system of manifest and direct control was speedily dismantled in the early 1960s by an atomization of land holdings and the work force. This radical shift, in many ways a reversion to the structures of the nineteenth century, occurred when for the first time Colombia was given an assured place in the U.S.A. sugar import quota, as a result of the exclusion of Cuban sugar following the Revolution. Militant and successful strikes by rural labour for wage increases seriously threatened production, and instead of continuing to expand and consolidate, the plantations now turned to smaller private contractors to provide cane and labour. By 1964, almost two-thirds of the cane milled came either from rented lands or from wealthy farmers growing cane on ten-year contracts, and about half the work to produce the Valley's sugar was done by contracted labourers working in small, unstable gangs at minimal wages, moving from one job and one small contractor to another. These workers were outside the trade-union structure, could not legally strike, and were ineligible for costly social security benefits.

The contraction of the land base of the local peasantry in the Puerto Tejada region, still practising bilateral partible inheritance, was also aggravated by the penetration of the capitalist mode of production and the modern technology of the 'green revolution'. The typical peasant mode of social organization is the *vereda* (neighbourhood) composed of several dispersed peasant households, centred on one or two *kulaks* or rich peasants, who possess a great surplus of land (around 50 hectares) above their subsistence needs. Beneath this tiny stratum lies a small class of 'middle peasants' who control about 7 hectares each, an amount which requires neither outside labour nor the seeking of outside sources of income. The vast bulk of the peasantry is made up of *minifundistas* or poor peasants with 1 hectare or less of untitled land, who gain a miserable living by working off their plots, either as *peones* for low wages but in easy conditions for the rich peasants (to whom they are usually related as kin), or as labourers hired by individual village labour contractors, themselves contracted by the plantations.[43]

Until recently, the basic peasant crops were cocoa and some coffee, with a few plantains as a staple food. These are all perennials; what is more, in this region they yield throughout the year (as does the sugar cane), being harvested and supplying a small cash income every two weeks. Cocoa and coffee each have two peak periods of production at distinct six-month intervals, so that the decline in the production of one is compensated for by the rise in the other, thereby neatly ensuring a fairly regular income. However, the incentives of modern technology (tractors, mechanization, fertilizers, and the new plant species) together with government encouragement and U.S. assistance[44] have led the rich and middle peasants to uproot their trees and plant strictly seasonal crops like soya beans and corn. These crops require heavy capital outlays and a seasonal pattern of work, and yield income only two or three times a year. This, plus the fact that natural drainage is poor (which is of little consequence to cocoa), has meant the ruin of an increasing number of peasants, whose land and labour subsequently find their way into the plantation sector. This process is further stimulated by the Valley's regional development agency, which through discriminated loans encourages the plantations to rent or contract plots as small as 6 hectares for the cultivation of sugar cane. Folk religion furthers this process. Funeral rites are the only ceremony left of any importance, and the outlay on this is so great and so obligatory that many poor peasant households are forced to sell out to cover these costs. Furthermore, partition of inheritance not only is partible in form but can cause extreme conflicts, as the pattern of serial monogamy and polygamy leads to diverse and rival claims which can take years to settle.

Traditionally, when there was a land surplus, work in the peasant sector was done through reciprocal sharing and exchange labour (*cambio de mano*). In the last forty years this has given way to wage contracts as the peasantry has become increasingly stratified into hierarchical kindreds of affinally related, serially polygamous males and females. By the 1950s, the socio-economic structure of the peasantry consisted basically of local hierarchies centred on a prominent middle-aged male, surrounded by a constellation of first- and second-cousin female-headed poor peasant households, bearing his offspring and supplying his labour, with the middle peasant households filling the gaps in between. As rich peasants converted their holdings from permanent to seasonal crops and acquired the use of tractors and labour-saving harvesters, so the poor female section of the population was forced to follow the males into day-labour wage work on the plantations. This transition was stimulated by the labour contractors, who greatly preferred women to men, since the former were more 'docile' and less likely to cause trouble over wage levels and working conditions. Since by now the female-headed and increasingly isolated household bereft of kin ties was emerging as the norm, the women's amenability was not surprising, as it was these women who had to bear the immediate and daily responsibility of feeding their variously fathered children.

In keeping with the formal decentralization of the plantations, the large landlords play only a marginal or indirect role in regional politics and local administration, a far cry from the situation of thirty years ago when the landlord *was* the state and his *mayordomo* the political *jefe*. Today, this is left to minor government officials, to the local directorates of the only two permissible political parties, and, above all, to the all-white *rosca*, which is the basic cell of the Colombian power structure. Literally meaning a ring, the *rosca* is an unofficial and informal association of power-brokers who congeal the power at their respective levels of operation, ascending from the municipal base through regional coalitions to the departmental and ultimately national level, with each stage having its respective *rosca*. The two-party political division throughout the country between Conservatives and Liberals only tenuously affects this network. In the words of a successful local politician, 'a *rosca* is a group of Conservatives and Liberals who are friends of the government and who receive or manipulate posts within it'. It is also simply referred to as 'those who command'. The landlords, who without exception live outside the immediate region, have no intimate dealings with the local *rosca* or with government officials (who, of course, are selected by the *rosca*). Instead they articulate directly with the highly centralized state apparatus at its highest levels in the more important regional as well as national centres. The plantations and surrounding slum towns are putrefying hovels, which they leave behind in the dusty wakes of their high-powered jeeps and armed police escorts, equipped with two-way radios in case of assault, which is commonly feared.

For the moment the toiling population may be pacified, but this is at the cost of severe but inchoate social tension and a fearfully wide moral disjunction between classes. Social control and labour requirements have been secured as a result of a large reserve army of landless poor and surrounding *minifundistas*. This surplus is a relatively new twentieth-century phenomenon in Colombian social history. The local natural population increase and the immigration of coastal subsistence people, of course, only create a 'surplus' given the prevailing political apportionment of the means of production. The social frustrations engendered by the economic – and personally humiliating – consequences of this large reserve army are to a certain extent defused by elaborate micro-divisions which tend to reduce class solidarity.

Despite the cruel incentives of poverty,[45] labour commitment is still low. Both poor peasants and landless day-labourers try to resist pro-letarian work whenever possible and stand far removed from the 'rational' cash-maximizing models of classical economics. Plantation workers aim at fixed goals, not accumulation, and they respond to wage increases by reducing output so long as they achieve their customary desires. Egalitarian folk norms, informal social levelling mechanisms, and a profound and complex awareness of the destruction of one's humanity posed by the commodity nature of the wage-labour market are firmly implanted in the culture of the Valley's poor. People who accumulate wealth are despised and feared as agents of the Devil, and sorcery is a common sanction against them.

While the local peasantry trust only in God and themselves for maintaining production on their plots, plantation workers are commonly believed to make contracts with the Devil to increase productivity even though they have to dissipate their hard-gained earnings immediately on luxury consumer items, and even though they will die in agony. Such money cannot serve as an investment by the workers, and all capital goods thus acquired are rendered barren. The land worked in this way is rendered as sterile as the work process itself; no ratoon or cane shoot, so it is said, will ever emerge from it until the land is freshly ploughed.

In contrast to the peasant consciousness, the conception of the plantation is that the previous balance of person and nature is reversed. Here there exists a totally alien relationship to land, tool, crop, and the social organization of production – so much human energy exchanged for so much cash. Here there is the possibility of increasing income from nature, but only through the illicit device of selling one's soul to the Devil. The attribution of evil to this new and ruthless type of exploitation of person and nature could hardly be clearer, given the cultural

idiom, and its contrast to the protestant ethic and the spirit of capitalism could barely be more profound.[46]

From the foregoing it should be obvious that the course of rural
proletarianization in the Cauca Valley has followed a pattern quite
different to that established in much of the 'developed' world of Western
Europe and North America, and that this is in good part due to the very
presence and activity of the 'developed' world, filtered as it has been by
the local socio-economic conditions.

The concentration of rural industry into plantations has been
accompanied by its organizational opposite as far as the work force is
concerned. The early move towards large trade unions has been forcefully replaced by the tendency to atomize the organization of labour
into that of small gangs regulated by labour contractors.[47] Furthermore
while proletarianization of the peasantry has been largely achieved
as an objective fact, it has not been subjectively accepted as correct or
proper by the wage workers themselves. Their understanding and moral
evaluation of this new mode of production are, in other words, at odds
with the ideology that normally, or ideally, should accompany that mode
of production. These neophytic proletarians critically contrast their new
objective situation as wage labourers with the drastically different mode
of production into which they were born, with which they still retain personal contact, and from which they have been wrenched.

NOTES

1. The field work on which this study is based was carried out during 1971 and
1972 and was made financially possible by grants from the Institute of Latin
American Studies, the University of London, and the Foreign Area Fellowship
Program. Historical data on the Arboledas' *haciendas* come from the Archivo Central
del Cauca, Popayán.
2. H. Tovar Pinzón, 'Estado actual de los estudios de demografía histórica en
Colombia', *Anuario Colombiano de Historia Social y de la Cultura* V (Bogotá, 1970),
pp. 65–140. J. Friede, *Los Quimbayas bajo la dominación española* (Bogotá, 1963).
3. James Ferguson King, 'Negro slavery in the Viceroyalty of New Granada' (unpublished Ph.D. dissertation, University of California at Berkeley, 1939), p. 219.
4. King, 'Negro slavery', p. 217; H. C. Lea, *The Inquisition in the Spanish dependencies*
(New York, 1908), pp. 462–516; A. de Sandoval, *De instauranda aethiopiom salute*
(Bogotá, 1956).
5. W. F. Sharp, 'Forsaken but for gold: an economic study of slavery and mining in
the Colombian Chocó, 1680–1810' (unpublished Ph.D. dissertation, University
of North Carolina at Chapel Hill, 1970), p. 276.
6. The distinction proposed by Eric R. Wolf and Sidney Mintz between *hacienda*
and plantation ('Haciendas and plantations in Middle America and the Antilles',

Social and Economic Studies VI, 3 (1957), pp. 380–412) was not observed by the people themselves in the Cauca Valley at this or at any other time, and accordingly I tend to follow the local practice of using the term '*hacienda*', except for the twentieth-century sugar mill/plantation complexes, which I call 'plantations' as they clearly come under these authors' definition of large-scale, profit-oriented agricultural enterprises with abundant capital and a dependent labour force.

7. G. Colmenares, *Haciendas de los jesuítas en el nuevo reino de Granada, siglo XVIII* (Bogotá, 1969), p. 124. The Colombian silver *peso* up to 1880 was on a par with the U.S. dollar.

8. All metal equipment was made by local blacksmiths from imported iron – a situation quite different from that in the second half of the nineteenth century, when even machetes were being imported from London!

9. At this time, 685 lb of fat were consumed annually: 200 lb to grease the mill, 420 for candles of general use, and 65 for candles for the big May *fiesta*.

10. Of the 200 hides per year, half went into harnesses for the drawing of ploughs, cane, and timber, and one-third was used in the construction of beds for the sick and slaves in childbirth; twelve were used for leather pack bags (*zurrones*), and ten were sold at one-sixth of a *peso* each.

11. This figure does not allow for the cost of buying slaves. Prices averaged around 400 *pesos* for an adult male and 300 *pesos* for a female for most of the period, declining greatly towards the end of the eighteenth century when the Crown had to institute a policy of lending capital to miners, which was very tardily repaid. See Fermín de Vargas, the eighteenth-century Colombian author, in his *Pensamientos políticos*, (Bogotá, 1944), and Sharp, 'Forsaken but for gold'. Both suggest an annual profit of 160 *pesos* per slave, although Sharp shows how extremely variable these profits were.

12. J. Jaramillo Uribe, *Ensayos sobre historia social Colombiana* (Bogotá, 1968), p. 22.

13. This also appears to have been the case on the Pacific coast at this time. Sharp, 'Forsaken but for gold', p. 265.

14. José María Arboleda Llorente, *El indio en la colonia* (Bogotá, 1948), p. 69.

15. J. P. Harrison, 'The Colombian tobacco industry from government monopoly to free trade: 1778–1876' (unpublished Ph.D. dissertation, University of California at Berkeley, 1951), pp. 39–40, 134.

16. H. A. Bierck, Jr, 'The struggle for abolition in Gran Colombia', *Hispanic American Historical Review* XXXIII, 3 (August 1953), pp. 365–86.

17. J. Arroyo, *Historia de la gobernación de Popayán*, 2nd edn. 2 vols. (Bogotá, 1955), vol. 2, p. 96.

18. Jaramillo Uribe, *Ensayos*, pp. 68–71.

19. G. Arboleda, *Historia de Cali*, 3 vols. (Cali, 1956), vol. 2, pp. 306–7.

20. J. León Helguera et al., 'La exportación de esclavos en la Nueva Granada', *Archivos* I, 3 (Bogotá, 1967), pp. 447–59.

21. E. Posada and C. Restrepo Canal, *La esclavitud en Colombia, y leyes de manumisión* (Bogotá, 1933), pp. 83–5.

22. S. Arboleda, *La república en america española* (Bogotá, 1972), p. 238.

23. Ibid., p. 331.

24. W. P. McGreevey, *An economic history of Colombia, 1845–1930* (Cambridge, 1971), p. 160. See also L. Scemarda, *Reise um die Erde in den Jahren 1852–1859*, 3 vols. (Berlin, 1863–5), vol. 3, pp. 324–32 (cited in P. J. Eder, *El fundador* (Bogotá, 1959), p. 410).

25. F. Pérez, *Jeografía física i política del estado del Cauca* (Bogotá, 1862), pp. 212–13.
26. Ibid., pp. 137–9.
27. E. Palau, *Memoria sobre el cultivo del cacao, del café y del té* (Bogotá, 1889), p. 28.
28. F. von Schenck, *Viajes por Antioquia en el año de 1880* (Bogotá, 1953), p. 54.
29. Compare Sidney Mintz's concepts of an 'opposition' and a 'proto-peasantry' in the social evolution of the Caribbean, and Nancy Solien González's formulation of 'neoteric societies' (Mintz, 'The question of Caribbean peasantries: a comment', *Caribbean Studies* I, 3 (1961); Solien González, *Black Carib household structure* (Seattle, 1969), p. 10).
30. J. P. Harrison, 'The evolution of the Colombia tobacco trade, to 1875', *Hispanic American Historical Review* XXXII, 2 (1952), p. 173.
31. J. V. Lombardi, *The decline and abolition of Negro slavery in Venezuela 1820–1854* (Westport, Conn. 1971), p. 53.
32. *Informe que el secretario de gobierno en el estado del Cauca presenta al gobernador* (Popayán, 1859), pp. 26–7.
33. Departamento Administrativo Nacional de Estadística, *Anuario estadístico de Colombia* (Bogotá, 1875), p. 139.
34. Palau, *Memoria*, pp. 9–13.
35. Eder, *El fundador*, pp. 111, 162.
36. Ibid., p. 395.
37. This mode of production seems to have been common for tobacco and other lowland crops. See Great Britain, Foreign Office, 'Report on the agricultural conditions of Colombia', *Diplomatic and Consular Reports on Trade and Finance, Annual Series*, vol. C, no. 446 (December 1888), p. 637.
38. Eder, *El fundador*, p. 439.
39. Ibid., p. 163.
40. P. J. Eder, *Colombia* (London, 1913), pp. 124–5.
41. The speed with which this was accomplished – during the period of the *Violencia* – deserves emphasis. A study of the number of peasant plots acquired by sugar plantations throughout the entire Valley (not just its southern section) between the years 1922 and 1953 reveals that a mere 169 plots smaller than 25 hectares were taken over during those thirty-two years (S. Mancini M., 'Tenencia y uso de la tierra por la industria azucarera del valle del Cauca', *Acta Agronómica* IV, 1 (Facultad de Agronomía, Palmira, Colombia), p. 30). In passing it should be pointed out that these figures, obtained as they are from land registry records, are bound to be under-estimations.
42. The owners of the plantations and mills are Colombian citizens. Nevertheless, foreign capital has played an important part, and its role appears to be increasing.
43. It is important to note that while the poor local peasants who enter the ranks of the plantations' labour force do so mainly as part-time contract workers, the coastal immigrants tend to find a place amongst the 'permanently' employed (*afiliados*).
44. U.S. Agency for International Development; Rockefeller, Ford, and Kellogg Foundations.
45. Clinical studies (based on height, weight, and physical signs) indicate that around one-half of the child population – fifteen years old or less – living in both town and countryside is suffering from mild to serious malnutrition.
46. This is clearly a striking case of the cultural recognition of the process referred to by Karl Marx and others as 'alienation'. It involves not just the feeling of opposition

or conflict between classes, but also fundamentally opposed world views, epistemologies, and moral systems.

47. Much of this process has been well described by Rolf Knight, *Sugar plantations and labor patterns in the Cauca Valley, Colombia*, Department of Anthropology, University of Toronto, Anthropological Series no. 12 (1972).

CHAPTER 17

The post–emancipation origins of the relationships between the estates and the peasantry in Trinidad

BRIAN W. BLOUET[1]

In 1848, nearly fifteen years after the abolition of slavery, Lord Harris, the governor of Trinidad, declared in a dispatch to the Colonial Office that 'a race had been freed, but a society had not been formed'. Harris was recognizing that although fundamental changes had been wrought in the basic rights of the black population 'little attention had been paid to any legislation having for its end the formation of a society on true, sound and lasting principles'.[2] The abolition of slavery had established a constitutional setting in which economic and social progress for the bulk of the population was now possible, but abolition alone could not promote that progress.

The abolition of slavery did not dissolve vested interests, established patterns of thought, or the unchallenged place of plantation owners and shareholders at the top of the hierarchy. Freedom in its basic sense did not mean for the black population freedom from the pressures and established advantages of a socio-economic system marked by massive gulfs in the distribution of wealth and privilege. Furthermore the termination of slavery did not itself bring about immediate changes in agricultural practices. The period of apprenticeship (1834–8) held the former slaves to the estates, and when release came the labouring population moved away from the plantations over a period of years. In Trinidad it would appear that labour shortages on the plantations did not become acute until the early 1840s.

As the labouring population moved off the plantations and began to establish itself as an independent peasantry it had to compete, within the framework of colonial society, with the established interests which had long controlled agriculture and land ownership. However, the evolution from an owner–slave situation to an estate–peasant relationship was a process which not only encompassed landowners of substance and former slaves but was also influenced by the government of Trinidad, the Colonial Office, the Colonial Land and Emigration Commissioners, anti-slavery societies, immigrant labourers, and the governments of those countries from which migrants emanated. The situation was multi-faceted and clearly liable to alteration of the loading of the constituent pressures. Whether or not a peasant was employed on an estate or held land from an estate was not necessarily important, since the larger landowners attempted to exert influences which had an impact upon the living conditions of peasants who were independent occupiers of land. In short, the plantation owners sought to control the legal bases of society in such a way as to preserve existing interests and privilege. In the light of the foregoing statement it is evident that the analysis of the relationships between large landowners and the peasantry cannot be undertaken without cognizance of a wide range of political, social, and economic variables. Much research on West Indian social and economic history in the nineteenth century is only just coming to fruition, and our knowledge of many socio-economic factors is still slight. Nevertheless it may be useful to review what can be discerned regarding the manner in which the major interest groups behaved in attempting to secure control of resources.

The planters

When the act to abolish slavery in British possessions was passed in 1833, West Indian planters turned their thoughts gloomily to the problem of how an adequate labour supply was to be maintained for the purpose of working the sugar estates. At first the West India Committee attempted to press the British government to sanction tough labour laws, and penalties for those leaving the plantations.[3] When it became clear that controls of this type could not survive the apprenticeship period, at least in the Crown colonies, planters in Trinidad worked as best they could to manipulate the local situation.

The predominant view amongst the planting class in Trinidad was that the slave population would abandon the estates and cease to constitute a reliable supply of labour. The immediate political task, as the planters saw the problem, was to arrange the land and labour laws of the colony to prevent the establishment of a class of small independent farmers and to keep the extensive Crown lands in the colony closed to smallholders, whether they be squatters or men with sufficient savings to purchase a few acres of land on which to establish a homestead. In preventing sales of small acreages of Crown land the pressure group was successful until 1847 and, indeed, succeeded at one point in getting the minimum size of lots to be disposed of doubled from 320 to 640 acres (approximately 130 to 260 hectares).[4] Even at £1 per acre, land in such parcels was only within reach of well-capitalized interests.

Unauthorized occupation of Crown lands or abandoned estates by those lacking benefit of title was a more difficult matter to curb. In 1838 an Order in Council had been issued which gave summary powers to stipendary magistrates in Trinidad, British Guiana, St Lucia, and Mauritius to remove unauthorized occupiers of land where such possession had not exceeded twelve months' duration. The measure proved ineffective in Trinidad, for there was not the necessary organization to gather evidence and initiate proceedings. William Burnley, a wealthy planter of the day, soon appreciated the difficulty and sought the opinion of a leading Trinidad barrister. Burnley was advised that the law was on the wrong footing in that it treated squatting as a private rather than a public offence.[5] Since the necessary acts would have violated some principles of English land law, the Colonial Office would have resisted sanctioning any legislation designed to bring about the change that Burnley desired. Nor could the planters tamper with the 1838 Order in Council which defined the powers of the stipendary magistrates when dealing with squatters, but they had a good chance of altering the procedures laid down in 1839 by which the Order was administered in the island, and they set about the task with some determination.

In September 1842, while the Chief Justice, Mr Scotland, was out of the island, the Legislative Council, on which the planters were heavily represented, passed revised forms of procedure which allowed much more in the way of summary eviction. The Governor apparently failed to appreciate exactly what the planting interest was about, but when the Chief Justice returned, he argued successfully to the Colonial Office that parts of the revised procedures were illegal.

In the same year the planters were able to persuade the Legislative Council to set up a Committee of Enquiry into the *Quantity of Land Occupied by Squatters*,[6] which gathered a great body of evidence to document the illegal occupation of Crown and private territory. This move backfired in that the information emphasized to the government of Trinidad and the Colonial Office the urgent need to devise a scheme for opening up the Crown lands to small settlers in an organized manner. James Stephen read the report of the Committee of Enquiry and was moved to comment, 'to create an artificial scarcity of land in Trinidad, is as hopeful a scheme as it would be to create an artificial scarcity of water in Holland'.[7] As a result Governor Macleod was given some encouragement by the Colonial Office to develop settlement schemes for smallholders, but the Colonial Lands and Emigration Commissioners raised sufficient objections to forestall the programme.

Little more was heard of land settlement schemes for a time, but in 1846, when Lord Harris arrived to take up the Governorship, he quickly devised a far-sighted rural development scheme which not only would have made Crown lands available in small lots at reasonable prices but would have laid the basic structure for the improvement of rural areas. The Governor's project was considered by the Colonial Office and the Colonial Lands and Emigration Commissioners and gained general approval. The planting interest was not to be entirely disregarded, for when the necessary legislation was passed in Trinidad, the terms on which land was to be disposed of were not as liberal as might have been suggested by the correspondence between Harris and the Colonial Office.[8] Shortly afterwards the price of Crown land was revised upwards, and it was decided to apply the proceeds to the costs of bringing in migrants,[9] whereas formerly the Governor had seen the land sale money as being earmarked for educational purposes and for the provision of basic services in the new villages which were laid out as a part of the settlement scheme.[10] Of course, the introduction of migrant labour would have the effect of helping to depress wages on plantations.

The reason for these important changes are not hard to find. The committee of the Legislative Council which dealt with the disposal of Crown land was heavily loaded with persons who enjoyed planting interests, and it is probable that they were able to use the worsening economic circumstances which marked the year 1847 as a lever in their argument. Harris was to regret the altered policy, at least in part, for in the following year he was lamenting that a 'wasteful and ill-regulated immigration has greatly assisted in promoting reckless speculation'.[11] What was more, many of the coolie immigrants were unemployed and came to require support from the government.[12]

In 1848 Harris's land settlement scheme was further undermined by economic circumstances and the selling off of small lots to labourers by speculators in uncultivated estate land.[13] By now the Governor had lost faith in many things, and his view of West Indian affairs was so different from that which he had held prior to leaving England that he presented his opinions to Grey by private letter rather than public despatch.[14] His view of the black population as workers was soured, and he commented, 'I hear of violence committed by planters or managers or overseers but my only surprise is that such cases do not happen daily.'[15] What the Governor did not add was that in 1847 wages for field labourers slumped by 25 to 30 per cent,[16] and that in 1848 they fell by 30 to 50 per cent.[17] In addition, many estates were months behind with payment to their workers. It is not surprising in these circumstances that Harris found that 'there can be no doubt that the Negro population is becoming both more disinclined to work on estates and more difficult to deal with when working and that any competition which has yet been brought to bear, has had little or no effect on them'.[18]

Throughout the period of difficulty in the late 1840s the Governor was exposed to the arguments of a group of influential planters who served on the Legislative Council. While economically the times were hard this group of men helped guide policy in such a way as to bring it into line with what the planters saw as their best interests in a bad situation. Although it is probable that many of Harris's schemes of improvement would have suffered in the economic recession, they would undoubtedly have fared better had the Governor received less opposition from self-interested men.

While the planting interests were well represented in the Legislative Council, the enactments of that body could be overruled by the Governor or disallowed in London by the Colonial Office. This constitutional limitation placed restraints on the forms of legislation which any interest group might hope to introduce successfully. Nevertheless there were many areas into which the Colonial Office would hesitate to reach. For example, the planting interest was highly effective in promoting legislation to allow the introduction of migrant labourers under contract. So influential were the major estate-owners and so important was the industry deemed to be that it was possible for the interest group to get the Trinidad treasury to meet a part of the costs of the migrant labour schemes, in spite of the fact that Lord Harris was of the opinion that the area under sugar should be determined by economic circumstances and not artificially maintained by subsidy.[19]

It can be argued that the allocation of scarce financial resources in the late 1840s was justifiable on the grounds that sugar production was the major economic activity on the islands, and that not to support it would cause widespread hardship. However, the sugar-estate interest group was able to exert an influence upon the local legislature which resulted in the provision of funds to support a part of the costs of immigration for many decades. It would seem that Howard Johnson's recent remarks to the effect that 'in the years following 1884 the indentured immigrant was used by the planting class to depress the wages of the estate labourer'[20] could apply equally to the post-emancipation period.

During that part of the nineteenth century which followed upon the abolition of slavery the planters haggled about wages, and about the rents of the huts and lands occupied by workers on the estates, but this was not the principal thrust of their activities in their relations with the peasantry. A major effort was made, via the Legislative Council, to control policy and the legal basis of society in such a way as to main-

tain and improve the position of the substantial estate-owners in an economic sense. The global economic trends were against the large sugar producers. Competition in world markets was fierce, and in the years after slavery they had to undergo the massive burden of adjusting from a credit to a cash economy. Yet in terms of preserving their position in Trinidad in relation to the peasantry, the planters were rather more successful than might have been anticipated, even if they did not achieve the form of *hacienda* society which would have been the outcome of the policies they were advocating.

Elsewhere in this volume Peter Eisenberg observes of the sugar region of Pernambuco in the nineteenth century that the planters 'remained dominant politically and followed their clear economic self-interest'. A similar conclusion could be drawn for Trinidad: it is as if monoculture plantation societies gave rise to political systems in which one interest group must inevitably be overwhelmingly dominant and must forestall the search for solutions which might ease economic and social problems.

The Colonial Office

As the institution of slavery was extinguished in the British empire, administrators at the Colonial Office could envisage problems arising as the newly created peasantry severed at least some links with the plantations. There was a widely held fear that when the former slaves were freed of labour obligations to the estates there would be a tendency for the peasantry to revert to subsistence activities and become widely scattered through the forests and savannahs of the island. It was to combat some facets of this supposed problem that Lord Howick wanted to impose a tax on land, particularly in British Guiana, Trinidad, and St Lucia, in such a way as to prevent a proliferation of smallholdings. The proposal was not well received by the likes of Henry Taylor[21] and James Stephen,[22] who saw it as a device which might be manipulated to create a dependent peasantry.

The fears of dispersion of the population were in part soundly based, and it is undoubtedly true that several disadvantages would be incurred in the process of rural development if a degree of control were not applied to the process of land settlement. Apart from the question of providing adequate titles to land occupied on a haphazard basis, the provision of roads and rural services becomes more complicated if the population is excessively dispersed. Recent work on the development of settlement patterns would tend to suggest that there is an initial phase of colonization during which random patterns emerge, followed by a competitive phase in which many of the earlier habitation sites decline and the population concentrates in a small number of centres.[23] In short, a planned settlement programme should be able to eliminate the first rather wasteful trial-and-error phase.[24]

There were then reasonable fears within the Colonial Office that a dispersion of population would lead to the wasteful utilization of human and physical resources. Whether such a dispersion would take place or not was another matter, and only James Stephen expressed strong doubts concerning the view that the former slaves would move into the un-occupied lands of the West Indian islands and become subsistence farmers. His opinion was expressed in the following terms:

In several West Indian islands there are large towns, with a great civic population in whom the migratory, land-occupying, passion has never been developed and could scarcely be roused into activity now. The stores of Kingston, George Town, and Spanish Town, are not only kept by a sort of colonial cockney (who abhors the wilderness) but contain allurements to exertion of which the whole rural populations have already felt the influence.[25]

Stephen concluded that the populations would remain close to the existing towns and villages, within reach of work when cash was required or desired. Although not borne out in all the West Indian islands, as far as Trinidad was concerned it was a remarkably accurate prediction, and it ran contrary to the predominantly held views in the colony and Whitehall.

The Colonial Office was generally concerned with problems of labour migration, working conditions, and land settlement within the colonial empire. The establishment of the Colonial Lands and Emigration Commissioners in 1841 reflected this interest, but it was a selective concern both topically and regionally. The Land Board could help with the creation of land settlement schemes on temperate grasslands but apparently never comprehended the conditions pertaining in the West Indies. The inputs of the Board to proposed settlement schemes for Trinidad probably did more harm than good. In the 1840s the Board was bound up with Wakefieldian concepts of labourers working to accumulate the money necessary to pay the 'sufficient price' prior to becoming independent farmers. This philosophy was for a time skilfully utilized by the planter William Burnley, in arguments presented to the Colonial Office which purported to show that the opening of the Crown lands to smallholders was contrary to the accepted theory and practice of land settlement.

The Government of Trinidad

During the nineteenth century the government of Trinidad was headed by a Governor appointed in London, normally on the advice of the Colonial Secretary. The Governors who served during the early post-emancipation period – Hill, Macleod, and Harris – all attempted to tackle the problems which existed between the planters and the peasantry. Hill worked hard to produce a viable relationship between the parties in the apprenticeship period and achieved some degree of success.[26] Hill's basic aims were to improve working conditions and educational facilities, although he fundamentally conceived of a black peasantry which was essentially dependent upon the plantations for a living.[27] It is true to say that in varying degrees the Governors mentioned above were influenced by the fact that a great part of the revenue of the colony was derived from the sugar industry, in one form or another, and they felt constrained not to take any action which might result in the diminution of income.

At the conclusion of apprenticeship (1838) there developed a considerable withdrawal of labour from the plantations together with the growth of untitled occupation of Crown land and uncultivated estate land. To meet the squatting problem Sir Henry Macleod conceived of a scheme for opening up the Crown lands to the peasant cultivator.[28] The project envisaged the construction of new roads with the dual object of improving communications and making accessible tracts of Crown land for settlement on smallholdings running back from the thoroughfares. Potential rural service centres were to be provided in the form of newly laid-out villages that were to be an integral part of the project.

A partial cause of the failure to adopt Macleod's ideas was the fact that they did not generate any enthusiasm with the Lands and Emigration Commissioners,[29] a body which tended to view the question of land settlement through the lenses of Wakefieldian theory and did not fully comprehend that the Trinidadian squatting problem was in existence and required some form of positive response.

Lord Harris devised a most far-sighted rural settlement scheme,[30] but as we have seen he was apparently induced to make it less liberal to the smallholder than he had originally intended. When in the 1847 financial crisis a local bank and a large merchant house with extensive interests in Trinidad collapsed, numerous plantations ceased operation, wages for labourers on estates were greatly reduced and the demand for land made available under Harris's scheme was swiftly curtailed (Figure 7).

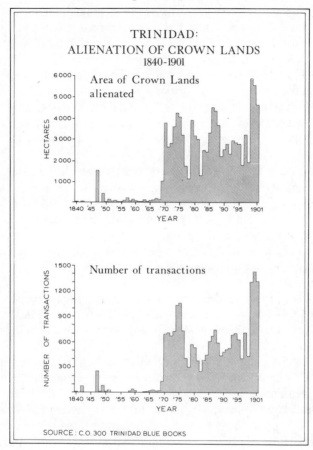

Fig. 7

For the next decade the labour requirements of the plantations were principally met by indentured labourers, while the peasants of African stock consolidated their position on the margins and in the interstices of the sugar-growing regions of the island. In 1863 the Governor was asked by the Secretary of State for the Colonies to comment upon the ideas of a Mr Guppy, warden of the North Naprina ward union, who had suggested that the present laws relating to the transfer of lands caused considerable expense.[31] The Governor was unimpressed, and Chief Justice Knox – a man not unconnected with the planting interest – submitted an opinion which held that the system then in operation worked well and at a moderate price. The opinion, however, was only valid in relation to transfers of large blocks of land, for some fees were levied upon all transfers and had a great impact upon the price of land sold in small tracts. The Colonial Office took notice of Mr Guppy's view and requested that the governor examine the question in greater detail. Whether this directive had a catalytic effect is difficult to say, but in the next few years the whole question of land transfers and Crown land sales was investigated with the result that a viable Crown land disposal policy was embarked upon, and land was made available in small parcels to the peasant cultivator and the farmer of modest means on the reasonable terms of £1 per acre.

By the early 1860s the agricultural frontier was once more expanding rapidly and squatting on Crown lands was on the upsurge.[32] It came to be recognized that the opening up of Crown lands would provide for a legitimate aspiration,[33] as well as achieving, in Carnarvon's words, 'a favourable grouping of the population'.[34] A longer-term objective was the encouragement of different types of cash crops (for example, cacao, coffee, cotton) and the expansion of the acreage devoted to food crops and pasture.[35]

The result of the re-evaluation of Crown land policy, a process which involved a number of governors and officials, was to make land available at £1 per acre with minimal costs and application procedures.[36] The necessary legislation was passed during the governorship of Arthur Hamilton Gordon in 1868, but not before the large landowning interests had made a determined, but abortive, attempt to emasculate the scheme in the legislature.[37] The 1868 legislation, and the administrative machine that was set up to supervise it, quickly brought squatting under control,[38] and by the end of the century it had become a thing of the past.[39]

Examination of Figure 7 will show that during the last third of the nineteenth century considerable acreages of Crown land were made available to the peasantry in relatively small lots. As far as it went this scheme, which benefited peasants of African and Indian stock, was excellent. But failure to wed the alienation of land to a comprehensive rural development programme resulted in the appearance of many of those difficulties which had been feared in the immediate post-emancipation years – a dispersed rural population which was lacking in adequate service centres and not sufficiently linked with the economy of the island. The West India Royal Commission of 1897 commented upon the problem of roads into the newly opened areas, and in 1930 the West Indian Sugar Commission again drew attention to this deficiency.[40] A. L. Jolly, in studies of peasant agriculture undertaken in the mid-1940s, was able to demonstrate the difficulties many smallholders had in marketing crops satisfactorily due to isolation problems.[41]

The ex-slaves

During the period of apprenticeship the majority of the former slaves remained upon the estates, but with the cessation of the obligations of apprenticeship a large percentage of the now free labourers moved off the plantations over a period of a few years. Some went to the towns; others bought plots of land with the money accumulated during apprenticeship;[42] and many squatted on Crown land or uncultivated estate lands. Within a short time the plantations were suffering a labour shortage.

The planters complained vociferously concerning the idleness of the black population, and many later commentators have represented this supposed idleness as a response and a reaction to slavery and the drudgery of forced field labour. However, the behaviour of the greatest part of the black population can also be seen as a reasonable economic response in view of the low wages offered and the uncertainty of payment.

It had been widely predicted that the cessation of apprenticeship would be shortly followed by the disappearance of the former slaves into the interior forests of the island where they would, in the parlance of the day, revert to barbarism. In contrast to many West Indian islands, for example Jamaica, events in Trinidad revealed a different pattern. Certainly the free labourers left the estates; a few moved deep into the forests, but the majority migrated a short distance, taking up residence on the margins of the already settled area. Many bought plots of land along the highways, crossroads being particularly favoured, at more than respectable prices from plantation owners.[43] Estates were selling off plots of land along thoroughfares at prices which ranged from £50 to £200 per acre.

The ex-slaves who settled close to the previously cultivated lands became small farmers growing provisions for the needs of their families and for sale. Most were prepared, on an occasional basis, to offer their labour to the adjoining estates. Overall, this behaviour was an intelligent response to circumstances. The withdrawal of labour pushed up its value; the production of cash crops rendered the ex-slave independent of the estates for a livelihood; and, perhaps above all, it was simply not worth while working upon the plantations. When James Stephen asked, 'who will work for wages when he can live in independence without them? Who will work for the low wages which a sugar planter can afford when he can satisfy all his wants by cultivating unoccupied ground?' he had defined the problem with some precision.[44] The plantations did not provide regular work even if, seasonally, wages were attractive; owners were often slow to pay; and in short, it was probably more secure to expend a smaller number of hours on a smallholding than to be an irregular wage-earner on an estate. Certainly it was more secure than living on an estate which adopted the 'odious system of tenancy at will'.[45] When the planting interest spoke of the evils of squatting and the idleness of the black population it was rationalizing a desire to work an underemployed labour force on terms which would pre-empt the rewards of increased productivity wholly for the estates. 'The disease is,' wrote Stephen, 'that sugar planting is not a pursuit profitable enough to yield wages to overcome the disinclination to work for them.'[46] Not unnaturally, the rural population saw the whole question of work, wages, and security from an entirely different viewpoint from that of the planters: unfortunately, the workers' view has had few chroniclers. Studies of present-day peasant economies frequently tend to show that 'a man who lives by selling his surplus subsistence products can expect an income comparable to that earned by a day labourer, with no greater risk'.[47]

The immigrants

The labour problems of the planters were relieved in no small degree by workers brought in from overseas. The sources of supply were various[48] and included West Africa, Madeira, India, China, North America, and other West Indian islands.[49] This last source was reported, probably inaccurately, to be supplying some two thousand persons per annum around 1860, although it was said that many of the new arrivals promptly squatted on Crown lands.[50] The major source of migrant labour during the period was the indentured worker from the Indian sub-continent. The migration from India to Trinidad was introduced in 1845, halted for a while in the early 1850s by the government of India, and then resumed until 1917, when the same authority brought about a cessation. The indentured worker was initially engaged on terms which at best provided the basic necessities of life.[51] The existence of the system of indentured labour had a marked impact upon the economics of estate management, and it influenced the labour demand and supply position and thus influenced the wages available to the un-obligated peasantry who chose to work upon the estates for only a part of the year.

The East Indians introduced by the indenture system were frequently allowed to raise provisions and even to keep livestock on some estates.[52] In 1847 the indentured labourer was given the option of taking Crown land rather than a return passage to India;[53] but this facility was later curbed, probably owing to planters' fears that it might encourage squatters from amongst the indentured estate labourers. The number of Indians becoming smallholders does not appear to have been great until a successful petition was made in 1869 to Governor Gordon by a group of time-expired labourers who wanted land in lieu of a passage.[54] From this time on, many Indians remained and were to have an important impact upon land utilization and population distribution throughout the cultivated portions of the island.[55]

During the early post-emancipation period the Indian was, in the words of Henry Mitchell, 'the plank which enabled the drowning planter to escape, to what may prove a desolate island, unless he recur largely to implemental culture and improved manufacture'.[56] Mitchell's opinion was sound but the planters remained wedded to the idea of cheap labour, to a degree which was detrimental to overall social and economic development.

Some consequences of the events of the post-emancipation period

In the last third of the nineteenth century, some promising trends began to appear in Trinidadian agriculture. Land was being made available to the small cultivator. The Indian migrant, who took up farming in his own right, was emphasizing provision crops, particularly rice, while cash crops other than sugar, like cacao, coffee, and rubber, were of increasing importance. Fruit-growers were benefiting from the establishment of a steamship connection with New York. The frontier of agricultural settlement was expanding, and the areas under sugar and cacao were undergoing a secular increase. Indeed, by the end of the century in terms of the value of exports cacao was to surpass sugar.

In the process of frontier expansion the small farmer and the peasant played a critical part. For example, in 1867 the district of Montserrat was largely occupied by squatters, some of Spanish extraction, and many growing cacao.[57] After the introduction of Governor Gordon's Crown land disposal scheme, titles were rapidly regularized and the area in cacao and cane greatly expanded. Many of the original settlers were bought out and estates established, the smaller agriculturalists moving on and taking up new lands. The Blue Book for 1883 contains the following comment: 'the supposed evil of establishing too large a peasant proprietory body, seems therefore to practically remedy itself, with advantage to all classes'.[58] Shephard is of the opinion that the Spanish element in the process of cacao cultivation was constantly moving on and bringing new areas into production, often on a contract basis for estates.[59]

Thus the process of frontier expansion began to assume recognizable forms: squatting, permanent clearing and cultivation of smallholdings, and assimilation into larger units. Broadly, the story is not dissimilar from that recorded on many agricultural frontiers in the nineteenth century or on such frontiers in Latin America at the present time.

Unfortunately, the Trinidad frontier was not illimitable. There were many areas which, owing to steep slopes, poor soils, or lack of adequate communications, were difficult to bring into contact with the economy. Inevitably the pinching of the frontier led, in this century, to a growth in the number of peasants who were unable to hold land in their own right or unable to acquire sufficient land to enlarge a landholding to a viable size.

The closing of the cacao frontier was dramatic. Rising prices had sired speculation, but in 1923 the world price of cacao slumped. Within a few years witches-broom disease appeared on the island. Much land went over from the production of cacao to that of sugar, and a curious string of relationships often developed to link the peasant and the sugar factory. The former cacao estate would rent land to peasants, stipulating that cane must be grown, at the same time that a contract was entered into with a sugar factory for all the cane produced on the land. The landlord collected all proceeds from the factory and deducted any rents due before paying the cane farmer.[60]

The shift from cacao to sugar in the 1920s reinforced another trend which had been developing since the late nineteenth century. Possibly because of the economics of sugar manufacture on the larger plantations which had emerged in the last quarter of the nineteenth century, estates began to encourage the independent cultivator of cane. Peasants engaged in this activity are referred to as 'cane farmers' and still form an important part of the structure of Trinidadian agriculture. Dayanand Maharaj dates the development of cane farming from the depression of the 1880s and sees the change as having given the sugar industry a 'dichotomous existence'.[61] Inevitably there are tensions in this relationship between plantations and peasants (and other cane farmers working rather more land than would qualify them for the apellation of 'peasant'), the most important problem being the price given to the smallholder for his crop.

The present difficulties of small farmers in Trinidad can be seen as a direct result of slavery, a plantation economy, and the measures taken in the post-emancipation period. Even the positive policies bear the defects of their origins. The Crown land disposal policy, owing to the small size of most of the transactions involved, was almost bound to lead to the development of a large class of peasant proprietors who lacked sufficient resources to operate either independently or efficiently. G. E. Young Sing, in a study of peasant farming in Trinidad, found the average size of holding in the sample she studied to be only 2.63 hectares and concluded that the greatest obstacle to diversification, efficiency, and mechanization was the size structure of land holdings.[62]

It is tempting to pontificate from amidst the resources of a well-stocked library and suggest that less immigration in the nineteenth century, larger land holdings for a smaller number of peasants, and more resources devoted to rural development would have avoided at least some of the current problems. But Howard Johnson has recently shown how effective the planting interest was in the late nineteenth century in keeping immigration at a high volume and preventing the financial resources of the colony from being devoted to forms of economic activity not connected with the sugar industry.[63]

Perhaps only one senior administrator in Trinidad in the nineteenth century really comprehended the breadth of the problems faced. Lord Harris, in the fine series of despatches he wrote in the first year of his rule,[64] was advocating what amounted to a broadly based rural development programme. Unfortunately, his judgements could not survive the economic, social, and political pressures of the time.

NOTES

1. The author wishes to thank the University of Nebraska and the Woods Foundation, Chicago for having made funds available to aid research. The following members of the Landlord and Peasant symposium made particularly helpful suggestions, many of which have been incorporated in this version of the paper: Olwyn Blouet, Michael Craton, Barry Floyd, Stephanie Goodenough, John McDonald, Lea McDonald, Janet Momsen, and James Walvin.

2. Public Record Office, London, Colonial Office (hereafter cited as 'CO') 295/162, Harris to Grey, 19 June 1848.

3. Grey Papers, Durham University, Minutes of Proceedings Between His Majesty's Government and the West India Body, London, 1833.

4. Donald Wood, *Trinidad in transition* (London, 1968) p. 94.

5. CO 295/138, Extract from a letter addressed to Mr Burnley by a leading barrister in that colony, communicated by William Burnley, 20 July 1842.

6. The report of the committee was returned to England in October (CO 295/137, Chichester to Stanley, 30 October 1842). The members of the committee were Charles Warner, T. B. Wylly, William Burnley, and John Losh.

7. CO 295/137, Chichester to Stanley, 8 October 1843. Minute by James Stephen, 24 November 1843.

8. CO 295/157, Harris to Grey, 2 July 1847.

9. Ibid.

10. CO 295/156, Harris to Grey, 16 January 1847.
11. CO 295/162, Harris to Grey, 19 June 1848.
12. Grey Papers, 108/9, Harris to Grey, 20 June 1848.
13. Grey Papers, 108/9, Harris to Grey, 24 March 1849.
14. Grey Papers, 108/9, Harris to Grey, 6 September 1849.
15. Ibid.
16. Grey Papers, 150/5/7.
17. Wood, *Trinidad in transition*, p. 125.
18. Grey Papers, 108/9, Harris to Grey, 6 September 1849.
19. CO 295/162, Harris to Grey, 19 June 1848.
20. Howard Johnson, 'Immigration and the sugar industry in Trinidad during the last quarter of the nineteenth century', *Journal of Caribbean History* III (1971), p. 70.
21. Grey Papers, 146/5, Memo on Lord Howick's plan for accompanying emancipation with a tax on land, 15 August 1832.
22. Grey Papers, 146/10, Mr Stephen on land tax as an accompaniment of emancipation, 7 July 1832.
23. J. C. Hudson, 'A location theory for rural settlement', *Annals of the Association of American Geographers* LIX (1969), pp. 365–81.
24. Brian W. Blouet, 'Factors influencing the evolution of settlement patterns', in P. J. Ucko, R. Tringham, and G. W. Dimbleby (eds.), *Man, settlement and urbanism* (London, 1972), pp. 3–15.
25. Grey Papers, 146/10, Mr Stephen on land tax as an accompaniment of emancipation, 7 July 1832.
26. W. L. Burn, *Emancipation and apprenticeship in the British West Indies* (London, 1937), while initially critical of Hill (p. 173), feels that apprenticeship in Trinidad 'worked as smoothly as anywhere' (p. 363).
27. CO 295/107, Hill to Glenelg, 11 September 1835.
28. CO 295/130, Macleod to Russell, 8 June 1840.
29. CO 295/138, Land Board to Stephen, 10 March 1842.
30. More detail on the schemes of Macleod and Harris was given by the present writer in a paper entitled 'African squatting in post-emancipation Trinidad', African Studies Association, 14th Annual Conference (Denver, 1971).
31. CO 295/224, Keate to Newcastle, 23 October 1863.
32. CO 295/232, Manners-Sutton to Cardwell, 23 October 1865.
33. CO 295/239, Memorandum of Trinidad Attorney-General, 23 February 1867.
34. CO 295/239, Carnarvon to the Governor of Trinidad, 20 August 1866.
35. CO 295/325, Rushworth to Cardwell, 19 June 1866, Rushworth's Memorandum relative to squatting and the management of the Crown lands.
36. Charles Warner, the Attorney-General of Trinidad, argued on the basis of construction costs that the price of land had to be at least £2 per acre to cover the expense of building the roads necessary to connect newly opened areas with the market. Warner was, of course, associated with the planting interest, but if he was attempting to reason up the price of land the exercise was undertaken with considerable skill (CO 295/234, Memorandum of Charles W. Warner, 23 February 1867).
37. J. K. Chapman, *The career of Arthur Hamilton Gordon* (Toronto, 1964), pp. 78–83.
38. CO 300/84, Report on Crown lands for the year 1873.
39. CO 300/107, Trinidad and Tobago blue book, 1896.

40. *Report of the West Indian Sugar Commission*, Cmd. 3517 (London, 1930), pp. 110–11.

41. A. L. Jolly, 'Peasant farming in two districts of the Oropouche Lagoon, June 1944–45', *Journal of Tropical Agriculture* XXV, 5 (1948), pp. 23–32, and 'Peasant agriculture: an economic survey on the La Pastora Land Settlement, Trinidad, May 1944–45', *Journal of Tropical Agriculture* XXIII, 5 (1946), pp. 137–45.

42. Between 1832 and 1849 'the number of proprietors increased from some 2000 to over 7000' (W. Emanuel Rivière, 'Labour shortage after emancipation', *Journal of Caribbean History* IV (1972), p. 15).

43. Parliamentary Papers, 1842, XXXIX, 379, Papers relative to the West Indies: resolutions of the sub-Committee of the Agricultural and Immigration Society. The pattern of settlement generated by the process described above was predominantly linear, a form of layout which is not always economical. For a discussion of this matter see G. E. Young Sing, 'Evolution of the present pattern of agricultural land use in the island of Trinidad in the West Indies' (unpublished Ph.D. thesis, Queen's University, Belfast, 1964).

44. CO 295/137, Chichester to Stanley, 8 October 1842, minute by James Stephen, 24 November 1843.

45. William G. Sewell, *The ordeal of free labour in the British West Indies*, 2nd edn (London, 1862), p. 110. Sewell was of the opinion that the system had been a major cause of labour's leaving the estates.

46. CO 295/137, Chichester to Stanley, 8 October 1842, minute by James Stephen, 24 November 1843.

47. Norman E. Whitten, Jr, *Class, kinship, and power in an Ecuadorian town* (Stanford, Calif., 1965), p. 87.

48. Wood, *Trinidad in transition*, contains a valuable account of these migratory patterns. Part II is particularly germane to the present discussion.

49. Migration of this latter type sometimes resulted in labour shortages on the island from which the migrant came, as in the case of Grenada. CO 101/96, C. E. Grey to Gladstone, 17 March 1846.

50. CO 295/239, Gordon to Buckingham, 8 June 1867, enclosure.

51. Judith Ann Weller, *The East Indian indenture in Trinidad* (Institute of Caribbean Studies, Río Piedras, Puerto Rico, 1968), pp. 58–63.

52. This aspect of estate life is not well documented with regard to Trinidad. See Weller, *East Indian indenture*, p. 64. In the case of British Guiana, a Commission of Enquiry was set up in 1870 to look into the conditions of the indentured labourers, and the report (CO 111/379 and 380) gives much interesting information on the nature of immigrant agriculture as practised on the estates. The commission was originally set up as a result of complaints laid by William Des Voeux, a former stipendiary magistrate in Guiana. His version of events is to be found in Sir G. William Des Voeux, *My colonial service*, 2 vols. (London, 1903).

53. Weller, *East Indian indenture*, p. 28.

54. Wood, *Trinidad in transition*, p. 274.

55. John P. Augelli and Henry W. Taylor, 'Race and population patterns in Trinidad', *Annals of the Association of American Geographers* L, 2 (1960), pp. 123–38.

56. CO 295/239, Gordon to Buckingham, 8 June 1867, Enclosure, Memorandum by the Agent General of Immigrants, Henry Mitchell.

57. CO 295/239, Gordon to Buckingham, 8 June 1867, Memoranda by Dr de Verteuil.

58. CO 300/94/Z3.

59. C. Y. Shephard, 'The cacao industry of Trinidad', *Journal of Tropical Agriculture* IX, 7 (1932), pp. 200–5.

60. C. C. Parisinos, C. Y. Shephard, and A. L. Jolly, 'Peasant agriculture: an economic survey of the Las Lomas district, Trinidad', *Journal of Tropical Agriculture* XXI, 5 (1944), pp. 84–99.

61. Dayanand Maharaj, 'Cane farming in the Trinidad sugar industry' (unpublished Ph.D. thesis, University of Edinburgh, 1969), p. 44. Howard Johnson, 'The origins and early development of cane farming in Trinidad, 1882–1906', *Journal of Caribbean History* V (1972), pp. 48–9, suggests a slightly earlier origin.

62. Young Sing, 'Evolution of the present pattern of agricultural land use in the island of Trinidad'.

63. Howard Johnson, 'Immigration and the sugar industry', p. 47.

64. See, for example, CO 295/155, Harris to Grey, 28 November 1846, and CO 295/155, Harris to Grey, 16 January 1847.

PART V

Postscript

The final chapter sets the preceding papers in the wider context of the general social and economic history of Latin America in the independence period, and in this way it provides a useful framework within which to place each of the individual essays. After a consideration of some of the theoretical problems underpinning any definition of the peasantry, Magnus Mörner poses some major questions concerning the nature of Latin American economic development and the attempts at diversification in the second quarter of the nineteenth century. His analysis of the differing characteristics of each of the major crops or crop/livestock combinations considered in this volume highlights some of the general theoretical issues raised in the Introduction. He stresses, for example, how the ecological and demographic variables associated with coffee production have allowed the development of a great variety of forms of social and economic organization and modes of production. This contrasts markedly with the case of sugar cultivation, where the technological imperative has been so much more compelling, and where a more uniform system of production and labour relations has been evolved. Clearly ecology and demography are two major explanatory variables to be considered in any analysis of the process of agrarian change. Their importance is emphasized in the final part of the discussion, on the evolution of the traditional *hacienda*, when Mörner considers the nature of the relations between 'landlords' and the internal and external peasantry.

CHAPTER 18

Latin American 'landlords' and 'peasants' and the outer world during the national period

MAGNUS MÖRNER

Introduction

Whatever interest has been shown to date in the agrarian history of Latin America has largely been concentrated on the colonial period. Even so, our present knowledge about Latin American rural society before Independence remains highly uneven and fragmentary. Only a few regions or districts have been researched in depth. Vital factors such as the movements of rural prices are largely unknown. Moreover, the dependence of scholars on Jesuit documentation illustrates the scarcity of other sources to explain the internal functioning of the large estate.[1]

The present volume therefore presents an ambitious and innovative approach and shows that there is indeed some significant ongoing research being conducted into the agrarian history of the last 150 years. Naturally enough, however, the contributions vary widely, in terms of approach, methodology, and sources; and naturally enough the coverage of regions and types of agricultural production is inevitably somewhat uneven. Some are studies on the macro-level, others on the micro-level. Yet, while far from all of them are actually written by historians, almost all illustrate the historical process of modernization within the agrarian sector of Latin America in the course of the nineteenth and twentieth centuries.

The aim of the present commentary will therefore simply be to place the papers in this volume, and others presented at the Cambridge conference, within a broader historical context, and to relate them to the actual state of historical research. In turn, this double purpose will imply an evaluation of the usefulness of these essays for comparative studies and as a basis for generalizations and theoretical models.

The concepts of 'landlord' and 'peasant'

No matter how familiar they may sound, several of the general concepts used throughout the literature (and, indeed, in the present volume) often imply different meanings and interpretations, which may render the general use of such terms quite misleading. I shall therefore briefly discuss two such concepts – those of 'landlord' and 'peasant'.

'Landlord' is in fact far from being a homogeneous concept. It covers highly traditional *hacendados* as well as modernizing agricultural entrepreneurs with a strong commercial orientation. It encompasses individual landowners, both resident managers and absentee rentiers, as well as national and foreign-owned corporations. Moreover, a tenant rather than the absentee landowner often plays the role of 'landlord' in the eyes of the rural population. Above all it seems that the various categories of 'landlords' differ widely in their mental outlook. Thus, reasonable generalizations about 'landlords' are difficult to make. One might question the usefulness of the term as an analytical tool.

'Peasant' appears to be even more ambivalent and vague a concept. Naturally, if 'peasant' or *'campesino'* is taken merely as synonymous with 'rural inhabitant', no problems arise. But what then is the use of the term for analytical purposes? If, on the other hand, the historian looks for an explanation in the rapidly swelling anthropological and sociological literature on 'peasants' he will soon find himself in a dilemma. True, most specialists conclude that 'peasant society' is distinguished from 'tribal society' as well as from 'farmers'. They agree that 'peasant' existence is characterized by a degree of subsistence as well as by the marketing of a surplus, and by autonomy as well as by dependency within the framework of a wider society. Thus, the appropriation of the surplus of the 'peasants' by a dominating group also becomes part of their characterization. But social scientists differ widely in their emphasis on the various features.[2] The historian should be aware that the aim of their efforts is no less than finding some kind of common denominator for *the majority of mankind through time*! One must ask, with George Dalton, if such grand generalizations really serve historical understanding. The role of the 'peasantry' in, for example, Western European medieval society was no doubt fundamentally different from that of 'peasantries' in national societies which are in the process of becoming industrialized and modernized.[3] In Latin America – the favourite ground for those looking for 'peasant' characteristics – there are various different 'peasantries'. One finds corporate 'peasants' producing mainly for subsistence as well as independent smallholders producing tropical export crops.[4] Thus the term 'peasant' has to be qualified in order to be of any analytical use at all.

To begin with, *ethnic origin* is usually possible to trace. There are 'peasants' of Indian origin and tradition, as well as *mestizo* and mulatto 'peasants' of European tradition, and descendants of African slaves or nineteenth-century immigrants from Europe or Asia who likewise exist on a 'peasant' level. There is no agreement among scholars, however, as to the moment when 'peasant' features became more relevant than the original ethnic characteristics. The use of the terms in the literature is completely arbitrary. The abolition of legal distinctions at the end of the colonial period could, of course, be used as a criterion. But it would be more realistic to consider instead the process of social change. This would imply different moments in the case of the various regions, and the timing would be far from easy to determine.[5]

The *social content* of the term is even more difficult to determine. When advancing his first definition of 'peasant' in 1955, Eric Wolf explicitly excluded those lacking effective land control – that is, tenants. In 1969, the same author included both tenants and sharecroppers as long as they mainly determined the mode of production. On the other hand, fishing populations and landless rural workers were excluded.[6] Other students prefer broader definitions. Teodor Shanin emphasizes that 'peasants' form a class but one of 'low classness'.[7] The historian does not have to concern himself with this sophisticated discussion. But he has to find out which social groups are, in fact, hidden behind that vague and ambivalent designation, 'peasant'. Rural groups so classified include members of landowning communities, independent smallholders, cash tenants, sharecroppers, labour tenants, resident and temporary wage labour, and squatters. The historian cannot take it for granted that the common links between these various groups have been more important historically than their differences and opposing interests.[8] Something vaguely called a 'peasant movement' may, in reality, reflect the interests and participation of only one or two of these groups.[9]

To summarize, the use of the concepts of 'peasant' and 'peasantry' appears to be useful from the point of view of the historian only in so far as information on ethnic origin as well as on socio-economic category is added.

The papers presented here deal with 'landlords' of two different varieties. There are individual *hacendados* of a more or less enterprising type, and there are large-scale corporate enterprises. The papers also discuss 'peasants' of different sorts. First, there are those settled *within* large estates on a sharecropper or labour-tenant basis. Secondly, we have those who are settled *outside* the estates but are periodically drawn upon as a source of seasonal or part-time labour. These latter include corporate Indian 'peasants' as well as different kinds of smallholders. How did relations develop between these parties – 'landlords', 'internal peasantry', and 'external peasantry' – under the impact of domestic or foreign de-

mands and the adoption of modern technology? It seems to me that this is
the key question presented by this book.

The neglected era (1825–1850)

The incorporation of Latin America within the world economy in a 'neo-
colonial' relationship is usually considered to have taken place from
the middle of the nineteenth century onwards. Yet it is strange that the
economic development of Latin America during the *second quarter* of the
century remains so little explored. For Andre Gunder Frank in his study
on Chile this was, indeed, a period of valiant attempts at national economic development. Because of Frank's fixed idea that Chile already found
itself in the grip of the 'capitalist system', however, he finds these
attempts to have been doomed to failure.[10] I am not going to discuss this
issue. Let me only state that Latin American diversification efforts during
the period 1825–50 deserve much more scholarly attention for offering
an alternative, viable or not, to subsequent trends. From our own present
perspective it can no longer be affirmed that the growth of the export
economies from the mid nineteenth century onwards necessarily spelled
socio-economic development.[11]

During the period 1825–50 western investors were notoriously unwilling to risk their capital in Latin America. We do not know if this was
due to the lack of stability in the Latin American countries or, rather,
to the inadequate capacity of the European economy itself at this early
stage of industrialization.[12] We do know, however, that European merchants succeeded in seizing control of the entire network of foreign
trade in Latin America.[13] At the same time as Church income and its
role as a source of rural credit declined, these merchants largely took
over that function.[14] The volume of foreign trade remained modest. The
period 1825–50 roughly corresponds to the 'B' phase of the first Kondratieff cycle established for industrialized economies.[15] Foreign interests were, above all, concerned with Latin America as an export
market for industrial consumer goods; in return they preferred bullion.
Not surprisingly, the Latin American countries therefore experienced a
clearly negative balance of trade, both officially and in reality if the
effect of contraband trade is duly taken into account.[16] Latin America
thus suffered from a lack of currency. The subsistence sector of the
Latin American rural economy probably expanded at this time;[17] this is
at least my impression from research on the Cuzco region in Peru.[18]

How did the large estates fare during this era? We know, of course,
about the boom in the Cuban sugar plantations which lasted until 1860.

But this was an exceptional phenomenon, to be explained by the comparative advantage enjoyed at this juncture by the slave-based cultivation of Cuba's fresh and fertile soils.[19] On the whole, early-nineteenth-century *haciendas* and plantations are known to us only as centres of social life, described by Fanny Calderón de la Barca and other travellers.[20] We ignore their profitability.

For this reason, David Brading's essay on some medium-sized maize-growing estates in the Mexican Bajío between 1700 and 1860 (chapter 2) appears especially noteworthy. Brading shows that, not very surprisingly, around 1800 the margin of profit of his sample was both uncertain and thin. Bajío landowners, according to this author, were soon faced with only three alternatives: modernization (by means of irrigation and a switch to wheat-growing), change from the position of landlord–rentiers to that of landlord–producers, or division of their estates into large farms. During the post-Independence depression the last phenomenon became particularly widespread in the area. Brading believes that the crisis of the large estates in this region was mainly due to the competition with smallholders and their own tenants in the maize market which drove corn prices down. But the decline of the traditional urban and mining markets should probably also be taken into account. Guanajuato and its surrounding *pueblos* and mines seems to have suffered a population decline from about 70,600 people in 1803 to 63,000 in 1854.[21]

Brading's paper is the only one in the present volume which is chiefly devoted to the period 1825–50. We clearly need much more research on land tenure, production, profitability, prices, labour organization, and so forth during this neglected era.

Latin America and the world economy during the latter part of the nineteenth century

Latin America was integrated within an increasingly dynamic world economy in the course of the *third quarter* of the nineteenth century, when it became its clearly defined function to export raw materials and foodstuffs. This crucial development was a consequence of the increased mobility of capital and population, greater technical knowledge, and improved transportation. It was triggered by the rising European demand during this period, which corresponds to the 'A' phase of the second Kondratieff cycle, abruptly ended by the crisis of 1873. World trade increased by leaps and bounds.[22]

During the *last quarter* of the century (1873–96), the economic expansion in Europe and the United States slowed down. But that of Latin

America and other extra-European areas continued at a more rapid rate. The foreign trade of the world's tropical countries grew by no less than 3.6 per cent yearly between 1883 and 1913.[23] Though it is often claimed that the terms of trade have been adverse for raw-material-exporting countries since the 1870s, recent studies suggest that they were indeed favourable from 1883 to 1926 or 1929.[24] Yet the trends in the foreign trade of some Latin American countries reflected the Kondratieff pattern. Peru experienced an upward trend between 1852 and 1876, followed by a downward trend until 1893.[25] In the case of Colombia, the mid-1870s appear as the watershed.[26] Economic expansion was facilitated by an extraordinary inflow of foreign capital, which was especially striking during the 1880s.[27] In this way, structural dependency was strengthened.

Celso Furtado claims that the impact of this whole process of economic change on the Latin American countries differed widely depending on their export specialization. In temperate countries with agricultural exports the expansion of trade in fact led to economic development. On the other hand, countries exporting the products of tropical agriculture on the whole barely developed economically. Economic expansion mainly strengthened the existing hierarchical social order, in itself a barrier against development. In the case of countries exporting the products of mining, the developmental role of trade expansion, according to Furtado, was virtually nil.[28]

There is only one article in this book which refers to Furtado's first group of countries. In his interesting study of the impact of the cereal boom on late ninteenth-century society in Santa Fe, Argentina (chapter 13), Ezequiel Gallo eloquently shows the developmental effects of wheat production as opposed to that of wool. However, it should be borne in mind that Gallo terminates his analysis at 1895, when Santa Fe wheat-growing suffered a severe crisis. As James Scobie has pointed out, the whole structure of Argentine wheat production now began to change, increasingly favouring the expansion of tenant farming.[29] The two other groups of countries mentioned by Furtado exemplify what is often termed the 'enclave' nature of so many export economies. The weakness of spread effects can be ascribed both to the organization of the plantation and mining sectors themselves and to the structural deficiencies of the surrounding national society.[30] As H. Myint sees it, the 'cheap labour policy' pursued for so long by plantation and mining enterprises has been especially baneful.[31] But one can also point, for example, to the extreme unevenness of income distribution within the entire national society.

Different types of tropical exports present considerable variations within this general theme. Furtado himself admits that the coffee production of the São Paulo region did play a great developmental role.[32] A student of Colombian economic history has found coffee exports to be much more favourable in developmental terms than, for instance, tobacco exports.[33] One has to bear in mind that coffee is a cash crop which does not necessarily require major capital outlays. Coffee production can be combined with the growing of foodstuffs. The harvesting and processing are rather simple. As a consequence, in certain circumstances it lends itself well to smallholder cultivation. It is also a pioneer's crop, because it can be grown on land only partly cleared, and because its high unit value makes heavy transport costs bearable. But the supply of coffee is quite inelastic, as the trees need several years to become productive. The impact of price fluctuations is also very heavy, both on producers and on the national or regional economy. Large plantations may be better prepared to withstand such uncertainties.[34]

As a consequence, the history of coffee production in Latin America presents great variety. In some areas very large plantations prevail, whilst in others middle-sized units or even *minifundia* predominate. The large slave-based coffee plantations in Brazil have been superbly described by Stanley Stein in his study on Vassouras in the Paraíba Valley, 1850–1900, and by Emilia Viotti da Casta in her work on those in São Paulo prior to the abolition of slavery.[35]

Thomas Holloway's paper on the coffee *colonos* of São Paulo (chapter 12) continues this story from the 1880s to the 1920s – that is, under a system of free labour. Holloway shows the evolution from sharecropping, by which the workers were at the mercy of nature and shifting coffee prices, to the system of *colono* contracts. Workers now received a fixed pay for their care of the trees, plus a harvest piece-rate and permission to grow subsistence crops. Workers – first-generation immigrants as a rule – could now feel more secure. Holloway claims that they were not infrequently able to accumulate savings which could be used for the purchase of farms. By 1920, immigrants owned a quarter of the rural properties of the State of São Paulo. Holloway's optimistic view is in striking contrast to the many accounts of immigrant misery based mainly on the reports of the Italian consuls. The author is unable to document the process of land acquisition by former *colonos*, however. Some of the immigrants who acquired land may have done so on their arrival; or, as Pierre Monbeig suggests, they may have worked as wage-earners in the city, leaving their families to care for the trees on the *fazenda* until they had saved the capital required.

In the Caribbean, coffee production was also originally slave-based. But, as Francisco Pérez de la Riva has pointed out, Cuban coffee plantations of the mid nineteenth century were usually small, and they were gradually taken over by sugar producers.[36] In post-Independence Haiti, on the other hand, coffee by mid-century had entirely replaced sugar as an export staple.[37] In Puerto Rico, coffee production, though no newcomer in the island, experienced its breakthrough between 1875 and 1885 – that is, after the demise of slavery.[38] In his paper on some aspects of Puerto Rican coffee production (see chapter 19), Carlos Buitrago Ortiz stresses the linkage between the merchant and the producer, both of whom were often Corsicans or Mallorcans. He also underlines the function of the plantation store as an instrument of social control. In Venezuela, as well, coffee started as a slave-based plantation crop in the late eighteenth century, gradually bypassing cocoa during the early part of the nineteenth century. From the 1830s onwards, under the impact of depressed prices, the planters became increasingly indebted. According to John Lombardi, slaves – who by then only constituted a minor part of the coffee plantation labour force – became especially valuable as collateral for short-term, high-interest commercial credits extended to landowners by their respective commission houses.[39] In the 1870s Venezuelan coffee expanded considerably but productivity remained low. How much this was due to scarcity of labour and how much, as Miguel Izard suggests, to the simplicity of contracts between *hacendados* and their *conuquero* labour tenants is unclear.[40]

In Colombia, coffee production was of little importance until the 1870s. From then onwards, however, its economic and social impact became increasingly important, especially in Antioquía and Caldas, where it became a smallholders' crop.[41] Both locational advantages and harvest techniques contributed to give Colombian coffee a reputation for quality that raised its price considerably. In this way, high transport costs became easier to endure.[42] Malcolm Deas's account (chapter 11) of the labour organization of a coffee *finca* in Cundinamarca, the district surrounding Bogotá, between 1870 and 1912 highlights some aspects of the production of coffee in a district which is far less well known than that of Antioquía. As distinguished from the small producers of western Colombia, the coffee estates in Cundinamarca were fairly large. This would, of course, make labour supply a more complicated matter. Deas stresses the relatively good bargaining position of labour, both permanent (day-work by *arrendatarios*) and temporary. If workers did not receive satisfactory wages they would simply go elsewhere, and then the harvest was lost. The aspirations of Colombian producers towards high quality made them especially dependent on careful and satisfied workers. As Deas points out, this feature stands in striking contrast to the extensive slave work at Vassouras described by Stein. A monograph of this latter type on Cundinamarca which also let us know more about land tenure, marketing, credit, and profitability would be extremely valuable.

The great variety of nineteenth-century coffee production in Latin America is also borne out by Ciro F. S. Cardoso's very substantial paper on the coffee *haciendas* of Costa Rica (chapter 7). In that country, land concentration gained momentum in the coffee areas from the 1850s onwards. Nevertheless most coffee land remained in the possession of very small producers. Labour was always scarce and relatively well paid. Though ready to work part-time for the *hacendados*, small producers tended to give priority to their own crops, so that the labour problem of the *haciendas* might occasionally become acute. Yet Cardoso underscores the high degree of social and economic control exercised by the large landowners, closely tied to British import interests ever since the 1840s, by means of their virtual monopoly of processing equipment and channels of commercialization, and through the extension of rural credit to smallholders. The formation and character of coffee domination in Costa Rica were strikingly different from those in Guatemala and El Salvador, where the expansion was more sudden and labour relations much more harsh. According to Cardoso, the smoothness of the process in Costa Rica was basically due to the country's poverty and the relative weakness of its institutions during the previous colonial era. In Guatemala and El Salvador, traditional structures were stronger and for a long time were opposed to the modernization represented by the coffee economy.[43]

It seems that the different alternatives for coffee production and the great historical and present importance of the crop constitute a formidable challenge for comparative studies. Why was large-scale production preferred in one case and not in another? What determined the use of this or that category of labour? Future studies ought to be prepared with a comparative application in mind; this implies the provision of a full range of data on all the more relevant variables.

A century of sugar production (1840–1940)

In the case of sugar cane, large-scale production units can be considered an inherent feature rather than an alternative. Even when smallholder producers do exist, they are bound to be under the effective control of the nearest sugar mill, because of the speed with which harvested cane has to be brought to the mill. Sugar cane cultivation tends to dominate the region where it was introduced and to be hard to replace by alternative cash crops. At the same time, as a result of sugar's need for fresh soils, producers in new areas tend to bypass those in older ones. Apart from a possible need for inputs of foodstuffs, sugar cane production usually appears strikingly isolated from other productive sectors.[45]

The crucial feature of the nineteenth-century cane sugar industry was, of course, the growing competition with beet sugar. Cane sugar's percentage of world production dropped dramatically between 1840 and 1890:

1840:	93.0 per cent
1850:	86.5 per cent
1860:	79.7 per cent
1870:	64.0 per cent
1880:	50.2 per cent
1890:	41.2 per cent

After an all-time high in 1814, sugar prices began to drop, and the decline was obvious from the 1840s onwards: a sharp fall to a still lower level took place in 1883. It should be noticed that the level of sugar consumption in the North Atlantic countries steadily rose from the early years of the nineteenth century until World War I.[46] The price drop during this era was therefore due to competition and to the loss of tariff protection in traditional markets and not to a decline in demand.

The demand for a large, disciplined labour force had been met for some three centuries by the importation of African slaves. With the coming of Emancipation, slavery disappeared in one region after another, between the 1830s and the 1880s. Several papers in this volume are devoted to post-Emancipation problems of labour supply on sugar plantations.

First, one explanatory feature has to be spelled out if the post-Emancipation situation is to be understood. Because of bitter experience, for fear of low wages, and for psychological reasons, ex-slaves usually desired to abandon their 'home' plantation as soon as they were legally free to do so.[47] But they were unable to satisfy this desire in areas where all the available land was already occupied by plantations. In north-eastern Brazil, for instance, the coast land was monopolized by the sugar estates, and the arid scrub-forest belt (*caatinga*) in the interior was not a very attractive alternative for settlement. The prospects were even gloomier for the ex-slaves on, let us say, the British Leeward Islands.

The small area of the territory, the virtual land monopoly enjoyed by the planters, and the density of the previous slave population left the freedmen without any choice at all. To avoid starvation they simply had to accept wages which were lower than their former maintenance costs as slaves.[48]

On the other hand, in the larger West Indian islands such as Jamaica and Trinidad, as well as in the Guianas, considerable space was left, outside the plantations, which lent itself to small-scale agriculture. Here, ex-slaves naturally preferred to establish themselves as independent smallholders, producing both for subsistence and sale, and at times for export. This phenomenon is already fairly well known to us, thanks to the contributions of Woodville Marshall, Gisela Eisner, Douglas Hall, Donald Wood, and Alan H. Adamson.[49] The paper presented here by Brian Blouet on Trinidad (chapter 17) complements the picture. Until 1847 the authorities there, under pressure from the planters, were able to prevent ex-slaves from buying Crown land. They could not prevent squatting, however. Yet Blouet, like Donald Wood, points out that the traditional image of 'lazy' blacks disappearing into the forest is a false one.[50] Most remained on the margins of settlement and were ready to accept part-time work on the plantations. Thus, 'labour shortage' was largely a question of the going wage rate. There is an interesting difference of emphasis between the two authors. Blouet underscores a violent slump in plantation wages which took place in connection with the financial crisis of 1847. Wood stresses that, in comparison with other Caribbean cane workers, those in Trinidad continued to be relatively well paid throughout the 1840s.[51] This relative advantage tended to harmonize with the pattern of workers' bargaining positions already outlined. It could be expressed thus: Trinidad planters, unlike so many others, were unable to pass on most of the cost of bleak market conditions to the workers. Blouet does go beyond Wood in his quantification of the alienation of Crown lands. This process, which gained momentum after 1868, benefited formerly indentured East Indian plantation workers as well as blacks. On the whole, it can be stated that slave emancipation in Trinidad and similar areas did imply a redistribution not only of property (slaves became their own owners) but also of income, although the majority continued to live on a very modest level.

In the 1840s the sugar production of the Cauca Valley in southern Colombia, where it had always been combined with placer gold mining, was still based on Negro slavery. In his extensive paper on the evolution of labour systems in this isolated inland area (chapter 16), Michael Taussig shows that the transition to 'free wage labour' in the 1850s, produced profound social and economic dislocations, at least for a time. The Arboleda plantation complex, for example, was obliged to resort to a form of black tenant labour (*concertaje*) which also encompassed a group of peasant pioneers who expanded cultivation into the virgin forest (*terrajeros*). Taussig states but does not prove that the *latifundia* also secured a labour force of resident *mestizo peones* from the central parts of the country. For some years, profits on the Arboleda estates actually rose, obviously in connection with a switch to the production of brandy. In the 1870s, however, a general decline set in. The subsequent re-organization and strengthening of the sugar-cum-cattle *latifundia* pattern was clearly related to the opening of the Panama canal and the Cali–Buenaventura railway in 1914. According to Taussig the defeat of the cocoa-producing 'peasant' sector was mainly a result of the *Violencia* of the 1950s. Without more data on production and market conditions, the many questions raised in Taussig's paper concerning the evolution of Cauca society will remain unanswered. In the view of a recent student, however, the basic characteristics today of the sugar industry in Cauca are the same as in other sugar-dominated regions.[52]

In Brazil, sugar exports suffered a sharp decline in volume between the 1880s and the first decade of the twentieth century, falling from a yearly average of 200,000 tons to only 64,000. Due to the drop in prices the income from sugar was even more reduced. Sugar's share in total Brazilian exports had already started to fall drastically in the 1860s.[53]

Yet on the regional level, in northeastern Brazil, sugar maintained its dominant position. As we have already explained, the land monopoly of the plantations made the bargaining position of labour very weak. Furthermore, as pointed out earlier by J. H. Galloway and emphasized in the papers by Peter Eisenberg and Jaime Reis (chapters 14 and 15), the transition from slave to 'free' labour in this region was a very slow and gradual one.[54] Sugar cultivation is hard and has always been based on male workers: this is a striking difference from, for instance, the culti-vation of cotton. Sugar planters everywhere therefore preferred to rely on the continuous imports of male slaves rather than favouring slave reproduction. Consequently, in the case of northeast Brazil the end of the slave trade around 1850 proved more crucial than the very abolition of slavery. At the same time, northeastern sugar planters, under the impact of declining prices and profitability, from the 1850s onwards sold a considerable proportion of their slaves to the booming coffee areas in the south. Instead, planters chose to impose labour obligations on the group of squatters (*moradores*) who were already settled on marginal plantation lands. After the abolition of slavery in 1888 most ex-slaves, for lack of employment alternatives, joined this group. Apart from the usufruct of parcels which provided their own subsistence, *moradores* were also paid for their work. Yet Eisenberg underscores the fall of real wages in rural Pernambuco from 1870 onwards.[55] The need for additional manpower at harvest time, a permanent feature in sugar cane production, was met by migrant workers (*corumbás*) from the drylands of the interior. As Eisenberg puts it, plantation owners were successful 'in transferring the losses suffered in export markets to the plantation work force in the form of depressed wages and poor working conditions'.[56] The two authors also pay attention to the role of the sharecroppers (*lavradores*), who without being secure in their own tenancies had to share the commercial risks of the landowners.

There is no reason to doubt the correctness of the general outline traced by Eisenberg, Reis, and Galloway. To attain further quantification on the macro-level may very well be out of the question. Yet one would like to have some studies on the micro-level, the better to evaluate the elements of change and continuity, such as the study which Sidney Mintz devoted to the history of a Puerto Rican sugar plantation from 1876 to 1949.[57] Would any documentation be available in northeast Brazil for such a purpose? Nor does the process of 'modernization' − that is, the divorce between the agricultural and industrial stages of the process of sugar production − appear completely clear. Unlike, for instance, the Cuban case, in Brazil government aid had to play the modernizing role in the northeast, Eisenberg asserts, because foreign capital and market protection could not be obtained.[58] Central sugar factories − *'usinas'* was the Brazilian term − arose, but by 1920 they had not yet achieved complete domination of the industry. The Brazilian *usinas* had acquired some lands of their own, but they also bought from independent producers of various sorts. This is another difference from the case of Cuba during the same period, so eloquently described by Ramiro Guerra y Sánchez.[59] If the character of production in the northeast remained heterogeneous, would not this reflect itself in a more diversified pattern of labour relations than that presented by our authors? Reis suggests that factory workers were much better off, which certainly is not surprising. But would not the conditions of the *usina* cane workers also differ from those of the labour of traditional planters and *lavradores*? Also, how great was the reduction in demand for labour due to mechanization and market difficulties? Finally, the coincidence that Eisenberg and Reis both concentrate on Pernambuco may increase the risk of generalizations that do not duly take into account, for example, the rather different pattern of Bahia.[60]

Nevertheless, as previously suggested by Furtado, it is obvious that in Pernambuco, at least, there was no redistribution of income in favour of labour after the abolition of slavery.[61] It is indeed likely that the material conditions of labour grew worse, while partial modernization essentially strengthened the existing socio-political structure.[62] Per capita income in the northeast seems to have declined from 1872 to 1900.[63]

The process of modernization had a much more violent character in northern Peru. Unlike the Brazilian case, the sugar expansion in this region from the 1880s onwards was due to a heavy input of English and American capital and was entirely oriented towards the world market. The concentration of land as well as of milling facilities was pushed forward by the need to reduce the cost of production during a long period of depressed world market prices.[64] World War I then ushered in a period of extreme price fluctuations – the boom that closed in 1920 and the precipituous decline after 1929. The nadir was reached in 1934.[65]

Peter Klarén's paper on sugar production in northern Peru from the 1870s to the 1930s (chapter 9) gives a perceptive account of the clash between these aggressive new sugar enterprises and the traditional 'plantocracy' as well as other strata of local society. By raising the price of milling little by little, the sugar companies forced planters to sell their lands to them. Independent smallholders were reduced to landless wage-earners. The device of *enganche*, long used in mining, was used to induce highland Indians to swell the ranks of the sugar proletariat. During World War I the costs of living of rural labour in Peru increased at a staggering rate. Real wages dropped and social conflict became acute in the sugar districts.[66] Klarén must be right in assuming that the origins of the Aprista movement are largely to be found in this explosive socio-economic situation. This would also give one of the clues to the socially heterogeneous, ideologically eclectic character of Aprismo. Rural and urban middle classes, smallholders, and workers had all been victimized by the powerful sugar interests which were backed by the national political system.[67]

Klarén himself suggests that the relation between the socially destructive modernization of the sugar industry and a 'radical' political movement in Peru has parallels elsewhere in the Americas, and his study suggests parallels with the cases of Emiliano Zapata's Morelos, of Cuba in the early 1930s as well as in 1959, and of Puerto Rico at the time of the rise of the Popular Democratic Party.[68] Other examples could be quoted, such as the politically important strikes and riots in the British West Indies between 1934 and 1938.[69] According to George L. Beckford's paper (see chapter 19), during that decade land monopoly in the hands of multinational corporations restricted peasant access to land at the same time that wages dropped and unemployment increased. Thus peasants were likely to join workers in any rebellion.[70] In any case, as Klarén is also aware, the very divergent preconditions make it hard to arrive at generalizations. Were the owners and the markets national or foreign? What was the character of labour supply and the extent of 'dislocation'? Also, if the case of Pernambuco suggests that 'halfway modernization' essentially strengthens the status quo, at what point does modernization stimulate a 'radical' political movement instead?

Furthermore, there are cases where no linkage can be discerned between the large-scale sugar industry and political radicalism. Like sugar production in nothern Peru, that on the southern coast of the Dominican Republic from the late nineteenth century onwards was tied to overseas markets and was highly capitalized and efficient. According to Harry Hoetink's paper (see chapter 19), there was no connection with previous slave plantations in this dry, irrigated area. In addition to a number of dispossessed small local cattle-breeders, sugar wage labour comprised domestic as well as external migrants. Because of the heterogeneous character of this labour force and because of seasonal unemployment, unionization was slow. Hoetink does not, however, pursue his account into the twentieth century. We are left to guess why conditions failed to produce any political radicalism to speak of. Was it because the sugar industry emerged without any plantation antecedents? Or was it merely because of the heavy-handed control of the post-Depression Trujillo regime?[71]

Ian Rutledge's paper (chapter 8) deals with a later period, 1930–43, and with sugar cane production for a domestic market, that of Argentina. Yet it illustrates the same need of the sugar enterprises for additional unskilled labour at harvest time which we have noticed in other essays. This labour demand brings pressure to bear on the traditional rural economy. Rutledge is able to show that in the case of northwest Argentina the sugar companies acquired Indian land merely as a tool to obtain labour. By using traditional, 'feudal' forms for labour service, 'capitalist' exploitation was furthered. One is often led to suspect the presence of such phenomena, but it is seldom so well shown as in Rutledge's contribution. It is worth while to observe, at the same time, that in this sugar area the decade of the 1930s was not a time of acute socio-political conflict. The Argentine sugar industry did not suffer from the Depression. On the contrary, advancing under national tariff protection, it experienced a steady, indeed spectacular, growth. This increase was

greater in Salta and Jujuy than in the original centre of sugar production, Tucumán. It has been suggested that the 'feudal' solution of the
problem of labour supply in Salta and Jujuy was partly responsible.[72]
'Indians' were free to remain on their lands during the slack season, so
that they could take care of their own subsistence without being a burden
on the estate.

To turn for a moment to another plantation crop – cotton – Henri
Favre, in his article (chapter 10), gives an account of a parallel phenomenon though with a different implication. In the Peruvian coastlands the
expansion of the cotton plantation had produced the same kind of 'dislocation' as sugar. According to Claude Collin Delavaud, seasonal cotton
labour was even more harshly exploited than on the sugar estates.[73]
Nevertheless, as Favre presents it, the seasonal migration from the Indian
communities of the highlands of central Peru to the cotton plantations,
from the 1880s onwards, may have worked to the Indians' own benefit.
These corporate 'peasants' eagerly volunteered for harvest work on the
coast. Favre finds an explanation in the process of internal stratification
in the Indian society, triggered by the penetration of 'white' and *mestizo*
elements.[74] Owing to this encroachment by outsiders, the traditional
system of autarky by means of ecological control over different kinds of
cropland was profoundly disturbed. Consequently, the more marginal
communities which retained a purer 'Indian' character could no longer
sustain themselves without recourse to outside work. According to
Favre, the seasonal labour on the coast gave those 'Indians' the money
they required to complement the economic basis for their traditional way
of life.

The evolution of the traditional hacienda

So far we have been concerned with the impact of plantation agriculture
on rural society. But some of the contributions included in this volume
also examine the evolution of the traditional grain-and-livestock *hacienda*
in countries dominated by mining exports.

Jane Benton (see chapter 19) presents an outline of the expansion of
the large estate in one of the most isolated and backward areas of contemporary Latin America, the highlands of Bolivia. There was no doubt
a profound change in the pattern of land ownership in Bolivia in the
course of the national period. In the 1840s Indian *comunidades* held a
clear majority of the rural population.[75] A century later, *comunarios*
were reduced to a rather small minority. By then most rural inhabitants
were serfs – *colonos* – on the large estates. Like most writers on Bolivia,

Jane Benton considers the presidency of Mariano Melgarejo (1864–71) to have been the crucial moment in this process of rural change. But she barely goes beyond the legal measures enacted in trying to explain the curious phenomenon of *hacienda* expansion. After all, the urban population was stagnant and small. Furthermore, its consumption of foodstuffs was to a great extent probably taken care of by imports, when the increasing income from mining exports permitted.[76] *Colonos* as well as *comunarios* were largely concerned with production for their own subsistence on the family plots they exploited. What we know is that the process of alienation of Indian lands was started by fiscal policy. Melgarejo's imposition of a tax on the *comunidades* to legalize their titles was the response to a financial emergency. The seriousness of the measure was reflected by a wave of *comunario* rebellions from 1868 to 1871.[77] More important, perhaps, is the fact that towards 1870 silver production suddenly increased. Bolivia's traditionally huge trade deficit was turned into a surplus. Hitherto, the government had relied to a great extent on the head-tax of *comunario* Indians for its revenues. From now on, these revenues were provided chiefly by taxes on mining and foreign trade. During the 1890s, when silver exports began to drop, Bolivia became instead one of the world's leading tin exporters.[78] In the world of politics, the tin oligarchy replaced the one supported by silver miners. In this connection there were widespread Indian rebellions from 1895 to 1900. Ramiro Condarco Morales suggests that these rebellions were largely a reaction against the land alienation which had taken place since the 1870s.[79] Until we know more about the actual process of alienation, it remains difficult to relate it to specific factors or trends. As Edmundo Flores points out, however, whatever the aims of the land-hungry *hacendados* were, they were actually left with only two choices: either to abstain from management in return for a fixed rent or to try to raise productivity somewhat by introducing innovations. In view of the abundance of labour such efforts were doomed to fail, because by custom *colonos* were fairly secure in their right of residence on the estate.[80]

Chile, like Bolivia, was a country where the *hacienda* system persisted in the shadow of an increasingly important mining industry. Yet the pattern of agrarian evolution differs widely. In various important studies on nineteenth-century rural Chile, as well as in his essay in this volume with Ann Hagerman Johnson (chapter 4), Arnold Bauer makes it clear that Chilean wheat exports to Europe made *hacienda* agriculture truly profitable during the period from 1865 to 1880.[81] During this interval, Chileans were able to exploit the combination of prices which were still high, drastically reduced transport costs, and the absence of other southern-hemisphere exporters. The expansion of wheat in Chile to meet this demand was not achieved by any change in production methods, nor by a territorial expansion of the *haciendas*. According to Bauer, the *haciendas* already held large expanses of unused land, which could now be put into cultivation. What happened was, above all, that the *hacienda* demand for rural labour increased. It was met partly by augmenting the labour obligations of labour tenants (*inquilinos*) and partly by recruiting part of the vagrant rural masses as seasonal labour. Cristóbal Kay, who in his paper (chapter 5) also studies the rural evolution of Chile, concludes that this period strengthened the *hacienda* rather than the 'peasant' sector. This can hardly be doubted.

However, the export boom soon drew to a close under the impact of falling world market prices and increased competition with other overseas markets. On the whole, Chilean agriculture from the 1890s onwards was restricted to the (albeit expanding) domestic market. At the same time, mineral exports experienced a spectacular rise.[82] The *haciendas* continued to slowly extend their acreage until the 1930s, and they maintained their grip on rural society. On the other hand, smaller holdings became fragmented, and the number of *minifundistas* increased. Real wages of rural workers may have fallen somewhat towards 1900.[83] Rural-to-urban migration became a large-scale movement much earlier in Chile than in other parts of Latin America.

Notwithstanding Bauer's many data and Kay's reflections, the reasons for the continued *hacienda* domination do not seem quite clear. It is worth while to observe that the large estates were able to practically monopolize rural credit. Yet, as Bauer points out, they barely used these means to invest in agriculture themselves. They did, on the other hand, in turn extend some credit to smaller producers, but on less generous terms. It is also clear that the *hacendado* benefited from inflation, a characteristic feature of the Chilean economy ever since the 1880s. But perhaps there were also other non-economic factors. Chilean *hacendados*, like those in many other countries, often exercised administrative and judicial functions at the local level. As Bauer has shown, they were also strongly represented at the parliamentary level. It would thus appear that the exceptional degree of 'political democracy' in Chile also helped to maintain the archaic rule by *hacendados* in the countryside.

Jan Bazant's article (chapter 3), on the relations between *haciendas* on the one hand and their permanent and temporary labourers, tenants, and sharecroppers on the other, presents a highly perceptive and important study of two *haciendas* in an area of northern Mexico. To evaluate it properly, Friedrich Katz's recent state-of-research report on labour conditions in Mexico during the Porfiriato should be consulted. I shall simply point out one striking feature – the way in which the Civil Code of 1871 was actually put to use by the *hacendados*. Their manipulation of the Code meant that the conditions of both tenants and resident workers were clearly undermined. The only ones actually to benefit from this change were the *aparceros* or sharecroppers.

The paper by Juan Martínez Alier (chapter 6), on the relation between *haciendas* and 'peasants' in the Peruvian Sierra during the 1940s and 1950s, is based on records which became available in the wake of the recent land reform. The paper deals with large commercial sheep *haciendas*. They used shepherds (*huacchilleros*) who, like *colonos*, enjoyed usufruct rights – in this case, free pasture for their own sheep. Martínez Alier's most provocative statement refers to the failure of the landowners to reach their modernizing objectives for 'lack of power'. They wanted to substitute cash wage labour for the traditional *huacchillero* system, which was no longer economical. But they failed because of the resistance that both the 'internal' and 'external peasantries' set up against their efforts at modernization. Martínez Alier also takes issue with the idea that *colonos* and *huacchilleros* were 'serfs', tied to the soil by their debts. He believes they were simply better off on the traditional basis than as cash wage-earners. This was why they resisted innovations and why eviction was a dreaded form of punishment.

Martínez Alier explicitly excludes demographic, commercial, and political factors from his analysis. Yet the issue of 'debt bondage' cannot possibly be understood without reference to demography. Devices for tying labour to the soil are needed only when manpower is scarce (from the point of view of landowners). This has certainly not been the case in the twentieth-century Peruvian Sierra. The conflict between 'landlords' and 'internal' and 'external peasantries' which is analysed by Martínez Alier should also be placed within a wider context. François Chevalier and Jean Piel have outlined how the archaic system of both *haciendas* and *comunidades* was already being challenged in the 1910s and 1920s.[84] The aggressive neolatifundism of this period was a consequence of the international demand for wool prior to 1918. The crisis which followed triggered a series of desperate Indian rebellions, which were ruthlessly crushed.[85] Over a longer perspective there can be no doubt that, in face of commercial latifundism, Indian *colonos* and *comunidades* were the weaker party.[86] For all its interest, Martínez Alier's evidence is only valid for a strictly limited period of time. Perhaps it is also conditioned by local circumstances.

Questions which remain

What was the relationship of 'landlords', 'internal peasantry', and 'external peasantry' in the course of the nineteenth and twentieth centuries? Let us summarize our impressions of the contributions in this volume in the light of this question, which was formulated at the beginning of the present article.

In the plantation areas we noticed the emergence of a new group of independent, individual 'peasants' in the wake of the abolition of Negro slavery. Blouet's paper presents the case of Trinidad; those of Jamaica and the Guianas are also fairly well known. On the other hand, Eisenberg's and Reis's contributions indicate that there must be special prerequisites for this phenomenon to occur. In order to explore the process further we should need more studies on post-abolition developments in those Latin American countries that used to harbour significant numbers of slaves. What were, for instance, the preconditions for 'peasant' exports to develop? This phenomenon is known in (for instance) Jamaica but it has clearly been much more frequent in African and Asiatic countries.[87]

The labour supply of the plantations is dealt with in some of the essays. The essential problem is how to analyse the mechanisms by which corporate Indian 'peasants' were attracted or drawn into the plantation system. Current generalizations about the destructive impact of this on traditional rural society are challenged in Favre's seminal contribution. His conclusion, that the modernization of coastal agriculture might actually work to the benefit of traditional community life in the interior, has to be tested by further research. On the other hand, Rutledge's contribution underlines the interest of plantation landlords in ensuring that their seasonal labour supplies were supported by their own traditional subsistence economy for part of the year. A considerable degree of compatibility between modernized plantations and traditional rural communities is indeed suggested. But there is also a need to explore the impact of the modernization of the plantations on increasing the standard-of-living gap between the resident labour force and seasonal workers. Partly thanks to unionization, the situation of the former was strikingly improved from the 1930s onwards; on the other hand, the 'cheap labour policy' was still pursued, it seems, with respect to seasonal labour.

The dynamics of the traditional grain-and-livestock *hacienda* appear more complex than those of the plantation. As Bauer and Johnson and Martínez Alier make clear, the process of land concentration at times took place within legal domains which had been established much earlier.

Where there was actually an expansion at the cost of Indian 'peasant' communities, as in Bolivia, the moving forces sometimes remain obscure. If there was no increase in demand, it would be most reasonable to consider land appropriation as a way for the elite to expand its basis of low-rent income without any investment of capital. But the possible relation with the mining economy would also have to be explored. In the early-twentieth-century Peruvian Sierra, the demand for wool lay behind neolatifundist aggressiveness. Corporate 'peasants' who were deprived of their land swelled rural-to-urban or rural-to-mining-district migration. Yet many corporate communities have survived up to the present, and they have been far less favoured by current land reform programmes than their *colono* brethren.

As far as the 'internal peasantries' of the *haciendas* are concerned, Bauer and Johnson and Kay make clear that in Chile their work obligations increased considerably under the impact of wheat exports. We learn less about what happened after the export boom. Was there an increase in sharecropping and tenancies? In any case, from the 1920s and 1930s onwards the rapidly increasing urban markets and the incipient mechanization produced, as Kay says, a further 'proletarianization' of rural labour. In the case of the central Peruvian Sierra, Martínez Alier claims that the 'internal' peasants succeeded in defeating the efforts of modernizing landowners to convert them into wage-earners. Though this fascinating hypothesis remains to be examined, it is clear that efforts at modernization of the traditional *haciendas* have become a rather frequent feature since the middle of the twentieth century. Because of the abundance of labour such efforts have tended to have disruptive social effects. The problem has now become the headache of the agencies carrying out national land reforms, as lucidly described by Kay.

We cannot reasonably expect the contributions contained in this book to provide 'models' or even to clearly indicate major trends. We are still only on the threshold of serious and systematic research concerning the evolution of Latin America's agrarian structure during the national period. But the papers form a highly suggestive sample of what serious studies, be they on macro- or micro-level, may reveal. While essential linkages and 'dependencies' do obviously exist between distant markets, 'landlords', and 'internal' and 'external peasantries', their relative importance and many of their social effects remain to be assessed. For example, what did a rise in the demand for an export crop mean in terms of employment for the 'external peasantry'? How did it change the relationship between demesne and 'internal peasant' agriculture? Did the subsequent rise in imports affect the two categories of 'peasants' in any perceptible way? How did the fluctuations of the export economy influence the degree of socio-political control exercised by the landlords over the rural population?

NOTES

1. This paper was first prepared for publication in 1973; therefore, the bibliographical references omit a number of more recent articles on the subject. For a review of the state of research up to that time, see my article 'The Spanish American *hacienda*: a survey of recent research and debate', *Hispanic American Historical Review* LIII (1973), pp. 183–216. More recent studies include William B. Taylor, 'Landed society in New Spain: a view from the south', *Hispanic American Historical Review* LIV,3 (1974), pp. 387–413. The impressive volume *Haciendas, latifundios y plantaciones en América Latina*, ed. Enrique Florescano (Mexico, 1975 – based on papers presented at a CLACSO seminar held in Rome in 1972), although it deals mainly with the colonial period, includes some noteworthy exceptions which cover the period under review here. An important state-of-research article of later date should also be particularly mentioned: Friedrich Katz, 'Labor conditions on *haciendas* in Porfirian Mexico: some trends and tendencies', *Hispanic American Historical Review* LIV,1 (1974), pp. 1–47.

2. See, for example, Eric R. Wolf, *Peasants* (Englewood Cliffs, N. J., 1966); John D. Powell, 'On defining peasants and peasant societies', *Peasant Studies Newsletter* I,3 (Pittsburgh, Pa., 1972), pp. 94–9; Teodor Shanin (ed.), *Peasants and peasant societies* (Harmondsworth, 1971), p. 240 and *passim*; George Dalton, 'Peasantries in anthropology and history', *Current Anthropology* XIII,3/4 (1972), pp. 385–415 (especially pp. 399–402). The strong ties of the 'peasants' to the land is often stressed, but Maria Pereira de Queiroz sensibly asks 'Does it really exist, or is it only a romantic interpretation of the townsman?' ('Expose de synthèse: les paysans-communautés et petits propriétaires', in CNRS, *Les problèmes agraires des Amériques Latines* (Paris, 1967), p. 763).

3. Dalton, 'Peasantries', tries to resolve the dilemma by distinguishing three stages in the evolution of European peasantries: feudal, early modern, and late modern. On the other hand, Eric Hobsbawm is content with a distinction between 'traditional' and 'modern' peasantries (Hobsbawm, 'Peasants and politics', *Peasant Studies Newsletter* I,3 (1973), pp. 109–14.

4. Eric R. Wolf, 'Types of Latin American peasantry', *American Anthropologist* LVII,3 (1955), pp. 452–71; Charles Wagley, 'The peasant', in John J. Johnson (ed.), *Continuity and change in Latin America* (Stanford, Calif., 1964), pp. 21–48; Dalton, 'Peasantries', p. 402; R. P. Schaedel, 'Etude comparative du milieu paysan en Amérique Latine', in CNRS, *Les problèmes agraires*, pp. 47–65.

5. According to Schaedel ('Etude comparative', p. 55), 'in the Andean highlands, and apparently also in Mexico, it was rare for descendants of the Spaniards, no matter how humble their origin, to be peasants themselves before the nineteenth century; on the contrary, in Chile, Colombia, and Venezuela, and in other regions where the indigenous population was neither sedentary nor dense, . . . there developed a local peasant community of impoverished *mestizos*'.

6. Wolf, 'Types of Latin American peasantry', pp. 453–4; and Wolf, *Peasant wars of the twentieth century* (New York, 1969), p. xlv.

7. Shanin (ed.), *Peasants and peasant societies*, p. 254. See also, for example, Henry A. Landsberger (ed.), *Latin American peasant movements* (Ithaca, N. Y., 1969), pp. 4–5; Aníbal Quijano Obregón, 'Contemporary peasant movements', in Seymour M. Martin and Aldo Solari (eds.), *Elites in Latin America* (New York, 1967), p. 335.

8. One should not exaggerate the differences, however, between the organization and economy of 'free' communities and those within traditional *haciendas*: see, for example, William E. Carter, *Aymara communities and the Bolivian agrarian reform* (Gainesville, Fla., 1964). On the other hand, the psychological differences between these two categories of 'peasants' may be profound: see, for example José María Arguedas and Alejandro Ortiz Rescanière, 'La posesión de la tierra: los mitos posthispánicos y la visión del universo en la población monolingue quechua', in CNRS, *Les problèmes agraires*, pp. 309–15.

9. See, for example, Pierre Vilar, 'Mouvements paysans en Amérique Latine', in *Enquête sur les mouvements paysans dans le monde contemporain (de la fin du XVIIIe siècle à nos jours)*, XIIIe Congrès International des Sciences Historiques (Moscow, 1970), pp. 76–96.

10. A. G. Frank, *Capitalism and underdevelopment in Latin America: historical studies of Chile and Brazil* (New York, 1969), pp. 55–66. See also Aníbal Pinto, *Chile: un caso de desarrollo frustrado* (Santiago, 1959). Both authors attempt to explain why development slowed up drastically after 1860, but they offer quite different interpretations.

11. Stanley J. Stein and S. J. Hunt, 'Principal currents in the economic historiography of Latin America', *The Journal of Economic History* XXXI (New York, 1971), p. 230.

12. Tulio Halperín Donghi, *Historia contemporánea de América Latina*, 2nd edn (Madrid, 1970), pp. 146–8.

13. A Swedish commercial agent who visited Chile, Peru–Bolivia, Ecuador, Colombia, and Venezuela observed that foreign trade was dominated everywhere by European merchants: Carl August Gosselman, *Informes sobre los estados sudamericanos en los años de 1837 y 1838* (Institute of Ibero-American Studies, Stockholm, 1962), pp. 60–1, 80, 105, 127, 153.

14. Arnold Bauer, 'The Church and Spanish American agrarian structure: 1765–1865', *The Americas* XXVIII (Academy of American Franciscan History, Washington, 1971), pp. 95–6.

15. Mario Hernández y Sánchez-Barba, 'Ciclos Kondratieff y modelos de frustración económica ibero-americana (siglo XIX)', *Revista de la Universidad de Madrid* XX,78 (1972), pp. 223–6.

16. Gosselman, *Informes*, p. 148, points out that Venezuela alone showed a positive trade balance. He hastens to add, however, that contraband imports annulled this surplus. For the effects of contraband trade see also M. Mörner, 'El comercio de Antioquia alrededor de 1830 según un observador sueco', *Anuario Colombiano de Historia Social y de la Cultura* 1,2 (Bogotá, 1964), pp. 317–32.

17. It should be noted, however, that national and local artisanry would soon suffer from the impact of foreign imports.

18. See M. Mörner, 'En torno a las haciendas de la región del Cuzco desde el siglo XVIII', in E. Florescano (ed.), *Haciendas, latifundios y plantaciones*, pp. 376–92.

19. See, for example, Franklin W. Knight, *Slave society in Cuba during the nineteenth century* (Madison, Wisconsin, 1970), pp. 18–21, 28–30; J. H. Parry and P. M. Sherlock, *A short history of the West Indies* (London, 1957), pp. 223–4.

20. F. Calderón de la Barca, *Life in Mexico, with new material from the author's private journals* (Garden City, N. J., 1966).

21. Keith A. Davies, 'Tendencias demográficas urbanas durante el siglo XIX en México', *Historia Mexicana* XXI,83 (Mexico, 1972), pp. 498–500. See also D. Brading and Celia Wu, 'Population growth and crisis: León, 1720–1860', *Journal of Latin American Studies* V,1 (Cambridge, 1973), pp. 1–36.

22. See, for example, Sanford Mosk's classic article 'Latin America and the world economy, 1850–1914', *Inter-American Economic Affairs* II (Washington, 1948), pp. 53–82; and Hernández y Sánchez-Barba, 'Ciclos Kondratieff', pp. 227–8.

23. W. Arthur Lewis, *Aspects of tropical trade, 1883–1965* (Wiksell Lectures 1969, Stockholm, 1969), p. 8.

24. Paul Bairoch, *Diagnostic de l'évolution économique du Tiers-Monde, 1900–1966* (Paris, 1967), pp. 141–55. This is contrary to Raúl Prebisch's famous statement.

25. Heraclio Bonilla, 'La coyuntura comercial del siglo XIX en el Perú', *Revista del Museo Nacional* XXXV (1967/8; published. Lima, 1970), pp. 159–87.

26. William Paul McGreevey, *An economic history of Colombia, 1845–1930* (Cambridge, 1971), pp. 99, 210.

27. J. Fred Rippy, *British investments in Latin America, 1822–1949* (Minneapolis, Minn., 1949), pp. 36–42.

28. Celso Furtado, *Economic development of Latin America: a survey from colonial times to the Cuban Revolution* (Cambridge, 1971), pp. 32–4.

29. James R. Scobie, *Revolution on the pampas: a social history of Argentine wheat, 1860–1910* (Austin, Texas, 1964), pp. 46–50. For a presentation of the state of research on Argentine and Uruguayan rural history see T. Halperín Donghi's and J. Oddone's accounts in *La historia económica en América Latina*, vols. 1 and 2 (Mexico, 1972). See also, for example, Roberto Cortés Conde, 'La expansion de la economía argentina entre 1870 y 1914 y el papel de la inmigración', *Caravelle: Cahiers du Monde Hispanique et Luso-Bresilien* X (Toulouse, 1968), pp. 67–88.

30. See, for example, the lengthy discussion in William P. Glade, *The Latin American economies: a study of their international evolution* (New York, 1969), pp. 251–70. On the 'enclave' theory, see also J. V. Levin, *The export economies: their pattern of development in historical perspective* (Cambridge, Mass., 1960). His main example is the Peruvian guano export industry.

31. H. Myint, *The economics of the developing countries*, 3rd edn (London, 1967), p. 63.

32. Furtado, *Economic development of Latin America*, p. 33.

33. McGreevey, *Colombia*, pp. 217–43. As Stein and Hunt ('Principal currents', p. 251) point out, an important task of economic historians will be to find out 'which types of primary exporting activities tend almost inevitably to create a set of social institutions reinforcing eventual stagnation, and which hold out substantially better development prospects'.

34. Joseph Grunvald and Philip Musgrove, *Natural resources in Latin American development* (Baltimore, Md. and London, 1970), pp. 305, 311.

35. Stanley J. Stein, *Vassouras: a Brazilian coffee county, 1850–1900* (Cambridge, Mass., 1957); Emília Viotti da Costa, *Da senzala à colônia* (São Paulo, 1966).

36. F. Pérez de la Riva, *El café: historia de su cultivo y explotación en Cuba* (Havana, 1944).

37. James G. Leyburn, *The Haitian people* (New Haven, Conn. and London, 1966), p. 85.

38. Juana Gil-Bermejo García, *Panorama histórico de la agricultura en Puerto Rico* (Seville, 1970), p. 204.

39. John V. Lombardi, *The decline and abolition of Negro slavery in Venezuela, 1820–1854* (Westport, Conn., 1971), pp. 95–111.

40. Miguel Izard, 'El café en la economía Venezolana del siglo XIX: estado de la cuestión', *Estudios* I (Valencia, Spain, 1973), pp. 230–6.

41. In the 1950s less than 7 per cent of Colombia's coffee production came from farms exceeding 50 hectares: McGreevey, *Colombia*, pp. 231–5. See also James J. Parsons, *Antioqueño colonization in western Colombia*, rev. edn (Berkeley and Los Angeles, Calif., 1968), pp. 60–8.

42. Robert C. Beyer, 'The quality of coffee: its Colombian history', *Inter-American Economic Affairs* II, 2 (Washington, 1948), pp. 72–80. Beyer's unpublished doctoral dissertation on the history of Colombian coffee production (University of Minnesota, 1947) has not been available to me for consultation.

43. See, for example, S. A. Mosk, 'The coffee economy of Guatemala, 1850–1918: development and signs of instability', *Inter-American Economic Affairs* IX, 3 (1955), pp. 6–20.

44. See the interesting viewpoints in Halperín Donghi, *Historia contemporánea*, pp. 300–2.

45. Grunvald and Musgrove, *Natural resources*, p. 348.

46. Noël Deerr, *The history of sugar* (London, 1950), vol. 2, pp, 490–1, 531–2.

47. See, for example, the graphic account in Stein, *Vassouras*, pp. 256–9.

48. David Lowenthal, *West Indian societies* (New York, London, and Toronto, 1972). I have discussed the subject in more detail in my article 'Legal equality – social inequality: a post-Abolition theme', *Revista Interamericana Review* III,1 (Puerto Rico, 1973), pp. 24–41. See also the perceptive analysis by Lloyd Best, 'Outlines of a model of pure plantation economy', *Social and Economic Studies* XVII,3 (Mona, Jamaica, 1968), pp. 294–6.

49. Gisela Eisner, *Jamaica, 1830–1930: a study in economic growth* (Manchester, 1961); Douglas Hall, *Free Jamaica, 1838–1865: an economic history* (New Haven, Conn., 1959); Alan H. Adamson, *Sugar without slaves: the political economy of British Guiana, 1838–1904* (New Haven, Conn. and London, 1972); Donald Wood, *Trinidad in transition: the years after slavery* (London and New York, 1968). For a definition of 'peasant' in the Caribbean context see Woodville K. Marshall, 'Notes on peasant development in the West Indies since 1838', *Social and Economic Studies* XVII, 3 (Mona, Jamaica, 1968), pp. 252–3.

50. Wood, *Trinidad in transition*, pp. 48–9.

51. Ibid., pp. 53–4. Wood takes up the crisis of 1847 at pp. 122–5.

52. Rolf Knight, *Sugar plantations and labor patterns in the Cauca Valley*, Department of Anthropology, University of Toronto, Anthropological Series no. 12 (1972).

53. Caio Prado Júnior, *História econômica do Brasil*, 2nd edn (São Paulo, 1962), p. 250. In 1851–60 sugar constituted 21.2 per cent of Brazil's total exports, in 1861–70 it was 12.3 per cent, and in 1891–1900 only 6.0 per cent. Hélio Schlitter Silva, 'Tendências e caraterísticas do comércio exterior do Brasil no século XIX', *Revista de História da Economia Brasileira* I,1 (São Paulo, 1953), p. 8.

54. In addition to the essays in this book, see J. H. Galloway, 'The last years of slavery on the sugar plantations of northeastern Brazil', *Hispanic American Historical Review* LI, 4 (1971), pp. 586–605; Peter Eisenberg, 'Abolishing slavery: the process on Pernambuco's sugar plantations', *Hispanic American Historical Review* LII, 4 (1972), pp. 580–97.

55. Eisenberg, 'Abolishing slavery', p. 597.

56. Eisenberg, p. 345 above. Reis asserts that after 1888 *moradores* were worse off than slaves in terms of consumption. At the same time he believes that when they were incorporated with the labour force, they became slightly less undernourished than earlier *moradores* had been.

57. Sidney Mintz, 'The culture history of a Puerto Rican sugar cane plantation, 1876–1949', *Hispanic American Historical Review* XXXIII,2 (1953), pp. 224–51. See also his book, *Worker in the cane: a Puerto Rican life history* (New Haven, Conn., 1960).

58. Eisenberg's recent book, *The sugar industry of Pernambuco, 1840–1910: modernization without change* (Berkeley, Calif., 1974), has not been available to me for consultation. According to Richard Graham, *Britain and the onset of modernization in Brazil, 1850–1914* (Cambridge, 1968), pp. 156–7, British-owned *usinas* made a considerable contribution to modernization within the sugar industry.

59. Ramiro Guerra y Sánchez, *Sugar and society in the Caribbean: an economic history of Cuban agriculture* (New Haven, Conn., 1964). It is a pity that Manuel Moreno Fraginals's excellent, provocative work, *El Ingenio: el complejo económico social Cubano del azúcar, I (1760–1860)* (Havana, 1964), has not been completed to cover the same period.

60. On Bahia, see Galloway, 'Last years of slavery', pp. 602–4.

61. Celso Furtado, *The economic growth of Brazil: a survey from colonial to modern times* (Berkeley and Los Angeles, Calif., 1965), pp. 150–2.

62. A moot question is, of course, how to assess the demise of the traditional 'plantocracy'. Gileno Dé Carli, *O progresso histórico da usina em Pernambuco* (Rio de Janeiro, 1962), deals with some aspects of this question.

63. Furtado, *Economic growth of Brazil*, p. 163.

64. Halperín Donghi, *Historia contemporánea*, pp. 308–9. For statistics on the volume and value of Peruvian sugar exports in the period 1900–38, see Emilio Romero, *Historia económica del Perú*, 2nd edn (Lima, n.d.), vol. 2, p. 211; and Table 38 above.

65. Deerr, *History of sugar*, vol. 2, p. 531. See also, for example, Simon G. Hanson, *Economic development in Latin America* (Washington, 1951), pp. 107–8.

66. A more detailed account can be found in Klarén's book, *La formación de las haciendas azucareras y los orígenes del APRA* (Lima, 1970); published in English as *Modernization, dislocation and Aprismo: origins of the Peruvian Aprista Party, 1870–1932* (Austin, Texas, 1973).

67. An enlightening diagram showing living costs, nominal wages, and real wages for Peruvian rural workers in the period 1912–28 can be found in Claes Brundenius, *Imperialismens ansikte: 400 år av underutveckling i Peru* (Lund, Sweden, 1972), p. 61.

68. That the modernization of the sugar industry in Morelos provided the backdrop of the Zapata revolt was made clear by François Chevalier, 'Un facteur décisif de la révolution agraire au Mexique: le soulèvement de Zapata (1911–1919)', *Annales ESC* I (Paris, 1961), pp. 66–82. See also John Womack, *Zapata and the Mexican Revolution* (New York, 1970).

69. See, for example, D. A. G. Waddell, *The West Indies and the Guianas* (Englewood Cliffs, N. J., 1967), pp. 94–5, 110.

70. See particularly K. W. J. Post, 'The politics of protest in Jamaica in 1938: some problems of analysis and conceptualization', *Social and Economic Studies* XVIII, 4 (Mona, Jamaica, 1969), pp. 374–90.

71. Hoetink's paper is based on his book *El pueblo dominicano, 1850–1900: apuntes para su sociología*, 2nd edn (Santiago, D. R., 1972). The first large-scale strike among

'Landlords' and 'peasants' and the outer world 481

the sugar workers took place in 1946; it was surprisingly successful: Jesús de Galíndez, *The era of Trujillo, Dominican dictator* (Tucson, Arizona, 1973), pp. 158–9. See also Franklin J. Franco, *República Dominicana: clases, crisis y comandos* (Havana, 1966), pp. 51–2.

72. Miguel Murmis and Carlos Waisman, 'Monoproducción agroindustrial, crisis y clase obrera: la industria azucarera tucumana', *Revista Latinoamericana de Sociología* V,2 (Buenos Aires, 1969), pp. 349–50.

73. Claude Collin Delavaud, 'Les consequences sociales de la modernisation de l'agriculture dans les haciendas de la côte nord du Pérou', in CNRS, *Les problemes agraires*, pp. 363–83, is an important, pioneering study.

74. This continuous process of penetration has been very little studied. M. Mörner, *La corona española y los foráneos en los pueblos de indios de América* (Stockholm, 1970), gives a general account for the colonial period.

75. José María Dalence, *Bosquejo estadístico de Bolivia* (Chuquisaca, 1851), pp. 234–5, makes a breakdown: *comuneros con tierras*, 48,295 families; *agregados con tierras*, 57,837; and *forasteros sin tierras*, 31,972. Thus there was a total of 138,104 families living in communities, as compared to some 80,000 *colono (arrendero)* families. But Dalence adds that these latter used to be much more numerous when there were still civil and ecclesiastical liens on property. He believes that *comunidades* were even less productive than *haciendas* (ibid., p. 274).

76. Even in Dalence's time, La Paz imported some of its food from Peru.

77. Ramiro Condarco Morales, *Zárate, el temible Willka: historia de la rebelión indígena de 1899* (La Paz, 1965), pp. 41–6.

78. Herbert S. Klein, *Parties and political change in Bolivia, 1880–1952* (Cambridge, 1969), pp. 5–6, 16, 31–4. Luis Peñaloza, *Historia económica de Bolivia*, 2 vols. (La Paz, 1953–4), vol. 2, p. 103, stresses the decline of silver prices during 1865–70; and he gives a table showing the percentage of national revenues derived from Indian tax during 1832–65 (ibid., vol. I, p. 288).

79. Condarco Morales, *Zárate*, pp. 46–9 and *passim*.

80. Edmundo Flores, 'Taraco: monografía de un latifundio del altiplano boliviano', *El Trimestre Económico* XXII, 85–8 (Mexico, 1955), pp. 211–12. Taraco was a *comunidad*, but President Ismael Montes himself forced the Indians to sell it to him in 1907.

81. Apart from his paper written with Ann H. Johnson for this book, Bauer has published the following: 'Expansion económica en una sociedad tradicional: Chile central en el siglo XIX', *Historia* IX (Santiago, 1970), pp. 137–235; 'Chilean rural labor in the nineteenth century', *The American Historical Review* LXXVI (Washington, 1971), pp. 1059–83; 'The hacienda El Huique in the agrarian structure of nineteenth-century Chile', *Agricultural History* XLVI, 4 (1972), pp. 455–70.

82. For a general analysis of sectoral growth, 1870–1899, see Marcello Carmagnani, *Sviluppo industriale e sottosviluppo economico: il caso cileno (1860–1920)* (Turin, 1971), pp. 128–32.

83. Bauer, 'Chilean rural labor', pp. 1079–80.

84. See François Chevalier, 'L'expansion de la grande propriété dans le Haut-Pérou au XXe siécle', *Annales ESC* XXI (Paris, 1966), pp. 815–31; Jean Piel, 'Le problème de la terre dans la region du Cuzco à l'époque contemporaine (fin 19e – début 20e siécle)', *Recherche Coopérative* no. 147 (Institute des Hautes Études de l'Amérique Latine, Paris, 1970), pp. 5–16, and his 'A propos d'un soulèvement rural Péruvien au début du vingtième siècle: Tocroyoc, 1921', *Revue d'Histoire Moderne et Con-*

temporaine XIV (Paris, 1967), pp. 375–405. An earlier period is outlined by Piel in 'The place of the peasantry in the national life of Peru in the nineteenth century', *Past and Present* no. 46 (Oxford, 1970), pp. 108–33.

85. See especially Piel, 'A propos d'un soulèvement', pp. 390–2.
86. Martínez Alier's account of the conflict between a modernizing landlord and shepherds of the traditional *huacchillero* type can be compared with what we know about an estate in southeastern Peru. Between 1953 and 1957, *colonos* there were deprived of many of their traditional rights: Gustavo Alencastre Montúfar, *Informe sobre la situación económico-social en Lauramarca* (Lima, 1957). See also M. H. Kuczynski Godard, 'Un latifundio del sur: una contribución al conocimiento del problema social', *América Indígena* VI, 3 (Mexico, 1946), pp. 257–74. Compare the pro-landlord interpretation of Cesar Augusto Reinaga, *En indio y la tierra en Mariátegui* (Cuzco, 1959), pp. 106–7.
87. See for example Myint, *Economies of developing countries*, pp. 38–52.

CHAPTER 19

Abstracts of other papers

Plantations, peasants, and proletariat in the West Indies:
an essay on agrarian capitalism and alienation

GEORGE BECKFORD

This paper explores the origins of rural poverty in the West Indies. Beckford's discussion of the transition from slavery to free labour illustrates many of the points brought out in Part IV of this book. In particular the author distinguishes between, on the one hand, the Leeward Islands – where the shortage of cultivable land threw the ex-slaves back onto the plantation system for subsistence – and, on the other hand, the larger territories, such as Jamaica, Trinidad, and Guyana, where the greater availability of land outside the plantation system provided the basis for the emergence of a peasant-farmer group from among the ranks of the ex-slaves.

The emancipation of the slaves in 1838 generally forced up the cost of labour in the West Indies, and together with certain other economic difficulties this change in the relations of production gave a strong impetus to the search for more efficient forms of production and an improved technology in the sugar industry. This development of a modern sugar industry in the latter part of the nineteenth century can be compared with the changes which were taking place simultaneously in other sugar-producing areas such as northeast Brazil and coastal Peru.

However, the condition of the rural sugar proletariat and the small farmer class remained extremely depressed, and major agrarian unrest occurred in 1865 (Jamaica), 1935 (St Kitts), and 1938 (Jamaica). Beckford argues that the peasant-farmer group played a key role in these rural revolts.

More recently, the development of trade unionism under a reformist leadership has won some limited economic and social advances for the rural workers, and migration from the rural areas has defused any serious social unrest. However, rural poverty remains widespread, and unemployment is growing. Beckford argues that if the peasantry once more are pushed down to the 'margin of survival' they may again provide the catalyst for serious unrest in the region, and in alliance with the rural proletariat they could bring revolutionary change to one or more of the countries of the West Indies.

(Note: This article has been published in full in George Beckford, *Small garden, bitter weed – roots of Caribbean poverty*, Institute of Social and Economic Research, University of the West Indies (Kingston, 1975).)

484

Abstracts of other papers

Domination and stagnation: a study of the Bolivian hacienda

JANE BENTON

An interesting comparison can be drawn between the agrarian histories of Mexico and Bolivia during the latter part of the nineteenth century. In both countries the predominantly Indian rural population was robbed of its communal lands and incorporated into an agricultural economy dominated by non-Indian landowners. But whereas in Mexico this process coincided with a general modernization of the economy and the development of fairly capitalistic forms of *hacienda* in certain areas, in Bolivia – as Jane Benton clearly demonstrates – the large estates created in the late nineteenth century remained extremely backward in both economic and social terms, to such an extent that it makes sense to refer to them as 'semi-feudal'. In particular, Jane Benton points out that the Bolivian landowner typically farmed only a very small proportion of his *hacienda* directly, and in the cultivation of this land he relied almost entirely upon *colonos* (unpaid labour tenants) rather than on wage labour.

In chapter 6 of this book, Juan Martínez Alier argues that labour tenancy in Peru was, at least in some cases, manipulated by the Indians in their own interests, but Jane Benton suggests that in the case of Bolivia there can be little doubt of the viciously exploitative nature of this system of labour tenancy. To illustrate this she gives a detailed account of a typical *hacienda* of the Lake Titicaca region in the early 1950s.

In contrast to many of the other studies in this book, which deal with the problems of social and economic change, Jane Benton emphasizes that any study of the Bolivian *hacienda* up to 1952 is essentially a study of stagnation and lack of change. Even after the widespread agrarian reform of the mid-1950s, many of the cultural and social consequences of the *hacienda* system persist and continue to plague Bolivian rural society.

The development of agrarian–commercial capitalism in Puerto Rico: some aspects of the growth of the coffee hacienda system, 1857–98

CARLOS BUITRAGO ORTIZ

Whereas most of the papers in this volume concentrate on the social and economic organization of different types of estate, the paper by Carlos Buitrago Ortiz deals extensively with the activities of a particular social group and their role in the economic changes taking place in mid-nineteenth-century Puerto Rico.

The author draws attention to the role of immigrant entrepreneurs from Corsica and Mallorca, and with the aid of substantial archival documentation he illustrates the economic activities of these immigrants in considerable detail. Particular attention is given to their role in the development of the coffee industry.

Some light is thrown upon the internal organization of the coffee *hacienda* by the author's references to two institutions, the *libreta de contabilidad* and the *tienda de despacho*. The former was a method of bookkeeping whereby the economic performance of individual workers was recorded; this in effect reflects the highly rationalized nature of the labour process in these coffee *haciendas*. The latter was a form of 'company store' in which the *hacendado* sold the basic necessities of life to his workers, apparently at a good rate of profit. Thus Buitrago Ortiz points out that the *hacendado* was not only the owner of the means of production but also a merchant, 'a seller of the means of consumption'.

Finally the author draws attention to the formation of a quasi-oligarchy within the *hacendado*–merchant class, towards the end of the nineteenth century. Based principally on the banking sector, this oligarchy tended to exert an increasingly dominant influence over the economy as a whole. Towards the end of his paper Buitrago Ortiz suggests that this group had various plans for the modernization of the economic infrastructure prior to the U.S. Occupation in 1898.

Recent developments in capitalist agriculture and agrarian struggles in Colombia

PIERRE GILHODES

Unlike the majority of the other essays in this volume, Pierre Gilhodes' paper deals with a relatively recent period of agrarian history. Describing the advances in capitalist agriculture from the mid-1950s onwards, Gilhodes draws attention to the recent large increase in production of those agricultural commodities pertaining to the capitalist or 'entrepreneurial' sector (sugar, cotton, irrigated rice, and so on) compared with the relatively poor record of the more traditional sectors of agriculture (extensive cattle-raising and coffee.)

He goes on to show how this development of capitalist agriculture created social and economic tensions in the countryside, leading to two major waves of rural unrest (1959–60 and 1969–70). One of the most important factors leading to peasant unrest was the failure of the agrarian reform law to meet the increased expectations of the peasantry which it helped to stimulate. Since the law stated that if previously unused land were brought into 'adequate cultivation' (which happened increasingly, as 'traditional' landlords let their land to capitalist farmers or started to farm it themselves) then it was no longer subject to agrarian reform, the peasants were thus frequently denied access to land, and feeling themselves betrayed they commenced a wave of land occupations.

Gilhodes makes some important criticisms of the tendency to sharply distinguish between 'peasant demands' (for land) and 'worker demands' (for wages), pointing out that in many concrete cases the same rural groups have been involved in both types of demands. In this sense Gilhodes stresses the fluctuating, intermediate position of the Colombian rural lower class – part peasant and part rural proletarian. Finally, the author discusses some of the possible future developments in Colombian rural society in the light of the expansion of these forms of capitalist agriculture.

Changes in the agrarian structure of the Dominican Republic in the nineteenth century

HARRY HOETINK

The Dominican Republic can be distinguished from some of the other sugar cane economies studied in this book, since slavery had already been abolished for over half a century when modern sugar plantations were established in the 1870s. The absence of slavery – and, for that matter, of any other form of forced labour – presents Hoetink with the opportunity to study some of the effects of the development of a modern sugar plantation economy in a relatively free labour market. Hoetink describes the processes whereby the older cattle ranching/cacao/coffee economy declined with the growth and expansion of the sugar cane economy. The small farms and ranches which were required by the sugar *centrales* for the expansion of their cane land were taken from their owners by fair means or foul, and as a result there emerged a growing army of landless agricultural labourers, dependent on the sugar plantations, albeit usually on a seasonal basis, for employment and income.

This proletarianization of the local rural population was accompanied by the immigration of workers from Haiti, Curaçao, and the British West Indies. Hoetink points out that the consequent cultural as well as social differences among the sugar plantation workers inhibited the growth of class-consciousness. The first strike which is recorded in the Dominican Republic occurred not in the sugar plantation area but on a railway project in the northern part of the country, where only native Dominican workers were employed.

Finally Hoetink emphasizes some tendencies towards romanticism in contemporary Dominican criticism of the sugar plantation economy. He points out that the yearning to return to a 'golden age' of economic autarky is based on a misunderstanding of the island's economic and political history.

Mythos and pathos: some unpleasantries on peasantries

ANTHONY LEEDS

This paper raises a number of basic theoretical issues about the nature of the peasantry relevant to the theme of this volume, some of which are discussed in the Introduction. Anthony Leeds makes a number of telling criticisms of some of the contemporary theorizing about peasants. He argues that in discussing this topic it is essential to distinguish between a 'person' (as a decision-maker) and a 'role' (as a socio-cultural entity). The distinction emphasizes that since roles are not genetic there is no inherent or necessary connection between a person and a role – only as institutional one – and that, in the absence of such a necessary connection, choice among roles is always, in principle, possible for persons, and its absence has an institutional and not a personal explanation (e.g. the 'peasant mentality'). Hence, individuals may be involved in a complex system of roles between which they can move to an extent which makes nonsense of some of the searching after an alleged peasant 'essence' or 'culture'. For example, a person (or aggregate of persons) may alternate among peasant, squatter, job-contracting, town-service, and rural-proletarian roles; such an alternation may occur not only within the lifetime of a single individual, but just as easily within a season, a week, or even a day. Indeed, Leeds argues that from a scientific point of view, *fixity within* a role is just as much in need of explanation as mobility. He further argues that no role stands alone. Both by its theoretical definition and by its actual social delimitation, any role or role set, as a charter of rights, duties, obligations, etc., necessarily entails 'alter' roles and role sets (rights over other, duties to others, and so on). Transactions take place between role and alter(s), and formal regularities of such transactions are called institutions. As a theoretical consequence, Leeds argues, no role such as 'peasant' can be understood without reference to its alter(s). A person's choice of role is governed by strategic considerations determined by the respective characteristics and situational determinants of time, place, and conditions, as of the market. As the conditions change, so also do the role and role alters, and hence too the institution. A similar argument holds true for the *person* commonly designated 'peasant'; in principle that person may strategically choose any alternative roles for his own ends. The limiting case is the absence of alternative roles for him to choose among, but this case must itself be explained.

In the second part of his paper, Leeds exemplifies the preceding theoretical arguments by reference to a case study of the historical pattern of rural change in the cacao-producing region of the State of Bahia, Brazil. From the ruins of the slave-plantation agrarian structure of the late nineteenth century, many ex-slaves and descendants of slaves struck out into the hinterland to create an agricultural frontier, establishing themselves for a time as squatters, producing partly for subsistence and incipiently for the commercial cacao market. In time, more powerful economic figures came to dominate the cacao industry by forcing the squatters off their lands and gradually converting them into a rural proletariat. Summing up the overall historical pattern, Leeds concludes that 'The general rule has been the elimination of the smallholders, the peripheralization of the residual ones, and the conversion of the several agrarian roles into the almost single one of wage labour.' From the point of view of the societal process, Leeds sees the major categories of agricultural labour as having been, sequentially, slaves, then squatters, and, today, their latter-day translations as rural proletarians and tenants. Though at each period each of these types of labour roles was dominant (along with their respective alter roles of slave-holder, plantation-owner, etc.), each period also had subsidiary roles for agricultural labour which presented some possibilities of choice for persons. The limitations on choice were governed by institutional aspects of role relations, especially restrictive sanctions. Clearly, this pattern of agrarian change is very similar to the general type discussed in Part IV of this volume. More specifically, the example studied by Leeds bears close similarities to the Colombian case described by Michael Taussig (chapter 17). Further, many of the empirical studies included in this volume provide examples of rural mobility in the context of broader, overall changes in the agrarian mode of production, such as the changes which Leeds treats here both theoretically and substantively.

'Gamonalismo' in the Andes: the central Sierra of Peru in 1950

JOSE R. SABOGAL-WIESSE

This paper describes in graphic detail the rural class structure of the central Sierra of Peru between the years 1947 and 1954, during which period the author was working in the region as a representative of the State Bank for Agricultural Credit. The paper opens with an account of the salt-mining industry, an industry which was in fact taken from the Indians of the central Sierra by the state, following the War of the Pacific in the nineteenth century. An apparatus of local bosses and officials was created in order to supervise the exploitation of this natural resource in the interests of the national ruling class, and various forms of direct and indirect coercion were used in order to recruit Indian labour for the salt mines.

Jose Sabogal-Weisse relates various accounts of the brutal treatment meted out to the Indians of the region by the *gamonales* – the white *hacienda* owners. Moreover he states that in many cases the Indian peasants were attached to the *haciendas* by forms of extra-economic coercion reminiscent of medieval serfdom.

However, the author also describes two major processes of change which were beginning to get under way in the central Sierra about this time. On the one hand, newer groups of landowners, often of middle-class origin, were expanding in the region, bringing with them more capitalistic forms of estate management. In one example described by the writer, a violent confrontation occurred between one of these new middle-class landowners and the Indians of a neighbouring community. The landowner in question successfully expropriated the Indians' traditional grazing lands by bringing in armed police, who murdered a number of Indians. On the other hand, the Indians themselves were beginning to experience a new independence, and growing numbers of them were breaking away from the archaic rural society of the Sierra by migrating to the coastal cotton plantations, where they could obtain money wages under freer working conditions. This outflow of labour from the central Sierra further weakened the pre-capitalist agrarian system of the region and undermined the rural class structure based on the principles of '*gamonalismo*'.

The impact of the Conquest of the Desert upon the Tehuelche of Chubut, Argentina – from hunters and gatherers to peasants

GLYN WILLIAMS AND JULIA GARLANT

Whereas the majority of the cases presented in this book deal with the conversion (or attempted conversion) of various types of peasantry into rural proletarians under the impact of a developing agrarian capitalism, Glyn Williams and Julia Garlant have studied the impact of colonial and capitalist institutions upon an indigenous society which anthropologists would regard as being 'primitive' rather than 'peasant'.

In contrast to those parts of Latin America previously dominated by the Incas and their vassal states, central and southern Argentina contained migrant populations of hunters and gatherers with little or no experience of the settled and hierarchical social order of a peasant-based civilization. For this reason, these small indigenous groups, which were both unwilling and unsuitable to serve as estate labour, had to be hounded and destroyed by the Argentine army to make the country safe for the waves of Europeans whose immigration was to follow shortly upon the 'Conquest of the Desert'.

The authors first describe early colonization attempts in Chubut province prior to the Conquest and then give an account of the campaign against the Indians and the process of land alienation which followed it. The latter part of the paper deals with the precarious economic and social position of the contemporary survivors of the Conquest. The authors show how the Indian has continued to suffer the alienation of his lands, the destruction of his own native culture, and the general marginalization of his economic position. It appears that many Indians have finally become converted into rural wage labourers working on the massive sheep *estancias* of the Patagonian region.

GLOSSARY OF
SPANISH AND PORTUGUESE TERMS
USED IN THE TEXT

Abrir montaña	Clearance of virgin land for agricultural colonization.
Acido fénico	Carbolic acid.
Acta de conciliación	Judicial compromise between parties to a dispute – typically, unions and employers – reached through mediation of government officials (Peru).
Administrador	Manager of a *hacienda*.
Afiliados	Full-time plantation workers (Colombia).
Afuerino	Wage labourer employed on a *hacienda* in Chile (the term means 'outsider': *afuerinos* were not permanently attached to the estate).
Agave	Juice from the *maguey* plant, used to distil *mezcal* (q.v.).
Agregado	Subsistence farmer allowed use of marginal land on a large estate, in return for occasional labour services and political support for the owner (Brazil); service tenant (Colombia).
Agricultor	General term for rural dweller, including proprietors, tenants, labourers, and the like; medium-size commercial farmers (Peru).
Aguardiente	Raw liquor distilled from sugar cane.
Alcalde	Mayor.
Aldea	Hamlet; small rural settlement (see also *caserío* and *villorio*).
A libreta	System of sale of commodities on credit in rural areas (see also *libreta de contabilidad*).
Allegado	Sub-tenant, generally related to an *inquilino* or *colono* and used by him to fulfil labour obligations to the landowner (Peru, Chile).
Almocrêve	Pack-horse driver (Brazil).
Alquilado	Seasonal labourer (Mexico).
Altiplano	High plateau of the Andes.
Anticipo	Advance on annual profits paid by the Corporación de la Reforma Agraria (CORA) to the members of *asentamientos* (Chile).

490

Apacheta	Pre-Columbian religious monument dedicated to *Pachamama* (q.v.) (Argentina).
Aparcero	Sharecropper.
APRA (Aprismo)	Peruvian political party (Alianza Popular Revolucionaria Americana), founded in the 1920s by Víctor Raúl Haya de la Torre.
Aprista	Adherent of APRA (q.v.).
Arreglarle un salario	Payment of wage supplement by an *inquilino* (q.v.) to his *peón reemplazante* (q.v.) to bring it up to the normal *peón* wage.
Arrendatario	Labour-service tenant on coffee estates (Colombia); tenant farmer on sheep ranch (Argentina); tenant farmer paying rent in cash or kind (Chile, Mexico).
Arrendatario de pastos	Renter of pasture belonging to a *hacienda* for grazing sheep (Peru).
Arrendero	Tenant on *hacienda* (Argentina).
Arrendire	Labour-service tenant in La Convención area of Peru.
Arriendo	Annual cash ground rent paid on cultivated land (northwest Argentina).
Arrimado	Labour-service tenant (Ecuador); squatter (Mexico).
Asedio externo	Pressure on *hacienda* lands exerted by peasants and others living outside the estate.
Asedio interno	Gradual encroachment by resident tenants, wage labourers, and others on *hacienda* resources.
Asentado	Former *inquilino* (q.v.), member of an *asentamiento* (q.v.) (Chile).
Asentamiento	Co-operative land settlement unit used in Chilean agrarian reform.
Asiento	Dwelling-place, settlement.
Ayllu	Village community, traditionally of pre-Columbian origin (Peru).
Bagazo	Dried cane fibre used for fertilizer (Colombia).
Bajo pueblo	Rural lower class.
Banguê	Small traditional sugar mill (Brazil).
Bangueseiro	Owner-operator of a *banguê* (q.v.).
Baracán	Homespun textiles (northwest Argentina).
Barracão	Plantation store (Brazil).
Beneficiador	Owner—operator of a coffee-processing plant.
Beneficio	Coffee-processing plant.
Bochinche	Brawl, quarrel (Colombia).
Bozal	Slave newly arrived from Africa (Colombia).
Bracero	Permanent or seasonal agricultural labourer.

Caatinga	Arid scrub and thorn brush of the *sertão* of north-eastern Brazil.
Cabildo	Local council; place where this council meets.
Cachaça	Cheap, low-quality rum (Brazil).
Cafetal	Coffee grove.
Cafetera	Female coffee-picker.
Camarada	Independent worker hired by coffee estates for daily wage (Brazil).
Camayo	Tenant or sharecropper (Peru).
Cambio de mano	Reciprocal labour service (Colombia).
Campesino	A peasant; any rural dweller who derives his main livelihood from agriculture.
Campiña	Countryside surrounding a town.
Cantina	*Hacienda* store (Peru).
Capellanía	Church mortgage on rural lands.
Caporal	Field overseer.
Carretero	Carter.
Casco	Main buildings of *hacienda* (Mexico).
Caserío	Hamlet; small rural settlement (see also *aldea* and *villorio*).
Casita	Small house for tenants, owned and maintained by the *hacienda* (Colombia).
Castas	Levels in system of ethnic stratification.
Catastro	Cadastral survey.
Caudillismo	Political system dominated by local bosses (*caudillos*).
Caudillo	Local political boss.
Cazador	Hunter.
Cebú	Breed of cattle well suited to tropical regions.
Censo	Church tax on land.
Central	Large modern sugar mill (Caribbean).
CERA (Centro de Reforma Agraria)	Co-operative structure established by the Agrarian Reform in Chile.
Cerco	Garden plot given to *inquilino* (q.v.) (Chile).
Chacarería	Vegetable cultivation.
Chacra	Small farm (Argentina); plot of land cultivated for his own use by service tenant on *hacienda* (Peru).
Chacrate	Sub-tenant on Peruvian highland *hacienda*; generally related to a *colono* (q.v.).
Chacrita	Diminutive of *chacra* (q.v.).
Chicha	Alcoholic drink made from maize, *quinoa*, etc.
Cholo	Acculturated Indian or *mestizo* (q.v.) (Peru).
Choza provisional	Temporary hut used to house seasonal labourers (Mexico).

Ckunza	Ancient language of the Atacama tribe (Argentina).
Colono	Service tenant on Andean *hacienda*; complex combination of daily, annual, and piece-work payments for labour on coffee *fazenda*, combined with non-monetary benefits (Brazil); sugar cane grower (Cuba).
Colono a larga distancia	Labour-rent tenants recruited from highland *haciendas* for use as seasonal harvest labour on lowland *haciendas* (Guatemala).
Comité campesino	Peasant committee; compromise between *asentamiento* and CERA (q.v.) (Chile).
Compadre	God-parent.
Comuna	Local administrative unit (Chile).
Comunario	Member of a *comunidad* (q.v.).
Comunero	Member of a *comunidad* (q.v.).
Comunidad	Freeholding rural community; sometimes required to conform to a set of legal norms to quality for legal recognition.
Concertado	Labour-service tenant (Colombia).
Concertaje	System of labour-service tenancy.
Conchabador	Labour contractor; another term for *contratista* (q.v.).
Conquistadores	Spanish conquerors.
Contrabandista	Smuggler.
Contratista	Labour contractor, recruiting workers for commercial estates, particularly sugar plantations.
Contrato de formação	A four-to-six-year contract to develop a coffee grove (Brazil).
Conuquero	Labour-service tenant (Venezuela).
Corral	Yard for domestic animals.
Corumbá	Seasonal migrant workers from the *sertão* (q.v.) of northeast Brazil.
Cosechera, Cosechero	Coffee-picker.
Costeño	Inhabitant of coastal region.
Criado	Domestic servant.
Criollo	Characteristic people or institutions of Spanish America.
Cuadra	Measure of land, equivalent to 1.57 hectares (Chile).
Cuadrero	Labour-service tenant (Ecuador).
Cuadrilla	Team of migrant labourers (Guatemala).
Cuadrilla de malhechores	Gang of outlaws.
Cuartel de peones	Housing for migrant coffee labourers.
Curso forzoso	Compulsory circulation of paper money.

Dependiente	Clerk on rural estate (Mexico).
Derecho de sereno y alumbramiento	Tax paid in urban areas for night-watchman and street-lighting services (Chile).
De rulo	Non-irrigated *hacienda* land.
Diezmo	Tithe on land and certain crops.
Ejido	Communal land holding.
Empleado	Administrative or technical worker on estate.
Empreitada	Jobbing contract using piece-rates (Brazil).
Empresa patronal	Demesne lands, worked directly by landowner.
Empresa rural	Commercial rural enterprise in general.
Encomienda	System of labour grants, originating with responsibility assigned to *conquistadores* (q.v.) for looking after the spiritual welfare of the Indians entrusted to them by the Crown.
Enganchado	Labourer hired by means of cash advances on his wages.
Enganchador	Labour contractor using *enganche* (q.v.) system.
Enganche	System of hiring labourers by means of cash advances.
Engenho	Traditional sugar mill (Brazil).
Engenho central	Modern sugar mill (Brazil).
Estancia	Commercial cattle or sheep ranch; term also applied to the traditional colonial estate (Argentina); dispersed rural settlement in highlands (Peru); stock-raising *hacienda* (northern Mexico).
Exención militar	Exemption from military service, secured by payment of a fee or tax.
Expediente de afectación	Dossier compiled by agrarian reform officials as part of process of expropriation of *haciendas* (Peru).
Faena	Unpaid, occasional Sunday labour, to fulfil communal duties.
Fazenda	Large estate (Brazil).
Fazendeiro	Owner or operator of a large estate (Brazil).
Finca	Farm.
Finquero	Owner or operator of a *finca* (q.v.).
Forastero	Seasonal worker (Chile).
Formador	Immigrant worker contracted by a coffee-planter for a certain number of years, to develop a new coffee grove (Brazil).
Fornecedor	Independent sugar cane grower (Brazil).
Fraccionamiento	Selling-off of a large estate in small lots (Mexico).
Fundito	A very small rural property, which may be as small as half a hectare (Chile).

Fundo	A small rural estate or farm (Chile).
Fundo rústico	Rural property in general.
Gamonal	A *hacienda* owner or operator (Peru).
Gañan	A rural wage labourer.
Gente decente	Middle or upper classes.
Gloria chupe	A special soup prepared for Easter Sunday (Peru).
Gobernador	Governor.
Goce	A piece of land allocated to each peasant member of a Centro de Reforma Agraria (see CERA) for his own private use (Chile).
Gratificación	A tip or bonus.
Guano	Natural fertilizer derived from deposits of bird droppings.
Habilitación	System of labour recruitment through cash advances.
Habilitado	Kind or money-paying tenant (Argentina).
Habilitador	Labour contractor or recruiting agent.
Hacendado	Owner of a large estate.
Hacienda	A large rural estate.
Hacienda estatal	A large state agricultural enterprise.
Herencia	A small peasant plot of land, resulting from subdivision through inheritance.
Hierbaje	Payment in kind to *hacienda* by *arrendatario* (q.v.) for use of pastures belonging to *hacienda*.
Huaccha	Sheep belonging to a tenant shepherd on a Peruvian Andean *hacienda* (Quechua).
Huacchillero	Shepherd on Peruvian Andean *haciendas* who has his own sheep grazing on pastures belonging to the *hacienda* (Quechua).
Huasipunguero	Labour-service tenant (Ecuador).
Huaso	Rural worker in general; a rustic (Chile).
Huerta	Garden or orchard (Mexico); land given to *arrendatarios* (q.v.) for growing their own food crops and raising small livestock (Colombia).
Indios forasteros	'Indians from other parts of the country', i.e. migrant workers.
Indiviso	Common lands.
Ingenio	Sugar factory or mill.
Ingenuo	A child born of a slave mother.
Inquilinaje	The use of *inquilinos* (q.v.) on rural estates (Chile).
Inquilino	A labour-service tenant resident on a large estate (Chile).
Inquilino de media obligación	A labour-service tenant who receives only half the normal land allotment for his own cultivation and

	therefore has only half the normal labour obligations to the estate (Chile).
Inquilino-mediero	A labour-service tenant who cultivates on a sharecropping basis (Chile).
Inquilino-peón	A cottage-garden labourer: a labour-service tenant who receives only a *cerco* as part-payment for his services (Chile).
Jefe	Chief.
Jornal	Daily wage payment.
Jornalero	Day-wage labourer.
Jornalero habilitado	A day-wage labourer contracted to work for an estate for a specified period of time (Guatemala).
Jornalero no habilitado	Day-wage labourer contracted at a special rate (Guatemala).
Junta de Catastro	Cadastral Survey Office.
Juez de paz	Justice of the Peace.
Keshwarr	Temperate valley lands (Peru).
Labor	A small estate, generally smaller than a *hacienda*.
Ladino	*Mestizo* or hispanicized Indian (the term refers to cultural rather than racial characteristics).
Latifundio(a)	Large traditional estate(s).
Latifundista	Owner of a *latifundio* (q.v.).
Lavrador	Sharecropper (Brazil).
Libre	Free black (Colombia).
Libreta	See *a libreta*.
Libreta de contabilidad	Work-sheet recording amount of work done on the estate, and labourer's debts with the estate store etc.
Maguey	Fibrous cactus plant which provides a juice used in the manufacture of *pulque* (q.v.).
Mandamiento	Forced labour draft.
Manta	Coarse cotton cloth.
Maquipurero	Day labourer on Andean *haciendas* in Peru (Quechua).
Marca	Trademark.
Mayordomo	Estate overseer or supervisor.
Mayordomo de cafeteras	Supervisor of coffee-pickers.
Media	Sharecropping tenancy.
Media paga	Supplementary wage paid by *inquilino* (q.v.) to his *peón obligado* or *peón reemplazante* (q.v.).
Mediero	Sharecropper.
Memoria	Report.
Merced	Royal property grant.
Mesero	Agricultural wage labourer contracted by the month (Guatemala).

Mestizo	Person of mixed European and Indian blood.
Mezcal	Alcoholic drink distilled from the *agave* juice of the *maguey* (q.v.).
Mezquite	Low wooded thicket and grassland vegetation of arid and semi-arid northern Mexico.
Miel	A form of sugar syrup used as the base for *guarapo*, an alcoholic beverage.
Milpa	Indian cornfield (Guatemala).
Milpero	Indian subsistence or semi-subsistence corn farmer.
Minifundia	Marginal or sub-marginal dwarf holding(s).
Minifundista	The owner or operator of a *minifundia*.
Mishipa	Livestock belonging to people living outside a *hacienda*, as opposed to *huaccha* (q.v.), sheep belonging to tenant-shepherds.
Mita	Forced labour levy for work in the mines and *obrajes* (workshops) during the colonial period in Spanish America; originally (in Inca times) a system of voluntary communal labour.
Monte oscuro	Dense jungle.
Morador	A squatter on plantation lands who, in return for a house site and a plot of land for food cultivation, is required to provide labour services (for which he is paid) to the estate-owner (Brazil); a tenant farmer, who rented pasture lands as well as a house plot and lands for cultivation (Mexico).
Mozo	General term for a labourer (Guatemala).
Muchachos	Literally 'boys': young men (with small families) who were paid only half the maize ration of the *sirviente acomodado* (q.v.) (Mexico).
Municipio	Municipality; the smallest politico-administrative unit.
Negro racional	An educated slave (Colombia).
Obligación	Labour obligation or duty.
Obligado	Extra hands required by the landowner, and provided by the *inquilino* to fulfil his labour service obligations.
Ocio	Idleness.
Orqo	Tundra zone of bare or partially snow-covered mountainsides (Peru).
Pachamama	'Mother-Earth', a religious figure (Quechua).
Pachaquero	Service tenant: a regional term used in parts of northern highlands of Peru, equivalent to *colono* (q.v.).
Palenque	Settlement of escaped slaves.
Palo Brasil	A dyewood, once significant in commerce.

Pampa criolla	The cattle-raising region of the Argentine *pampas*, where the population was predominantly Argentine-born.
Pampa gringa	Cereal growing areas of the *pampas* of Santa Fe, populated largely by people of foreign birth (*gringos*).
Panela	A rough, low-quality sugar.
Paña	Cotton-picking season (Peru).
Parceiro	Sharecropper (Brazil).
Parcela	A sub-division of estate lands; a parcel or plot of land.
Parcelización	Process of land division.
Parceria	Sharecropping (Brazil).
Participación	A share in profits.
Partidario	Kind- or money-paying tenant (Ecuador).
Pastaje	Payment to landlord of rent for grazing livestock on estate lands (see also *hierbaje*).
Patrón	Term applied to the owner and/or administrator of a *hacienda* by the estate workers and tenants; a boss.
Peón	A general agricultural wage labourer.
Peón acasillado	A labour-service tenant (Mexico).
Peón ambulante	A seasonal labourer.
Peón eventual	A seasonal labourer (Mexico).
Peón obligado	A *peón* whose labour the *inquilino* (q.v.) was required to supply to the *hacienda* all the year round; the *peón obligado* was paid with the food ration normally reserved for the *inquilino* (Chile).
Peón permanente comun	Ordinary landless wage worker on a *hacienda*; in addition to his wage he could buy maize rations at a fixed concessionary price (Mexico).
Peón reemplezante	Same as *peón obligado* (q.v.).
Peón sedentario	Same as *inquilino-peón* (q.v.).
Peón temporal	Seasonal labourer.
Picardía	Knavery.
Pieza	Slave (Colombia).
Piloncillo	Brown, unclayed sugar (Mexico).
Pisaje	Ground rent; also known as '*el piso*' – 'the floor'.
Pisante	Sub-tenant on Peruvian Andean *haciendas*; generally related to a *colono* (q.v.).
Pizca	Maize harvest.
Planilla	Record- or work-sheet.
Plátano	Plantain-tree.
Pliego de petición	Labour petition, generally for higher wages.
Posesión	Piece of land occupied by an *inquilino* on a *hacienda* (Chile).

Prófugo	Fugitive indebted or contracted tenant or worker from a *hacienda*.
Propios de los pueblos	Municipal common lands (Costa Rica).
Protocolo	Register of property transactions.
Proveeduría	Company store operated by some *haciendas*; equivalent to *cantina* or *tienda de raya* (q.v.).
Puchuruna	Sub-tenant on a Peruvian Andean *hacienda*; generally related to a *colono* (q.v.).
Pueblo	Town.
Pulpería	*Hacienda* store.
Pulque	Alcoholic drink made from the *maguey* (q.v.).
Puna	High windswept grasslands of the Andean region.
Quina	Quinine.
Quinoa	Cereal crop grown at high altitudes in the Andes.
Ración	Allowance (generally of maize).
Ración cosechada	Allowance in kind from the harvest.
Ración de tierra	Land allocation to *inquilino* (q.v.).
Ramonear	Poor grazing on *haciendas* (Chile).
Ranchería	A small settlement or hamlet (Mexico).
Ranchero	Owner of a *rancho* (q.v.).
Rancho	A large farm or small estate (Mexico); the outlying section of a large estate (Mexico); mud and straw huts used by dwellers in the *pampas* (Argentina).
Rapadura	Crude, low-grade sugar (Brazil).
Recaudo	Weekly ration, covering all types of food except maize, beverages, and tobacco.
Reducción	Spanish colonial policy of grouping scattered Indian populations into nucleated settlements.
Regalía	Non-monetary perquisites given by estate to *inquilinos* (q.v.).
Regalía p'a chacra	Land lent to *inquilinos* for vegetable-growing.
Regalía p'a trigo	Land allocation for wheat.
Regalía tierra	Area of land given to *inquilino* by estate for cultivation of his own food crops.
Reserva	Area of land which the owner of a *hacienda* expropriated under Chilean Agrarian Reform law was allowed to retain for his own use: not to exceed 80 'basic' hectares.
Rosca	Basic cell or unit of the Colombian power structure; literally the 'ring'.
Rulo	See *de rulo*.
Safra	Sugar cane harvest (Brazil).
Satjata	Sub-tenant of Peruvian Andean *hacienda*; generally related to a *colono* (q.v.).

Senhor de engenho	The owner of a traditional sugar mill (Brazil).
Serrano	Inhabitant of the Sierra (Peru).
Sertão	The arid backlands of northeast Brazil.
Servicios personales	Personal services which Indians subject to *encomienda* (q.v.) were obliged to render to the Spanish *encomendero*.
Sindicato	Syndicate, trade union.
Sirvientes acomodados	Permanent labourers resident on an estate; they formed the upper stratum of the *sirvientes permanentes* and were paid a free *ración* (q.v.) of maize in addition to a monthly wage (Mexico).
Sirvientes permanentes	Permanent servants or agricultural labourers on an estate (Mexico).
Sobre-peón	A wage labourer supplied by an *inquilino* (q.v.) to provide part of the *inquilino*'s labour rent on the landlord's estate.
Socio	Ex-*voluntario* (q.v.), member of an *asentamiento* (q.v.).
Sub-delegación	Political division within a department (Chile).
Tablón	Area of coffee groves (Costa Rica).
Tagua	Vegetable ivory.
Taita	Quechua term of respect ('father') used by highland Indians in Peru.
Talaje	Pasture grazing rights on a *hacienda* (Chile).
Tarea	The work to be completed by a labourer on a *hacienda* in one day; a task or unit of work.
Temporadista	Seasonal migrant worker (Guatemala).
Terraje	A variation of the *concertaje* system of labour-service tenancy.
Terrajero	A variant of the *concertado* labour-service tenant; used for expanding cultivation into virgin forest (Colombia).
Terrazguero	A labour-service tenant (Colombia); another term for an *arrendatario* (q.v.) (Mexico).
Terreno baldío	Common or uncultivated ('waste') lands.
Terrenos censitarios	Tithe lands.
Tienda de despacho	Company store on a *hacienda*.
Tienda de raya	Same as *tienda de despacho* (q.v.).
Tierra caliente	Hot tropical lands, lying below 500 metres.
Tierra fría	Cold highland areas in the tropics, lying above approximately 2,500–3,000 metres.
Tierra pública	Public lands.
Tierras de caballería	Lands lying outside the *tierras de legua* (q.v.) (Costa Rica).

Tierras de legua	All lands located within a certain distance from major urban centres (Costa Rica).
Tierra templada	Temperate lands in the tropics, lying between 500 and 2,500 metres.
Tlachiquero de mezcal	Distiller of *mezcal* (q.v.).
Toma	Land invasion; seizure of an estate by peasants.
Torrante	Migrant labourer.
Tortilla	Maize pancake; the basic item of diet in many parts of Latin America.
Trabajador	Common labourer: the same as *peón permanente comun* (literally a 'worker').
Trabajador libre	Free worker.
Trabalho assalariado	Wage labour (Brazil).
Trato	Same as *Tarea* (q.v.).
Troje	*Hacienda* granary or storage barn.
Tuna	The fruit of the *maguey* plant.
Usina	Large modern sugar factory (Brazil).
Usineiro	Owner or operator of an *usina* (Brazil).
Vago	Vagrant.
Villorio	Hamlet; small rural settlement; or simply a group of houses (see also *aldea* and *caserío*).
Vereda	Neighbourhood.
Voluntario	Free wage labour.
Yanacona	Kind- or money-paying tenant (Peruvian coastal regions); labour-service tenant (Sierra of Peru).
Yanapacuc	Sub-tenant of Peruvian highland *hacienda*; generally related to a *colono* (q.v.) of the *hacienda*.
Yanapakoj	Same as *Yanapacuc*.
Yanapero	Labour-service tenant (Ecuador).
Zafra	Sugar cane harvest.
Zona da Mata	The moist coastal lowlands of northeast Brazil, a major sugar-growing region.
Zurrón	Leather pack-bag.

WEIGHTS AND MEASURES

1 *manzana* = 0.69 hectare (Central America)
1 *cuadra* = 1.57 hectares (Chile)

IN SAN LUIS POTOSÍ, MEXICO:

1 *almud* = 7.6 litres
1 *fanega* = $\frac{1}{2}$ *carga* = 12 *almudes* = 91 litres

1 *almud* of maize land (1 *almud de tierra de sembradura*) =
c. 3,000 sq. metres
1 *fanega de tierra de sembradura* = 3.6 hectares

IN THE BAJÍO OF MEXICO:

1 *fanega de sembradura* = c. 7 hectares
1 *caballería* = 6 *fanegas de sembradura*

1 *caballería* = between 42.5 and 45 hectares (depending on location)
Sitio de estancia de ganado menor = 18 *caballerías* = c. 780 hectares
Sitio de estancia de ganado mayor = c. 41 *caballerías* = c. 1,750 hectares

1 *arroba* = 25 lb
1 *quintal* = 4 *arrobas* = 100 lb = 46 kilogrammes
1 *alqueire* = 50 litres

8 *reales* = 1 *peso*
1 *peso* = 100 *centavos*

BRAZIL:

1,000 *reis* = 1 *milreis* (written '1$000')
10$500 = 10 *milreis, 500 reis*

NOTES ON CONTRIBUTORS

ARNOLD BAUER is Associate Professor of History at the University of California at Davis. He has lived, worked, and studied for several years in Mexico and Chile, has written a number of articles for various journals, and is the author of *Chilean rural society* (Cambridge, 1975).

JAN BAZANT is Professor of History in the Centro de Estudios Históricos, Colegio de Mexico. He has written a number of articles on Mexican history and is author of *Los bienes de la iglesia en Mexico (1856–75)*, published in English as *Alienation of Church wealth in Mexico* (Cambridge, 1971).

GEORGE BECKFORD is Professor of Economics at the University of the West Indies, Jamaica. He is the author of numerous articles on the problems of economic, and particularly agricultural, development in the Caribbean, and of *Persistent poverty: underdevelopment in plantation economies in the Third World* (New York and London, 1972). His most recent publication is *Small garden, bitter weed – roots of Caribbean poverty* (Kingston, 1975).

JANE BENTON is a Lecturer in Political and Tropical Geography at the North Staffordshire Polytechnic. She has worked in Guyana and in Bolivia, where she conducted field research into the comparative problems and consequences of agrarian reform in freeholding and ex-*hacienda* communities.

BRIAN BLOUET is Professor of Geography at the University of Nebraska. He holds degrees from the University of Hull and taught at the University of Sheffield prior to emigrating to North America. His research interests include the historical geography of the Caribbean, the evolution of settlement patterns, and the diffusion of agricultural innovations in the British empire and Commonwealth.

DAVID BRADING graduated with his B.A. from Cambridge and his Ph.D. from London. He has been Assistant Professor of History at the University of California at Berkeley, and Associate Professor at Yale. Currently he is Lecturer in Latin American History and Director of the Centre of Latin American Studies, University of Cambridge. Apart from various articles in the *Hispanic American Historical Review*, *Journal of Latin American Studies*, and *Historia Mexicana*, he has published two full-length studies, *Miners and merchants in Bourbon Mexico, 1763–1810* (Cambridge, 1971), and *Los orígenes del nacionalismo mexicano* (Mexico, 1973). At present he is working on a book about *haciendas* and *ranchos* in the Mexican Bajío, 1700–1860.

CARLOS BUITRAGO ORTIZ is Professor of History in the Departamento de Ciencias Sociales, Universidad de Puerto Rico. He has published several studies of the social and economic history of Puerto Rico.

CIRO F. S. CARDOSO graduated in history at the Universidade Federal de Rio de Janeiro and received his doctorate from the Institut des Hautes Etudes de l'Amérique Latine, Paris. He is currently Professor of History at the University of Costa Rica and Director of the Central American Social Science Research Programme. His publications include a number of articles on socio-economic problems and the mode of production in Latin America, with particular reference to slave societies.

MALCOLM DEAS is a Fellow of St Antony's College, Oxford, and teaches Latin American history in the Department of History and the Centre of Latin American Studies, University of Oxford. His particular interests are the modern political and socio-economic history of Colombia, where he spends long periods on field research.

KENNETH DUNCAN graduated from Edinburgh University and has studied at the University of Cambridge, where he was a member of the Department of Land Economy and the Centre of Latin American Studies. He has carried out field research in El Salvador and Guatemala, where he worked on the problems of migrant labour, and in Belize, where he examined the social and economic organization of communities of shifting cultivators.

PETER L. EISENBERG holds degrees in History from Yale, Stanford, and Columbia Universities. He has taught at Rutgers University and the University of the West Indies, and is currently Professor of History at the Universidade Estadual de Campinas in São Paulo. Apart from a major study, *The sugar industry of Pernambuco, 1840–1910: modernization without change* (Berkeley, Calif., 1974), he has written a number of articles on Brazilian history. At present he is working on the demographic history of nineteenth-century Brazil.

HENRI FAVRE received his doctorate in Sociology from the University of Paris and is now Professor at the Institut des Hautes Etudes de l'Amérique Latine, and Director of the Research Programme on Latin American Indian peasant societies, Centre National de la Recherche Scientifique, Paris. He has carried out extensive field work in Chiapas, Mexico, and in the central and southern Sierra of Peru. He is the author of a number of studies, including *Changement et continuité chez les Mayas du Mexique* (Paris, 1970) and some thirty articles.

EZEQUIEL GALLO, who is currently Director of the Instituto Torcuato Di Tella, Buenos Aires, was formerly a Research Fellow of St Antony's College, Oxford, and Lecturer in Sociology at the University of Essex. Apart from a number of articles dealing with various aspects of the social and economic history of Argentina, he has written *La formación de la Argentina moderna* in collaboration with Roberto Cortes Conde.

JULIA GARLANT has studied at the University of Oxford and at Tulane University, where she completed the M.A. course in Latin American Studies.

PIERRE GILHODES is Professor of Political Science at the Centre d'Etude des Relations Internationales of the Fondation Nationale des Sciences Politiques, Paris. He has published several studies on the agrarian situation in Colombia, including *Las luchas agrarias en Colombia* (Medellin, 1972) and *La question agraire en Colombie, 1958–71* (Paris, 1974).

COLIN HARDING received his B.A. and B.Litt. in Latin American Studies from the University of Oxford. After spending three years in Peru, where he collaborated in the collection and organization of the archives of the Centro de Documentación Agraria, he was for a time a Research Officer at the Centre of Latin American Studies, University of Cambridge. He is now one of the editors of *Latin American Newsletters*.

HARRY HOETINK is Professor of Sociology and Director of the Institute of Caribbean Studies at the Universidad de Puerto Rico. He has published a considerable number of articles on the Caribbean and is the author of *El pueblo dominicano, 1850–1900* (Santo Domingo, 1972).

THOMAS H. HOLLOWAY received his M.A. and Ph.D. from the University of Wisconsin and has lived for considerable periods in Panama, Colombia, and Brazil. He is now Assistant Professor of Latin American History at Cornell University, where he is preparing a full-length study on immigrant labour and social mobility in rural São Paulo. Apart from several articles he is the author of the monograph *The Brazilian coffee valorization of 1906: regional politics and economic dependence* (Madison, Wisconsin, 1975).

ANN HAGERMAN JOHNSON is a graduate student and research assistant in History at the University of California, Davis. She is currently working on internal migrations in Chile from 1850 to 1970.

CRISTOBAL KAY is at present a Lecturer in Development Studies in the Department of International Economic Studies, University of Glasgow. Prior to this he was for several years a Fellow of the Centre for Socio-Economic Studies (CESO) at the University of Chile. He has published a number of articles on the agrarian systems of Latin America and on agrarian reform in Chile.

PETER KLAREN, who received his B.A. from Dartmouth College, and his Ph.D. in History from the University of California at Los Angeles, is currently Associate Professor of History at the George Washington University in Washington. His book *La formación de las haciendas azucareras y los orígines del Apra* (Lima, 1970) was published in English by the University of Texas Press in 1973. Currently he is engaged on a comparative agrarian history of Peru and Mexico in the nineteenth and twentieth centuries.

ANTHONY LEEDS is presently Professor of Anthropology at Boston University. He has published widely on many aspects of the sociology and social anthropology of Latin America; he is particularly concerned with urban sociology.

JUAN MARTINEZ ALIER, formerly a Research Fellow at St Antony's College, Oxford, is now a Lecturer in the Department of Economics at the Universidad de Barcelona. He is the author of two full-length studies, *Labourers and landowners in southern Spain* (London, 1971) and *Haciendas, plantations and collective farms – studies on agrarian class societies: Cuba and Peru* (London, 1975), as well as a number of articles and reviews.

MAGNUS MÖRNER is the Director of the Institute of Latin American Studies, Stockholm, and has been Visiting Professor at a number of American universities on a number of occasions. In addition to his major studies, *Race mixture in the history of Latin America* (Boston, 1967) and *La corona española y los foráneos en los pueblos de Indios de America* (Stockholm, 1970), he has written a large number of articles and reviews covering many aspects of the social and economic history of Latin America.

JAIME REIS is currently a Lecturer in Economic History at the University of Glasgow, having previously taught at Vanderbilt University and been a Research Fellow at the Institute of Latin American Studies, University of Glasgow.

IAN RUTLEDGE, after taking his B.A. and Ph.D. in economics at the University of Cambridge, was for some years Lecturer in Rural Sociology at Wye College and the Institute of Latin American Studies, University of London. He now works in deepest Yorkshire.

JOSE R. SABOGAL-WIESSE teaches at the Universidad Nacional Agraria La Molina in Lima and is an agronomist and sociologist. He has worked widely throughout Latin America on the problems of agrarian reform.

MICHAEL TAUSSIG is Assistant Professor of Anthropology at the University of Michigan, Ann Arbor. He has carried out several years' field work in southwest Colombia, and with Anna Rubbo has written *Esclavitud y libertad en el Valle del Cauca*, a local history which combines archival research with oral history and is mainly aimed at a peasant readership. At the moment he is working on a book concerned with the ideological reactions to the spread of rural capitalism in Latin America.

GLYN WILLIAMS is a Lecturer in Sociology in the Department of Social Theory and Institutions at the University College of North Wales. He has carried out extensive field work in Patagonia and has published several articles on the Tehuelche and on the Welsh Colony in Patagonia.

Subject index

507

faenas (*cont.*)
  Peru, 148, 260
Farias brothers, owners of Bocas *hacienda*, 74
farmers, independent: in cereal-growing
  areas, Arg, 332, 460; *see also* tenant
  farmers
'farming type' approach to study of agrarian
  capitalism, 13
farms: Arg: family-sized, in cereal-growing
  areas, 325, 333–4; Chile: distribution
  of, by size, 128
fazendas (large estates, Braz), 307, 308–9,
  310–11
Felipe, Pedro, Indian tenant on *hacienda*,
  Mex, 35
Fernández y Montealegre and Fernández y
  Salazar, coffee export firms, CR, 189
Fernandini *haciendas*, Peruvian Andes, 145,
  147, 149, 150, 152, 157, 159
fertilizers, for coffee plantations, 185
feudalism in Latin America?, 3, 4–5
fiestas: on Arboleda estates, Col, 404, 411,
  421; of mountain villages, Peru, 265
fincas (estates, Col), 269
fincas de recreo (present-day holiday places,
  Col), 275, 293
firewood, tenants' rights to: Chile, 106–7,
  120; Col, 413; Mex, 36, 37
flax cultivation, Arg, 326
flour-milling, Arg, 334
foodstuffs:
  Braz: prices of (1860s and 1870s) 358
  Chile: black market in (from 1972), 129–30
  Col: harvest labour partly paid in, Santa
    Bárbara *hacienda*, 280, 282; shortage of,
    during *Mil Días* war, 284
  production of, reduced by spread of coffee
    plantations: CR, 185, 195–6; Peru, 239,
    250
forasteros sin tierras, Bol, 481
foreign trade of Latin America: (1825–5),
  458; (1850–73), 459; (1873–96), 459–60
forests: clearing of, for cultivation, (Braz)
  310–11, (CR) 196; of San Diego
  hacienda, Mex, 60; planting of, by
  mountain villages, Peru, 263
formadores: contracts with, for planting new
  coffee bushes, Braz, 311
fornecedores (independent sugar planters, Braz),
  350
France: exports to, 189, 231; immigrants
  from 180
Freedmen's Bureau, USA, 360
Frei, Eduardo, President of Chile, 123
fruit-growing: Chile, 85; Trin, 447

fundos (estates, Chile), 85–6, 92, 100;
  labour force of, 95–7
funeral rites of peasants, Col, 428

Gaitán, Liberal leader, Col: assassination of
  (1948), 426
Galinski, Andrés, mine and *ingenio* owner,
  Arg, 226
gamonales (*hacienda* owners, central sierra of
  Peru), 488
gañanes: *peones*, Mex, 37; relatives of *inquilinos*, Chile, 97
Garcia brothers, owners of Bocas *hacienda*
  (1899), 79
General López department, Arg, 333, 334
genocide, by *conquistadores* in Col, 397, 400
George Town, Guyana, 441
Germany: immigrants from, 180, 302, 314;
  trade with, 189
Gildemeister and Co., trading house, Lima,
  236, 237
Gildemeister family, sugar planters, Peru,
  233, 234, 236, 237
gloria chupe, traditional Easter Saturday
  soup, Huancavelica, 263
goats
  Mex, 33, 34, 36, 39, 49; *mayordomo's*
    rights to milk for cheese, in rainy
    season, 35; of tenants, rent for
    pasturage of, 70, 71, 76, 77
  woodland fenced against, mountain villages,
    Peru, 263
gobernadores, 257
goces (pieces of land allotted to workers on
  CERAs, Chile), 129, 131
gold mines
  Arg highlands, 209, 210
  Col, Cauca Valley: worked by slaves, 397,
    398, 400, 402, 403–4, 465; as market
    for agricultural produce, 402, 405, 465;
    profits from, 406; state of, after aboli-
    tion of slavery, 410, 417; transfer of, to
    foreign companies, 399
  CR, 182
Gordon, A. H., Governor of Trin, 444, 447
Grace Co., trading house, Peru, 233;
  purchase of sugar plantations, 236–7
Graham, Rowe and Co., trading house, Peru,
  236, 237
grain, *see* cereals
grain storage, on *haciendas*, Mex, 31, 38, 43,
  68, 80
Grande de San Ramón, Río, CR, 167
Guadeloupe, West Indies, 341
Guadelupe, CR, 170

516 *Subject index*

illiteracy *(cont.)*
    Braz: among Pernambuco sugar workers, 388
immigrants
    Arg: in centre and south, dispossessing
        hunter–gatherers, 489; to cereal-growing
        areas, 14, 300, 324–5, 330; to cereal
        and wool areas, 335; predominance of
        Italians in, 328, 332
    Braz, to coffee areas, 16, 299, 302–5; as
        colonos, 308–12; geographical mobility
        of, 303, 304–5, 317; government
        subsidy to, 306; social mobility of, 312–19
    CR, 179–80, 182
    Dominican Republic, 486
    Puerto Rico, 462, 484
    see also indentured labour
import substitution, Arg sugar industry as
        example of, 205
imports, Col (1860s), 419, 420
Incañán, Peru, 259
income: of free labourers, sugar plantations,
        Pernambuco, 381–4; from gold mining,
        Arboleda family, Col, 406; of rural
        properties, central Chile (1854, 1874),
        86, 87, (distribution of) 88, 89
indentured labour: Cuba, 348; Peru, 154–5,
        232, 241, (revolts of) 246, 252; Trin,
        344, 439, 446–7, 465
India, indentured labourers from, 344, 446–
        7, 465
Indians (Amerindians): Conquest, and
        population of, 14, 397–8; hunter–
        gatherer groups of, 27, 323, 489;
        remains of pre-Conquest culture of,
        209–10; resilience of cultural life of,
        161; *see also individual groups*
indigo cultivation, Col, 285, 292, 399, 419
indios forasteros, Peru, 154
indiviso lands, Col, *see* 'common lands'
industrial establishments and workshops,
        Santa Fe Province, Arg (1870, 1895),
        328; numbers and size of, in cereal and
        wool areas, 336
industrialization: Braz coffee areas, 352, 360;
        Mex (Monterrey), 79
inflation, Chile: benefits *hacendados*, 472
ingenios (sugar factories)
    Arg, 210; political power of owners of,
        211–15, 220; purchases of land by
        owners of, to obtain labour force, 211,
        216–21
    Braz: *see engenhos, usinas*
    Peru: modernization of, 235, 237
ingenuos (children born of slave mothers,
        Braz), 356, 357

inheritance, laws of: Col, 427, 428; Mex, 28, 54
inquilinos (labour-service tenants, Chile), 94,
        95–7, 106–7, 111; changes in situation
        of, 11–12, 98, 472; cost per day of
        labour of (1965), 119; earnings of, 120,
        121; percentage of, in population
        (1935–65), 115; percentage of culti-
        vated land held by, and of production by
        (1955–65), 114, 116; proletarianization
        of, 113–23; under land reform, 124,
        125, 126
inquilinos peones, 112
inquilinos medieros, earnings of, 121
interest rates: CR, 173; very low in colonial
        period, 406
Iquique, Chile, 233
Irapuato, Mex, 33
Irazú volcano, CR, 167
Iriondo department, Arg, 337
irrigation
    Arg, lack of water for, Catamarca province,
        221
    Chile, 83, 85, 95
    Mex, 47, 80; for sugar, 60, 61; for
        vegetables, 45, 65; for wheat, 32, 65
Iruya department, Arg, 217
Istla *hacienda*, Mex, 31
Italy, immigrants from: Arg, in cereal areas,
        300, 328, 332; Braz, in coffee areas,
        299, 302, 461–2, (as property owners)
        314–17, (social mobility of) 312–13
Izquierdo, Salvador, owner of El Principal
        hacienda, Chile, 134

Jalisco state, Mex, 46, 47
Jalpa *hacienda*, Mex, 32, 47, 55
Jamaica, 445, 465, 474, 483
Japan: immigrants from, Braz, 302; in-
        dentured labour from, Peru, 241
Japio *hacienda*, Col, 402, 404–5, 409, 410,
        411–15, 419, 420, 421, 423
Jaú, Braz, 313
Jesuits: expulsion of, (Col) 402, 404, 411,
        (Peru) 232; as source of agrarian history, 455
Jequetepeque Valley, Peru, 232
Johnson, Andrew, President of USA, 360
jornaleros
    day labourers: CR, 178, 181; Mex,
        transformation of *peones permanentes*
        into, 74–5, 79
    seasonal workers, Guatemala, 10
Juchitlan el Grande *hacienda*, Mex, 33–6
juez de composiciones, and land titles in
        Bajío, 28, 29
juez de paz, 257

peasants (*cont.*)
    than wage labourers, Chile, 120, 121,
    446; incorporation of, into plantation
    system, 474; in Latin American sense,
    133; proletarianization of, *see* prole-
    tarianization; relations of landlord and,
    474–6; in traditional agriculture, tendency
    to oust capitalist landowners, 31; *see also*
    smallholders
    Arg: Catamarca, subdivision of holdings of,
    221; Santa Catalina, as proprietors,
    208–9
    Chile: conflict between collective economy
    and, 129, 132; conflict between land-
    lords and, in *hacienda* system, 103–6;
    divisions among, created by land re-
    form, 125–6; extension of franchise to
    (1950s), 122; limited re-emergence of,
    on expropriated estates, 11, 22, 129,
    131
    Col, Cauca Valley: dispossession of (1910
    onwards), 423–7; outlaw black
    peasants, 407–8; rich, middle, and
    poor, 427–8
    Guyana, after abolition of slavery, 483
    Peruvian highlands, 16, 18; accommoda-
    tion of, to wage labour, 204
    Trin, after abolition of slavery, 435, 436,
    442–7 *passim*, 448–9, 474
Pénjamo, Mex, 30, 32, 46
peones: Chile (wage labourers), 96, 97; Col,
    399, (white or *mestizo*) 413, 466; CR,
    178, 181; Mex, 30, 31, 37, 59, (maize
    ration of) 53, 68; Peru, 257–8
peones ambulantes, peones forasteros, and
    peones temporales, see seasonal labour
peones obligados or *peones reemplazentes*,
    supplied by *inquilinos*, Chile, 107, 112,
    115, 117
peones permanentes comunes, Mex, 67, 68;
    become *jornaleros* (by Civil Code, 1871),
    74–5; debts of, 69; impoverishment of,
    79
Péréz Galvez, Juan, owner of Bocas
    hacienda, Mex (1844), 65
Pernambuco state, Braz, sugar production in
    compared with Cuba, 343, 345, 347–50,
    363, 462
    economic crisis in, 345–54
    modernization of, 345, 354, 369–71, 469;
    government subsidies for, 350–1, 352,
    467; and labour relations, 389–93; and
    social structure, 361, 371, 372–80;
    and welfare of population, 380–8
    social crisis in, at abolition of slavery,

354–62, 440, 468
Peronists, Arg, 216, 217
Peru, 13, 15, 228, 398
    Chilean occupation of, 229, 232, 458
    foreign trade of, 460
    Grace Contract between Britain and (1889),
    248
    guano industry of, 185, 231, 232
    migration to, from Chile, 99
    movement of peasants to higher lands in,
    204, 253–67, 470
    Odria period in (1948–56), 144
    oncenio period in (1919–30), 243, 248
    production relations in Andean *haciendas*
    of, 141–64, 475, 482, 484
    purchase of coffee from CR by, 189
    sale of slaves to, from Col (1843), 409
    social and economic consequences of
    modernization of sugar industry in
    (1870–1930), 204, 229–52, 468
    wheat exports from Chile to, 106, 134
Pichetti, Alberto, mine and *ingenio* owner,
    Arg, 226
Pichetti, Pirquitas y Compañia, Arg, 214, 226
piece-work payment (*tarea, trato*)
    on coffee estates: Braz, 307–8, 309–10;
    Col, 280, 282, 413; CR, 181
    in wheat-exporting period, Chile, 113
pigs, on *haciendas* in Mex, 39, 49
Pijao Indians, Col, 408
Pilchaca, Peru, 259
piloncello (unrefined sugar), sold by San Diego
    hacienda, 60
Pirquitas mine, Arg, 226
pisaje (ground rent paid by *arrendatorios*,
    Mex), 63, 64, 70, 71, 72, 78; raising
    of, 76, 77
Piura department, Peru, 229, 231, 232
plague, bubonic, Braz, 388
plantains, Col: in Cauca Valley, 403, 410,
    (staple of free black peasants) 417, 428;
    on coffee plantations, 282–3
plantation economy
    change from slave to capitalist form of,
    6, 16–17
    cheap labour policy of, 460, 474
    distinguished from *hacienda* economy, 5–6,
    7
    labour in, 9–10; highland peasant labour
    for, 15–16, 18, (Arg) 203–4, (Peru)
    240–7
    not necessarily producing for export
    market, 205
    see also sugar cultivation, coffee cultiva-
    tion

Subject index

Author index

Endnote numbers are in brackets: 227(30) = p. 227, note 30.
Main references are in italic type.

Aban, Leopoldo, *227(30)*
Accioli Lins, Presciano de, *394(13)*
Adams, Richard, 8, *19(26)*, 266(2)
Adamson, Alan H., 465, *479(49)*
Affonso, A., *137(61)*, *138(76)*
Alberti, Giorgio, 153, *163(10)*, *164(31)*
Alencastre Montúfar, Gustavo, *482(86)*
Alers, J. Oscar, *164(31)*
Althusser, L., 266(1)
Alvarado, Eduardo, 181
Alvarez Beltrán, Carlos, *249(9)*
Anderson, C. W., 2, *18(1)*
Araya Pochet, Carlos, 182, *200(33)*
Arboleda, G., *433(19)*
Arboleda, S., *433(22)*
Arboleda Llorente, José María, *432(14)*
Arguedas, José María, *477(8)*
Arrighi, Giovanni, *228(57)*
Arroyo, J., *432(17)*
Augelli, John P., *451(55)*
Azuela, M., *81*

Bachmann, Carlos, *249(12)*
Bairoch, Paul, *478(24)*
Balandier, G., 266(1)
Baldwin, Robert, *325-6*, *340(2)*
Balibar, E., 266(1)
Ballesteros, M., *135(29)*
Balmaceda, J., *134(13)*
Baraona, Rafael, 84, *100(3)*, 103, 133(2), *134(10)*, *136(40)*, 145, 146
Barbosa Lima Sobrinho, A. José, *362(4)*
Bardella, Gianfranco, 239 (table), *250(23)*
Barraclough, Solon, *128* (table), *138(76)*, *139(81)*
Barreto, Lêda, *367(61)*
Barreto, Tobias, *394(8)*
Barros Wanderley, José M. de, *395(34)*
Bauer, Arnold, 11, *20(31)*, 21, *101(15)*, 110, *134(11,16)*, *135(22, 23)*, 146, *163(9)*, 300, *471–2*, 474, 475, *477(17)*, *481(81)*
Bazant, Jan, 21, *57(42, 44)*, *80(1)*, 146, *162(8)*, 300, *472–3*

Beckford, George, *340(5)*, 469, *483*
Best, Lloyd, *479(48)*
Bello, José María, *396(42)*
Bello, Júlio, *365(51)*, *393(2)*
Benton, Jane, *470–1*, *484*
Bernstein, Henry, *340(5)*
Bertram, G. W., *340(5)*
Beyer, Robert C., 297, *479(42)*
Bierck, H. A., Jr, *432(16)*
Biolley, Paul, *201(44)*
Blouet, Brian, *344*, *450(24, 30)*, 465, 474
Boeke, J. H., *18(1)*
Boman, Eric, *208–10*, *225(2)*
Bonilla, Heraclio, *478(25)*
Boorstein Couturier, Edith, *81*
Borde, Jean, *56(7)*, *101(7)*
Brading, David, 21, *56(11)*, 300, 459, *478(21)*
Brevis, O., *139(82)*
Brown, Manon, *138(70)*
Buarque de Holanda, Sergio, *320(12)*, *364(29)*
Buescu, Mircea, *365(42)*
Buitrago Ortiz, Carlos, 462, *484–5*
Bulnes, Francisco, *58(55)*
Buntig, A. J., *226(9)*
Burgess, Eugene W., *250(19)*
Burn, W. L., *450(26)*
Bustamente Roldán, Dario, *297(17)*

Cabello, Mario, *152–3*
Calderón de la Barca, Fanny, 459, *478(20)*
Calle, Rigoberto, 157, *162(5)*
Calvo, Joaquín Bernardo, 178, 179 (table), 186, *198(21)*
Camacho Roldán, Salvador, 298
Camargo, José Francisco de, *321(25)*
Campello, Samuel, *396(48)*
Campoletti, R., *342(13)*
Carcano, M. A., *340(1)*
Cardoso, Ciro, F. S., 22, *463*
Carmagnani, M., *135(23)*, *481(22)*
Carranza Solis, Jorge, *200(38)*
Carter, William E., *477(8)*
Carvalho de Morais, João Pedro, *320(15)*

530

Author index

535

DATE DUE

.cLEAN, TORONTO FORM #38-297